Instructor's Manual

to accompany

CONCEPTUAL
Physical
Science

SECOND EDITION

Paul G. Hewitt

John Suchocki

Leslie A. Hewitt

Addison
Wesley
Longman

Menlo Park, California • Reading, Massachusetts
New York • Harlow, England • Don Mills, Ontario
Amsterdam • Madrid • Sydney • Mexico City

Sponsoring Editor: Sami Iwata
Publishing Assistant: Bridget Biscotti-Bradley
Production Supervisor: Larry Olsen
Cover Designer: Yvo Riezebos

ISBN 0-321-03536-4

12 13 14 15 —VG—03 02

2725 Sand Hill Road
Menlo Park, California 94025

Contents

Acknowledgements

For many of the ideas in the first edition of this manual, which carry to this second edition, we remain thankful to Charlie Spiegel.

For contributions to physics ideas we thank Chuck Stone, and we remain thankful to William J. Beaty, Howie Brand, Debra Brice, Romulo Broas, Jim Court, Peter Crooker, Paul Doherty, Marshall Ellenstein, Ken Ford, Ken Ganezer, Charlie Hibbard, Jerry Hosken, John Hubisz, Ron Lindemann, Chelcie Liu, Graham Robertson, Pablo Robinson, Josip Slisko, Paul Tipler, David Wall, and David Willey, and Larry Wolfe.

For contributions to chemistry ideas we are remain grateful to Bob Asato, Carl Baer, Ted Brattstrom, Richard Brill, Mauri Ditzler, Doris Kolb, Kenneth Kolb, Michael Reese, Robert Ricci, Erwin Richter, Bassam Shakhashiri, and Pearl Takeuchi.

For help with suggested lectures to Part 7 we are most grateful to Bob Abrams. We are especially indebted to CCSF geology/physics instructor Jim Court for sharing his lecture notes. For ideas on the atmosphere, we thank meteorologist Robert Baruffaldi. We are grateful to those whose own books served as principle references for Part 7: Edward Tarbuck and Fredrick K. Lutgens of Illinois Central College, Brian J. Skinner of Yale University, and Stephen J. Porter of the University of Washington. For meteorology ideas we are indebted to Don Ahrens.

And for helping with astronomy we thank Richard Crowe, John Hubisz, Tenny Lim, Forrest Luke, and Marshall Mock.

For assisting in page makeup we are grateful to Lillian Lee.

Introduction

This manual describes a way to teach physical science conceptually. It helps tie physics, chemistry, and geology to the student's personal experience in the everyday world, so your students learn to see physical science not as a classroom or laboratory activity, but as a part of everyday living. People with a conceptual understanding of physical science are more alive to the world, just as a botanist taking a stroll through a wooded park is more alive than most of us to the trees, plants, flora, and the life that teems in them. The richness of life is not only seeing the world with wide open eyes, but knowing what to look for. This puts the physical science instructor in a very nice role — being one who points out the relationships of things in the world about us. Such an instructor is in a good position to add meaning to students' lives.

Your influence goes beyond the students you face in class, for it is passed on to others through them. Many of your students will become teachers in elementary school, where they must feel good about science as they impart science to their students. In our profession, we can never tell where our influence stops. It will touch younger people in their precious years, when the world "out there" is wonderful and exciting. It will touch kids who wonder about stars, clouds, wind, rocks, electronic and mechanical gadgets, plants, animals, and food. Science courses have too often been the "killer courses" in schools. Let *Conceptual Physical Science* not be one of them! The rigor in tilling a field has more to do with the depth of the plow setting, than the field itself. *Conceptual Physical Science*, with the plow not too deep and not too shallow, can be a favorite and meaningful course for your students.

On Class Lectures

Many students are justly dissatisfied if a lecture seems remote from the chapter being studied, or if the lecture is a verbatim presentation of it. A successful lecturer avoids both of these extremes. A lecture can provide additional examples and explanations to chapter material. Educational research strongly shows that students learn from what they already know. This finding supports what we all know — that knowledge is aquired layers at a time, each layer depending on the layer underneath — hence the emphasis on *analogies* in the text. In your teaching too, the authors strongly recommend you use analogies whenever possible. You may find that your students are an excellent source of new analogies and examples to supplement those in the text. A productive class assignment is:

> Choose one (or more) of the concepts presented in the reading assignment and cite any illustrative analogies or examples that *you* can think of.

This exercise not only prompts your students to relate the concepts being learned to their own experiences, but adds to your future teaching material.

We can paraphrase William James, who stated that "wisdom is knowing what to overlook," and say that good teaching is knowing what to omit. It is important to distinguish between what to skim over and what to dig into. Too often an instructor will spend precious class time digging into non-central and non-essential material. How nice for the student when class time is stimulating and the material covered is central and relevant.

This text begins with physics, with its supply of equations. These are important in a conceptual course — not as a recipe for plugging in numerical values, but as a guide to thinking. The equation tells the student what variables to consider in treating an idea. In physics, for example, how much an object accelerates depends not only on the net force, but on mass as well. The formula $a = F/m$ reminds one to consider both quantities. Does gravitation depend on an object's speed? Consideration of $F \sim mM/d^2$ shows that it doesn't, and so forth. The problem sets at the ends of many chapters involve computations that help to illustrate concepts rather than challenge your students' mathematical abilities. They are fewer in number than excercises, to avoid course emphasis on number crunching.

A note of caution: Please don't overwhelm your students with excessive written homework! (Remember those courses you took as a student where you were so busy with the chapter-end material that you didn't get into the chapter material itself?) The exercises are numerous only to provide you a wide selection to consider. Depending on your style of teaching, you may find that posing and answering exercises in class makes a successful lecture.

New to this edition are answers and solutions to odd-numbered exercises and problems that appear for students in the Practice Book. Answers to all exercises and problems are in this manual (pages 161 to 260). These are suitable for copying and posting or distributing, or whatever. It's your course.

In lecture we think that before moving on to new material it is important to provide the student with a self check after important ideas and concepts are presented. We do this by posing the following, after presenting an idea and supporting it with examples: "If you understand this — if you really do — then you can answer the following question." Then we pose the question slowly and clearly, usually in multiple-choice form or such that a short answer is called for, and ask the class to make a response — usually written. Then we ask them to look at their neighbors' papers, and depending on the importance of the question, we ask them to briefly discuss it with their neighbors (at the beginning of the course we add that if their neighbors aren't helpful, to sit somewhere else next time).

Several of this type questions in a lecture brings the students into an active role, no matter how large the lecture section. It also clears misconceptions before they are carried along into new material. We call these questions, CHECK QUESTIONS, in the suggested lectures on the following pages of this manual. The check-question procedure may also be used to *introduce* ideas. A discussion of the question, the answer, and some of the misconceptions associated with it, will get more attention than the same idea presented as a statement of fact. And one of the nice features of asking for neighbor participation is that it gives you pause to reflect on your delivery. Such reflections can be very worthwhile!

We strongly recommend lecture notes. Even quite abbreviated notes will remind you of points you wish to cover in your lecture — which can be glanced at during your check-your-neighbor interludes. Such notes insure you don't forget main points, and a mark or two will let you know next time what you missed or where you stopped. A sample of the notes used by the physics author for Chapter 2 is shown above.

Getting students to come to class prepared is a perennial problem. Rather than preach to your students about the value of coming to class prepared, or the value of taking their education seriously, a remedy to consider is to give frequent quizzes. Hugh Hickman of Hillsborough Community College in Florida, and Suk Hwang of the University of Hawaii at Hilo, practice the extreme — a quiz each and every class meeting — with great success! Hugh gives a single problem quiz at the end of each class, that covers something just lectured about. Suk gives a single question quiz at the beginning of each class, on reading material for the following lecture. Attendance in these classes runs close to 100%, and students are generally favorable about the policy. Suk reports that his testing process takes less than five minutes per lecture. He assigns a grade to the sheets, with brief comments, and returns them. But the grades do not count at all to the final course grade. He is out front with his class when he tells them that the only purpose of the quizzes is to increase the probability of coming to class having first read the assigned reading material. Suk claims that because students abhor returning blank sheets, or dislike not being able to correctly answer the simple questions, they DO the reading assignment. Evidently a well-answered paper, even though it doesn't count to the final grade, is sufficient reward for the student. Hugh reports that the response to his daily quizzes has been favorable "beyond belief". We now do the same. The practice is in keeping with what we all know: the best ideas are often the simplest.

A sample NEXT-TIME QUESTION page is shown on the following page. These can be photocopied and used on display boards to capture attention and create discussion. They can also be made into OHP transparencies to be used as a brain teaser for homework and for class discussion. So conclude your lessons with them in class as ties to the next class meeting, or post them in the hallway for all to ponder.

The PRACTICE BOOK, in the opinion of the authors, is the strongest component of the Conceptual Physical Science package. The practice sheets are excellent in-class cooperative-learning activities. Or if time doesn't permit, they serve well as a tutor on the side for after-class activities. At CCSF the Practice Book is carried in the student book store as "recommended but not required" and used by about one-third of our students. New to this edition are answer sheets at the back of the book (as well as answers to the odd-numbered exercises and problems from the textbook).

The Conceptual Physical Science package of text and ancillaries lend themselves to teaching by way of the 3-stage LEARNING CYCLE, developed by Robert Karplus of UC Berkeley more than 25 years ago.

EXPLORATION— giving all students a common set of experiences that provide opportunities for student discussion. Activities are mainly in the *Laboratory Manual*.

CONCEPT DEVELOPMENT — lectures, textbook reading, doing practice sheets from the *Practice Book*, and class discussions.

APPLICATION — doing end-of-chapter Exercises and Problems, Next-Time Questions, and experiments from the *Laboratory Manual*.

Implementing the learning cycle involves delaying the presentation of content until the students have experienced the phenomena via an activity. Before a lecture on Archimedes' Principle, for example, students first get their hands wet by dunking objects in containers of water to experience displacement, buoyancy, floating, and sinking. A lecture that follows this recent first-hand experience has more learning hooks for catching information. Learning stems from their own experience. Learning-cycle activities are generally short. If your students meet once per week in lab, you can follow up an experiment on material they have covered with one or two short activities that set the stage for next week's topic.

Most suggested lectures in this manual require more than one class period, depending on your pace of instruction and what you add or omit. Instructors have their own teaching styles, and we present our lecture notes only to show what works for us (more question asking and less professing — we pose many more check questions than the samples in this manual). Whatever your teaching style, you may find these suggested lectures quite useful, and a means to jump off and develop your own non-computational way of teaching.

Please bring to our attention any errors you find in this manual, in the textbook, or its ancillaries. We welcome correspondence suggesting improvements in the presentation of physical science, and we answer mail [Pghewitt@aol.com; Lahewitt@aol.com; and Jasuchocki@aol.com] or c/o Addison Wesley Longman, 1 Jacob Way, Reading, MA 01867. Good luck in your course!

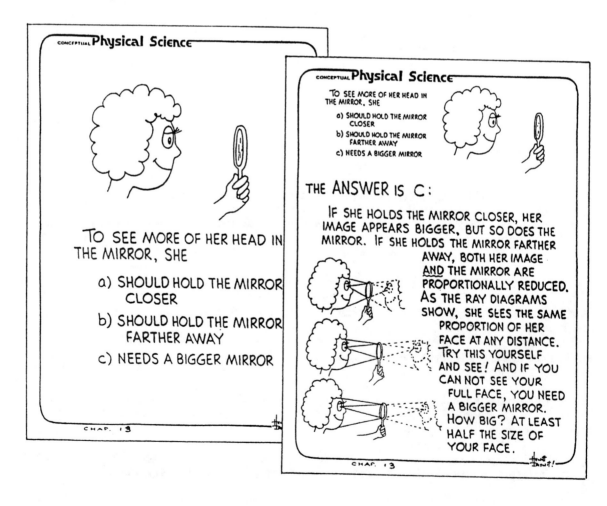

CONCEPTUAL PHYSICAL SCIENCE
ANCILLARIES

In addition to this Instructor's Manual, you should have the NEXT-TIME QUESTIONS book, printed TEST BANK, and TestGen-EQ Computerized Testing Software for Windows or Mac. Ancillaries available for student purchase include the LABORATORY MANUAL by Hewitt, Suchocki, and Hewitt, and the practice sheets in the PRACTICE BOOK, by the same authors. To obtain any of these ancillaries, contact your Addison-Wesley-Longman representative or regional sales office.

NEXT-TIME QUESTIONS (0-321-03539-9): These are in book form, on 8-1/2 x 11 standard pages. If you use an overhead projector, you can make transparencies from them to display at the end of your lectures. Or you can simply post them as is for your students as homework, or as food for thought. Each question has a cartoon and is hand lettered. On the back side of each question is an answer sheet, with the question reduced and repeated (as shown on facing page 4). Display each at the appropriate time. There are 143 next-time-questions, some for every chapter.

TEST BANK (0-321-03535-6) and the **TestGen-EQ COMPUTER TESTING SOFTWARE** (Win: 0-321-03533-X; Mac: 0-321-03534-8): The Test Bank has more than 2000 multiple-choice questions, with a much fewer number of short-answer exercises. They are rated by three levels of difficulty as well as by emphasis on mathematical or conceptual understanding. The software provides options to scramble questions, print different versions of a test, edit questions and answers, or add to and modify existing question files. It contains all of the items provided in the printed Test Bank. Documentation for the test-generating software and a description of how it works is contained in an accompanying booklet.

LABORATORY MANUAL (0-321-03531-3): The laboratory manual, 218 pages, by Hewitt, Suchocki, and Hewitt, is rich with simple activities to precede the coverage of course material, as well as experiments that apply course material. Instructions and answers to most of the lab questions are included in this manual, beginning on page 261.

Conceptual Physical Science PRACTICE BOOK (0-321-03531-3): This book of 90 practice sheets that helps students develop concepts is very different from traditional workbooks that are seen as drudgery by students. These are insightful and interesting activities that prompt your students to engage their minds and DO physical science. Used in class, they are ideal for cooperative learning. Out of class they play the role of a tutor. The book is low priced so it can be offered as a suggested supplement to the text in your student bookstore. Reduced practice pages with answers are at the back of the book, along with answers to the odd-numbered exercises and problems from the textbook.

Transparency Acetates (0-3212-03532-1) features more than 100 important figures from the text, which are available to qualified adopters from your Addison Wesley Longman rep.

VIDEOTAPES: For the physics part of *Conceptual Physical Science* is a video lecture series of 34 tapes *Conceptual Physics Alive!* for sale that features Paul Hewitt's classroom lectures while teaching Conceptual Physics at the University of Hawaii in 1989-1990. Also available for qualified adopters is a 1993 video tape of 28 physics and chemistry demonstrations performed by John Suchocki, which may be used in-class for such demos as the hard-to-do Bed of Nails and the Firewalk. Many of the demos offer a modest forum of ideas for classroom instruction. Also available is a more recent set of two videotapes that features two students exploring physical science principles (especially chemistry) in the kitchen and beyond. The 35 plus segments average over 3 minutes each. Like the demonstration video, they can be used either in or out of the classroom. Filmed in 1998, these segments are scheduled as part of the upcoming video lecture series *Conceptual Chemistry Alive!* that features John Suchocki. The tapes will accompany his soon to be printed solo text *Conceptual Chemistry*. Contact your Addison Wesley Longman sales rep for info on these videotapes.

CHALKBOARD ILLUSTRATION TECHNIQUES

I vividly remember as a student how annoyed I was with a professor who couldn't draw a simple cube in his lectures. He'd make an attempt, step back and look at it, wipe part of it from the board and patch it here and there with no improvement whatever, continue wiping and patching and finally settle for a "cube" with non-parallel sides. I thought, "He's forever overloading us with homework assignments that take up entire weekends and he won't take a few minutes of his own time to learn how to draw a simple cube." The professor probably never did learn to draw a cube and may still be bumbling at the board at cube-drawing time. If he were as inept in some physics topic during lecture he'd feel quite compelled to clean up his act in short order. But not so with "art." I think many instructors feel they are "scientists, not artists," and therefore have no responsibility to improve the "art" that is part of their lectures, or is avoided in their lectures. Unfortunately, they likely overestimate the effort required to draw well, and underestimate the value of drawing well. Only a small amount of practice is all that is required.

A step-by-step method for drawing a cube is shown at the right. The important thing is keeping the vertical lines vertical, and the other two sets of lines parallel to one another. Simply draw a "square" tilted for perspective, draw its twin slightly displaced, then connect the two with four parallel lines. For a finishing touch, wipe away part of the lines to indicate which lines are behind.

When my friend and colleague Dave Wall joined the physics faculty at CCSF about 15 years ago, he sat in on my conceptual physics class and was most impressed with my chalkboard illustrations — not that they well especially well drawn, but that they were drawn quickly. (Before getting into physics, I was a professional signpainter and silkscreen printer, and an amateur cartoonist, so I brought a talent for chalkboard illustrations with me into the teaching profession.) Dave told me that he wished he had a talent for drawing that he could bring to his lectures. He wanted very much to be a good classroom lecturer, for

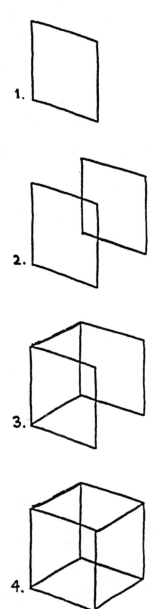

1.

2.

3.

4.

WIPE AWAY BACKGROUND LINES WITH FINGER!

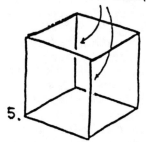

5.

he knew that instructors who are good in class have altogether more satisfying careers than instructors who somehow don't connect with their classes. He was more than willing to put whatever effort was required to improve his instruction, so when I told him I'd give him a couple of lessons in drawing, he was estatic. I asked him to first select cartoons in comic strips from the Sunday newspaper that he would most like to be able to draw. So he brought in Andy Capp. I had Dave copy Andy Capp on the chalkboard. Why copy? Because Andy Capp's creator spent many years developing the few lines that show how Andy Capp walks — the posture, the position of the legs and feet, the arms and hands, all the result of not only a great talent, but years of embellishment. Better to start with a rendition of Andy Capp and have the "lines right" than to begin at ground zero. When Dave had some semblance of Andy Capp on the board, I asked him to copy his own drawing, using less lines. Then the same again until he had something better. So my advice to Dave and to all of you is to begin by copying the work of the professionals. Then after you can do that, add your own touch of "originality." Dave was bolstered by the surprise that he could draw after all, and from that semester on, has been and is a very proficient chalkboard illustrator.

Stick figures are easiest to draw. Excellent stick figures by Eric Rogers are shown in his classic text, "Physics For The Inquiring Mind," Princeton University Press, 1960. If you learn to draw a few of these, you'll be doing yourself and your students a service. You can go one step further and use double lines for a full figure, as shown. Either way is effective.

The number of basic drawings that I do in my classes is surprisingly small — less than a dozen. Variations on a few basic drawings results in many drawings. For example, both a person running along the street and a person pitching a ball, with minor changes, are one basic drawing. This is shown on the following pages, on the step-by-step illustrations that I suggest you copy a few times on a chalkboard. Take your time with them and after you can make your own renditions, then work on speed. If after much practice your drawings take too long to draw, try stick figures, for effectiveness depends not on how well your drawings look, but on the quickness with which you draw them. You're highly successful when you can casually draw an illustration at about the pace you write a formula on the board. So give these a try, then try copying your favorite comic strip figures. Good Energy!

Draw Me ... Step by step!

1.   2.   3.   4.   5.   6.   7.   8.

8

Draw Me ... Step by step!

1.

2.

3.

4.

5.

6.

7.

8.

9.

10.

9

Draw Me ... Step by step!

Prologue: About Science

Mathematics and Scientific Measurements
The Scientific Method
The Scientific Attitude
Science, Art, and Religion
Science and Technology
Physics, Chemistry, Geology, and Astronomy

Much of this prologue can be regarded as a personal essay by the authors, and hence is not a chapter. Unlike other texts that begin with the customary treatment of measurements, significant figures, and system of measurements (that are anything but exciting to most students) we begin with the early role of measurements of the Earth, Moon, and Sun, by Erathosthenes and Aristarchus. This high-interest treatment, which was featured in the Prologue of the First Edition, has been scrapped in this edition. It made the Prologue too long, and unfortunately, placing it at the beginning of the astronomy material in Part 8 also found it making the chapter too long. But alas, at the 11th hour we found room for it at the end of the *Conceptual Physical Science Practice Book*—pages 209-212. See more on this treatment in the excellent book *Physics for the Inquiring Mind*, by Eric Rogers, 1960, Princeton University Press (which was a main resource to me when I first started teaching).

The roots of science are found in every culture. The Chinese discovered printing, the compass, and rockets; Islam cultures developed algebra and lenses; mathematicians in India developed the concept of zero and infinity. This text, nevertheless, emphasizes western science. Science did advance faster in western rather than eastern cultures, largely because of the different social and political climates. While early Greeks in an era of experimental democracy and free thinking were questioning their speculations about the world, their counterparts in the more authoritarian eastern parts of the world were largely occupied in absorbing the knowledge of their forebearers. In regions like China, absorbing this knowledge was the key to personal success. So scientific progress in eastern cultures was without the early period of questioning that accelerated the scientific advances of Europe and Eurasia. In any event, it is important to emphasize throughout your course that science is a human activity that answers questions of human interest. It is done by and for humans.

You may consider elaborating on the idea about the possible *wrongness* **versus** **rightness** of ideas; a practice that characterizes science. This is generally misunderstood, for it is not generally a criterion in other disciplines. State that it is the prerogative of science, in contrast to the speculative procedures of philosophy and metaphysics, to embrace only ideas that can be tested and to disregard the rest. Ideas that can't be tested are not necessarily wrong — they are simply useless insofar as advancement in scientific knowledge is concerned. Ideas must be verifiable by other scientists. In this way science tends to be self-correcting.

Expand on the idea that **honesty in science** is not only a matter of public interest, but is a matter of self interest. Any scientist who misrepresents or fudges data, or is caught lying about scientific information, is ostracized by the scientific community. There are no second chances. The high standards for acceptable performance in science, unfortunately, do not extend to other fields that are as important to the human condition. For example, consider the standards of performance required of politicians.

Distinguish between *hypothesis, theory, fact*, and *concept*. Point out that theory and hypothesis are not the same. A **theory** applies to a synthesis of a large body of information. The criterion of a theory is not whether it is true or untrue, but rather whether it is useful or non useful. It is useful even though the ultimate causes of the phenomena it encompasses are unknown. For example, we accept the theory of gravitation as a useful synthesis of available knowledge that relates to the mutual attraction of bodies. The theory can be refined, or with new information it can take on a new direction. It is important to acknowledge the common misunderstanding of what a scientific theory is, as revealed by those who say, "But it is not a fact; it is *only* a theory." Many people have the mistaken notion that a theory is tentative or speculative, while a fact is absolute.

Impress upon your class that a **fact** is not immutable and absolute, but is generally a close agreement by competent observers of a series of observations of the same phenomena. The observations must be testable. Since the activity of science is the determination of the most probable, there are no absolutes. Facts that were held to be absolute in the past are seen altogether differently in the light of present-day knowledge.

By **concept**, we mean the intellectual framework that is part of a theory. We speak of the concept of time, the concept of energy, or the concept of a force field. Time is related to motion in space and is the substance of the Theory of Special Relativity. We find that energy exists in tiny grains, or quanta, which is a central concept in the Quantum Theory. An important concept in Newton's Theory of Universal Gravitation is the idea of a force field that surrounds a material body. A concept envelops the overriding idea that underlies various phenomena. Thus, when we think "conceptually" we envelop a generalized way of looking at things.

Prediction in science is different from prediction in other areas. In the everyday sense, one speaks of predicting what has not yet occurred, like whether or not it will rain next weekend. In science, however, prediction is not so much about what *will* happen, but about what *is* happening and is not yet noticed, like what the properties of a hypothetical particle are and are not. A scientist predicts what can and cannot happen, rather than what will or will not happen.

Science and technology — In discussions of science and technology and their side effects, a useful statement is: *You can never do just one thing.* Doing *this* affects *that.* This is similar to "there is never just one force" in discussions of Newton's third law.

"Any sufficiently advanced society is indistinguishable from magic." Arthur C. Clark

Science and religion Einstein said "Science without religion is deaf; religion without science is blind." The topic of religion in a science text is rare. We treat it briefly only to address what is foremost on many student's minds. Do religion and science contradict each other? Must one must choose between them? We hope our very brief treatment presents a satisfactory answer to these questions. Your feedback on this matter will be appreciated.

With regard to science courses and liberal arts courses, there is a central factor that makes it difficult for liberal arts students to delve into science courses the way that science students can delve into liberal arts courses — and that's the vertical nature of science courses. They build upon each other, as noted by their prerequisites. A science student can take an intermediate course in literature, poetry, or history at any time, and in any order. But in no way can a humanities student take an intermediate physics or chemistry course without first having a foundation in elementary physics and mathematics. Hence the importance of this conceptual course.

Except for the measurements by early Greek scientists, we do not lecture about Prologue material and instead assign it as reading. It can be omitted without interfering with the following chapters.

Two activities in the **Conceptual Physical Science Laboratory Manual** complement this chapter. They are *Tuning up the Senses*, which enhances perception, and *Making Cents*, which introduces the use of a massing balance and the making of a simple graph.

There is one page for this material in the **Next-Time Questions** book.

A teacher's influence knows no bounds — Our immortality begins with our students!

Motion

I

Speed
Galileo Galilei (1564—1642)
Speed is Relative
Velocity
Velocity Vectors
Acceleration
Free Fall
How Fast
How Far
Link to Sports — Hang Time
Hang Time

DO NOT SPEND TOO MUCH TIME ON THIS CHAPTER!! Doing so is the greatest pacing mistake in teaching physics! Time spent on kinematics is time not spent on why satellites don't fall, why high temperatures and high voltages (for the same reason) can be safe to touch, why rainbows are round, why the sky is blue, and how nuclear reactions keep the Earth's interior molten. Even if you don't get into chemistry, geology, and astronomy, too much time on this chapter is folly. Make the distinction between speed, velocity, and acceleration, plant the seeds for the idea of inertia, and move quickly to Chapter 2. (We typically spend only *one* class lecture on this chapter without vectors, and two periods with vectors.) **By all means, avoid the temptation to get into the classic motion problems that involve 90% math and 10% physics!** Too much treatment of motion analysis can be counter productive to stimulating an early student interest in physical science. Tell your class that you're skimming the chapter so you'll have more time for more interesting topics in your course — let them know they shouldn't expect to master this material, and that mastery will be expected in later material (that doesn't have the stumbling blocks of kinematics). Its okay not to fully understand this first part of your course. As stated earlier: *Just as wisdom is knowing what to overlook, good teaching is knowing what to omit.*

Vectors as a physics tool go back only about 100 years—introduced by Oliver Heaviside in England and developed by Gibbs in USA.

My good friend Chelcie Liu teaches instantaneous velocity by supposing the velocity of free fall is measured with a pair of photogates. The photogates will record the time difference as the falling object falls between them. Knowing the distance between the gates and the time, the average speed is calculated. But it is the average speed, mind you! How does this average speed compare with the instantaneous speed of the object as it falls within the gates? It depends on how close the gates are to each other. As the gates are brought closer and closer together, the range of instantaneous speeds is closer to the average speed. And in the limit, where we approach zero space between the gates, the average speed and the instantaneous speed are one in the same. So a bit of conceptual calculus!

Some tidbits from Peter J. Brancazio, physics prof and sports buff from Brooklyn College in New York (*Just a Second*, March 91, Discover):

• Carl Lewis has run 100 m in 9.92 s. At this speed Carl covers 10.1 m per second. But because he starts from rest and accelerates up to speed, his top speed is more than this — about 10% over his average speed.

• Downhill skiers attain speeds of 70 to 80 mph on winding runs inclined about 10 - 15°. A speed of 70 mph is 102.7 ft/s, which means a skier covers 10.3 ft in 0.1 s. Even quicker are speed skiers, who ski slopes inclined up to 50° at speeds up to 139 mph or 204 ft/s. At this speed a skier could cover the length of a football field in 1.5 s. (This is faster than a skydiver falls in spread-eagle position.)

• Baseball pitchers such as Roger Clemens and Nolan Ryan can throw a baseball nearly 100 mph. Since the pitcher's mound is 60.5 feet from home plate, the ball takes less than 1/2 second to get to the batter. Due to the pitcher's reach, actual distance is about 55 feet. Because

13

of air drag, a 95 mph ball slows to about 87 mph, giving a travel time of 0.41 s. On average it takes 0.2 s for a batter to get his bat from its cocked position up to speed in the hitting zone, so he must react to the pitcher's motion in a quarter-second or less, beginning his swing when the ball is only a little more than half the distance to the plate. These abilities and reflexes are rarities!

• Michael Jordan's hang time is less than 0.9 seconds (discussed in the box *Hang Time* in the text). Height jumped is less than 4 feet (those who insist a hang time of 2 s are way off, for 1 s up is 16 feet — clearly, no way!). A neat rule of thumb is that height jumped in feet is equal to four times hang time squared $(d = g/2 \ (T/2)^2 = g/2 \ T^2/4 = g/8 \ T^2 = 4 \ T^2)$.

I feel compelled to interject here (as I mean to stress all through this manual) the importance of the "check with your neighbor" technique of teaching. Please do not spend your lecture talking to yourself in front of your class! The procedure of the "check with your neighbor" routine keeps you and your class together. I can't stress enough its importance for effective teaching!

Take care about being seduced by the wonderful tools of graphical analysis. Like the astronomer whose love is more for telescopes than stars, many instructors are more enamored with ticker timers, sonic rangers, and computers, than the concepts they illustrate. A big reason for kinematics getting overtime. We instructors love graphical analysis. But I think students, given a choice between learning to plot motion graphs and learning to analyze rainbows, would prefer rainbows. If there is time left at the end of the course, after "rainbows," why not then bring out the ticker timers and computer graphing tools?

The first page of the **Practice Book** treats the distinction between velocity acquired and distance fallen for free fall via a freely-falling speedometer-odometer. The second page treats constant velocity and accelerated motion, and the third introduces vectors and the elegant but simple parallelogram rule. Students *do* learn from these, in class or out of class, so whether you have your students buy their own from your bookstore or you photocopy select pages for class distribution, get these sheets to your students.

The activity in the **Laboratory Manual**, *Reaction Time* makes very nice use of the equation $d = 1/2gt^2$. Quite worthwhile. Perchance you feel you have time to teach graphical analysis, be sure to consider the lab *Graphing with Sonar*, which features the sonic ranger device. This is conceptual graphing at its best, and if not done as a lab experiment, can be demonstrated as part of your lecture. Only in Appendix II of the Lab Manual is motion described with graphs.

There are 5 questions for this chapter in the **Next-Time Questions** book. As stated earlier, use these as a way to close your lectures, or post them for viewing. After your students are sufficiently teased, show the answers.

The distinction between velocity and acceleration, and how vectors combine and are resolved, are prerequisite to the following chapters on mech-anics.

SUGGESTED LECTURE PRESENTATION

Start by holding up the textbook and remarking on its vast amount of information. A look at the table of contents shows there is much to cover. Whereas some material will be covered in depth, some will not. State that they will come to feel quite comfortable with an understanding of much of the content, but not all. There isn't time for a thorough treatment of all material. So rather than bear down at the beginning of your course and end up racing over material at semester's end, you're going to do it the other way around, and race through Chapter 1 to have time for more interesting physics later! Rather than tilling this soil with a deep plow setting, you're going to skim it and dig in later.

Your first question: What means of motion has done more to change the way cities are built than any other? [Answer: The elevator!]

Explain the importance of simplifying. That motion is best understood if you first neglect the effects of air drag, the effects of buoyancy, spin, and the shape of moving objects — that beneath these are simple relationships that might otherwise be masked by these considerations, and that these *relationships* are what Chapter 1 and your lecture are about. Add that by completely neglecting the effects of air resistance not only exposes the simple relationships, but is a reasonable assumption for heavy and compact (dense) objects traveling at moderate speeds; e.g., one would notice no difference between the rates of fall of a heavy rock dropped from the classroom ceiling to the floor below, when falling through either air or a complete vacuum. For a feather and heavy objects moving at high speeds, air resistance does become important, and will be treated in Chapter 2.

Mention that there are few pure examples in physics, for most real situations involve a combination of effects. There is usually a "first order" effect that is basic to the situation, but then there are 2nd, 3rd, and even 4th or more order effects that interact also. If we begin our study of some concept by considering all effects together before we have studied their contributions separately, understanding is likely to be difficult. To have a better understanding of what is going on, we strip a situation of all but the first order effect, and then examine that. Only when that is well in hand, then we proceed to investigate the other effects for a fuller understanding.

My lectures never cover all that is in a chapter, which I leave to reading. In any discussion of Galileo, emphasize that he asked *how* things move, not *why* they move.

> DEMONSTRATION: Here's a simple and nice one: Drop a sheet of paper and a book, side by side. Of course the book falls faster, due to its greater weight compared to air drag. (Interestingly, the air drag is greater for the faster-falling book — an idea you'll return to in Chapter 2.) Now place the paper against the lower surface of the raised horizontally-held book and when you drop them, nobody is surprised to see they fall together. The book has pushed the paper with it. Now repeat with the paper on *top* of the book and ask for predictions and neighbor discussion. Then surprise your class by refusing to show it! Tell them to try it out of class! (Good teaching isn't giving answers, but raising good questions — good enough to prompt wondering. Let students discover that the book will "plow through the air" leaving an air-resistance free path for the paper to follow!)

Speed, Velocity, and Acceleration Define speed, writing its equation in longhand form on the board while giving examples — automobile speedometers, etc. Similarly define velocity, then acceleration. State there are three controls in an automobile that make the auto accelerate. Ask for them (accelerator, brakes, and steering wheel). State how one lurches in a vehicle that is undergoing acceleration, especially for circular motion, and state why the definition of velocity includes direction to make the definition of acceleration all-encompassing. Talk of how without lurching one cannot sense motion, giving examples of coin flipping in a high-speed aircraft versus doing the same when the same aircraft is at rest on the runway.

Vectors Begin by stating that if one were to be sitting next to a physicist on a long bus ride, and the physicist were attempting to explain some physical idea on the back of an envelope, that the physicist would likely make extensive use of little arrows. These little arrows, that illustrate size and direction, are part of a physicist's language. They are *vectors*. Then explain how vectors make the ground speed of an airplane flying in the wind easier to understand — flying with the wind, against the wind, and then cross wind. Avoid information overload by avoiding cases that aren't parallel or at right angles to the wind. Notice the text confines vectors to those for velocity. Take care if you introduce force vectors at this point. Force and velocity vectors in a vector diagram is an invitation to confusion — what you don't need at this point in your course.

Units for Acceleration Give numerical examples of acceleration in units of kilometers/hour per second to establish the idea of acceleration. Be sure that your students are working on the examples with you. For example, ask them to find the acceleration of a car that goes from rest to 100 km/hr in 10 seconds. It is important that you not use examples involving seconds twice until they taste success with the easier kilometers/hour per second examples. Have them check their work with their neighbors as you go along. Only after they get the hang of it, introduce the units meters/second/second in your examples to develop a sense for the units m/s^2.

Falling Objects If you round 9.8 m/s^2 to 10 m/s^2 in your lecture, you'll more easily establish the relationships between velocity and distance. Later you can then move to the more precise 9.8 m/s^2, in accord with the following chapters.

> CHECK QUESTION: If an object is dropped from an initial position of rest from the top of a cliff, how *fast* will it be traveling at the end of one second? (You might add, "Write the answer on your note paper." And then, "Look at your neighbor's paper — if your neighbor doesn't have the right answer, reach over and help him or her — talk about it." And then possibly, "If your neighbor isn't very cooperative, sit somewhere else next time!")

After explaining the answer when class discussion dies down, repeat the process asking for the speed at the end of 2 seconds, and then for 10 seconds. This leads you into stating the relationship $v = gt$, which by now you can express in shorthand notation. After any questions, discussion, and examples, state that you are going to pose a different question — not asking for how *fast*, but for how *far*. Ask how far the object falls in one second. Ask for a written response and then ask if the students could explain to their neighbors *why* the distance is only 5 m rather than 10 m. After they've discussed this for almost a minute or so, ask "If you maintain a speed of 60 km/hr for one hour, how far do you go?" — then, "If you maintain a speed of 10 m/s for one second, how far do you go?" Important point: You'll appreciably improve your instruction if you allow some thinking time after you ask a question. Not doing so is the folly of too many instructors. Then continue, "Then why is the answer to the first question not 10 meters?" After a suitable time, stress the idea of *average* velocity and the relation $d = vt$.

Show the general case by deriving on the board $d = 1/2 \ gt^2$. (We tell our students that the derivation is a sidelight to the course — something that will be the crux of a follow-up physics course. In any event, the derivation is not something that we expect of them, but is to show that $d = 1/2 \ gt^2$ is a reasoned statement that doesn't just pop up from nowhere.)

CHECK QUESTION: How far will a freely falling object that is released from rest, fall in 2 seconds? In 10 seconds? (When your class is comfortable with this, then ask how far in 1/2 second.)

To avoid information overload, we restrict all numerical examples of free fall to cases that begin at rest. Why? Because it's simpler that way. (We prefer our students understand simple physics than be confused about not-so-simple physics!) We do go this far with them.

CHECK QUESTION: Consider a rifle fired straight downward from a high-altitude balloon. If the muzzle velocity is 100 m/s and air resistance can be neglected, what is the *acceleration* of the bullet after one second? (If most of your class say that its *g*, you're on!)

What we do *not* do is ask for the time of fall for a freely-falling object, given the distance. Why? Unless the distance given is the familiar 5 meters, algebraic manipulation is called for. If one of our teaching objectives were to teach algebra, this would be a nice place to do it. But we don't have time to present this stumbling block and then teach how to overcome it. We'd rather put our energy *and theirs* into straight physics!

Hang Time As strange as it first may seem, the longest time a jumper can remain in air is less than a second. It is a common illusion that jumping times are more. Even Michael Jordan's best *hang time* (the time the feet are off the ground) is 0.9 second. Then $d = 1/2 \ gt^2$ predicts how high a jumper can go vertically. For a hang time of a full second, that's 1/2 s up and 1/2 s down. Substituting, $d = 5(0.5)^2 = 1.25$ m (which is about 4 feet)! So the great athletes and ballet dancers jump vertically no more than 4 feet high! Of course one can clear a higher fence or bar; but one's *center of gravity* cannot be raised more than 4 feet in free jumping. In fact very few people can jump 2 feet high! To test this, stand against a wall with arms upstretched. Mark the wall at the highest point. Then jump, and at the top, again mark the wall. For a human being, the distance between marks is at most 4 feet! We'll return to hang time for running jumps when we discuss projectile motion in Chapter 4.

NEXT-TIME QUESTION: For OHT or posting. Note on the next page a sample reduced page from the *Next-Time Questions* book, full 8-1/2 x ll, just right for OHTs. At least one of these Next-Time Questions, each with answer on the back, is available for every chapter in the text. Consider displaying NTQs in some general area outside the classroom — perhaps in a glass case. This display generates general student interest, as students in your class and those not in your class are stimulated to think physical science. After a few days of posting, then turn the sheets over to reveal the answers. That's when new NTQs can be displayed. How better to adorn your school corridors! Because of space limitations, those for other chapters are not shown in this manual.

[State the usefulness of solving the "Bikes and the Bee" problem with the formula $d = vt$. The key to solving this problem is considering time *t*. Whether or not one thinks about time should not be a matter of cleverness or good insight, but a matter of letting the formula dictate the variables to consider in handling an idea. The *v* is given, but the time *t* is not. The formula instructs you to consider time. Formulas are important in guiding our thinking about things.]

Throughout your course, consider posing questions like, "How many steps would you take if you walked from your city to a particular neighboring city — and how long would it take to make the trip?" Such order-of-magnitude guesstimates, called "Fermi questions" (after the physicist Enrico Fermi who posed them often to his students) are much more stimulating than problems that list variables and ask for specific unknowns. Like, "How many piano tuners are there in Chicago?" One has to make guesses about how many people in one hundred have pianos, how often pianos need to be tuned, how many people live in Chicago, how many pianos can be tuned per day, and so on. One can then check the "Yellow Pages" to see the closeness of the estimate. Others include estimating the amount of rubber that comes off a tire per revolution — the weight of water that falls on your city when rainfall is reported as so many inches in say an hour — how many cars per hour can pass through a certain tunnel per hour if the speed limit is 35 mph — whether or not Los Angeles could be supplied by trucking in water. if its water supply were cut off — how many toothpicks can be made by a tree, and how many trees are needed to keep Americans supplied for toothpicks in one year — if you read 300 words per minute, how many books could you read in a year if you read for an hour and a half per day?

At the risk of overstressing the obvious, your course will be much more successful when you make use of the ancillaries — particularly the Practice Sheets, and the Next-Time Questions as sampled below. If you're an overhead-projector person, then make use of the OHTs that come with this program. And check out the videos of physics and chemistry lectures, which are great whenever you're absent from class. The videotapes also make a valued prize to students when you let them borrow them for home viewing.

CONCEPTUAL **Physical Science**

WHEN THE 10 km/h BIKES ARE 20 km APART, A BEE BEGINS FLYING FROM ONE WHEEL TO THE OTHER AT A STEADY SPEED OF 30 km/h. WHEN IT GETS TO THE WHEEL, IT ABRUPTLY TURNS AROUND AND FLIES BACK TO TOUCH THE FIRST WHEEL, THEN TURNS AROUND AND KEEPS REPEATING THE BACK-AND-FORTH TRIP UNTIL THE BIKES MEET, AND ⸚SQUISH!⸚

10 km/h .... 30 km/h .... 10 km/h

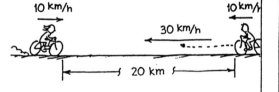

|← 20 km →|

QUESTION

HOW MANY KILOMETERS DID THE BEE TRAVEL IN ITS TOTAL BACK-AND-FORTH TRIPS ?

CHAP. 1

CONCEPTUAL **Physical Science**

WHEN THE 10 km/h BIKES ARE 20 km APART, A BEE BEGINS FLYING FROM ONE WHEEL TO THE OTHER AT A STEADY SPEED OF 30 km/h. WHEN IT GETS TO THE WHEEL, IT ABRUPTLY TURNS AROUND AND FLIES BACK TO TOUCH THE FIRST WHEEL, THEN TURNS AROUND AND KEEPS REPEATING THE BACK-AND-FORTH TRIP UNTIL THE BIKES MEET, AND ⸚SQUISH!⸚

QUESTION

HOW MANY KILOMETERS DID THE BEE TRAVEL IN ITS TOTAL BACK-AND-FORTH TRIPS ?

10 km/h .... 30 km/h .... 10 km/h

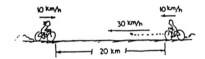

|← 20 km →|

SOLUTION:

LET THE EQUATION FOR DISTANCE BE A GUIDE TO THINKING :

$$d = \bar{v}\,t$$

WE KNOW $\bar{v}$ = 30 km/h, AND WE MUST FIND THE TIME t. WE CONSIDER THE SAME TIME FOR THE BIKES AND SEE IT TAKES 1 HOUR FOR THEM TO MEET, SINCE EACH TRAVELS 10 km AT A SPEED OF 10 km/h. SO,

$$d = \bar{v}\,t = 30\ km/h \times 1\ h = 30\ km$$

THE BEE TRAVELED A TOTAL OF 30 km.

CHAP. 1

2

Newton's Laws of Motion

Newton's First Law of Motion
    Mass
        | Isaac Newton (1642—1727) |
Newton's Second Law of Motion
    When Acceleration is Zero — Equilibrium
    When Acceleration is g — Free Fall
    When Acceleration is Less than g — Nonfree Fall
Newton's Third Law of Motion

Acceleration, inertia, and falling objects as introduced in Chapter 1, are further developed in this chapter. In the treatment of Newton's 1st law the distinction between mass and weight is emphasized, but very little attention is given to units of measurement. (Because we think time spent on this is better spent on physical science concepts.) A brief treatment of units and systems of measurement is provided in Appendix A.

It is useful to represent magnitudes with numerical quantities from time to time. An option that sometimes better makes the point is the exaggerated symbol technique that is shown on text page 46 and later in following chapters.

This chapter is central to the study of mechanics. It is reinforced with 5 exercises from the student **Practice Book.** You may or may not be interested in the *Force-Vector Diagrams* sheet, but it's a must if you treat problem solving.

There is an activity/experiment pair, *Dropping and Dragging, I* and *II*, in the **Laboratory Manual** to complement this chapter. The pair is the classic cart pulled across the table by a falling weight — first qualitatively, then quantitatively. Specific instructions are *not* given for doing these, the intent being that students devise.

There are more than a dozen **Next-Time Questions** for this important chapter — so you can use different ones in different semesters.

You may find that this most central part of classical mechanics and the following suggested lecture may span 3 or 4 class periods.

SUGGESTED LECTURE PRESENTATION

Newton's 1st Law Begin by pointing to an object in the room and stating that if it started moving, one would reasonably look for a cause for its motion. We would say that a force of some kind was responsible, which would seem reasonable. Tie this idea to the notion of force maintaining motion as Aristotle saw it. State that a cannonball remains at rest in the cannon until a force is applied, and that the force of expanding gases drives the ball out of the barrel when it is fired. But what keeps the cannonball moving when the gases no longer act on it? This leads you into a discussion of inertia. In the everyday sense, inertia refers to a habit or a rut. In physics it's another word for laziness, or the resistance to change as far as the state of motion of an object is concerned. Roll the ball along the lecture table to show its tendency to keep rolling. Inertia was first introduced by Galileo's with his inclined plane experiments.

DEMONSTRATION: Show that inertia refers also to objects at rest with the classic *table-cloth-and-dishes demonstration.* [Be sure to pull the tablecloth slightly downward so there is no upward component of force on the dishes!] We precede this demo with a simpler version, a simple block of wood on a piece of cloth — but with a twist. We ask what the block will do when we suddenly whip the cloth toward us. After a neighbor check, we surprise the class when they see that the block has been stapled to the cloth! This illustrates Newton's zeroth law — be skeptical. Then we follow up with the classic tablecloth demo. Don't think the classic demo is too corny, for your students will really love it.

(Of course when we show a demonstration to illustrate a particular concept, there is almost always more than one concept involved. The tablecloth demo is no exception, which also illustrates impulse and momentum (Chapter 3 stuff). The plates experience two impulses; one that first involves the friction between the cloth and dishes, which moves them slightly toward you. It is brief and very little momentum builds up. Once the dishes are no longer on the cloth, a second impulse occurs due to friction between the dishes and table, which acts in a direction away from you and prevents the dishes from sliding toward you. This brief impulse brings the dishes to rest. Done quickly, the brief displacement of the dishes is hardly noticed. Is inertia really at work here? Yes, for if there were no friction in the demo, the dishes would strictly remain at rest.

DEMONSTRATION: Continuing with inertia, do as Jim Szeszol does and fashion a wire coat hanger into an m shape as shown. Two globs of clay are stuck to each end. Balance it on your head, with one glob in front of your face. State you wish to view the other blob and ask how you can do so without touching the apparatus. Then simply turn around an look at it. It's like the bowl of soup you turn only to find the soup stays put. Inertia in action! (Of course, like the tablecloth demo, there is more physics here than inertia; this demo can also be used to illustrate rotational inertia and the conservation of angular momentum.)

A useful way to impart the idea of mass and inertia is to place two objects, say a pencil and a piece of chalk, in the hands of a student and ask for a judgment of which is heavier. The student will likely respond by shaking them, one in each hand. Point out that in so doing the student is really comparing their inertias, and is making use of the intuitive knowledge that weight and inertia are directly proportional to each other.

Mass vs. Weight: To distinguish between mass and weight compare the efforts of pushing horizontally on a block of slippery ice on a frozen pond versus lifting it. Or consider the weightlessness of a massive anvil in outer space and how it would be difficult to shake, weight or not weight. And if moving toward you, it would be harmful to be in its way because of its great tendency to remain in motion. The following

demo (often used to illustrate impulse and momentum) makes the distinction nicely:

DEMONSTRATION: Hang a massive ball by a string and show that the top string breaks when the bottom is pulled with gradually more force, but the bottom string breaks when the string is jerked. Ask which of these cases illustrates weight. [Interestingly enough, it's the weight of the ball that makes for the greater tension in the top string.] Then ask which of these cases illustrates inertia. [When jerked, the tendency of the ball to resist the sudden downward acceleration, its inertia, is responsible for the lower string breaking.] This is the best demo we know of for showing the different effects of weight and mass.

DEMONSTRATION: An unforgettable follow-up to the previous demo is lying on your back and having an assistant place a blacksmith's anvil on your stomach and then striking it rather hard with a sledge hammer. The principles here are the same as the ball and string demo. Both the inertia of the ball and the inertial of the anvil resist the changes in motion they would otherwise undergo. So the string doesn't break, and your body is not squashed. (Be sure that your assistant is good with the hammer. When I, Paul Hewitt, began teaching I used to trust students to the task. In my fourth year the student who volunteered was extra nervous in front of the class and missed the anvil entirely — but not me. The hammer smashed into my hand breaking two fingers. I was lucky I was not harmed more.).

Relate the idea of tightening a hammer head, Figure 2.3, with the bones of the human spine, and how as a result of jostling all day, we are a bit shorter at night. Ask your students to find a place in their homes that they can't quite reach before going to bed — a place that is one or two centimeters higher than their reach. Then tell them to try again when they awake the next morning. Unforgettable, for you are likely instructing them to discover something about themselves they were not aware of!

DEMONSTRATION: Follow the hammer bit with a broom handle or wooden dowel that fits rather snugly in a hole through a few-kilogram wooden block. When held as shown, they stay together due to friction. Strike the top

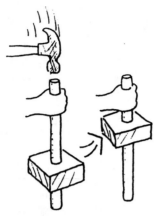

of the dowel with a hammer and voila, the block climbs the handle! The block tends to stay put while the handle suddenly moves downward. More inertia in action.

DEMONSTRATION: Do as Marshall Ellenstein does and place a metal hoop atop a narrow jar. On top of the hoop balance a piece of chalk. Then whisk the hoop away and the chalk falls neatly into the narrow opening. The key here is grabbing the hoop on the inside, on the side farthest from your sweep. This elongates the hoop horizontally and the part that supports the chalk drops from beneath the chalk. (If you grab the hoop on the near side, the elongation will be vertical and pop the chalk up into the air!)

Stand facing a wall and jump up. Then ask why the wall does not smash into you as the earth rotates under you while you're airborne. Relate this to the idea of a helicopter ascending over San Francisco, waiting motionless for 3 hours and waiting until Washington DC. appears below, then descending. Hooray, this would be a neat way to fly cross country! Except, of course, for the fact that the "stationary" helicopter remains in motion with the ground below. "Stationary" with respect to the stars, means it would have to fly as fast as the earth turns (what jets attempt to do!).

Newton's 2nd Law Briefly review the idea of acceleration and its definition, and state that it is produced by an imposed force. Write this as $a \sim F$ and give examples of doubling the force and the resulting doubling of the acceleration, etc. Introduce the idea of net force, with appropriate examples — like applying twice the force to a stalled car gives it twice as much acceleration — three times the force, three times the acceleration.

Units of Force—Newtons: I suggest not making a big deal about the unfamiliar unit of force—the newton. I simply state it is the unit of force used by physicists, and if students find themselves uncomfortable with it, simply think of "pounds" in its place. Relative magnitudes, rather than actual magnitudes, are the emphasis of conceptual physics anyway. Show a 1-kg mass and then suspend it from a spring scale. If the scale is calibrated in newtons, it will read 9.8 N. If the scale is calibrated in pounds it will read 2.2 pounds. State that you're not going to waste good time in conversions between units (students can do enough of that in one of those dull physics courses they've heard about).

CHECK QUESTION: Which has more mass, a 1-kg stone or a 1-lb stone? [A 1-kg stone has more mass, for it weighs 2.2 lb. But we're not going to make a big deal about such conversions. If the units newtons bugs you, think of it as a unit of force or weight in a foreign language for now!]

Shift to *static* examples, where the net force is zero as evidenced by zero acceleration. Hold an object at rest in your hand, say a 1-kg mass that weighs 9.8 N, and ask what is the net force on the object. Be sure they distinguish between the 9.8 N gravitational force on the object and the zero net force on it — as evidenced by its zero acceleration. Then suspend the same object from a spring scale and show the 9.8-N reading. The scale is pulling up on the object, with just as much force as the earth is pulling down on it. Pretend to step on a bathroom scale. Ask how much gravity is pulling on you. This is evident by the scale reading. Then ask what the net force is that acts on you. This is evident by your absence of acceleration. Consider two scales, one foot on each, and ask how each scale would read. Then ask how the scales would read if you shifted your weight more on one than the other. Ask is there is a rule to guide the answers to these questions. Before answering, go into the following skit.

Signpainter Skit: Draw on the board the sketch to the left below, which shows two painters on a painting rig suspended by two ropes. Step 1: If both painters have the same weight and each stands next to a rope, the supporting force in the ropes will be equal. If spring scales, one on each rope, were used, the forces in the ropes would be

evident. Ask what the scale reading in each rope would be in this case. [The answer is each rope will support the weight of one man + half the weight of the rig — both scales will show equal readings.] Step 2: Suppose one painter walks toward the other as shown in the sketch at below, which you draw on the chalkboard (or show via overhead projector).Will the reading in the left rope increase? Will the reading in the right rope

decrease? Grand question: Will the reading in the left rope increase exactly as much as the tension in the right rope decreases? And if so, how does either rope "know" about the change in the other rope? After neighbor discussion, be sure to emphasize that the answers to these questions lie in the framework of Newton's second law, $a = F_{net}/m$. Since there is no acceleration, the net force must be zero, which means the upward support forces supplied by the ropes must add up to the downward force of gravity on the two men and the rig. So a decrease in one rope must necessarily be met with a corresponding increase in the other. (This example is dear to my heart. When I was a signpainter and before I had any training in physics, my sign-painting buddy, Burl Grey, posed this question to me. He didn't know the answer, nor did I. That was because neither he nor I had a model for analyzing the problem. We didn't know about Newton's second law, and therefore didn't think in terms of zero acceleration and a corresponding zero net force. How different one's thinking is when one has or does not have a model to guide it. If Burl and I had been mystical in our thinking, we might have been more concerned with how each rope "knows" about the condition of the other. This is the approach that intrigues many people with a nonscientific view of the world.)

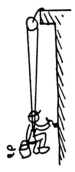

SKIT: Harry the painter swings year after year from his boson's chair. He weighs 500 N and the rope, unknown to Harry, has a breaking point of 300 N. Ask the class if the rope should break when attached as shown to the left. One day Harry is painting near a flagpole

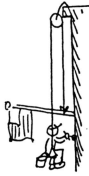

and to be different, he ties the free end of the rope to the flagpole instead of to his chair. Why was this Harry's last day on the job?

Forces at an Angle: The text doesn't treat the tensions in ropes at an angle. Ample cases are developed in the Practice Book. As a demonstration support a heavy weight with a pair of scales as shown. Show that as the angles are wider, the tensions increase. This explains why one can safely hang from a couple of strands of vertical clothesline, but can't when the clothesline is horizontally strung. Interesting stuff.

DEMONSTRATION: Have two students hold the ends of a heavy chain. Ask them to pull it horizontally to make it as straight as possible. Then ask what happens if a bird comes along and sits in the middle (as you place a 1-kg hook mass on the middle of the chain!). What happens if another bird comes to join the first (as you suspend another 1-kg mass)? Ask the students to keep the chain level. Now what happens if a flock of birds join the others (as you hang additional masses). This works well!

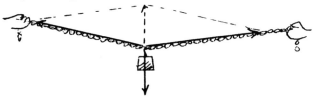

Explain the above via the parallelogram rule (as shown in the Practice Book, pages 3 - 9). The chain must be directed slightly upward to provide the needed vertical components to offset the weight.

Nonaccelerated Motion Continue to cases of zero acceleration and zero net force for moving things. Drag a block at constant velocity across your lecture table. Acknowledge friction, and how the force of friction must exactly counter your pulling force. Show the pulling force with a spring balance.

CHECK QUESTION: (similar to the one on page 39 in the text) Suppose in a high-flying airplane the captain announces over the cabin public address system that the plane is flying at a constant 900 km/h and the thrust of the engines is a constant 80,000 newtons. What is the acceleration of the airplane? [Answer: Zero, because velocity is constant.] What is the combined force of air resistance that acts all over the plane's outside surface? [Answer: 80,000 N. If it were less, the plane would speed up; if it were more, the plane would slow down.]

Friction Continue your activity of pulling the block across the table with a spring balance. Show what happens when you pull harder. Your students see that when the pulling force is greater than the friction force, there is a net force greater than zero, as evidenced by the observed acceleration. Show different constant speeds across the table with the same applied force, which shows that friction is not dependent on speed. Distinguish between static and sliding friction, and show how a greater force is needed to get the block moving from a rest position. Show all this as you discuss these ideas. Cite the example in the book about skidding with locked brakes in a car [where the distance of skid for sliding friction is greater than static friction, where lower braking application results in non-sliding tires and shorter sliding distance]. Discuss the new Automatic braking systems (ABS) now available on cars.

After you have adequately discussed friction and the idea of net force, pose the following (Be careful that your class may not be ready for this, in which case you may confuse rather than enlighten):

CHECK QUESTION: If one were able to produce and maintain a constant net force of only 1 newton on the Queen Mary ocean liner, what would be its maximum speed? [Give multiple choices for an answer: a) 0 m/s; b) 1 m/s; c) less than 1 m/s; d) about 10 m/s; e) almost the speed of light!] In the following discussion, the key concept is net force. Point out the enormous applied forces necessary to overcome the enormous water resistance at high speeds, to yield a net force of 1 newton; and the meaning of acceleration — that every succeeding second the ship moves a bit faster than the second before. This would go on seemingly without limit, except for relativistic effects which result in (e) being the correct answer.

Falling Objects Point out that although Galileo introduced the idea of inertia, discussed the role of forces, and defined acceleration, he never tied these ideas together as Newton did in his second law. Although Galileo is credited as the first to demonstrate that in the absence of air resistance, falling objects fall with equal accelerations, he was not able to say why this is so. The answer is given by Newton's 2nd law.

SKIT: Hold a heavy object like a kilogram weight and a piece of chalk with outstretched hands, ready to drop them. Ask your class which will strike the ground first if you drop them simultaneously. They know. Ask them to imagine you ask the same of a bright youngster, who responds by asking to handle the two objects before giving an answer. Pretend you are the kid judging the lifting of the two objects. "The metal object is heavier than the chalk, which means there is more gravity force acting on it, which means it will accelerate to the ground before the chalk does." Write the kids argument in symbol notation on the board. $a \sim F$. Then go through the motions of asking the same of another child, who responds with a good argument that takes inertia rather than weight into account. This kid says, after shaking the metal and chalk back and forth in his or her hands, "The piece of metal is more massive than the chalk, which means it has more inertia than the chalk, which means it will be harder to get moving than the chalk. So the chalk will race to the ground first, while the inertia of the metal causes it to lag behind." Write this kid's argument with, $a \sim 1/m$. State that a beauty of science is that such speculations can be ascertained by experiment. Drop the weight and the chalk to show that however sound each child's argument seemed to be, the results do not support either. Then bring both arguments together with $a \sim F/m$, Newton's 2nd Law.

Relate your skit to the case of falling bricks, Figure 2.13, and the falling boulder and feather, Figure 2.14. Once these concepts are clear, ask how the bricks would slide on a frictionless inclined plane, then illustrate with examples such as the equal times of a fully loaded roller coaster and an empty roller coaster making a complete run. In the absence of friction effects, the times are the same. Cite the case of a Town Car and Civic rolling down a hill in the absence of friction. By now you are fielding questions having to do with air resistance and friction. (Avoid getting into the buoyancy of falling objects — information overload.)

DEMONSTRATION: After you have made clear the cases with no friction, then make a transition to practical examples that involve friction — leading off with the dropping of sheets of paper, one crumpled and one flat. Point out that the masses and weights are the same, and the only variable is air resistance. Bring in the idea of net force again, asking what the net force is when the paper falls at constant speed. (If you left the Chapter 1 demo of the falling book and paper on top of it unexplained, reintroduce it here.)

CHECK QUESTIONS: What is the acceleration of a feather that "floats" slowly to the ground? The net force acting on the feather? If the feather weighs 0.0N, how much air resistance acts upward against it?

These questions lead into a discussion of the parachutists in Figure 2.16. When the decrease of acceleration that builds up to terminal velocity is clear, return to the point earlier about the Town Car and Civic rolling down an incline, only this time in the presence of air resistance. Then ask whether or not it would be advantageous to have a heavy cart or a light cart in a soap-box-derby race. Ask which would reach the finish line first if they were dropped through the air from a high-flying balloon. Then consider the carts on an inclined plane.

The "Principle of Exaggeration:" In discussing the effects of air resistance on falling objects, it is useful to exaggerate the circumstance so that the effects are more clearly visualized. For example, in comparing the falls of a heavy and a light skydiver, ask your students to substitute the falling of a feather for the light person, and the falling of a heavy rock for the heavy person. It is easy to see that the air resistance plays a more significant role for the falling feather than for the falling rock. Similarly, but not as much, for the falls of the two skydivers.

For your information, the terminal velocity of a falling baseball is about 150 km/h (95 mi/h), and for a falling ping pong ball about 32 km/h (20 mi/h).

Newton's 3rd Law Begin by reaching out to the class and stating, "I can't touch you, without you touching me in return — I can't nudge this chair without the chair in turn nudging me — I can't exert a force on a body without that body in turn exerting  a force on me — In all these cases of contact there is a *single* interaction between *two* things— contact requires a *pair* of forces, whether they be slight nudges or great impacts, between *two* things. This is Newton's 3rd Law of motion. Then state the law and support it with examples.

A good one is to extend your hand and show the class that you can bend your fingers upward only very little. Show that if you push with your other hand, and thereby apply a force to them, or have a student do the same, they will bend appreciably more. Then walk over to the wall and show that the inanimate wall does the same (as you push against the wall). State that everybody will acknowledge that you are pushing on the wall, but only a few realize the fundamental fact that the wall is simultaneously

pushing on you also — as evidenced by your bent fingers!

Do as Linda E. Roach does and place a sheet of paper between the wall and your hand. When you push on the paper, it doesn't accelerate — evidence of a zero net force on the paper. You can explain that in addition to your push, the wall must be pushing just as hard in the opposite direction on the paper to produce the zero net force. Linda recommends doing the same with an inflated balloon, whereupon your class can easily see that both sides of the balloon are squashed.

CHECK QUESTION: Identify the action and reaction forces for the case of a bat striking the ball.

Discuss walking on the floor in terms of the single interaction between you and the floor, and the pair of action and reaction forces that comprise this interaction. Contrast this to walking on frictionless ice, where no interaction occurs. Ask how one could get off a pond of frictionless ice. Make the answer easy by saying one has a massive brick in hand. By throwing the brick there is an interaction between the thrower and the brick. The reaction to the force on the brick, the recoiling force, sends one to shore. Or without such a convenient brick, one has clothing. Or if no clothing, one has air in the lungs. One could blow air in jet fashion. Exhale with the mouth facing away from shore, but be sure to inhale with the mouth facing toward shore.

CHECK QUESTION: Identify the force that pushes a car along the road. [Interestingly enough, the force that pushes cars is provided by the road. Why? The tires push on the road, action, and the road pushes on the tires, reaction. So roads push cars along. A somewhat different viewpoint!]

Most people say that the Moon is attracted to the Earth by gravity. Ask most people if the Earth is also attracted to the Moon, and if so, which pulls harder, the Earth or the Moon? You'll get mixed answers. Physicists think differently than most people on this topic: rather than saying the Moon is attracted to the Earth by gravity, a physicist would say there is an attractive force between the Earth and the Moon. There is an important difference here.

Asking if the Moon pulls as hard on the Earth as the Earth pulls on the Moon is similar to asking if the distance between New York and Los Angeles is the same as the distance between Los

Angeles and New York. Rather than thinking in terms of two distances, we think of a single distance *between* New York and Los Angeles. Likewise there is a single gravitational interaction *between* the Earth and the Moon.

Support this point by showing your outstretched hand where you have a stretched rubber band between your thumb and forefinger. Ask which is pulling with the greater force, the thumb or the finger. Or, as you increase the stretch, which is being pulled with more force toward the other — the thumb toward the finger or the finger toward the thumb. After neighbor discussion, stress the single interaction between things that pull on each 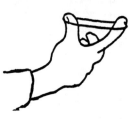 other. The Earth and the Moon are each pulling on each other. Their pulls on each other comprise a single interaction. This point of view makes a moot point of deciding which exerts the greater force, the Moon on the Earth or the Earth on the Moon, or the ball on the bat or the bat on the ball, et cetera. Pass a box of rubber bands to your class and have them do it.

Consider a tug of war where scales are at opposite rope ends. Ask your class if it is possible for the scales to have different readings when participants pull. The answer is no. Both scales will have the same readings at any time, no matter how the ropes are pulled!

Have a tug-of-war in your classroom between males with *shoes removed*, only socks, and females with rubber-soled shoes. The fact that the females win aptly demonstrates that the team to win is the team that exerts more force on the floor!

Discuss the firing of a bullet from a rifle, as treated in the chapter. Illustrate Newton's 3rd Law with a skit about a man who is given one last wish before being shot, who states that his crime demands more punishment than being struck by a tiny bullet, who wishes instead that the mass of the bullet match the magnitude of his crime (being rational in a rigid totalitarian society), that the mass of the bullet be much much more massive than the gun from which it is fired — and that his antagonist pull the trigger!

 Drop a sheet of paper and then punch it in midair. State that the heavyweight champion of the world couldn't hit the paper with a force equaling the weight of his arm — that he can't exert any greater force on the paper than the paper can exert on him.

Philosophically we know that if you try to do one thing, something else happens as a result. So we say you can never do only one thing. In this chapter we similarly see that you can never have only one force.

NEXT-TIME QUESTION: Home Project 4 — Show this before the class with the string from the spool directed over the top of the spool.

The spool, not surprisingly, rolls in the direction of the pull. Ask which way it would roll if the string were directed from the bottom of the spool (as shown in the sketch accompanying Home Project 4).

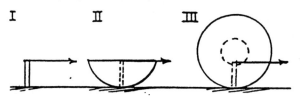

Step I. On the board sketch a wooden peg standing upright. Make an arrow at the top of the peg as shown, which represents a string being pulled toward the right. Ask the class which way the peg will topple.

Step II. Sketch two "wings" on both sides of the peg so that it will roll rather than topple. Ask the class which way it will roll when pulled.

Step III. Sketch a "cap" on the top, effectively sketching a side view of the spool. Again question the class.

If you pull the string upward, there is a point where it doesn't roll at all, but slides, and beyond that elevation the spool will roll in the opposite direction. The explanation for this involves torques, which for brevity is a topic not treated in the textbook. 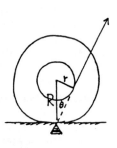 Interestingly enough, the critical angle for this is when the string extends to the point of spool contact with the table, as the sketch shows. Then there is no torque. You might refer to a torque as a "twisting force."

3
Momentum and Energy

This chapter begins by picking up where chapter 2 leaves off. Newton's 2nd and 3rd Laws lead directly to momentum and its conservation. We emphasize the impulse-momentum relationship with applications to many examples which have been selected to catch the students' interest. In presenting your own, the exaggerated symbol technique as shown in Figures 3.2, 3.3, 3.4, and 3.7 is suggested. Draw a comparison between momentum conservation and Newton's 3rd Law in explaining examples such as rocket propulsion. You might point out that either of these is fundamental — i.e., momentum conservation may be regarded as a consequence of Newton's 3rd Law, or equally, Newton's 3rd Law may be regarded as a consequence of momentum conservation.

Little Andrea Wu's question about the behavior of balls in the swinging balls apparatus in the Part 1 opener on page 11 is entertained in this chapter. In answer to the question, "Why can't two balls be raised and allowed to swing into the array, and one ball emerge with twice the speed?" be careful. Momentum would indeed be conserved if this were the case. But the case with different numbers of balls emerging never happens.

Why? Because *energy* would not be conserved. For the two-balls-one-ball case, the KE after would be twice the KE before impact. KE is proportional to the square of the speed, and the conservation of both momentum and KE cannot occur unless the numbers of balls for collision and ejection are the same.

A system is not only isolated in space, but in time also. When we say that momentum is conserved when one pool ball strikes the other, we mean that momentum is conserved during the brief duration of interaction when outside forces can be neglected. After the interaction, friction quite soon brings both balls to a halt. So when we isolate a system for purposes of analysis, we isolate both in space and in time.

David Wiley, physics professor at the University of Pennsylvania at Johnstown, has pointed out that only about 60 to 75% the PE of a drawn bow goes into the KE of an arrow, depending on the type of bow — the rest heats the bow. Likewise, only about 30% of the energy of firearms is transferred to the bullets they fire. The rest heats the gun. This poses a problem with sustained fire in machine guns, where the bore thermally expands so bullets no longer take the rifling and tip over and over in flight just as though they were fired from a smooth bore. Hence the water cooling for machine guns.

There are seven exercises for this chapter in the **Practice Book**. Of particular importance is the one on *Systems* — excellent for understand both Newton's third law and momentum conservation. Expect your students to find Page 20, *Energy and Momentum*, more challenging than other practice sheets.

The **Laboratory Manual** has a simple activity for impulse-momentum, *By Impulse*, that serves well as a lecture demo, and an experiment on energy conservation, *Energy Ramp*.

There are five **Next-Time Questions** for this chapter.

SUGGESTED LECTURE PRESENTATION

Momentum Begin by stating that there is something different between a Mack truck and a roller skate — they each have a different inertia. And that there is still something different about a moving Mack truck and a moving roller skate — they have different momenta. Define and discuss momentum as inertia in motion.

CHECK QUESTION: After stating that a Mack truck will always have more inertia than an ordinary roller skate, ask if a Mack truck will always have more momentum than a roller skate.

Cite the case of super tankers that normally cut off their power when they are 25 or so kilometers from port. This is because of their huge momentum (due mostly to their huge mass), which requires about 25 kilometers of water resistance to bring them to a halt.

Impulse and Momentum Derive the impulse-momentum relationship. In Chapter 1 you defined acceleration as $a = \Delta v/t$ (really Δt, but you likely used t as the "time interval"). Then later in Chapter 2 you defined acceleration in terms of the force needed, $a = F/m$. Now simply equate; $a = a$, or $F/m = \Delta v/t$, with simple rearrangement you have, $Ft = \Delta mv$. (as in the footnote, page 54.)

Then choose your examples in careful sequence: First, those where the object is to increase momentum — pulling a sling shot or arrow in a bow all the way back, the effect of a long cannon for maximum range, driving a golf ball. Second, those examples where small forces are the object when decreasing momentum — pulling your hand backward when catching a ball, driving into a haystack versus a concrete wall, falling on a surface with give versus a rigid surface. Then lastly, those examples where the ob-

ject is to obtain large forces when decreasing momentum — karate — more properly called *tae kwon do.*

Point of confusion: In boxing, one "follows through" whereas in karate one "pulls back". But this is not so — a karate expert does not pull back upon striking his target. He strikes in such a way that his hand is made to bounce back, yielding up to twice the impulse to his target (just as a ball bouncing off a wall delivers nearly twice the impulse to the wall than if it stuck to the wall).

CHECK QUESTION: Why is falling on a wooden floor in a roller rink less dangerous than falling on the concrete pavement? [Superficial answer: Because the wooden floor has more "give." Emphasize that this is the beginning of a fuller answer—one that is prompted if the question is reworded as follows:] Why is falling on a floor with more give less dangerous than falling on a floor with less give? [Answer: Because the floor with more give allows a greater time for the impulse that reduces the momentum of fall to zero. A greater time for Δ momentum means less force.]

The loose coupling between railroad cars (Exercise 8) makes a good lecture topic. Discuss the importance of loose coupling in bringing a long train initially at rest up to speed, and its importance in braking the train as well. (I compare this to taking school load in proper sequence, rather than all at once where for sure one's wheels would simply spin.)

Conservation of Momentum Distinguish between external and internal forces and lead into the conservation of momentum. Show from the impulse-momentum equation that no change in momentum can occur in the absence of an external net force.

DEMONSTRATION: Perform momentum conservation with an air-track.

Defining Your System Momentum is not conserved in a system that experiences an external net force. Consider a cue ball that makes a head-on collision with an 8- ball at rest. If the system is taken to be only the 8-ball at rest, then we isolate it with a dotted border around it, sketch I. So long as no outside force acts on it, there will be no impulse on it and no change in its momentum. But when the cue ball strikes it, there is an

26

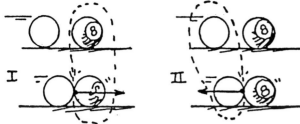

outside force and an impulse on it. Its momentum changes as it speeds away with the speed of the incident cue ball. Or take the system to be the cue ball, sketch II. Initially it has momentum mv. Then it strikes the 8-ball and its momentum undergoes a change. The reaction force by the 8-ball brings it to a halt. Now consider the system of both balls, sketch III. Before collision the momentum is that of the moving cue ball. When the balls strike, no outside force acts, for

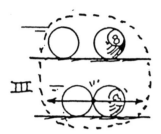

the interaction is between the balls, both parts of the same system. So no impulse acts on the system and no change in momentum of the system occurs. In this case momentum is conserved. It is the same before and after the collision. Again, the momentum of a system is conserved only when no external impulse is exerted on the system.

Consider a dropped rock in freefall. If the system is taken to be the rock, sketch IV, then momentum is not conserved as it falls because an external force acts on the system (its vector is seen to penetrate the dotted border of the system). This external force, gravity, produces an impulse on

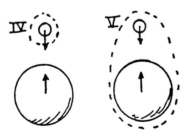

the rock that changes its momentum. If the system is instead considered to be the rock + the entire world, sketch V, then the interaction between the rock and the Earth is internal to the system (there is no penetrating vector). For this larger system, momentum is conserved. Momentum is always conserved if you make your system big

enough. The momentum of the universe is without change.

System definition is nicely treated on page 14 in the Practice Book.

Numerical examples of lunch time for the fish, like Problem 2, should clarify the vector nature of momentum — particularly for the case of the fishes approaching each other.

Bouncing Discuss bouncing and how Lester Pelton made a fortune from applying some simple physics to the old paddle wheels.

DEMONSTRATION: This one by Rich Langer of Beaumont High School in St. Louis, MO, who uses a toy dartgun and computer-disc box. Tape some toothpicks to one side the box, so the suction-cup dart shot against it won't stick to it. First fire the dart against the smooth side of the box. The dart sticks and the box slides an observed distance across the table. Then repeat, but with the box turned around so the dart hits the toothpick side. When the dart hits, it bounces. Note the appreciably greater distance the box slides!]

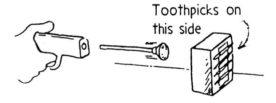

Toothpicks on this side

Or do as Fred Bucheit does and fashion a pendulum using the "happy-unhappy" rubber balls, and let them swing into an upright board. When the less-elastic ball makes impact, with very little bounce, the board remains upright. But when the more-elastic ball makes impact, it undergoes a greater change in momentum as it bounces. This imparts more impulse to the board, and it topples.

Energy Begin your treatment of energy by standing on a chair against a wall with an extended heavy pendulum bob held at the tip of your nose. Say nothing. Release the bob and let it swing out, then back to your nose. Don't flinch (you don't have to!) Then comment on your confidence in physical laws and lead into potential and kinetic energy (PE & KE). If you don't actually do this, describing the demo still has merit.

Work Define work and compare it to previously treated impulse. In both concepts, a force is extended — in time for impulse, in distance for work. Return to previous examples of drawn slingshots and long cannons, where the added length produced greater speeds. We can describe this speed and mass in terms of two concepts — momentum and energy. Failure to distinguish between these two gave rise to much controversy in Europe after the time of Newton. (The concept of KE was after Newton's time.)

Potential Energy Return to your pendulum (or description of your pendulum). Show how work is done to elevate it. In its elevated position it has a capacity for doing work on whatever it strikes when released. Discuss the equation PE = mgh.

CHECK QUESTIONS: Does a car hoisted for lubrication in a service station have PE? How much work is required to raise it twice as high? Three times as high? How much more PE will it have in these cases?

Kinetic Energy Relate force × distance to ΔKE to examples of pushing a car, and then braking to a stop. Show how twice the speed results in four times the stopping distance.

Work — Energy Theorem: When discussing whether or not work is done, be sure to specify *done on what*. If you push a stationary wall, you may be doing work on your muscles (that involve forces and distances in flexing), but you do no work on the wall. Key point: if work is done on something, then the energy of that something changes. Distinguish between the energy one expends in doing things, and the work that is actually done on something.

CHECK QUESTION: When a car slows down due to air drag, does its KE decrease? [Most certainly!]

CHECK QUESTION: Which is greater, 1 joule or 1 newton? [Whoops! The comparison is silly, for they're units of completely different things—work and force. An idea about the magnitude of 1 joule is that it is the work done in vertically lifting a quarter-pound hamburger with cheese (approx. 1 N) one meter.

Energy Conservation Return to your pendulum. Explain how the KE and hence, the speed of the bob at the bottom of its swing is equal to the speed it would have if dropped vertically through the same height.

CHECK QUESTION: Refer to Figure 3.14 in "inclines" a and b: how does the speed of the ball compare at ground level when released from equal elevations? [It is impressive that the speeds will be the same. The lesser acceleration down the sloped ramp is compensated by a longer time. But return to the situation and ask how the *times* to reach the bottom

compare and be prepared for an incorrect response, "The same!" Quip and ask if the colors and temperatures will also be the same. Straightforward physics can be confusing enough!]

DEMONSTRATION: Preview electricity and magnetism and bring out the horseshoe magnet hand-cranked generator that lights up the lamp. Have student volunteers attest to the fact that more work is needed to turn the crank when the lamp is connected than when it is not. Then relate this to Exercise 30.

We follow through on the fuel economy bit (remember we used to say "mileage" in the pre-SI days?) with escalators in a department store. Even though the escalator is in operation, more electrical energy is consumed when you add to its load. The motor "knows" when you get on and when you get off. It does work to pull you up to the next floor. So strictly speaking, you'll save electrical energy if you walk up the stairs rather than ride the escalator. And as for riding the escalator down, do so and feel good about it, for friction aside, you'll be doing work *on* the escalator, relieving the work the motor does, and you'll be saving electrical energy. Pushed to the idealistic extreme with friction aside, at least, this is really be the case!

Go over the check question on page 70 of the text — very important. (We pose the same question on exams, which to the student is the *definition* of what's important!) With a 500-N drag force to overcome, ideal fuel economy is 80 km per liter. As a side point, gas economy is increased when tires are inflated to maximum pressures, where less flattening of the tire occurs as it turns. The very important point of this exercise is the upper limit possible.

We extend this idea of an upper limit to the supposed notion that certain gadgets attached to automobile engines will give phenomenal performance — so much in fact, (tongue in cheek) that the oil companies have gobbled up the patents and are keeping them off the market. Charlatans stand ready to benefit from this public perception, and offer the public a chance to invest in their energy producing machines. They prey on people who are ignorant of or do not understand the message of the energy conservation law. You can't get something for nothing. You can't even break even, because of the inevitable transformation of available energy to heat.

Matter is frozen energy, as will be briefly discussed in Chapter 30 — $E = mc^2$.

Power Distinguish between energy and power. The power of the space shuttle, as mentioned in the text, makes a good example. Note the rate at which fuel is consumed in text Figure 3.19 — like emptying a swimming pool in 20 s!

Note that one pays for energy when the electric bill comes. And the units of energy used by power utilities is power × time; kW × hr. So 1 kW·hr is the energy consumed at the rate of 1 joule per second for a period of 1 hour.

Efficiency It should be enough that your students become acquainted with the idea of efficiency, so we don't recommend setting the plow setting too deep for this topic. The key idea to impart is that of useful energy. To say that an incandescent lamp is 10% efficient is to say that only 10% of the energy input is converted to the useful form of light. All the rest goes to heat. But even the light energy converts to heat upon absorption. So all the energy input to an incandescent lamp is converted to heat. This means that it is a 100% efficient *heater* (but not a 100% device for emitting light)!

The concept of systems is nicely shown in this Practice Sheet.

Systems

Momentum conservation (and Newton's 3rd law) apply to *systems* of bodies. Here we identify some systems.

1. When the compressed spring is released, Blocks A and B will slide apart. There are 3 systems to consider here, indicated by the closed dashed lines below — System A, System B, and System A+B. Ignore the vertical forces of gravity and the support force of the table.

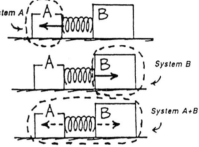

a. Does an external force act on System A? (yes) (no)

Will the momentum of System A change? (yes) (no)

b. Does an external force act on System B? (yes) (no)

Will the momentum of System B change? (yes) (no)

c. Does an external force act on System A+B? (yes) (no)

Will the momentum of System A+B change? (yes) (no)

2. Billiard ball A collides with billiard ball B at rest. Isolate each system with a closed dashed line. Draw only the external force vectors that act on each system.

System A

System B

System A+B

a. Upon collision, the momentum of System A (increases) (decreases) (remains unchanged).

b. Upon collision, the momentum of System B (increases) (decreases) (remains unchanged).

c. Upon collision, the momentum of System A+B (increases) (decreases) (remains unchanged).

3. A girl jumps upward from the Earth's surface. In the sketch to the left, draw a closed dashed line to indicate the system of the girl.

a. Is there an external force acting on her? (yes) (no)

Does her momentum change? (yes) (no)

Is the girl's momentum conserved? (yes) (no)

b. In the sketch to the right, draw a closed dashed line to indicate the system [girl + Earth]. Is there an external force due to the interaction between the girl and the Earth that acts on the system? (yes) (no)

Is the momentum of the system conserved? (yes) (no)

4. A block strikes a blob of jelly. Isolate 3 systems with a closed dashed line and show the external force on each. In which system is momentum conserved?

5. A truck crashes into a wall. Isolate 3 systems with a closed dashed line and show the the external force on each. In which system is momentum conserved?

thanx to Cedric Linder

14

4
Gravity and Satellite Motion

Show the 15-min NASA film *Zero g* — of footage aboard Skylab in 1978, narrated by astronaut Owen Garriott, which reviews Newton's laws. Excellent and entertaining!

For brevity, Kepler's laws are not covered in this chapter (but are later in Chapter 27).

The text treats tides in terms of forces rather than fields. In terms of the latter, tidal forces are related to differences in gravitational *field* strengths across a body, and occur only for bodies in a non-uniform gravitational field. The gravitational fields of the Earth, Moon, and Sun, for example, are inverse-square fields — stronger near them than farther away. The Moon obviously experiences tidal forces because the near part to us is in a stronger part of the Earth's gravitational field than the far part. But even an astronaut in an orbiting space shuttle strictly speaking experiences tidal forces because parts of her body are closer to the Earth than other parts. The micro differences produce **microtides**. Farther away in deep space, the differences are less. Put another way, the Earth's gravitational field is more uniform farther away. The "deepness" of a deep-space location can in fact be defined in terms of the amount of microtides experienced by a body there. Or equivalently, by the uniformity of any gravitational field there. There are no microtides in a body located in a strictly uniform gravitational field.

If there are microtides of an astronaut in orbit, would such microtides be even greater on the Earth's surface? The answer is yes. How about **biological tides**? Micro-tides in human bodies are popularly attributed to not the Earth, but the Moon. This is because popular knowledge cites that the Moon raises the ocean an average of 1 meter each 12 hours. Point out that the reason the tides are "stretched" by 1 meter is because part of that water is an Earth diameter closer to the Moon than the other part. In terms of fields, the near part of the Earth is in an appreciably stronger part of the Moon's gravitational field than the far part. To the extent that part of our bodies are closer to the Moon than other parts, there would be lunar microtides — but enormously smaller than the microtides produced by not only the Earth, but massive objects in one's vicinity.

Is there any way to distinguish between a gravity-free region and orbital free-fall inside the space shuttle? It turns out there is. Consider a pair of objects placed side by side. If the shuttle were floating in a gravity-free region, the two objects would remain as placed over time. Since the shuttle is in orbit around the Earth, however, each floating object is in its own orbit about the Earth's center in its own orbital plane. All orbital planes pass through the center of the Earth and intersect, which means the two objects will collide by the time the shuttle makes a quarter orbit — a little more than 20 minutes! If the pair of objects are placed one in front of the other, with respect to their direction of motion, there will be no such effect since they are in the same orbital plane. If the objects are one above the other, however, they will migrate in seemingly strange ways relative to each other because they are in distinct orbits, beginning with equal KEs but different PEs. Gravity makes itself present to astronauts by the strange secondary effects that are not directly related to weight. (More on this in *Weightlessness and Microgravity*, by David Chandler, The Physics Teacher, May, 91.)

The inverse-cube nature of tidal forces follows from subtracting the tidal force on the far side of a body from the tidal force on the near side. Consider a kilogram of water on the side of the Earth nearest the Moon that is gravitationally attracted to the Moon with a greater force than a kilogram of water on the side of the Earth farthest from the Moon. The difference in force per kilogram of mass, $\Delta F/m$, which we'll call the tidal force T_F is

$$T_F = F_{d+R} - F_{d-R}$$
$$= GM[\frac{1}{(d+R)^2} - \frac{1}{(d-R)^2}] = \frac{4GMdR}{(d^2-R^2)^2}$$

where M is the Moon's mass, $(d + R)$ is the distance to the far side or Earth, $(d - R)$ is the distance to the near side.

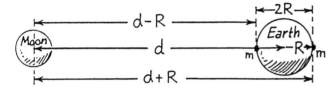

When d is very much greater than R, then $(d^2 - R^2)^2$ is very nearly equal to d^4. Then the inverse-cube nature of tidal force is evident, for

$$T_F \sim \frac{4GMR}{d^3}.$$

Some interesting results occur when calculating the tidal force of the Moon on planet Earth. T_F is 2.2×10^{-6} N/kg. In contrast T_F for an overhead Moon on a person on the Earth is about 3×10^{-13} N/kg, some hundred million times weaker because of the tiny differences in pulls across the body. The tidal force of the Earth on the same person is 6×10^{-6} N/kg, more than the Moon's influence. And as the text reports, the tidal force due to a 1-kg mass held 1 m above your head is about 200 times more effective as the Moon! Have those who believe the tidal effects of planets influence people make the calculations themselves.

Solar photon force: To a small extent, sunlight affects satellites, particularly the large disco-ball-like satellite LAGEOS, which wobbles slightly in its orbit because of unequal heating by sunlight. The side in the Sun radiates infrared photons, the energy of which provides a small, but persistent, rocket effect as the photons eject from the surface. So a net force some 100 billion times weaker than gravity pushes on the satellite in a direction away from its hot end. LAGEOS

has 426 prism-shaped mirrors. By reflecting laser beams off its mirrored surface, geophysicists can make precise measurements of tiny displacements in the Earth's surface.

The **Practice Book** has 6 exercises for on this chapter. The concluding one on page 28 provides an overview of mechanics.

In the **Laboratory Manual** is *Bullseye*, an interesting experiment featuring projectile motion.

Note 7 **Next-Time Questions** for this chapter.

SUGGESTED LECTURE PRESENTATION

Begin by briefly discussing the simple codes and patterns that underlie the complex things around us, whether musical compositions or DNA molecules, and then briefly describe the harmonious motion of the solar system, the Milky Way and other galaxies in the universe — stating that the shapes of the planets, stars, and galaxies, and their motions are all governed by an extremely simple code — a pattern. Then write the gravitational equation on the board. Give examples of bodies pulling on each other to convey a clear idea of what the symbols in the equation mean and how they relate.

G If you explain the force constant G, consider the analogous constant of proportionality π for the circumference and diameter of a circle. Students learn from analogies!

Inverse-Square Law Discuss the inverse square law and go over Figures 4.4 and 4.6 or their equivalents with candlelight or radioactivity.

Plot to scale an inverse-square curve on the board, showing the steepness of the curve — 1/4, 1/9, and 1/16, for twice, three times, and four times the separation distance occur rather "suddenly." This is shown in Figure 4.4. (You'll return to this curve when you explain tides.)

CHECK QUESTIONS: How is the gravitational force between a pair of planets altered when one of the planets is twice as massive? When both are twice as massive? When they are twice as far apart? When they are three times as far apart? Ten times as far apart?

CHECK QUESTION: If the Sun were somehow suddenly plucked from its location to a position infinitely far away, describe the effect on the Earth's orbit in the following ten-minute interval. [For the first 8 minutes, the Earth would continue as though the Sun were still there, for "gravity" travels at the speed of light, and the Sun is 8-light minutes away. Then after 8 minutes, the Earth would move off in a straight line, deviated only by the influence of other planets, mainly Jupiter.]

Tides Begin your treatment of tides by asking the class to consider the consequences of someone pulling your coat. If they pulled only on the sleeve, for example, it would tear. But if every part of your coat were pulled equally, it and you would accelerate — but it wouldn't tear. It tears when one part is pulled harder than another — or it tears because of a *difference* in forces acting on the coat. In a similar way, the spherical Earth is "torn" into an elliptical shape by differences in gravitational forces by the Moon and Sun.

Misconceptions About the Moon In case you are not covering Part 8 in your course (or even if you are) this is an appropriate place for you to dispel two popular misconceptions about the Moon. One is that since one side of the Moon's face is "frozen" to the Earth, it doesn't spin like a top about its polar axis; and two, that the crescent shape commonly seen is *not* the Earth's shadow. To convince your class that the Moon spins about its polar axis, simulate the situation by holding your eraser at arms length in front of your face. Tell your class that the eraser represents the Moon and your head represents the Earth. Rotate slowly keeping one face of the eraser in your view. Show that from your frame of reference, the eraser doesn't spin as it revolves about you — as evidenced by your observation of only one face, with the backside hidden. But your students occupy the frame of reference of the stars (each of them *is* a star). From their point of view they can see all sides of the eraser as it rotates because

it spins about its own axis as often as it revolves about your head. Show them how the eraser, if not slowly spinning and rotationally frozen with one face always facing the same stars, would show all of its sides to you as it circles around you. You'd see one face, then wait 14 days to view the backside. The Moon has a spin rate that is the same as its revolution rate. (*Why* the Moon is frozen with one face always toward Earth is explained in Chapter 28, page 684.)

Misconception 2: Draw a half Moon on the board. The shadow is along the diameter and is perfectly straight. If that were the shadow of the Earth, then the Earth would have to be flat, or be a big block shape! Discuss playing "flashlight tag" with a suspended basketball in a dark room that is illuminated by a flashlight in various locations. Ask your class if they could estimate the location of the flashlight by only looking at the illumination of the ball. Likewise with the Moon illuminated by the Sun!

Sketch the picture below on the board and ask what is wrong with it. [Answer: The Moon is in a daytime position as evidenced by the upper part of the Moon being illuminated. This means the Sun must be above. Dispel notions that the crescent shape of the Moon is a partial eclipse by considering a half Moon and the shape of the Earth to cast such a shadow.]

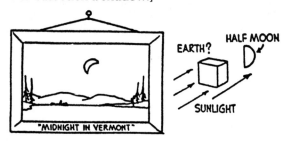

Tides and the Inverse-Square Law (Optional) A roughly plotted graph of the gravitational force on an object near the Earth's surface, versus distance from the Earth, is useful in explaining tidal forces. Make a chalkboard sketch like this and show the inverse-square decline with distance.

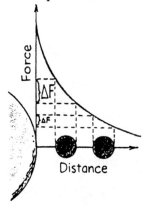

Back to Tides Consider tides via the accelerating ball of Jell-O as in the text. Equal pulls result in an undistorted ball as it accelerates, but unequal pulls cause a stretching. This stretching is evident in the Earth's oceans, where the side nearest the Moon is appreciably closer to the Moon than the side farthest away. Modify your graph of grav force vs distance to that of the Sun on the board.

Understanding this inverse relationship explains why closeness is so important for tides. Your graph shows that the size of ΔF rather than F

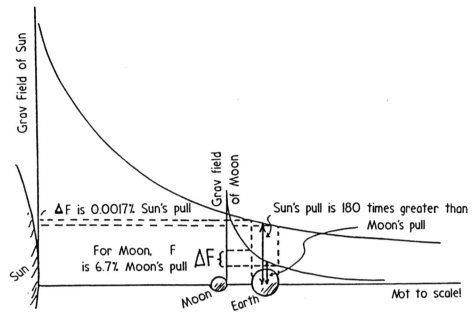

itself is responsible for tidal effects. Hence the greater attraction of the distant Sun produces only a small *difference* in pulls on the Earth, and compared to the Moon makes a small contribution to the tides on Earth.

Explain why the highest high tides occur when the Earth, Moon, and Sun are aligned — at the time of a new and a full Moon.

Discuss tides in the molten Earth and in the atmosphere.

Amplify this graph with a comparison of ΔFs for both the Sun and the Moon as shown above. Clearly ΔF is smaller for the larger but farther Sun.

CHECK QUESTION: Consider the tiny tidal forces that DO act on our bodies, as a result of parts of our bodies experiencing slightly different gravitational forces. What planetary body is most responsible for microtides in our bodies? [The Earth, by far. When we are standing, there is a greater difference in Earth gravity on our feet compared to our heads than the corresponding differences in gravity due to farther away planetary bodies.]

Weight and Weightlessness Discuss weightlessness and relate it to the queasy feeling your students experience when in a car that goes too fast over the top of a hill. State that this feeling is what an astronaut is confronted with all the time in orbit! Ask how many of your class would still welcome the opportunity to take a field trip to Cape Canaveral and take a ride aboard the shuttle. What an exciting prospect!

Projectile Motion Roll a ball off the edge of your lecture table and call attention to the curve

it follows. The ball is a projectile — acted on only by gravity. Discuss the "downwardness of gravity, and how there is no horizontalness to it, and therefore no horizontal influence on the projectile. Consider Figures 4.15 to 4.17.

Independence of Horizontal and Vertical Motion Pose the situation of the horizontally-held gun and the shooter who drops a bullet at the same time he pulls the trigger, and ask which bullet hits the ground first.

DEMONSTRATION: Show the independence of horizontal and vertical motion with a spring-gun apparatus that will shoot a ball horizontally while at the same time dropping another that falls vertically. Follow this up with the popular "monkey-and hunter" demonstration.

Point to some target at the far side of your classroom and ask your class to imagine you are going to project a rock to the target via a slingshot. Ask if you should aim at the target, above it, or below it. Easy stuff. Then ask your class to suppose it takes 1 second for the rock to reach the target. If you aim directly at the target, it will fall beneath and miss. How far beneath the target would the rock hit (supposing the floor weren't in the way)? Have your students check with their neighbors on this one. Then ask how far above should you aim to hit the target. Do a neighbor check on this one. Now you're ready to discuss Figure 4.18 on page 88.

Point out that the relationship of the curved path of Figure 4.18 and the vertical distance fallen, $d = 5t^2$, of Chapter 1. Stress that the projectile is falling beneath the straight line it would otherwise follow. This idea is important for understanding satellite motion.

Hang Time Revisited Return to your Chapter 1 discussions of hang time, and explain that jumping time in a stationary bus and jumping time in a fast-moving bus is the same. Likewise for a running jump. Once a jumper leaves the ground, forward motion has no effect whatever on hang time. One might argue that in running, one is able to exert more force against the ground and hence increase the vertical component of velocity at liftoff, and this is usually the case. But the point to be made is that once off the ground, hangtime is determined only by the initial vertical component of motion — period. This topic is bound to elicit discussion — Can a skateboarder jump higher when the skateboard is moving? Can one on an airliner in the sky jump higher than when the plane is at rest on the runway? Interesting material!

Discuss Figure 4.25 on page 91 and ask for the pitching speed if the ball traveled 30 m instead of 20 m. (Note the vertical height is 5 m. If you use any height that does not correspond to an integral number of seconds, you're diverting your focus from physics to algebra.) More important is considering greater horizontal distances — great enough for the curvature of the Earth to make a difference.

Satellite Motion Sketch "Newton's Mountain" and consider the longer and longer time intervals for greater and greater horizontal speeds. Ask if there is a "pitching speed" or cannonball velocity large enough so the time in the air is forever. Not literally "in the air", which is why the cannon is atop a mountain that extends above the atmosphere. The answer of course is yes. Fired fast enough the cannonball will fall around the world rather than into it. You're into satellite motion.

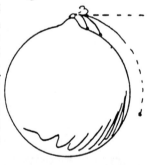

Calculating Satellite Speed An effective skit that can have your class calculating the speed necessary for close earth orbit is as follows: Call attention to the curvature of the Earth, Figure 4.27. Consider a horizontal laser standing about a meter above the ground with its beam shining over a level desert. The beam is straight but the desert floor curves 5 m over an 8000 m or 8 km tangent, which you sketch on your chalkboard (or overhead projector). Stress this is not to scale:

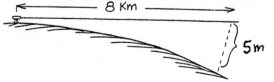

Now erase the laser and sketch in a super cannon

Consider a cannonball fired at say, 2 km/s, and ask how far downrange will it be at the end of one second. A neighbor check should yield an answer of 2 km, which you indicate as below. But it doesn't really get to this place, you say, for it falls beneath the straight line because of gravity. How far? 5 m if the sand weren't in the way. Ask if 2 km/s is sufficient for orbiting the Earth. Clearly not, for the cannonball strikes the ground. If the cannonball is not to hit the ground, we'd have to dig a trench first, as you show on your sketch, which now looks like this:

Continue by considering a greater muzzle velocity, say 4 km/s, so the cannonball travels 4 km in one second. Ask if this is fast enough to attain an Earth orbit. Student response should indicate that they realize that the cannonball will hit the ground before 1 second is up. Then repeat the previous line of reasoning, again having to dig a trench, and your sketch looks like this:

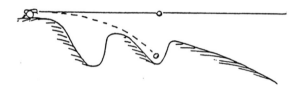

Continue by considering a greater muzzle velocity — great enough so that the cannonball travels 6 km in 1 second. This is 6 km/s. Ask if this is fast enough not to hit the ground (or equivalently, if it is fast enough for Earth orbit!) Then repeat the previous line of reasoning, again having to dig a trench. Now your sketch looks like this:

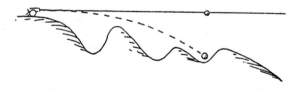

You're almost there: Continue by considering a muzzle velocity great enough so the cannonball travels 8 km in one second. (Don't state the velocity is 8 km/s here as you'll diminish your punch line.) Repeat your previous reasoning and note that this time you don't have to dig a trench!

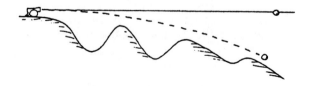

After a pause, and with a tone of importance, ask the class with what speed must the cannonball have to orbit the Earth. Done properly, you have led your class into a "derivation" of orbital speed about the Earth with no equations or algebra.

Acknowledge that the gravitational force is less on satellites in higher orbits so they do not need to go so fast. (Speed for circular orbit is $v = \sqrt{GM/d}$, so a satellite at 4 times the Earth's radius needs to travel only half as fast, 4 km/s.)

DEMONSTRATION: Swing a bucket of water in a vertical circle and show that the water doesn't spill. All your students have seen this demonstration, which is usually used to illustrate centripetal or centrifugal force (not covered in the text). But show it anyway — they'll love it! The important point of the demo is your explanation: Explain that the water at the top of the swing DOES fall, and the execution of the swing is such that the bucket is made to fall at least as fast as the water. This is why the water doesn't spill. In a similar way, the orbiting space shuttle DOES fall. It falls at the same "rate" as the Earth below curves, so remains above its surface. Analogies are the way to teach!

Moving Perpendicular vs Moving Non-Perpendicular to Gravity Back to your sketch the cannon on "Newton's mountain". Simulate a cannonball fired horizontally and curving to the ground. You've established that a cannonball with a speed of 8 km/s will trace a circular path and orbit the Earth. You now will show why gravity does not increase the speed of the cannonball in circular orbit: Suppose the cannonball leaves the cannon at a velocity of say 1 km/s. Ask the class whether the speed when it strikes the ground will be 1 km/s, more than 1 km/s, or less than 1 km/s (neglecting air resistance). The answer is that it strikes at more than 1 km/s, because gravity speeds it up. (Toss your keys horizontally from a one-story window and catching them would pose no problem. But the same toss horizontally from the top of a tall building would pose a real problem in catching. Ask if a person below would care to catch them!) Suppose the firing speed is now 4 km/s. Repeat your question: Will it be traveling faster, slower, or 4 km/s when it hits the ground? Again, faster, because it moves in the direction of the gravitational field. [Caution: Do not draw a trajectory that meets the Earth's surface at a point beyond the half-way

mark (unfortunately, the Zero-g film makes this error). Why? Because the parabolic path is actually a segment of a Keplerian ellipse. Half way around puts it all around!] Now draw the circular trajectory that occurs when the firing speed is 8 km/s. Ask if the speed increases, decreases, or remains the same after leaving the cannon. This time it remains the same. Why? Neighbor checking time!

Before answering the question, pose the case of rolling a ball along a bowling alley. Does gravity pull on the ball? [Yes.] Does gravity speed up or slow down the ball? [No.] Why? The answer to this question is the answer to the satellite question. [In both cases, the ball criss-crosses gravity — with no component of the gravitational field in the direction of motion. No change in speed, no work, no change in KE, no change in PE. Aha! The cannon ball and the bowling ball simply coast.

Circular Orbits Erase the mountain from your sketch of the world and draw a huge elevated bowling alley that completely circles the world. Show how a bowling ball on such an alley would gain no speed because of gravity. But now cut part of the alley away, so the ball rolls off the edge and crashes to the ground below. Does it gain speed after falling in the gap? [Yes, because a component of its motion is in the direction of the Earth's gravitational field.] Show how if the ball moves faster it will fall farther before crashing to the ground. Ask what speed would allow it to clear the gap (like a motorcyclist who drives off a ramp and clears a gap to meet a ramp on the other side).

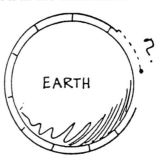

[8 km/s, of course.] Can the gap be bigger at this speed? Sketch a gap that nearly circles the world when you ask this question. Then ask, what happens with no alley? And your class sees at 8 km/s no supporting alley is needed. The ball orbits the Earth.

Elliptical Orbits Back to Newton's Mountain. Fire the cannonball at 9 km/s. It then overshoots

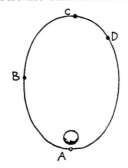

a circular path. Your sketch looks like the one here. Ask, at the position shown, is the cannonball moving at 9 km/s, more than 9 km/s, or less than 9 km/s. And why? After a neighbor check, toss a piece of chalk upward and say you toss it upward at 9 m/s. When it's half way to the top of its path, is it moving 9 m/s, more than 9 m/s, or less than 9 m/s? Equate the two situations. [In both cases the projectile slows because it is going against gravity.]

Continue your sketch and show a closed path — an ellipse. As you draw the elliptical path, show with a sweeping motion of your arm how the satellite slows in receding from the Earth, moving slowest at its furthermost point, then how it speeds in falling towards the Earth, whipping around the Earth and repeating the cycle over and over again. Move to a fresh part of the chalkboard and redraw with the mountain at the bottom, so your sketch is more like Figure 4.35. (It is more comfortable seeing your chalk moving slowest when farthest coincides with the direction "up" in the classroom. We quip that Australians have no trouble seeing it the first way.)

Sketch in larger ellipses for still greater cannon speeds, with the limit being 11.2 km/s, beyond which the path does not close — escape speed.

Work-Energy Relationship for Satellites You already have sketches on the board of circular and elliptical orbits. Draw sample satellites and then sketch in force vectors. Ask the class to do likewise, and then draw component vectors parallel and perpendicular to instantaneous directions of motion. Then show how the changes in speed are consistent with the work-energy relationship.

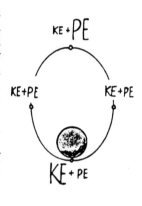

Escape Speed Distinguish between ballistic speed and sustained speed, and that the value 11.2 km/s refers to ballistic speed. (One could go to the Moon at 1 km/s, given a means of sustaining that speed and enough time to make the trip!) Compare the escape speeds from different bodies via Table 4.1.

Maximum Falling Speed The idea of maximum falling speed, page 100, is sufficiently interesting for elaboration. Pretend you throw your car keys from ground level to your friend at the top of a building. Throw them too fast and they continue by your friend; throw them too slow and they never reach her. But if you throw them just right, say 11 m/s, they just barely reach her so she has only to grab them at their point of zero speed. Question: It took a speed of 11 m/s to get the keys up to her — if she simply drops them, how fast will they fall into your hands? Aha! If it takes a speed of 11.2 km/s to throw them to her if she is somewhat beyond Pluto, and if she similarly drops them, how fast will they fall into your hands? Now your students understand maximum falling speed.

Recap of Satellite Motion You can wind up your brief treatment of satellite motion and catch its essence via the following skit: Ask your students to pretend they are encountered by a bright youngster, too young to have much knowledge of physics and mathematics, but who nevertheless asks why satellites seem to defy gravity and stay in orbit. You ask what answer could correctly satisfy the curiosity of the kid, then pose the following dialogue between the kid and the students in your class (you're effectively suggesting how the student might interact with the bright kid). Ask the kid to observe and then describe what you do, as you hold a rock at arm's length and then simply drop it. The kid replies, "You dropped the rock and it fell to the ground below," to which you respond, "Very good — now what happens this time?", as you move your hand horizontally and again drop the rock. The kid observes and then says, "The rock dropped again, but because your hand was moving it followed a curved path and fell farther away." You continue, "Very good — now again —" as you throw the rock still farther. The kid replies, "I note that as your hand moves faster, the path follows a wider curve." You're elated at this response, and you ask the kid, "How far away will the rock hit the ground if its curved path matches the curved surface of the Earth?" The kid at first appears very puzzled, but then beams, "Oh — I get it! The stone doesn't hit at all — it's in Earth orbit" Then you interrupt your dialogue and ask the class, "Do YOU get it?" Then back to the kid who asks, "But isn't it really more complicated than that?", to which the answer is NO. The essential idea of satellite motion IS that simple.

(While you're on the subject of circles, you might ask why manhole covers are round. The answer is so some moron type doesn't drop them accidentally into the manhole. If they were square, they could be tipped up on edge and dropped through the hole on a diagonal. Similarly with ovals. But a circular hole will defy the most determined efforts. Of course there is a lip around the inside of the manhole that the cover rests on, making the diameter of the hole somewhat less than the diameter of the cover.)

CHECK QUESTIONS: Go over the Mechanics Review on page 28 in the **Practice Book**. If they don't use $a = F/m$ as a guide, expect most to miss the question about maximum acceleration.

5

Fluid Mechanics

The depths of the ocean as well as the expanse of outer space are of current interest, yet liquids are seldom studied in introductory physical science classes anymore. Perhaps this is because Archimedes' Principle and the like are too far from the frontiers of present research. But because much of the science here is more than 2000 years old is no reason it shouldn't be in your course. Liquids are a very real part of your students' everyday world.

It is well known that falling from great heights into water has much the same effect as falling to solid ground. Less well known are the new "water saws," with pressures of about 5500 lb/in^2 used for cutting through armor-plate steel.

The dedicated teacher walking on broken glass with bare feet in his classroom on page 130 is Marshall Ellenstein. Marshall has been a contributor to Hewitt's books for years and is the editor of the video series *Conceptual Physics Alive!*

As a sidelight, whereas water in a vessel exerts a pressure proportional to its depth, such isn't the case for a vessel of sand or other particles. For a granular material, the pressure at the base reaches a maximum at a certain elevation and remains there. That's why sand trickles at a nearly constant rate through the narrow opening separating two glass bulbs in an hourglass. Contact forces between grains transfer weight to the container's walls, which bear the extra load.

In student laboratory exercises, it is more common to work with mass density than with weight density, and floating or submerged materials are more often described in units of mass rather than weight. Displaced liquid is also described in units of mass rather than weight. This is why buoyant force in this chapter is treated as "the weight of so many kilograms," rather than "so many newtons." The expression of buoyancy in terms of mass units should be more in keeping with what goes on in lab.

An impressive buoyancy demo by John Suchocki: Place about 8 grams of dry ice in a large (several cm) uninflated balloon. Tie the balloon. Immediately set it on a digital balance reading to the nearest milligram. As the balloon inflates (over a few minutes) the balance readout plummets at a rate of about 2 mg/sec. The scale will finally read about 2.4 grams less, assuming the balloon inflates to about 2 liters (density of air is about 1.2 g/L).

Oceans tidbit: The Atlantic is getting wider, the Pacific narrower.

The section on Boyle's Law avoids distinguishing between absolute pressure and gauge pressure. Charles' Law is not covered, and is referenced only to a footnote.

The **Practice Book** features two sheets on Archimedes' Principle.

The **Laboratory Manual** has two activities and two experiments on liquids and gases.

There is a whopping dozen plus **Next-Time Questions** — again, enough to use fresh ones in succeeding semesters.

SUGGESTED LECTURE PRESENTATION

Density Measure the dimensions of a large wooden cube in cm and find its mass with a pan balance. Define density = mass/volume. (Use the same cube when you discuss flotation in the next chapter.) Some of your students will unfortunately conceptualize density as massiveness or bulkiness rather than massiveness per bulkiness, even when they give a verbal definition properly. This can be helped with the following:

CHECK QUESTIONS: Which has the greater density, a cupful of water or a lakeful of water? A kilogram of lead or a kilogram of feathers? A single uranium atom or the world?

I jokingly relate breaking a candy bar in two and giving the smaller piece to my friend who looks disturbed. "I gave you the same density of candy bar as I have."

Contrast the density of matter and the density of atomic nuclei that comprise so tiny a fraction of space within matter. From about 2 gm/cm^3 to 2×10^{14} gm/cm^3. And in a further crushed state, the interior of neutron stars, about 10^{16} gm/cm^3.

Area-Volume In this chapter we discuss volume and area, as evident in the units gm/cm^3 and N/m^2. Emphasize the relationship between area and volume as Chelcie Liu does by showing the following: Have a 500-ml spherical flask filled with colored water sitting on your lecture table. Produce a tall cylindrical flask, also of 500 ml (unknown to your students), and ask for speculations as to how high the water level will be when water is poured into it from the spherical flask. You can ask for a show of hands for those who think that the water will reach more than half the height, and those who think it will fill to less than half the height, and for those who guess it will fill to exactly half the height. Your students will be amazed when they see that the seemingly smaller spherical flask has the same volume as the tall cylinder. To explain, call attention to the fact that the *area* of the spherical flask is considerably smaller than the surface area of the cylinder. We see a greater area and we unconsciously think that the volume should be greater as well. Be sure to do this. It is more impressive than it may first seem.

Force versus Pressure Begin by distinguishing between force and pressure. Illustrate with examples: Somebody pushing on your back with a force of only 1 N — with a pin! As you're lying on the floor, a 400-N woman stands on your stomach — perched atop spike heels! Indian master lying on a bed of 1000 nails — apprentice considering starting with one nail! Why the importance of jewel bearings (remember them, old timer?) in watches, diamond stylus (still around!) in record players, rounded corners on tables, sharp blades on cutting knives, and the absurdity of standing tall while pointing your toes downward when caught in quicksand.

Have students compare in their hands the weights of a small steel ball and a large Styrofoam ball, and after agreeing that the little ball is heavier, weigh them and show the Styrofoam ball is heavier! Another example of pressure (on the nerve endings).

Liquid Pressure Liquid pressure = density × depth: After a few words about density, you may want to derive or call attention to the derivation of this relationship (footnote on page 114).

DEMONSTRATION: Pascal's Vases (similar to Figure 5.4) — rationalize your results in terms of the supporting forces exerted by the sloping sides of the vases. [That is, in the wide sloping vase, the water pushes against the glass, and the glass reacts by pushing against the water. So the glass supports the extra water without the pressure below increasing. For the narrow vase that slopes outward near the bottom, the water pushes up against the sloping glass. By reaction, the glass pushes down on the water, so the pressure at the bottom is as if water were present all the way to the surface.]

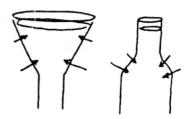

Ask why your heart gets more rest if you sleep in a prone position versus sitting up. Call attention to the fact that when swimming, the pressure one feels against the eardrums is a function of only depth — that swimming 3 meters deep in a small pool has the same effect as swimming 3 meters deep in the middle of a huge lake.

CHECK QUESTION: Would the pressure be greater swimming 3 m deep in the middle of the ocean? (Then compare the densities of fresh and salt water.)

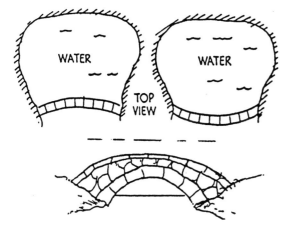

Ask why dams are built thicker at the bottom, and after discussing Figure 5.5 sketch the top view of a couple of dams on the board and ask which design is best. Then relate this to the shape of stone bridges (which actually need no mortar), and the arched shape of the tops of windows in old brick buildings. Another illustration is the concave ends of large wine barrels.

Buoyant Force Show that a consequence of pressure being depth dependent is the phenomenon of buoyancy. Sketch Figure 5.8 on the board. Follow this up with a sketch and explanation of Figure 5.13.

DEMONSTRATION: Show how an overflow can enables the measure of an object's volume. Ask how one could measure a quarter of a cup of butter in a liquid measuring cup using this method.

DEMONSTRATION: Archimedes' Principle, as shown in Figure 5.12.

Point out that because a liquid is incompressible (practically incompressible, as the volume of water decreases by only 50 one-millionths of its original volume for each atmosphere increase in pressure, or equivalently, for each addition 10.3 m in depth) its density is not depth dependent. The density of water near the surface is practically the same as the density far beneath the surface. You may wish to acknowledge that some variation occurs due to temperature differences. Usually a student will inquire about waterlogged objects which lie submerged yet off the bottom of the body of water. Such objects are slightly denser than the warmer surface water and not quite as dense as the cooler water at the bottom. Stress that this is unusual and that objects appreciably denser than water always sink to the bottom, regardless of the depth of the water. Scuba divers do not encounter "floating" rocks near the bottoms of deep bodies of water!

CHECK QUESTION: Two solid blocks of identical size are submerged in water. One block is lead and the other is aluminum. Upon which is the buoyant force greater?

After discussion, try this one:

CHECK QUESTION: Two solid blocks of identical size, one of lead and the other of wood, are put in the same water. Upon which is the buoyant force greater? [This time the BF is greater on the lead, because it displaces more water than the wood that floats!]

CHECK QUESTION: What is the buoyant force on a ten-ton ship floating in fresh water? In salt water? In a lake of mercury? [Same buoyant force, but different *volumes* displaced.]

The unit "ton" may be taken to mean a metric tonne, the weight of 1000 kg, or the British ton, 2000 lbs. Either interpretation is sufficient in treating the idea involved.

Archimedes and the King's Crown Eureka was the solution to whether or not the king's crown was adulterated with silver. When immersed in water, a measure of the volume of water displaced gives the volume of the crown. If more water is displaced by the crown than by a mass of gold of equal weight, this indicates the presence of an alloy.

Flotation Discuss boats and rafts and the change of water lines when loaded.

CHECK QUESTIONS: What is the approximate density of a fish? Of a person? What can you say of people who can't float?

DEMONSTRATION: Cartesian diver (inverted partially filled small bottle submerged in a larger flexible plastic bottle that you squeeze to increase and decrease the weight of water in the small bottle to make it rise and fall).

Discuss the compressibility of the human body in swimming — how the density of most people a meter or two below the surface of the water is still less than the density of water, and that one need only relax and be buoyed to the surface. But that at greater depths, the greater pressure compresses one to densities greater than the density of water, and one must swim to the surface. Simply relaxing, one would sink to the bottom! Relate this to the Cartesian diver demonstration. Also state why one cannot snorkel with a tube that goes deeper than a half meter or so.

Side point: Contrary to those old Tarzan movies, you cannot sink in quicksand. Quicksand is the name given to a mass of sand particles that are supported by circulating water rather than by each other. Its density is greater than the density of human bodies, so you can float on it. If you struggle, you'll unfortunately succeed in digging yourself deeper in. So if you're ever stuck in it, keep yourself still until you stop sinking (you will), and then use slow swimming motions to get yourself into a horizontal position and then roll onto the ground.

DEMONSTRATION: (By Sean Elkins and suggested by Marshall Ellenstein.) Place a Ping Pong ball a couple of inches below the surface of a glass container of puffed rice. Then place a golf ball on top of the puffed rice. Shake the container and say the magic words "physics." The golf ball and Ping Pong ball soon changes places — the golf ball "sinks" and the Ping Pong ball "floats."

Floating Mountain Box Isostacy is the concept wherein high structures like mountains are lighter and "float" on a denser substructure in the Earth — Archimedes' principle for rocks.

Weight of Air Hold out an empty drinking glass and ask what's in it. It's not really empty, for it's filled with air, and has weight. It is common to think of air as having very little mass, when the truth is air has a fairly large mass — about 1.25 kilogram for a cube one meter on a side (at sea level). The air that fills your bathtub has a mass of about 0.5 kilogram. We don't feel the weight of this mass only because we are immersed in an ocean of air. A plastic bag full of water, for example, has a significant weight, but if the bag is taken into a swimming pool it weighs nothing (Figure 5.22). Likewise for the surrounding air. A bag of air may have a fairly large mass, but as long as the bag is surrounded by air, its weight is not felt. We are as unconscious of the weight of air that surrounds us as a fish is unconscious of the weight of water that surrounds it.

CHECK QUESTION: Open the door of a refrigerator and inside is a large lonely grapefruit. Which weighs more, the air in the frig or the grapefruit? [The inside volume of a common refrigerator is between 1/2 and 3/4 m^3, which corresponds to nearly a kilogram of cold air (about 2 pounds). So unless the grapefruit is more than a 2-pounder, the air weighs more.]

The Atmosphere Draw a circle as large as possible on the chalkboard, and then announce that it represents the Earth. State that if you were to draw another circle, indicating the thickness of the atmosphere surrounding the Earth to scale, that you would end up drawing the same line — for over 99% of the atmosphere lies within the thickness of the chalk line! Then go on to discuss the ocean of air in which we live.

DEMONSTRATION: While discussing the preceding, have a gallon metal can with a bit of water in it heating on a burner. When steam issues, cap it tightly and remove from the heat source. Continue your discussion and the collapsing can will interrupt you as it crunches. If you really want to impress your class, do the same with a 50-gallon drum! [The explanation is that pressure inside the can or drum decreases as cooling occurs and the steam condenses. Atmospheric pressure on the outside produces the crunching net force on the can or drum.]

DEMONSTRATION: Here's a goodie! Heat some aluminum soda pop cans on a burner, empty except for a small amount of water that is brought to a boil to make steam. With a pot holder or tongs, pick up a can and quickly invert it into a basin of water. Crunch! The atmospheric pressure immediately crushes the can with a resounding WHOP! Very impressive. [Condensation of the steam and vapor occur and the interior pressure is reduced. This occurs even when the temperature of the water bath into which the can is inverted is nearly boiling temperature. What happens is a "flypaper effect" — water molecules in the vapor state condense when they encounter the water into which they're placed — even hot water. You'll show this demo again when you discuss the reason for the condensation cycle in a steam turbine — to decrease the back pressure on the turbine blades.]

Atmospheric Pressure While this is going on, state that if you had a 30-km tall bamboo pole of cross section 1 square cm, the mass of the air from the atmosphere in it would amount to about 1 kg. The weight of this air is the source of atmospheric pressure. The atmosphere bears down on the earth's surface at sea level with a pressure that corresponds to the weight of 1 kg per square cm. (Remember the old days when we could talk about plain old 14.7 lb/in^2? Since the unit of force is now the newton and the unit of area is the square meter, conceptualizing atmospheric pressure is less simple than before. Nevertheless, continue with the following description.) To understand the pressure of the atmosphere in terms of newtons per square meter, ask your class to imagine a 30-km tall sewer pipe of cross section 1 square m, filled with the air of the atmosphere. How much would the enclosed air weigh? The answer is about 10^5 N. So if you draw a circle of one square meter on the lecture table, and ask what the weight is for all the air in the atmosphere above, you should elicit a chorus, silent or otherwise of "10^5 N!" If your table is above sea level, then the weight of air is correspondingly less. Then estimate the force of the air pressure that collapsed the metal can — both for a perfect vacuum and for a case where the pressure difference is about half an atmosphere.

Estimate the force of the atmosphere on a person. You can estimate the surface area by approximating different parts of the body on the board — leg by leg, arm by arm, etc. (This can be quite funny, if you want it to be!)

DEMONSTRATION: This great one from John McDonald of Boise State University consists of a square sheet of soft rubber with some sort of handle at its center. A 50-gram mass hanger poked through its center works well. Toss the rubber sheet on any perfectly flat surface — best on the top of a lab stool. Picking the rubber up by a corner is an easy task, because the air gets under it as it is lifted. But lifting it by the middle is another story. As the middle is raised, a low-pressure region is formed because air cannot get in. The rubber sheet behaves as a suction cup, and the entire stool is lifted when the handle is raised.

DEMONSTRATION: Whap a toilet plunger or other suction cup on the wall. (Instruct your class to inquire with their neighbors to see if there is a consensus as to the reason.)

Barometers State that a better vacuum source than sucking would remove much more air, and if all the air were removed, a very large column of water would be needed to balance the atmosphere on the other side. This would be about 10.3 m, but depends a little on today's atmospheric pressure. Such devices made up the first barometers. They are impractically large, so mercury is instead commonly used. Since mercury is 13.6 times as dense as water, the height of water needed to balance the atmosphere is 1/13.6 of 10.3 m = 76 cm. If you have the opportunity, construct a mercury barometer before the class.

CHECK QUESTION: How would the barometer level vary while ascending and descending in the elevator of a tall building? [You might quip about the student who was asked

to find the height of a building with a sensitive barometer who simply dropped it from the top and measured the seconds of fall — or who exchanged it with the builder of the building for the correct information.]

Discuss ear popping in aircraft, and why cabin pressure is lower than atmospheric pressure at high altitudes.

DEMONSTRATION: As the sketch shows, try sucking a drink through a straw with two straws; one in the liquid and the other outside. It can't be done because the pressure in your mouth is not reduced because of the second straw (although with some effort a bit of liquid can be drawn). Invite your students to try this, and to share this (and other ideas!) at parties.

DEMONSTRATION: The siphon. Careful! Many instructors have found in front of their classes that they misunderstood the operation of a siphon. The explanation does not have to do with differences in atmospheric pressures at the ends of the tube, but with the difference in liquid pressures in the short and long sides of the bent tube. Unless the long end of the tube exceeds 10.3 m, atmospheric pressure acting upwards against the liquid in the tube is greater than the downward pressure of liquid. The situation is analogous to pushing upward against the bottom ends of a see-saw with unequal pushes. Liquid in the short end of the tube is pushed up with more net force than the liquid in the long end of the tube. (Or it's analogous to a chain hanging over a peg, with one end longer and heavier than the other end.)

Boyle's Law Discuss Boyle's Law. At the risk of information overload you may or may not want to get into the differences between absolute and gauge pressures. (I avoid it in the text.)

Buoyancy of Air Hold your hands out, one a few centimeters above the other, and ask if there really is any difference in air pressure at the two places. The fact that there is can be demonstrated by the rising of a helium-filled balloon of the same size! The balloon rises only because the atmospheric pressure at its bottom is greater than the atmospheric pressure at its top. Pressure in the atmosphere really is depth dependent!

CHECK QUESTION: Which is greater, the buoyant force on the helium-filled balloon, or the buoyant force on you? [Assuming the balloon has less volume than you, there is more buoyant force on you.] Discuss why.

Interestingly enough, atmospheric pressure halves with every 6 km increase in elevation, so a freely expanding balloon becomes twice as big with each 6 km rise. Does this increase the buoyant force? No, because the displacement of twice as much half-as-dense air has the same weight!

CHECK QUESTION: A large block of Styrofoam and a small block of iron have identical weights on a weighing scale. Which has the greater mass? [Actually the Styrofoam has the greater mass. This is because it has a greater volume, displaces more air, and experiences a greater buoyant force. So it's weight on the scale is its "true weight," minus the buoyant force of the air, which is the case for all things weighed in air. The fact that it reads the same on the scale as the iron means it must have more mass than the iron. (A lobster that walks on a bathroom scale on the ocean bottom has more mass than the reading indicates.)]

CHECK QUESTION: What would happen to the bubbles in a beer mug if you dropped the mug of beer from the top of a high building? Would the bubbles rise to the top, go to the bottom, or remain motionless with respect to the mug? [First of all, you'd likely be apprehended for irresponsible behavior. As for the bubbles, they'd remain motionless relative to the mug, since the local effects of gravity on the beer would be absent. This is similar to the popular demo of dropping a cup of water with holes in the side. When held at rest the water spurts out, but drop it and the spurting stops.]

Bernoulli's Principle Introduce Bernoulli's principle by blowing across the top surface of a sheet of paper, Figure 5.33. Follow this up with a variety of demonstrations such as making a beach ball hover in a stream of air issuing from the reverse end of a vacuum cleaner or a Ping-Pong ball in the airstream of a hair dryer.

DEMONSTRATION: Line a cardboard tube with sandpaper and sling a Ping-Pong ball sidearm. The sandpaper will produce the friction to make the ball roll down the tube and emerge spinning — you'll see that the ball breaks in the correct direction. Point out that paddles have a rough surface like the sand-paper for the same reason — to spin the ball when it is properly struck — that is, to apply "English" to the ball.

DEMONSTRATION: Place a pair of upright empty aluminum soft drink cans on a few parallel straws on your lecture table. Blow between the cans and they roll toward each other. Or do the same with the nearby cans suspended by strings. A puff of air between them makes them click against one another, rather than blowing them apart as might be expected. [Some people avoid Bernoulli's principle because in some cases, like plane flight, there are alternate models to account for the forces that occur. These clicking cans, however, are straight Bernoulli!]

DEMONSTRATION: Swing a Ping-Pong ball taped to a string into a stream of water as shown in Figure 5.39. Follow this up with the shower curtain bit of page 124.

42

6
Thermal Energy

The concept of heat flow between temperature differences provides some background to the concept of current flow between electric potential differences in Chapter 9. Here we introduce the concept of KE/molecule, *temperature,* which is analogous to the later concept of PE/charge, *voltage.* Both high temperatures and high voltages are ordinarily harmful only when large energies are transferred in a relatively short time (that is, when large power is transferred). The white-hot sparks of the 4th-of-July sparkler held by little Terrance Jones on page 133 have very high temperatures, but their energies are very small. So they are quite harmless. Similarly, a balloon rubbed on your hair may have thousands of volts, but the energy stored is very small. Energy per molecule or energy per charge may be high, but if the molecules or charges involved are small in number, the energy content is also small. Aside from the parallels between heat and electricity, the chapter serves as a prerequisite only for the two following chapters dealing with heat transfer and thermodynamics.

In the text, temperature is treated in terms of the kinetic energy per molecule of substances. Although strictly speaking, temperature is directly proportional to the kinetic energy per molecule only in the case of ideal gases, we take the view that temperature is related to molecular translational kinetic energy in most common substances. Rotational kinetic energy, on the other hand, is only indirectly related to temperature, as is illustrated in a microwave oven. There the

H_2O molecules are set oscillating with considerable rotational kinetic energy. But this doesn't cook the food. What does is the translational kinetic energy imparted to neighboring molecules that are bounced from the oscillating H_2Os like marbles that are set flying in all directions when they encounter the spinning blades of fans. If neighboring atoms did not interact with the oscillating H_2O molecules, the temperature of the food would be no different before and after the microwave oven was activated. Temperature has to do with the translational kinetic energy of molecules. Degrees of freedom, rotational and vibrational states, and the complications of temperature in liquids and solids are not treated. Next course!

Quantity of heat is spoken of in terms of calories, a departure from the SI unit, joules. Note that heats of fusion and vaporization of water are in calorie units. We find the SI units 334.88 kJ/kg and 2.26 MJ/kg too conceptually difficult compared to the 80 and 540 calories that many students are familiar with in chemistry courses. If you're a 100% SI type, a footnote on page 153 gives the SI units, and you can lecture with SI units and point out the very few places where the units calories occur.

The definition of the calorie, page 139, implies that the same amount of heat will be required to change the temperature of water $1°C$ — whatever the temperature of the water. Although this relation holds true to a fair degree, it is not exactly

43

correct: a calorie is precisely defined as the amount of heat required to raise a gram of water from 14° to 15° Celsius.

The exaggeration of the volume vs temperature scale in Figure 6.16 should be pointed out, for it is easy for a student to erroneously conclude that a great change in the volume of water occurs over a relatively small temperature change. Despite the warning in the following page, some students will interpret the volume at 0°C to be that of ice rather than ice water.

Regelation is treated conventionally in the text — in terms of added pressure that crushes ice crystals. This explanation, however, is controversial; that added pressure and crushing of the crystals is insufficient to explain the melting and refreezing of ice. Perhaps we could "ice skate" on most any solid material near its melting temperature. The box on *Snowballs and Ice Skating* may or may not be changed in later printings.

If you wish to introduce the idea of distribution curves in your course, this is a good place to do it. Treat the cooling produced by evaporation with plots of relative numbers of molecules in a liquid vs their speeds, as show below, and show how the distribution shifts as

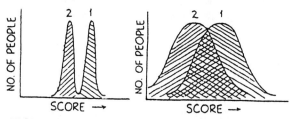

NARROW-MINDED PERCEPTION BROAD-MINDED PERCEPTION

the faster-moving molecules evaporate. You may wish to point to the bell-shapes distribution curves that represent the distributions of so many things, from molecular speeds to examination scores to people's IQ scores. Regrettably, many people tend to regard such distributions not as bell-shaped, but as spikes. This makes a difference in attitudes. For example, suppose you compare the grade distributions for two sections of your course, Group 1 and Group 2, and that the average score for Group 1 is somewhat greater than that for Group 2. For whatever reason, Group 1 outperforms Group 2. With this information can we make any judgment about individuals from either group? One who looks at these distributions as spiked shaped behaves as if he can make such a judgement — he'll say (or not say but think) that individuals from Group 1 are "better" than particular individuals from Group 2. On the other hand, one who thinks in

terms of the broad shape of the bell shaped distribution will not make any assumptions about such individuals. He is well aware of the region of overlap in the two distribution curves. His attitude toward individuals from either group is unbiased by unwarranted prejudice. Hence the difference between narrow-mindedness and broad-mindedness!

This chapter introduces the concepts of evaporation, condensation, melting, and freezing, which will be treated in more detail in Part 6 — Chemistry.

There are three exercises for this chapter in the **Practice Book**.

There are 7 experiments in the **Laboratory Manual** that go with this and other Part 2 chapters.

Next-Time Questions features some 6 for this chapter.

By now it is hoped that the "Check-Your-Neighbor" technique of is a major part of your lecture method. Take pity on students who sit through lectures where the instructor poses questions that he or she immediately answers without involving the students, who are passive observers rather than participants in the learning process. Pose check questions before you move onto new material.

SUGGESTED LECTURE PRESENTATION

Begin by asking what the difference is between a hot cup of coffee and a cold cup of coffee. Think small for the answer: The molecules in the hot cup of coffee are moving faster — they are more energetic. Heat and temperature have to do with the kinetic energies of the molecules in substances. Heat and temperature are different: To begin with, **heat** is energy that is measured in joules, or calories. **Temperature** is measured in degrees. More on this soon.

Temperature Calibration
Describe how the increased jostling of molecules in a substance result in expansion and show how this property underlies the common thermometer. Draw a sketch of an uncalibrated thermometer on the board, with its mercury vessel at the bottom, and describe how the energy of jostling molecules is transferred from the outer environment to the mercury

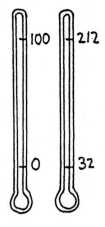

within. If placed in boiling water, energy of the jostling water molecules would be transferred to the mercury, which would expand and squeeze up the tube. State that one could make a scratch on the glass at this level and label it 100. And then describe how, if placed in a container of ice water, the molecules of mercury would give energy to the cold water and slow down, contract, and fall to a lower level in the tube. One could again make a scratch and call this point zero. Then, if 100 equally-spaced scratches are made between the two reference points, one would have a centigrade thermometer.

In a vein of humor draw a second uncalibrated thermometer on the board and repeat your discussion (in abbreviated fashion) of placing it in boiling water. State that the upper level needn't be called 100, that any number would do so long as all thermometers were calibrated the same. Ask the class for any random number. Someone will say 212. Then casually acknowledge the 212 response and write that on your diagram. Repeat the bit about placing the instrument in ice water and state that the position on the scale needn't be called zero, that any number would do. Ask for a random number. You'll have several students volunteer 32, which you graciously accept. The class should be in a good mood at this point, and you briefly discuss the two scales and lead into the idea of absolute zero and the Kelvin scale. (Name after "Lord Scale?")

Did Fahrenheit have a fever on the day he calibrated his temperature scale? Was a 1.4° above normal responsible for his placement of the 100° mark where he wished to be the standard for 100°? Your class may wish to speculate how he placed his zero.

CHECK QUESTION: Which has the largest degrees, a Celsius thermometer or a Fahrenheit thermometer? [Celsius.]

CHECK QUESTION: True or false: Cold is the absence of fast-moving molecules. [False; cold refers to very slow-moving molecules, not their absence.]

Absolute Zero Review the temperature scales and lead into the thermodynamic temperature scale. To lead into an understanding of the absolute temperature scale, begin by considering the ordering of a piece of hot apple pie in a restaurant and then being served cold pie — ice cold pie, at $0°C$. Suppose you ask the waiter to put the pie in the oven and heat it up. How hot? Say twice as hot. Question: what will be the temperature of the pie? Move your class to the "check-your-neighbor" routine. Change your

mind about the $0°C$ initial temperature of the piece of pie, and ask if the problem is easier if you begin with, say, a $10°C$ piece of pie. Tell your class to beware of neighbors who say the problem is simplified, and the answer is (wrongly) $20°C$. This should spark interest. Now you're ready for "Celsius, the Village Tailor" story.

Celsius, the Village Tailor Hold a measuring stick against the wall of the lecture room (so that the bottom of the vertically-oriented stick is about 1 meter above the floor) and state that you are Celsius, the village tailor, and that you measure the heights of your customers against the stick, which is firmly fastened to the wall. You state that there is no need for the stick to extend to the floor, nor to the ceiling, for your shortest and tallest customers fall within the extremities of the stick. Mention that all tailors using the same method could communicate meaningfully with each other about the relative heights of their customers providing the measuring sticks in each shop were fastened the same distance above the "absolute zero" of height. It just so happens that the distance to the floor, the "absolute zero," is 273 notches — the same size notches on the stick itself. Then one day, a very short lady enters your shop and stands against the wall, the top of her head coinciding with the zero mark on the measuring stick. As you take her zero reading, she comments that she has a brother who is twice her height. Ask the class for the height of her brother. Then ask for the temperature of the twice-as-hot apple pie. When this is understood, ask why the pie will not *really* be $273°C$. Or that for the initially $10°C$ pie, the temperature will not really be $293°C$. [Considerable heat has gone into changing the state of the water in the pie, which accounts for it being "dried out." If you wish to avoid the change of state factor, begin your discussion with the temperature of something such as a piece of metal that will not change state for the temperature range in question.]

Thermal Energy Distinguish internal energy from temperature. A neat example is the 4th of July type sparklers, even if you've mentioned it earlier. The sparks that fly from the firework and strike your face have temperatures in excess of 2000°C, but they don't burn. Why? Because the thermal energy of the sparks is extremely low. It is the amount of energy you receive that burns, not the ratio of energy/molecule. Even with a high ratio (high temperature), if a relatively few molecules are involved, the energy transfer is low. (Again, this is similar to the high voltage of a balloon rubbed against your hair. It may have thousands of volts, which is to say thousands of joules per charge. But if there are a relatively small number of charges, the total energy they carry is small.)

Heat Distinguish between *heat* and *temperature*. Heat has to do with energy flow while temperature is a ratio of energy per molecule. They are very different. A Fourth-of-July-type sparkler emits sparks with temperatures exceeding 2000°C, but the heat one receives when one of these sparks lands on ones face is very small. High temperature means a high ratio of heat per molecule. The *ratio* and the *amount* of heat energy transferred are different things. Relatively few molecules comprise the tiny bit of white-hot matter that makes up the sparks of the sparkler. (Later you'll invoke a similar argument when you discuss the small energy associated with the high voltage of a charged van de Generator or party balloon rubbed on your hair.)

CHECK QUESTION: How are the sparks from a sparkler that strike your skin akin to tiny droplets of boiling water striking your skin? [Both have high temperatures, but safe levels of thermal energy to transfer to your skin.]

Thermal Energy Distinguish between *heat* and *thermal energy*. Thermal energy is loosely referred to as heat energy, although by definition, heat is the energy that flows from one place to another by virtue of a temperature difference. Thermal energy is the total molecular energies, kinetic plus potential, internal to a substance. Heat is thermal energy in transit.

Quantity of Heat Define the calorie, and distinguish it from the Calorie, the concern of people who watch their diet.

Specific Heat Capacity Lead into a distinction between the difference between calories and degrees, and the concept of specific heat capacity by asking your class to consider the difference in touching an empty iron frying pan that has been placed on a hot stove for one minute (ouch!) and doing the same with a frying pan of water. With the water, you could place your hand in it safely even if it were on the stove for several minutes. Ask which has the higher temperature, the empty pan or the one filled with water. Clearly, it is the empty pan. Ask which absorbed the greater amount of energy. The answer is the water-filled pan, if it was on the stove for a longer time. The water has absorbed more energy for a lesser rise in temperature! Physics and chemistry types have a name for this idea — specific heat capacity, or for short, specific heat. Cite the different specific heat capacities of cooked foods, of a hot TV dinner and the aluminum foil that can be removed with bare hands while the food is still too hot to touch.

Water's High Specific Heat Cite examples of water's high specific heat — hot water bottles on cold winter nights, cooling systems in cars, and the climate in places where there is much water. With the aid of a large world map, globe, or chalkboard sketch, show the sameness of latitudes for England and the Hudson Bay, and the French and Italian Rivieras with Canada. State how the fact that water requires so long a time to heat and cool, enables the Gulf Stream to hold thermal energy long enough to reach the North Atlantic. There it cools off. But if the water cools, then according to the conservation of energy, something else has to warm. What is that something? The air. The cooling water warms the air, and the winds at that latitude are westerly. So warmed air moves over the continent of Europe. If this weren't the case, Europe would have the same climate as regions of northern Canada. A similar situation occurs in the United States. The Atlantic Ocean off the coast of the eastern states is considerably warmer than the Pacific Ocean off the coast of Washington, Oregon and California, yet in winter months the east coast is considerably colder. This has to do with the high specific heat of water and the westerly winds. Air that is warmed by cooling water on the west coast moves landward and gives mild winters to Washington, Oregon, and California. But on the east coast, this warmed air moves seaward, leaving the east coast frigid in winter months. In summer months, when the air is warmer than the water, the air cools and the water warms. So summer months on the west coast states are relatively cool, while the east coast is relatively hot. The high specific heat of water serves to moderate climates. The climates on islands, for example, are fairly free of temperature variations. Even San Francisco, a peninsula that is close to being an island, has the most stable climate of any city in continental America.

4°C Water To lead into the idea of water's low density at 4°C you can ask if anyone in class happens to know what the temperature at the bottom of Lake Michigan was on a particular date, New Year's eve in 1905, for example. Then for the bottom of Lake Tahoe in California for any other date. And for another, until many are responding "4°C".

CHECK QUESTION: Ask the same for the bottom of a rain puddle outside the building, and be prepared for some to say 4°C.

Then ask why 4°C was the right answer for the deep lakes but the wrong answer for puddle. Then go into the explanation as given in the book — how the microscopic slush forms as the freezing temperature is approached, yielding a net expansion below 4°C. (We haven't done this, but we have thought of showing a Galileo-type thermometer in class — a small flask with a narrow glass tube filled with colored water, so changes in temperature would be clearly evident by different levels of water in the narrow tube. Then surround the flask with perhaps dry ice to rapidly chill the water. The water level drops as the temperature of the water decreases, but its rate slows as it nears 4°C, and then the direction reverses as cooling continues. This expansion of the water is due to the formation of "microscopic slush." The level of water observed, as a function of time, yields a graph similar to that of Figure 6.16.)

Ice Formation on Lakes Discuss the formation of ice, and why it forms at the surface and why it floats. And why deep bodies of water don't freeze over in winter because all the water in the lake has to be cooled to 4°C before colder water will remain at the surface to be cooled to the freezing temperature, 0°C. State that before one can cool a teaspoon full of water to 3°C, let alone 0°C, all the water beneath must be cooled to 4°C and that winters are neither cold or long enough for this to happen in the United States.

Thermal Expansion (Note the order differs from the text — in lecture we keep running with water) State that steel lengths expand about 1 part in 100,000 for each 1°C increase in temperature. Show a steel rod and ask if anybody would be afraid to stand with their stomach between the end of the rigidly held steel rod and a wall while the temperature of the rod is increased a few degrees. This is a safe activity, for the slight expansion of the rod would hardly be noticeable. Now ask for volunteers for a steel rod several kilometers in length. This is much different, for although the rate of change in length is the same, the total change in length could well impale you! Then discuss the expansion joints of large structures (Figures 6.11 and 6.12).

DEMONSTRATION: Place the middle of a bimetallic strip in a flame to show the unequal expansions of different metals, and the subsequent bending.

Point out that different substances expand or contract (length, area, and volume) at their own characteristic rates [coefficients of expansion]. Cite examples such as the need for the same expansion rate in teeth and teeth fillings; iron reinforcing rods and concrete; and the metal wires that are encased in glass light bulbs and the glass itself. Provision must be made when materials with different expansion rates interact; like the piston rings when aluminum pistons are enclosed in steel cylinders in a car, and the rockers

on bridges (Figure 6.11), and the overflow pipe for gasoline in a steel tank.

CHECK QUESTION: How would a thermometer differ if glass expanded with increasing temperature more than mercury? [Answer: The scale would be upside down, because the reservoir would enlarge (like the hole enlarged in the heated metal ring) and mercury in the column would tend to fill it up with increasing temperature.]

NEXT-TIME QUESTION: Ask your students to place an ice cube in a glass of ice water at home, and compare the water level at the side of the glass before and after the ice melts. Ask them to account for the volume of ice that extends above the water line after it melts. The answer to the original question is, of course, that the level remains unchanged. This can be explained from the principles learned in Chapter 5. The floating ice cube displaces its own weight of water, so if the cube weighs say a newton, then when placed in the glass, one newton of water is displaced and the water level rises. If it is first melted and then poured in the glass, again the water line would be higher, but by one newton, the same amount. More interesting is to account for the volume of floating ice that extends above the water line. The ice expanded upon freezing because of the hexagonal open structures of the crystals. Ask the class if they have any idea of how much volume all those billions and billions of open spaces constitute. Their combined volume is essentially that of the part of ice extending above the water line! When the ice melts, the part above the water line fills in the open structures as they collapse. Discuss this idea in terms of icebergs, and whether or not the coastline would change if all the floating icebergs in the world melted. The oceans would rise a bit, but only because icebergs are composed of fresh water. (They form above sea level and break off and then fall into sea [Chapter 24].) The slight rise is more easily understood by exaggerating the circumstance — think of ice cubes floating in mercury. When they melt, the depth of fluid (water on mercury) is higher than before. [Exaggeration of factors is a useful technique in "greater-than, equal-to, or less-than type" questions!]

Take note that ocean levels also rise due to thermal expansion. If you had a water-filled test tube that was 2 miles high (the average depth of the ocean), even a slight increase in temperature would raise the level of water appreciably. Similarly, a warmer ocean means a higher ocean and quite different coastlines in many places! (Too often we attribute rising oceans only to ice-cap melting.)

If your lecture breaks about here, consider the following:

NEXT-TIME QUESTION: Exercise 16 (The size of the hole in the iron ring when heated): Many students will correctly reason that the thickness of the ring will increase, but they will then conclude that the hole becomes smaller. When you treat the answer, consider cutting the ring into 4 quadrants, and put the pieces into a hot oven. They all expand. Now bring them back together to form a ring. This should make it clear that the hole expands when the ring is heated. More simply, the circumference as well as the thickness and every other dimension increases. Support this by demonstration and by the examples of opening a stuck metal jar lid by placing it under hot water, and the fitting of iron wheel rims on wooden wagon wheels by first placing the slightly smaller iron rims into the blacksmith's fire.

NEXT-TIME QUESTION: Problem 3, the ring around the earth.

Evaporation Begin by citing the familiar case of leaving the water when bathing and feeling chilly in the air, especially when it is windy. Explain the cooling of a liquid from an atomic point of view, and reinforce the idea of temperature being a measure of the average molecular kinetic energy, and acknowledge molecules that move faster and slower than the average.

CHECK QUESTION: Why does cooling occur in the water of a leaky canvas water bag? [Water seeps through the canvas. More faster-moving molecules leak and vaporize, leaving less energy per molecule behind.]

CHECK QUESTION: Cite at least two ways to cool a hot cup of coffee. [You can increase evaporation by blowing on it or pouring it into the saucer to increase the evaporating area. You can cool it by conduction by putting silverware in it, which absorbs heat and provides a radiating antenna.]

Sketch a bell-shaped distribution curve on the board to represent the wide array of molecular speeds in a container of water. The peak of the curve represents the speeds that correspond to the temperature of the water. (It is not important to distinguish here between the mean speed, the rms speed, and the most probable speeds.) Stress the many lower and higher speeds to the left and right of the peak of your curve at any moment in the water. Which molecules evaporate? The fast ones, which you clip from the right hand tail of your curve. What is the result? A shift toward the left of the peak of the curve — a lowering of temperature. [Actually, this approach is highly exaggerated, for the molecules that do penetrate the surface and escape into the air have energies that correspond to 3400K! See Paul Hewitt's article on page 492 of *The Physics Teacher*, October, 1981.]

The relatively strong bond between water molecules (hydrogen bonding) prevents more evaporation than presently occurs. It also enhances condensation. [This idea is explained in detail in Chapter 17.]

Condensation If evaporation is a cooling process, what kind of process would the opposite of evaporation be? This is condensation, which is a warming process.

CHECK QUESTION: Why is it that many people after taking a shower will begin drying in the shower stall before getting outside. [While still in the shower region, appreciable condensation offsets the cooling by evaporation.]

Make the point that a change of state from liquid to gas or vice versa is not merely one or the other. Condensation occurs while evaporation occurs and vice versa. The net effect is usually what is spoken about. If you haven't shown the collapsing can demo in your atmospheric pressure lecture, now is a good time. A better time, however, is in the next chapter when you discuss the condensation cycle of a steam turbine — that the condensation reduces the back pressure on the turbine blades.

Make clear just what is cooling when evaporation occurs. To say that one thing cools is to say that another warms. When a hot cup of coffee cools by evaporation, the surrounding air is warmed. Conservation of energy reigns!

Boiling Discuss boiling and the roles of adding heat and pressure in the boiling process. A tactic we use throughout our teaching is to ask the class members to pretend they are having a one-to-one conversation with a friend about the ideas of physics. Suppose a friend is skeptical about the idea of boiling being a cooling process. We tell our class just what to say to convince the friend of what is going on. We tell them to first point out the distinction between heating and boiling. If the friend knows that the temperature of boiling water remains at 100°C regardless of the amount of heat applied, point out that this is so because the water is cooling by boiling as fast as it is being warmed by heating. Then if this still is not convincing, ask the friend to hold his or her hands above a pot of boiling water — in the steam. Your friend knows the hands will be burned. But burned by what? By the steam. And where did the steam get its energy? From the boiling water; so energy is leaving the water — that's what we mean by cooling! Bring in the role of pressure on boiling, and illustrate this with the pressure cooker.

CHECK QUESTIONS: In bringing water to a boil in the high mountains, is the time required to bring the water to a boil longer or shorter than at sea level? Is the time required for cooking longer or shorter? (Preface this second question with the statement that you are posing a different question, for any confusion about this is most likely due to failing to distinguish between the two questions.)

DEMONSTRATION: Evacuate air from a flask of water that is at room temperature, enough so that the water in the flask will boil from the heat of the students' hands as it is passed around the classroom. [Take care that the flask is strong enough so that it doesn't implode!]

Geyser Explain how a geyser is like a pressure cooker. Discuss the operation of a coffee percolator.
Boiling and Freezing at the Same Time This must be seen to be appreciated!

DEMONSTRATION: The triple-point demonstration, Figure 6.27. [A film loop or short video should be made of this impressive demo for those who don't have the equipment!]

Melting and Freezing

DEMONSTRATION: Regelation of an ice cube with a copper wire. (The wire must be a good heat conductor for this to work, for when the water immediately above the wire refreezes, it gives up energy. How much? Enough to melt an equal amount of ice immediately under the wire. This energy must be conducted through the thickness of the wire. Hence this demo requires that the wire be an excellent conductor of heat. Common string, for example, won't do.)

Energy and Changes of Phase Ask if it is possible to heat a substance without raising its temperature, and why a steam burn is more damaging than a burn from boiling water at the same temperature. In answering these, discuss the change of phase graph of Figure 6.29, and relate this to Figure 6.28. After citing examples of changes of phase where energy is absorbed, cite examples where energy is released — like raining and snowing. People sometimes say that it is too cold to snow. Explain that this statement arises from the fact that the process of snowing warms the air!

Ask about cooling a room by leaving the refrigerator door open, and compare it to putting an air conditioner in the middle of a room instead of mounting it in a window. Ask what the result would be of mounting an air conditioner backwards in a window.

Air Conditioning In view of the ozone-destroying chemicals used as refrigerants, cite present efforts you are acquainted with in developing alternative systems. One approach introduced in mid 1992 by ICC Technologies in Philadelphia uses ordinary water in place of chlorofluorocarbons, with reports of providing cooling for a small fraction of the energy of conventional systems. The device utilizes the evaporation condensation cycle with a new type of desiccant, or drying agent, that chills air without increasing its humidity. Alternative air conditioning systems will likely be in the forefront of news on new technologies. It's needed.

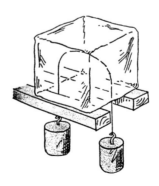

7

Heat Transfer and Thermodynamics

This chapter begins with conduction, convection, and radiation of heat with emphasis again on bodies of water and the atmosphere, which will be treated again in Part 7. The section on radiation serves as some background to later chapters on light.

Firewalking. Charlatans still cite firewalking as overcoming nature. James Randi interestingly points out that when a charlatan is exposed, the outrage of his or her victims is most frequently aimed at the one who strips away the mask. And on the matter of nonsense, it seems unlikely that there will ever be a claim so whacky that at least one PhD physicist cannot be found to vouch for it. There are fringies in every group—ours included.

Paul Doherty point out that unlike the decrease in temperature with distance about a hot coal or two, above a bed of coals the temperature remains fairly constant, like the constant electric field near a plane of charges.

There is only one practice sheet for this chapter in the **Practice Book**.

A choice of 7 experiments on heat transfer are in the **Laboratory Manual**.

Next-Time Questions features 7.

SUGGESTED LECTURE PRESENTATION

Conduction Begin by asking why pots and pans have wooden or plastic handles, why one can safely touch wood at a high temperature — then discuss conduction from an atomic point of view, citing the role of the electrons in both heat and electrical conductors. You might demonstrate the oldie of melting wax on different metal rods equidistant from a hot flame, and illustrate relative conductivities. Other materials can be compared in their ability to conduct heat, like newspaper when having to sleep out-of-doors. Discuss the poor conductivity of water, which ties to the previous lecture where you discussed the $4°C$ temperature of the bottom of deep lakes all year round.

DEMONSTRATION: Do Home Project 1 with ice wedged at the bottom of a test tube. Some steel wool will hold the ice at the bottom of the tube. It is impressive to see that the water at the top is brought to a boil by the flame of a burner while the ice below barely melts!

DEMONSTRATION: Do Home Project 3 and wrap a piece of paper around a thick metal bar and attempt to burn it in the flame. The paper does not reach its ignition temperature because heat is conducted into the metal.

DEMONSTRATION: Extend the previous demo and place a paper cup filled with water in the flame. Again, the paper will not reach its ignition temperature and burn because heat from the flame is conducted into the conductor — this time water. Water is not *that* poor a conductor — its high specific heat comes into play here also (this is Exercise 13.)

Discuss the poor conductivity of air, and its role in insulating materials — like snow. Discuss thermal underwear, and how the fish-net open spaces actually trap air between the skin and the undergarment. Discuss double-window thermopane. Cite the case of the manufacturer in the midwest who sent a shipment of thermopane windows by truck over the Rocky Mountains only to find that all the windows broke at the higher altitude. The atmospheric pressure between the panes was not matched by the same pressure outside. Ask if the windows "imploded" or "exploded".

Convection and rising Warm Air Illustrate convection by considering the case of rising warm air. Discuss Figure 7.5. An analogy is a drunk who is moving haphazardly in the middle of a large dance floor where there is a "gradient" of people, crowded near the bandstand, and sparse toward the opposite end of the room. If the drunk rambled around for a few minutes, wouldn't you be most prone to find him on the side of the room farthest from the crowded bandstand? You can sketch this situation on the board, your sketch being essentially that of Figure 7.5.

CHECK QUESTION: Why does smoke from a cigarette rise and then settle off?

CHECK QUESTION: Why does helium rise to the very top of the atmosphere? Why doesn't it settle like the smoke? [Aha, helium is a much lower mass atom than molecules in air, and thus has a much higher average speed than other molecules. So it rises, but unlike the smoke particles that lose speed as they collide with neighboring molecules, the helium doesn't lose speed.]

After explaining that for the same temperature, the relatively small mass of helium is compensated for by a greater speed at whatever temperature and altitude, state that helium is not found in the air but must be mined from beneath the ground like natural gas. (The helium nucleus is the alpha particle that emanates from radioactive ores.) This idea of faster-moving helium underscores the relationship of kinetic energy to temperature. Stress it.

Expanding Air Cools Depart from the order of topics in the text and first treat the warming of compressed air. The familiar bicycle pump offers a good example. Why does the air become warm when the handle is depressed. It's easy to see that the air molecules speed up when the pis-

ton slams against them. A Ping-Pong ball similarly speeds up when a paddle hits it. Now, consider what happens to the speed of a Ping-Pong ball when it encounters a receding paddle! Can your students see that its rebound speed will be less than its incident speed? Now you're ready to discuss the cooling of expanding air and compare this to the case of the slowing Ping-Pong balls with molecules that are on the average receding from one another.

Here's a great one: Have everyone in class blow against their hands with open mouths. Their breaths feel warm. Then repeat with mouth openings very small. Their breaths are remarkably cooler (Figure 7.6). They **experience** first hand that expanding air *really does* cool!

DEMONSTRATION: Heat water in a pressure cooker, remove the cap and place your hand in the expanding steam that is ejected to show the cooling of expanding air, as co-author Leslie's mom does in Figure 7.7. Mixing of water vapor with the outside air also contributes to this cooling. Cite that the students don't see steam as such, for the steam is actually not visible. The cloud they see is not steam but condensed water vapor — and considerably cooled at that!

Discuss the role of convection in climates. Begin by calling attention to the shift in winds as shown in Figure 7.10. This leads you into radiation, the heat from the sun.

Warm at the Equator; Cold at the Poles You may want to discuss why the earth is warmer at the equator than at the poles, and get into the idea of solar energy per unit area. A neat way to do this is to first draw a large circle on the board that represents the earth (like the one below, only without the sun's rays at this point). Ask for a neighbor check and speculate why it is warm near the equator and cold at the poles. To dispel the idea that the farther distance to the poles is the reason, do the following:

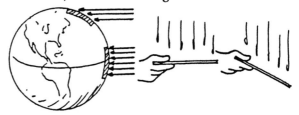

SKIT: Ask the class to pretend there is a vertical rainfall, into which you reach out your window with two sheets of paper — one held horizontally and the other held at an angle as shown. You bring the papers inside as a friend strolls by and inquires what you're doing. You remark that you have been holding the sheets of paper out in the rain. Your friend sees that the horizontally held paper is much wetter and asks why. You repeat with both papers held outward as before, and your friend says, "Oh, I see why. You're holding the tilted sheet further away from the clouds!" Ask your class if you are holding it farther away from the overhead clouds. The answer is yes. Ask if this is the reason the paper is not as wet. The answer is no!

Radiation Discuss the radiation one feels from red hot coals in a fireplace. And how the radiation decreases with distance. Consider the radiation one feels when stepping from the shade to the sunshine. Amazing! The heat is not so much because of the Sun's temperature, because like temperatures are to be found in the torches of some welders. One feels hot not because the Sun is hot, but because it is *big*. Comfortably big!

Acknowledge that everything emits radiation — everything that has any temperature. But everything does not become progressively cooler because everything absorbs radiation. We live in a sea of radiation, everything emitting and everything absorbing. When emission rate equals absorption rate, temperature remains constant. Some materials, because of their molecular design, emit better than others. They also absorb better than others. They're easy to spot, because they absorb visible radiation as well and appear black. (Whereas color affects both emission and absorption in the visible part of the spectrum, for the infrared a dominant role is played by the surface texture — polished versus dull.)

Everyone knows that the Sun radiates, and most people know the internal energy of the Sun has to do with nuclear processes—namely thermonuclear fusion. But relatively few people know that the same holds for planet Earth. The Earth's radiation, terrestrial radiation, is less intense and lower in frequency, but is nonetheless the same—electromagnetic radiation. And the source of Earth's heat is also radioactive processes—but radioactive decay of uranium, thorium, and potassium rather than fusion. Expand on these ideas—Figure 15.10 and one of the Next-Time Questions.

It is terrestrial radiation rather than solar radiation is directly responsible for the warmth of the air around us. Air is primarily warmed by the Earth, which is an important reason we don't freeze at night when we're not in the Sun's light.

Acknowledge the role of smudgepots in an orchard. They create a cloud close to the ground, which enables terrestrial radiation a means of absorption and reradiation back to the ground. This results in a longer cooling time for the ground to cool, enabling more time to survive the night without freezing until sunlight comes to the rescue the following morning. Three cheers for terrestrial radiation!

We live in a sea of radiation, everything emitting and everything absorbing. When emission rate equals absorption rate, temperature remains constant. Some materials, because of their molecular design, emit better than others. They also absorb better than others. They're easy to spot, because they absorb visible radiation as well and appear black.

DEMONSTRATION: Make up and show the black hole in the white box, as shown by Helen Yan in Figure 7.16. (Helen is a physics instructor at CCSF. Those of you familiar with *Conceptual Physics*, Editions 5, 6, and 7, may recall the earlier black and white photo of Helen showing the same box when she was Paul Hewitt's 21-year-old student teaching assistant in 1983.)

DEMONSTRATION: Pour hot water into a pair of vessels, one black and the other shiny silver. Ask for a neighbor check as to which will cool faster. Have thermometers in each that you ask a student to read aloud at the beginning and a few minutes later. (You can repeat this demo with initially cold water in each vessel.)

Explain the frost in the above-freezing mornings bit, page 167.

First Law of Thermodynamics Introduce the first law of thermodynamics by citing the findings of Count Rumford: that when cannon barrels were being drilled and became very hot, that it was the friction of the drills that produced the heating. Recall the definition of work, *force ×distance*, and cite how the metal is heated by the frictional force × distance that the various parts of the drill bit move. Have your students rub their hands together and feel them warm up. Or warm part of the chair they sit on by rubbing.

Follow this up with the account of Joule with his paddle wheel apparatus and his measuring the mechanical equivalent of heat. Of interest is Joule's attempt to extend this experiment to a larger scale while on his honeymoon in Switzerland. Joule and his bride honeymooned near the Chamonix waterfall. According to Joule's conception of heat, the gravitational potential energy of the water at the top should go into increasing the internal energy of the water when at the bottom. Joule made a rough estimate of the increased difference in water temperature at the bottom of the waterfall. His measurements did not substantiate his predictions, however, because considerable cooling occurred due to evaporation as the water fell through the air. Without this added complication, however, his predictions would have been supported. What happens to the temperature of a penny, after all, when you slam it with a hammer? Likewise with water. Emphasize that the first law is simply the law of energy conservation for thermal systems.

Adiabatic Processes Cite the opposite processes of compression and expansion of air and how each affects the temperature of the air. It's easy to see that compressing air into a tire warms the air; and also that when the same air expands through the nozzle in escaping, it cools. Discuss cloud formation as moist air rises, expands, and cools.

CLASS DEMONSTRATION: Blow on your hands first with wide-open mouth, and then with puckered lips so the air expands. Adiabatic cooling!

If you have a model of an internal combustion engine, such as is shown in Figure 7.20, strongly consider showing and explaining it in class. Many students likely have little idea of the process. (Isn't it amazing that automobile engines are as quiet as they are?)

Second Law Introduce the second law by discussing Exercise 29 on page 181, about immersing a hot tea cup in a large container of cold water. Stress that if the cup were to become even warmer at the expense of the cold water becoming cooler, the first law would not be violated. You're on your way with the second law.

According to my friend Dave Wall who many years ago worked in the US patent office, the greatest shortcomings of would-be inventors was their lack of understanding the laws of thermodynamics. The patent office has long been besieged with schemes that promise to circumvent these laws. This point is worth discussion, which you can direct to Carnot's efficiency equation and its consequences, like why better fuel economy is achieved when driving on cold days. [Remember in pre-SI days we talked of "mileage" — now it's fuel economy, because "kilometerage" just doesn't have the right ring yet.]

Steam Turbine Explain the steam-turbine cycle of Figure 7.22. The box on Thermodynamics Dramatized shows a demonstration you should show. This is the best demo I know of to answer the question as to why the condensation cycle in a steam turbine. The accompanying reduction in pressure is very dramatic. WHOP! Very impressive. Do this first by inverting cans into a cold basin of water. It is evident that condensation of the steam and vapor on the inside takes place, pressure is correspondingly reduced, and the atmospheric pressure on the outside crunches the can. Then repeat but this time invert cans into a basin of very hot water, just short of the boiling temperature. Crunch again, but less forceful than before. Steam molecules stick to the water surface, hot or cool, like flies sticking to fly paper. [If you do this with hot water just short of boiling, you'll still get a crunch, tho less violent. If you do this in boiling water, then there is no crunch. Lead your class into the explanation wherein the *net* effect is no change, as condensation of steam is met with just as much vaporization from the boiling water.]

CHECK QUESTION: Temperatures must be expressed in kelvins when using the formula for ideal efficiency, but may be expressed in either Celsius of kelvins for Newton's law of cooling. Why? [In Carnot's equation, ratios are used; in Newton's law of cooling, only differences.]

CHECK QUESTION: Now there are new "electronic bulbs" that use a quarter of the energy that standard bulbs use to emit the same amount of light (these bulbs generate a radio signal that mixes with the same gas used in conventional fluorescent lamps). Can it be said that these bulbs generate less heat? [Yes, of course.]

CHECK QUESTION: Common incandescent lamps are typically rated only 5% efficient, and common fluorescent lamps are only 20% efficient. Now we say that incandescent lamps are 100% heat efficient. Isn't this contradictory? [5% and 20% efficient as *light* sources, but 100% efficient as *heat* sources. All the energy input, even that which becomes light, very quickly becomes heat.]

NEXT-TIME QUESTION: Those who missed the expansion of the ball and ring question can mend their ways with this one: Consider the gap in a piece of metal in the shape of a C. When the metal is heated, will the gap get wider or narrower? [Wider, as is seen better if it is first cut into several sections, then rearranged when all parts have expanded.]

Entropy Conclude your treatment of this chapter with your best ideas on entropy — the measure of messiness. Woody Allen, in one of his recent movies has a crude but memorable way of stating the law of entropy: "Given enough time, everything turns to shit!"

Chicanery If any of your students want to acquire large sums of money by preying on the ignorance of the public, there may still be enough people left that don't know their physics who may be willing to shell out $300 each to learn how to walk barefoot on red-hot coals. Do as chemistry co-author John Suchocki demonstrates in Figure 7.2 and use wood coals of low heat conductivity. Different woods will give different results. After the surfaces of coals with a low heat conductivity give up their heat, it will take a sufficient time before appreciable thermal energy from the inside reheats the surface. Lead your walkers to believe they are apart from nature, do not tell them about physics, and above all, do not have them walk on red-hot rocks or stones (unless you get that $300 first). Don't fret taking the $300, for that's a small violation of ethics compared to your robbing them of a rational view of the world — not that they had one to begin with, but you *are* leading them further astray. To gain community respect, consider incorporating and calling yourself a church.

Do you want your students to read chapter material _before_ coming to class? Then reward them for doing so! Give them a quickie quiz at the outset of each class — or if not every class, then frequently at unannounced times. My students know they'll be quizzed on the chapter-end *Review Questions* of the assigned chapters. They *do* come to class prepared. Common sense — reward the behavior you want!

8
Electricity

Here we begin with electrostatics, continue on to electric current, and end with electric power. There's easily enough material here for two or more chapters. This is heavy stuff, so unless you're going to spend more than a week or so on this chapter, you may want to set your plow setting near the surface. This material should be supported with lecture demonstrations.

For electrostatics, you'll want charging apparatus such as rubber and glass rods, silk and cat's fur or the equivalent, the electrophorus (a metal plate charged by induction that rests on a sheet of Plexiglas which has been charged with cat's fur, or equivalently, a pizza pan that rests on a charged phonograph record), the Whimshurst machine (electrostatic generator), and the Van de Graaff generator.

For electric currents you simply must use an automobile storage battery with extended terminals as shown here. The extended terminals are simply a pair of rigid rods, welding rods or simply pieces of thick wire. They are easily inserted and removed if female connectors are permanently fastened into the battery terminals. Also fasten alligator clips to the ends of three short lengths of wire fastened to lamps of equal resistance. This is a MUST!

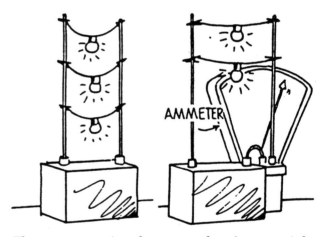

There are practice sheets on *electric potential, series circuits, parallel circuits,* and *combination series-parallel combination circuits* in the **Practice Book**.

There is an electrostatics activity, *Charging Up,* in the **Laboratory Manual.**, and 3 activities on simple circuits. One activity, *Cranking Up I,* precedes the quantitative version of the same, *Cranking Up II,* both of which feature a *Genecon* or other hand-held generator.

There are 6 **Next-Time Questions.**

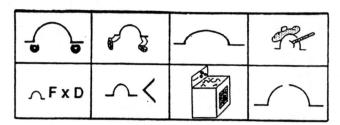

If you're into puns in your lectures on rainy days, Marshall Ellenstein has a few pictorial puns on the symbol for resistance that he and coworkers Connie Bownell and Nancy McClure came up with ("Ohmwork" or $\Omega F \times D$, *Physics Teacher* magazine, Sept 91, page 347). A few are shown above:

Answers in order are: Mobile Ohm; Ohm Run; Ohm Stretch; Ohm Sick; Ohmwork; Ohmless; Ohm on the Range; Broken Ohm.

The order of topics in the lecture sequence below departs somewhat from the order of topics in the chapter. The ideas of each demo flow nicely to the next. Have your lecture table set up with rods, pith ball, and charging demos at one end of the table, then an electrophorus, then a Whimshurst or whatever electrostatic machine, and finally the Van de Graaff generator. Then your lecture begins at one end of the table and proceeds in order to the opposite end. It is possible to do electrostatics in one lecture, and electric currents in another.

SUGGESTED LECTURE PRESENTATION

Electrical forces Begin by comparing the strength of the electric force to gravitational force — billions of billions of times stronger. Acknowledge the fundamental rule of electricity: That *like charges repel and unlike charges attract*. Why? Nobody knows. Hence we say it is fundamental.

Electric Charges Electrical effects have to do with electric charges, minus for the electron and plus for the proton. Discuss the near balance that exists in common materials, and the slight imbalance when electrons transfer from one material to another. Different materials have different affinities for electrons, which explains why charge transfers from fur to rubber when rubbed. It also explains why its painful for people with silver fillings in their teeth to chew aluminum spitballs. Silver has more affinity for acquiring electrons than aluminum. The mildly acidic saliva in your mouth facilitates a flow of electrons, which when transmitted to the nerves of your teeth produce that familiar unpleasant sensation. Discuss **charging**.

DEMONSTRATION: Bring out the cat's fur, rubber and glass rods, and suspended pith

balls (or their alternatives). Explain the transfer of electrons when you rub fur against rubber rod (and silk against glass). Explain what it means to say an object is electrically charged, and discuss the **conservation of charge**.

Rubbing a rubber rod on cat's fur or a glass rod on silk illustrates charging by friction, but charge separation can occur without friction, by the simple contact between dissimilar insulating materials. In this case charge simply peels from one material to another, like dust is peeled from a surface when a piece of sticky tape is peeled from it.

DEMONSTRATION: Show the effects of electrical force and **charge by induction** by holding a charged rod near the ends of a more-than-a-meter-long wooden 2 x 4, that balances and easily rotates sideways at its midpoint on a protrusion such as the bottom of a metal spoon. You can easily set the massive piece of wood in motion. This is quite impressive!

DEMONSTRATION: Rub a balloon on your hair and show how it sticks to the wall. Draw a sketch on the board (Figure 8.6) and show in induction how the attracting charges are slightly closer than the repelling charges. Closeness wins and it sticks! (Induction will be treated in great detail in Chapter 18, *Chemical Interactions.*)

DEMONSTRATION: Charge the electrophorus, place the insulated metal disk on top of it, and show that the disk is not charged when removed and brought near a charged pith ball. Why should it be, for the insulating surface of the electrophorus has more grab on the electrons than the metal plate. But rest the plate on the electrophorus again and touch the top of the plate. You're grounding it (producing a conducting path to ground for the repelling electrons). Bring the plate near the pith ball and show that it is charged. Then show this by the flash of light produced when the charged metal plate is touched to the end of a gas discharge tube — or a fluorescent lamp. Engage neighbor discussion of the process demonstrated. Only after this is generally understood, proceed to the next demo.

DEMONSTRATION: Move up the lecture table to the Whimshurst machine, explaining its similarity to the electrophorus (actually a rotating electrophorus!). Show sparks jumping between the spheres of the machine and so forth, and discuss the sizes (radii of curvature) of the spheres in terms of their capacity for storing charge. [The amount of charge that can be stored before discharge into the air is directly proportional to the radius of the sphere.] Fasten a metal point, which has a tiny radius of curvature and hence a tiny charge storing capacity, to one of the Whimshurst spheres and demonstrate the leakage of charge.

If you wish to expand upon charge leakage from a point, you might simplify it this way: On the surface of an electrically charged flat metal plate, every charge is mutually repelled by every other charge. If the surface is curved, charges on one part of the plate will not interact with charges on some distant part of the plate because of the **shielding** effect of the metal — they are "out of the line of sight" of each other. Hence for the same amount of work or potential, a greater number of charges may be placed on a curved surface than on a flat surface. The more pronounced the curvature, the more shielding and the more charge may be stored there. To carry this idea further, consider a charged needle. Under mutual repulsion, charges gather to the region of greatest curvature, the point. Although all parts of the needle are charged to the same electric potential, the charge density is greatest at the point. The **electric field** intensity about the needle, on the other hand, is greatest

about the point, usually great enough to ionize the surrounding air and provide a conducting path from the charge concentration. Hence charge readily gathers at points and readily leaks from points. DEMONSTRATE this leakage and the reaction force (ion propulsion) with a set of metal points arranged to rotate when charged. This is the "ion propulsion" that science fiction buffs talk about in space travel. Interestingly enough, this leaking of charge from points causes static with radio antennas; hence the small metal ball atop automobile antennas.

Discuss **lightning rods** and show how the bottoms of negatively charged clouds and the resulting induced positive charge on the surface of the Earth below are similar to the electrophorus held upside down; where the charged Plexiglas plate is analogous to the clouds and the metal plate is analogous to the Earth. After sketching the charged clouds and Earth on the chalkboard, be sure to hold the inverted electrophorus pieces against your drawing on the board in their respective places. Discuss the lightning rod as a preventer of lighting while showing the similar function of the metal point attached to the metal point attached to the Whimshurst machine. [Notice that one idea is related to the next in this sequence —

very important, as the ideas of electricity are usually difficult to grasp the first time through. So be sure to take care in moving through this sequence of demonstrations and their explanations.]

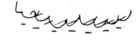

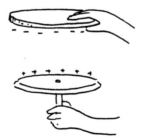

Benjamin Franklin's kite, by the way, was not struck by lightning. If it had, he would likely have not been around to report his experience. Franklin showed that the kite collected charges from the air during a thunderstorm. Hairs on the kite string stood apart, implying that lightning was a huge electric spark.

After establishing the idea that charge capacity depends on the size and curvature of the conductor being charged, advance to what your students have been waiting for: **The Van de Graaff generator** (for humor, invented by Robert Generator).

DEMONSTRATION: When showing the long sparks that jump from the dome of the generator to the smaller grounded sphere, do as Bruce Bernard suggests and hold a lightning rod (any sharp pointed conductor) in the vicinity of the dome and the sparking will stop. Bring the lightning rod farther away and the frequency of sparking will resume.

DEMONSTRATION: Set a cup of puffed rice or puffed wheat on top of the Van de Graaff generator. Your students will like the fountain that follows when you charge it. Or do as Marshall Ellenstein does and place a stack of aluminum pie plates on the dome and watch them one by one levitate and fly away. Then snuff out a match by holding it near the charged dome. Introduce (or reintroduce) the idea of the **electric field** at this time, the aura of energy that surrounds all charged things. Compare electric and gravitational fields.

Electric Fields and Potential Fields are called "force fields" because forces are exerted on bodies in their vicinity, but a better term would be "energy field," because energy is stored in a field. In the case of an electric field, any charges in the vicinity are energized. We speak about the potential energy that electrically charged bodies have in a field — or more often, the potential energy compared to the amount of charge — **electric potential**. Explain that the field energy, and correspondingly the electric potential, is greatest nearest the charged dome and weaker with increased distance (**inverse-square law**).

DEMONSTRATION: Hold a fluorescent lamp tube in the field to show that it lights up when one end of the tube is closer to the dome than the other end. Relate this to potential difference, and show that when both ends of the fluorescent tube are equidistant from the charged dome, light emission ceases. (This can be effected when your hand is a bit closer to the dome than the far end of the tube, so current does not flow through the tube when the dome discharges through you to the ground. There is no potential difference across the tube and therefore no illuminating current, which sets the groundwork for your next lecture on electric current.)

The Van de Graaff generator nicely illustrates the difference between **electric potential energy** and **electric potential**: Although it is normally charged to thousands of volts, the amount of charge is relatively small so the electric potential energy is relatively small. That's why you're normally not harmed when it discharges through your body. Very little energy flows through you. In contrast, you wouldn't intentionally become the short-circuit for household 110 volts because although the voltage is much lower, the transfer of energy is appreciable. Less energy per charge, but many many more charges! [All this is analogous to thermal energy — high temperature may or may not be associated with high or low thermal energy. Recall the white hot sparks of the fireworks sparkler — similarly, high energy per molecule, but not many molecules. Both the high-temperature sparkler and the high-voltage generator are relatively harmless.]

Your electrostatics lecture should end with the Van de Graaff demo and discussion of electric fields, potential energy, and potential. The following question is a bridge to your next lecture on electric currents.

NEXT-TIME QUESTION: Why does current flow when one end of the fluorescent tube is held closer to the charged Van de Graaff generator, but not when both ends are equidistant? [The simplified answer you're looking for at this point is that the close end is in a stronger part of the field than the far end. More energy per charge means more voltage at the near end. With a voltage difference across the tube, you get a current. When both ends are equidistant, there is no voltage difference across the tube, and no current. This leads into electric current. Strictly speaking, the current path is more than simply between the ends of the tube; it goes through you also and to ground where it returns to the generator.]

Flow of Charge; Electric Current Define electric current and relate it to the lighting of the lamp via the Van de Graaff Generator from your previous lecture. Explain this in terms of current being directly proportional to a difference in voltage. That is, one end of the lamp was in a stronger part of the energy field than the other — more energy per charge on one end than the other — more voltage at one end than the other. Write on the board *Current ~ voltage difference.* (You're on your way to Ohm's law. Strictly speaking, the voltage term in Ohm's law implies the difference in potential, so voltage difference is redundant. But it underscores a point that may be missed, so go for it.) [A high moment in my life was a conversation with Richard Feynman about teaching physics conceptually, and the topic of redundancies in teaching electricity came up. Feynman advised me to put concepts above grammar, and go for redundancies when they underscore a point — so current flows in a circuit!]

Voltage Sources Relate voltage to the idea of electrical pressure. Emphasize that a *difference* in electric potential must exist — or as above, a voltage difference. Cite how a battery provides this difference in a sustained way compared to suddenly discharging a Van de Graaff generator. Generators at power plants also provide a voltage difference across wires that carry this difference to consumers. Cite examples of voltage differences in cases of birds sitting on bare high-voltage wires, walking unharmed on the third rail of electric-powered train tracks, and the inadvisability of using electric appliances in the bathtub.

Discuss the function of the **third prong on electric plugs** (that it provides a ground wire between the appliance and the ground, Figure 8.23). The ground prong is longer than the pair of flat prongs. Why? (So it will be first to be connected when plugging it into a socket, establishing a ground connection slightly before the appliance is electrically connected. This path to ground prevents harm to the user if there is a short circuit in the appliance that would otherwise include the user as a path to ground.)

When a power line falls near you, don't walk from it—hop with both feet together. Why? Because there may be a voltage difference across the ground. If one foot is anchored to a voltage much different than where your other foot is, you could be electrocuted.

Discuss **electric shock** and why electricians put one hand behind their back when probing questionable circuits [to prevent a difference in potential across the heart of the body]. Discuss how being electrified produces muscle contractions that account for such instances as "not being able to let go" of hot wires, and "being thrown" by electric shock.

Electrical Resistance Introduce the idea of electrical resistance, and complete Ohm's law. Compare the resistances of various materials, and the resistances of various thickness of wires of the same metal. Call attention to the glass supports on the wires that make up high-voltage power lines; the rubber insulation that separates the pair of wires in a common lamp cord.

Ohm's Law Complete your chalkboard equation by introducing resistance and you have Ohm's law.

DEMONSTRATION: Connect two or three lamps to a battery and relate the current, as viewed by the emitted light, to the voltage of the battery and the resistance of the lamps. (Be sure the lamps are not bright enough to make viewing uncomfortable). Interchange lamps of low and high resistance, relating this to the brightness of the lamps.

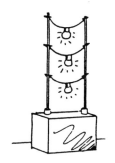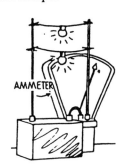

DC and AC Discuss the differences between DC and AC. Compare the DC current that flows in a circuit powered with a battery to the AC current that flows in a household circuit (powered by a generator). A hydrodynamic analogy for AC is useful: Imagine powering a washing-machine agitator with water power. Verbally describe with gestures a pair of clear plastic pipes connected to a paddle wheel at the bottom of the agitator, fashioned so water that sloshes to and fro in the pipes causes the agitator to rotate to and fro. Suppose the free ends of the plastic pipe are connected to a special socket in the wall. The socket is powered by the power utility. It supplies no water, but consists of a couple of pistons that exert a pumping action, one out and the other in, then vice versa, in rapid alternation. When the ends of the pipe containing water are connected to the pistons, the water in the pipes is made to slosh back and forth: power is delivered to the washing machine. There is an important point to note here: The **source** of flowing substance, water or electrons, is supplied by you. The power company supplies no water, just as the power utilities supply no electrons! The greater the load on the agitator, the more energy the power company must deliver to the action of the alternating pistons, affording a visual model for household current — especially with the transparent plastic pipes where your students can "see" the sloshing water!

Speed of Electrons in a Circuit To impart the idea of how DC current travels in a circuit, use the following analogy. Ask the class to suppose that there is a long column of marchers at the front of the room, all standing at rest close together. Walk to the end of this imaginary column and give a shove to the "last person." Ask the class to imagine the resulting impulse traveling along the line until the first marcher is jostled against the wall. (Or use the analogy of loosely coupled railroad cars.) Then ask if this is a good analogy for how electricity travels in a wire. The answer is no. Such is a good analogy for how sound travels, but not electricity. Cite how slowly the disturbance traveled, and how slowly sound travels compared to light or electricity. Again call attention to the column of marchers and walk to the far end and call out, "Forward march!" As soon as the command reaches each individual, each steps forward. The marcher at the beginning of the column, except for the slight time required for the sound to get to her, steps immediately. State that this is an analogy for electricity. Except for the brief time it takes for the electric *field* set up at the power source to travel through the wire, nearly the speed of light, electrons at the far end of the circuit respond immediately. State that the speed at which the command "forward march" traveled is altogether different from how fast each marcher moved upon receiving that command — and that the velocity of the electric signal (nearly the speed of light) is quite a bit different than the drift velocity of electrons (typically 0.01 cm/s) in a circuit.

CHECK QUESTION: When turning the key to start a car, electrons migrate from the negative battery terminal through the electric network to the starter motor and back to the positive battery terminal. Estimate the time required for electrons to leave the negative terminal, go through the circuit, and return to the battery? Less than a millisecond? Less than a second? About a second or two? Or about a day? (Class interest should be high when you announce the latter answer!)

Ask for an estimate of the number of electrons pumped by the local power plant into the homes and industries locally in the past year. [zero] Stress the idea that power plants sell not electrons, but energy. Discuss the origin of electrons in electric circuits.

Electric Power Distinguish between energy and power. Electric power is usually expressed in kilowatts, and electric energy in kilowatt-hours. Use an actual electric bill to make your point. Note that a kilowatt-hour is 1000 joules per second times 3600 seconds, or 3600 kJ.

Electrical Circuits We recommend introducing series and parallel circuits using only equal resistances. Use small lamps of equal resistance connected to short wires with alligator clips at their ends for easy connection to the extended terminals of the auto battery described earlier. Three lamps are sufficient. Sketches are repeated for emphasis.

DEMONSTRATION: Connect the ends of one of the lamps directly to the battery terminals. It glows, evidence of current flow. Then insert the rods and repeat. It glows as before. Slide the lamp farther up the rods and its glow is the same. It is easily accepted that the 12-volt potential difference between the terminals is also established along and across the full length of the rods. State how the rods could extend across campus and someone far away could similarly light up a lamp. State how the resistance of the rods is very small compared to the resistance of the lamp filament. Compare the rods to a long lamp cord. Then to power lines from power plants to consumers. Take your time with these ideas, for they are central!

Series Circuits

DEMONSTRATION CONTINUED: Attach two lamps in series via alligator clips. Before connecting the double lamp circuit to the rods, ask for a neighbor check about the relative brightness of light. [Since the resistance is doubled, the current is halved and the brightness diminished — brightness is "less than half" because most of the energy is going to heat and not light. The effects of heat can be discerned for low currents when no light is seen.] Point out that the voltage across each lamp is 6 volts when connected in series. Repeat the process for three lamps in series, where three lamps share the 12 volts, and describe the reduced current in terms of Ohm's law. This is even more effective if you connect a lecture-size ammeter to your circuit.

Parallel Circuits

DEMONSTRATION CONTINUED: Now connect a pair of lamps in parallel. Before making the second connection, ask for a neighbor check about the relative brightnesses. It's easy to see that the voltage across each lamp is not reduced as with the series connection, but each is impressed with a full 12 volts. [Nearly a full 12 volts; line voltage diminishes with increased current through the battery — perhaps information overload at this stage of learning.] Repeat with 3 lamps after a neighbor check. Ask about the "equivalent resistance" of the circuit as more lamps are attached in parallel (or the equivalent resistance to people flow when more cash registered are opened in a supermarket). The smaller resistance is consistent with Ohm's law. An ammeter between one of the rods and the terminal shows line current, which is seen to increase as lamps are added. I see this as the simplest and most visually comprehensible demo of parallel circuits.

CHECK QUESTION: Consider two resistors to be connected in a circuit. Which will have more resistance, if they are connected in series or in parallel? [A series connection will have more resistance, regardless of the values of resistance; the equivalent resistance of a parallel connection will always be less than that of the smaller resistor.]

Home Circuits and Fuses Discuss home lighting circuits. Draw a simple parallel circuit of lamps and appliances on the board. Estimate the current flowing through each device, and point out that it makes no difference how many of the other devices are turned on. Show on your diagram the currents in the branches and in the lead wires. Show where the fuse goes and describe its function. Then short your circuit and blow the fuse.

Overloading Discuss the consequences of too many appliances operating on the same line, and why different sets of lines are directed to various parts of the home. Most home wiring is rated at 30 amperes maximum. A common air conditioner uses about 2400 watts, so if operating on 120 volts the current would be 20 amps. To start, the current is more. (Why the starting current is larger would be premature to explain here — if it comes up you can explain that every motor is also a generator, and the input electricity is met with a generated output that reduces the net current flow.) If other devices are drawing current on the same line, the fuse will blow when the air conditioner is turned on, so a 220-volt line is usually used for such heavy appliances. Point out that most of the world operates normally at 220 - 240 volts.

Whenever you consider an equation, point out that when you change one side, you change the other. This is an important lesson that goes beyond physical science -- you can never change only one thing!

9

Magnetism

Like the previous chapter, this is a meaty chapter and could easily be two chapters. It focuses on the important features of simple magnets and electromagnetic induction, and avoids such complications as the distinctions between ferro and para magnetism, reactances, back emf, Lenz's law, and the left and right hand rules that normally serve to overwhelm your students. An important function of the chapter is to implant the idea of transferring energy from one place to another without means of physical contact. The chapter should be supported with various lecture demonstrations of electromagnetic induction, such as those in the figures of the chapter.

Make iron-filing permanent displays by spraying water on iron filings on a paper atop a magnet. The rust strains will leave a permanent impression of the magnetic field. (This idea from Matt Keller.)

American Journal of Physics editor Robert Romer of Amherst College reports his fascination with a compass on subways (The Physics Teacher, Feb. 93). Rather than simply pointing north, the compass dances erratically in response to the strong DC that varies as the cars maneuver. Magnetic fields some 20 times larger than the Earth's are produced by DC in the wires, and the 600-V third rail that carries current — often in excess of 5000 A. Changes in field direction are noted when the cars brake by using motors as generators, feeding energy back into the third

rail. If your students ride subway or other electric cars, urge them to note the effects of the currents on small hand-held compasses!

A new radiation belt was discovered in 1993, a tourous of anomalous cosmic rays making up a third radiation belt within the inner belt of protons. The outer belt is electrons.

This chapter serves as a background for the study of light.

There are two practice sheets in the **Practice Book**.

In the **Laboratory Manual** there is one activity on magnetic fields. Electromagnetic induction is part of the activity-experiment pair, *Cranking Up I* and *II*, in that they feature a hand-held generator.

There are 4 **Next-Time Questions**.

The suggested lecture will probably span two or three class periods.

SUGGESTED LECTURE PRESENTATION

Magnetic Force Begin by holding a magnet above some nails or paper clips on your lecture table. State that the nails or clips are flat on the table because every particle of matter in the whole world is gravitationally pulling them against the table. Then show that your magnet outpulls the whole world and lifts the nails or clips off the table.

Show that iron is not the only ferromagnetic substance. Certain Canadian nickels and quarters (1968 to 1981 which are pure nickel) are easily attracted to a magnet. The United States 5 cent piece is no longer pure nickel, is 75% copper, and won't respond to a magnet.

Magnetic Poles Show how a bar magnet affects a large lecture compass and discuss magnetic poles. Similar to the fundamental rule of electricity, *like poles repel and opposite poles attract.*

Magnetic Fields Show field configurations about bar magnets with the use of an overhead projector and iron filings (as per Figures 9.3 and 9.5 in the text). Simply lay a magnet on the glass surface of the projector and cover it with a sheet of plastic, and sprinkle iron filings over the plastic. Acknowledge the alignment of **magnetic domains** in the magnet material.

Magnetic Induction Explain magnetic induction, and show how bringing a non-magnetized nail near a magnet induces it to become a magnet and be attracted. Then contrast this with an aluminum rod — discuss unpaired electron spins and magnetic domains. Compare magnetic induction (Figure 9.9) to the electric induction shown in Figure 8.6 back on page 189. Stress the similarities of electrically inducing charge polarization and magnetically inducing the alignment of magnetic domains.

Electric Currents and Magnetic Fields Discuss the source of magnetism — the motion of charges (Figure 9.6 in the text). All magnetism starts with a moving electric charge: in the spin of the electron about its own axis (like a top), in the revolution about the nuclear axis, and as it drifts as part of an electric current.

DEMONSTRATION Place a lecture compass near a wire and show the deflection when current is passed through the wire.

The magnetic field is actually a relativistic "side effect" or "distortion" in the electric field of a moving charge. (Einstein's paper on special relativity, after all, was entitled, *On the Dynamics of Moving Charges.*)

Side point: When the magnetic field about a current-carrying wire is undesirable, double wires are used, with the return wire adjacent to the wire. Then the net current for the double wire is zero, and no magnetic field surrounds it. Wires are often braided to combat slight fields where the cancellation is not perfect.

Electromagnets Call attention to the circular shape of the magnetic field about a current-carrying wire (Figures 9.10, 9.11 and the photos of field lines of Figure 9.12). It's easy to see how the magnetic field is bunched up in a loop of current-carrying wire, and then in a coil of many loops. Then place a piece of iron in the coil and the added effect of aligned domains in the iron produces an electromagnet.

DEMONSTRATION: Make a simple electromagnet in front of your class. Simply wind wire around a spike and pick up paper clips when you put a current through the wire. Mimic the operation of a junk yard magnet, where the clips are dropped when the current is turned off.

DEMONSTRATION: Show your department's electromagnets, and your superconducting electromagnets!

If you have an electromagnetic levitator, discuss the train application when you are fascinating your students with its demonstration. The idea of a **magnetically-levitated train** was described in 1909 by Robert Goddard, an American better known for inventing the liquid-fueled rocket. Although Europe and Japan now have the lead in this field, the first modern design for a maglev train comes from Americans, nuclear-engineer James R. Powell, and particle-acceleration physicist Gordon T. Danby. They were awarded a patent in 1968 for their design.

Whatever the present variations in design, once the train is levitated there is no mechanical friction to contend with, so only modest force is needed to accelerate it. Fixed electromagnets along the guideway alternately pull and push by switching polarity whenever one of the train's propulsion magnets passes it. The phased switching is timed by computers under the control of the driver to accelerate or decelerate the train, or simply keep it moving. Various designs have the overall result of propelling the train like a surfboard riding a wave. Speculation by co-inventor Danby is that future travel in partially evacuated tubes will permit cross-country passage in about an hour. Maglev trains may play a large role in transportation in the coming century.

Magnetic Force on Moving Charges

DEMONSTRATION: Show how a magnet distorts the electron beam of an oscilloscope or TV picture. Stress the role of motion.

Discuss the motion of a charged particle injected into a magnetic field perpendicularly, and explain how it will follow a circle. The perpendicular push is a centripetal force that acts along the radius of its path. Briefly discuss cyclotrons and bevatrons, with radii ranging from less than a meter to more than a kilometer.

Magnetic Force on Current-Carrying Wires Simple logic tells you that if forces act on electrons that move through a magnetic field, then forces act on electrons traveling through a wire in a magnetic field.

DEMONSTRATION: Show how a wire jumps out of (or into) a magnet when current is passed through the wire (Figure 9.17). Reverse current (or turn wire around) to show both cases.

If you have a large lecture galvanometer, show your class the coil of wire that is suspended in the magnetic field of the permanent magnet (Figure 9.19). The same is found in ammeters and voltmeters. Now you are ready to extend this idea to the electric motor.

DEMONSTRATION: Show the operation of a DC demonstration motor.

Earth's Magnetic Field Discuss the field configuration about the Earth and how cosmic rays are deflected by the magnetic field lines. In discussing pole reversals, add that the magnetic field of the Sun undergoes reversals about every eleven years.

Biomagnetism Acquaint yourself with the latest findings regarding magnetic field sensing by living things. Bacteria, bees, and pigeons are mentioned briefly in the text.

Magnetic Resonance Imaging (MRI) This is treated as a side topic in the Link-To box on page 220, the now widely used application in medicine; particularly as a method of cancer detection. An external alternating magnetic field is applied to the part of the body of a patient to be examined. Slight differences in the natural frequencies of magnetic quadrapole moments of atomic nuclei, commonly protons, due to the environment of neighboring atoms are detected by a "magnetic echo." The resonant signals from the nuclei of atoms in living cells differs slightly for cancerous tissue and is picked up by a sensitive magnetometer. Why the name change from NMR to MRI? The word *nuclear*, honey! Its simply out with the public, who are phobic about anything with the dreaded word nuclear. Another reason for conceptual physical science for the common student!

Electromagnetic Induction Up to this point you have discussed how one can begin with electricity and produce magnetism. The question was raised in the first half of the 1800s; can it be the other way around — can one begin with magnetism and produce electricity? Indeed it can, enough to light entire cities with electric lighting! Now you produce your galvanometer, magnet, and wire loop — conspicuously well away from your previous electric power source.

DEMONSTRATION: Plunge a magnet in and out of a single coil, as in Figure 10.23, and show with a galvanometer the current produced. This is nice with a large lecture demonstration galvanometer.

This need not be mysterious, for it follows from the deviations of electrons in a magnetic field. Invoke the argument shown previously in Figure 9.15. [Electrons are moved across the magnetic field lines when you push the wire downward, and they experience a sideways force. This time there *is* a path for them and they move along the wire.] Then repeat with the wire bent into two coils — twice the effect. Many coils (Figure 9.24), many times more current.

DEMONSTRATION: Drop a small bar magnet through a vertically held copper or aluminum pipe. It will take appreciably longer to drop through than an unmagnetized piece of iron (which you show first). The explanation is that the falling magnet constitutes a changing magnetic field in the metal pipe. It induces a voltage and hence a current flow in the conducting pipe. The magnetic field set up by the current loops repel the falling magnet and account for its slow fall. Electromagnetic induction! [The magnetic field so induced opposes the change in the original field — Lenz's law. If the induced field enhanced the change in the original field, the falling magnet would be attracted rather than repelled and increase in its acceleration and gain more KE than its decrease in PE. A conservation of energy no no!] (This demo is a kit available from Pasco Scientific Co.)

Faraday's Law We have seen that charges moving in a magnetic field experience forces. In the last chapter, the force deviated the direction of electrons, both in a free beam and traveling along a wire, in which case the wire was deviated. Now we see that if we push electrons that are in a wire into a magnetic field, the deviating force will be along the direction of the wire and current is induced. Another way to look at this is to say that *voltage* is being induced in the wire. The current then, is an outcome of that voltage. Faraday states that the voltage induced in a closed loop equals the time rate of change of the magnetic field in that loop. Another way of looking at induction. So rather than saying current is induced, Faraday says voltage is induced, which produces current.

DEMONSTRATION: Show the assorted demonstrations with the classical Elihu Thompson Electromagnetic Demonstration Apparatus. With the power on, levitate an aluminum ring over the extended pole of the Elihu Thompson device.

CHECK QUESTION: Do you know enough physics to state how much electromagnetic force supports this 1-newton aluminum ring (assuming the ring weighs 1 N)? [Answer: 1 N, not particularly from a knowledge of electromagnetic forces, but from knowledge about forces in general that go back to Newton's laws. Since the ring is at rest and not accelerating, the upward electromagnetic force (in newtons!) must be equal to the downward force of gravity.]

DEMONSTRATION: With the power off, place the ring at the base of the extended pole. When you switch on the power the current induced in the ring via electromagnetic induction converts the ring into an ac electromagnet. (By Lenz's law, not developed in the text, the polarity of the induced magnet is always such to oppose the magnetic field imposed.)

CHECK QUESTION: Do you know enough physics to state whether or not the electromagnetic force that popped the ring was more, equal to, or less than the magnetic force that produced levitation earlier? [Answer: More, because it accelerated upward, evidence the upward force was more than the weight. This is also understandable because the ring was lower and intercepting more changing magnetic field lines.]

As interesting examples of electromagnetic induction, consider Exercises 24, 25, and 26 (smart traffic lights, airport metal detectors, and earthquake detectors).

Emphasize the importance of this discovery by Faraday and Henry, and how its application transformed the world. Isn't it difficult to imagine having no electric lights — to live in a time when illumination after the Sun goes down is by candles and whale-oil lamps? Not so long ago. In older cities many buildings still have pre-electric light fixtures: gas and oil lamps.

State that underlying all the things discussed and observed is something more basic than voltages and currents — the induction of *fields*, both electric and magnetic. And because this is true we can send signals without wires — radio and TV — and furthermore, energy reaches us from the Sun, sunlight.

Generators and Alternating Current Point out that strictly speaking generators do not generate electricity — nor do batteries. What they do is pump a fluid composed of electrons. As stressed in the previous chapter, they don't make the electrons they pump. The electron fluid is in the conducting wires.

DEMONSTRATION: Return to the motor demo and show that when you reverse the roles of input and output, and apply mechanical energy, it becomes a generator. Light a bulb with the hand-cranked generator and show how the turning is easier when the bulb is loosened and the load removed. Allow students to try this themselves during or at the end of class.

Compare motor and generator — in principle the same. When electric energy is put in it converts it to mechanical — motor. When mechanical energy is put in it converts it to electrical energy — generator. In fact, a motor acts also as a generator and creates a "back voltage" [back emf] and an opposing current. The net current in a motor is the input current minus the generated back current. The net current in a power saw will not cause its overheating and damage to its motor windings — so long as it is running and generating a back current that keeps the net current low. But if you should jam the saw so that it can't spin, without the back current generated by the spinning armature, the net current is dangerously high and can burn out the motor.

It is interesting that electric motors are used in diesel-powered railroad engines. The combustion engine cannot bring a heavy load from rest, but an electric motor can. Why? Because when the armature is not turning, the current in the windings is huge, with a corresponding huge force. As both the train and the motor gain speed, the back current generated by the motor brings the net current in the motor down to non-overheating levels.

Stress the fact that we don't get something for nothing with electromagnetic induction, and acknowledge Figure 9.25. This can be readily felt when lamps powered with a hand-cranked or a bicycle generator are switched on. Each student should experience this. The conservation of energy reigns!

Power Production Continue with a historical theme: With the advent of the generator the task was to design methods of moving coils of wire past magnetic fields, or moving magnetic fields past coils of wire. Putting turbines beneath waterfalls, and boiling water to make steam to squirt against turbine blades and keep them turning — enter the industrial revolution.

Transformers Explain the operation of a transformer. (I remember as a student being very confused about the seeming contradiction with Ohm's law — the idea that when voltage in the secondary was increased, current in the secondary was decreased.) Make clear that when the voltage in the coil of the secondary and the circuit it connects is increased, the current in *that* circuit also increases. The decrease is with respect to the current that powers the *primary*. So $P = iV$ does not contradict Ohm's law!

DEMONSTRATION: With a step-down transfer, weld a pair of nails together. This is a spectacular demonstration when you first casually place your fingers between the nail ends before they make contact, and after removing your fingers bring the points together allowing the sparks to fly while the nails quickly become red and white hot.

Cite the role of the transformer in stepping down voltages in toy electric trains, power calculators, and portable radios, and the role of stepping up voltages in TV sets and various electrical devices, and both stepping up and stepping down voltages in power transmission.

Field Induction Point to the similarity of the field induction laws of Faraday and Maxwell — how a change in either field induces the other. This concept led Einstein to the development of his special theory of relativity. Einstein showed that a magnetic field appears when a purely electric field is seen by a moving observer, and an electric field appears when a purely magnetic field is seen from a moving vantage point.

Because of the electric and magnetic induction of fields in free space we can "telegraph" signals without wires — hence radio and TV — and furthermore, we shall see that because of field induction, there is light.

10

Sound Waves

Some instructors begin the study of the physics part of physical science with waves, vibrations, and sound — topics that have greater appeal to many students than mechanics. Your course could begin here, and you could pick up mechanics later. A useful feature of the text is that for a large part, chapters can stand alone .

This chapter lends itself to interesting lecture demonstrations: a ringing doorbell inside a vacuum jar being evacuated — the easily seen vibrations of a tuning fork illuminated with a strobe lamp — resonance and beats with a pair of tuning forks mounted on sound boxes — and the 8-mm film loop of the "Tacoma Narrows Bridge Collapse".

Forced vibrations, resonance, and interference provide a very useful background for the same concepts applied to light in the following two chapters.

For more about dolphins and ultrasound, see *Mind In The Waters*, by J. McIntyre, pp 141, 142. Sierra Club Books, San Francisco, 1974.

For a very impressive demonstration of measuring sound speed, see the article *A Visual Measurement of the Speed of Sound* by Loren M. Winters (North Carolina School of Science and Mathematics, Box 2418, Durham, NC 27715), in *The Physics Teacher* (Vol. 31, May 1993). An upright black disk about the size of an LP record is rotated about 50 cps in view of the class. On the disk is painted a radial white line that will show when illuminated with a pair of strobe units. Two strobe-flash units, each triggered by sound, illuminate the spinning disc at slightly different times when the source of sound is closer to one unit than the other. The setup can be arranged so that the images make an easy to see right angle (while the disc rotates a quarter turn). Knowing the differences in distances to the triggers from the sound source, and the time it takes the disk to make a quarter turn, the speed of sound is easily calculated. A great demo!

There are two practice sheets in the **Practice Book**.

There are 3 activities that go with this chapter in the **Laboratory Manual**. One of them, *Sound Off*, makes a great lecture demonstration, as described here.

There are 4 **Next-Time Questions**.

SUGGESTED LECTURE PRESENTATION

Vibration of a Pendulum Demonstrate the periods of pendula of different lengths, and compare the strides of short and tall people, and animals with short and long legs. Giraffes certainly run at a different stride than dachshunds!

Wave Description Move a piece of chalk up and down, tracing and retracing a vertical straight line on the board. Call attention to how "frequently" you oscillate the chalk, and tie this to the definition of frequency. Also discuss the idea of amplitude. With appropriate motions, show different frequencies and different amplitudes. Then do the same while walking across the front of the board tracing out a sine wave. Show waves of different wavelengths.

DEMONSTRATION: Show waves on a Bell Telephone torsion type wave machine (if you're fortunate enough to have one).

DEMONSTRATION: In jest, do as Tom Gordon at Bronx High School does and suspend a harmonica from a spring, bob it up and down, and ask, "What do we have here?" Answer: Simple "harmonica" motion!

Swing a pendulum to and fro and discuss the reciprocal relationship between frequency and period: $f = 1/T$, and $T = 1/f$. Or $fT = Tf = 1$.

Distinguish between wiggles in time — vibrations, and wiggles in space and time — waves. Stress the sameness of the frequency of a wave and the frequency of its vibrating source.

Wave Speed Explain or derive the *wave speed = frequency × wavelength* formula. Support this with examples, first the freight car question on page 256, and then the water waves as in Problem 2, and then lead into electromagnetic waves as suggested in Problem 3. Calculate the wavelength of one of your local popular radio stations. If you discuss electromagnetic waves, be sure to contrast them with longitudinal sound waves and distinguish between them. You may refer ahead to the family of electromagnetic waves in Figure 11.3 on page 259.

Transverse and Longitudinal Waves

DEMONSTRATION: You and a student hold the ends of a stretched spring or a slinky and send transverse pulses along it, stressing the idea that only the disturbance rather than the medium moves along the spring. Shake it and produce a sine wave. Then send a stretch or compression down the spring, showing a longitudinal pulse, and wave. After some discussion, produce standing waves.

Origin of Sound Begin by stating that the source of sound or all wave motion, is a vibrating object. Ask your class to imagine a room filled with Ping Pong balls and that you hold a giant Ping Pong paddle. When you shake the paddle to and fro you set up vibrations of the balls. Ask how the frequency of the vibrating balls will compare with the frequency of the vibrating paddle. Sound is understood if we "think small."

DEMONSTRATION: Tap a large tuning fork and show that it is vibrating by dipping the vibrating prongs in a cup of water. The splashing water is clear evidence that the prongs are moving! (Small forks do not work as well.)

DEMONSTRATION: Hold an aluminum rod (a meter long or so) horizontally at the midpoint and strike one end with a hammer. You will create vibrations that travel and reflect back and forth along the length of the rod. The sustained sound heard is due to energy "leaking" from the ends, about 1% with each reflection. So at any time the sound inside is about 100 times as intense as that heard at the ends. (This is similar to the behavior of light waves in a laser.) Shake the rod to and fro as Paul Doherty does for the Doppler effect.

DEMONSTRATION: Rub some pine pitch or rosin on your fingers and stroke the aluminum rod. If you do it properly, it will "sing" very loudly. Do this while holding the rod at its midpoint and then at different places to demonstrate harmonics. (Of course you practiced this first!)

Nature of Sound in Air

DEMONSTRATION: Ring the doorbell suspended in a bell jar that is being evacuated of air. While the loudness of sound diminishes, discuss the movement of sound through different media — gases, liquids, and solids. Ask why sound travels faster in warm air — then faster through moist air.

Media That Transmit Sound Discuss the speed of sound through different media — four times as fast in water than in air — about eleven times as fast in steel. The elasticity of these materials rather than their densities accounts for the different speeds. Cite how the American Indians used to place their ears to the ground to hear distant hoofbeats. And how one can put the ear to a track to listen for distant trains.

Speed of Sound Discuss the speed of sound and how one can estimate the distance from a lightning storm.

Compute or state that a radio signal takes about 1/8 second to go completely around the world, while in the same time sound travels about 42.5 meters. Pose the following: Suppose a person attends a concert that is being broadcast over the radio, and that he sits about 45 m from the stage and listens to the radio broadcast with a transistor radio over one ear and the non-broadcast sound signal with the other ear. Which signal will reach his ear first? The answer is that the radio signal would reach his ear first, even if the radio signal traveled around the world before reaching his radio!

Reflection of Sound Bats and echoes, charting of the ocean bottom, reverberations in the shower, and acoustics in music halls — go to it.

Refraction of Sound Explain refraction with a chalkboard drawing similar to Figure 10.13. As an example different than the sound of the bugle waking the dog, consider the temperature inversion over a lake at night, and how one can hear whispers of people on the opposite side of the lake. You may want to follow this up with the similar case of refraction by wind, where wind speed is greater higher up than near the ground.

A useful medical application of sound refraction is ultrasound technology (Figure 10.14), especially in examining the unborn children in pregnant women. Fortunately, the method appears to be relatively free of dangerous side effects.

The most fascinating example of reflection and refraction of sound is the dolphin. Dolphins have been doing all along what humans have just learned to do. Add to the boxed material about dolphins, that unlike humans, dolphins breathe voluntarily. They cannot be put to sleep for medical operations because they will cease breathing and die. They are subject to drowning, as any mammal is. When in trouble other dolphins hold the troubled dolphin at the surface so breathing can take place. When sick, they will beach themselves so they won't drown. Many shipwrecked sailors owe their lives to dolphins who have beached them. Fascinating creatures!

Forced Vibrations, Natural Frequency Tap various objects around you and explain what is happening at the atomic level — that crystalline or molecular structures are made to vibrate, and that due to the elasticity and bonding of the material constituents, natural modes of vibration are produced. Objects have their own characteristic frequencies. The organs of humans have a natural frequency of about 7 hertz.

Resonance

DEMONSTRATION: Show resonance with a pair of tuning forks, explaining how each set of compressions from the first fork push the prongs of the second fork in rhythm with its natural motion. Compare this to pushing somebody on a playground swing. Illuminate the forks with a strobe light for best effect!

When you are adjusting the frequency of one of your tuning fork boxes, by moving the weights up or down the prongs, call attention to the similarity of this with tuning a radio receiver. When one turns the knob to select a different station, one is adjusting the frequency of the radio set to resonate with incoming stations.

Cite other examples of resonance — the chattering vibration of a glass shelf when a radio placed on it plays a certain note — the loose front end of a car that vibrates at only certain speeds — crystal wine glass shattering by a singer's voice, — troops breaking step in bridge crossing.

Conclude your treatment of resonance with the exciting film loop "The Tacoma Narrows Bridge Collapse". This short film is by far the most impressive of the physics films. (It is included in *Sound and Vibrations II*, in the *Conceptual Physics Alive!* videotape.)

Interference Introduce interference by sketching a sine wave on the board — actually a water wave. Then superpose another identical wave on it and ask what happens. Nothing spectacular, simply a wave of twice the amplitude. Now repeat and superpose the second wave a half-wavelength out of step. State that physicers don't say "out of step," but "out of phase." Same thing.

DEMONSTRATION: Play a stereo radio, tape or CD player, on a mono setting and demonstrate the different quality of sound when the speakers, set apart from each other, are out of phase. I have mine connected to a DPDT switch to flip the phase. Do as Meidor does in Figure 10.22 and face the stereo speakers toward each other, at arm's length apart. Flip one speaker out of phase and gradually bring them closer. The volume of sound fades dramatically as they are brought face to face. Interference. This may likely be one of the more memorable of your demos.

The question may arise as what happens to the sound energy when sound cancels. Interestingly enough, each radio loudspeaker is also a microphone. When the speakers face each other they "drive" each other, inducing back voltages in each other that cut the currents down in each. Thus energy is diminished, but not canceled.

DEMONSTRATION: Show the reason for speakers mounted in boxed enclosures by producing a bare speaker connected to a music source. The sound is "tinny". State why; that as compressions are produced by one side of the speaker cone, rarefactions are produced by the other. Superposition of these waves results in destructive interference. Then produce a square piece of board (plywood or cardboard) close to a meter on a side with a hole the size of the speaker in its center. Place the speaker at the hole and let your class hear the difference in the fullness of the sound that results. You have diminished the superposition of waves that previously canceled. The effect is dramatic.

I kid around about my keen ability to completely cancel sound by striking one tuning fork and then the other at precisely the time to produce cancellation. When I do this I quickly grab and release the prongs of the sounding fork while not really making contact with the second. It is especially effective for students who weren't watching carefully. I exclaim that when I'm lucky enough to achieve complete cancellation on the first try, I never repeat it. Is this real science? No, but it's a mood elevator so that my students are receptive to the real science I discuss the rest of the time.

Beats Acknowledge you were kidding around before about producing interference with the pair of tuning forks, but now you're for real with them. Strike the slightly different frequency forks and hear the beats. This is even nicer when your students see an oscilloscope trace what they hear.

Doppler Effect Introduce the Doppler Effect by throwing a ball, perhaps sponge rubber or Styrofoam, around the room. In the ball you first place an electronic whistle that emits a sound of about 3000 Hz. Relate this to the sound of a siren on a fire engine (Figure 10.29) and radar of the highway patrol. [Note that sound requires a medium; radar is an E&M wave and doesn't.]

Wave Barriers, Bow Waves, and Shock Waves Describe the Doppler effect via the bug in water sequence as treated in the text. From this lead into bow and shock waves. After sketching Figures 10.30, 10.32, and 10.33, ask the class to consider the waves made by two stones thrown in the water. Sketch the overlapping waves as shown above. Ask where the water is highest

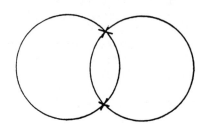

above the water level, then indicate the two places where the waves overlap with X's. Then show that this is what happens with a bow wave, that a series of such overlaps make up the envelope of many circular waves forming a V-shape. Then discuss the shock waves produced by super-sonic aircraft.

The analogy between bow waves in water and shock waves in air is very useful. Questions raised by students about shock waves and the sonic boom can be effectively answered by translating the question from one of an aircraft in the air to one of a speedboat knifing through the water, a much easier-to-visualize situation.

If you wish to go further with shock waves than is treated in the text, consider explaining how the speed of an aircraft can be estimated by the angle of its shock wave (shock waves are visible, Figure 10.34), for light is refracted in passing through the denser air).

Shock Wave Construction Construct a shock wave on the board by the following sequence: first place your chalk on the board anywhere to signify time zero. Draw a meter-long horizontal line, say to the right, to represent how far an aircraft has traveled in a certain time. Suppose it travels twice the speed of sound (Mach 2). Then during the time it travels your one meter, the sound it made initially has traveled half this distance, which you mark on the midpoint of your line. State that the initial sound has expanded spherically, which you represent two-dimensionally by drawing a circle as shown. Explain that this circle represents only one of the nearly infinite circles that make up the shock wave, which you draw. The shock wave should be a 60 degree wedge (30 degrees above your horizontal line, and 30 degrees below). The next line you draw is important: draw the radius of the circle, from its center to a point

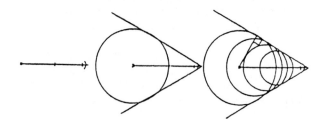

tangent to the shock wave. Explain how the speed of the craft is simply the ratio of the horizontal line to this radial distance. (If your students are science students, at this point and not before, introduce the sine function). Now your test of all this: Construct a shock wave of different angle on the board and ask your class to estimate the speed of the craft that generated it. In making constructions, working backwards now, the most common student error is constructing the right angle from the horizontal line rather than from the shock wave line that is tangent to the circle.

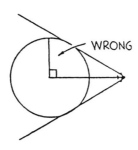

Such geometrical constructions are the subject of this chapter's activity in the **Practice Book**.

Musical Sounds Bring out the oscilloscopes, the audio oscillator, microphones, loudspeakers, and musical instruments.

Pitch, Loudness, and Quality Wave forms can be displayed on the screen of an oscilloscope. An audio oscillator connected to a loudspeaker and an oscilloscope will demonstrate the relationships between pitch, frequency, and wavelength, and between amplitude and loudness. You can speak into the loudspeaker and display a wave pattern on the oscilloscope screen, showing that the loudspeaker serves as a microphone. (It may or may not be appropriate to briefly discuss the electromagnetic induction that takes place in the electromagnet of the loudspeaker at this point.) The wave forms of various musical instruments can be displayed and compared on the oscilloscope screen. Show the different harmonics for the same notes played on different instruments. Discuss quality.

If you display a decibel meter, show that for mid-range frequencies a decibel is the just-noticeable sound level difference that humans can detect.

Demonstrate Chladni figures with a fastened metal plate, violin bow, and fine sand (or if you still have Ealing film loops around, show the one on Chladni figures). Discuss nodes and antinodes.

Musical Instruments Although *standing longitudinal waves* are not treated in the text, you may wish to introduce this topic and relate it to musical instruments. If so, begin by demonstrating the resonance of standing air columns with a resonance water tube (a long glass tube partially filled with water, the level of which can be adjusted by raising or lowering an external reservoir). Hold a vibrating tuning fork over the open tube and adjust the water level until the air in the tube resonates loudly to the sound being sent into it by the fork. Show and explain that several heights will result in resonance. Measure the wavelengths of a high and a low frequency sound. Consider doing as Paul Hickman does and drop a couple of Alka Selzer tablets into the water. The air column above soon is filled with CO_2 and the tone of the reverberating sound undergoes a marked change. Relate the relative sizes of the respective sound cavities to the relative sizes of musical instruments; the bigness of a bass fiddle, and the smallness of a piccolo. These ideas underlie the tones one produces when blowing over the top of a soda pop bottle.

II

Light Waves

Note that the "depth of the plow" in the treatment of light is respectably deep. The aim is not to separate and name categories such as transmission, reflection, and absorption, but to get into the physics. Your students will get into some good physics in this chapter — and understand it. Understanding more than you may expect, and discovering more than you thought there was, is a real joy of learning. So this should be an enjoyable chapter — why some instructors opt to begin their physical science course here.

In this chapter we introduce a model of the atom in which electrons behave as tiny oscillators that resonate or are forced into vibration by external influences. If you haven't preceded light with a study of sound, and if you haven't demonstrated resonance with a pair of tuning forks, do it now, for the tuning fork model is used in the text to account for selective reflection and transmission of light

We continue to refer to color primarily by frequency rather than wavelength, in effort to reduce the number of terms students must learn to understand concepts. There is a trend toward using wavelength in nanometers (Angstroms are "out") for the color spectrum, probably because there seems to be evidence that the color sensitive elements of the retina-optic-nerve-brain system are more reasonably a function of wavelength than frequency due to velocity variation. There is a trend to terahertz (THz) in place of exponential notation for visible light frequencies.

If you haven't shown your class the black hole that appears in a box with white interior, back in the heat chapters (Figure 7.13, p.171) do it now. It nicely illustrates the "color" black.

Be sure to mount three floodlights on your lecture table, red, green, and blue, of shades such that all three overlapping produce white on a white screen. Then stand in front of the lamps, illuminated one at a time and show the interesting colors of the shadows, as is shown by the shadows of the golf ball in Figure 11.17. Impressive! Included is a sample of Paul Hewitt's three-lamps demo lecture that he gives to the general public.

The three overlapping primary colors is featured in the **Practice Book**. There are also sheets on interference, pinhole image formation, and polarization.

There is an activity on polarization in the **Laboratory Manual**.

There are 5 **Next-Time Questions** for this chapter.

SUGGESTED LECTURE PRESENTATION

If you have already delved into E&M from Chapter 9 with your class, then begin your lecture with **Begin 1** that follows. If you're jumping into light without having covered E&M, then jump ahead to **Begin 2**.

Begin 1: Electromagnetic Waves Usually I begin my lecture by asking the class to recall my recent demonstration of charging a rubber rod with cat's fur and how when I brought it near a charged pith ball, I produced action at a distance. When I moved the charged rod, the charged ball moved also. If I gently oscillate the rod, the ball in turn oscillates. State that one can think of this behavior as either action-at-a-distance or the interaction of the ball with the space immediately around it — the electric field of the charged rod. For low frequencies, the ball will swing in rhythm with the shaking rod. But the inertia of the ball and its pendulum configuration makes response poor for any vigorous shaking of the rod (that's why it's best not to actually show this, but to only describe it and go through the motions as if the equipment were present — you avoid the "that's the way it would behave" situation). You can easily establish in your students' minds the reasonableness of the ball shaking back and forth in response to the shaking electric field about the shaking rod. Carry this further by considering the ball to be simply a point charge with negligible mass. Now it will respond in synchronous rhythm with the shaking rod. Increase the frequency of the shaking rod and state that not only is there a shaking electric field about the rod, but because of its changing, there is a also different kind of field.

CHECK QUESTIONS: What kind of field is induced by the shaking rod? What kind of field in turn, does this induced field induce? And further in turn, what kind of field does this further induced field induce? And so on.

Begin 2: Electromagnetic waves Begin by stating that everybody knows that if you placed the end of a stick in a pond and shook the stick back and forth, you'd generate waves across the water surface. But what everybody doesn't know is that if you shook a charged rod back and forth in free space, you'd generate waves also. Not waves of water, or even waves of the medium in which the stick exists, but waves of electric and magnetic fields. You'd generate *electromagnetic waves*. Shaking the rod at low frequencies generates radio waves. Shaking at a million billion times per second generates waves one could see in the dark. For those waves would be seen as light.

Electromagnetic Spectrum Continue by stating that, strictly speaking, light is the only thing we see. And to understand what light is, we will first try to understand how it behaves. Call attention to the rainbow of colors that are dispersed by a prism or by raindrops in the sunlight. We know white light can be spread into a spectrum of colors. Ask your students to consider the world view of little creatures who could only see a tiny portion of the spectrum, creatures who would be color blind to all the other parts. Their world view would be very limited. Then state that we are like those little creatures, in that the spectrum of colors we can see are a tiny portion of the *electromagnetic spectrum* (Figure 11.3)— less than a tenth of one percent! We are color blind to the other parts.

Buckminster Fuller put it well when he stated that ninety-nine percent of all that is going to affect our tomorrows is being developed by humans using instruments that work in ranges of reality that are nonhumanly sensible. The instruments of science have extended our view of the other parts. These instruments are not microscopes and telescopes, for they enable closer viewing of the part of the spectrum we are familiar with. It is the infrared detecting devices, microwave and radio receivers, that allow us to explore the lower-frequency end of the spectrum, and ultraviolet, X-ray, and gamma-ray detectors that let us "see" the higher-frequency end. What we see with unaided eyes is a tiny part of what's out there in the world around us.

CHECK QUESTION: Where does sound fit in the electromagnetic spectrum? [It doesn't of course!]

CHECK QUESTION: A photographer wishes to photograph a lightning bolt, and comes up with the idea of having the camera triggered by the sound of thunder. A good idea or a poor idea? [Very poor, for light travels about a million times faster than sound. By the time the sound of thunder arrives, the lightning bolt is long gone!]

CHECK QUESTION: So the speed of light is finite; does this mean your image in the mirror is always a bit younger or a bit older than you? [Older, but of course not by very much!]

Transparent Materials Recall your earlier demonstration of sound resonance (or if you haven't done this, demonstrate now the resonance of a pair of tuning forks mounted on sounding boxes (Figure 11.4)). The tuning fork demo provides important experience for your students in understanding the interaction of light and matter. In some cases light strikes a material and rebounds — reflection (next chapter). In cases where light continues through the material, we say the material is *transparent.*

DEMONSTRATION: Show the swinging balls apparatus that is usually used to illustrate momentum and energy conservation. Here you are showing that the energy that cascades through the system of balls is analogous to light energy cascading through transparent matter. Just as the incident ball is not the same ball that emerges, the incident "photon" of light upon glass is not the same photon that emerges through the other side. Although too difficult to see, slight interaction times between balls produces a slight time delay between incidence and emergence of balls. Likewise for light.

Point out the value of **scientific models**, in understanding physical phenomena. Hence the discussion of cascading balls, tuning forks, and imaginary springs that hold electrons to the nuclei of atoms. A model is not correct or incorrect, but useful or nonuseful. Models must be refined or abandoned whenever they fail to account for various aspects of a phenomenon.

CHECK QUESTION: Compared with the speed of light in a vacuum, why is the speed of light less in transparent materials such as water or glass? [According to the model treated in the text, there is a time delay between the absorption of light and its re-emission. This delay serves to decrease the average speed of light in a transparent material.]

Another analogy for light traveling through glass is the average speed of a basketball moving down a court. It may fly through the air from player to player at one constant speed, but its average speed down the court depends on the holding time of the players. Carrying the analogy further, different materials have different players, and although the instantaneous speed of light is always the same, the average speed depends on both the number of players encountered, and the holding time of each player.

On the subject of glass, it's interesting to note that we see through it for the same reasons we see through water. Its internal structure is not the regular crystalline latticework of most solids, but is essentially random like that of liquids. Whereas conventional liquids have a freezing point at which they become solid, liquid glass gets stiffer as it cools. (Window panes that are thicker at the bottom were likely thicker on one end to begin with, and were simply mounted with heavy sides down. The flow is not perceptible.)

Opaque Materials State that light generally has three possible fates when incident upon a material: (1) reflects, (2) is transmitted through the material, or (3) is absorbed by the material. Usually a combination of all three fates occurs. When absorption occurs, the vibrations given to electrons by incident light are often great enough

to last for a relatively long time, during which the vibratory energy is shared by collisions with neighboring atoms. The absorbed energy warms the material.

CHECK QUESTION: Why in the sunlight is a black tar road hotter to the touch than a pane of window glass? [Sunlight is absorbed and turned into internal energy in the road surface, but transmitted through the glass to somewhere else.]

For the record, we say that ultraviolet light cannot penetrate glass. Hence you cannot get a sunburn through glass. But *some* ultraviolet light does pass through glass — long wavelength ultraviolet light, which has insufficient energy to cause a sunburn. Most sunlamps *aren't* made of ordinary glass — they're made of quartz or special UV-transparent glass.

Color What first made Isaac Newton a famous physicist was not his contributions to mechanics, but to light. He was the first to explain the colors produced by a prism held in the sunlight. White light, after all, is all the colors "smudged" together.

Selected Reflection Discuss the oscillator model of the atom, and the ideas of forced vibration and resonance as they relate to color, as you display different colored objects. A red object, for example, reflects red. It absorbs the other colors. Resonance is *not* occurring for red, by the way, for the resonant frequencies are being *absorbed*. (I was mixed up about this point for years!)

Selective Transmission Similarly for colored glass — the resonant frequencies are absorbed and becomes the internal energy of the transparent material. The frequencies to pass through the glass are those away from the resonant frequencies. Frequencies close to resonance undergo more interactions with the molecules and take longer to travel than frequencies far from resonance. Hence different colors have different speeds in transparent materials. (If not, no rainbows, as we shall see in the following chapter!)

Mixing Colored Light How many colors are there in the spectrum? Although we commonly group the colors into seven categories, red, orange, yellow, etc., there are an infinite number of colors. The "in-between" colors are not mixtures of their neighboring colors. The red-orange between red and orange, for example, is not a mixture of red and orange but is a distinct frequency present in sunlight.

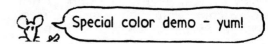 Special color demo - yum!

74

SPECIAL LECTURE/DEMO ON COLOR LIGHT ADDITION

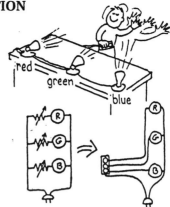

This narration with three colored lamps, red, green, and blue, each a meter or so apart in front of a white surface, is great for a general audience The narrator holds dimmer switches for each lamp and has an assistant stand between the lamps and screen. The narrator can stand in the light, but if it's a classroom, students like to see "one of their own" in the light for a change. Although dichro-color flood lights are quite vivid, any red, green, or blue flood lamps , or even colored gels in front of white lamps, works fine. Common wall-switch dimmers vary brightness [Wiring diagram is as shown.]

White light from the sun or an incandescent lamp is composed of the spectral colors. The reds are the lowest frequencies, the greens the middle, and the blue and violet the highest. Color vision is the result of three types of cones sensitive to the three colors, red, green, and blue. Color television uses combinations of only these three primary colors to produce the color spectrum. Note the white light where the red, green, and blue lamps overlap.

[Project all three lamps at once on the screen to show white]

Lets look at these colors one at a time.

[Project red on screen; then green]

Note that red and green overlap to produce yellow. Is that surprising? What is the average of red + green? What's between red and green in the spectrum? Yellow! So red light and green light produce yellow light.

[Project blue atop red and green]

And all three produce white light.

[Person walks into the crossed beams]

Note that she is illuminated just as if white light was shining upon her. You can't tell the difference—except for the shadows! Where the colors overlap, different colors are produced. Can these colors be understood? Yes they can, if we look at their role one at a time.

[Shine only red light and step into beam]

Note that both the person and the screen is red. But the shadow is black. Black, strictly speaking, isn't a color. It's the absence of light. And the shadow region is a region with no light—so it's dark. No mystery here. But watch the color of the black shadow when I turn on the green light.

[Turn on green light, so red and green are on]

Note that the black shadow is now green. That makes sense. Green light is falling on the formerly dark area. And note that the green light casts a shadow. If the red light weren't here, what color would it be?

[Turn off the red light so black shadow from green lamp appears]

No color! Black.

[Turn back the green so red and green shine]

So we see the shadow from the green lamp is red, because red light shines on it. No mystery here. And look at the background—yellow. As we expect from the average of red + green. Now let's focus our attention on one of these shadows, say the red one when I turn on the blue light.

[Turn on the blue, so all 3 are shining]

We see the red shadow turns a different color—the average of red + blue—**magenta**—bluish red—the color of Bougainvillea blossoms! And look at the former green shadow. With blue added, it's now a bluish green—**cyan**—the color of tropical seas. And we see a third shadow, the one cast by the blue lamp. It's not black because there are two colors shining on it. We see the color is **yellow**. Why is the color of this shadow yellow? In other words, what are the colors that shine on the shadow produced by the blue lamp? Check your neighbor!

We've seen that red, green, and blue overlap to produce white light. We call these three colors the **primary colors**. The three types of cones in our retinas are sensitive to these colors. Question time: Is it possible for *two* colors to produce white?

Will red + green = white? No, we've seen that red + green = yellow.
Will green + blue = white? No, we've seen that green + blue = cyan.
Will red + blue = white? No, we've seen that red + blue = magenta.
Is there some other color that when combined with red = white? Check your neighbor!

The answer is cyan. And why not, for cyan, after all, is the combination of green + blue. So cyan + red = white. Colors are logical.

We call any two colors that add to produce white, **complimentary colors**. We say red and cyan are complementary colors. Put this algebraically: Red + cyan = white. Question: By the same algebra, what is white - red? Check your neighbor! Let's try it.

[Turn down the red light from the overlapping three, and leave cyan]

This brings us to some interesting physics. Water is a strong absorber of infrared radiation—that's light with a lower frequency than red. Different materials absorb different frequencies of light, which is why we see so many different colors around us. It turns out that water not only absorbs infrared, but also absorbs visible red. Not a lot, which is why a glass of water appears without color. But the red absorbed by a larger body of water, like the ocean, means that when white light from the sun shines on it and is reflected, some of that white light isn't there anymore. The red is absorbed, which is why the ocean is cyan. A white piece of paper near the surface of water still looks white, because only a little bit of red is absorbed by the time it reaches the paper. But if the white paper is deeper, it looks greenish blue. If it's very deep, it's a vivid greenish blue—cyan. Sunlight that reaches the bottom of the sea has no more red in it. A lobster that looks red at the surface, looks black at the bottom, for there is no red light to show its redness. At the bottom of the sea, a red-painted object and a black-painted object look alike.

We have a nearly white sun because it emits all the visible frequencies. The distribution of frequencies is not even, however, and since more red is emitted than violet, the sun is a yellowish white. But the sky is blue. Why is the sky blue? Well this is another story; let's discuss the short version.

When sunlight hits the molecules in the earth's atmosphere, light is **scattered**. Have you ever seen the demonstration where sound is scattered off a tuning fork? When you hit one fork and the sound travels across the room and interacts with another tuning fork of the same frequency, what happens? The answer is, the second fork is set into vibration.

In a sense, it *scatters* the sound from the first fork. The same demonstration can be done with bells. Tuning forks and bells scatter sound. Molecules similarly scatter light waves—at select frequencies. Everything has its own natural frequency. Consider two bells—a large one and a small one.

If we strike the large one it goes "bong". If we strike the small one it goes "ting". We all know that large bells ring with low frequencies, and tiny bells ring with high frequencies. Similarly with light waves. Small molecules, or small particles, scatter high frequencies; large particles scatter low frequencies. So what is the atmosphere composed of? Tiny molecules. And what color of sunlight do these tiny particles scatter? High-frequency; blue! So we have a blue sky.

We look at the clouds and they are white? What does this tell you about the size of particles that make up a cloud? Check your neighbor! The answer is, an assortment of particle sizes. Different particle sizes scatter different colors, so the whiteness of a cloud is evidence of a wide variety of particle sizes. If white light falls on a cloud, it looks white. If the particle sizes grow in size so that they absorb rather than reflect light, then the cloud is dark—and we have a rain cloud.

Now at sunset, or sunrise, clouds are not white. Even the sun is not white. The sun is reddish yellow—orange—low frequency light. Why is the sun this color? Watch what happens when I subtract the higher frequencies from white light.

[From the 3 shining lamps, turn down the blue lamp]

All the blue is gone. The white light has turned yellow. If the atmosphere is thick enough, some of the greens are scattered as well.

[Turn down the green lamp, but not all the way]

And we have a yellowish red—the color of sunsets. The passage through the atmosphere at sunset is not long enough to scatter all the mid frequencies, so we don't normally see the sun as a deep red. But there is an event where only a deep red survives atmospheric scattering. And that happens during the **eclipse of the moon.**

Exactly what is happening during a lunar eclipse? The earth casts a shadow on the moon.

[Show via OHP or chalkboard how earth is between sun and moon, and show the lens effect of the earth's atmosphere—how rays of light refract through the earth's atmosphere and cast upon the moon. So the moon is not completely dark. The small amount of light that falls on it has traveled through twice as much air as one sees at sunset, so all the blues and greens are scattered. The result? A deep red!]

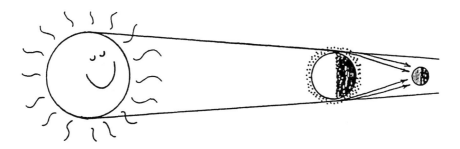

[Turn the green lamp off, leaving only red on the screen]

So poetically enough, the redness of the moon is the refracted light from all the sunups and sunsets that completely circle the earth!

Why Water is Greenish Blue Water absorbs infrared. It also absorbs visible light up into the red end of the color spectrum. Take away red from white light and you are left with the complimentary color — cyan. You can demonstrate this with all three lamps illuminating the white screen. When you turn down the red lamp, the screen turns cyan — the color of the sea! A piece of white paper deep in the water looks cyan. There is no red left in the sunlight to make it white. A red crab and a black crab have the same appearance on the ocean floor.

Why the Sky is Blue Compare the molecules in the atmosphere to tiny bells, that when struck, ring with high frequencies. They ring mostly at violet, and next at blue. We're better at hearing blue, so we "hear" a blue sky. On the other hand, bumble bees and other creatures that are good at seeing violet see a violet sky.

LECTURE SKIT — PART 1; Blue sky: Put a variety of six tuning forks at one end of your lecture table — calling their "colors" — a "red" one, "orange" one, "yellow" one, etc., to a "violet" one. Ask what "color" sound they would hear if you struck all the tuning forks in unison. Your class should answer, "White." Then suppose you have a mirror device around the forks so that when you "strike" them again, a beam of sound travels down the length of your lecture table. Ask what color they will hear. Several might say "White" again, but state that if there is no medium to scatter the beam that they will hear nothing (unless, of course, the beam is directed toward them). Now place a tray of tuning forks at the opposite end of your lecture table (the tray I use is simply a 2 × 4 piece of wood, about a third meter long, with about a dozen holes drilled in it to hold a dozen tuning forks of various sizes). Ask your class to pretend that the ends of your lecture table are 150 million km apart, the distance between the Earth and the Sun. State that your tray of assorted tuning forks represents the Earth's atmosphere — point to the tuning forks, calling out their colors; a blue one, a violet one, a blue one, a blue one, a red one, a blue one, a violet one, a blue one, a green one, a blue one, a violet one, and so forth emphasizing the preponderance of blue and violet forks. Your tray of forks is perpendicular to the imaginary beam from the Sun (to simulate a noonish thin atmosphere). Walk to the Sun end of the table and again pretend to strike the forks and show how the beam travels down the table and intercepts and scatters from the atmospheric tuning forks in all directions. Ask what color the class hears. Since blue is predominantly scattered, you have a blue sky, especially if they're a bit deficient in hearing violet.

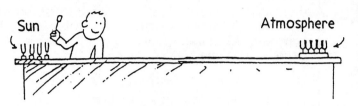

Why Sunsets are Red

PART 2; Red Sunset: Sketch a rendition of Figure 11.22 on the board and show that at sunset the sunlight must travel through many kilometers of air to reach an observer — that blue light is scattered all along these kilometers. What frequencies survive, you ponder. Then back to your Sun and Earth forks on the lecture table. Select a student (a cooperative one, of course) from the class to sit beside the tray of Earth forks. State to the class that your volunteer represents an Earth observer. Place the observer's ear next to the tray of tuning forks (still perpendicular to the length of the lecture table and "Sun rays").

Forks like this for a "thin" atmosphere.

Repeat your procedure from Part I and ask what color the class hears as the sunlight strikes the forks. Again, they say blue. Ask your volunteer what color he or she heard (while whispering "white" to avoid embarrassment). "White," your volunteer states, to which you acknowledge explaining that most of the Sun's white light penetrated the forks, as sunlight does when you stare at it when the Sun is high in the sky. Now conspicuoulsy rotate the tray of forks 90° to represent the Earth's thicker atmosphere at sunset. Go back to the Sun forks which you pretend to strike. Down the table comes the beam, which you follow. Whap, into the Earth's atmosphere where most of it scatters throughout the classroom. Again, ask the class what color they "hear." "Blue" is the answer. Correct. Now you ask your volunteer what color he or she heard. "Orange," is the answer! Your demonstration has been a success. For humor, by "experiment" you have proved your point. Your student volunteer has simply heard a composite of the lower-frequency left-over colors after the class received most all the higher-frequency blues. So those nice colors at sunset are what? Left-over colors. Put another way, you can say the orange of the sunset is the complementary color of the blue-violet sky.

Scattering is the haphazard reradiation of light. Electromagnetic waves "rock" electrons in air molecules, producing forced vibration. The vibrating electrons then radiate electromagnetic waves in all directions — not just the direction of the incident light. Violet is scattered most but we see blue more than violet mainly because our eyes see blue better than violet. Larger particles, like ashes from volcanic emissions scatter longer wavelenth light. When red is scattered, what survives travel in the air is light of higher frequencies. Then the Sun and Moon take on a bluish tint. Question: Why does smoke from a campfire look blue against trees, but yellowish against the brightness of the sky?

Why the Moon is Red During a Solar Eclipse
This is discussed in Chapter 28, and a view of the red Moon shown in Figure 28.13. It is also featured as a Chapter 28 Next-Time Question, in the Next-Time Questions Book. As stated in the special lecture, begin with all lamps fully illuminated, then turn down the blue and green lamps until only red survives. Only red passes through the "lens" of the Earth's atmosphere to shine on the eclipsed Moon.

DEMONSTRATION: Shine a beam of white light through a colloidal suspension of a very small quantity of instant nonfat dry milk in water, to show the scattering of blue and transmission of orange.

Why Clouds Are White Small particles scatter high frequencies. Larger molecules and particles also scatter lower frequencies (like larger bells ring at lower frequencies). Very large ones ring in the reds. In a cloud there are a wide assortment of particles — all sizes. They ring with all colors. Ask why clouds are white! (Cumulus clouds, composed of droplets, are white because of the multitude of particle sizes, but higher-altitude cirrus clouds are composed of ice crystals, which like snow, reflect all frequencies.) When drops become too big, they absorb rather than scatter light, and we have a dark rain cloud. (And the rain cleans the sky of particles that make for a whitish sky, and the cleaner sky is a more vivid blue.)

CHECK QUESTION: Sometimes the sky is not blue, but whitish. Why is it sometimes whitish, and what does your answer have to do with the variety of particle sizes in the atmosphere at these times? [Of course your double question leads directly to the answer of a wide variety of particle sizes — Question for you: Isn't the question technique preferable than simple statements of fact?]

Diffraction Introduce diffraction with the following demonstration.

DEMONSTRATION: Pass some index cards with razor slits in them throughout the class. Show a vertical show-case lamp or fluorescent lamp separated into three segments by colored plastic: red, clear, and blue. Have your students view the diffraction of these three segments through the slit, or through a slit provided by their own fingers. Note the different fringe spacings of different colors.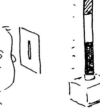

Interference Diffraction fringes are produced by interference, introduced in the pervious chapter with sound. Review this by sketching the overlapping of water waves on the board, like that shown in Figure 12.26. Point out that interference is a property of light waves, sound waves, and ALL kinds of waves.

Prepare your class for your laser demonstration by holding a piece of glass with an irregular surface (shower door glass, sugar bowl cover, crystal glassware) against a laser and show the interference pattern on a screen. Be sure to hold the glass steady so the pattern is fixed. Then make a sketch similar to Figure 11.32 on the board to explain the fringes (a dark area is the result of waves meeting out of phase; a bright area where waves meet in phase).

DEMONSTRATION: This is a great one! With the lights out, shine laser light through the same irregular piece of glass and display beautiful interference patterns on the wall, but this time while you make slight movements of the glass. I do this in rhythm with music (Bach's Suite Three in D.) Your students will not forget this demonstration!

DEMONSTRATION: Set up a sodium lamp and show interference fringes due to reflection from a pair of glass plates with a toothpick or bit of paper in between to separate them slightly. Press lightly on the top plate and show the changed interference pattern.

The practice sheet that treats Figure 11.33 should be helpful at this point. Pass around diffraction gratings if available.

Interference Colors by Reflection from Thin Films

Bubble time! Your class will be delighted if you show a display of giant bubbles (made with a wide hoop in a wide tray of bubble solution — a mixture of equal amounts of Joy or Dawn dishwashing liquid, glycerin, and water). Point out that the film of the soap bubble is the thinnest thing seen by the unaided eye — 5000 times thinner than a human hair or cigarette paper. The smallness of light waves is sensed here also. Emphasize the need for two surfaces for interference colors, and why the film should be thin (Exercise 35).

Go through the text explanation of interference colors seen from splotches of gasoline on a wet street. Treat a single wave of blue light, first from only a single surface where one would see a blue reflection. This would be the case with no gasoline film on a water surface. Then draw a second surface, that of the thin film of gasoline and show that the proper thickness (1/4 wave) will produce cancellation of the blue light. Ask how many students have ever seen gasoline films illuminated with blue light. None. But sunlight, yes. And when sunlight is incident the blue part is canceled. The complementary color of blue, yellow, is what is seen.

CHECK QUESTION: Why are interference colors not seen from gasoline spilled on a dry surface? [Only one plane reflecting surface is present.]

Polarization   Distinguish between polarized and nonpolarized light.

DEMONSTRATION: Tie a rubber tube to a distant firm support and pass it through a grating (as from a refrigerator or oven shelf). Have a student hold the grating while you shake the free end and produce transverse waves. Show that when the grating "axis" and the plane of "polarization" are aligned, the wave passes. And when they are at right angles, the wave is blocked.

Crossed polaroids with another sandwiched between, as shown by Ludmila Hewitt in Figure 11.43 is a dandy. Second only to the sailboat sailing into the wind, it is my favorite illustration of vectors. The explanation for the passage of light through the system of three polaroids is not given in the chapter, but is indicated in Figure C-12, Appendix C (repeated here more quantitatively).

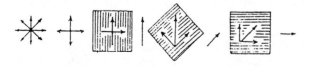

[For an ideal polarizer, 50% of nonpolarized incident light is transmitted. That is why a Polaroid passes so little light compared to a sheet of window pane. The transmitted light is polarized. So in the above diagram, only the electric vector aligned with the polarization axis is transmitted; this is 50% of the incident light transmitted by the first sheet. The magnitude of this vector through the second sheet is 50% cos ø, where ø is the angle between the polarization axes of both sheets, and (50% cos ø) cos Θ of the original vector gets through the third sheet, where O is the angle between the polarization axes of the second and third sheet. The intensity of light is proportional to the square of the emerging vector (not treated in the textbook). In any event, the polarizers are less than ideal, so less than this actually gets through the three-sheet system.]

After explaining how the light that reflects from nonmetallic surfaces is polarized in a plane parallel to the surface (by drawing an analogy of skipping flat rocks off a water surface only when the plane of the rock is parallel to the water surface), draw a couple of pair of sunglasses on the board with the polarization axes as shown on page 308 and ask which are the best for reducing road glare. (If you want to discuss the viewing of three-dimensional slides and movies, you'll have a transition to such by the third choice of sunglasses with polaroids at right angles to each other.)

Colors by Transmission Through Polarizing Materials

DEMONSTRATION: The vivid colors that emerge from cellophane between crossed Polaroids makes a spectacular demonstration. Have students make up some 2 × 2 inch slides of cut and crinkled cellophane mounted on Polaroid material (which can be obtained inexpensively from Edmund Scientific Co.). Place in a slide projector and rotate a sheet of Polaroid in front of the projecting lens so that a changing montage of colors is displayed on the screen. Also include a showing of color slides of the interference colors seen in the everyday environment, as well as of microscopic crystals. This is more effective with two projectors with hand dissolving from image to image on the screen. Do this in rhythm to some music, and while you're at it, shine a laser on a vibrating mirror stuck to a bare speaker cone, and you'll have an unforgettable lecture demonstration!

12

Properties of Light

Reflection is highlighted by the half-size mirror problem, Exercises 3 through 6, which nicely illustrate one of the valuable things about your course — that the richness in life is not only seeing the world with wide open eyes, but in knowing what to look for. Concepts in this chapter provide a lot of guidance in this respect.

Paul Doherty makes rainbows that his students can study first hand at the Exploratorium. You can too. Your giant water drop is a glass sphere filled with water. Cut a hole that's slightly larger than your sphere in a piece of white cardboard. Shine a bright beam of light from a slide projector or the sun through the hole so that the beam illuminates the entire water drop. The drop will project a colored circle of light onto the cardboard screen around the hole you have cut. If at first you don't see a circle of light, move the screen closer to the drop, as Paul shows to the right! (See his article on rainbows in the Exploratorium quarterly, *Exploring* (Summer 92).Thanx Paul!

Courtesy Exploratorium

I owe the conical treatment of the rainbow to one of Cecil Adams' syndicated newspaper columns, *The Straight Dope.*

The half-size mirror problem, Exercises 3, 4, and 5, nicely illustrate one of the valuable things about your course—that the richness in life is not only seeing the world with wide open eyes, but in knowing what to look for. Concepts in this chapter provide a lot of guidance in this respect.

Not covered in the text or ancillaries is the **green flash**, the momentary flash of green light that is sometime seen when the sun sets. A simple explanation is that the atmosphere acts as a prism, but upside down, so that white light of the sun is dispersed with blue on top, green near the top, and red on the bottom. At the moment of setting, the red is cut off by the earth, the blue is removed by scattering, and green survives to give the famous green flash.

An explanation of why a rainbow is bow-shaped is aided with this simple apparatus that is easily constructed: Stick three colored dowels into a sphere of clay, Styrofoam, wood, or whatever that represents a raindrop. One dowel is white, one violet, and the other red, to represent incident white light and refracted red and violet. The angles between dowels is shown in the sketch. A student volunteer crouching in front of your chalkboard shows the class how the only drops that cast light to him or her originate in drops along a bow-shaped region. (More on this in the lecture below.)

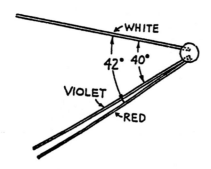

Quantum physics is introduced at the end of this chapter. Much of the confusion about quantum physics has to do with the questions one asks. The answers one gets often depends on the way the question is asked. This is illustrated by the two monks who wished to smoke in the prayer room of a monastery. The first monk wrote a letter to his superior asking if it was permissible to smoke while praying. The answer was a resounding no. The second monk wrote a letter to his superior asking if it was permissible to pray while smoking. The answer was a resounding yes — one can pray always. In a sort of similar way, many of the perplexities of quantum physics have to do with the way questions are asked, and more particularly with what kind of questions are asked. For example, asking for the energy of a hydrogen atom in its first excited state has a definite answer, accurate to one part in 10^{12}. The answer to asking exactly when the electron makes its transition to the ground state, on the other hand, is probabilistic. The probabilistic answers to such questions foster the false notion that there are no exact answers at the quantum realm. Questions appropriate to the quantum realm, however, are crisply and precisely answered by quantum mechanics.

There are 3 practice sheets of this chapter in the **Practice Book**.

The **Lab Manual** has two activities and one experiment to complement this chapter.

There are a dozen **Next-Time Questions**.

SUGGESTION LECTURE PRESENTATION

Begin by pointing out that light from a point source follows the inverse-square law (first treated in Chapter 4, and later for Coloumb's law in Chapter 8). A camera flash is a point source, obeys the inverse-square law, something not understood by people who attempt to take pictures of far-away nighttime scenes with flash cameras — like snapping long-distance shots at a

nighttime concert, or a night view of a distant city. I cite the airline passenger I saw some years ago taking flash shots of a distant dark city below through the aircraft window! Cite how light from the flash spreads out on both the outgoing and return trip to the camera, consequently delivering very little light to the camera. And if through a window, how the light reflected from the window overwhelms what little light would survive the round trip anyway.

On the subject of flash photography, cite the futility of using a flash to take pictures of slides or a movie projected on a screen in a dark room. Of course, the flash overwhelms the image projected and the picture ends up showing a blank white screen. (This seems to not have been known by the many teachers who were flashing away at slides shown by cartoonist Gary Larson at an NSTA conference several years ago!)

Law of Reflection Anybody who has played pool is familiar with the law of reflection — angle of incidence equals angle of rebound. Likewise for light. Sketch Figure 12.2 on the board and carefully show how image and object distance are the same. Call attention to the curved mirrors of Figure 13.3 and stress that the law reigns in whatever small region a light ray strikes. Likewise with **diffuse reflection**. Relate the diffuse reflections from a road surface and how on a rainy night the surface becomes a mirrored surface. Instead of sending light back to the driver as from a rough dry surface, the wet mirrored surface sends the light forward (making glare for oncoming motorists). That's why it's difficult to see the road in a car on a rainy night.

It is commonly thought that a plane mirror reverses left and right, but not up and down. This is perplexing until it is realized that a mirror does not reverse left and right. What it does reverse is front and back. The axes drawn next to the photo of Marjorie in Figure 12.3 illustrate this.

Refraction Do not fail to emphasize the cause of refraction: a change in the speed of light in going from one medium to another. The slowing of light in transparent mediums was established in Chapter 11. The analogy of the wheels rolling onto the grass lawn (Figure 12.8) shows that bending of path is the result of this change of speed. This is reinforced in *Practicing Physics*.

Cite common examples of refraction: shallower looking pools, distorted viewing in fish tanks, and the operation of lenses, as we shall soon see. The most interesting, perhaps, are mirages. With chalkboard diagrams, show how gradual refraction, caused by a gradually changing air density, produces such phenomena as the displaced Sun at sunset (and consequently a longer day, Figure 12.13), and the mirages of Figures 12.14, 12.15, and 12.16.

Dispersion Now that you've established refraction as a result of changes in light speed, it follows that different speeds of different frequencies of light in transparent materials refract at different angles. This is dispersion, nicely illustrated with a prism.

Rainbows Amplify the section on rainbows, and liken them to viewing a cone held with its apex to the eye. The deeper the misty region, the more intense the rainbow appears. The cone bit explains why the rainbow is round. Another is via the ball-and-sticks demo.

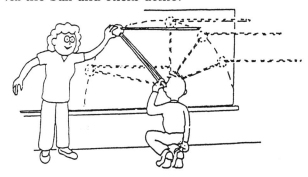

DEMONSTRATION: Show the rainbow-sticks apparatus described earlier and compare it to the rainbow schematic drawing of Figures 12.18 and 12.19. The white stick represents incoming white light, and the red and violet sticks the refracted rays. Have a student volunteer crouch in front of the board as shown in the sketch. Place the ball near the chalkboard so the white dowel is perpendicular to the board (from the Sun at the horizon for simplicity). Position the free end of the violet dowel so that it nearly meets the volunteer's eye. State that a drop at this location refracts violet light to the eye. The question follows: are there other locations that will also refract violet light to the eye? Move the "drop" to other locations along the board while keeping the white dowel perpendicular to the board. It is easy to see that refracted violet from drops farther away miss the eye altogether. The only locations that send violet light to the eye are along a bow — which you trace with violet or blue chalk. This is easy to do if the students holds the end of the violet dowel near the eye while you scribe the arc in compass fashion.

CHECK QUESTION: With the ball and dowels positioned at the top of the bow, ask where the volunteer must look to see red — above the

violet, or below? [Above (2° to be exact).] Show this by moving the "drop" up, whereupon the red dowel lines up with the eye. Complete your demo by sweeping this wider bow with red chalk.

Enlist a second volunteer to crouch in front of the board at a different position. Show how this volunteer must look to different drops in the sky to see a rainbow. Ask the class if the two volunteers see the same rainbow. [No, each sees his or her own personal rainbow!] Do as Marshall Ellenstein does and quip that when one person says to another, "Look at the beautiful rainbow," an appropriate response is, "Move over and let me see!"

Rainbows cannot be seen when the Sun is more than 42 degrees in the sky because the bow is below the horizon where no water drops are to be seen. Hence rainbows are normally seen early and late in the day. So we don't see rainbows in midday in summer in most parts of the world (except from an airplane, where they are seen in full circles).

Point out a significant yet commonly unnoticed feature about the rainbow — that the disk segment bounded by the bow is appreciably brighter than the rest of the sky. This is clearly shown in Figure 12.22. The rainbow is similar to the chromatic aberration around a bright spot of projected white light.

Show Paul Doherty's rainbow from a sphere of water (described before this suggested lecture).

Extend rainbows to the similar phenomenon of the halo around the Moon. Explain how the halo is produced by refraction of moonlight through ice crystals in the atmosphere. Note the important difference: whereas both refraction and internal reflection produce rainbows, only refraction produces halos. And whereas the observer is between the Sun and the drops for seeing a rainbow, the ice crystals that produce halos are between the observer and the Moon. Moonlight is refracted through ice crystals high in the atmosphere — evidence of the coldness up there even on a hot summer night.

Total Internal Reflection

DEMONSTRATION: Show examples of reflection, refraction and total internal reflection with the usual apparatus — light source (laser), prisms, and a tank of water with a bit of fluorescene dye added.

(You may notice that at the critical angle, some light skims the surface of the water. This is because your beam is slightly divergent, so where the central axis of the beam may be at the critical angle and reflect back into the medium, part of the beam is slightly beyond the critical angle and refracts.)

Ask your class to imagine how the sky would look from a lake bottom. For humor, whereas above water we must turn our heads through 180 degrees to see from horizon to horizon, a fish need only scan twice the 48 degree critical angle to see from horizon to horizon — which is why fish have no necks!

Fibre Optics Show some examples of light pipes. Discuss some of the many applications of these fibers, or "light pipes," particularly in telephone communications.

The principle underlying fiber optics is similar to a boy scout signaling Morse code in flashlight to a distant friend. In fiber optics, computers fire lasers that turn on and off rapidly in digital code. Current lasers send about 1.7 billion pulses per second to optical detectors that receive and interpret the information. AT&T researches in mid 1992 sent some 6.8 billion pulses per second over a 520-mile fiber optic cable.

Today glass fibers as thin as a human hair carry 1300 simultaneous telephone conversations, compared to the only 24 that can be carried per conventional copper cable. Signals in copper cables must be boosted every 4 to 6 kilometers, whereas re-amplification in light-wave systems occurs every 10 to 50 kilometers. For infrared optical fibers, the distance between regenerators may be hundreds or perhaps thousands of kilometers. Fibers are indeed very transparent! For several years it was thought that the hairs in the fur of polar bears were optical fibers for UV. Not so, according to several follow-up studies.

Lenses The explanation of lenses follows from your demo of light deviating through a prism. Whereas a study of lenses is properly a laboratory activity, all the ray diagrams in the world are of little value unless paired with a hands-on experience with lenses. So if a laboratory experience is not part of your course, I would recommend lenses be treated very briefly if at all in lecture.

DEMONSTRATION: Show examples of converging and diverging lenses. A white light source will do, but a neat source of light is a laser beam that is widened by lenses and then directed through a mask of parallel slits. Then parallel rays of light are incident upon your lenses.

DEMONSTRATION: Simulate the human eye with a spherical flask filled with water and a

bit of fluorescene dye. Paint an "iris" on the flask and position appropriate lenses in back of the iris for normal, farsighted and near-sighted vision. Then show how corrective lenses placed in front of the eye put the light in focus on the retina.

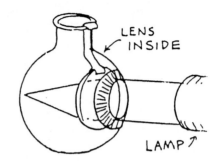

Exercise 30 about the sheet of lenses that supposedly direct more solar energy into a swimming pool makes a good lecture topic.

Seeing Light: The Eye An interesting tidbit not in the chapter is the explanation for the seemingly luminous eyes of nocturnal animals such as cats and owls at night. It turns out there are reflective membranes located in back of the rods in the animals' eyes, which provide a "second chance" for the animal to perceive light that initially misses the rods. This arrangement, common in night predators, gives excellent night vision. Hence also the reflection from their eyes when light is shone on them.

Discuss the function of the rods and three types of cones in the retina of the eye, and how color cannot be perceived in dim light, and how the colored stars appear white to us whereas they show up clearly colored with camera time exposures. (I show a colored slide that I took of the stars, and discuss the curved lines encircling the north star, and get into a discussion of how long the camera shutter was held open.)

In discussing color vision, point out that in a bullfight, the bull is angry not at the redness of the cape that is flaunted before him, but because of the darts that have been stuck into him! Whereas a frog is "wired" to see only motion, so it is also on the periphery of human vision. Discuss the fact that we see only motion and no color at the periphery of our vision.

DEMONSTRATION: Stand at a corner of the room and shake brightly colored cards, first turned backward so the color is hidden and students can adjust their head positions (somewhat facing the opposite corner of the room). When they barely see the moving cards, turn them over so the color shows. They'll see the cards, but not their colors. Try with different colors. This goes over well, and is quite surprising!

The box on lateral inhibition, page 303, is just one more reminder to your students that they should be careful about believing firmly in what appears to be true. By obstructing the edge between the rectangles, a whole different picture is presented. Our eyes do indeed deceive us from time to time. We should always be open to new ways to look at what we consider is real.

Wave-Particle Duality   Cite the flavor of physics at the turn of the century, wherein many in the physics community felt that the bulk of physics was in the can and only applications and engineering were left.   And then along came Einstein and Max Planck, who fell through cracks that turned out to be Grand Canyons! Quantum mechanics was born.

The particle nature of light is best demonstated with the photoelectric effect.

DEMONSTRATION: Demonstrate the photoelectric effect by placing a freshly polished piece of zinc on an electroscope and illuminate it with an open carbon arc lamp (no glass lens). To focus the beam, use a quartz lens (to pass the UV). Show that a positively charged electroscope will not discharge when the light shines on the zinc plate. But that a negatively charged electroscope will quickly lose its charge, showing that the negative charges (electrons) are ejected from the zinc surface by the light. Show the blockage of UV light by placing a piece of glass in the path of the light beam. This is evidenced by the stopping of the discharge process. If you have a quartz prism, pass the light through a slit, then through the prism, and onto the zinc.   Show that the negatively-charged electroscope discharges only when the portion of the spectrum beyond the violet end strikes the zinc plate.

Discuss how light travels in bunches of light — *photons*, whose energies are directly proportional to their frequencies — $E \sim f$. We will return to this relationship when we study spectra in the next chapter. Conventional thinking about light is that it is wavelike in traveling from place to place, but particle-like when incident upon matter, as evident in various **double slit experiments**. It travels like waves and lands like particles. Note the photon-by-photon buildup of the photograph of Figure 12.45.

Discussion of the wave-particle duality sets the stage for the brief treatments of quantum physics in following chapters.

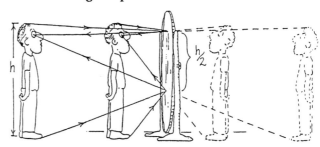

NEXT-TIME QUESTIONS: Be sure to ask for the minimum size mirror bit, Exercises 3 and 4. Don't be surprised if many miss them, and don't be surprised to find some students won't believe the answers [half size with distance not mattering]. Most may correctly get the first part, the half-size answer, but miss the second. Perhaps like the visual illusion of hands remaining the same size when viewed at different distances (from the Practice Sheet "Inverse-Square Law," page 27 in the Practice Book), their belief in their uninvestigated answer is so strong, that they will not see what is there unless it is explicitly pointed out to them. And that, of course, is our role. In any event, when you discuss the answer, consider bringing into class a full-length mirror or pass a few small mirrors among your students. It may be worth the extra effort.

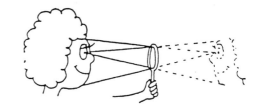

Structure of the Atom

The treatment of atoms in this chapter is basic, and provides a good background for all following chapters.

Atomic spectra is introduced in this chapter, which extends the treatment of light from Part 4. Excitation between the various simplified energy levels of the Bohr model of the atom explains the emission of light. Note that this is quite a different model of light emission compared to the oscillator model we introduced in Chapters 11 and 12. Subtle oscillations of the electron shells underscore light being reflected or transmitted. Excitation is not subtle, and is a different process — electrons make transitions from one electron shell to another. There are two different models of behavior here. One suits the processes of reflection and transmission of light, and the other suits the way light is emitted from a light source to begin with. Neither of the two atomic models presented is intended to convey a picture of what atoms are "really doing," but instead are simplified representations that are useful for conceptualizing how atoms behave. You may comment on the nature of a model in physical science here; namely that a model is not "right" or "wrong", but "useful" or "nonuseful." No scientific models are carved in stone.

Students are quite familiar with glow-in-the-dark strips used as head gear or necklaces, popular in dance spots. Or glow-in-the-dark key rings, activated by light. For the record, these phosphorescent materials contain calcium sulfide, activated by bismuth, with additional traces of copper, silver, or lead. These materials are harmless, and very different from the old zinc sulfide materials impregnated with trace amounts of radium to supply alpha particles for stimulation.

This chapter introduces quantum mechanics, via the classic wave-particle duality. Much of this confusion is failing to see that light behaves as a wave when it travels in empty space, and lands like a particle when it hits something. It is mistaken to insist it must be both a particle and a wave at the same time. This is not the case, despite some writers who try to make this mysteriously profound. What something *is* and *what it does* are not the same. Another misconception fostered in popular and not-so-popular literature is that quantum theory is non-deterministic and that it is acausal. Solutions to the fundamental quantum equation are unique, continuous, and incorporate the principle of causality. Another misconception is that quantum theory reveals nature as a game of probability. Although some predictions about certain quantities are sometimes probabilistic, it doesn't follow that the predictions of quantum mechanics are necessarily uncertain. Quantum mechanics, in fact, leads to extremely accurate results (it predicts for example, the energy of the hydrogen atom in its ground state to one part in 10^{12}). Whether quantum mechanics gives definite or probabilistic answers to questions depends on the nature of the questions. For questions inappropriate to the quantum level, quantum mechanics gives probabilistic answers. For appropriate questions, its answers are definite. See more on this in the Reference Frame essay, *Ask a Foolish Question...* by Herman Feshback and Victor Weisskopf in the October 88 issue of *Physics Today*.

The philosophical implications of quantum mechanics is left to your lecture. At minimum you might warn your class that there are many people who have much to say about quantum physics who don't understand it. Quantum physics does not come in the neat package that Newtonian physics comes in, and is not all sewed up like other less complex bodies of knowledge. It is an ill-understood theory. Because it works so well it is a widely respected theory. We should be wary of pseudo scientists who attempt to fit their own theories into the cracks of quantum mechanics, and ride on the back of its hard-earned reputation.

This chapter has one practice sheet in the **Practice Book**.

Two excellent experiments in the **Laboratory Manual** are *Thickness of a BB Pancake* and *Oleic Acid Pancake*. The first nicely leads into the second, and time permitting, both may be combined.

There are 2 **Next-Time Questions**.

SUGGESTED LECTURE PRESENTATION

Begin by posing the situation of breaking a boulder into rocks, rocks into stones, stones into pebbles, pebbles into gravel, gravel into sand, sand into powder, and so forth until you get to the fundamental building block — the atom. Relate how from the earliest days of science people wondered how far the idea of breaking boulders into stones, pebbles, sand, powder, and so on, would go. Does it ever end? Hundreds of years ago, people had no way of finding out, and they instead carried on with philosophical speculation. Not until "modern" chemistry in the late 1700s did people begin to get indirect evidence of some basic order in the combinations of things. The first real "proof" that there were atoms was given by Einstein in 1905, the same year he published his paper on relativity. He calculated what kind of motion there ought to be in Brownian motion, based on ideas we've considered already, like energy and momentum conservation, and the idea of heat as atomic motion. Many of the "heavies" in physics at that time didn't believe in atoms until Einstein's work.

Smallness of Atoms Give examples to convey the idea of the smallness of the atom, i.e., an atom is as many orders of magnitude smaller than a person as an average star is larger than a person — so we stand between the atoms and the stars. The size of an atom is to the size of an apple as the size of an apple is to the size of the Earth. So if you want to imagine an apple full of atoms, think of the Earth, solid-packed with apples.

CHECK QUESTION: Ask what an atom would "look like" if viewed through a vertical bank of about 40 high-powered optical microscopes stacked one atop the other. [It turns out they wouldn't have an appearance, at least not in the range of frequencies we call light. The atom is smaller than the wavelength of light.]

The electron beam in the electron microscope has the properties of high-frequency light. Matter has a wave nature — the distinction between particles and waves at the atomic level is "fuzzy"— "solid" particles seem to be congealed standing waves of energy.

Recycling of Atoms You can lead into the idea of more molecules in your lungs than there are breaths of air in the world with the following: State that if you put a drop of ink in a bathtub full of water, that you (the students) know that in a short time you can sample any part of the water and find ink in it. The atoms of ink spread out. We can get an idea of how small atoms are from this fact: There are more atoms in a thimbleful of ink than there are thimblefuls of water in the Atlantic Ocean. That means if you throw a thimbleful of ink into the Atlantic Ocean and give it enough years to mix uniformly, and then dip anywhere in the ocean with a thimble, you'll have some atoms of ink in your sample. You may want to discuss Problem 1 at this point and demonstrate its solution. (Note that the data for this problem concerns all the oceans of the world, not just the Atlantic.) By now your class is ready for the more interesting bit about breaths of air in the atmosphere. Relate this to Problem 2 and the statement made by little Manuel Hewitt on page 313.

The Electron and Electrical Forces The electron is the carrier of negative charge in the atom. Discuss the relative distances between positive and negative charges in neighboring atoms and the role of the electric forces in molecular structure. (You're discussing the implications of Coulomb's law at short distances — combined with the ideas you previously discussed in your treatment of tides and tidal forces, namely the importance of relative distances.) Discuss the role of electrical forces in preventing us from oozing into our chairs and so forth. Ask the class to imagine that the lecture table is a large magnet, and that you wear magnetic shoes that are repelled by the table you "stand" on. Ask them to imagine whether or not a sheet of paper could be passed between your shoes and the table. For there is a space there. Then state that on the submicroscopic scale that this is indeed what happens when you walk on any solid surface. Only the repelling force isn't magnetic, it's electric! Discuss the submicroscopic notion of things touching. Acknowledge that under very special circumstances the nucleus of one atom can physically touch the nucleus of another atom — that this is what happens in a thermonuclear reaction.

DEMONSTRATION Show a cathode ray tube (Figure 13.5) and its bending by a magnet.

The Atomic Nucleus Discuss the nuclear model of the atom as advanced by Rutherford, and the subsequent planetary model of Bohr. Stress the emptiness of the atom and the tiny domin of the atomic nucleus, which leads into the fact that solid matter consists mostly of empty space. State how our bodies are 99.999% empty spaces, and how a particle, if tiny enough and not affected by electrical forces, could be shot straight through us without even making a hole! Making a direct hit with an atomic nucleus or an electron is as improbable as making a direct hit with a planet or the sun if you throw a gravity-free dart from outer space at the solar system. Both the solar system and an atom are mostly empty space. Walk through a beam of neutrons and very few if any will interact with your body. Still smaller neutral particles called neutrinos, the most elusive yet most numerous and fastest of all particles, pass though us every moment. But they do so without consequence, for only very rarely, perhaps once or so per year, do any make a bull's-eye collision with any of our atomic nuclei. They freely pass through the entire earth with rare inter-actions. (Interestingly enough, the neutrino flux from the 1987 supernova was so enormous that about 1 out of every 240 people on earth absorbed one of its neutrinos. This tidbit from John Learned, University of Hawaii.)

Protons and Neutrons Schematically show the hydrogen atom, and add a proton and neutrons to build a helium atom, and then a lithium atom, and so on. Discuss atomic number, and the role that the number of protons play in the nucleus in dictating the surrounding electron configuration. Call attention to and briefly discuss the periodic table that is located inside the front cover of the text. Point out that the atomic configurations you sketch on the board are simply models, not to be taken as visually correct. For example, if the nuclei were drawn to scale they would be scarcely visible specks. And the electrons don't really "orbit", as your drawings suggest — such terms don't seem to have much meaning at the atomic level. It would be more precise to say they "swarm", or are "smeared", around the central nuclei. Add that the configuration of electrons and their interactions with each other is basically what the field of chemistry is about.

Atomic Spectra Much of what we know about atoms is from the light they emit. Using the Bohr model, explain energy levels with the following analogy: Hold a book above the lecture table and drop it. Then hold it higher and drop it again. State that the potential energy you supplied to the book was converted to kinetic energy and then to sound energy. State that the higher you boost the book before dropping it, the louder the sound. State that a similar thing happens in the case of atoms. Parallel your book example and consider the case of an electron being boosted to a higher orbit in an atom. Just as a screen door that is pushed open against a spring snaps back and produces sound, the displaced electron snaps back to its ground state and produces light. It emits a throbbing spark of light we call a *photon*. Show that when it is boosted to higher levels, it emits a higher-frequency photon upon de-excitation. Introduce the relationship $E \sim f$ for the resulting photons. Discuss the variety of energy-level jumps for a simple atom.

CHECK QUESTION: Two photons are emitted as a result of the transitions shown on the board. If one photon is red and the other blue, which is which? [Be sure to draw the shorter wavelength for the greater transition, from the second level to ground state, and the longer wavelength for the smaller transition from level one to ground.]

DEMONSTRATION: Show the spectra of gas discharge tubes. Either use a large diffraction grating that you hold in front of the tube (I use one the size of a sheet of typing paper, Edmund Scientific Co.), or pass small gratings among the class, so the spectral lines can be observed.

Cite examples of the uses of spectrometers — how very minute quantities of materials are needed for chemical analysis — note their use in fields as diverse as chemistry and criminology.

Consider going beyond the book treatment and distinguish between *emission* and *absorption* spectra. Cite that a century ago, the chemical composition of the stars were thought to be forever beyond the knowledge of humankind — and now today we know as much about their composition as we do the Earth's.

Emphasize the discreteness of the lines from atoms in the gaseous state. Consider going beyond the book treatment and lead into the idea of excitation in an incandescent lamp, where the atoms are in the solid state. Why do we get a continuous spectrum from a solid lamp filament, but spectral lines from the same atoms in the gaseous state? The answer is that in the crowded condition the energy levels interact with one another and produce a smudged distribution of frequencies rather than discrete frequencies characteristic of the gaseous state. It's like the difference between the tone of bells that are struck while packed together in a box, and their tone when suspended apart from one another. The distribution of frequencies of atoms in the solid state make up the standard radiation curve, which you can approximate by sketching a bell-shaped curve on the board. Where the curve peaks indicates the temperature of the source of light. Hence the difference between red hot, white hot, and blue hot sources — stars, for example. The peak of the curve is the peak frequency, which is proportional to the absolute temperature of the source — $f \sim T$ (this is the equation that explains the greenhouse effect, where the frequency of light emitted by the hot Sun is proportionally higher than the frequency of reradiation emitted by the Earth's relatively cool surface).

CHECK QUESTION: Hold up an obviously broken light bulb and ask if it is presently emitting energy. [Sure is, as is everything — its temperature is simply too low for the corresponding frequency to tick our retinas.]

Get into the idea of the infrared part of the spectrum. Show in a sequence of radiation curves on the board how an increase in temperature brings the curve "sloshing over" into the lower frequency portion of the visible spectrum — hence the red hotness of a hot poker. Show how an increase in temperature brings the curve into the visible spectrum, producing white light. Show why a hot poker does not become green hot, and how sharp the curve would have to be to produce green without sloshing into the other frequencies which result in white light.

Conceptual Models Young's explanation of the double-slit experiment is based on the wave model of the nature of light; Einstein's explanation of the photoelectric effect involves a model of light in which light is composed of particles. The effectiveness of one model or another doesn't invalidate the other model, particularly in this instance where the models are used to describe completely different phenomena. Models are not to be judged as being "true" or "mistaken"; models are useful or nonuseful. The particle model of light is useful in making sense of the details of the photoelectric effect, whereas the wave model of light is not useful in understanding these details. Likewise, the wave model of light is useful for understanding the details of interference, whereas the particle model is not useful. The effectiveness of one model over

another means simply that: one model is more useful than another. This effectiveness doesn't mean that one model is correct and the other invalid. As we gather more data and gain new insights, we refine our models.

Particles as Waves Like others, de Broglie was in the right place at the right time, for the notion of particles having wave properties was at hand. De Broglie showed Planck's constant again with his formula that relates the wavelength of a "matter wave" with its momentum. So matter, like light, has wave properties. When incident upon a target its matter nature is evident. We don't ordinarily notice the wave nature of matter because the wavelength is so extremely small.

Electron waves are evident in the electron microscopes that were common before the advent of the scanning tunneling microscopes. Discuss the electron wave-cloud model of the atom, and the **uncertainty principle**, what it means and what it doesn't mean.

Quantum physics is concerned with the extremely small. Today's physicists are involved in exploring extremes: the outer limits of the fast and the slow, hot and cold, few and many, and big and small. In a light sense it can be said that everything in the middle is engineering.

The chapter treats the matter-wave concept that gives a clearer picture of the electrons that "circle" the atomic nucleus. Instead of picturing them as tiny BBs whirling like planets, the matter-wave concept suggests we see them as smeared standing waves of energy — existing where the waves reinforce, and nonexisting where the waves cancel (Figures 13.17 and 13.18). Electrons form probability clouds (Figure 13.19), and orbitals (Figures 13.20 and 13.21) that are distinctly different than the planetary paths of the Bohr atom. The purpose of models is not to provide visual pictures of the atom, but to enable predictions of atomic behavior.

The philosophical implications of quantum mechanics is left to your lecture. At minimum you might warn your class that there are many people who have much to say about quantum physics who don't understand it. Quantum physics does not come in the neat package that Newtonian physics comes in, and is not all sewed up like other less complex bodies of knowledge. It is still an incomplete theory. It is a widely respected theory, however, and we should be wary of pseudo scientists who attempt to fit their own theories into the cracks of quantum mechanics, and ride on the back of its hard-earned reputation.

14
The Atomic Nucleus

What keeps the Earth's interior molten, makes volcanoes hot, and warms hot springs? Nuclear power! It is the energy of radioactivity that heats the earth's interior.

On page 334 of the text it is stated that a couple of round-trip flights across country exposes one to as much radiation one receives in a normal chest X ray. More specifically, a dose of 2 millirems is typically received in flying across the United States in a jet. This is the same dose received annually from those old luminous dial wristwatches.

The high-flying British-French SST, the Concorde, was equipped with radiation detectors that signaled the pilots when a level of 10 millirems per hour was reached (during a solar flare, for example). The pilots were required to descend to lower altitudes at 50 millirems per hour. According to a report by the British government after a year of Concorde operation, none of the alarms had ever gone off. Concorde pilots are limited to 500 hours flying time per year, compared to 1000 hours for crews on conventional aircraft.

Cosmic radiation at sea level imparts 45 millirems annually, and radiation from the earth's crust imparts about 80 millirems. Living in a concrete or brick house makes this figure slightly higher, for these materials contain more radioactive material than wood. The total annual dose is about 150 millirems, when radiation of 25 millirems from the body itself are included. This makes up about 56% of the radiation the average person encounters, the rest being mainly medical and dental X rays.

To find significant radiation, we need only look into the human body. We, like all living creatures since time zero are radioactive. Most of the atoms in our bodies are hydrogen, and some of the hydrogen is tritium blown to earth by the solar winds. A person of 75 kg, for example, contains 45 billion tritium atoms, producing a decay rate of about 100 per second. These are replenished by the liquids we drink, the food we eat, and the air we breathe. The 75-kg person also contains 75×10^{25} carbon atoms, 75×10^{13} of which are C-14. Of these radiocarbon atoms, 3000 decay every second, which are also replenished. The number of radioactive rubidium-87 atoms in the body is 25×10^{20} with a beta decay of about 100 every second. Potassium-40 atoms number some 30×10^{20} with a higher decay rate. All tolled, about 8600 radioactive atoms decay in our body between two heart beats. We are now and always have been, truly radioactive!

The damage of radiation is probabilistic. It is also cumulative. A gamma quantum either hits a DNA molecule at one of its sensitive sites, initiating cancer by the replication of the

90

damaged pattern, or it does not. One person out of 2000 at the age of 55 years is going to be killed by the radioactivity of their own body. (The total risk of dying from cancer is about 20%, and that of dying anyway is exactly 100%.)

Common smoke detectors in the home make use of the very low dose of about 2 microcuries of americium-241, used to make the air in the detector's ionization chamber electrically conductive. When smoke enters the chamber it inhibits the flow of electricity, which activates the alarm. The lives saved each year by these devices number in the thousands (which dwarfs the numbers seriously harmed by radiation).

Bernard Cohen at the University of Pittsburgh has found from worldwide data that the incidence of cancer is smaller at places with higher than average radiation. His conclusions are that *a radiation dose of 10 - 20 mSv/year seems to suppress the risk of cancer!* (The SI unit for radiation dose is the *sievert*, Sv.)

Recent studies of survivors of the Nagasaki atomic bomb made by Sohei Kondo (Tokyo) support this conclusion. Kondo found that the probability of getting leukemia, lung cancer and colon cancer as a function of dose drops at first, has a minimum at about 20 - 50 mSv, and increases linearly only above 100 mSv. Those people who survived after receiving a modest dose at Hiroshima and Nagasaki lived on average four years longer than the control population!

Conjecture is that the mass of antibodies that increase in the body as a result of radiation may activate the defense (repair enzyme and antibody production) against oxidative attacks. A small dose may increase the immunity against carcinogens. Apparently we can defend ourselves biologically against doses below some threshold, but cannot against stronger or multiple attacks. Interesting.

The material on fission and fusion is of great technological and sociological importance. Nuclear bombs are not avoided in the applications of nuclear energy, but the emphasis of the few applications discussed in the chapter is on the positive aspects of nuclear power and its potential for improving the world. Much of the public sentiment against nuclear power has to do with a distrust of what is generally not understood, and with the sentiments against centralized power, rather than with the technological pros and cons. In this climate, we have a responsibility to provide our students with an understanding of the basics physics of nuclear power. In your physical science class, an appropriate slogan is spoken by our cartoon friend at the right.

Note that in this text, the energy release from the opposite processes of fission and fusion is approached from the viewpoint of decreased mass rather than the customary treatment of increased binding energy. Hence the usual binding energy curve is "tipped upside-down" in Figure 14.27, and shows the relationship of the mass per nucleon versus atomic number. We consider this way conceptually more appealing, for it shows that any reaction involving a decrease in mass releases energy in accordance with mass-energy equivalence. By any reaction is meant chemical reactions as well!

Mass-energy can be measured in either joules or kilograms (or in ergs or grams). For example, the kinetic energy of a 2-gram beetle walking 1 cm/s = 1 erg, and the energy of the Hiroshima bomb = 1 gram. So we can express the same quantity in essentially different units. How big is an erg? That's about the energy expended by a mosquito doing a single pushup. [Let's hope you're not making a big deal out of units of measurement in your course, for it's using time that is better spent on explaining the many concepts of physical science.]

Nuclear waste need not plague future generations indefinitely, as is commonly thought. Teams of scientists are presently designing devices in which long-lived radioactive atoms of spent reactor fuel can be turned into short-lived, or non radioactive, atoms. See "Will New Technology Solve the Nuclear Waste Problem?" in *The Physics Teacher*, Vol. 35, Feb. 97.

One of my general lectures that makes sweeping generalizations about fusion power and an idealized description of a fusion torch is available on videotape, *The Fusion Torch and Ripe Tomatoes*. It goes into a speculative and entertaining scenario of a follow-up device to the fusion torch — a replicator, similar to that described by Arthur C. Clark in his 1963 book, *Profiles of the Future*. Contact an Addison-Wesley-Longman rep for information on this 45-minute videotape, or contact the producer, Craig Dawson, at Media Solutions in San Francisco (415) 665 1077.

A radiation sequence similar to that in Figure 14.12 is in the **Practice Book**. Two others feature nuclear and fission-fusion reactions.

There are 3 activities in the **Laboratory Manual**.

There are 8 **Next-Time Questions**.

91

Begin by asking what is the source of energy that keeps the Earth's interior molten; that makes volcanoes hot, and hot springs warm? Radioactivity in the Earth's material, from its very beginning. Radioactivity is nothing new and is as natural as hot springs and geysers. When electricity was harnessed in the last century, people were fearful of it and its effects on life forms. Now it is commonplace, for its dangers are well understood. We are at a similar stage with regard to anything called nuclear. Even the very beneficial medical science *nuclear magnetic resonance* (*NMR*) has undergone a name change to *magnetic resonant imaging* (*MRI*). Why? "I don't want *my* Aunt Minnie near any *nuclear* machine!"

Hundreds of thousands of Americans live in houses that have a yearly radiation dose from radon in the ground equal to the dose residents living in the vicinity of Chernobyl received in 1986 when one of its reactors exploded and released radioactive materials into the environment (Scientific American, May, 88). This is not to say it is unharmful to live in the vicinity of radon emission, but to say that radioactivity is not a modern problem and not a byproduct of science per se. It's been with us since day 1.

X Rays and Radioactivity   Begin by comparing the emission of X rays with the emission of light, showing that X rays are emitted when the innermost electrons of heavy elements are excited. Then discuss medical and dental applications of X rays, citing the newer photographic films now available that permit very short exposures of low intensity, and therefore safer dosages. Cite also the fact that the eye is the part of the body most prone to radiation damage — something that seems to be ignored by many dentists when making exposures of the teeth (and inadvertently, the eyes). (Why not eye masks as well as chest masks?)

Alpha, Beta, and Gamma Rays   Distinguish between alpha, beta, and gamma rays. Which of the three rays is most like an X ray? If you've covered electricity and magnetism, ask if the rays could be separated by an electric field, rather than the magnetic field depicted in Figure 14.1.

Effects of Radiation on Humans Radiation has for decades been acknowledged as not good for anybody, but we can't escape it. (Recent studies, interestingly and surprisingly, indicate however, that a little radiation is good for you — apparently because of its effect in alerting the immune system!)   Radiation is everywhere.

However, we can take steps to avoid unnecessary radiation. Radiation, like everything else that is both damaging and little understood, is usually seen to be worse than it is. You can alleviate a sense of hopelessness about the dangers of radiation by pointing out that radiation is nothing new. It not only goes back before science and technology but before the Earth came to be. It goes back to day 1. It is a part of nature that must be lived with. Good sense simply dictates that we avoid unnecessary concentrations of radiation.

The Nucleus   Everybody is interested in quarks. Nobody has ever seen one, but it's a fact they exist. Go quarks!

Isotopes   Less exotic than quarks, but make the point that isotopes are associated with all atoms, not just radioactive ones. Distinguish between isotopes and ions. Start with the isotopes of hydrogen (Figure 14.9) and then discuss the isotopes of uranium (which will be important later in the chapter).

Why Atoms are Radioactive   This continues from your discussion of the nucleus. Make the point that although neutrons provide a sort of nuclear cement, too many of them separate the protons and lead to instability. The nuclear fragments of fission are radioactive because of their preponderance of neutrons.

Half Life   Radioactive decay is somewhat like making popcorn. You never know when any individual kernel of popcorn is going to pop. But when it does, it's irreversibly changed. The rate of popping can be described by the time it takes a given amount to pop. Likewise with radioactive decay, where we describe decay rate in terms of half life. Talk of jumping half way to the wall, then half way again, then half way again and so on, and ask how many jumps will get you to the wall.   Similarly with radioactivity.   Of course, with a sample of radioactivity, there is a time when all the atoms undergo decay. But measuring decay rate in terms of this occurrence is a poor idea if only because of the small sample of atoms one deals with as the process nears the end of its course. Insurance companies can make accurate predictions of car accidents and the like with large numbers, but not so for small numbers. Dealing with radioactive half life at least insures half the large number of atoms you start with.

CHECK QUESTIONS: If the radioactive half-life of a certain isotope is one day, how much of the original isotope in a sample will still exist at the end of two days? Three days? Four days?

Radiation Detectors Discuss and compare the various detectors of radiation. Particle tracks similar to those of the cloud chamber are the bubble-chamber tracks of Figure 14.14, and in the chapter opener photo on page 332. Ask your class to venture a reason for the spiral shapes instead of the circular or helical shapes that a magnetic field would produce — of course the track is there only because of an interaction with the liquid hydrogen, friction of sorts. The conceptually nice bubble chamber is fading fast and arrays of fine wires in concert with fast computers have taken their place.

DEMONSTRATION: Show a cloud chamber (Figure 14.13) in action.

Natural and Artificial Transmutation of Elements Introduce the symbolic way of writing atomic equations. Write some transmutation formulas on the board while your students follow along with their books opened to the periodic table insert. A repetition and explanation of the reactions shown on pages 342 - 346 is in order, if you follow up with one or two new ones as check questions. Be sure that your class can comfortably write equations for alpha decay before having them write equations for beta decay, which are more complex because of the negative charge. Your treatment is the same for both natural and artificial transmutations.

Radioactive Isotopes Acknowledge the use of these in so many common devices. One is the ionization smoke detectors where particles of smoke are ionized as they drift by a beta emitter to complete an electric circuit that sounds the alarm. Ironically while many people fear anything associated with *nuclear* or *radioactivity*, these devices save thousands of lives each year.

Carbon Dating Pose the Check Question on page 345 as a lecture skit, after explaining the nitrogen-carbon-nitrogen cycle. The idea of the archeologist in the cave adds interest to the idea.

NEXT-TIME QUESTION: With the aid of the periodic table, consider a decay-scheme diagram similar to the one shown in Figure 14.12, but beginning with U-235 and ending up with an isotope of lead. Use the following steps and identify each element in the series with its chemical symbol. What isotope does this produce? [Pb-207]

1.	Alpha	5.	Beta	9.	Beta
2.	Beta	6.	Alpha	10.	Alpha
3.	Alpha	7.	Alpha	11.	Beta
4.	Alpha	8.	Alpha	12.	Stable

Nuclear Fission Briefly discuss the world atmosphere back in the late 30s when fission was discovered in Germany, and how this information was communicated to American physicists who urged Einstein to write his famous letter urging President Roosevelt to consider its potential in warfare. The importance of the fission reaction was not only the release of enormous energy, but the ejected neutrons that could stimulate other fissions in a chain reaction. In the practice of writing equations from the previous chapter, write the reaction shown in mid-page 348 on the board and discuss its meaning. To give some idea as to the magnitude of the 200,000,000 eV of energy associated with one fission reaction, state that New York City is powered by water falling over Niagara Falls, and that the energy of one drop over the falls is 4 eV; the energy of a TNT molecule is 30 eV, the energy of a molecule of gasoline oxydizing is 30 eV. So 200,000,000 eV is impressive (Note here we don't say 200 Mev, because we're comparing it to 30 ev — the comparison is missed if students are to compare 200 Mev to 30 ev — unclear numbers). Discuss the average 3 neutrons that are kicked out by the reaction and what a chain reaction is (Figure 14.19). Discuss critical mass, and a nuclear device, simplified in Figure 14.20.

Nuclear Reactors A piece of uranium or any radioactive material is slightly warmer than ambient temperature because of the thermal activity prodded by radioactive decay. Fission reactions are major nuclear proddings, and the material becomes quite hot — hot enough to boil water and then some. Make clear that a nuclear reactor of any kind is no more than a means to heat water to steam and generate electricity as a fossil fuel plant does. The principle difference is the fuel used to heat the water. You could quip that nuclear fuel is closer to the nature of the Earth than fossil fuels, whose energies come from the Sun.

Discuss the mechanics of a reactor via Figure 14.21.

Plutonium Show the production of plutonium via the equation suggested by Figure 14.23. Make this two steps, from U-238 + n Np-239. Then by beta decay Np-239 to Pu-239. Neptunium's half live of 2.3 days quickly produces plutonium, with a half life of 24,000 years. Acknowledge that to some degree all reactors produce plutonium.

Breeder Reactors Reactors designed to maximize the production of plutonium are the breeder reactors. Make clear that they don't make something from nothing, but merely convert a nonfissionable isotope of uranium

(U-238) to a fissionable isotope of plutonium (Pr-239).

Mass-Energy Relationship It would be helpful if students have studied relativity at this point, but a brief discussion of what $E = mc^2$ says and what it doesn't say (midchapter 30 in the textbook) should suffice. This is the crux of your lecture — the *why* of nuclear power.

Begin by supposing that one could journey into fantasy and compare the masses of different atoms by grabbing their nuclei with bare hands and shaking the nuclei back and forth. Show with hand motion, holding an imaginary giant nucleus, how the difference might appear in shaking a hydrogen atom and a lead atom. State that if you were to plot the results of this investigation for all the elements, that the relationship between mass and atomic number would look like Figure 14.26, (which you draw on the board). Ask if this plot is a "big deal?" The answer is "no," it simply shows that mass increases with the number of nucleons in the nucleus. No surprise.

Distinguish between the mass of a nucleus and the mass of the nucleons that make up a nucleus. Ask what a curve of mass/nucleon versus atomic number would look like — that is, if you divided the mass of each nucleus by the number of nucleons composing it, and compared the value for different atoms. If all nucleons had the same mass in every atomic configuration, then of course the graph would be a horizontal line. But the masses of nucleons differ. The interrelationship between mass and energy is apparent here, for the nucleons have "mass-energy", which is manifest partly in the "congealed" part which is the material matter of the nucleons, and the other part which we call binding energy. The most energetically bound nucleus has the least mass/nucleon (iron). Go into the nucleon shaking routine again and demonstrate how the nucleons become easier to shake as you progress from hydrogen to iron. Do this by progressing from the student's left to right the full length of your lecture table. Indicate how they become harder to shake as you progress beyond iron to uranium. Then draw the curve that represents your findings, and you have Figure 14.26 on the board. Announce that this is the most important graph in the book!

From the curve you can show that any nuclear reaction that produces products with less mass than before reaction, will give off energy, and any reaction in which the mass of the products is increased is a reaction that will require energy. Further discussion will show how the opposite processes of fission and fusion release energy.

CHECK QUESTIONS: Will the process of fission or fusion release energy from atoms of lead? Gold? Carbon? Neon? (Be careful in selecting atoms too near atomic number 26 in this exercise — for example, elements slightly beyond 26 when fissioned will have more massive products, that extend "up the hydrogen hill"; elements near 26 when fused will combine to elements "up the uranium hill". Acknowledging this point, however, may only serve to complicate the picture — unless, of course, a student brings it up in class.)

State how the graph can be viewed as an pair of "energy hills" on both sides of a valley, and that to progress "down" the hill is a reaction with less mass per nucleon and therefore a gain in energy.

Nuclear Fusion: By way of the energy-hill-valley idea, there are two sides to go down. Going from hydrogen down to iron is even steeper— more mass "defect" in combining light nuclei than splitting heavy ones. This combining atomic nuclei is nuclear fusion—the energy releasing process of the Sun and the stars.

CHECK QUESTION: Will the process of fission or fusion release energy from the nucleus of iron? [Neither! Iron is the nuclear sink; either process results in "going up the hill," gaining rather than losing mass.]

Discuss the latest developments in *inertial confinement fusion*, which includes not only fusion induced by lasers, but also by electron beams and ion beams. Explain how in each case a small fuel pellet is "ignited" to yield a thermonuclear microexplosion, and that the greatest problem to overcome other than obtaining significant energies is the precise timing of laser firings. (As of this writing the Shiva and Nova lasers at Lawrence Livermore Labs have both achieved fusion burns, but not sustained burns. Problems have had to do with characteristics of the fuel pellets and the stability of the supporting optics. Sustained fusion by lasers is presently a 21st Century hope.)

Box on Fusion Torch and Recycling A discussion of the prospects of fusion power is most fascinating. With all the inputs students get from the prophets of doom, it is well to balance some of this negativity with some of our positive prospects. Abundant energy from controlled fusion is one such positive prospect, which should concern not only physicists, but economists, political scientists, sociologists, ecologists, psychologists, and the everyday person on the street. Particularly exciting is the prospect of the fusion torch, which may provide a means of recycling material and alleviate the scarcity of raw material — not to mention the sink it could provide for wastes and pollutants. Ideally, all unwanted wastes could be dumped in the fusion torch and vaporized. Atoms could be separated into respective bins by being beamed through giant mass spectrographs. Point out that the fusion torch may never come to be — but not because technology won't progress to such a point, but because it most likely will progress further. If the past is any guide, something even better will make idea of 25 years ago obsolete. Whether or not the fusion torch is around the corner, the more important questions to consider are how this or comparable achievements will affect the life of people. How will people interact with one another in a world of relatively abundant energy and material? Admittedly, we know that abundant energy and material will not solve all the major problems, but it will mark an end to the scarcity that has always been a foundation of the governance of past and the present civilization — a scarcity that has shaped the institutions governing the respective civilizations. The institutions of tomorrow's world will surely be unlike those we have known to date.

This is a time of transition — an exciting time to be alive! Particularly for those who are participating in the transition — for those who have not lost nerve and retreated from knowledge into irrationality in its many generally-respected forms. Ask how many of your students would prefer living in the past?

15

Elements of Chemistry

This chapter serves as an introduction to the language of chemistry and its submicroscopic perspectives. It is designed to set the foundation for the subsequent chemistry chapters: 16 through 21. Because it is the introductory chapter, you should consider performing a large number of lecture demonstrations, such as the ones suggested here.

There are 2 practice sheets that supplement this chapter in the **Practice Book**.

Laboratory Manual activities and experiments that supplement this chapter include "Tubular Rust," "Collecting Bubbles," "Sugar Soft," and "Chemical Personalities."

SUGGESTED LECTURE PRESENTATION

15.1 About Chemistry As a preface to Part VI you might start by discussing the prevalence of chemical goods as presented in the box "The Impact of Materials". Be sure to note that chemistry is a "material science." To follow up, you may also discuss where chemistry stands relative to other sciences. Ask your students: "Which is the most complex science: physics, chemistry, or biology?" The answer, of course, is <u>biology</u> for it is the application of chemistry to living organisms. Chemistry, in turn, is the application of physics. In this sense, chemistry is the "Central Science" situated between physics and biology. Go to any biology lab and you'll see chemistry on the chalkboard. Go to any chemistry lab and you'll see physics on the chalkboard. (What might you see on the chalkboard of a physics laboratory?)

15.2 Phases of Matter—A Molecular View Particles of a solid are fixed and can only vibrate relative to one another (hold your two fists together while giving them a vibrating motion). Particles in a liquid, on the other hand, are able to tumble over one another much like a bunch of marbles in a plastic bag (tumble your fists over each other). Particles in the gaseous phase are moving so rapidly that they separate from one another altogether (Rapidly bring your two fists together and bounce them off each other).

DEMONSTRATION: Show how gaseous molecules do not stick to one another because of their great velocities. Lightly toss a small magnet against an upright metal surface, such as a metal cabinet or door. Observe how the magnet sticks (Be sure to use the right kind of magnet—some will tend to roll). Throw the magnet again, this time with enough velocity such that it bounces.

DEMONSTRATION: To show how gases occupy much more volume than do solids or liquids, crush some dry ice and use a powder funnel to add some to a balloon as per Figure 15.4. Place the expanding balloon in a tub of warm water for a more rapid effect. In talking about phase changes you may find that the water directly beneath the dry-ice containing balloon has frozen. Be sure to identify the dry-ice as solidified carbon dioxide having nothing in common with water ice except for its solid phase. Note how the dry ice "sublimes" directly from the solid to gaseous phase. Snow does the same thing, especially high on mountain tops where it is sunny and dry. To integrate this demonstration with physics, let the dry ice containing balloon expand while resting on a digital balance. Beforehand, ask your students whether the mass readings will increase, decrease, or remain the same. Of course, as the buoyant force on the balloon becomes greater, the digital read-out becomes less—noticeable so! Remind students that the scale is really measuring weight and is only calibrated to mass.

Not discussed in the text is a special class of liquids called **liquid crystals**. These materials consist of rod-shaped molecules that align with one another in an orderly array. This array is unlike the solid crystalline phase only in that the particles are not held in fixed orientations—they can still tumble around one another like wooden matches in a matchbox. Liquid crystals have many uses, most notable in the displays of wristwatches and calculators.

If you have previously discussed plane polarized light (Chapter 12), then you're in a position to explain the operation of liquid crystal displays (LCD's). Light will not normally pass through two polarizing filters set perpendicular to each other. Sandwich the right kind of liquid crystal between these filters, however, and light will pass. This is because the liquid crystal has the property of rotating plane polarized light by 90°. In the liquid crystal display, light passes through the front filter to become polarized, then rotates as it passes through the liquid crystal, which permits it to pass through the second filter. The light is reflected off of a mirror backing, and then passes back through the filters to an observer who sees light (Figure A).

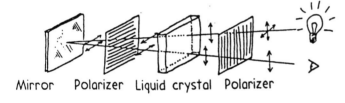

Mirror   Polarizer   Liquid crystal   Polarizer

Figure A

When a voltage is applied to the liquid crystal it loses the ability to rotate plane polarized light, and light can no longer pass through the polarizing filters (Figure B).

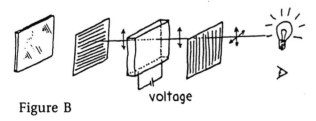

voltage

Figure B

When the voltage is confined to a particular region, only that particular region becomes dark. Build regions that look like numbers, letters, or whatever, and you have the liquid crystal display used for watches, calculators, laptop computers, et. al. Use a polarizing filter to show how the light coming from an LCD is polarized.

15.3 Physical and Chemical Properties
This section will be most meaningful to students after they have had the opportunity to investigate physical and chemical properties on their own in the laboratory. The main difference between a physical and chemical change is that only a chemical change involves the production of a new material. Distinguishing between the two in the laboratory, however, is not easy because in both cases there are changes in physical attributes. The aim of the laboratory should be to help students to recognize evidence that suggests one or the other.

Because physical and chemical properties are such broad concepts, almost any chemistry demonstration can be performed within their context. Here are some of the chemistry author's favorites.

DEMONSTRATIONS: Demonstrate the physical properties of liquid nitrogen by quick freezing flowers, balloons, etc. Here's a new one: solidify liquid nitrogen by placing about 100 mL inside a bell jar and reducing the pressure with a good vacuum pump. Demonstrate the physical properties of metallic sodium (can be cut with a knife) then throw a small amount (less than a pea-size) into some phenolphthalein containing water to demonstrate chemical change. (Metallic sodium is very hazardous as it reacts violently with water to form sodium hydroxide and combustible hydrogen gas. It should be stored under mineral oil or kerosene) Flash paper from your local magicians shop also works well for demonstrating chemical change. A crowd favorite is to blow soap bubbles using methane gas. Since methane is less dense than air (a physical property), the bubbles rise. Dim the lights and ignite one of the bubbles (a chemical property) with a butane lighter. CAUTION: only ignite bubbles that are still relatively far from the ceiling.

DEMONSTRATION: Stuff some iron wool cut from a cleansing pad at the bottom of a test tube. Rinse the wool with a little acetic acid (vinegar). Invert the test tube in a beaker of water and let stand through the lecture period (or for at least 20 minutes). Water will climbed up into the test tube as oxygen reacts with the iron to form rust. For more details see the laboratory activity Tubular Rust. As a variation, as some steel wool and vinegar to a 250 mL round bottom flask. Stretch a balloon of about the same size over the mouth of the flask and wait. Within a couple hours the balloon will be sucked inside the flask and inflated backwards!

CHECK QUESTION: Does the wool gain or lose mass as it rusts?

CHECK QUESTION: Will the iron continue to rust after the water level stops rising inside the test tube?

DEMONSTRATION: Collect a gas by the displacement of water as per the laboratory activity "Collecting Bubbles". You can get the tubing to form a J-hook at one end by inserting a paper clip. Add vinegar by the capful to the baking soda (restopper the flask quickly) to form the water displacing carbon dioxide. Stopper the inverted gas-filled flask and bring it over to a lit candle. Unstopper the flask allowing the carbon dioxide, which is heavier than air, to extinguish the flame.

DEMONSTRATION: React baking soda and vinegar in a tall drinking glass. Let settle. Because the carbon dioxide is heavier than the air it remains within the glass. Dip a lighted match within the carbon dioxide containing glass to demonstrate that chemical property of carbon dioxide.

DEMONSTRATION: React a 3% hydrogen peroxide solution with bakers yeast in a bowl. Poke the resulting bubbles with a red-hot wood splint to demonstrate the formation of oxygen.

15.4 Elements, Compounds, and Mixtures
This section presents the modern definition of an *element*: a substance that contains only one kind of atom. A *compound* results when different types of atoms bond to one another. At this point, elemental and chemical formulas are introduced.

It should be emphasized that chemical compounds are uniquely different from the elements from which they are made. Sodium and chlorine, for example, are toxic, but sodium chloride is essential for good health. Review the segment "The reaction between sodium and chlorine" from the CPS physics and chemistry demonstration video for possible inclusion in your lecture. Many different compounds can be produced out of a smaller variety of elements. This is what gives rise to the diversity of materials around us.

DEMONSTRATION: Show how sugar is not an example of an element. Under a fume hood or in a well ventilated area add a milliliter of concentrated sulfuric acid (the fresher the better) to about an inch of sugar in a long test tube. A cork will be useful to have to minimize the amount of smoke generated. As you await the chemical reaction discuss the term "carbohydrate", which tells us that sugar is made of carbon and water. Hold the test tube with a test tube holder—it gets hot enough to turn the escaping water into steam. Wear safety glasses. This is a good one to perform at the *end* of your lecture as a burnt sugar smell may permeate.

DEMONSTRATION: Tell students that carbon is an example of an element for it cannot be broken down into simpler components—it consists of only carbon atoms. You may point to its location on the periodic table. Water, on the other hand, is still a compound. Prove this by subjecting the water to electrolysis and collect the resulting the hydrogen and oxygen. If you are unable to set up electrolysis equipment you might simply invert a 9 V battery into a glass of salt water. Caution students that this is a good way of ruining a battery. Discard the battery.

In nature, it's rare that elements or compounds are found in a purified state. Instead we find them mixed together. The components of a mixture can be separated ("purified") based upon differences in physical properties.

DEMONSTRATION: Hold out a cup of water and add to it a piece of chalk. Announce that you have just created a mixture. Ask students how you might separate the components of this mixture. As you pour the water through your fingers alert students to the fact that you are separating based upon differences in physical properties—at room temperature water is a liquid while chalk is a solid. Show how this same principle applies to a distillation set-up. Distilling water away from food coloring works well.

DEMONSTRATION: Pour liquid nitrogen into an empty soda can held up by a clamp. The oxygen in the surrounding air will condense along the sides of the soda can much as water vapor condenses along the sides of a filled soda can just pulled from the refrigerator. Ask your students if they see evidence to indicate that the drips off the soda can containing liquid nitrogen are *not* drips of water.

DEMONSTRATION: Before lecture, boil down a large glass of tap water in a clean beaker. Scrape the residual contents from the bottom of the beaker into a small vial. During lecture, hold out the vial and describe what you did. Encourage students to do the same at home using kitchenware. Ask them if the contents represent "concentrated water" or "not concentrated water". A successful answer is: "That's not water at all. That's the material that was in the water. Argh!" Comment on the box "What's in a Glass of Water". You might label your vial as "'Your state's or your community's drinking water", for example, "Hawaiian drinking water". Suggest to students the possibility of selling such vials abroad with the directions "Just add distilled water".

17.5 Classification of Matter This section is most useful for summing up many of the concepts presented in this chapter.

CHECK QUESTION: Impure water can be purified by
(a) removing the impure water molecules.
(b) removing everything that is not water.
(c) breaking down the water to its simplest components.
(d) adding some disinfectant such as chlorine.

This important check question is in the text but should also be presented during lecture. Students have many misunderstandings about the term "pure", which is understandable considering how it is commonly used, often erroneously, in advertising. Contrast what is meant by 100% pure water verses 100% pure apple juice—one is fictional, and the other is set by definition. Contrast the terms "pure" and "purified".

DEMONSTRATION: Separate orange juice into the pulp and the juice using a centrifuge. Talk about how the same technique is used to separate the components of blood.

When you were a student, maybe struggling to make financial ends meet, did you ever dream that students of today would pay for bottled drinking water? And not cheap! Compare the prices of bottled drinking water with the prices of other drinks in your local store. Don't be surprised to find that some brands of water are more costly than the same volume of apple juice! Is this a public fear of contaminated drinking water? Or a distrust of consumer items in general? Or merely a trendy fad? What do your students say about this?

16

The Periodic Table

Organizing the Elements
| Link to History |
| Dmitri Mendeleev — Father of the Periodic Table |
Metals, Nonmetals, and Metalloids
Atomic Groups and Periods
| Chlorine in Water |
| Transition Metals in Society |
Noble Gas Shells
   Inner Shell Shielding
| Link to Relativity |
| Why Gold is the Color Gold |
Periodic Trends
   Atomic Sizes
   Ionization Energies
   Electron Affinity

Chapter 16 can be divided into two parts. The first part, Sections 16.1 through 16.3, introduces organization of the periodic table. It shows how a single column listing of the elements transforms into the general form of the periodic table. The properties and uses of individual elements are then described according to atomic group number. In the second part, Sections 16.4 and 16.5, the remarkable organization of the periodic table is explained conceptually using the noble gas shell model. Through this model, students see how electrons are arranged around the nucleus. The model is quite simplified, but for the physical science student it is very practical. Applying the shell model, students can visualize the concepts of atomic size, ionization energy, and electron affinity. Coverage of this shell model also sets the stage for a deeper understanding of electronegativity and chemical bonding as addressed in Chapter 17.

The 3-dimensional periodic tables seen in this chapter and on the Conceptual Physical Science poster were adapted from the article "Materials Reshaping Our Lives", which appeared in the December 1989 issue of National Geographic.

There are 2 practice sheets that supplement this chapter in the **Practice Book**.

SUGGESTED LECTURE PRESENTATION

16.1 Organizing the elements Ask your students for various ways that the elements might be listed in a single vertical column. Three rea-sonable answers include: alphabetically, by mass, and by atomic number. Choose the latter and present the transparency of Table 16.1 on an overhead projector. Obscure the atomic radius and ionization energy columns with two sheets of paper. State that alongside the atomic number it would be interesting to list a property of each element. Reveal the atomic radius of each element one at a time starting with hydrogen. Ask students to look for any trends. Explain that another interesting property to look at is ionization energy, which is the amount of energy required to remove an electron from an atom. Reveal the ionization energy column and note its similarities to the atomic radius column. Use this transparency of Figure 16.1, which includes additional elements, to summarize these similarities. Note how elements on this transparency may be grouped by the interval in which they appear. Circle these intervals.

A vertical listing is too long to fit on a single page. It is far more convenient to break the column into a series of horizontal rows. Make an overhead transparency of the art piece shown on facing page 101. Note to your class how elements directly above and below one another happen to share similar physical and chemical properties. All the elements in the first vertical column, for example, are metals (hydrogen behaves as a metal at very high pressures) that tend to lose one electron and tend to react with water. Similarly, all the elements in the second column are metals that tend to lose 2 electrons...every one except for helium. At this point remove the helium with an Exacto knife or a single edge razor blade (gets

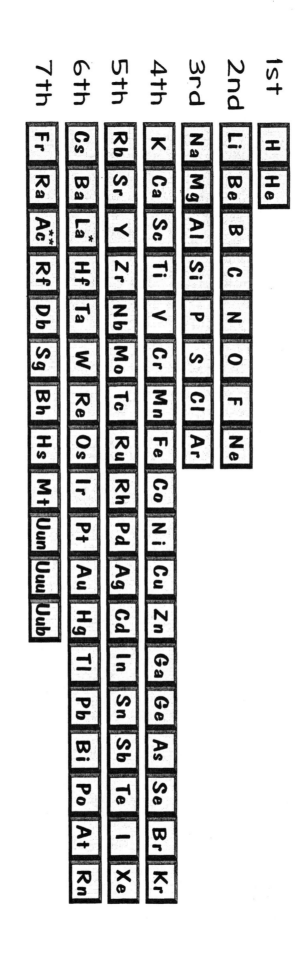

1st
2nd
3rd
4th
5th
6th
7th

H	He																
Li	Be												B	C	N	O	F	Ne
Na	Mg												Al	Si	P	S	Cl	Ar
K	Ca	Sc	Ti	V	Cr	Mn	Fe	Co	Ni	Cu	Zn	Ga	Ge	As	Se	Br	Kr
Rb	Sr	Y	Zr	Nb	Mo	Tc	Ru	Rh	Pd	Ag	Cd	In	Sn	Sb	Te	I	Xe
Cs	Ba	La*	Hf	Ta	W	Re	Os	Ir	Pt	Au	Hg	Tl	Pb	Bi	Po	At	Rn
Fr	Ra	Ac**	Rf	Db	Sg	Bh	Hs	Mt	Uun	Uuu	Uub						

101

the class, every time!). You're looking for order and helium simply doesn't fit...except for that helium is an inert gas as are neon and argon (place helium directly above neon). Continue the discussion by noting that while helium, neon, and argon have a lot in common, they have nothing in common with the iron, ruthenium, osmium, or hassium listed directly below. Likewise, fluorine and chlorine have little to do with manganese and technetium. In fact this whole block (point to the p-block elements) is rather out of place. Slice out the p-block group elements (boron and aluminum through neon and argon) and slide them along with helium to the right such that all the noble gases are aligned. Point out that with this arrangement all elements directly above or below one another share similar physical and chemical properties. Note the noble gases of group 18 and the precious metals of group 11. Students should now understand the general outline of the periodic table. How the inner transition metals get to the bottom of the periodic table is discussed in Section 16.3.

It is at this point you want to bring the periodic tables grand organization to the student's attention. Use the Transparency for Figure 16.2 to show the periodic trends of atomic size and ionization energy.

Mock Quiz: Go back to a wall-sized periodic table and remind the students that atoms of elements to the upper right tend to be the smallest while the atoms of elements to the lower left tend to be the largest. Now ask the students which is a larger atom: Sulfur, S, or Arsenic, As? Ideally the class responds that the sulfur atom is larger. Mockingly inquire of the students how they knew the answer, and in the same breath: "Gee, you must have memorized all the properties of all the elements of the periodic table to be able to answer a question like that." Pick two more elements that are on a lower left to upper right diagonal and ask again. Comment on how you are able to pick elements by random and they're *still* able to answer! Your grand finale, of course, is to point out that the periodic table is like a book. We don't memorize books—we learn to read them. Likewise with the periodic table. "As a student of physical science, you are here to learn how to read the periodic table. Let's begin..."

16.2 Metals, Nonmetals, and Metalloids One of the more apparent organizations of the periodic table is by metals, nonmetals and metalloids. Your discussion here will likely be brief. The main intent should be to identify metals, nonmetals, and metalloids by their physical properties. The theme of the periodic table's

organization is carried well by pointing out the greater electrical conducting properties of germanium versus silicon as presented in the text.

16.3 Atomic Groups and Periods The text's discussion of the periodic table does not go into sufficient detail to account for the traditional method of numbering the atomic groups, e.g. 1A, 2A, 3B, etc. For this reason we follow the numbering system recommended by IUPAC, e.g. 1 through 18. Certainly, there are reasons for the traditional method, which you may care to discuss.

This section presents the opportunity for much descriptive chemistry. A good way to enhance your lectures is to bring to class many samples of different elements and to perform chemical reactions with elements.

Atomic Group Discussions and Demonstrations

Group 1: If you were unable to show the properties of sodium metal in chapter 15, here's your second chance. Drop a small amount (less than a pea-size) into a beaker of water containing phenolphthalein pH indicator to demonstrate its reactivity. Contrast the reactivity of sodium with two other group 1 elements, lithium, and potassium (Exercise extra caution when adding these metals, especially potassium, to water. Hydrogen gas is produced, which is often ignited by the heat of reaction. Sodium hydroxide, which turns the solution alkaline, is also produced. These metals must be stored under kerosene or mineral oil. Wear protective clothing and safety glasses). Alternatively, you'll find this demonstration on the accompanying Conceptual Physical Science video *Physics and Chemistry Lecture Demonstrations.*

If your students will not be performing flame tests of group 1 and 2 elements in the laboratory, you might consider demonstrating these flame tests. See the procedure described in the experiment "Bright Lights". Chloride or nitrate salts of lithium (scarlet), sodium (yellow), potassium (purple), strontium (red), and barium (green) are most impressive. These materials give the color to fireworks. Interestingly enough, fireworks had little or no color prior to the discovery of these compounds in the late 1800's.

Group 2: In a plastic weigh boat (5" × 5") mix 10 grams of sand with 3.33 grams of lime (calcium oxide). Stir in 5 mL of water to create a thick paste of brick mortar. Use universal pH paper to note its alkalinity. Measure its weight and ask the class to predict whether the mortar will weigh more or less after it hardens. [As is discussed in the text, hardening cement mortar gains mass as it absorbs carbon dioxide from the air. Chemically, the calcium oxide reacts with water to form calcium hydroxide (slaked lime). This material, in turn, absorbs carbon dioxide to form calcium carbonate, limestone, which is reinforced by sand particles. As CO_2 is absorbed, water is lost. Since carbon dioxide is more massive than water, the mortar gains weight. Protective clothing and safety glasses should be worn as calcium oxide is a powerful dehydrating agent and is irritating to skin. Avoid breathing any calcium oxide dust. Calcium hydroxide is very caustic and should be handled with care. Interestingly, calcium hydroxide is the active ingredient of many hair removal products.]

It is always interesting to burn a small ribbon of magnesium. The brightness of the flame is impressive. If you can find some "Magicube" flash bulbs, this reaction can be used to demonstrate the conservation of mass principle. First demonstrate how the magnesium strip is "consumed" as it burns. Ask students if matter was destroyed. Point out the magnesium strips inside one of the flash bulbs and ask whether the bulb should weigh more or less after being ignited. Weigh the bulb before and after igniting it with a 9 V battery and wire leads. Despite the intense heat, the bulbs are thick enough to contain all the reactants and products.

Groups 3-10: Transition Elements: Compare various transition elements in their metallic state to the some of the highly colored compounds they form. Search your stockroom for examples such as: iron III nitrate, $Fe(NO_3)_3$ (orange); cobalt II nitrate, $Co(NO_3)_2$ (purple); nickel II nitrate, $Ni(NO_3)_2$ (green). Many pigments consist of transition element compounds.

Group 13 & 14: Students should recognize that elements in the same atomic group don't always share similar properties. With group 13 and 14, for example, upper elements are nonmetallic while lower elements are metallic. The statement that elements in the same group often share many properties is a broad generalization with numerous exceptions.

Aluminum is commonly thought of as an inert metal. In fact, aluminum is quite reactive, especially in a powdered form. The reaction between powdered aluminum and ammonium perchlorate, NH_4ClO_4, for example, is used to lift the space shuttle into orbit (See Section 20.2). Powdered aluminum also reacts with rust, Fe_2O_3, to form molten iron in the "thermite" reaction, which is demonstrated in the Conceptual Physical Science Demonstrations Video. Aluminum also reacts rapidly with atmospheric oxygen to form relatively inert aluminum oxide, Al_2O_3. Interestingly enough, you do not touch aluminum. Instead, you touch a very thin, transparent, and protective coat of aluminum oxide. Tear a piece of aluminum foil and the freshly exposed aluminum immediately transforms into aluminum oxide. A piece of aluminum foil ground up in a sealed container lacking oxygen — in a vacuum, for example — will burn spontaneously as it is exposed to atmospheric oxygen.

Place a sample of the group 13 element gallium, Ga, in a sealed vial and pass it around the class. The warmth from students hands will cause this intriguing metal to melt (m.p. 30 °C). Interestingly, gallium, like water, is one of those rare materials that expands upon freezing. Also, the compound gallium arsenide, GaAs, is a remarkable semiconductor used to make integrated circuits that operate up to five times faster than silicon circuits. Gallium arsenide, however, is relatively expensive to produce.

Display molecular models of graphite, diamond, and buckminsterfullerene. Mention how carbon is unique from all other elements in that it is able to bond with itself repeatedly. An astounding variety of materials can be produced when carbon also forms bonds to elements such as hydrogen, oxygen, and nitrogen. These are the organic compounds discussed in Chapter 21.

Group 15: Comment to your students that you need not bring nitrogen to class for it's already there—air is almost 80% nitrogen. As an exciting alternative (if you haven't done so already), bring in a Dewar of liquid nitrogen. The last element in group 15 is bismuth, Bi, which is the heaviest of the nonradioactive elements. Crystals of bismuth are iridescent and quite beautiful. Bismuth salts make the active ingredient of Pepto-Bismol. The great atomic mass of these salts assists in their ability to "soothe and coat" the digestive tract.

Group 16: Along with showing the properties of liquid nitrogen you might demonstrate the properties of liquid oxygen. The boiling point of oxygen (-183 °C) is higher than that of nitrogen (-196 °C). So, liquid oxygen can be generated by flowing gaseous oxygen into a container immersed in liquid nitrogen. Clamp a large test tube and immerse it into about a liter of liquid nitrogen in a Dewar flask. Connect one end of rubber tubing to the valve of an oxygen tank and the other end to about 30 cm of glass tubing. Place the free end of the glass tubing into the test tube and open the valve to allow a gentle flow of oxygen. In a few minutes about 20 - 30 mL of liquid oxygen can be collected. Transfer the liquid oxygen to an unsilvered Dewar flask to show its pale blue color (water quickly condenses on the outside of the test tube obscuring the oxygen from view). To show the effects of high concentrations of oxygen, pour several milliliters of the liquid into a 250 mL beaker and then quickly toss in a smoldering wood splint. The splint will rapidly catch fire. Substances that do not combust under ordinary conditions, such as clothing, can be quite flammable in such high concentrations of oxygen. Open flames, therefore, are particularly dangerous and caution should be exercised.

Sulfur has the elemental formula S_8. The chemical structure of the most stable allotrope of sulfur is that of an eight-membered ring, which has the shape of a crown. Heat several grams of sulfur in a crucible over a Bunsen burner flame. At 119°C the sulfur will melt. Then, as the temperature rises above 150°C the ring structure breaks apart and the melt becomes viscous due to tangling of the sulfur chains. The chains recombine upon cooling. Pour the viscous melt into water and the sulfur will appear back in its original form. (Is this a physical or chemical change???) Note how elemental sulfur is not the same as hydrogen sulfide, which is a chemical compound that gives the smell of rotten eggs. As was discussed in Chapter 15, chemical compounds are uniquely different from the elements from which they are composed.

Group 17: The halogens iodine and bromine may be shown for their different phases. Keep them in sealed containers. The sublimation and deposition of iodine may be presented as a demonstration (but only under a fume hood!), but it is also presented in the CPS lab "Chemical Personalities".

Group 18: Blow soap bubbles using various noble gases. The rate at which noble gases heavier than helium fall is directly proportional to their masses. Ask your students why this is so (See Chapters 4 and 5). If you don't have any argon available, it is interesting to note that carbon dioxide is only 4 amu more massive than is argon. You may also choose to demonstrate several noble gas containing discharge tubes (See the CPS lab "Bright lights")

16.4 Noble Gas Shells For a cursory introduction to chemistry you may consider skipping the noble gas shell model presented in Sections 16.4 through 16.5. For a deeper understanding of chemistry, however, the student should be provided a working model that explains not only the organization of the periodic table but the nature of chemical bonding. This is provided by the atomic shell model, which, because of its visual nature, is both conceptual and appealing to students.

Begin with the analogy of musical notes as is described in the text. Add to this that electrons be-

have as though they are arranged about the atomic nucleus in a series of 7 concentric shells. Also, be sure to qualify this model as a simplification of a more accurate, but more complex model (atomic orbitals), which may be explored in a follow-up chemistry course.

For your information only, the following table shows the atomic orbitals contained in each shell. These orbitals are grouped together according to their energy levels in a multielectron atom, not according to their principle quantum numbers.

Shell	Orbitals	Electron Capacity
First	1s	2
Second	2s, 2p	8
Third	3s, 3p	8
Fourth	4s, 3d, 4p	18
Fifth	5s, 4d, 5p	18
Sixth	6s, 4f, 5d, 6p	32
Seventh	7s, 5f, 6d, 7p	32

Concerning the capacities of various shells, you may be asked "Why the numbers 2, 8, 8, 18...? Why not other numbers?" The short answer is that there is no reason — it's just an observation. The long answer has to do with the number of dimensions in our universe. If there were more or less than the ones we have (three dimensions plus the dimension of time), then these numbers would be different.

You might wish to show students how to draw a shell model using the following steps. Not all students, however, will catch on. Thus, you should also announce that a series of concentric circles work just as well. Show how this is so by drawing concentric lines onto the transparency for Figure 16.15b.

1. Draw a diagonal guideline in pencil. Then, draw a series of 7 semicircles. Note how the ends of the semicircles are not perpendicular to the guideline. Instead, they are parallel to the length of the page (Figure A).

2. Connect the ends of each semicircle with another semicircle such that a series of concentric hearts is drawn. The ends of these new semicircles should be drawn perpendicular to the ends of the previously drawn semicircles (Figure B).

3. Now the hard part. Draw a portion of a circle that connects the apex of the largest vertical and horizontal semicircles as in Figure C.

4. Now the fun part. Erase the pencil guideline drawn in step 1, then add the internal lines, as shown in Figure D, that create a series of concentric shells.

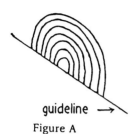
guideline →
Figure A

Figure B

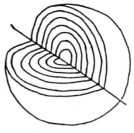
Figure C

Figure D

Point out the various electron capacities of each shell and how this corresponds to the organization of the periodic table. Define valence electrons and show how electrons can be represented using arrows. In your discussion, you may wish to refer to "the arrangement of electrons in an atom" as the "electron configuration". Through the shell model, however, the symbolic notations of $1s^2$, $2s^2$, $2p^6$, etc., are avoided.

CHECK QUESTION: How many valence electrons are unpaired in the sodium atom? [answer: 1] How many in the sodium ion, Na^{1+}? [answer: none]

Inner Shell Shielding is the process of inner shell electrons weakening the attraction between outer shell electrons and the nucleus. The diminished nuclear charge is referred to as the *effective nuclear charge*. Please check out the practice sheet entitled "Effective Nuclear Charge and the Shell Model." If students don't have access to the Practice Book, consider creating an overhead transparency of this particular practice sheet.

16.5 Periodic Trends This section serves as a check on how well the students understand the shell model. After reviewing this section, test student comprehension by asking for the relative sizes of various ions.

CHECK QUESTION: Which should be larger, the lithium ion, Li^{1+}, or the lithium atom, Li? How come? [Answer: the lithium ion has electrons only in the first shell, while the lithium atom has electrons in both the first and second shell. The lithium atom, therefore, should be larger. In fact, the lithium ion has a radius of 60 picometers while the lithium atom has a radius of 152 picometers.]

CHECK QUESTION: Which should be larger, a chlorine ion, Cl^{1-}, or an argon atom, Ar? How come? [Answer: both these species have the same electron configuration but the effective nuclear charge in the outermost shell of argon is greater, so electrons are pulled in closer to the nucleus. The chlorine ion, Cl^{1-}, therefore, should be larger. In fact, the chloride ion has a radius of 181 picome

ters while argon has a radius of about 94 picometers.]

Electron Affinity
The discussion of electron affinity here sets the stage for a deeper understanding of chemical bonding in Chapter 17. Consider that a driving force for the formation of a chemical bond is the affinity that atoms have for additional electrons. In a covalent bond, atoms acquire additional electrons by sharing. In an ionic bond, one atom has so much more of an affinity for electrons that ions are formed.

Even a perfectly neutral atom can have an affinity for an additional electron. The hydrogen atom, for example, definitely prefers to have a negative charge, rather than be neutral. Its electron affinity is -72.4 kJ/mol, which means that you have to *expend* 72.4 kJ worth of energy to remove that extra electron from one mole of hydrogen atoms. Some other interesting electron affinity values are given below. Positive electron affinities mean that the neutral atom prefers not to have an additional electron. Use these values to question your students' understanding of the shell model.

Electron Affinities (kJ/mol)

H -72.4	O -142	F -322	He +21
Li -59.8	S -201	Cl -348	Ne +29
Na -53.1		Br -324	Ar +35
K -48.3			Kr +39
			Xe +41

CHECK QUESTION: Why are all the electron affinities for noble gases positive? [The shells of noble gases are filled. An additional electron would have to go into the next shell outwards where it is completely shielded from the nucleus.]

CHECK QUESTION: Why is the electron affinity of the potassium atom less than that of the lithium atom? [Both lithium and potassium should have an effective nuclear charge in the outermost shell of about +1. The outer shell of potassium, however, is farther way from the nucleus, hence, the effective nuclear charge is less.]

17

Chemical Bonding

Metals and Alloys
Ionic Bonds
Covalent Bonds
    Metallic, Ionic, and Covalent Bonds Compared
Covalent Bond Polarity
Molecular Polarity
| Link to Cooking — Heating Bonds and Molecular Polarity |

A central theme for this chapter is how the periodic table can be used to gain insight into the nature of chemical bonding. Students who are familiar with the noble gas shell model of Chapter 16 will have insight as to why it is that oxygen has an affinity for two additional electrons or that hydrogen has an affinity for only one additional electron. The chapter is written, however, with the understanding that the noble gas shell model may not have been covered. In such cases, students need only be taught how it is that many atoms tend to attract additional electrons. We call this *electron affinity*. How many electrons an atom attracts is a function of its position in the periodic table.

There are 3 practice sheets that supplement this chapter in the **Practice Book**.

Laboratory Manual activities and experiments that supplement this chapter include "Molecular Polarity," and "Molecules by Acme."

SUGGESTED LECTURE PRESENTATION

17.1 Metals and Alloys After describing the nature of the metallic bond and the applications of alloys, prepare and alloy in class with the following demonstration:

DEMONSTRATION: Heat a zinc coated penny in the flame of a Bunsen burner or a propane torch. Within a few seconds, the zinc will alloy with the copper to form a stunning gold-colored brass. Alloy several of the pennies and pass them around class after they have cooled. Post 1982 pennies can be heated further to separate the internal zinc from the copper (now brass) coating. Heat until blistering occurs and then "shake" the internally melted zinc into a crucible. This, too, should be passed around after cooling. The zinc coated pennies should be fabricated in advance. The following procedure shouldn't take more than 30 minutes from start to finish. Prepare about 200 mL of a 6 M solution of

either sodium hydroxide, NaOH, or potassium hydroxide, KOH. (Note: the KOH dissolves in water much quicker than the NaOH.) Because this solution is very caustic, wear protective clothing and safety glasses. Fill the bottom of the beaker with granulated zinc and then bring the solution to a boil. At this point carefully drop in a half-dozen or so pennies. Pennies in contact with the zinc will be electroplated with the zinc. Use tongs carefully to flip and stir the pennies to guarantee they are all electroplated. After a few minutes of boiling, remove the electroplated zinc pennies using the tongs. Rinse the pennies thoroughly. At this point you may wish to create more zinc pennies for future demonstrations. For clean-up, allow the solution to cool and then pour the concentrated NaOH or KOH solution into a larger beaker filled with water to dilute. The solution can then be poured down the drain with plenty of flushing. Alternatively, label and store the solution for future use. Rinse the zinc granules thoroughly, allow to dry, and store for future use. Note: if your zinc coated pennies are stored in contact with one another, much of the zinc coating will fade away—store the zinc coated pennies separate from each other.

17.2 Ionic Bonds A good way to start a discussion of ionic bonds is to develop Figure 17.6 on the chalk board. Draw the sodium atom first with 11 electrons. Ask the class what happens when you take one of the electrons away. Keep track of the net charge below the atoms as is shown if Figure 17.6. Show the symbol notation of the sodium ion, Na^{1+}, above the diagram. Similarly, draw a chlorine atom to the right of the sodium atom first with 17 electrons. Ask class what happens when you add an electron. Keep track of the net charge and then show the symbol notation of the chloride ion, Cl^{1-}, just to the right of the Na^{1+}. By this time you should have the complete rendition of Figure 17.6 on the board. Colored chalk works well. Talk about the coulomb attraction that must occur between these two oppositely charged ions. Then point out that we give this Coulomb force a name. We call it the *ionic bond*.

CHECK QUESTION: One chlorine ion may be attracted to a sodium ion, but can two?

Answer: Yes, provided the second chlorine ion approaches from another angle. Draw the second chlorine ion on the opposite side of the sodium ion already drawn. Ask students if any additional chlorine ions may be attracted to this sodium ion. As they answer "yes" draw chlorine ions above and below the sodium ion. You should mention that electric fields are three dimensional so chlorine ions may also approach from outside the plane of the board. Ask then how sodium ions might feel about all these chlorine ions. Oppositely charged ions packed together in such an orderly three dimensional fashion form an *ionic crystal*. Interestingly enough, the macroscopic dimensions of a crystal are the consequence of this atomic packing. Sodium and chlorine ions pack in a cubic orientation, hence, table salt crystals are cubic. (Salt manufacturers have discovered that under the proper conditions cubic salt crystals will coalesce into the shape of a hollow pyramid. This dietetic "flaked" salt occupies greater volume so that less salt is used per shake. Also, flaked salt is thought to be more easily tasted by the tongue because it has a greater surface area per crystal.)

Note the types of ions that elements tend to form relative to the periodic table. If you were able to cover the noble gas shell model of Chapter 16, ask your students why the trend?

An important consideration is that the ions of any ionic bond must balance each other electrically. For example, if one ion carries a double charge and the second ion carries a single charge, then the ratio of ions can no longer be 1:1. Rather, there will need to be twice as many of the singly charge ion. There is a Conceptual Physical Science Practice Sheet that covers this issue.

17.3 Covalent Bonds Illustrate how two kids may be held together by their mutual attraction for toys they share. In this analogy, the kids represent protons and the toys represent electrons. To keep it accurate, the kids should be nasty to each other (protons repel protons) and each have one toy (bonding electron) to share. Show how the analogy relates to the hydrogen molecule. Point out that in a covalent bond there are no ions involved but that the force holding the two atoms together is still electrical. This level of understanding satisfies most students. You may be asked, however, how it is that two repelling

electrons can be squeezed together in between two hydrogen atoms. To answer this question you may want to refer the student to the noble gas shell model of Chapter 16 where paired valence electrons are discussed.

Point out that covalent bonds primarily involve those elements toward the upper right hand side of the periodic table. These are the elements with high electron affinities. Also address the unique feature of multiple covalent bonds. The term molecule should then be introduced as a group of atoms held together by covalent bonds. Check to see who was listening by announcing the following question:

CHECK QUESTION: Are atoms made of molecules or are molecules made of atoms?

The term "molecule" was introduced in the early 1800's by the French chemist Gay-Lussac in his work with the principle of combining volumes (no longer discussed in this edition). During this time very few believed in the existence of atoms, and even fewer in the existence of groups of atoms — molecules. Ask students if it's possible to see a single molecule. You will surprise those who haven't read the chapter yet by noting that a diamond is an example of a macromolecule. Show the molecular model of a diamond. A large model (1 ft^3) built from miniature pieces should be placed on the overhead projector and twirled for a dramatic effect. Note the "tunnels" as they appear on screen.

Ask your students to think both carefully and critically about the "family" analogy given at the end of this section. You may want to come back to this analogy when in Chapter 18 you get to discuss what happens to covalent and ionic compounds when dissolved in water.

17.4 Covalent Bond Polarity The applications of bond polarity are far reaching. They are discussed here and then explored much further in Chapter 18 Molecular Interactions.

In the **Practice Book** on page 75 see the practice sheet "Bond Polarity and the Shell Model." This practice sheet stems from a lecture skit that you may wish to apply here. You may or may not involve the shell model in your presentation. The two key points to address are:

1) Different atoms have different "pulling powers". This pulling power, also known as electronegativity, is a function of how strongly the atomic nucleus is able to pull on the valence electrons. The greater the pulling power of an atom, the greater its ability to pull bonding electrons closer to itself.

2) An atom that pulls electrons closer to itself will be slightly negative in charge because of the greater amount of time that electrons spend on that side of the bond.

Wrap up your discussion of covalent bond polarity by comparing it to the ionic bond. That all ionic bonds have some covalent character and that all polar covalent bonds have some ionic character is a useful unifying concept. Covalent bonds and ionic bonds are just two extremes of the same thing: atoms held together by some distribution of electrons.

17.5 Molecular Polarity We highly recommend that students have experience in the laboratory working with molecular models before being introduced to this material. (See "Molecules by Acme" in the *Laboratory Manual*). Any previous experience they have with vector addition will also be useful.

A good order of examples to choose is as described in the text: carbon dioxide, CO_2, followed by boron trifluoride, BF_3, followed by water, H_2O. The overhead transparencies of Figures 17.28, 29 and 33 may prove particularly useful. The more examples you can perform in class the better. Consider using the tetrafluoroethylene and 1,1-difluoroethylene as shown in the in-chapter questions of this section.

An assumption has been made in presenting Table 17.1, namely, that students understand the concept of boiling. Be sure they do by asking the following:

CHECK QUESTION: When water boils, water molecules
  (a) break down into hydrogen and oxygen.
  (b) separate from one another.
  (c) become lighter in mass.
  (d) All of the above.

Finish the chapter with the following demonstration, which makes for a good transition to the subsequent chapter on molecular interactions.

DEMONSTRATION: Charge a balloon by rubbing it on your hair. Hold the balloon to a thin stream of falling water (from a buret works nicely). The negative charge of the balloon attracts the dipoles of the water. Next pull out a balloon of a different color and lie by saying it is made out of a different type of polymer that actually forms a positive charge upon being rubbed over hair. Ask the class what will happen when you hold it up to the thin stream of water. Tease them jokingly. If you're in the mood, we suggest not answering this question until next time you meet. You'll find this and other "next-time" questions in the **Next-Time Questions** book.

18
Molecular Mixing

The chapter begins by defining and showing examples of four types of molecular interactions. They are presented in order of decreasing strength. Subsequent sections apply the concepts of molecular interactions to commonly encountered phenomena.

There are 2 practice sheets that supplement this chapter in the Conceptual Physical Science **Practice Book.**

Laboratory Manual activities and experiments that supplement this chapter include "Crystal Clear," "Circular Rainbows," "Sugar and Sand," and "Sugar Soft," "Home Sugar Brew."

SUGGESTED LECTURE PRESENTATION

Types of Molecular interactions Start by distinguishing between chemical bond and molecular interaction. Both involve electrical forces of attraction, but chemical bonds are over 100 fold stronger and hold atoms together in a molecule. Molecular interactions hold molecules together in groups. (Be careful with the semantics: "what holds a molecule together" and "what holds molecules together" may be easily confused.) Review the concept of the molecular dipole to be sure your students understand it before going further. Use water as an example.

Ion-Dipole Use the transparency of Figure 18.2 to show how many water molecules are required to break apart the sodium chloride ionic bond.

DEMONSTRATION: If this demo was performed in the previous chapter, here's your second chance. Bring a charged rod, balloon, or comb near a thin stream of running water (a buret works very well) and note the bend in the stream as it is attracted to the charge.

Dipole-Dipole Discuss the dipole-dipole interaction, which is fairly straight-forward. Note how the hydrogen bond is simply a relatively strong dipole-dipole interaction.

DEMONSTRATION: Fill two burets, one with 50.00 ml of water, and the other with 50.00 mL of 95% ethanol. Ask the students what volume will be obtained when the two liquids are combined. Drain the two liquids simultaneously into a 100 mL volumetric flask (use a permanent marker to calibrate the last three milliliters). A total of only 98.0 mL will be obtained. Tell the students to "Check their neighbor" for an explanation. [Answer (by analogy): At a dance hall 50 men by themselves and 50 women by themselves occupy a given amount of floor space. Bring the men and women together, however, and they occupy a total floor space that is less than the sum of the floor space they occupied while by themselves. Similarly, water and ethanol molecules are attracted to one another, hence, they are able to contract into a volume less than the sum of their volumes alone.]

Dipole-Induced Dipole Electrons in a molecule are not static. Instead they are continually moving around. In a polar molecule, the electrons, on average, are found closer to one side. In a nonpolar molecule, the electrons, on average, are distributed evenly across the whole molecule. Because the electrons in a nonpolar molecule are not held in place they can be shuffled to one side or the other upon the application of an electric force. Draw Figure 18.5 on the chalkboard to show how the permanent dipole of a water molecule induces a temporary dipole in an oxygen molecule. Point out how the oxygen dipole exists only so long as the water is present. It is the dipole-induced dipole interaction that permits small quantities of nonpolar substances such as oxygen and carbon dioxide to dissolve in water.

CHECK QUESTION: There are dipole-induced dipole forces of attraction between oil and water molecules. So, why don't the two mix? [Answer: They do mix, but like oxygen and carbon dioxide, only to a very small extent because water molecules have such a great preference for other water molecules.]

Here is an analogy you might use to explain why it is that oil and water form two different phases. Say at a party there are two kinds of people, those who like to talk and share ideas and those who are stone-faced and would rather say nothing. Mix these two types of people together and soon the talkative people are on one side and the stone-faced people on the other. It's not that there is a repulsion between the talkative people and the stone-faced people. In fact, there may be a weak attraction — some people need to be *induced* into a conversation. There is, nonetheless, a greater force of attraction between talkative people and this is what pulls them together to the point that they exclude most of the stone-faced people. Similarly, water is too attracted to itself by the stronger dipole-dipole interactions to the point that it excludes most of the oil molecules.

NEXT-TIME QUESTION: Due to ion-dipole interactions, a thin stream of water bends towards a charge rod. Will a thin stream of hexanes, a very nonpolar organic solvent, also bend towards the charged rod? [Answer: Yes, and it does so by way of ion-induced dipole interactions.]

Induced Dipole-Induced Dipole On the average, electrons in a nonpolar molecule or atom are distributed evenly. But electrons are perpetually moving around and at times more may be grouped to one side. This is the nature of a "momentary" dipole. A momentary dipole, albeit weak, is able to induce dipoles in neighboring molecules or atoms just as a permanent dipole can. The induced dipole can then, in turn, induce dipoles in other molecules or atoms. Since all the molecules or atoms are nonpolar, it is unclear as to who induced whom first. So, the interaction is simply called "induced dipole-induced dipole", rather than "momentary dipole-induced dipole."

Interestingly enough, the same argument about momentary dipoles applies to molecules with permanent dipoles. Due to the random motion of electrons a permanent dipole may at one instant be slightly stronger or slightly weaker. So, induced dipole-induced dipole interactions occur between water molecules too, as do dipole-induced dipole interactions. These weaker interactions, however, are overshadowed by the stronger dipole-dipole interaction.

The less volume electrons occupy, the less of a tendency they will have to congregate to one side — because of greater electrical repulsions. This means that smaller atoms, such as fluorine, exhibit weaker induced dipole-induced dipole interactions than do larger atoms, such as iodine. At this point in lecture you may wish to introduce the term "polarizability", which is the degree to which an atom can be polarized. Fluorine has a low polarizability, while iodine has a great polarizability.

LECTURE SKIT: Explain that atoms with great polarizability are soft, that is, electrons can easily be pushed to one side or the other. Pull out two marshmallows and demonstrate how this polarizability makes it easy for the two to stick to each other (take a small bite out of each marshmallow and stick them together). Explain that if the electrons are compressed into a smaller volume then, because of electron-electron repulsions, the atom becomes less polarizable, that is, the electrons cannot easily be pushed to one side. This makes for a very hard atom. (In one of your pants or dress pockets have a marshmallow and a piece of white chalk that has been carved into a small sphere. Reach into your pocket, grab the chalk and press it into the marshmallow with your index finger. Lift out the marshmallow using your other fingertips and hold it toward the students so that they do not see the chalk. Clasp both hands together and appear to squeeze the marshmallow. Facial expressions help. With sleight of hand hold the compressed marshmallow—the small piece of chalk—up for all students to see while with your other hand you sneak the marshmallow into your other pocket.) Explain that you have a second marshmallow to compress in your other pocket. (In your other pocket have a second piece of spherical chalk. Perform the same sleight of

110

hand to create a second "compressed" marshmallow.) Show how these "harder atoms" do not stick to each other as do the "softer atoms." As a follow up, point out that this is why very few things ever stick to Teflon, which is a polymer saturated with nonpolarizable (hard) fluorine atoms (Transparency Figure 18.11).

Although a single induced dipole-induced dipole interaction is relatively weak, many of them can make for a strong interaction. Demonstrate the Velcro analogy given in the text using short and long pieces of Velcro. The interaction between two methane molecules is like that between two short pieces of Velcro. The interaction between two gasoline molecules is more like that between two long pieces of Velcro (Transparency Figure 18.12).

18.2 Solutions

DEMONSTRATION: Before lecture, fill a 500 mL graduated cylinder to the 500 mL mark, then find out how much sugar must be added so that the volume of solution reaches the brim of the cylinder. Add 500 mL of warm water to the graduated cylinder. Tell the students that you are going to dissolve a bunch of sugar in this water. Ask them whether the volume should increase, decrease, or stay the same. Pour the water into the beaker and mix in the sugar until it dissolves. Pour the solution back into the graduated cylinder. Slow down as you approach the 500 mL mark. Many students will be surprised for they will confuse this demonstration with a previous one where you mixed 50 mL of water with 50 mL ethanol. It's even more surprising to see the solution fill to the brim. Explain that matter does not cease to occupy volume even when it's dissolved. Also, explain how this demo and the previous one are not contradictory. In both cases, greater volumes were obtained— 98 mL is greater than 50 mL, just as 520 mL is greater than 500 mL.

Use the transparencies of Figure 18,17 to illustrate what happens when sugar dissolves in water. Note that when a covalent compound dissolves, it dissociates into individual molecules. When an ionic compound dissolves, it dissociates into individual ions.

CHECK QUESTION: The ionic bond is easily broken apart by water molecules. The covalent bond, on the other hand, is not. How come? [Answer: The ionic bond has great electrical charge that attracts polar water molecules. Covalent bonds tend to be more neutral.]

A pitfall to this section is that there are many, many terms associated with solutions. A Practice Sheet has been designed to help students with these many terms. Behind each term lies a concept. Guide your students towards these concepts and away from memorization. There is much to see here on the molecular level.

The *mole* is introduced in this section. It is used to define *molarity*, a common unit of concentration. How the value of one mole, 6.02×10^{23}, is obtained is explored in Section 19.5 *Avogadro's Number and the Mole*. The molarity is used again in Section 20.3 for defining the pH of a solution.

18.3 Solubility

DEMONSTRATION: Float a Styrofoam coffee cup in a petri dish full of acetone placed on the overhead projector. Flippantly ask the students if they can see the Styrofoam cup melting. Ask the question again and again until they realize it's not melting at all. So cried the Wicked Witch of the East "I'm dissolving! I'm dissolving!" For the pure humor of it cut out a small circle of yellow paper and place it in the middle of the remaining deformed Styrofoam. Use a spatula to place the "fried egg" on a paper towel while saying: "Chemistry is aiming to serve. How would you like your egg? Sunny side up?"

Many students are still reminded of the early 1990's movie "The Abyss" as they read or hear about the applications of perfluorocarbons. In this movie there is a scene were an aquanaut is required to breathe perfluorocarbons saturated with oxygen. On this note you might comment about movies that contain good science verses movies that contain bad science. For example, in "Star Wars" the opening scene shows a colossal imperial starship passing overhead with deafening thunder — bad science. Then came the movie "Aliens", which touted: "In space (pause) no one can hear you scream"—good science! Thankfully, for a number of recent movie producers there has been a focus on getting the science "as right as possible". Three notable examples include "Apollo 13", "Contact", and "Deep Impact".

Solubility and Temperature If your students will not be making crystal in the laboratory (See the lab "Crystal Clear" in the **Laboratory Manual**), then you may wish to demonstrate the making of a supersaturated solution of sugar. Set it up for the formation of crystals and set it aside so that the class can observe the crystal growth over the next several weeks. For quicker crystallization, prepare a solution of supersaturated copper sulfate, Cu_2SO_4.

Solubility of Gases Perform the following demonstration to so that tap water does indeed contain dissolved gases.

DEMONSTRATION Fill a large beaker with warm tap water and let it stand at room temperature while you lecture. Note the bubbles that adhere to the inner sides of the beaker. Ask the student where the bubbles came from and what they contain? For further experimentation, perform the same demonstration in two beakers side-by-side. In one beaker use warm water from the faucet. In the second beaker, use boiled water that has cooled down to the same temperature. The process of boiling *deaerates* the water, that is, removes the atmospheric gases. Chemists sometimes need to use deaerated water, which is made simply by allowing boiled water to cool in a sealed container. Ask your students why don't fish live very long in deaerated water?

18.4 How Soap Works Draw soap molecules surrounding grime to illustrate how soap works. Point out the induced dipole-induced dipole interactions between the nonpolar tail of soap and the grime, and the ion-dipole interactions between the polar head of soap and water. Note that your drawing is a cross-section of a spherical conglomeration, also known as a *micelle*. Time permitting, you might take this a step further and draw a lipid bilayer in the shape of a circle. Note that this is a cross-section of a 3-dimensional conglomeration known as a *cell*. Point out the aqueous inner chamber. Add proteins to the bilayer and call it a membrane. Throw in a cellular nucleus some organelles and call it living tissue.

18.5 Hard Water and Soap Scum Show how soap molecules bind to calcium ions and discuss the disadvantages of hard water. The following demonstration shows how indicator chemicals can be used to assess a water sample's hardness.

DEMONSTRATION Place a multi-well see-through well-plate on the overhead projector. Add 1 mL of distilled water to one well, 1 mL of tap water to a second, and 1 mL of a solution concentrated with calcium carbonate in a third (use ocean water if available). If well-plates are not available, you can use test-tubes. To each of these samples add one drop of a pH=10 buffer solution. Follow with one drop of "Eriochrome Black T" indicator solution. This indicator turns a reddish color

upon binding to calcium or magnesium ions. In the absence of these ions, the indicator remains a dark sky blue color, as should be seen with the distilled water. To qualitatively assess the amount of calcium and magnesium (hence the hardness of the water) add drops of 0.002M solution of EDTA to the samples. The EDTA has an even greater affinity for the calcium and magnesium ions than does the Eriochrome Black T and actually removes these ions from this indicator ultimately turning the solution from red to sky blue. If there are a lot of calcium and magnesium ions present, it will take a lot of drops of EDTA to free them all from the Eriochrome Black T. (A more concentrated solution of EDTA might thus be needed.) Count the number of drops that must be added to the concentrated calcium carbonate solution and compare that to the number of drop required for the tap water solution. You might have students bring in samples of their own drinking water for this qualitative testing. This activity may be quantitated by calibrating against a calcium solution of known concentration, say 200 ppm. To an additional well-plate add some Dowex ion exchange resin. Mix the tap water through the resin and then ask students what they might expect to see upon addition of the Eriochrome Black T. Test the calcium/magnesium absorbing powers of a given small quantity of the resin.

18.6 Surface Tension and Capillary Action An interesting example of surface tension (not in the text) involves the tallness of trees. When a single water molecule evaporates from the cell membrane inside a leaf, it is replaced by the one immediately next to it due to cohesive forces between water molecules. A pull is created on the column of water, which is continuous from leaves to roots. Water can be lifted to 100 meters in this way, to the height of the largest trees. Biology types call this effect *transpiration*.

DEMONSTRATION: Place a water-filled petri dish on the overhead projector (the wider the petri dish the better). Get a needle to float on its surface. Ask a student volunteer to touch the wet end of a bar of soap to the water. Soap molecules spreading across the surface may actually push the needle sideways. Eventually, surface tension is disrupted and the needle drops into the water. Try this demo, as all your demos, beforehand. Some soaps work better than others.

19
Chemical Reactions

The Chemical Equation
Energy and Chemical Reactions
   Catalysis
      | Stratospheric Ozone and CFC's |
Chemical Equilibrium
     | Link to the Environment — Equilibrium in Nature |
Relative Masses of Atoms and Molecules
   Atomic and Formula Masses
   Avogadro's Number and the Mole

Here is the meat and potatoes of chemistry.

There are 4 practice sheets that supplement this chapter in the **Practice Book**.

The experiment "Mystery Powders" supplements this chapter in the **Laboratory Manual**.

SUGGESTED LECTURE PRESENTATIONS

19.1 The Chemical Equation The chemical equation is used to depict the chemical reaction. Significant features of the chemical equation are presented in this section. The importance of having a balanced chemical equation should be related back to the conservation of mass principle presented here.

A good way to keep the art of balancing chemical equations low key in your quizzes and exams is to present an equation and simply ask whether or not it is balanced. Learning how to balance chemical equations is good mental exercise, but it is not a prerequisite for subsequent sections.

A methodology explored in the practice sheet on page 81 in the *Practice Book* is as follows:

1. Focus on balancing only one element at a time. Start with the left-most element and modify the coefficients such that this element appears on both sides of the arrow the same number of times.

2. Move to the next element and modify the coefficients so as to balance this element. Do not worry if you incidentally unbalance the previous element. You will come back to it in subsequent steps.

3. Continue from left to right balancing each element individually.

4. Repeat steps 1 - 3 until all elements are balanced.

Six reasonable equations you might try balancing with your class — reviewing techniques as you go along — are:

$$3\,O_2 \rightarrow 2\,O_3$$
$$4\,Cr + 3\,O_2 \rightarrow 2\,Cr_2O_3$$
$$2\,SO_2 + O_2 \rightarrow 2\,SO_3$$
$$2\,N_2O \rightarrow 2\,N_2 + O_2$$
$$2\,NO + O_2 \rightarrow 2\,NO_2$$
$$3\,HNO_2 \rightarrow HNO_3 + 2\,NO + H_2O$$
$$2\,N_2H_4O_3 \rightarrow 2\,N_2 + O_2 + 4\,H_2O$$

When dealing with odd and even subscripts, as in $O_2 \rightarrow O_3$, it's useful to "barrow the opposite subscript as the coefficient". In this manner, the subscript of O_3 is used as the coefficient of O_2, and vice versa. Alternatively, an extra oxygen atom might simply be added to the left side: $O + O_2 \rightarrow O_3$. This is illegal, however, because it alters the identity of the reactants (O is not O_2). A way around this is to use a fraction of a coefficient, such as 1/2, which gives $1/2\,O_2 + O_2 \rightarrow O_3$, which can also be written as $3/2\,O_2 \rightarrow O_3$. The fraction of oxygen can be corrected by multiplying every term by 2, which gives: $2(3/2)\,O_2 \rightarrow 2(\,O_3\,)$, which equals: $3\,O_2 \rightarrow 2\,O_3$. This alternative approach is useful in balancing the equation given in Exercise #2.

19.2 Energy and Chemical Reactions It takes energy to break a chemical bond, and energy is released when a chemical bond is formed. The analogy with magnets is quite useful. Students easily recognize that it takes energy to pull two magnets apart. Similarly, they can be led to understand that energy is released when two magnets come together (in the form of kinetic energy or heat from the collision). Holding with the principle of the conservation of energy, the amount of energy required to break a bond is equal to the amount of energy released when a bond is formed.

Show how there is a net release of energy when water is produced from hydrogen and oxygen. Write the equation on the board using chemical structures rather than chemical formulas. This makes for a conceptual presentation because students can actually see the bonds that are to be broken and the ones that are to be formed. Summarize the data of Table 19.1.

Show how energy is a product in an exothermic reaction and a reactant in an endothermic reaction. Cite examples of both.

DEMONSTRATION: Show how the formation of crystals is an exothermic reaction. Sporting goods stores and science supply companies sell hand-warmers (instant hot packs) that typically consist of a super-saturated solution of sodium acetate. The bending of a small metal disk inside the plastic pouch initiates crystallization with the production of heat.

Concerning an explanation of the chemical hot-pack: Particles set loose from the bent metal disk initiate the formation of anhydrous sodium acetate $C_2H_3O^- Na^+$ (s). Interestingly enough, this step is endothermic, requiring about 16 kJ/mole. This may seem odd since there is the ionic bond *forming* between the sodium and acetate ions. This bond forms, however, at the expense of *breaking* the many ion-dipole interactions that hold the sodium and acetate ions in solution. In the second step, water molecules pull toward the solidifying anhydrous salt to form the hydrate complex. During the rapid crystallization the water seems to vanish, being replaced by crystals. Students may wonder where the water went. The answer is that the water is now organized within the crystal lattice such that there are three water molecules for every unit of sodium acetate, $C_2H_3O^- Na^+ \cdot 3 H_2O$ (s). The formation of sodium acetate trihydrate from anhydrous sodium acetate releases about 37 kJ/mole. The total amount of energy released from this reaction, therefore, is about 21 kJ/mole.

Pedagogically, there are at least three approaches to say what is happening. The first is most demanding: review the explanation given above. The second approach is more basic: crystallization is an exothermic process since it involves the formation of bonds among molecules or ions (the bonds are formed as the molecules or ions pack together). The third approach is a twist of the truth: tell students that energy is released upon the formation of ionic bonds. Present the following equation:

$$C_2H_3O^- (aq) + Na^+ (aq) \rightarrow C_2H_3O^- Na^+ (s) + ENERGY$$

Strictly speaking, this is only true when the reactants are in a gaseous phase. Ignoring the effects of water, however, helps students to focus on the main concept — that energy is always released upon the formation of a chemical bond.

CHECK QUESTION: Is the hot-pack reusable? How so? [Answer: Yes, the hot-pack is reusable, provided energy is put back into the system to separate the chemical bonds. This is done by placing the solidified hot-pack in boiling water. Point out that the heat being felt by the hot-pack today is the heat that was added to it last night while on the stove. The hot-pack does not create energy — it simply stores it for later use.]

DEMONSTRATION: Show the electrolysis of water as an example of an endothermic reaction. As you move on to further discussions, continue the electrolysis so as to collect a test tube full of hydrogen gas. DON'T FORGET THE ELECTROLYSIS IS STILL RUNNING! When appropriate, ignite the hydrogen with a match. A small flame will burst out of the tube with a fairly loud pop. This, of course, is the exothermic formation of water that was discussed previously. If possible, save this dramatic reverse reaction for the beginning of your discussion of chemical equilibrium.

Some endothermic reactions can absorb energy from their immediate surroundings. (If students don't believe there's a lot of heat available at room temperature, ask them to compare it to the amount of heat available in a room kept to -10°C). The dissolution of many salts provide good examples.

	$\Delta H_{formation}$
$C_2H_3O^- (aq) + Na^+ (aq) \rightarrow C_2H_3O^- Na^+ (s)$	+16 kJ/mole
$C_2H_3O^- Na^+ (s) + 3 H_2O (l) \rightarrow C_2H_3O^- Na^+ \cdot 3 H_2O (s)$	-37 kJ/mole
NET: $C_2H_3O^- (aq) + Na^+ (aq) \rightarrow C_2H_3O^- Na^+ \cdot 3 H_2O (s)$	-21 kJ/mole

DEMONSTRATION: Fill two clear plastic cups half-way full with warm water. Pour the water back and forth between cups. Ask students why you are doing this while you do it. (Your answer: Just the kind of thing they might expect a chemist to do. Hmm?) Then ask them if they would believe that the water in each of the cups was at the same temperature. (Sure, because of the mixing.) Ask a student volunteer to verify this fact. Show on the chalkboard that an endothermic reaction occurs when sodium nitrate dissolves in water since it is separated into sodium and nitrate ions (note the breaking of the ionic bond):

$$Energy + NaNO_3 \rightarrow Na^+ (aq) + NO_3^- (aq)$$

Ask a student volunteer to close his or her eyes as you mix several scoops of sodium nitrate into one of the cups. (Dry the outsides of the cups) Carefully hand the two cups to the eyes-closed volunteer and ask him or her to judge to which one the sodium nitrate had been added. The student will choose the colder cup. Refer students to Home Project #1. (For your information: Warm water is used because we are more sensitive to changes in its temperature.) The saltpeter used to make homemade ice cream is a mixture of sodium nitrate and potassium nitrate. Potassium nitrate has a greater enthalpy of dissolution (gets colder) than sodium nitrate, but its solubility in water is significantly less. Commercial cold-packs use ammonium nitrate because it's cheaper and much more soluble in water. Its enthalpy of dissolution is greater than that of sodium nitrate, but less than that of potassium nitrate. Ammonium nitrate can be used in this demonstration, however, as a solid it is a powerful oxidizing agent and forms explosive mixtures with chloride salts. Aqueous solutions of ammonium nitrate are relatively safe to handle, except that they can irritate the skin.)

NEXT-TIME QUESTION: Salt lowers the melting point of ice, but at the same time the temperature of the ice
   a) increases.
   b) also decreases.
   c) remains the same.

[Answer: The melting point of ice decreases because salt ions interfere with the packing of water molecules. The temperature of the ice, however, decreases as it loses energy to the breaking of ionic bonds in salt.]

Catalysis Show how chlorine atoms catalyze the destruction of atmospheric ozone. See the box Atmospheric Ozone and CFC's.

DEMONSTRATION Dip a hot platinum wire into a solution of hydrogen peroxide. The platinum will catalyze the decomposition of the hydrogen peroxide. The enzymes in Baker's yeast, which is more readily available than platinum, will do the same thing.

19.3 Chemical Equilibrium Under the right conditions, all chemical reactions are reversible. Start by referring to the case where water is broken down into hydrogen and oxygen and then converted back into water.

DEMONSTRATION: In a well ventilated room or fume hood, add a couple drops of concentrated nitric acid to a penny or strip of copper in a 125 mL Erlenmeyer flask, which is sitting in petri dish of water. (The water helps to cool the reaction thereby preventing a build up of steam and condensation in the flask). Immediately seal the flask with a well fitting rubber stopper. Repeat this procedure so that you now have two sealed Erlenmeyer flasks containing brown nitrogen dioxide. Discuss the equilibrium between NO_2 and N_2O_4 that is occurring in each of the flasks (See text). Note how NO_2 is a dark brown gas, while N_2O_4 is a colorless gas. A mixture of the two is light brown.

Use the department store analogy to explain the fundamentals of equilibrium and that equilibrium can be altered by changing the conditions (holding a sale, for example). Ask the following check question:

CHECK QUESTION: Is the formation of N_2O_4 an exothermic or endothermic reaction? (Draw the structures on the board using brown chalk for NO_2 and blue or white chalk for the N_2O_4) [Answer: Exothermic, since it involves the formation of a chemical bond.]

Draw energy as a product to the above equation: $NO_2 + NO_2 \rightarrow N_2O_4 + Energy$. Ask students what might happen if energy were added to N_2O_4. (The energy serves to break the nitrogen-nitrogen bond.) Show how the reverse reaction occurs by drawing a second arrow that points to NO_2. (What is a reactant and what is a product depends upon your point of view!) Ask students what might happen to the color of a mixture of NO_2 and N_2O_4 if it were heated.

DEMONSTRATION: Place one of the 125 mL Erlenmeyer flasks containing NO_2/N_2O_4 in a beaker of boiling water. Observe that it gets darker. Ask students what might happen if energy were taken *away* from the equilibrium (Less available energy for splitting N_2O_4 molecules, and as NO_2 molecules slow down they have an easier time joining. The N_2O_4 concentration increases). Place the second 125 mL flask in a bucket of ice water (add salt to the ice water to bring the temperature to below 0°C - students will appreciate the application of the recently learned concept). The contents of the flask will get lighter. (See Figure 19.7) Switch the flasks to show the reversibility of the reaction. (After class, release the NO_2 in a fume hood.)

19.4 Relative Masses of Atoms and Molecules
The essence of stoichiometry are distilled into this and the following section. For instructors on a fast-track through chemistry, these sections are not recommended. For those who are willing and able to cover these sections, the goal is to clue students into how chemists get a literal handle on atoms and molecules when atom and molecules are so incredibly small.

Begin your discussion with the idea that measuring equal masses of different substances does not mean you have the same number of each. Use the golf ball/Ping Pong ball example given in the text plus numerous other examples. Only when the student firmly understands these examples is he or she ready to apply the concept to chemistry.

Atomic and Formula Masses After presenting formula masses it's useful to stress the difference between the amu and the gram. You'll find that the end-of-chapter exercises 19 through 23 are useful to ask of your students in class. Try these also:

CHECK QUESTION: What is the approximate mass of a single water molecule in amu? [18.02 amu]

CHECK QUESTION: What is the approximate mass of a single water molecule in grams? [The answer will have to come from the students' notes: 2.83×10^{-23} grams.]

19.5 Avogadro's Number and the Mole
This section can be tied into the beginning of Part V where the smallness of atoms was discussed. Atoms are so small. They are so very small—so small that we commonly weigh them not by the millions, trillions, quadrillions but by the Avogadro's number's worth. Emphasize that with one mole of a substance there are 6.02×10^{23} units of that substance.

After you've developed the concept of Avogadro's number, summarize by showing the Transparency of Figure 19.16. To follow-up, you might ask the following questions:

CHECK QUESTION: Which has a greater mass, 12.04×10^{23} molecules of hydrogen, H_2, or 12.04×10^{23} molecules of water, H_2O? [Answer: All water molecules are more massive than all hydrogen molecules. Given the same number of molecules, water will have more mass.]

CHECK QUESTION: Which has a greater number of molecules, 16.00 grams of water, H_2O, or 2.02 grams of hydrogen, H_2? [Answer: These are the molecular masses of these substance, therefore, they both contain one mole of molecules.]

CHECK QUESTION: What is the approximate mass of 12.04×10^{23} molecules of water, H_2O, in grams? in amu? [Answer: 32.00 grams. Amu's are so very small that there are so very many of them in a large quantity such as 32 grams. If 1.661×10^{-24} grams equals 1 amu, then by setting up a ratio we can find how many amu there are in 32.00 grams: 1.93×10^{25} amu.]

Summarize the chapter by noting all that chemistry and cooking have in common.

CHECK QUESTION: Which of the following culinary processes involve chemistry:
   a) whipping cream
   b) baking bread
   c) stir frying
   d) boiling an egg

[Answer: All of them! Whipping cream is the preparation of a suspension. Baking bread involves the rising of bread with CO_2 from yeast fermentation. With stir frying, organic flavorings are extracted into a nonpolar oil solvent. When an egg is placed in boiling water, protein molecules are broken and reoriented.]

20
Acid, Base, and Redox Reactions

This new chapter for the second edition was developed by expanding two sections that appeared in the first edition. Various applications were then integrated. These applications include the topics of acid rain, basic oceans, buffer solutions, photography, batteries, fuel cells, and corrosion.

There are 2 practice sheets that supplement this chapter in the Conceptual Physical Science **Practice Book.**

Laboratory Manual activities and experiments that supplement this chapter include "Sensing pH," and "Upset Stomach."

And of course, there are alway insightful **Next-Time Questions** to give follow through to this and other chapters of the book.

SUGGESTED LECTURE PRESENTATIONS

An opening lecture should start with an overview of the two types of reactions presented in this chapter. While the acids/base reactions involve the transfer of a hydrogen ion, H^+, the redox reactions involve the transfer of an electron, e^-. Be sure to point out how the hydrogen ion and the proton are one in the same.

20.1 Acids and Bases Defined Begin by discussing the many commercial applications of acids and bases. Point out how economists judge the economic strength of nations based upon the quantities of these materials produced.

The Arrhenius definitions of acids and bases are treated only briefly. Emphasis is placed on the more general Bronsted-Lowry definition. The acronym BAAD given in the footnote is useful tool for many students.

It's best not to say that a chemical is an acid or that it is a base. Students are quickly confused when they find that in one instance a chemical, such as water, is an acid, and in another it is a base (perhaps they are reminded of the wave-particle duality of the electron). It is far better to say that a chemical behaves as an acid, or that it behaves as a base. When a chemical donates a hydrogen ion it behaves as an acid, when the same chemical accepts a hydrogen ion it behaves as a base.

On the chalkboard it's useful to show the movement of the hydrogen ion from one molecule to the other. Draw the symbol for hydrogen on a piece of paper, which may be taped to the board. Show how the acid donates the hydrogen ion by transferring the paper between reactants. Likewise, note how the base accepts the hydrogen ion. For example:

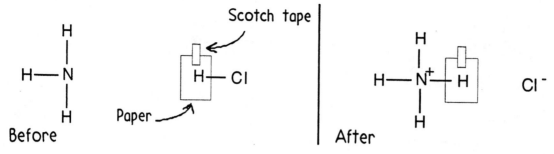

Before | After

This visualization helps students to recognize which chemicals in an equation are behaving as acids and which are behaving as bases. Also, students get the sense that products are, in fact, made from the reactants, despite that they are both seen at once in the chemical equation. The reversibility of acid/base reactions can be visualized by using two pieces of paper containing the symbol for hydrogen (as shown in the example at the bottom of this page).

Salt: The Ionic Product of an Acid and a Base Define the chemist's use of the terms "salt" and "neutralization reaction." Draw Figure 20.4 on the chalkboard while emphasizing how it is that, upon neutralization, negative and positive atoms come together. The transparency for the cocaine figure allows the opportunity to discuss the differences between a "free base" and a "salt". Note the reasons for the great harm provided by inhaling vapors of cocaine in its free base form, also known as crack.

20.2 Acid Strength Different chemicals have different personalities. Some are quite forceful about donating the hydrogen ion (strong acid), while others are more timid (weak acid). What determines the strength of an acid is complicated and not discussed in the text. It's more important that the physical science student focus on the effect acid strength has on the position of equilibrium. With a strong acid, ionic products predominate. With a weak acid, non-ionic reactants predominate.

DEMONSTRATION: Use a light bulb equipped with electrodes as seen in Figures 20.5 and 20.6 to demonstrate the proportion of ions found in solutions of strong and weak acids. Begin with distilled water. Pour sodium chloride into the distilled water to show how the intensity of light increases with the number of ions. Draw the equilibrium for HCl on the board and have students predict the

brightness of the bulb. Repeat the same for acetic acid. (Use 1 M solutions.) Follow up by showing that tap water is a weak conductor of electricity.

Water as an Acid and a Base Since acidity and basicity are <u>behaviors</u>, it makes sense that some chemicals might do both.

20.3 Acidic, Basic, or Neutral The product of the hydronium ion concentration, $[H_3O^+]$ and the hydroxide ion concentration, $[HO^-]$, is equal to a constant, K_W, which is 1.0×10^{-14}. This necessarily means that if the concentration of one goes up, then the concentration of the other must come down. As an analogy, show how $10 \times 10 = 100$. If you were to increase the first 10 to 50, then the second 10 would have to reduce to 2 in order to maintain the constant. Conceptually, we can understand how this happens by a close examination of Figure 20.7. If you're going for that conceptual depth, you may wish to use the transparency for Figure 20.7 and discuss it in class.

Note that K_W is a very small number. This means that the concentrations of hydronium and hydroxide ions are very small. By definition, in an acidic solution $[H_3O^+] > [HO^-]$, in a basic solution $[H_3O^+] < [HO^-]$, and in a neutral solution $[H_3O^+] = [HO^-]$.

20.4 The pH Scale Spend a few minutes reviewing the logarithm (See box) before defining pH. Note that when the pH changes by 1, the hydronium ion concentration changes by a factor of 10.

CHECK QUESTION: What's the pH of a 0.5 M solution of HCl? How about a 1.0 M solution? A 2.0 M solution? [Answers: 0.301; 0; -0.310. Students will be surprised that negative pH values are possible. The lower limit of pH depends on the solubility of acid. A saturated solution of hydrochloric acid is 12.0 M, which corresponds to a pH of -1.08.

Many chemicals change color with pH. These chemicals, which are usually organic, can serve as pH indicators. You'll note that pH indicators are not discussed in the text. The stage is set, however, to present pH indicators as a demonstration:

DEMONSTRATION: (Home project #2) Shred a quarter of a head of red cabbage into a 1000 mL beaker half full of boiling water. Boil for several minutes. Strain the cabbage while collecting the broth, which contains the pH indicator. Distribute the solution into 5 clear plastic cups, which may be illuminated from below using an overhead projector. Add small amounts of the following chemicals to give various pH's: Lysol toilet bowl cleanser (HCl), white vinegar, water, baking soda, bleach.

Some dyes used to make color paper are also pH sensitive. Certain brands of goldenrod colored paper, for example, turn bright red when dipped in a solution of sodium hydroxide.

DEMONSTRATION: Submerge a pH electrode in a glass of water and then using a straw, blow bubbles into the water. The carbon dioxide of your breath will bring the water to a pH of 5. Ask the class whether they think you really have acid breath. While the pH meter is set up, be sure to submerge the electrode in a glass of cola. Another favorite is to stir campfire ashes into water and see the pH rise to above 10. As was discussed in Chapter 16, alkaline ashes were once used to make soap. Recall that the term alkaline is derived from the Arabic term for ashes: al-quali.

DEMONSTRATION: Add a drop of phenolphthalein to a few milliliters of water in a test tube. Make the solution slightly alkaline by adding a small amount of sodium carbonate , Na_2CO_3. The solution will turn pink. Point out that by adding an acid the pH drops and the pink color will disappear (Phenolphthalein indicator changes color at about a pH of 7). Demonstrate by adding a drop of acid, such as hydrochloric acid or vinegar. Repeat the same procedure in a second test tube this time using a straw to blow in carbon dioxide from your breath.

20.5 Acid Rain and Basic Oceans Having studied through Sections 20.1 through 20.4, students should have little difficulty in understanding and appreciating this environmentally-oriented section. All three of the illustrations in this section appear as overhead transparencies.

20.6 Buffers Some physiologic applications of acid-base reactions are presented here. The take-home message for students should be that a buffer solution contains an acidic component that neutralizes any incoming base along with a basic component that neutralizes any incoming acid.

DEMONSTRATION: Fill a large test tube three quarters full with water. Add a couple drops of phenolphthalein indicator along with a small amount of sodium carbonate (enough to turn the solution pink and then some). Cover the test tube and shake to mix. Pour half of the solution into a second test tube. To one of the two test tubes add less than a mL of pH 7 through 9 buffer solution. To the non-buffered test tube add drops of 0.1 M hydrochloric acid. Have the students count the drops until the solution turns colorless. Do the same for the second test tube. Note the difference in the number of drops. Note also that the buffer is eventually exhausted. Have the students describe what is happening chemically as you add the acid. Play with the system prior to class time to make sure you have workable proportions. The reverse procedure of adding 0.1 M NaOH to water buffered from pH 5 to 7 can also be explored. Furthermore, the same demonstration can be done using red cabbage juice in place of the water plus phenolphthalein.

20.7 Oxidation-Reduction Reactions Elements have a tendency to lose or gain electrons. To help students remember which is oxidation and which is reduction you might introduce the mnemonic: LEO the lion goes GER (Loss of Electrons is Oxidation and Gain of Electrons is Reduction). In your treatment of this section highlight the many applications of redox reactions.

DEMONSTRATION: Show how copper and zinc electrodes generate the current that drives the "Potato Clock."

DEMONSTRATION: Recruit students to bring in samples of tarnished silver for this most well-received in-class demonstration, which also makes for a good laboratory activity or home project. Silver tarnish is an outer coating of silver sulfide, Ag_2S, formed when silver reacts with trace quantities of airborne hydrogen sulfide, a smelly gas produced naturally by the digestion of food in living beings. Silver atoms in silver sulfide have lost electrons to sulfur atoms. Convert silver atoms back to their elemental state by restoring their electrons. Sulfur atoms won't relinquish electrons to silver, but with the proper connection, aluminum atoms will. Add about a liter of water and several heaping tablespoons of baking soda to an aluminum pan that has been scoured clean. If you don't have an aluminum pan, use aluminum foil at the bottom of another pan. Bring the water to boiling and remove it from the heat source. Slowly immerse a tarnished piece of silver; you'll see an immediate effect as the silver and aluminum make contact. (Add more baking soda if you don't.) Also, as silver is brought back to its elemental state, hydrogen sulfide is released back into the air. You'll smell it! The baking soda serves to remove a thin and transparent coating of aluminum oxide, which normally coats aluminum and thus prevents direct contact. The baking soda also serves as a conductive ionic solution to permit the passage of electrons from the aluminum to the silver. Ask students what advantage this approach has over polishing the silver with an abrasive?

DEMONSTRATION: Bring in a single lens reflex camera and wax paper to class to demonstrate the optical principles of the camera as per the photograph shown in the box on photography. Explain how the chemistry of the film permits a permanent "capture" of the image seen.

20.8 Electrochemistry

DEMONSTRATION: Place a shiny nail half-way into a solution of copper sulfate. It's a show stopper!

DEMONSTRATION: Continue on the lines of the previous demo by building a crude galvanic cell in class. A sensitive amp meter, zinc and copper electrodes, beakers, and a copper sulfate solution work quite well. For the salt bridge you can use a paper towel wet with the copper sulfate solution.

Once the principles of these demonstrations are understood, students are ready to look at the various designs of batteries, fuel cells, and electrolysis. The take-home message is that putting chemicals that like to lose electrons in contact with chemicals that like to gain electrons generates an electric current provided the electric circuit is complete.

20.9 Oxidizing Powers of Oxygen This section provides a great opportunity to wrap up concepts learned in this and in previous chapters, such as periodic trends. Encourage students to work through the practice sheet on oxidations and reductions (Practice Book page 91). Consider even creating an overhead transparency of this Practice Sheet helping students work through it during class. A good final note is one that points to our respiration as a form of combustion. Oxygen has a great affinity for electrons. This, in turn, has led to the fascinating chemistry of life.

21

Organic Chemistry

The structures of organic compounds and their physical and chemical properties are introduced in this chapter. Much of the chapter is descriptive, however, you will also find the application of previously learned concepts such as molecular interactions and acid/base chemistry.

There are 2 practice sheets that supplement this chapter in the Conceptual Physical Science **Practice Book**.

Laboratory Manual activities that supplement this chapter include "A Roping Experience," and "Name That Recyclable."

SUGGESTED LECTURE PRESENTATION

Carbon is quite unique in the number of ways it is able to bond with itself and other elements. Using a molecular modeling kit show the wide variety of structures possible from six carbon atoms alone (leave out the hydrogen atoms to facilitate switching between structures). Note how each configuration has a different set of physical and chemical properties. Introduce an oxygen atom to show an even greater variety of compounds.

With organic chemicals, carbon and hydrogen atoms provide a relatively inert framework to which reactive atoms, such as nitrogen and oxygen, may attach. These added atoms give the organic chemical much of its character — much like ornaments on a tree. We begin by studying the carbon-hydrogen framework.

21.1 Hydrocarbons Hydrocarbons come in all three phases. Blow some soap bubbles using methane (or propane) to demonstrate the gaseous phase (methane bubbles will rise, but propane bubbles will sink). Bring in some hexanes or gasoline to show the liquid phase. The solid phase is seen with plastics such as high or low density polyethylene, polypropylene, or polystyrene. The recycle codes for these plastics is as follows: HDPE, 2; LDPE, 4; PP, 5; PS, 6 (Lab Activity, *Name that Recylable*). The phase of a hydrocarbon is a function of its molecular mass (See Table 21.1).

Show what is meant by a structural isomer. Introduce the term *conformation* and contrast it to what is meant by *configuration*, which refers to how the atoms are connected. Use the human body as an analogy. The configuration of the arm is such that the wrist bone is connected to the ulna bone, the ulna bone is connected to the elbow bone, etc. The conformation refers to how the bonds are oriented within a particular configuration. Again, using the human body as an analogy, the whole arm is one configuration, which can have a wide variety of different conformations (extend your arm and twist it about). Go through examples so that students can recognize when two structures are either different configurations, or different conformations of the same configuration.

CHECK QUESTION: How many different configurations are shown (next page)? Which ones, if any, are different conformations of the same configuration?

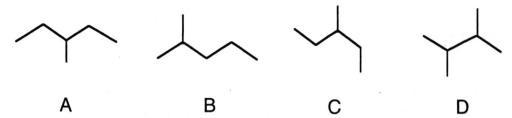

A   B   C   D

Alert students to the massive quantities of hydrocarbons consumed every day and to the issues addressed in the box *Construction or Combustion*.

21.2 Unsaturated Hydrocarbons When students hear the term "unsaturated" they are likely to think of unsaturated fats. "Saturated" means that a carbon atom is saturated with hydrogen atoms, that is, bonded to a maximum number. Only single covalent bonds appear in saturated hydrocarbons. The hydrocarbons discussed in the previous section are all saturated. "Unsaturated" means that there are fewer than a maximum number of hydrogen atoms bonded to carbon. This occurs when double or triple bonds are present. Relating this to one's diet, the hydrocarbon portion of saturated fat molecules consist of only single bonds. The hydrocarbon portions of unsaturated fats, however, contain multiple bonds, usually the one or more double bonds. The reason that unsaturated fats are better for our health is that double bonds are more chemically reactive, hence, easier to metabolize. You might tell your students that the double bond is like a handle that the body grabs to help move the molecule through the digestion process. In general, the better a molecule flows through our bodies, the less harmful it is.

Higher octane gasolines not only contain hydrocarbons with a greater degree of branching, they also contain a higher proportion of unsaturated hydrocarbons, which burn quite efficiently.

21.3 Non-Carbon Atoms in Organic Molecules "Heteroatom" is the common term used by organic chemists to describe nitrogen, oxygen, chlorine, or any other non-carbon/non-hydrogen atoms in an organic molecule. As an alternative you might consider the term "added-atom", as in: The added-atoms give an organic molecule its character.

21.4 Alcohols, Phenols, Ethers, and Amines In society, the words "alcohol" and "ethanol" are used interchangeably. From a chemical point of view, however, alcohols are a class of organic compounds, of which ethanol is one example. Define the alcohol as an organic molecule containing the hydroxyl functional group.

CHECK QUESTION: Since water consists of a hydroxyl group bonded to a hydrogen atom can it be classified as an alcohol? [No. Alcohols are organic molecules, which by definition contain carbon. Since there is no carbon in water, it cannot be classified as an alcohol.]

Alcohol molecules are attracted to one another primarily by the dipole-dipole interactions between hydroxyl groups. The more hydroxyl groups in an alcohol, the greater the molecular interactions.

DEMONSTRATION: Write on the chalkboard the chemical structures for ethanol, ethylene glycol, and glycerol. Ask students to predict the order of boiling temperatures. Then produce three unlabelled vials, each containing one of the above alcohols. Ask students to identify them. Point out how viscosity is also a function of the strengths of molecular interactions.

Show how ethers are structurally related to alcohols. You might do this with a molecular modeling kit. It is interesting to note that a new class of compounds is produced simply by changing the arrangement of atoms. Since they lack the oxygen-hydrogen dipole, ethers are much less soluble in water and their boiling temperatures are lower.

DEMONSTRATION: Contrast the miscibility of ethanol and diethyl ether with water. First define miscibility as the ability of two substances to form a single phase. Pour equal amounts of water into two graduated cylinders. Have the class note the volume levels. Mix in a drop of water soluble food coloring. Pour the same quantity of ethanol to one of the containers and the same quantity of diethyl ether to the other. Cover the tops with parafilm and mix (You will note a pressure build up as you mix the water and ether). The water and ethanol form a single liquid phase. The water and ether, however, form two liquid phases. Note the volume level of the water in the water/ether cylinder and ask the class to explain any discrepancies. That some of the ether has dissolved in the water can be demonstrated by pouring the two phases into a separatory funnel and collecting the lower aqueous phase. Have a student volunteer note the odor of this ether containing water.

Low molecular mass amines have a characteristic bad odor. Inform your students that this is why you have not brought any samples to show them. Higher molecular mass amines, however, do not have such characteristic odors.

NEXT-TIME QUESTION: Higher molecular mass amines do not give off the characteristic bad odor released by lower molecular mass amines. Why not? [We can only smell that which reaches our nose. In order for a scent to reach our nose it must be in a gaseous phase. Lower molecular mass amines have fewer chemical interactions, hence, they are more volatile, which means that the molecules readily escape into the gaseous phase. Higher molecular mass amines, on the other hand, have strong chemical interactions that hold the molecules to the solid or liquid phases which we cannot smell.]

Show how amines can act as bases by accepting the hydrogen ion. The hydrogen ion is attracted to the lone pair of electron on the nitrogen atom. You might show where these electrons come from by drawing the shell model for nitrogen.

DEMONSTRATION: Show how to extract caffeine from coffee. Pour a strong cup of coffee into a large separatory funnel. Bring the coffee to a pH of about 9 or 10 by adding drops of a solution of sodium hydroxide. Pour some methylene chloride, CH_2Cl_2, (about a third the volume of the coffee) into the funnel. Stopper the funnel, invert it and open the stopcock to release any pressure. Close the stopcock and shake the contents. After two layers settle collect the lower methylene chloride layer in a beaker. Hold the beaker up for the class to see while you explain how it contains the caffeine. Ask students how they might get the caffeine back into an aqueous phase. Brewed coffee contains from 18-15 milligrams of caffeine per oz. Decaffeinated coffee is made by extracting whole coffee beans with organic solvents, usually methylene chloride. The beans are then steamed to remove residual solvent, then dried and roasted to bring out flavor.

21.5 Carbonyl-Containing Organic Molecules
Before introducing these new classes of compounds, remind your students that they are only to focus on the diversity of organic chemicals, and not on the details of their structures, physical and chemical properties.

DEMONSTRATION: Bring to class samples of some of the more pleasantly fragrant aldehydes such as the ones listed in Figure 21.24.

CHECK QUESTION: Most of the aspirin consumed today is synthetically produced from crude oil. How is this aspirin different from aspirin derived from the willow tree? [There is no difference. They are exactly the same. Neither one is either better or worse.]

21.6 Modified Natural Polymers
A good theme to carry through this and the following section is how the physical properties of a polymer are a consequence of the chemical structure of its component monomers. Properties to focus on include density, hardness, and glass transition temperature.

DEMONSTRATION: In a fume hood, set fire to a Ping Pong ball. Talk about the impracticality of using such a material as movie film.

21.7 Synthetic Polymers

DEMONSTRATION: Synthesize a strand of nylon following the procedure given in the laboratory activity *A Roping Experience*.

22
Rocks and Minerals

This chapter introduces Geology with an emphasis on definitions and description of processes. The specialized vocabulary may mean some memory work. We suggest that memorization be kept to a minimum (open book exams will prompt this). More important than the introduced basic vocabulary, is the appreciation of the more interesting aspects of rocks and minerals. Nurturing a wide overview should not be hampered by definitions and memorization. How you till your soil determines where student effort is placed.

Key words that appear in this chapter very frequently are: *mineral, sedimentary, metamorphic, igneous, magma,* and *lava,* and key words that appear less frequently are *batholith, intrusive, extrusive, sill, pluton, clastic, dike, feldspar,* and *andesite.* This is some

indication of their importance. It helps to mention and provide a list of words you think students should be able to define, and to test by matching or multiple choice rather than by recall.

The box on Asbestos merits elaboration. Humans have been ingesting asbestos since time zero. It has always been in the air and water, the amounts being little different today than centuries ago. The prevalent form of asbestos, relatively harmless chrysotile, is tarred with association to the dangerous amphibole crocidolite. The two minerals differ in composition, color, shape, solubility, and persistence in human tissue. Chrysotile, $Mg_6Si_4O_{10}(OH)_8$, is a white serpentine mineral that tends to be soluble and disappears in tissue. Crocidolite, $Na_2(Fe^{3+})_2(Fe^{2+})_3SiO_{22}(OH)_2$, is blue in color, is relatively insoluble, and persists in tissue. Only about 5% of the asbestos in place in the United States is crocidolite. Much of North American asbestos comes from chrysotile mines in Quebec, which have been operating since before 1900 and have produced about 40 million tons of chrysotile. Needless to say, lax mining practices resulted in large amounts of chrysotile dust in the surrounding air. Wives of miners who lived near the mines were heavily exposed. But four epidemiological studies of Quebec chrysotile mining localities show that lifelong exposure of women to dust from nearby mines caused no statistically significant excesses in asbestos related disease. The panic to remove all types of asbestos reflects the absence of science. A multibillion dollar program is in full swing, without starting with an accurate assessment of the problem. (Check the Yellow Pages for the alarmingly large numbers of lawyers in the asbestos claim business.) More about this in the March 1990 *Science* editorial, "The Asbestos Removal Fiasco", October 1995 *Environmental Geology* article "The Schoolroom Asbestos Abatement Program" and July 1997 *Scientific American* article "Asbestos Revisited".

For interesting articles on volcanoes and volcanic eruptions please see:
Exploring Loihi: The Next Hawaiian Island, Parks, Noreen. *Earth,* September, 1994.
Cooking Up a Volcano, Milstein, Michael. *Earth,* April, 1998.
Return to Mount St. Helens, Pendrick, Daniel. *Earth,* April, 1995.

For a special report on oil production and the energy crisis please see:
Preventing the Next Oil Crunch, various authors. *Scientific American,* March, 1998.

For your own information, the USGS compiles a list of *Selected references on rocks, minerals, and gemstones* Write to:

U.S. Geological Survey
Geologic Inquiries Group
907 National Center
Reston, VA 22092
(703) 648-4383

The list has three sections: selected guides for rockhounds and hobbyists, general references for all ages, elementary school to adult, and periodicals.

An identification book on rocks and minerals is very helpful for this chapter. I like *Simon & Schusters Guide To Rocks and Minerals.* Another very interesting book is *The Practical Geologist,*by Dougal Dixon. This book contains helpful hints for things to do.

Many successful geology lectures emphasize the showing of slides. Not only is your presentation visual, but it is ordered by the slides you select.

SUGGESTED LECTURE PRESENTATION

Begin by citing how physical science has been taught thus far; by considering ideal cases. In the physics of falling objects, the air was neglected; in the chemistry of molecular interactions, molecules were treated in isolation, which is seldom the case in the real world. And now we study rocks and the minerals that compose them. We see minerals in collections and in textbook photographs as individual crystals, showing all of the form, luster, and other properties we will study. But most minerals are actually irregular blobs in rocks. Onward!

Remind students that recall of definitions learned in physics and chemistry is assumed., e.g. element and a compound, solid, liquid and gas, acid and base, density, pressure, heat and hydraulics.

Rocks Encourage your students to bring in small samples of rocks they collect while studying the geology part of this course. In doing so you are reinforcing the idea that Earth Science is a hands-on, observation-based activity. Rock samples of the different rock groups (igneous, sedimentary, and metamorphic) are also required for the laboratory exercises.

Minerals Atoms make up molecules; minerals make up rocks. Formation of minerals depends on the pressure and temperature at the time of formation. Hence minerals can be indicators of conditions at the time and place of origin.

Key concepts are: The difference between a rock and a mineral is somewhat like that between a compound and an element, but more like the difference between a mixed and a pure substance. Minerals are commonly thought of as metals: the single elements gold, silver, lead, copper, zinc and aluminum. Most minerals, however, are compounds of different elements. When a mineral is considered to be of economic value, a rock rich in that mineral is considered to be an ore body.

Composition of a mineral depends on what's available at the time of formation. Greatest effect of composition on physical properties is ion size, which affects packing and so affects structure.

Packing of atoms in a mineral depends on the relative size of atoms. Closer packing leads to stronger bonds which influence the physical properties of the mineral.

Overall **charge** must be zero. For example, halite: Na^{+1} and Cl^{-1} must be combined 1:1. Fluorite: Ca^{+2} and F^{-1} must be combined 1:2.

Rate of mineral growth depends on how often the right atom can get to a spot where it is likely to stay. This depends on concentration and mobility of components—viscosity and flow restriction.

Remind your students that minerals or the products of minerals can be found just about everywhere. In fact, minerals have contributed greatly to our present technologic culture—practically every manufactured product contains materials obtained from minerals. The world of human-made articles depends on the elements obtained from minerals. Ask your students to think of some common articles made up of minerals, ask them to list the articles. Suggest a survey of their immediate surroundings—the classroom, home, or work place. Have a class discussion about the common articles they have found.

Instructors have saved time, kept it simple, and involved students in hands-on activities by using a few readily available materials; e.g. pieces of chalk, candy, china, coal, glass, metal, wood, and so on. Involving students encourages their imagination and creativity, but avoid busy work.

DEMONSTRATION: Check the cleavage properties of calcite, which exhibits perfect cleavage in three directions. Align a screwdriver in direction of a cleavage plane and hit with a hammer. The calcite should break into two pieces, each piece displaying rhombohedral cleavage planes. Then wrap one piece of calcite in cloth or newspaper. Hit with hammer. Unwrap and show the numerous pieces each displaying the rhombohedral cleavage planes. Be careful not to hit the calcite too hard, for calcite will crumble.

Crystal **shape** reflects internal structure—this can provide a link to the Chemistry section.

CHECK QUESTION: In how many ways can we tell a genuine diamond from an imitation? [By determining cleavage, hardness, density, and any of the many physical and chemical properties].

While on the subject of precious minerals, distinguish between 10 and 24 karat gold. The proportion of pure gold in an alloy is thus: Pure gold is 24 karat; 10 karat is 10/24 pure, or 10 parts pure gold by weight and 14 parts of other metals.

Building Blocks of Rock-Forming Minerals
Begin this Section by referring to Table 22.4 and the Periodic Table of Elements in the front inside cover. For example, are you going to refer to silicates, oxides, carbonates, sulfides, and sulfates primarily by name, or primarily by formula, or by both? Formulas for feldspars can be very complicated.

Refer back to the chapters in chemistry and the different bonding mechanisms of the chemical elements. Illustrate that the internal arrangement of atoms in a mineral is determined by the charges on the atoms and more importantly by the size of the atoms involved. The atoms need to fit with one another in order to form a stable bond.

The two most abundant elements, oxygen and silicon, combine with other cations to form the most common mineral group, the silicates. The silicon-oxygen (SiO_4) tetrahedron is the common building block of the silicates. It has four oxygen atoms (O^{2-}) with a single silicon atom (Si^{4+}) at the center. The tetrahedron has an excess charge of -4 and is not stable. To satisfy the charges, the tetrahedron acts as a simple anion (-) and forms a bond to a cation (+). Another way to satisfy the negative oxygen charge is by polymerization, the linking of tetrahedra to form chains, sheets, and various network patterns.

CHECK QUESTION: If a particular mineral has a consistent shape, why don't all crystals of a given mineral look the same? [Different growth rates may be in different directions. Many crystals run out of room to grow, and fill whatever space is available. Well-formed crystals develop only when space is available, OR when a particular mineral's "crystallizing power" is much greater than the surrounding minerals (e.g. garnets surrounded by muscovite in a schist).]

Most silicate minerals form when molten rock cools. Thus with minor exceptions, all the igneous rock forming minerals are silicates. In addition, some silicate minerals may represent the weathered products of pre-existing silicate minerals. Still other silicate minerals are formed under the extreme pressures associated with metamorphism. Silicate minerals are divided into two groups based on the presence or absence of iron. Minerals containing iron and/or magnesium in their structure are referred to as ferromagnesium silicates, whereas minerals with an absence of iron and/or magnesium are simply referred to as non-ferromagnesium silicates. To help in lecture and lab work the following information is provided. This information is not included in the text — too much information may lead to overload.

Ferromagnesian Silicates (the dark-colored minerals)

Olivine and garnet are the two chief groups of silicates built of isolated tetrahedra. Olivine, predominant in basaltic rocks of the oceanic crust and rocks of the upper mantle, is olive-green to yellowish brown in color, has a glassy luster, and a conchoidal fracture. Garnet, characteristically found in metamorphic rocks of the continental crust, is most often brown to deep red in color. Both have a glassy luster and conchoidal fracture.

Pyroxenes and amphiboles are silicates made of continuous chains of silicate tetrahedra. Pyroxenes are built from single chains; amphiboles are built of double chains. Most are dark green to black in color and have good cleavage parallel to the silicate chain. The bonds are weaker across these surfaces than the bond between silicon and oxygen. The two differ in cleavage angle, pyroxenes cleave at a 90° angle, and amphiboles at 60° and 120° angles. Pyroxene is dominant in dark colored igneous rocks formed by basaltic lavas and intrusives. Pyroxene commonly alters to amphibole during late stages of crystallization of igneous rocks and during metamorphism.

Biotite a member of the mica family, has a sheet-like silicate tetrahedra as a basic building unit. The bond between the sheets is weaker than the bond holding the tetrahedra together within the sheet. Hence biotite, like other micas, has excellent cleavage in one direction. Biotite is black due to its iron content, and occurs in a variety of geologic environments. Biotite is a characteristic mineral in igneous rocks such as granite and granitic pegmatites.

Non-ferromagnesian Silicates (the light-colored minerals)

Muscovite, also a member of the mica family, has the same sheetlike structure of biotite, but has a lighter color. Muscovite occurs in a variety of geologic environments from igneous, metamorphic, and sedimentary. It is a common to abundant mineral in almost every type of metamorphic schist.

Quartz is the only mineral consisting entirely of silicon and oxygen. Quartz belongs to a network in which all the oxygen atoms in each SiO_4 tetrahedron are shared with neighboring tetrahedra, producing a stable, strongly bonded structure. As a result, quartz is hard, resistant to weathering, and displays no cleavage—quartz has a conchoidal fracture. Generally colorless unless affected by impurities, quartz characteristically forms six sided, hexagonal, crystals. Quartz is a common and abundant mineral occurring in a great variety of geological environments. It is present in many igneous and metamorphic rocks where it is a major constituent of granitic pegmatites. In sedimentary rocks, quartz is the major constituent of sandstone.

Feldspar is the most common mineral in the Earth's crust. It accounts for about 60 percent of all minerals in the continental crust, and together with quartz comprises about 75 percent of the volume of the continental crust. The structure of feldspar is very similar to the shared oxygen network found in quartz, except that some silicon atoms are replaced by aluminum atoms. Feldspars are relatively hard, have two planes of cleavage meeting at 90° angles, and vary in composition. There are two types of feldspars, alkali-feldspars ($KAlSi_3O_8$ to $NaAlSi_3O_8$) and plagioclase-feldspars ($NaAlSi_3O_8$ to $CaAlSi_3O_8$). Members of both of these groups are given individual names. Most alkali-feldspars are light in color (for example the alkali-feldspar orthoclase is usually light to salmon pink in color). Most plagioclase feldspars range in color from white to gray. The only sure way to distinguish between the two types of feldspars is by looking for parallel lines, striations, on the cleavage faces. Only plagioclase feldspar has striations. As rock-forming minerals, feldspars are widely distributed and very abundant. They are found in igneous, metamorphic, and, more rarely sedimentary rocks.

Point out that the igneous, metamorphic and sedimentary rock classifications are not mutually exclusive, because, over long periods of time, the same material may be subjected repeatedly to all the different processes. Refer students to the plate tectonic application of the rock cycle.

Igneous Rocks
This is a good place to show *Fire Under the Sea*. Remind students that the key concepts of composition, structure, and process of formation are identical to those introduced in the physics and chemistry parts of this text. Students often have a way of mistakenly thinking that, because each scientific discipline has its own

vocabulary and area of concern, science courses have little in common. This not only makes learning more difficult, but also may prevent students from enjoying the beauty and majesty of science as a single universe of knowledge and process.

Six minerals make up the great bulk of all igneous rocks—the minerals are quartz, feldspars, micas, amphiboles, pyroxenes, and olivine. Therefore, the chemical elements contained in these minerals are the principal chemical elements in magmas. They are Si, Al, Ca, Na, K, Fe, Mg, H, and O. With O as the most abundant anion, we express the compositional variations in terms of oxides with SiO_2 as the most abundant oxide for controlling the properties of magma. In a general sense, there are three compositionally distinct types of magma. The first type, basaltic, contains 50% SiO_2, the second type, andesitic, about 60%. The third type, rhyolitic, referred to in the text as granitic to avoid introducing extra terms, contains about 70% SiO_2. Of all igneous rocks in the crust (oceanic and continental combined) approximately 80% forms from basaltic magma, 10% from andesitic magma, and 10% from granitic magma.

Of note for the water content of the different magmas: From the text, water content of a rock affects its melting point. Rocks with a high water content have a lower melting point because water dissolves in the magma. Rocks with a low water content have a higher melting point and therefore require higher temperatures to melt.

CHECK QUESTION: Can buildings that are constructed of granite be called fireproof? Why or why not? [No. Although granite will not ignite like wood, granite has a high water content. So if heat steams away the moisture, the stone may weaken and crumble.

NEXT-TIME QUESTION: When a volcano erupts under the sea, does all the lava freeze instantly when it hits the sea water. If not, why not? [Everything we learned about latent heat, thermal conductivity and convection applies for both the water and the rock. The tremendous changes in location and temperature of a lot of rock and water take a lot of time!]

Sedimentary Rocks
An interesting thing about sediment is that it takes time for grains in water to settle. In general, smaller grains settle slower; larger grains settle faster; grains don't settle when water moves fast. Relate the settling of grain particles

to inertia. Larger grains have more mass and thus more inertia; larger grains are the first to settle out. Large grains get broken into small ones; small grains coalesce into big ones.

DEMONSTRATION: An inexpensive small package of concrete mix consisting of cement, sand and gravel, and a pan can show interesting properties of a rock mix. A home owner doing a little patching of a wall may want to separate the gravel and have just sand and cement left. (This is known as a "neat" mix.) We can do this easily; no water required. Just cover the pan bottom with an inch or more of mix, and tap the pan sharply. Will the gravel go to the bottom, stay where it is, or go to the top, where it can easily be removed? Why? [Gravel goes to the top, due to mean density and sufficient impact.]

The process of weathering occurs by mechanical means, chemical means, or both together. The process of erosion is simply transportation of sediment. Terms like "clastic" and "lithification" can be omitted when time is short. Just how you apportion time between studying alluvial fans, glacial erosion, streams, beaches and all the other sedimentary environments can depend pretty much on where your campus is located. Being able to observe these things is best, and next comes good films and videotapes.

The section on fossils is of interest to many students. Lectures on fossilization are better off as a hands-on approach. If you have samples of fossils let the students learn by observation.

Metamorphic Rocks
Metamorphic rocks are rocks that have been changed from their original state. Mechanical deformation by itself produces the least significant type of metamorphism. The general effect of mechanical deformation produces rocks that are flattened and elongated with a decrease in grain size. Recrystallization usually produces a change in mineral assemblage. The general effect of recrystallization produces rocks with an increase in grain size.

Once again the study of metamorphic rocks can be highlighted depending on your location. Students in Pennsylvania may know what a slate roof is like, and be interested in knowing that old-time blackboards were made of a big slice of slate. Billiard table tops were made that way too!

The vocabulary of metamorphic rock types and their characteristics is covered in the laboratory section on identification of rocks. Use your discretion as to its importance for text material.

Students often learn better by hands-on experience.

The Rock Cycle
This section is a summary and review of this chapter. Should a situation arise when there is just not enough time available to cover all the material, careful reading of this section, together with a short quiz, should give students the key concepts.

Activity Projects
Students need to do the Activity Projects in the Lab Manual, and the practice sheets in the Practice Book. Students can work in groups to prepare a joint report.

Suggested Discussion Techniques for the Exercises

Exercises 1, 2, 10, and 12: These exercises are best done in class recitation. Give every student a chance to speak, either from their own experience or from what friends and family have told them. Many students are from, or have visited, other parts of the country (and the world) where they observed geology. This is an opportunity for students to get to know each other, and in this descriptive, observational, speculative subject we can develop people who learn how to enjoy our beautiful world! For 12, try to get a student team to research National Geographic articles for class discussion.

Exercise 17: The class can be divided into groups to bring in small samples of the different types of feldspar, clay minerals, or of quartz. If some students complain you're treating them like children, you can tell them that most great geologists did what children do, and collected pretty stones. Remind them of what Newton said about pebbles near the end of his life.

Exercises 37 and 38: Here is an excellent opportunity for a research assignment based on library data. For example, students can research mineralogy, litigation, health hazards, old and recent newspaper articles, and various uses of asbestos to name just a few.

Selections from the other exercises can be assigned to develop technical writing skills. Much of geology depends on written field notes that need to be read by others before editing or typing. Assure students that they will rarely be expected to remember how to spell many of the long, unfamiliar words so common in geology. A short matching or multiple choice quiz can assess this information and evaluate how well each student is absorbing the concepts.

Some instructors have found that it is worth while to take 10 to 20 minutes to allow students to state briefly their major field and to suggest what aspects of geology are more relevant or of interest to them. Many students become interested in geology because of their love for the outdoors or concern for the environment.

23
The Earth's Internal Processes

This chapter is the most "physical" of the geology chapters. Waves have their application in seismology and the study of the Earth's interior. Mechanics and thermodynamics are the foundations of convection in the core and mantle, plate tectonics, and structural geology. Even though some of the physics isn't mentioned by name, here's your opportunity to tie in earlier parts of the course and show how a great deal of geology is applied physics.

This chapter opens with speculation of digging a hole completely through the Earth, which is simply a pedagogical way of turning the students attention to the Earth's interior. For the record, the deepest hole drilled was by the Soviets, who reached a depth of some 12 kilometers. The second deepest hole drilled is still (1993) in process, in southern Germany. A great surprise was the unexpected large amount of water at depths below 3 kilometers. After drilling more than 3 km of dry rock, water was found in abundance — water saltier than the ocean water. At 4 km, gas-rich, calcium-sodium-chloride brine twice as concentrated as seawater was found in abundance. The hole, 7.5 km deep in mid 1993, is scheduled to go a depth of 10 km. Cost? Some third of a billion dollars. (More on this in *Science*, p. 295, Vol. 261, July 93.)

The USGS has put out several animated computer disks using Hypercard. The disks show earthquake effects and fault motion. To order contact:

U.S. Geological Survey
Book and Open-file Report Sales
Denver, CO. 80225
(303) 236-4476

Fault Motion Loma Prieta, Open-File report 89-640 A and B
Faulting of the Earth, Open-file Report 90-257 A and B
Volcano Model, Open-file Report 91-115 A and B
Earthquake Effects, Open-file Report 92-200B
Make Your Own Earth and Tectonic Globes, Open-file Report 93-380-A
Northridge, California Earthquake, Open-file Report 94-214
Ocean Trenches, Open-file Report 96-76

There are many great articles about Earth's internal properties. Although it has recently gone out of print, one of my favorite magazines is *Earth*. Please consider:

Earthquakes in the Stable Continental Crust. Johnston, Arch, and Kantner, Lisa. *Scientific American*, March 1990.
Ancient Floods of Fire. White, Robert. *Natural History*, April 1991.
How Faults Shape the Earth. Bykerk-Kauffman, Ann. *Earth*, July 1992.
Cruise an Ancient Oceanic Rift Valley. Dombrowski, Phil. *Earth*, July 1992.
Roof of the World. Waters, Tom. *Earth*, July 1993.
Journeys in Iceland. Flanagan, Ruth. *Earth*, July, 1994.

The Mid-Cretaceous Superplume Episode.
Larson, Roger. *Scientific American,* February,
   1995.
Inner Earth Revealed. Vogel, Shawna. *Earth,*
August, 1995.
Burial of Radioactive Waste Under the Seabed.
Hollister, C., and Nadis, S. *Scientific
   American,* January, 1998.

For an interesting article on the Earth's magnetic field and migratory animals please see:

Earthly Attraction. Grossman, D., and Shulman, S. *Earth,* February, 1995.

There are several practice pages to supplement this chapter in the **Practice Book.**

There are also several lab activities in the **Laboratory Manual.**

SUGGESTED LECTURE PRESENTATION

Depart from the order of the chapter and begin in high gear with the idea of the continents floating over the globe like ice floes in the Arctic Sea. Where the ice sheets rise highest above the sea, is where they're also the thickest and where they extend deepest into the water. Likewise for the continents, which in a sense are floating upon the mantle. We are all certainly aware of changes that occur suddenly, like during an earthquake or the collapse of a building. But we aren't as aware of these changes if they occur in slow motion. The changes in geology that build mountains and wear them down to nubs are more spectacular than those of the greatest earthquakes — the change simply eludes us because it extends over long periods of time.

MOTIVATIONAL QUESTION: We understand that coal deposits are the ancient remains of vegetation trapped beneath the Earth's surface. And we find coal deposits in Antarctica, a place certainly too cold for vegetation. How can coal deposits exist in this cold place? [Antarctica wasn't always at the south pole. It was at one time far from the poles, where the climate was warm enough for vast vegetated regions. Onward to continental drift.]

Continental Drift and Plate Tectonics
Many people have looked at a world map and noticed how South America and Africa look like they "fit" together like jigsaw puzzle pieces. (I remember noticing this as a child—and that the idea created my initial interest in science.) This is also where Alfred Wegener started his theory

of continental drift, and a good place to begin a lecture because it starts the student thinking from the point of discovery. The fact that Wegener backed this up with geologic, climatic, and biologic evidence didn't help him convince his contemporaries. However, when the theory of sea-floor spreading arrived in the 1960s Wegener's original lines of evidence were revived, and he was shown to be one of the great creative thinkers and synthesizers of our time. H.H. Hess provided the missing piece, the driving force, by showing that sea floor spreads at **divergent** boundaries. Later work by others hinted at subduction zones (**convergent** boundaries). Because mid-ocean ridges are quite long, and, since they are on a sphere, spreading cannot occur at equal rates along the whole ridge. Hence, the ridge becomes "offset" and segmented. **Transform faults** provide the mechanism that accommodates the different spreading rates by "transforming" motion between ridge segments. Interestingly, it was first thought that these transform faults were actually the cause of the offset ridge segments. This makes the transform fault appear to have the opposite sense of strike-slip motion that they really do (see practice sheet on plate boundaries).

CHECK QUESTION: Okay, so the continents drifted long ago. How do we know whether or not they are still drifting? [Ask people who live along the plate boundaries, where earthquakes are quite common, if the plates are still moving.]

Hot spots Showing a map of the Hawaiian Islands and the Emperor Seamounts chain as an excellent way to illustrate the effects of a plate moving over a hot spot. Another great one is the Yellowstone—Snake River Plain hot spot. For a very long time North America has been riding over this hot spot and it has produced the volcanic rocks of the Snake River Plain and the amazing Yellowstone National Park. This can be clearly seen on a geologic map of the region.

Continental Collision One of the most amazing things about geology is geologic time and the power of erosion. The Appalachian mountains were produced by the same process that formed the Himalayas: continental collision. The Himalayas formed when India crashed into Asia, and they are still rising. The Appalachians formed about 250 million years ago when North America collided with Gondwanaland (an amalgamation of Africa, South America, Antarctica, India, Australia, New Zealand, and southeast Asia). The Appalachians were likely as high and grand as the Himalayas, but now look at them! Two hundred and fifty million years has worn them down to a nub.

CHECK QUESTION: Floating icebergs often collide and crunch into one another. Do the Earth's plates similarly collide? [Ask inhabitants of the Himalaya and Andes regions this question. If they don't know the answer, it's because the events that produced the high mountains occurred over long periods of time, and in "slow motion" as discussed earlier.]

CHECK QUESTION: Except for the observations in deep mines, how do we know any details about the Earth's interior? [How we know about the details of the Earth's interior is not altogether different than how a bat knows about the details of a dark cave. Onward to seismic waves.]

Not only does a bat know details of caves it can't "see", dolphins sense the details of the ocean bottom in the middle of the night. In the same way, Earth scientists probe the Earth's interior. They do so by studying seismic waves. In your lectures, consider picking up on the distinction between transverse and longitudinal waves (Chapter 10), but going further into the details of seismic waves is getting away from the essence of the chapter, and should be avoided (the text conveys enough material on seismic waves for a physical science class). An interesting point to make is that one of the ways in which Earth scientists learned so much about the Earth's interior was the Cold War. During the height of the Cold War numerous underground tests conducted by the former Soviet Union were of great concern to the free world. To more closely monitor these tests, an extensive network of sensitive seismographs was installed around the world. The seismograms from this monitoring allowed a closer examination of the Earth's interior — a boon to Earth scientists. Thus political conflict resulted in a tremendous gain in science.

Earth's Internal Layers
The Core The core-forming process has a name that I have always found amusing, "the iron catastrophe." The story goes like this: A popular theory of the formation of the terrestrial planets is called *cold accretion*. The planets formed when many stony and metallic meteorites, gases, dust, etc. clumped together due to gravitational attraction. Heat from radioactive decay initiated melting. Molten rock and molten metal are largely immiscible, so the Earth's own gravity resulted in the migration of denser molten metal toward the center of the planet. A hypothesized consequence of this is that the speed of the Earth's rotation increased due to more mass in the center, much like a spinning ice skater increases her speed when she draws her arms close to her body. This increase

in speed provides a mechanism for the *daughter theory* of our Moon. The theory states that the Moon was formed from molten Earth material that was either thrown off the Earth during this increase in rotational speed or from one or more "splashes" caused by large meteorites crashing into the still-molten Earth. Nice story! (Other theories for the Moon include (1) the *sister theory* (formed at the same time), and, (2) capture of "wandering" celestial body.)

CHECK QUESTION: Do Earth scientists REALLY KNOW that the Earth's center is iron? [No, they don't really know, with the assurance they know the composition of the Earth's crust. But all studies of the Earth's interior support the hypothesis that the center of the Earth is indeed iron. We assume it is and go from there. If it turns out we are wrong, then we make adjustments and update our knowledge base. Science progresses by assuming a hypothesis that is consistent with all the known data while holding the door open to other theories if it turns out that a better explanation comes up.]

The Mantle Convection in the mantle is and has been the driving force of plate tectonics, which in turn has created every mountain range on Earth. Very dynamic indeed. Also, the mantle is "a girl's best friend" (really a jewelry store's best friend!) because all gem quality diamonds are formed in the intense pressure environment of the mantle. The diamonds are later brought near the Earth's surface by rare, explosive volcanic eruptions called *kimberlite pipes*.

CHECK QUESTION: How big are the molecules that make up a diamond? [This is a review of Chapter 17 material: A diamond is an example of one molecule — as big as the particular diamond itself!]

The Crust The crustal surface is where we see the dynamics of our planet. The concept of isostasy can be explained by a floating iceberg. Most of the mass of an iceberg is below the water line much like the mass of continental land. Tall mountain ranges have most of their mass below the surface.

CHECK QUESTION: If you wish to drill a hole through the Earth's crust, where would you drill to succeed with the shortest hole? [The ocean floor.]

Structural Geology Here's where mechanics comes into the picture — compression (reverse and thrust faults, folds), tension (normal faults), and shearing (strike-slip faults). The rug example in the text is an easy demonstration in the classroom, and it gets students involved. To repeat the text here a bit, suppose you had a throw rug on your floor, with your friend standing on one end. If you push the rug toward your friend while keeping it on the floor, a series of ripples, or **folds**, develop in the rug. This is what happens to the Earth's crust when it is subjected to compressive stress. We can compare the ripples created on the rug to folding of rocks on the Earth's surface—both are generated by compressive stresses. Explain that if the compressive force overcomes the mechanical strength of the rock, thrust or reverse faults form to accommodate the compression.

Suggested Techniques for the Exercises

Exercises 21, 22, 28, and 33: can all be answered as a discussion while looking at a map of the world. Interaction and discussion between students helps learning. Have students ask their neighbor about these questions, and work in small groups.

Exercise 36: Discussion about tsunamis is very brief in the text. Students can research newspaper and magazine articles to find out more about tsunami occurrences. *Earth* magazine lists recent geologic events such as earthquakes, tsunamis, and volcanic activity in every January, May, September issue.

24
Water and Surface Processes

This chapter focuses on the Earth's freshwater supply—groundwater, surface water, and water locked in glacial ice packs—as well as the vast reservoir of ocean water.

For a great article on the Ogallala Aquifer see

Wellspring of The High Plains. *National Geographic* March 1993.

Earth magazine has excellent articles about all areas of geology. Articles regarding glaciers include:

Field Trip : New York — Take a Geologic Look *Earth* March 1992
Probing an Iceberg Barrier *Earth* May 1992
Roof of the World — How the Himalayas Change our Climate
Earth July 1993

Suggested articles about the oceans and ocean floor:

Life's Undersea Beginnings. Cone, Joseph. *Earth*, July, 1994.
The Oceans Salt Fingers. Schmitt, Raymond. *Scientific American*, May, 1995.
The Seafloor Laid Bare. Yulsman, Tom. *Earth*, June, 1996.
Panoramas of the Seafloor. Pratson, L., and Haxby, W. *Scientific American*, June, 1997.

Suggested articles for student assignments:
Water, Water, Everywhere, How Many Drops to Drink? Macleish, William.
World Monitor, December 1990, pp. 54-58.
Threats to the World's Water, Maurits la Riviere, J.W. *Scientific American*,   September 1989
The Kesterson Syndrome, Harris, Tom. *The Amicus Journal*, Fall 1989
The Lower Depths, Brown, Michael. *The Amicus Journal*, Winter 1986
A Problem That Cannot be Buried, Magnuson, E. *Time*, Oct. 14, 1985

There are several activities on groundwater flow, stream flow, and glacial flow in the **Practice Book**, and several lab activities on groundwater and contamination problems in the **Lab Manual**.

SUGGESTED LECTURE PRESENTATION

Begin with the following observation and questions: If we dig a hole in the ground and then fill it with water, the water soon seeps into the ground and is gone. Then we look at a lake or pond. Why doesn't water there similarly seep into the ground? Is there plastic or something beneath the bottom that prevents draining? State that these questions are not correctly answered by most people — who are only vaguely aware of what groundwater and water tables are about. One with a knowledge of water tables realizes the interesting reason that lakes don't (ordinarily) drain and a hole dug in the ground that is then filled with water (ordinarily) does. The pond or lake doesn't drain simply because it intersects the water table. When you dig a hole in the ground that is above the water table, of course the water soon drains downward. Knowing about groundwater changes the way we look at our surroundings. The person educated in geology sees the world quite differently.

Groundwater Continue by pointing out that most of the Earth's fresh water (aside from water tied up in the polar ice caps) resides underground. These underground "reservoirs" of water account for about 98.56% (0.80% of which is soil moisture) of the Earth's fresh water, or about 0.62% of the Earth's total water. However, if we consider groundwater that is economically available (shallow groundwater; certainly no deeper than one kilometer) groundwater plus soil moisture equals 97.04% of the Earth's fresh-water resources. Since soil moisture isn't exploitable as a water resource, about 95.39% of our available fresh water is beneath the ground. Students may wonder why the groundwater percentage goes down when we consider only shallow groundwater. Remind them that we changed our focus to "available" freshwater. The percentage of surface freshwater has not changed but the total has, so the fraction that is underground is now smaller. Groundwater is an important source of fresh water for people, agriculture, livestock, and industry. As the population grows so will dependence on groundwater. Groundwater can be found just about anywhere below the Earth's surface.

CHECK QUESTION: Why aren't soil moisture and deep groundwater available as a freshwater resource? [Soil moisture resides in the unsaturated zone under negative pressure (i.e. less than atmospheric pressure). If a pump were operating in the unsaturated zone it would pump only air. Deep groundwater is simply too expensive to bring to the surface (due to pumping costs). It is cheaper to get water from other sources.]

DEMONSTRATION: Absorption of water by different soil or rock materials. Have a student dip a sugar cube half way into colored water. Explain that the sugar cube is not completely solid and contains many open pore spaces. These pore spaces become saturated when a cube is dipped in water. Have four students fill four beakers with different soil/rock materials—sand, clay, small pebbles, and garden soil. Fill the beakers with measured amounts of water. The amount of water added gives the porosity of the soil/rock material.

In the western United States groundwater is the primary source of water for drinking, domestic use, and agriculture. In many areas groundwater literally brings life to the region.

Population growth and industrial and agricultural production produce quantities of waste that are frequently greater than the environment can handle. The contamination of subsurface waters is of primary concern. Have students research articles about waste disposal techniques. Two widely used techniques include deep-well injection of liquid wastes and sanitary landfills for solid wastes. Your class can discuss the pros and cons of the different techniques. Contamination is also caused by leakage from ponds and lagoons used by larger waste-disposal systems, and by leaching of animal wastes, fertilizers, and pesticides from agricultural soils.

In discussing the problems of groundwater and surface water contamination, end on a positive note. Try to get into what can be done to better the situation. Encourage students to look for the solutions to the problems in their readings.

Surface Water This section concentrates on the effect of stream flow on the land surface. It is the erosive work of rivers that gouges out canyons and whittles away solid rock. Rivers shape the landscape. Emphasize that rivers do their work by three processes: erosion, transportation, and deposition.

You may refer back to the Rock Cycle to show the process of erosion. Use the term WETS—Weathering, Erosion, Transportation, Sedimentation. (Note: Sedimentation = deposition—the physical process of laying down sediment, and precipitation—the chemical and biochemical means of sediment cementation.)

In general, erosion is extensive where rivers move swiftly and transport great quantities of sediment; and deposition takes place where the streams slow down. The amount of sediment the river can carry depends on the speed of the current which in turn determines the erosive power of the river. Running water can swiftly carry off soil as well as uncompacted sand and gravel. Water rich in dissolved substances can also chemically erode river channels. A river can carry a great amount of sediment in a short period. The Mississippi River transports more than 440 million tons of silt, clay, and sand in an average year. It is no wonder that over a course of a few million years, the Mississippi River Delta has moved from Cairo, Illinois to its present location near the city of New Orleans, Louisiana. The Mississippi River transports enough debris to move its delta six miles seaward every century!

More recently, the great flood of 1993 has altered the map of the Midwest. Flooding of the Mississippi River has erased towns, made islands out of peninsulas, and forged new river channels. The 1993 flood event is excellent for class discussion. Students can research effects of flooding on the land, groundwater, wells, and transportation links. A question to ponder—How does this affect sedimentation in the Mississippi River Delta? Is there a noticeable increase in the delta's extension?

DEMONSTRATION: Purchase 3 feet of 6 inch diameter nonporous, flexible, plastic tubing (similar to the type used for drainage). Cut the tube to make a U-shaped trough. Fill the trough with coarse sand. Step 1: Hold the trough in a slanted position over a large empty pan. Pour water, a trickle at a time, on the sand at the upper end. Water flowing at a slow steady rate carries small grains of sand with it to the pan. The larger, heavier sand grains remain in the trough. Step 2: Repeat step 1 but pour the water at a faster rate (more force). Both the small and large grains should wash down into the pan. Step 3: Raise and lower the trough to see the effect of slope. Step 4: Place a large rock in the middle of the flow of water to see the effect it has on the deposition of sediments. Step 5: Bend the trough into gentle and tight curves to see the effect of stream velocity, erosion, and deposition.

Rivers and streams are greatly affected by their gradient. The steeper the gradient the faster the flow, the greater the energy. The obvious role of gravity has led to a widespread misconception—that rushing mountain streams flow swiftly, while broad rivers roll along slowly. In fact, water velocity often increases downstream

despite the loss of steep gradient. One reason has to do with friction and efficiency. In the headwater regions, where the gradient is steep, water moves through small narrow boulder strewn channels. Although the water moves swiftly it is slowed down both externally, by the force of friction from contact with boulders and the narrow channel, and internally within the turbulent water itself. As the water moves downstream, the channel widens and deepens as it accommodates more water. Deepening and widening of the channel thereby reduces some of the factors of friction and increases the streams efficiency. Wider and deeper channels permit water to flow more freely and hence more rapidly. Another reason is that the number of tributaries to the mainstream increases as we move downstream. If the cross-sectional area of the main stream doesn't increase much, the water velocity will increase.

Glaciers and Glaciation Glaciers are powerful agents of transformation as they erode the land surface and then deposit great quantities of debris.

Glaciers and the polar ice caps account for about 77 percent of the Earth's total fresh water supply. Most of this glacial ice (98%) is found in the polar regions where the intensity of solar radiation is greatly reduced as the Sun's rays strike the Earth at an oblique angle. Since the energy is dispersed over a great area, it does not act to effectively heat the Earth's surface. The remaining 2 percent of the Earth's glacial ice is distributed around the world in locations of high elevations.

The Oceans This section on oceans focuses on landforms — landforms on the ocean floor as well as land forms adjacent to the shoreline. If Chapters 22 and 23 have already been covered, students should have little difficulty in discussing land features of the ocean basins. Because waves dominate beach processes, the section on waves relates directly to shoreline landforms. Ocean waves and wave refraction also provide a link to physics and the study of waves discussed in Chapter 10.

Suggested Techniques for the Exercises

The end of chapter exercises are meant to be more challenging than the review questions. Please don't overload the students by assigning too many. Because this chapter focuses on water and the processes of flow, some of these exercises assume prior knowledge of physics and chemistry.

Exercise 2: This is a difficult question and may be assigned if Chapter 26 and/or 27 have already been covered.

Exercise 20: This is a good question if you decide to lecture about the Mississippi River (see comments above). Students need not know the amount of sediment carried by the river, all they need to know is that the Mississippi River transports a lot of material to its delta. Students may refer to the section on delta environments in Chapter 22. Since the flooding of the Mississippi River in summer 1993, a good discussion might be about the floods effect on the delta. Did the flooding produce noticeable change in the delta region?

Exercise 22: Students may need to refer to the section on sedimentary desert environments in Chapter 22 to answer the question about wind.

25
A Brief History of the Earth

This chapter focuses on the many stages of the development of life and tectonic events that have occurred throughout the Earth's long history. Getting students to gain some grasp of the immensity of geologic time is your challenge.

For what it's worth, consider these memory aids for the Earth's periods and epochs.
Periods of the Paleozoic: Campbell's Old Soup Does Make Peter Pale.
Periods of the Mesozoic and Cenozoic: Triple Junctions Create Terrible Quandaries.
Epochs of the Cenozoic: Put Eggs On My Plate Please Honey.

For a great article on early life please see:
Burgess Shale Faunas and the Cambrian Explosion, Morris, Conway. *Science*, Oct 20, 1989.

For interesting articles on evolution please see:
Climate and Evolution: First Steps into the Human Dawn, Boaz, Noel. *Earth* March, 1992.
Captured in Amber, Grimaldi, David. *Scientific American*, April, 1996.
Early Homind Fossils from Africa, Leakey, M., and Walker, A., *Scientific American*, June 1997.
Origins—Special Edition, various authors. *Earth*, February, 1998

Dinosaurs Take Wing, Ackerman, Jennifer. *National Geographic*, July, 1998.
The Dawn of Humans, Berger, Lee. *National Geographic*, August, 1998.

There are several activities on relative and radiometric age dating in the **Practice Book**.

There are no lab activities or experiments for this chapter in the **Laboratory Manual**.

SUGGESTED LECTURE PRESENTATION

It has been said that children can't really appreciate history, because their own experience of time is too limited for them to have an appreciation of any time scale. A fully conscious insect with a few-hour life span similarly would have no idea that the plant or tree it feeds upon has a "short" life cycle that fits in the life cycles of other life forms that utilize trees. "Short" to us, that is. Upon casual observation, even we are not fully aware of the actions of plants and trees. Because their activities are in "slow motion" we do not see that vegetation is every bit as violent as animals in maintaining their hierarchical positions in the food chain. Even slower and more violent are the Earth's geological processes. Like the insect with the few-hour life span, we are not aware of long-term changes—unless we study out surrounding very carefully—which is what this course is about!

So we begin by looking into the Earth's time scale. Draw a long line on the chalkboard. Then segment the line into twelve equal pieces to represent the months of the year, going from January to December. In the various sections mark off the time for the different events. Some of the dates used are not known with great precision (especially early dates). So I am providing the dates used in developing this time line.

Jan 1—the origin of the Earth. (4.6 billion years ago)

Mar 5 —Earliest Earth rocks. (3.8 billion)

Mar 29—first simple life and photosynthesis. (3.5 billion)

July 26—free oxygen begins to accumulate in the atmosphere. (2.0 billion)

Sept 3—first green algae and organisms with a nucleus. (1.5 billion)

Nov 18—the proliferation of life—the beginning of the Paleozoic Era. (544 million)

Nov 21—first fish; the first vertebrate. (505 million; Cambrian-Ordovician boundary)

Nov 28—life on land (plants). (423 million; mid-Silurian)

Dec 3—amphibians move to land. (360 million; Devonian-Carboniferous boundary)

Dec 14—first mammals. (226 million; mid-Triassic)

Dec 14 to Dec 26—the age of the dinosaur. (215 to 66 million; mid-Triassic to end of Cretaceous)

Dec 31 at 11:50 p.m.—Humans emerge. (90,000 years ago)

Dec 31, fourteen seconds before midnight—the birth of Christ. (33 B.C.)

Dec 31, two seconds before midnight—the Declaration of Independence. (1776)

Dec 31, about one second before midnight—the start of the Industrial Revolution. (1800)

Follow this up with the analogy: If the age of the Earth is the length of the Golden Gate Bridge (about 6000 ft long), then 600 years of civilization is 0.1 inch (about the thickness of a car key)! Whereas most fields of study are concerned with no more than the car key, geologists are concerned with the whole bridge! (Or carrying this further, cosmologists are concerned with the bridge and its more than 2-mile long on ramp!)

Early (European) thoughts about geologic history

Before ~ 1500 (pre-Renaissance)—strictly biblical.

~ 1500 DaVinci (Italy) —Questioned the flood as the cause of fossils.

~1670 Nicolaus Steno —Superposition, Original Horizontality, Lateral Continuity

Robert Hooke —Looked at fossils with a microscope; suggested fixed life span for species; questioned flood.

~1785 James Hutton/John Playfair (Scotland) —Uniformitarianism, etc.

~1800 William Smith (England)—Map completed in 1815, plus table of strata; general ideas about correlation of fossils.

W. Smith/G. Cuvier (France) Principle of faunal succession (oldest fossils are in lowest strata). Principle of faunal assemblages (strata with similar fossils are similar age).

Principles plus lots of detailed descriptive work led to relative time scales (which are always in the process of being revised).

Early attempts at establishing absolute time scale

1654 Archbishop Ussher (Ireland): Added up life spans of old testament characters; Earth was created in 4004 B.C., on October 26 at 9 a.m. (apparently he wasn't into significant figures!). Very influential for about 150 years, and is still cited.

~1760 Buffon (>100 years later) 75,000 years based on cooling rate of Earth's iron core.

~1850 Kelvin (Scotland) 20-40 million years, based on cooling of Earth.

Kelvin ~ 18 million years, and Helmholtz 20-40 million years, both based on radiation from Sun, assuming energy from gravitational contraction.

~1893 Walcott ~75 million years, based on total thickness of strata.

1899 Joly ~90 - 100 million years, based on salt accumulation in the ocean.

During this time radioactivity was discovered by Becquerel (France), x-rays by Roentgen (Germany), and radium was isolated by Curie (France). In 1905 Rutherford suggested the use of radioactivity for dating. In 1950 Libby (USA) developed C-14 dating.

Contemporary thoughts about geologic history
How amazing we know any details about a history so vast. We are able to date events of Earth's history principally by two methods of dating: *relative dating*, and more recently, *radiometric dating*.

Relative Dating tells us the sequence that events occurred—if one event happened before another event. Generalizations concerning contacts of rock masses —where two rock masses are in contact with one another, the younger rock mass is the one that 1) contains fragments of the other, 2) sends tongues or branches into the other,

3) bakes or alters the other, 4) cuts across the layers or structures of the other, 5) overlies the other. Point out that an object must exist before anything can happen to it.

Radiometric Dating gives us the absolute age of rock. Radiometric dating is a refinement of relative time. This section can be tied to radioactivity as described in Chapter 15. Point out that the age of the Earth is not estimated by analyzing rocks that formed 4.6 billion years ago. Instead scientist have dated certain meteorites which presumably coalesced at the same time as the Earth. The processes of erosion, volcanism and plate tectonics have effectively obliterated all traces of the Earth's early history.

CHECK QUESTION: The Earth is some 4.6 billion years old, yet the oldest rocks only date back to 3.7 billion years. Why don't we find rocks dated at 4.6 billion years? [The material that may have formed any rocks 4.6 billion years ago has been mixed back into the stew that made up the Earth's surface that long ago.]

The Precambrian comprises over 85 percent of the Earth's history. In this time the Earth's surface cooled, which allowed the formation of lithospheric plates. The development of photosynthesis generated free oxygen and the beginning of primordial life forms.

CHECK QUESTION: From where did the oxygen that makes a large part of the Earth's early atmosphere originate? [Mainly from the waste products of plant life.]

CHECK QUESTION: From where did the oxygen that makes a large part of today's atmosphere originate? [Mainly from the waste products of plant life.]

The Paleozoic Era marks the first abundant fossil evidence of life. The significant occurrences of the Paleozoic include the emergence of many diverse life forms and the formation of the supercontinent of Pangaea.

The Mesozoic Era is the age of the reptile. The subject of dinosaurs has always been of general interest. If there is a natural history museum in your area, try to get a field trip together. Even the movie "Jurassic Park" generates interesting discussions. For instance, were dinosaurs warm blooded or cold blooded? The main goal is to get students interested — a spark may lead to a fire. Science is an ongoing process and at present we don't know all the answers. The world is like a big puzzle, with each piece an answer to a question. The puzzle is incomplete. The main points of the Mesozoic Era include the rise and fall of the dinosaurs, the appearance of the first mammals, and the break up of Pangaea.

The Cenozoic Era is the age of the mammals, and is the Era in which humans evolved. For a more biological and cultural approach (integration) discuss how people from various areas around the world are different.

Point out that humans, like other species from previous geologic time, adapt to the environment to survive. But humans do more than adapt — they also change the environment. Humans can be a geologic force. This ties in to the problems of water contamination discussed in Chapter 24.

Relate your discussion about the Pleistocene to the effects of glacial erosion. Point out that there have been several glacial and interglacial periods in the present ice age. Many people do not realize that we are still in an ice age. An ice age can be defined as a time period when continental scale glaciers (such as the polar ice caps) are present. You may remark about the Little Ice Age—the period of cold between the 15th and 19th Century. The Little Ice Age is depicted in the paintings of ice skaters by Flemish artists. Point out that glacial advances are accompanied by a drop in sea level, due to water taken up by glacial ice.

Suggested Techniques for the Exercises

Exercise 3: Assign this exercise first then follow with practice sheet on Relative Time.

Exercise 6: This can be an interesting question for class discussion. Have students discuss with their neighbors the reasons for the decrease of uranium and increase of lead. Relate this to the conservation of mass. If the concept of conservation of mass is true, how can the amount of lead change? This is a good "check" question to see if students understand both the concept of radiometric dating and the conservation of mass.

26
The Atmosphere, The Oceans, and Their Interactions

Evolution of the Earth's Atmosphere and Oceans
Components of the Earth's Atmosphere
  Vertical Structure of the Atmosphere
Solar Energy
  The Seasons
  The Solar Constant
  Terrestrial Radiation
  The Greenhouse Effect and Global Warming
  | Global Warming |
Components of the Earth's Oceans
  Physical Structure of the Ocean
Driving Forces of Air Motion
Global Circulation Patterns
  Upper Atmospheric Circulation
  Oceanic Circulation
    Surface Currents
    Deep-Water Currents
  | The El Niño Condition |

The Earth is powered by the radiant energy of the Sun, which because of the Earth's curvature, is spread unevenly over its surface. This unevenness of solar energy generates circulations in the atmosphere and on the surface below. Because of the Earth's tilt and corresponding uneven distribution of energy during the year, our planet undergoes seasonal change. The atmosphere filters harmful UV radiation, charged particles, and space debris from reaching the Earth's surface, The atmosphere offers protection as it balances the amount of energy the Earth receives and re-emits. These surface energy balances give rise to global patterns of temperature, winds and ocean currents—the topics covered in this chapter.

For articles about climate change consider:
The Changing Atmosphere, Graedel, Thomas. *Scientific American*, Sept. 89.
The Changing Climate, Schneider, Stephen. *Scientific American*, Sept. 89.
El Niño Strikes Again. Davidson, Keay. *Earth*, June, 1995.
Living Planet. Vogel, Shawna. *Earth*, April, 1996.
Blame it on the Sun. Penvenne, Laura. *Earth*, August, 1996.
The Iron Hypothesis. Dopyera, Caroline. *Earth*, October, 1996.
Engineering a Cooler Planet. Flanagan, Ruth. *Earth*, October, 1996.

A note of optimism on the ozone layer: Apparently the wide-scale publicity given to the polar ozone hole has resulted in the slowdown of production of CFCs and halons, with resulting decreases of these ozone-killing chemicals in the ozone layer (*Nature*, Aug 93). 1993 findings are far less grave than earlier findings. Concentrations of CFC-11 dropped from an annual average of 11 parts per trillion from 1985 to 1988 to 3 parts per trillion in 1993. For CFC-12, the growth rate dropped from 20 parts per trillion in 1985-88 to 11 parts per trillion in 1993. In any event, recovery of the layer will be a slow process. Under an agreement signed by 87 countries in November 1992 in Copenhagen, the manufacture of CFCs was to be phased out by the end of 1995, while halon manufacture was to stop by the end of 1993. It was dire news of spreading of the ozone hole in 1991 that prompted voluntary speeding up of phase-outs by major manufacturers of CFCs and halons. Most post-1994 cars, for example, have non-CFC air conditioning systems. Science and public policy can work well together.

There is one page on *Wave Motion* in the **Practice Book.**

Try to do both *Solar Power I* and *Solar Power II* in the **Laboratory Manual.**

SUGGESTED LECTURE PRESENTATION

Begin by asking your class where the atoms come from that make up the material that composes a tree? Many think that tree material originates from the ground. [So a massive tree should be in the middle of a hole?] Not so, except for a few minerals and much of the water it takes into its substance, trees get most of their building material from the *air*. When CO_2 impinges on a tree leaf, it is pulled in. The leaf is able to pull the carbon from the molecule and discharge the refuse — the oxygen. How is it able to pull this feat off? By the energy of sunlight! So the next time you take a breath of air, be thankful for the existence of trees. No trees, no oxygen! Wood is composed of mainly hydrogen and carbon. Wood, like us, is a hydrocarbon. And where does the tree get its hydrogen? From water. Again, sunlight provides the energy to make the separation. And what happens when you burn the wood of the tree? It cycles back to its original form, CO_2, which forms when oxygen is energetically slammed against the carbon as in a fire. So the energy of the fire is simply the stored energy of sunlight. Interesting stuff.

The Evolution of the Earth's Atmosphere and Oceans So where did the early atmosphere come from? Trees? No, from miniature trees of a sort — from green algae — which dates back to the late Precambrian. Like all higher forms of green plants that followed, the algae developed the ability of photosynthesis, the byproduct of which is guess what? Oxygen!

Evidence of early atmospheric compositions are obtained by core samples from the polar ice caps. Tiny air bubbles trapped within the ice are then analyzed for composition. By taking samples from different layers Earth scientists can determine when the air was last floating around in the atmosphere (analogous to dating layers of sedimentary rock!)

Tie in the evolution of the Earth's atmosphere and oceans to the eruption of surface volcanoes and the outside bombardment of interplanetary comets—for both processes contributed. Once the atmosphere and oceans formed, life emerged on the Earth.

Components of the Earth's Atmosphere If we make a tall stack of foam-rubber bricks, the bricks at the bottom will be more squashed than the bricks at the top. So it is with the atmosphere. The densest part of the atmosphere is at the Earth's surface (or in mines below). Most of the atmosphere is near the Earth's surface because of gravity. So it is the force of gravity on

molecules of air that holds most of the atmosphere from going off into space. (If gravity were less, like on the Moon, molecular speed caused by solar energy would be greater than escape velocity and no atmosphere would be maintained.) The atmosphere thins with altitude and ultimately becomes indistinguishable from the background gas in space. So there is no upper "surface" of the "ocean of air" like there is on the ocean of water.

CHECK QUESTION: When a helium-filled balloon is released in the air, how high does it go? Does it leave the Earth's atmosphere? [It doesn't get very high before it bursts, usually within sight. Why does it burst? Because surrounding air pressure decreases with height allowing the balloon to grow until it ruptures. Special balloons for high-altitude measurements can achieve altitudes into the stratosphere without bursting — another story.]

Solar Energy and the Seasons Do the flashlight demonstration suggested in the text. Take the demonstration one step further by bringing in a globe and showing the wide distribution of light at the poles and the concentration of light at the equator. Relate seasons to the Earth's tilt. New Englanders who revel in the fall foliage and others who enjoy the seasonal cycle can be thankful that the polar axis is inclined at 23.5 degrees to the orbit plane (the ecliptic). Draw the sketch below on the board, first with only the two positions of the Earth at the far left and far right. Ask which of these two positions represents winter months and which represents summer months. Encourage neighbor discussion.

Once it is clear that winter is at the left, show the position of the Earth in autumn and in spring. Shift the position of the Sun closer to the Earth in winter, for this is actually the case. From your drawing, your class can see why Northern Hemisphere types enjoy an extra week of spring and summer! Southern Hemisphere types are compensated by a somewhat milder climate year round due to the greater amount of ocean in the Southern Hemisphere (80% as compared to about 60% for the Northern Hemisphere).

Long and Short Wave Radiation and the Greenhouse Effect Compare the window glass of the florist's greenhouses to the water vapor and carbon-dioxide window glass of the Earth's atmosphere. Relate the section on solar and terrestrial radiation back to concepts covered in Physics, section 7.3. Short waves easily penetrate the Earth's atmosphere whereas long waves do not (they are reflected back to the Earth thus they warm the Earth). Emphasize that among the atmospheric gases, water vapor plays the largest role in confining the Earth's heat. Although increased levels of carbon dioxide have impacted the Earth's atmosphere, more information is needed before we can identify the major causes of global warming. Recent studies, for example, indicate that hurricanes kick appreciable amounts of carbon dioxide from the ocean into the atmosphere. Emphasize and reemphasize that the Earth has undergone many climatic changes during her long history (see box on global warming). How much human activities affect these changes is usually overestimated in the media.

State that terrestrial radiation rather than solar radiation is directly responsible for the warmth of the air around us. Air is primarily warmed by the Earth, which is an important reason we don't freeze at night when we're not in the Sun's light. Three cheers for terrestrial radiation!

Interesting point: The Earth is always "in equilibrium" whether it is overheating or not. At any higher temperature produced by global warming, the Earth simply radiates more terrestrial radiation. Income and outgo match in any case; the important consideration is the temperature at which this income and outgo match.

As an interesting side point that has to do with adjusting to heating, cite how a frog cannot discern small changes in temperature, and if sitting comfortably in a pan of water that is slowly heated on a stove, it will make no effort to jump out of the water as temperature increases. It will just sit there and be cooked. But this is not limited to frogs. According to accounts given by cannibals who cook their victims in large pots of water, the same is true of humans. This was a sad fact some 25 years ago in Mill Valley, CA, where water in a hot tub gradually overheated (due to a faulty heater) and resulted in the death of the unsuspecting and drowsy occupants. You can compare this to other cases where if adverse conditions are increased gradually, humans will tolerate what otherwise would be completely unacceptable to them: smog, noise, pollution, crime, and so on.

Components of the Earth's Oceans
Similar to the atmosphere, the ocean can be divided into layers—the surface layer, the transitional layer, and the deep layer. In each of these layers salinity, temperature, and density vary. Although these variations contribute to the flow of water, the underlying cause of water movement relates back to the atmosphere and the uneven distribution of solar energy.

Driving Forces of Air and Water Motion
Consider a non spinning world with a uniform surface and without clouds. Then you have a world with very little air and water movement and a world without weather. For it is the unequal heating of the Earth's surface that produces the fluctuations in the atmosphere. Give the world a spin and you'll get meandering waves moving west-east just below the poles. You now have a world with jet streams.

The processes of the pressure gradient force, Coriolis force, and frictional force operate on both the atmosphere as well as the ocean. Emphasize the connections between these two fluids—what effects one effects the other. Atmospheric circulation assists in the important transfers of energy and mass on Earth Together, Earth's atmospheric and oceanic circulations represent a vast heat engine powered by the Sun.

Suggested Techniques for the Exercises

Exercises 7 and 8: Relate these questions back to the class demonstration using the flashlight and the globe.

Exercise 16: Use the globe to illustrate this question. Remember the only change is the absence of global spin. What other factors contribute to wind? [unequal heating due to distribution of solar intensity, unequal heating due to absorbency of heat by land and water cover.]

Exercises 20, 21, 22: With the 1998 occurrence of El Niño, these questions could provide an opportunity for great discussion. They can also be used to encourage student research.

Exercises 27, 28, 29: These questions on ocean salinity can be assigned after this easy class demonstration.

DEMONSTRATION: Fill a large basin with fresh water. Fill a large container (clear soda bottles work nicely) with fresh water, fill another large container with salt water (salt concentration can vary, but keep track of amount of salt added.) One at a time, submerge the water filled containers into the basin. Measure the amount of water displaced by the fresh water filled container. Measure the amount of water displaced by the salt water filled container. Compare the amount of displacement. The salt water filled container should displace the volume of the salt added.

27
Weather

What do most people talk about in casual conversations? The weather, of course. This chapter provides some scientific insights that underlie the weather. Chapter 8 on Thermodynamics and Chapter 26 on Atmosphere and Ocean Interactions provide useful although not mandatory background.

Articles regarding meteorology include:
As the World Breathes: The Carbon Dioxide Cycle, Zaburunov, Steven. *Earth* Jan. 92.
Under the Ozone Hole, Vogel, Shawna. *Earth* Jan. 93
Tornadoes. Davies-Jones, Robert. Scientific American, August, 1995.
Tornado Troopers. Pendrick, Daniel. Earth, October, 1995.
Hurricane Mean Season. Pendrick, Daniel. Earth, June, 1996.
Lightning Control with Lasers. Diels, Jean-Claude, et al. *Scientific American*, August, 1997.
Lightning Between Earth and Space. Mende, Stephen, et al. *Scientific American*, August, 1997.

The textbook discusses the energy release that accompanies the condensation of water in the atmosphere. It doesn't discuss the mechanism for this energy release. Interestingly enough, H_2O molecules simply give most of their KE to the air during their last collision before condensation. The details are shown in the three sketches below.

Consider two pairs of molecules, say with equal KEs before collision (Sketch 1). After collision, individual KEs may be quite unequal, for molecules that transfer much of their KE to others are left with corresponding less KE of their own (Sketch 2). So far, there is no change in the air's total KE score. But if the slower molecules happen to be H_2O, they are candidates for condensation if their next collisions are with other H_2Os that have similarly just given most of

144

their KE to neighboring molecules (Sketch 3). Upon condensation of the slow-moving H_2Os, other molecules remaining in the air have an increase in average KE. Voila! *H_2O molecules transfer KE to the surrounding air during their last collision while in the gaseous phase*—the collision that immediately precedes condensation. The energy gained by the air is the well-known heat of vaporization—about 540 calories per gram of condensed H_2O for an ambient temperature of 100°C. It's greater for lower temperatures (molecules bopped to high speeds in a low-speed environment gain more energy than molecules bopped to the same high speeds in higher-speed environments). So all things being equal, a rainy day really is warmer than a cloudy day.

There are two activities on Weather Patterns in the **Practice Book**.

In the **Laboratory Manual** are two experiments on finding the energy output of the Sun, *Solar Power I* and *Solar Power II*.

SUGGESTED LECTURE PRESENTATION

Expansion and Compression of Air Ask if it would be a good idea on a hot day when going for a balloon ride to only wear a T-shirt. Or would it be a good idea to bring warm clothing? A glance at Figure 27.3 will be instructive. You're into the *adiabatic expansion* of rising air in our atmosphere (recall from Chapter 8 that adiabatic means *without heat input or output.*)

But better than words, have your students blow on their hands and feel the warmth of their breath. Then repeat, with lips puckered so the air expands on the way to their hands. Coolness! Likewise for rising air, which cools by about 10°C for each 1-km rise. And what happens to air that descends? Warmness! The air is compressed and its temperature rises (Chinooks).

Discuss the check question in the text about yanking down a giant dry-cleaner's garment bag from a high altitude and the changes in temperature it undergoes. (It's helpful to consider parcels of air as if they were blobs in giant plastic tissue bags — good for visualizing processes.) Then follow this with the second footnote about aircraft heating, which is of considerable interest: but don't assume that because it's in the text that you can't introduce it to your class as if it were brand new information. (We're past that stage, thinking that everything really interesting in the text is absorbed by our students in their reading — or are our students really less scholarly than yours?)

There is more to Chinook winds than is cited in the text. As Figure 27.4 suggests, warm moist air that rises over a mountain cools as it expands, and then undergoes precipitation where it gains latent heat energy as vapor changes state to liquid (rain) or solid (snow). Then when the energetic dry air is compressed as it descends on the other side of the mountain, it is appreciably warmer than if precipitation hadn't occurred. Without the heat gain by the air in precipitation, air would cool in expanding and warm the same amount in compressing, with no net increase in temperature.

Discuss temperature inversion and the role it plays in air pollution; or at least in confining air pollution. On the matter of pollution, we find now that even rain is polluted. Acid rain has wreaked havoc with the environment in many parts of the world. Interestingly enough, pure rain water is naturally acidic. Ever-present carbon dioxide dissolves in water vapor to form carbonic acid. Decomposing organic matter, volcanoes, and geysers can release sulfur dioxides that form sulfuric acid. Lightning storms can cause nitric acid formation. The environmental problem of acid rain is compounded by fossil fuel combustion that produces acid-producing compounds. Almost humorously, it isn't the destruction of forests or poisoning of wildlife that has evoked the loudest public outcry — acid rain dulls the high-tech finishes on automobiles, and *that*, for John Q. Public, is going too far!

Condensation in the Atmosphere An interesting way to present the condensation of water vapor to droplets is the following: Ask why a glass containing an iced drink becomes wet on the outside, and why a ring of moisture is left on the table. You can inject a bit of humor here and state that the reason has to do with — then pause and write a big 27.1 on the board. Then ask why the walls of the classroom would become wet if the temperature of the room were suddenly reduced. State that the answer is — then underline your 27.1 . Ask why dew forms on the morning grass, and state the answer is — another underline for 27.1 . Ask why fog forms, and how the clouds form, and back to your 27.1. By now your class is wondering about the significance of 27.1. Announce you're discussing Figure 27.1 , and with class attention and interest go on to discuss the formation of fog and clouds (and even rain, hail, and snow). [Snow crystallizes from vapor; hail is rain that freezes when tossed upward, often repeatedly, by strong updrafts.]

Condensation is enhanced by the presence of ions, dust, or tiny particles that act as the nuclei of droplets. London became much foggier when coal burning provided more particles in the air to initiate condensation.

Cloud formation So air expands as it rises, and therefore cools. What happens to the water molecules in air that cools? Condensation! If it happens high up in the sky, it's called a cloud. If condensation happens down near the ground, it's called fog. So remember the three Cs: Cooling — Condensing — Clouds.

CHECK QUESTION: Why does cooling air condense? [See Figure 27.1, or recall from Chapter 17 that the polar characteristics of water molecules makes them tend to stick to one another, as seen when water drops bead on a surface. In warm air they are moving too fast to stick when they collide. Like a couple of magnets thrown at each other, they fly off in different directions when they bounce. But toss the magnets slowly and they'll stick when they meet. Likewise for H_2O molecules in the air. Slow-moving water molecules stick—condensation.]

CHECK QUESTION: Why are clouds predominantly over mountain ranges, rather than above adjoining valleys? [Any moist air that blows against the mountains is swept upward, and then it's the three Cs!]

CHECK QUESTION: Why are clouds so prevalent over islands—even those without mountains to provide updrafts? [When exposed to sunshine, land warms more than water (recall water's high specific heat capacity in Chapters 6 and 17). So moist air blowing over the relatively warm land is heated. When it warms it expands and becomes buoyant and rises. Then it's the three Cs!]

(Hey, three CHECK QUESTIONS IN A ROW — by now you've likely noticed that some of your most successful lectures occur when you pose intriguing questions instead of professing! Most of the questions you pose pop up spontaneously, and those appearing here are merely samples.)

DEMONSTRATION: If you haven't done so previously, show the very dramatic demo of condensation as shown on page 174 in the textbook — the aluminum can collapse.

Evaporation Change of phase was treated earlier in Chapters 6 and 17. Here we consider the effects of phase changes in the atmosphere. Phase change infers a corresponding energy change. Interesting examples are:

• Cooling produced by an air conditioner
• Warming produced by a heat pump (an air conditioner "turned backward")
• Spraying of crops when frost threatens
• Freeze-dried products (including coffee)

CHECK QUESTION: Is evaporation greater over warm water or cold water? [Evaporation is greater above warm water, for greater molecular motion pops more of them from the water. Thus evaporation is greater over oceans in warm regions (warm air holds more moisture than cool air) than over oceans in cold polar regions (which is also one reason why there is little snowfall in the polar regions).

It is interesting to note that raindrops evaporate as they fall toward the Earth's surface, so they need to be relatively large in order to reach the Earth's surface. If they are not large enough, they evaporate in the atmosphere forming *virga* (streams seen under clouds).

There are two interesting effects of energy transfer in rainfall. The key concept is that energy is absorbed by something that changes phase from solid to liquid to gas, and energy is released by something that changes the other way; from gas to liquid to solid. Consider water vapor condensing to form rain drops. Energy is released by the H_2O (discussed before the suggested lecture presentation), tending to warm the air. But when rain falls, considerable evaporation occurs. If drops evaporate entirely on the way down, then no net energy transfer occurs. When rainfall does reach the ground, which wins, cooling or warming? Pose this as a check question. [For rain that reaches the ground, the net effect is warming — until it again evaporates. Interesting material!]

Conclude Earth Science with your best shots on *storms* — thunderstorms, tornadoes, hurricanes — the works!

146

28
The Solar System

Consider writing this on the board when you begin your study of astronomy:

"Man must rise above the Earth, to the top of the atmosphere, and beyond; for only then will he fully understand the world in which he lives."

Socrates

This is the time to bring your class to a planetarium, if possible. Or give a slide show and invite your colleagues in astronomy to give an illustrated guest lecture with his or her best slides. If you have one or two portable telescopes and the time in the evening, you might consider a class "star party" and discuss the universe out-of-doors. Some instructors do this with telescopes, hot dogs, and soft drinks.

An excellent 10-minute film that makes an excellent tie from the solar system, galaxies, and the universe, discussed briefly in the preceding chapter, to the atom — comparing sizes as powers of ten is *Powers of Ten*, by Charles and Ray Eames, and narrated by Philip Morrison. (Pyramid Films, 1978).

Britannica's *Halley: A Comet Returns* (30 min), is a great film on comets, which change so much each time they sweep the Sun. Interesting stories of the alleged effects of comets on people are presented. Another good film about solar system members is NASA's *Mars: The Viking Mission* (25 min), which depicts the spectacular Martian landscape and some of the techniques used by NASA to explore the solar system.

A great computer program that among many things traces the paths of planets in the solar system is *Dance of the Planets*, by ARC Incorporated, P.O. Box 1995, Loveland, Colorado, 80539 (1-800-759-1642).

There is a practice page on eclipses in the **Practicing Physical Science** book.

There is one activity and one experiment in the **Laboratory Manual** for this chapter. The activity is ellipse construction via pencil, string, and pins — no big deal. But the experiment is a dandy — measuring the diameter of the Sun by measuring the diameter of Sunballs, the images of the Sun cast by a pinhole illuminated by the Sun. The idea is at the beginning of the book, in the Prologue. Its execution is here, near the end of the book. Go for it, it's one of my favorites!

SUGGESTED LECTURE PRESENTATION

Begin by challenging your class to give convincing information to support the notion that the world is not flat, but round. Students "know" the Earth is round and in motion around the Sun, but how many are prepared to defend these beliefs? Their belief is usually based on faith in a teacher, in a book, in an astronomer, or in programs they have watched on TV — but rarely upon evidence. Interestingly, there is much evidence that the Earth is flat, and not in motion at all!

What is the direct evidence for a round Earth? Does it appear round when you drive across the country? Does it appear round from a high-flying plane? And how does one know whether or not pictures taken from space are authentic? How does one know whether or not the space ventures by astronauts were not "Hollywood?"

The Moon Don't be disheartened if you find that there are students in your class who don't know that the Moon can be seen in the daytime. Suggest they look for it during the daytime near the first or third quarter. Ask on which side of the Sun should they look for the Moon at these times. Be sure all your students make observations of the Moon for several weeks. Observations night after night will show that at the same time each evening the Moon is farther to the east among the stars.

> CHECK QUESTION: Often when viewing the crescent of the Moon, the shadowed part is not completely dark, but is quite visible. Why? [Earthshine! The dark face of the Moon is basking in earthshine, the reflection of which we see as the dark part of the Moon in the Sun's shade.]

The gravity lock of the Moon on the Earth such that one side always faces us may need further explanation, for the explanation of Figure 28.5 cites two concepts not covered earlier in the text: torque and center of mass. The center of mass of the Moon is in its geometric center (assuming symmetrical structure). The center of gravity, with respect to the Earth, is displaced toward the Earth from its center of mass. This is because the nearer side of the Moon interacts with more force than the far part — it "weighs" more. So like a compass, any off-axis orientation with the force field results in a torque that aligns it.

Cratering is a notable feature of the lunar surface. Point out that the craters are often many times larger than the meteorites that caused them. A unit of energy from a munitions explosion causes the same size crater as the same unit of kinetic energy from a falling object. If you toss a baseball into mud, you'll produce crater shapes not unlike those seen on the Moon. Different impact speeds will produce different shaped craters, with depth-to-width ratios much the same as those produced by meteorites. Of course, the many craters made on the Earth when the Moon's were occurring have now been covered.

Particularly fascinating is the discovery of water on the Moon. From Clementine 1994 data and two years of careful analysis, ice has been discovered on the Moon's poles. In January 1998, Lunar Prospector III found more and stronger evidence for ice at the lunar poles. This is good news for future travelers who won't have to bring a supply of drinking water when they visit our nearest celestial neighbor.

Color of the Moon The redness of the eclipsed Moon is an interesting extension of the redness of Sunsets. Understandably, the red is most predominant near the edge of the Earth's shadow, and in the center may be completely dark. Hence we say the eclipsed Moon sometimes appears red. In discussing Moon color, the question often arises about the "Blue Moon. The term "Blue Moon," for what it's worth, is the name given to the second full Moon that appears in a calendar month. Since the lunar cycle is 29.5 days and the average month is 30 days, there will be times when the 29.5-day cycle fits within a calendar month. This happens every 2.7 years, on the average. So the blue Moon doesn't have to do with physics or astronomy. However, the term "Blue Moon" also refers to the different phenomenon that does involve physics: That's when the Moon's disk appears bluish, which occurs when the Earth's atmosphere contains particles 0.8 to 1.8 microns in diameter, slightly larger than the wavelength of visible light. Such particles, produced by forest fires or volcanoes, scatter red light while allowing the blue through (just the opposite of red getting through blue scattering to produce red Sunsets).

Phases of the Moon Be prepared to find out (if you haven't already) that many students in your class think the crescent Moon is so because of the Earth's shadow on it. A survey before the chapter is covered may reveal this. (If the survey shows the same students believing this after you have covered the chapter, then...egad!)

> DEMONSTRATION: Play flashlight tag. Suspend a large ball above your lecture table, turn out the lights, and illuminate the ball with a flashlight from different parts of the room. Phases of the ball are easily seen, and the phases of the Moon forever understood

by those who disappointed you on your survey. Learning has occurred! Or toss Styrofoam balls, about 6 cm in diameter or larger, to your class. Let them move the balls around their heads to see the changing phases as you shine the light on them.

Sunspots are dark because they are cooler than the surrounding regions. Their darkness has to do with the contrast of hotter regions. If you put a 7.5-watt light bulb and a 100-watt lightbulb at the ends of your lecture table, they both look rather bright. Bring them together, and the 7.5-watt bulb looks darker when held in front of the brighter 100-watt bulb. (In a similar way, the black you see on a TV screen is actually no blacker than the "gray" face when not lit up. It looks black in contrast to the brightness of the illuminated part.)

The Planets People who talk about visiting Mars usually have no idea of how far away it is. They may remember that it is supposed to take two years to reach it, but how far away is it? It is not a short hop away on a spaceship. Scaling of the solar system is a worthwhile activity.

A magnetometer on the spacecraft Surveyor detected in Sept 97 a weak magnetic field about Mars, one eight-hundreth that of Earth's surface. Perhaps the field was stronger in the past, in which case it would have played a role in shielding living material from the solar wind and cosmic rays.

Uranus is barely perceptible to the naked eye in a clean dark sky. In ancient times, without photographic film and time exposures that betray movement in the skies, Uranus went unnoticed as a planet. Nobody noticed that it wandered.

Scale of the Solar System Consider scaling the solar system down to the size of a football field, where the Sun is on the goal line and Earth on the 2-yard line (leaving some room for Mercury and Venus). Mercury would then be on the 2-foot line, and Venus on the 4-foot line. Beyond Earth, Mars would be on the 3- yard line, Jupiter on the 10-yard line, Saturn on the 20-yard line, Uranus on the 40-yard line, Neptune on the 60-yard line, and Pluto on the 80-yard line. On this scale, the nearest star would be 1000 miles away!

ACTIVITY: Integrate planetary sizes and distances into the student's experience by scaling 1 foot = one million miles. Then the Sun is close to the size of a basketball. The planets are small objects that can be held in the hand. Calculate the sizes and distances of one or two planets with your students, and let them calculate others. The Earth, for ex-

ample, would be 93 feet away from the basketball, easy to set off as paces. Ask for a volunteer for each of the other planets. Whoever volunteers for Pluto (average distance some 3800 million miles) will have to pace 3800 feet away; across town!

Meteorites How have scientists established the age of the Earth as 4.5 billion years? By rock samples? No, any rocks that existed in early Earth have long ago subducted to magma and to become part of the rock cycle (Chapter 22). We date the Earth not by Earth rocks, but by dating meteors, which presumably coalesced at the same time as the Earth. Geologists love meteors!

Meteor showers dump an estimated 360 to 6000 tons of cosmic dust on the Earth each year. Annual meteor showers occur when the Earth passes through streams of material formed from the outgassing of a comet's nucleus as it nears perihelion. Micrometeorites do not incandesce like larger meteorites because their large surfaces compared to their masses allows them to radiate heat very rapidly. So they pass through the atmosphere relatively unchanged. It turns out the Earth appears to be under a constant rain of micrometeorites. Collecting them can be done by the sticky side of ordinary Scotch tape upon a rooftop exposed to the clear sky. Investigation of the tape after several hours of exposure can be done by microscope, where the tape is sandwiched between microscope slides. At a magnification of about 100, airborne dust, pollen, and various types of industrial pollution are evident on the tape. Micrometeorites appear as metallic nickel-iron spheres. You'll need to be proficient at identifying nickel-iron compounds to increase the likelihood of extraterrestrial origin. More of these should be found, of course, during times of meteor showers. To learn more about this technique, see the article *Chasing Meteors with a Microscope* in the Junior College Science Teacher, May 1993.

Comets The text states that the orbits of comets extend far beyond the orbit of Pluto. This is true for most comets, but not the shorter periodic comets like Halley's (76 years), which orbits the Sun well within the solar system. The majority of comets discovered each year are the long-period comets that take 100,000 to 1 million years to complete a solar orbit. Most of their times are beyond the orbit of Pluto, at distances of 40,000 to 50,000 AU from the Sun — about one-fifth the way to the nearest star. The textbook does not treat the Oort cloud, the proposed reservoir of cometary nuclei.

We anxiously await the findings of the JPL team that includes our friend Tenny, in their quest to link up with Comet Tempel 1.

29

The Stars

This chapter is a brief overview of the life of stars, galaxies, with some flavor of black holes and brief mention of quasars — standard stuff. Although most all scientists accept astronomy and condemn astrology, it is embarrassing to note that astronomy attracts more adherents than astronomy — in this so called rational age of human history. Check the horoscope section of your newspaper. Incredible!

Whereas astronomy is predominantly an observational science that relies on complex techniques and time sequences that are difficult for a lecture or textbook to impart, consider class time viewing the better suited depictions available on select films, TV tapes, and computer programs. Consider the following:

NASA's films "Flight of Apollo 11" (29 min), which shows the dynamics of the solar system, star systems, and galaxies. NASA's "Space Shuttle: A Remarkable Flying Machine" (31 min) illustrate Kepler's and Newton's laws.

TV tape from the Nova series "Lives of the Stars" (60 min) presents stellar evolution in super compressed time, with characteristics of the Sun, white dwarfs, neutron stars, and black holes.

A great little book with many teaching tips is *West's Great Ideas for Teaching Astronomy*, by West Publishing Company, 1989. Some of the ideas in the suggested lecture below come from this dandy book.

Martin Gardner addresses what may perk up in your class — the public fascination with *fads and fallacies in the name of science*, in his book of the same name. Exposing hoaxes perpetrated by pranksters, publicity seekers, and psychotics is made difficult by what Gardner calls, semi-lies. An observer sees a balloon but is convinced it is a saucer. Others are skeptical and this irritates him. So to convince them, he adds details, or exaggerates what he has seen. He may do this without being aware of it, and later recall the episode not as he saw it, but as he "told it". This well-known human failing is likely involved in much of the pseudo science that proliferates.

A practice sheet on stellar parallax is in the **Practice Book**.

Two activities, *Reckoning Latitude* and *Tracking Mars* are in the **Laboratory Manual**. *Tracking Mars* is a dandy, where students plot the orbit of Mars from measurements of the sky in Tycho Brahe's time. Data of the position of Mars begins with the Julian calendar and continues with the Gregorian calendar, which is in current use. Ask your students what happened between October 5 and October 14 in 1582; the answer is nothing! These dates simply didn't exist when the change was made from the Julian to Gregorian calendars!

This is where you take your students to a planetarium, and where you show slides.

SUGGESTED LECTURE PRESENTATION

Begin by relating the statement by the philosopher Auguste Compte more than a hundred years ago; that humankind, despite advances in science, would never know much about the distant stars — certainly not their chemical compositions. Considering the information available to Compte and his contemporaries at that time, the conjecture was reasonable, for the great distance of the stars seemed certainly to put information about them out of reach. What Compte didn't realize, however, is that the light emitted by those stars, quite within reach, contained much information about their makeup. Starlight betrays the elements that emit it, as the soon-to-come science of spectroscopy showed. That we know so much about stars is incredible — and the present time is the golden age for astronomers, who are presently finding more about them each decade than was ever known previously. Gone are the eyepieces on telescopes that once viewed the visible part of the spectrum. In their places are receptors for the nonvisible parts of the spectrum — from radio waves to X rays. The field of astronomy is aburst with excitement these days. It goes far beyond describing how the sky looks by explaining how it got to be as it is.

Constellations Discuss the constellations, and the big dipper in particular, and Polaris. Every student should be able to locate Polaris in the night sky. Explain why Polaris is directly overhead only at the pole, and how and why it is seen lower in the sky the closer one gets to the equator (the subject matter of the activity *Reckoning Latitude* in the Lab Manual).

CHECK QUESTION: Polaris is stationary above the Earth's north pole and is a guide to all in the northern hemisphere. Why are there no "stationary stars" above [your city]?

Ask your class to pretend they are on a merry-go-round in motion, viewing lamps on the stationary ceiling overhead. Further suppose they took time exposure photographs of the lamps above. What would the photos look like?

Confronting Astrology To confront astrology, better than lecturing in an authoritarian manner, do as Stephen Pompea of the University of Arizona does and try the following experiment: Ask students NOT to consult a horoscope for three days. During this period, students keep a daily diary of their feelings and moods. They may also make note of how their financial and love lives are going, since this is a major aspect of horoscopic predictions. In class, distribute the 36 horoscopes of the three-day period, but with the Sun signs removed and the order scrambled. Students must then find the three that best describe their days. Then a comparison between their answers and the "correct" horoscopes is made to see if the predictive power of astrology is significant.

Interestingly enough, due to precession of the Earth about its axis, with a period of 26,000 years, the Sun is about one and a half astrological signs off those of 3000 years ago, when astrology was born. During the last 3000 years the Earth has wobbled about 1.5 constellations along the zodiac.

Astrology was an important stepping stone to science. It went beyond physical speculations and certainly emphasized observation, progressed to processes of experimentation, and to logical reasoning, which are now cornerstones of science. Interestingly, science advanced faster in western rather than eastern cultures, largely because of the different social and political climates. While early Greeks in an era of experimental democracy and free thinking were questioning their speculations about the world about them, their counterparts in eastern parts of the world were largely occupied in absorbing the knowledge of their forebears. Absorbing this knowledge was the key to personal success. So the progress in science in regions like China were without the period of questioning that accelerated the scientific advances of Europe and Euroasia.

Stellar Distances — Parallax How do we know the distances to stars? The only direct way is by parallax, which you'll want to explain. Begin by having students hold a finger at arm's length in front of their faces and looking with one eye at the position of the finger with respect to the background. Then have them switch eyes. Parallax! The parallax is easily seen because the finger is relatively close to the eye. The parallax of more distant objects is more difficult to see, as can be seen by judging the distance of something a few meters distant, and then something many meters distant. Cite the importance of the distance between one's eyes — the baseline. At any given moment, the largest baseline for finding parallax among the stars is the Earth's diameter. Stars viewed from one side of the Earth can be compared to the same stars viewed at the opposite side of the Earth. A still larger baseline that takes a 6-month interval to utilize is the diameter of the Earth's orbit about the Sun. Have your students do the practice sheet on parallax at this point.

Interestingly, the most distant objects we can detect are about 20-30 billion light years away.

Ever wonder why a chicken or pigeon bobs its head while it walks? Ronald Stoner of Bowling Green University ties the chicken walk to stellar parallax. Here's how: While the chicken's body moves forward, the head remains momentarily fixed as if anchored in space. This is because a chicken's eyes are on the sides of its head, not suited for parallax viewing. Vision for the chicken is monocular. So the chicken gauges distances to objects in its sight by the shifts of the objects against the background with succeeding steps. Images on the retina of the chicken are compared when the head moves through a standard difference (one step). Astronomers likewise measure distances to the stars by noting shifts of images of stars on photographic plates when the telescope moves though a standard difference (one half Earth orbit around the Sun). So just as a chicken compares the image of something in the foreground with the background between steps, an astronomer does much the same with foreground and background stars between 6-month intervals.

Stellar Masses — Binary Stars Binary stars offer the astronomer the only direct means of determining the mass of a star (Box in text). About half the stars in the sky are binaries. Do as Gene Maynard of Radford University does and attach a pair of Styrofoam balls of different diameters (and masses) with plastic sticks to model binary star systems. Balance on a finger to illustrate the center of mass, and the center about which the stars circle each other. The relative sizes of orbit about the center of mass is easily seen to relate to the relative masses.

Stellar Evolution Just as a child cannot see the aging of friends from babies to adults, the astronomer cannot see stellar evolution directly. But the child can see the various ages of other children, adults, and elderly people, even though seeing the transition for any one person is not possible. The direction of time is evident. Just as a baby in no way resembles its form as an elderly person, changes in a star throughout its lifetime are similar. Young stars do not resemble mature stars, and in no way resemble dead stars.

H-R Diagram Compare the H-R diagram to a similar diagram of human heights versus weights for a group of people. There will be a "main sequence" where most individuals will be. Those above the line might be classified as giants; those below as dwarfs. Although we can't see these giants and dwarfs directly, we can deduce some of their characteristics indirectly. Likewise with stars in the H-R diagram.

Stardust Chris Impey at the University of Arizona points out that the composition of humans is quite different from the composition of the universe as a whole. Of every 10,000 atoms in the Sun, 7400 are H, 2440 are He, only 3 are C, 2 are N, 5 are O, and 150 all other elements. But of the same 10,000 atoms in Melissa's body (Figure 29.22), or anyone's body, 6500 are H, 2 are He, 2000 are C, 500 are N, 900 are O, and 100 all other elements. Our bodies are cinders formed in the residue of stellar collapses in a universe that is overwhelmingly H and He. It is important to stress that the cinders came from previous generations of stars — before the Sun formed. (Melissa is the daughter of good friends, Dennis and Tai McNelis, of Somerville, MA.)

Black Holes When you toss garbage into a garbage disposal without putting the lid on, much material goes into the drain but some pieces come flying out considerably faster than they went in. Likewise for matter that encounters a black hole. Black holes, named by physicist John Archibald Wheeler, are collapsed stars that eat their own light. Contrary to science fiction stories, they're non-aggressive in that they don't reach out and swallow innocents at a distance.

Spiral Galaxies Invite your students to make their own model of a spiral galaxy the next time they have a cup of coffee, as Stephen Pompea at the University of Arizona does with his students. Simply stir the coffee before adding a little cream — the cream will take a shape not unlike a spiral galaxy. Fluid flow in a cup of coffee approximates the flow on a much larger scale, just as wind tunnel tests on tiny airplanes predict the behavior of larger ones in larger air flows. (There is more on this in P. Stevens' book, *Patterns in Nature*.)

Space is stretching out, carrying the galaxies with it. Early waves of light have been stretched out to now be microwaves.

30

Relativity and the Universe

This concluding chapter begins with cosmology, is concerned mainly with special and general relativity, and ends on a cosmological theme. The ideas of relativity are perhaps the most exciting in the book — and also the most difficult to comprehend. Regardless of how clearly and logically this material is presented, students will find that they do not "understand" it in a manner that satisfies them. This is understandable for so brief an exposure to a part of reality untouched by conscious experience. The intention of this chapter is to develop enough insight into relativity to stimulate further student interest and inquiry.

Time is one of those concepts we are all familiar with yet are hard pressed to define. A simple yet less than satisfying way to look at it is like our definition of space; that which we measure with a measuring stick — and time; that which we measure with a clock. Or has been quipped, time is nature's way of seeing to it that everything doesn't happen all at once!

Relativistic momentum, rather than relativistic mass, is treated in this edition. The previous edition, and some physics textbooks, speak of *relativistic mass*, given by the equation $m = m_0 / \sqrt{1 - (v^2/c^2)}$. This idea is now losing favor to the somewhat more complex idea of relativistic momentum. One problem with the idea of increased mass is that mass is a scalar: it has no direction. When particles are accelerated to high speeds, their increase in mass is directional. Increase occurs in the direction of motion in a manner similar to the way that length contraction occurs only in the direction of motion. Moving mass is, after all, momentum. So it is more appropriate to speak of increases in momentum rather than mass. Either treatment of relativistic mass or relativistic momentum, however, leads to the same description of rapidly moving objects in accord with observations.

This is the longest chapter in the book, too long to include material that has been relegated to the Practice Book — "The Twin Trip." Be sure your students try this activity, which completely bypasses the equations for time dilation and the relativistic Doppler effect. The reciprocity of relativistic Doppler frequencies for approach and recession stems only from Einstein's 1st and 2nd postulates and is established without the use of a single mathematical formula. This is detailed in the 4-step classroom presentation in the following suggested lecture. [This reciprocal relationship does not hold for sound, where the "moving" frame is not equivalent to the "rest" (relative to air) frame. If the ratio of frequency received to frequency sent for hearing in the rest frame is 2, the ratio for hearing in the moving frame is 3/2 (clearly not 2!). For sound, the speed as well as the frequency depends on the motion of the receiver.] From this and the simple flash-counting sequence, time dilation follows without the use of any mathematical formulas. The results of the twin-trip flash sequence agree with Einstein's time dilation equation. So this treatment is completely independent of the time dilation equation and the relativistic Doppler equation! (Who says that good physics can't be presented without high-powered math?)

If your class is in a more mathematical mood, you may wish to show an alternative approach to The Twin Trip and consider straightforward time dilation plus corrections for the changing positions of the emitting or receiving body between flashes. Instead of bypassing the time dilation equation, use it to show that at 0.6c, 6-minute flash intervals in the emitting frame compute to be 7 1/2-minute flash intervals in the receiving frame. The flashes would *appear* at 7 1/2-minute intervals if the ship were moving crosswise, neither approaching or receding, such that each flash travels essentially the same distance to the receiver. In our case the ship doesn't travel crosswise, but recedes from and then approaches the receiver — so corrections must be made in the time interval due to the extra distance the light travels when the spaceship is receding and the lesser distance the light travels when the ship is approaching. This turns out to be 4 1/2 minutes;

$$\Delta t = \frac{\text{extra distance}}{c} = \frac{0.6c \times 7\,1/2\,\text{min}}{c} = 4\,1/2\,\text{min}$$

So when receding, the flashes are seen at 7 1/2 + 4 1/2 = 12-min intervals; when approaching, the flashes are seen at 7 1/2 - 4 1/2 = 3-min intervals. The results of this method are the same as those of the 4-step conceptual presentation in the following suggested lecture.

Our 12-minute animated film, *Relativistic Time Dilation*, amplifies the section on The Twin Trip. It is part of the video tape of relativity in Hewitt's *Conceptual Physics Alive!* series. Contact an Addison Wesley Longman rep for availability.

The three most important theories of physics in the 20th century are the special theory of relativity (1905), the general theory of relativity (1915), and the theory of quantum mechanics (1926). The first and third theories have been focal points of interest and research since their inceptions, yet the second, general relativity, has been largely ignored by physicists — until recently. New interest stems from many of the new astronomical phenomena discovered in recent years — pulsars, quasars, black holes, and compact x-ray sources, all of which have indicated the existence of very strong gravitational fields that could be described only by general relativity. The move is now on to a quantum theory of gravitation that will agree with general relativity for macroscopic objects.

One important point to make is that relativity doesn't mean that everything is relative, but rather that no matter how you view a situation, the physical outcome is the same. There is a general misconception about this. Point out that

in special and general relativity that fundamental truths of nature look the *same* from every point of view — not different from different points of view!

We measure velocities with rods and clocks; rods for space, and clocks for time. In our local environment, rods and clocks are no different when in different locations. In a larger environment in accord with general relativity, however, we find that space and time are "warped". Rods and clocks at appreciably different distances from the center of the Earth are affected differently. Accordingly, gravitation can be seen as the effects of a curved space-time such that the motion of objects subject to what we call the gravitational force is simply the result of objects moving freely through curved space-time.

John Mallinckrodt of Claremont College asks his class the following question: If relative *motion* can alter the measurements made by rods and clocks, might it also be possible for different *locations* (in space and time) to alter such measurements? Then he compares the observations of two observers at rest to each other — one just inside a window on a second floor of an apartment building, and the other on the sidewalk below. Both observers use rods and clocks to make their measurements. Consider a refrigerator accidentally pushed off the roof of the building. The first observer (by the window) uses her rods and clocks to measure the time it takes for the refrigerator to travel the short distance between the top and bottom of her window. From her measurements she infers a velocity. The second observer on the sidewalk does the same with his rods and clocks just before the frig hits the ground. They of course measure entirely different velocities. The guy on the ground measures a larger downward velocity than the woman in the window and, when they compare notes, conclude that the refrigerator was accelerating downward. John asks someone in class to play the role of Isaac Newton and explain this observation — that a *force* acted on the falling refrigerator. Quite incredible back then (and to many theoreticians now!) that the Earth somehow exerts a force on the refrigerator without even touching it! Is it any less preposterous an idea to suppose the rods and clocks used by the observers were affected differently by their differing distances from the center of the Earth? (Out of fairness to Isaac, you should point out that he himself found the idea of a gravitational force exerted through the void of space to be a particularly absurd idea.)

And here's the 21st Century. Very shortly the theories of special and general relativity, quantum mechanics, nuclear power, the theory of the Big Bang, computers, and DNA will be seen of things of the twentieth century. As the 21st Century progresses, what will power automobiles? Where will electricity come from? What will the climate be? How will wars be fought? What will happen to borders? Instructors today don't have the answers to these questions. Perhaps it is our moral duty as instructors to educate our students to orient, anticipate, decide, and to act. What they most need to learn is the process of learning itself.

An oldie but goody student reference for general relativity is *Physical Foundations of General Relativity*, by D.W. Sciami, a Doubleday Science Study Series (S-58) paperback (1969).

There are two practice exercises on special relativity in **Practice Book**. One is "The Twin Trip," a four-pager that usually is included in the various editions of the physics textbook *Conceptual Physics*. We set it aside here since Chapter 30 is already our longest chapter. The other practice page is a follow-up exercise of clocking the same trip.

Not surprisingly, there are no activities or experiments on special or general relativity in the **Laboratory Manual**.

Because of the interest in physical science that relativity generates, this chapter may be treated earlier in the course.

SUGGESTED LECTURE PRESENTATION

The Big Bang Most astroscientists subscribe to the Big Bang theory, called the "standard model." Point out that the model doesn't picture an explosion in space, like a giant firecracker going off, but rather an explosion of space itself — not at some time in the past, but at the beginning of time itself. This is heavy stuff — and intriguing stuff. The dullest lecturer has the attention of his or her class with any discussion of the beginning of the universe! The chapter begins on this theme, and ends on this theme. You're now set to discuss the natures of space and time.

Space-Time An interesting way to look at how space and time are related to the speed of light is to think of all things moving through space-time at a constant speed. When movement is maximum through space, movement in time is minimum. When movement in space is minimum, movement in time is maximum. For example, something at rest relative to us moves not at all in space; consequently it moves in time at the maximum rate of 24 hours per day. On the other hand, when something moves "at

the speed of light" (or qualified, *near* the speed of light) relative to us, it moves at its near maximum speed in space, and moves near zero in time — from our point of view, it doesn't age.

Special Relativity After discussing Einstein and a broad overview of what special relativity is and is not, point out somewhere along the line that the theory of relativity is grounded in *experiment*, and in its development it explained some very perplexing experimental facts (constancy of the speed of light, muon decay, solar energy, the nature of mass, etc.). It is not, as some people think, only the speculations of one man's way of thinking.

First Postulate The laws of physics are the same in all uniformly moving reference frames. A bee inside a fast-moving jet plane executes the same flying maneuvers regardless of the speed of the plane. If you drop a coin to the floor of the moving plane, it will fall as if the plane were at rest. Physical experiments behave the same in all uniformly moving frames. This leads, most importantly, to the development of special relativity, to the speed of light that is seen to be the same for all observers. There is no violation of common sense in this first postulate. It rules out any effect of uniform motion on any experiment, however. For any observed effect violates this postulate and the foundation of relativity.

Second Postulate Stand still and toss a piece of chalk up and down, catching it as you would when flipping a coin. Ask the class to suppose that in so doing that all measurements show the chalk to have a constant average speed. Call this constant speed c for short. That is, both they and you see only one average speed for the tossed chalk. Then proceed to walk at a fairly brisk pace across the room and again toss the chalk. State that from your frame of reference you again measure the same speed. Ask if the speed looked any different to them. They should respond that the chalk was moving faster this time (because of the horizontal component of motion). Ask them to suppose that their measurement yielded the *same* previous value. They may be a bit perplexed, which again is similar to the perplexed state of physicists at the turn of the century. On the board, write with uniformly sized letters

$$c = \frac{SPACE}{TIME}$$

This is the speed as seen by you in your frame of reference. State that from the frame of reference of the class, the space covered by the tossed chalk appeared to be greater, so write the word

SPACE in correspondingly larger letters. Underline it. State that if they see the same speed, that is, the same ratio of space to time, then such can be accounted for if the time is also measured to be greater. Then write the enlarged word TIME beneath the underline, equating it to *c*. Analogy: Just as all observers will measure the same ratio of circumference to diameter for all sizes of circles, all observers will measure the same ratio of space to time for electromagnetic waves in free space.

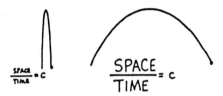

Space Travel Speculate on the idea of "century hopping," the future version of today's "jet hopping." In this scenario future space travelers may take relatively short trips of a few years or less and return in decades, or even centuries. This is, of course, pending the solution to two present problems: rocket engines and sufficient fuel supplies for prolonged voyages, and a means of shielding the radiation that would be produced by impact of interstellar matter.

The Centrifuge Follow this up with this interesting but fictitious example to show that one needn't go far in space for significant time dilation: Suppose that one could be whirled in a giant centrifuge up to relativistic speeds without physical injury. Of course one would be crushed to death in such a case, but pretend that somehow one is physically unaffected by the crushing centripetal forces (the fictitiousness of this example). Then cite how one taking a "ride" in such a centrifuge might be strapped in his seat and told to press a button on the seat when he or she wishes the ride terminated. And suppose that after being whirled about at rim speeds near the speed of light the occupant decides that 10 minutes is enough. So he or she presses the button, signaling those outside to bring the machine to a halt. After the machine is halted, those outside open the door, peer in, and ask, "Good gosh, what have you been doing in there for the past 3 weeks!" In the laboratory frame of reference, 3 weeks would have elapsed during a ten-minute interval in the rotating centrifuge. Motion in space, rather than space itself is the key factor.

Length Contraction Hold up a meter stick, horizontally, and state that if your students made accurate measurements of its length, their measurements would agree with your own. Everyone would measure it as 1 meter long.

People at the back of the room would have to compensate for its appearing smaller due to distance, but nevertheless, they would agree it is 1 meter long. But now walk across the room holding the meter stick like a spear. State that your measurements and those of your students would differ. If you were to travel at 87% the speed of light, relative to the class, they would measure the stick to be half as long, 0.5 m. At 99.5% the speed of light, they would see it as only 10 cm long. At greater speeds, it would be even shorter. At the speed of light it would contract to zero length. Write the length-contraction formula on the board:

$$L = L_0 \sqrt{1 - (v^2/c^2)}$$

State that contraction takes place only in the direction of motion. The stick moving in spear fashion appears shorter but it doesn't appear thinner.

Contraction is indicated in Figures 30.9 and 30.10. The check question on the same page about the rectangular billboard emphasizes the directional nature of length contraction.

The Mass-Energy Relationship
Write $E = mc^2$ on the board, the most celebrated equation of the twentieth century. It relates energy and mass. Every material object is composed of energy—"energy of being." This "energy of being" is appropriately called *rest energy*, which is designated by the symbol E. (Some instructors label this E_0, to distinguish it from a generalized symbol E for total energy. Since we're concerned only with rest energy here, there isn't a need for the subscript.) So the mass of something is actually the internal energy within it. This energy can be converted to other forms, light for example.

On the 4 1/2 million tons of matter that is converted to radiant energy by the sun every second: that tonnage is carried by the radiant energy through space, so when we speak of matter being "converted" to energy, we are merely converting from one form to another—from a form with one set of units perhaps, to another. Because of the mass and energy equivalence, in any reaction that takes into account the whole system, the total amount of mass + energy does not change.

Discuss the interesting idea that mass, every bit as much as energy, is delivered by the power utilities through the copper wires that run from the power plants to the consumers.

With the advent of special relativity, the two conservation laws of mass and energy meld into one — the conservation of mass/energy. For brevity, the combined conservation principle is often called simply the "conservation of energy."

From a long view, the significance of the twentieth century will be most likely seen as a major turning point with the discovery of the $E = mc^2$ relationship. It may be interesting to speculate what the defining equations of future centuries might be.

Relativistic Momentum: State that if you push an object that is free to move, it accelerates in accord with Newton's 2nd law, $a = F/m$. As it turns out, Newton originally wrote the 2nd law not in terms of acceleration, but in terms of momentum, $F = \Delta p/\Delta t$, which is equivalent to the familiar $F = ma$. Here we use the symbol p for momentum. $p = mv$. In accord with the momentum version of Newton's 2nd law, push an object that is free to move and we increase its momentum. The acceleration or the change-of-momentum version of the 2nd law give the same result. But for very high speeds, it turns out that the momentum version is more accurate. $F = \Delta p/\Delta t$ holds for all speeds, from everyday speed to speeds near the speed of light—as long as the relativistic expression of momentum is used.

Write the expression for relativistic momentum on the board:

$$p = \frac{mv}{\sqrt{1 - (v^2/c^2)}}.$$

Point out that it differs from the classical expression for momentum by the denominator $\sqrt{1 - (v^2/c^2)}$. A common interpretation is that of a relativistic mass $m = m_0/\sqrt{1 - (v^2/c^2)}$, multiplied by a velocity v.

Show how for small speeds the relativistic momentum equation reduces to the familiar mv (just as for small speeds $t = t_0$ in time dilation). Then show what happens when v approaches c. The denominator of the equation approaches zero. This means that the momentum approaches infinity! An object pushed to the speed of light would have infinite momentum and would require an infinite impulse (force × time), which is clearly impossible. Nothing material can be pushed to the speed of light. The speed of light c is the upper speed limit in the universe.

A good example of the increase of either mass or momentum for different relative speeds is the accelerated electrons and protons in high-

energy particle accelerators. In these devices speeds greater than 0.99c are attained within the first meter, and most of the energy given to the charged particles during the remaining journey goes into increasing mass or momentum, according to your point of view. The particles strike their targets with masses or momentum thousands of times greater than the physics of Newton accounts for. Interestingly enough, if you traveled along with the charged particles, you would note no such increase in the particles themselves (the v in the relativistic mass equation would be zero), but you'd measure a mass or momentum increase in the atoms of the "approaching" target (the crash is the same whether the elephant hits the mouse or the mouse hits the elephant).

Cite how such an increase must be compensated for in the design of circular accelerators such as cyclotrons, bevatrons, and the like, and how such compensation is not required for a linear accelerator (except for the bending magnets at its end).

Cars, planes, and even the fastest rockets don't approach speeds to merit relativistic considerations, but subatomic particles do. Particles are routinely pushed to speeds beyond 99% the speed of light whereupon their momenta increase thousands of times more than the classical expression mv predicts. This is evidenced when a beam of electrons directed into a magnetic field is appreciably deflected from its normal path. The greater its speed, the greater its "moving inertia" — its momentum, and the greater it resists deflection (Figure 30.11). High-energy physicists must take relativistic momentum into account when working with high-speed subatomic particles in atomic accelerators. In that arena, relativity is an everyday fact of life.

The Correspondence Principle Show your students that when small speeds are involved, the relativity formulas reduce to the everyday observation that time, length, and the masses of things do not appear any different when moving. That's because the differences are too tiny to detect.

Its important to point out that the effects of relativity don't "switch on" at some special speed, but are present for all speeds. Its simply that at everyday speeds, the effects are so small as to be negligible. The graph of Figure 29.8 illustrates this — relativistic effects become appreciable for speeds greater than about 3/4 the speed of light.

The Twin Trip (from the Conceptual Physical Science Practice Book) The "Twin Trip" nicely illustrates time dilation, and dramatizes the potential of relativity as a major factor to be reckoned with for future spacefarers. You have a choice of a short treatment of this or a longer more detailed treatment. The short treatment begins without fanfare and as a matter of fact presents the half rate of flashes seen when a ship approaches (Figure 2 in the Practice Book) and the doubled rate seen when the ship recedes (Figure 3). The fact that the half rate and doubled rate are reciprocals is not developed. For the vast majority of students this should be fine. More sophisticated students may be uneasy with this and wish to see this reciprocal relationship developed. This is the longer treatment. This longer treatment is shown by the 4 steps below. For the shorter treatment, jump ahead to paragraph 2, with the * on the facing page.

We will in effect bypass the derivation of the relativistic Doppler effect, namely,

$$f = f_o \sqrt{\frac{1 + v/c}{1 - v/c}}$$

with the following four-step conceptual presentation:

Step 1: Consider a person standing on Earth directing brief flashes of light at 3-min intervals to a distant planet at rest relative to the Earth. Some time will elapse before the first of these flashes reaches the planet, but since there is no relative motion between the sender and receiver,

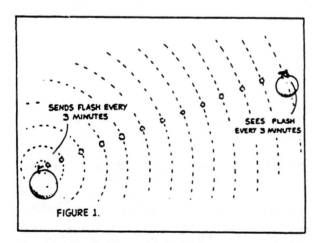

FIGURE 1.

successive flashes will be observed at the distant planet at 3-min intervals. While you are making these remarks, make a sketch on the board of Fig. 1.

Step 2: How frequently would these flashes encounter an observer in a fast-moving spaceship traveling between the Earth and the planet? Although the speed of the flashes would be measured by the spaceship to be *c*, the frequency of flashes would be greater or less than the emitting frequency depending on whether the ship were receding or approaching the light source. After supporting this idea with some examples of the Doppler effect (car horns, running into versus away from a slanting rain, etc.) make the supposition that the spaceship recedes form the light source at a speed great enough for the frequency of light flashes to decrease by half — so they are seen from the ship only half as often, at 6-min intervals. By now your chalkboard sketch looks like Fig. 2.

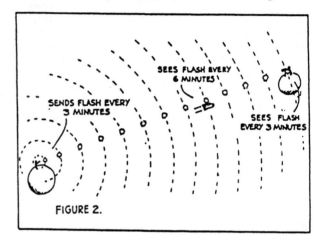

FIGURE 2.

Step 3: Suppose further that each time a flash reaches the ship, a triggering device activates a beacon on the ship that sends its own flash of light toward the distant planet. According to a clock in the spaceship then, this flash is emitted every 6 min. Since the flashes from Earth and the flashes emitted by the spaceship travel at the same speed *c*, both sets of flashes travel together, and an observer on the distant planet sees not only the Earth flashes at 3-min intervals, but the spaceship flashes at 3-min intervals as well (Fig. 3). At this point you have established that 6-min intervals on the approaching spaceship are seen as 3-min intervals on the stationary planet.

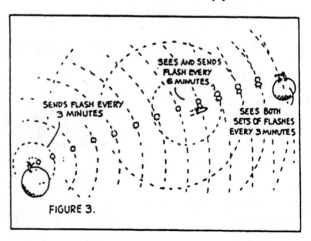

FIGURE 3.

Step 4: To establish that the 6-min flashes emitted by the spaceship are seen at 12-min intervals from the Earth, go back to your earlier supposition that 3-min intervals on Earth are seen as 6-min intervals from the frame of reference of the receding ship. Ask your class: If instead of emitting a flash every 3-min, the person on Earth emits a flash every 6-min, then how often would these flashes be seen from the receding ship? And then ask if the situation would be any different if the ship and Earth were interchanged — if the ship were at rest and emitted flashes every 6 min to a receding Earth? After a suitable response erase from your chalkboard drawing all the flashes emitted form the Earth. Replace the Earth-twin's light source with a telescope while asking how often the 6-min flashes emitted by the moving spaceship are seen from Earth. Class response should show that you have established the reciprocity of frequencies for the relativistic Doppler effect without a single equation. This is summarized in Fig. 4.

to Earth observers? [at 12 min apart]. What time is it on Earth when the 10th flash is received? [Two hours later!] The ship quickly turns around and continues homeward, again sending 10 flashes at 6-min intervals. When the 10th flash is emitted, another hour passes for the ship and its total trip time is 2 hours. But ask how often the incoming flashes occurred to Earth types. [at 3-min intervals] Ten incoming 3-min flashes take only 30 min, Earth time. So from the Earth frame of reference the spaceship took a grand total of 2 1/2 hours.

During your discussion, summarize this on the board as shown.

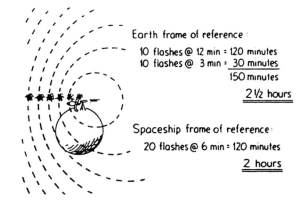

Earth frame of reference:
10 flashes @ 12 min = 120 minutes
10 flashes @ 3 min = 30 minutes
150 minutes
2 1/2 hours

Spaceship frame of reference:
20 flashes @ 6 min = 120 minutes
2 hours

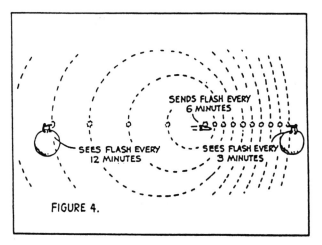

SENDS FLASH EVERY 6 MINUTES

SEES FLASH EVERY 12 MINUTES

SEES FLASH EVERY 3 MINUTES

FIGURE 4.

Note that you have employed Einstein's postulates in the last two steps, that is, the second postulate in Step 3 (constancy of the speed of light) and the first postulate in Step 4 (equivalence of the Earth and ship frames of reference).

Whether you have established this reciprocity from the Doppler equation or from the preceding four steps, you are now ready to present the twin trip and demonstrate time dilation while also presenting a resolution to the so-called twin paradox.

*With a sketch of Fig. 4 above in an upper corner of your board, make a sketch of a sender on Earth on the main part of the left side of your board. Let your chalkboard eraser be the ship which you move away from Earth (as suggested in the sketch). State the ship sends 10 flashes at 6-min intervals. At the 10th flash 1 hour has passed for the ship. Ask how these 6-min intervals appear

Depending on lecture time, switch frames of reference and repeat the similar sequence suggested by Practice Book page 133 where the flashes are emitted from Earth and viewed by the moving ship. Same results.

General Relativity Toss a ball and it curves due to gravity. Fire a high-powered rifle and the bullet also curves — the same amount in the same time, which is difficult to notice when the distance it curves is small compared to the distance from the rifle. Shine a light beam from a flashlight and it too curves (Figure 29.17). We don't notice the curve because the distance it travels is so great compared to the distance it curves. The curving of light was not evident until the eclipse photos taken during the early part of the century, when much of the world was amidst World War I. Note Figure 30.22.

Light bends because the space it traverses bends. Relate this bending of space to Figures 30.17—30.20.

Stress the importance of the local effects of relativity, both special and general, as always happening to "the other guy." There are no differences in our perception of time, distances, mass, or gravity in our own frame of reference.

Our Expanding Universe The Universe is like a giant refrigerator, forever cooling itself by its continued expansion. We are today surrounded by the embers of the big bang, the ash that remains after of billions of years of expansion and cooling. The heat of the big bang survives today as an afterglow of 2.7 K radiation that permeates the universe. In addition the light chemical elements are the product of nuclear ractions that took place during the first few minutes — the condensation of the primordial soup.

Scientists today know more about conditions of the universe 1 second after the big bang, than they do about predicting local weather? Why? Because the early universe is much simpler than the weather!

While big-bang necleosynthesis is responsible fo only a small fraction of the chemical elelments, it is nonetheless the origin of more than 98% of the known matter in the cosmos. Only 3 elements were produced in the big bang — H, He, and Li. The cosmic inventory also included electrons and their antiparticles with a thick soup of neutrinoes and antineutrinos. For every 8 photos there were 6 electrons, 6 positorons, 9 neutrinos, and 9 antineutrios. one electron for each proton, so the mix was electrically neutral — all in thermal equilibrium. (Read Guth's *The Inflationary Universe* for more on this.)

At least 90% of the matter in the universe is dark; invisible, and can be tetected only by its gravitational pull on visible matter. The dark matter cannot be composed of protons and neutrons. How interesting that most of the material that makes up the universe is not present in our periodic table of the elements!

Students are always fascinated with discussion of the possible oscillating mode of the universe. You can get class interest into high gear with speculations as to the possibility of past and future cycles. After discussion, you can end your class on a high note by doing the following: State that you wish to represent a single cycle with the positions of the chalk you are holding in your hand above the lecture table. Place the chalk on the table and let that represent the time of the primordial explosion. Then as if the chalk were projected upward, raise the chalk to a point just above your head and state that this position represents the point where the universe momentarily stops before beginning its inward collapse — then move your hand slowly down, speeding up and back to its starting point — the completion of one cycle. Then hold the chalk a foot or so above the table, to a point corresponding to where we are today — a point representing about 15 to 20 billion years from the beginning of the cycle. Holding the chalk steady, and purposefully, ask where the chalk should be positioned to represent the dawning of civilization. Then move the chalk very intently to a position less than a quarter of an inch below the present point. State that that's where we were, and this is where we are, as you move the chalk back to the present position. Still holding it there, ask for a speculation of where humankind will be and what the world will be like when we move to ... and then raise the chalk upward about a quarter of an inch. That point, of course, represents a time on Earth that we can't begin to comprehend. It is conceivable that by then we will have evolved to beings with so powerful an intelligence as to be completely beyond present human imagining — to a point that by today's standards would be deemed God-like.

The continued evolution of humankind holds much promise.

1   Motion

Answers to Exercises

1. False. Charlie may drive his car around the block at constant speed, but not at constant velocity, because he must change his direction at the corners.

2. Your fine for speeding is based on your instantaneous speed; the speed registered on a speedometer or a radar gun.

3. Yes, velocity and acceleration need not be in the same direction. A car moving north that slows down, for example, accelerates toward the south.

4. Yes, again, velocity and acceleration need not be in the same direction. A ball tossed upward, for example, reverses its direction at its highest point while its acceleration g remains constant (this idea will be explained further in Chapter 4). Note that if a ball had zero acceleration at a point where its speed is zero, its speed would *remain* zero. It would sit still at the top of its trajectory!

5. You would not have to lean to compensate for uniform motion. You would lean only to compensate for *changes* in motion — for accelerated motion. If the car is moving with constant acceleration, velocity would be changing constantly and you would lean into the direction of the acceleration. If the car gains in speed, you'd lean forward; if braking, you'd lean backward; if rounding a curve, you'd lean into the curve. Once this leaning posture is assumed, however, no further adjustment would be necessary as long as the acceleration doesn't change.

6. Carol is correct. Harry is describing speed. Acceleration is the time rate of change in speed — "how fast you get fast," as Carol asserts.

7. Only on hill B does the acceleration decrease with time, for the hill becomes less steep as motion progresses. When the hill levels off, acceleration will be zero. On hill A, acceleration is constant. On hill C, acceleration increases as the hill becomes steeper.

8. The streaks are slanted because they are the resultant of the vertical motion of the down-falling rain and the horizontal motion of the car window. An angle of 45° tells us that both components are equal, which means the car travels at the speed of the falling rain. (Because of air resistance, raindrops normally have a constant speed by the time they reach the ground.)

9. Ground speed = $\sqrt{120^2 + 90^2} = \sqrt{22500} = 150$ km/h.

10. The acceleration is zero, for no change in velocity occurs. Whenever the change in velocity is zero, the acceleration is zero. If the velocity is "steady," "constant," or "uniform," the change in velocity is zero. Remember the definition of acceleration!

11. The acceleration of free fall at the end of the 5th, 10th, or any number of seconds will be g. Its *velocity* has different values at different times, but since it is free from the effects of air resistance, its *acceleration* remains a constant g.

12.

Time (*in seconds*)	Velocity (*in meters/second*)	Distance (*in meters*)
0	0	0
1	10	5
2	20	20
3	30	45
4	40	80
5	50	125
6	60	180
7	70	245
8	80	320
9	90	405
10	100	500

13. Since acceleration = 10 m/s^2, speed would increase 10 m/s each second. (See Table 1.2, page 22.) (Using 9.8 m/s^2 changes these values by 2%.)

14. Distances would be successively larger and larger since the average speed each second is larger. (See Table 1.3, page 24.)

15. Whether up or down, the rate of change of speed with respect to time is 10 m/s^2 (or 9.8 m/s^2), so each second while going up the speed decreases by 10 m/s (or 9.8 m/s). Coming down, the speed increases 10 m/s (or 9.8 m/s) each second. So when air resistance can be neglected, the time going up equals the time coming down (like running movie film backward.)

16. Both will strike the ground below at the same speed. That's because the ball thrown upward will have the same initial speed when it returns to its starting position — the same as the ball thrown downward.

17. If air resistance is not a factor, its acceleration is the same 9.8 m/s^2 regardless of its initial velocity. Thrown downward, its velocity will be greater, but not its acceleration.

18. Its acceleration would actually be less if the air resistance it encounters at high speed retards its motion. (We will treat this concept in detail in Chapter 2.)

19. The ball on B finishes first, for its average speed along the lower part as well as the down and up slopes is greater than the average speed of the ball along track A.

20. (a) Yes; (b) Yes; (c) Yes for its speed at the top is the same as the speed of ball A, and its speed at the bottom is greater still—so the average speed of the ball on the slopes is greater than the speed of ball A along the straight-away. (d) Since ball B moves faster down and up the slopes, and faster along the lower straight-away, it has the greater average speed. (If you chose "both the same" as your original answer to Exercise 19, change it to "Ball B." Although both balls end up with the same speed as they leave the ramps, their *average* speeds are different!)

Chapter 1 Problem Solutions

1. From $v = \frac{d}{t}$, $t = \frac{d}{v}$. We convert 3 m to 3000 mm, and t = $\frac{3000 \text{ mm}}{1.5 \text{ mm/year}}$ = 2000 years.

2. From $d = 1/2\ gt^2 = 5\ t^2$, $t = \sqrt{d/5} = \sqrt{(0.6)/5} = 0.35$ s. Double for a hang time of 0.7 s.

3. $a = \frac{change\ in\ velocity}{time\ interval} = \frac{-100 \text{ km/h}}{10s} = -10$ km/h·s. (The vehicle decelerates at 10 km/h·s.)

4. Since it starts going up at 30 m/s and loses 10 m/s each second, its time going up is 3 seconds. Its time returning is also 3 seconds, so it's in the air for a total of 6 seconds. Distance up (or down) is $1/2\ gt^2 = 5 \times 3^2 = 45$ m. Or from $d = vt$, where average velocity is $(30 + 0)/2 = 15$ m/s, and time is 3 seconds, we also get $d = 15$ m/s $\times$ 3 s = 45 m.

5. (a) The velocity of the ball at the top of its vertical trajectory is instantaneously zero.
   (b) One second before reaching its top, its velocity is 10 m/s.
   (c) The amount of change in velocity is 10 m/s during this 1-second interval (or any other 1-second interval).
   (d) One second after reaching its top its velocity is -10 m/s — equal in magnitude but oppositely directed to its value 1 second before reaching the top.
   (e) The amount of change in velocity during this (or any) 1-second interval is 10 m/s.
   (f) In 2 seconds, the amount of change in velocity is 20 m/s.
   (g) The acceleration of the ball is 10 m/s^2 before reaching the top, when reaching the top, and after reaching the top. In all cases acceleration is downward, toward the Earth.

6. Using $g = 10$ m/s^2, we see that $v = gt = (10$ m/s$^2)(10$ s$) = 100$ m/s;
$$v = \frac{(v_{beginning} + v_{final})}{2} = \frac{(0 + 100)}{2} = 50 \text{ m/s, downward.}$$
We can get "how far" from either $d = vt = (50$ m/s$)(10$ s$) = 500$ m,
or equivalently, $d = 1/2 \, gt^2 = 5 \, (10)^2 = 500$ m.
(Physics is nice...we get the same distance using either formula!)

7. $v = gt = (10$ m/s$^2)(8$ s$) = 80$ m/s.
The average speed of fall is 40 m/s, so $d = vt = (40$ m/s$)(8$ s$) = 320$ m;
or $d = 1/2 \, gt^2 = 5 \, (8^2) = 320$ m.

8. $a = \dfrac{change \; in \; velocity}{time \; interval} = \dfrac{[50 \text{m/s} - 0]}{10\text{s}} = 5 \text{ m/s}^2.$

9. How fast: at $a = 20$ m/s^2, $v = at = (20$ m/s$^2)(1$ s$) = 20$ m/s.
How far: $d = 1/2 \, at^2 = 1/2 \, (20$ m/s$^2)(1$ s$)^2 = 10$ m.
Note these values make sense, for they are simply twice those if the acceleration were half as much, 10 m/s^2.

10. From $d = 1/2 \, gt^2 = 5 \, t^2$, $t = \sqrt{d/5} = \sqrt{(0.6)/5} = 0.35$ s. Double for a hang time of 0.7 s. For jumping height in feet, where g is 32 ft/s^2, a neat rule of thumb is *height jumped is equal to four times hang time squared* (d = g/2 (T/2)^2 = g/2 T^2/4 = g/8 T^2 = 32/8 T^2= 4 T^2). Or, hang time is the square root of the height jumped divided by 4. So a 2-ft jump gives a hang time of 0.7 s (the square root of 2/4 or 1/2).

2 Newton's Laws of Motion

Answers to Exercises

1. Shake the boxes. The box that offers the greater resistance to acceleration is the more massive.

2. When carrying a heavy load there is more mass involved; more tendency to remain moving. If a load in your hand is moving toward a wall, its tendency is to remain moving when contact is made. This tends to squash your hand if its between the load and the wall — an unfortunate example of Newton's lst law in action.

3. A massive cleaver is more effective in chopping vegetables because its greater mass contributes to greater tendency to keep moving as the cleaver chops through the vegetables.

4. Although the amount of air space the car occupies changes (its volume), neither the mass nor the weight of a junked car change when it is crushed.

5. Ten kilograms weighs about 100 N on the Earth (weight = mg = 10 kg ×10 m/s2 = 100 N; or using g = 9.8 m/s^2, weight = 98 N). On the Moon it would weigh 1/6 of 100 N = 16.6 N. The mass would be 10 kg everywhere.

6. Mass in kilograms is weight in pounds divided by 2.2 (if we are at the Earth's surface). One's weight in newtons is found by multiplying one's weight in pounds by 9.8/2.2. For example, if you weigh 100 pounds, your mass is 100/2.2 = 45.45 kg. Your weight in newtons is 100 (9.8/2.2) = 445.5 N. Once mass is determined, find weight by using the defining relationship, Wt = mg.

7. An object in motion tends to stay in motion, hence the discs tend to compress upon each other just as the hammer head is compressed onto the handle in Figure 2.3. This compression results in people being slightly shorter at the end of the day than in the morning. The discs tend to separate while sleeping in a prone position, so you regain your full height by morning. This is easily noticed if you find a point you can almost reach up to in the evening, and then find it is easily reached in the morning. Try it and see!

8. A stone will fall vertically when released from rest. If it is dropped from the top mast of a moving ship, the horizontal motion is not changed as the stone falls. We will see in Chapter 4 when we study projectile motion that the path of the stone will be parabolic as seen from a frame of reference at rest. If air resistance is not a factor, and the ship doesn't accelerate while the stone falls, it will move as far horizontally as the ship moves in the same time, and hit the same place it would hit if the ship were at anchor. From the frame of reference of the moving ship, the stone falls in a vertical straight line path.

9. The *net* force on the wagon, your pull plus friction, is zero.

10. When you drive at constant velocity, the zero net force on the car is the resultant of the driving force that your engine supplies against the friction drag force. You continue to apply a driving force to offset the drag force that would otherwise slow the car.

11. If an object has no acceleration, we can conclude that no *net* force acts on it. There may be any number of impressed forces, but if the object does not accelerate their resultant will be zero.

12. To see why the acceleration gains as a rocket burns its fuel, look at the equation $a = F/m$. As fuel is burned, the mass of the rocket becomes less. As m decreases, a increases! There is simply less mass to be accelerated as fuel is consumed.

13. When standing on a floor, the floor pushes upward against your feet with a force equal to that of your weight. This upward force (called the *normal force*) and your weight are oppositely directed, and since they both act on the same body, you, they cancel to produce a net force on you of zero — hence, you are not accelerated. (Be careful here, the normal force is not the reaction to your weight — your weight is the world pulling on you, and reaction to this is you pulling on the world. See the next exercise.)

14. It is greater. The Earth must push up on you with a force greater than the downward force of gravity so that there is a net upward force to accelerate you.

15. When you stop suddenly, your velocity changes rapidly, which means your acceleration of stopping is enormous. By Newton's second law, this means the force that acts on you is enormous. Application of a huge force is what hurts you.

16. The scale will read half her weight. [In this way, the net force (upward pull of left rope + upward pull of right rope - weight) = 0.]

17. In the left figure, Harry is supported by two strands of rope that share his weight (like the little girl in the previous exercise). So each strand supports only 250 N, below the breaking point. Total force up supplied by ropes equals weight acting downward, giving a net force of zero and no acceleration. In the right figure, Harry is now supported by one strand, which for Harry's well-being requires that the tension be 500 N. Since this is above the breaking point of the rope, it breaks. The net force on Harry is then only his weight, giving him a downward acceleration of g. The sudden return to zero acceleration changes his vacation plans.

18. The forces must be equal and opposite because they are the only forces acting on the person, who obviously is not accelerating. Note that the pair of forces do *not* comprise an action-reaction pair, however, for they act on the *same* body. The downward force, the man's weight, *Earth pulls down on man*; has the reaction *man pulls up on Earth*, not the floor pushing up on his feet. And the upward force of the floor on the man's feet has the reaction of man's feet on the floor, not the interaction between the man and Earth. [If you find this confusing, you may take solace in the fact that Newton himself had trouble applying his 3rd law to certain situations. Apply the rule, A on B; B on A, as in Figure 4.20.]

19. The scale will read 100 N, the same it would read if one of the ends were tied to a wall instead of tied to the 100-N hanging weight. Although the net force on the system is zero, the tension in the rope within the system is 100 N, as shown on the scale reading.

20. When held at rest the upward support force equals the weight of the apple and the net force is zero. When released, the upward support force is no longer there and the net force is the weight of the apple, 1 N. (As the apple picks up speed air drag will reduce the net force.)

21. (a) Two force pairs act; weight, which is the Earth's pull on the apple (action), and the apple's pull on the Earth (reaction). Hand pushes apple upward (action), and apple pushes hand downward (reaction). (b) If air drag can be neglected, one force pair acts; Earth's pull on apple, and apple's pull on Earth. If air drag counts, then air pushes upward on apple (action) and apple pushes downward on air (reaction).

22. High-speed meteorites grazing the Earth's atmosphere burn up because of friction against the air.

23. Rate of gain in speed (acceleration), is the ratio weight/mass (Newton's second law). In free fall, only the force due to gravity acts on a body — its weight. Since weight is proportional to mass, the ratio weight/mass is the same whatever the weight of a body. So all freely falling bodies undergo the same gain in speed — g (illustrated in Figures 2.13 and 2.14). Although weight doesn't affect speed in free fall, weight does affect falling speed when air resistance is present (non-free fall).

24. A stick of dynamite nor anything contains force. We will see later that a stick of dynamite contains "energy," which is capable of producing forces when an interaction of some kind occurs.

25. If the dog wags its tail (action), the tail will in turn wag the dog (reaction). How noticeable this is depends on the relative masses of the dog and the tail being wagged!

26. When the barbell is accelerated upward, the force exerted by the athlete is greater than the weight of the barbell (the barbell, in turn, pushes with greater force against the athlete). When acceleration is downward, the force supplied by the athlete is less.

27. When you pull up on the handle bars, the handle bars in turn pull down on you. This downward force is transmitted to the pedals.

28. Both the Earth and satellite *pull on each other* with 1000 N. So the satellite exerts the same 1000 N force on the Earth — but in the opposite direction as the pull of the Earth on the satellite.

29. The strongman can exert only equal forces on both cars, just as your push against a wall equals the push of the wall on you. Like-wise for two walls, or two freight cars. Since their masses are equal, they will undergo equal accelerations and move equally.

30. In accord with Newton's 3rd law, if the Earth pulls down on your body, your body will pull up equally on the Earth.

31. Like the answer to Exercise 29, the force on each cart will be the same. But since the masses are different, the accelerations will differ. The twice-as-massive cart will undergo only half the acceleration of the less massive cart. The less massive cart will spring apart with twice the speed of the more massive cart.

32. The friction is 200 N, which cancels your 200-N push to yield the zero net force that accounts for the constant velocity (zero acceleration). Although the friction force is equal and oppositely directed to the applied force, the two do *not* make an action-reaction pair of forces. That's because both forces *do* act on the same object — the crate. The reaction to your push on the crate is the crate's push back on you. The reaction to the friction of the floor on the crate is the friction of the crate acting on the floor.

33. In accord with Newton's 3rd law, the force on each will be of the same magnitude. But the effect of the force (acceleration) will be different for each because of the different mass. The more massive truck undergoes less change in motion than the Civic.

34. The forces on each are the same in magnitude, and their masses are the same, so their accelerations will be the same. They will slide equal distances of 6 meters to the midpoint.

35. The twice-as-massive person will undergo half the acceleration and slide half as far as the less massive person — that is, 4 m for the more massive person, and 8 m for the less massive person [so their combined sliding distance equals the 12 m].

36. The winning team pushes harder against the ground. The ground then pushes harder on them, producing a net force in their favor.

37. The terminal velocity attained by the falling cat is the same whether it falls from 50 stories or 20 stories. Once terminal velocity is reached, falling extra distance does not affect the speed. (The low terminal velocities of small creatures enables them to fall without harm from heights that would kill larger creatures.)

38. (a) No. Air resistance is also acting. By free fall is meant free of all forces but gravity. A falling object may experience air resistance; a freely falling object experiences only the force due to gravity. (b) Yes. Although getting no closer to the Earth, the satellite is falling (more about this in Chapter 4).

39. Just before a falling object reaches terminal velocity, its weight is slightly more than air resistance. When air resistance increases to equal weight, then terminal velocity is attained. After terminal velocity is attained, weight and air resistance have the same magnitudes.

40. As acceleration of fall decreases, the rate of increasing speed gets less. This doesn't mean the speed gets less! Speed increases, but not as quickly.

41. Acceleration decreases because the net force acting on the falling object decreases. Why does the net force decrease as speed increases? Because air drag increases with increasing speed, and air drag is opposite to the downward force of gravity.

42. Air resistance is not really negligible for so high a drop, so the heavier ball does strike the ground first. [This idea is shown in Figure 2.17.] But although a twice-as-heavy ball strikes first, it doesn't fall twice as fast as Aristotle's followers believed.

43. The heavier tennis ball will strike the ground first for the same reason the heavier parachutist in Figure 2.16 strikes the ground first. Note that although the air resistance on the heavier ball is small compared to the weight of the ball, it is greater than the air resistance that acts on the other ball. Why? Because the heavier ball falls faster and encounters more air in any instant.

44. The acceleration at the top or anywhere else in free fall is 10 m/s^2 (or 9.8 m/s^2), downward. The velocity of the rock is momentarily zero, but the rate of change of velocity is still there. Or better, by Newton's 2nd law, the force of gravity acts at the top as elsewhere; divide this net force by the mass and you have the acceleration of free fall. That is, $a = F_{net}/m = mg/m = g$.

45. (a) Suzie will encounter an air resistance equal to her weight when she reaches terminal velocity, which will be about 500 N. (b) After the chute is open she will also encounter an air resistance equal to her weight — 500 N. (c) Answers are the same, but it should be noted that without the large area of the opened parachute, her terminal velocity is much greater before she opens the chute. The same amount of air resistance is achieved for much less speed when the chute is open.

46. Open ended.

Chapter 2 Problem Solutions

1. Friction is 4000 N. Since the bear is not accelerating, the net force on it is zero. So the downward force, its weight, is balanced by the same upward force of friction.
   Weight = mg = (400 kg)(10 m/s^2) = 4000 N.

2. **a.** F_{net} = 30 N + 20 N = **50 N**, in the direction of the forces.

   b. F_{net} = 30 N - 20 N = **10 N**, in the direction of the 30-N force.

   c. $F_{net} = \sqrt{30^2 + 20^2} = \sqrt{1300} =$ **36.1 N**, between the two at 45° to either force.

3. For $a = 0$, $F_{net} = 0$, so 600 N - 400 N = 200 N
   $$200\ N - X = 0$$
   $$X = \textbf{200 N} \text{ (so a force of 200 N opposite to the 600-N force is needed)}$$

4. **a.** $F_{net} = ma = 0$, because $a = \Delta v/\Delta t = 0$(no change in speed). so $F_{net} = \textbf{0}$.
   b. F_{net} = 100 N - f = 0, so f = **-100 N**.

5. The acceleration of each is the **same**: $a = F/m = 2\ N/2\ kg = 1\ N/1\ kg = 1 m/s^2$.[Incidentally, from the definition that 1 N = 1 kg·m/s^2, you can see that 1 N/kg is the same as 1 m/s^2.]

6. For the jumbo jet: $a = \dfrac{F}{m} = \dfrac{4(30\ 000N)}{30\ 000\ kg} = \textbf{4 m/s}^2$.

7. $a = \dfrac{F_{net}}{m} = \dfrac{20\ N - 12\ N}{2\ kg} = \dfrac{8\ N}{2\ kg} = \textbf{4 m/s}^2$.

8. F = mg= 1 kg (9.8 m/s^2) = **9.8 N**

9. Net force (downward) = ma = (80 kg)(4 m/s^2) = 320 N. Gravity is pulling him downward with a force of (80 kg)(10 m/s^2) = 800 N, so the upward force of friction is 800 N – 320 N = **480 N**.

10. $a = \dfrac{F_{net}}{m} = \dfrac{mg - R}{m} = \dfrac{g}{2}$

    $mg - R = \dfrac{mg}{2}$ $\qquad\qquad R = mg - \dfrac{mg}{2} = 490\ N - 245\ N = \textbf{245 N}$

3 Momentum and Energy

Answers to Exercises

1. One important reason a wine glass survives a fall on a carpet is that the carpet has more "give," which means the time during which the glass is brought to a halt during impact is extended. This extended time is compensated by a reduced force in the impulse upon the glass.

2. Supertankers are so massive, that even at modest speeds their motional inertia, or *momenta*, are enormous. This means enormous impulses are needed for changing motion. How can large impulses be produced with modest forces? By applying modest forces over long periods of time. Hence the force of the water resistance over the time it takes to coast 25 kilometers sufficiently reduces the momentum.

3. This is another illustration of the previous exercise. The time during which momentum decreases is lengthened, thereby decreasing the jolting force of the rope.

4. The impulse required to stop the momentum of a heavy truck is considerably more than the impulse required to stop a skateboard moving with the same speed. The force required to stop either, however, depends on the time during which it is applied. Stopping the skateboard in a split second results in a certain force. Apply less than this amount of force on the moving truck and given enough time, the truck will come to a halt.

5. When the moving egg makes contact with a sagging sheet, the time it takes to stop it is extended. More time means less force, and a less-likely broken egg.

6. Impact with a boxing glove extends the time during which momentum of the fist is reduced, and lessens the force. A punch with a bare fist involves less time and therefore more force.

7. When a boxer hits his opponent, the opponent contributes to the impulse that changes the momentum of the punch. When punches miss, no impulse is supplied by the opponent — all effort that goes into reducing the momentum of the punches is supplied by the boxer himself. This tires the boxer. This is very evident to a boxer who can punch a heavy bag in the gym for hours and not tire, but who finds by contrast that a few minutes in the ring with an opponent is a tiring experience.

8. Without this slack, a locomotive might simply sit still and spin its wheels. The loose coupling enables a longer time for bringing the entire train up to momentum, requiring less force of the locomotive wheels against the track. In this way, the overall required impulse is broken into a series of smaller impulses. This loose coupling is very important for braking as well.

9. To get to shore, the person may throw clothing. The momentum of the clothing will be accompanied by the thrower's oppositely-directed momentum. In this way, one can recoil towards shore. (One can also blow, like a jet or a rocket.)

10. Momentum will be conserved because the force due to the spring is internal to the two-cart system. So by momentum conservation, both carts will have equal and opposite momenta after the spring is released. Since the heavier cart has twice the mass, it will have half the speed of the lighter cart.

11. The large momentum of the spurting water is met by a recoil that makes the hose difficult to hold, just as a shotgun is difficult to hold when it fires birdshot.

12. Whether or not momentum is conserved depends on the system. If the system in question is you as you fall, then there is an external force acting on you (gravity) and momentum increases, and is therefore not conserved. But if you enlarge the system to be you and the Earth that pulls you, then momentum is conserved, for the force of gravity on you is internal to the system. Your momentum of fall is balanced by the equal but opposite momentum of the Earth coming up to meet you! (See the Practice Sheet on page 14 of the Practice Book.)

13. By Newton's 3rd law, the force on the Mack truck is equal in magnitude and opposite in direction to the force on the Civic. The time of impact on each is also the same, so the magnitude of force, impulse, and change in momentum will be the same for each. The Civic undergoes the greater acceleration because its mass is less.

14. Cars brought to a rapid halt constitute a change in momentum, and a corresponding impulse. But greater momentum change occurs if the cars bounce, with correspondingly greater impulse and therefore greater damage. Less damage results if the cars stick upon impact than if they bounce apart.

15. We assume the equal strengths of the astronauts means that each throws with the same speed. Since the masses are equal, when the first throws the second, both the first and second move away from each other at equal speeds. Say the thrown astronaut moves to the right with velocity V, and the first recoils with velocity $-V$. When the third makes the catch, both she and the second move to the right at velocity $V/2$ (twice the mass moving at half the speed, like the freight cars in Figure 3.9). When the third makes her throw, she recoils at velocity V (the same speed she imparts to the thrown astronaut) which is added to the $V/2$ she acquired in the catch. So her velocity is $V + V/2 = 3V/2$, to the right — too fast to stay in the game. Why? Because the velocity of the second astronaut is $V/2 - V = -V/2$, to the left — too slow to catch up with the first astronaut who is still moving at $-V$. The game is over. Both the first and the third got to throw the second astronaut only once!

16. Yes, momenta can cancel but energies cannot. The answers are different because momenta are vectors (and can therefore cancel) whereas energies are scalars (do not involve directions) and cannot cancel.

17. When a rifle with a long barrel is fired, more work is done as the bullet is pushed through the longer distance. A greater KE is the result of the greater work, so of course, the bullet emerges with a greater velocity. (It might be mentioned that the force acting on the bullet is not constant, but decreases with increasing distance inside the barrel.)

18. (a) The work being done on the falling object is the force of gravity × falling distance.
    (b) The impulse that changes its momentum is the force of gravity × time of fall.

19. Yes, the increase in momentum of the skydiver toward the Earth is equal to the increase in momentum of the Earth moving toward the skydiver. Of course the impulse on the Earth supplied by the skydiver has a negligible effect on the enormously massive Earth. When both skydiver and Earth are considered as one system, the two forces are within the system, cancel out, and there is no net change of momentum for the system skydiver-Earth.

20. The PE of the drawn bow as calculated would be an overestimate, (in fact, twice its actual value) because the force applied in drawing the bow begins at zero and increases to its maximum value when fully drawn. It's easy to see that less force and therefore less work is required to first draw the bow halfway, than to draw it the second half of the way to its fully-drawn position. So the work done is not *maximum force × distance drawn*, but *average force × distance drawn*. In this case where force varies directly with distance (and not as the square or some other complicated factor) the average force is simply equal to the initial force + final force, divided by 2. So the PE is equal to the average force applied (which would be half the force at its full-drawn position) multiplied by the distance through which the arrow is drawn.

21. The KE of the tossed ball relative to occupants in the airplane does not depend on the speed of the airplane. The KE of the ball relative to observers on the ground below, however, is a different matter. KE, like velocity, is relative. So is PE. See the answer to question 2 on page 65 of the text.

22. If an object has KE, then it must have momentum — for it is moving. But it can have potential energy without being in motion, and therefore without having momentum. And every object has "energy of being," — as is stated in the celebrated equation $E = mc^2$. So whether an object moves or not, it has some form of energy. If it has KE, then with respect to the frame of reference in which its KE is measured, it also has momentum.

23. If KEs are the same but masses differ, then the ball with smaller mass has the greater speed. That is, $1/2\ Mv^2 = 1/2\ mV^2$. Likewise with molecules, where lighter ones move faster on the average than more massive ones. (We will see in Chapter 6 that temperature is a measure of average molecular KE — lighter molecules in a gas move faster than same-temperature heavier molecules.)

24. Agree with the first friend because after the collision, the bowling ball does have greater momentum than the golf ball. We can see this as follows. Before collision, the momentum of the system of two balls is all in the moving golf ball. Call this 1 unit. Then after collision, the momentum of the rebounding golf ball is nearly -1 unit. The momentum (not the speed!) of the bowling ball will have to be nearly +2 units. Why? Because of momentum conservation: Only then will the total momentum before collision (+1) = the total momentum after collision (+2 -1 = +1). (The golf ball, however, has the greater KE, very nearly as much as it had before impact. The KE of the bowling ball is very small, because its speed is very small and the speed is squared in the KE equation. So although the bowling ball may have nearly twice the momentum of the golf ball, it has only a small fraction of its KE.)

25. The KE of a pendulum bob is maximum where it moves fastest, at the lowermost point; PE is maximum at the uppermost points; When the pendulum bob swings by the point that marks half its maximum height, half its energy is PE and the other half KE (in accordance with energy conservation: total energy = KE + PE).

26. If the ball is given an initial KE, it will return to its starting position with that KE and hit the instructor. (The usual classroom procedure is to release the ball from the nose at rest. Then when it returns it will have no motional energy to bump the nose.)

27. No work is done on the bob by the string because the string tension is everywhere perpendicular to the path of the bob. There is no component of this string tension along the bob's path. But gravity is another story. The force of gravity acts downward, producing a component that does lie along the bob's path. It is this component of force that is responsible for the changing speed of the bob. Interestingly, the only place where there is no component of gravitational force on the bob is at the very bottom of its path. If it is moving, it overshoots this point. If the bob is at rest, it remains at rest here.

28. The design is impractical. Note that the summit of each hill on the roller coaster is the same height, so the PE of the car at the top of each hill would be the same. If no energy were spent in overcoming friction, the car would get to the second summit with as much energy as it starts with. But in practice there is considerable friction, and the car would not roll to its initial height and have the same energy. So the maximum height of succeeding summit should be lower to compensate for the work done by the roller coaster car in overcoming friction.

29. Both will have the same speed because both have the same PE at the ends of the track — and therefore same KEs. This is a relatively easy question to answer because *speed* is asked for, whereas the similar question in Chapter 1 (Exercise 19) asked for which ball got to the end sooner. The question asked for *time* — which meant first establishing which ball had the greater average speed.

30. Yes, a car burns more gasoline when its lights are on. The overall consumption of gasoline does not depend on whether or not the engine is running. Lights and other devices run off the battery, which "run down" the battery. The energy used to recharge the battery ultimately comes from the gasoline.

31. Your friend may not realize that matter itself is congealed energy, so you tell your friend that much more energy in its congealed form is put into the reactor than is put out by the reactor. Less than one percent of the fission fuel is converted to energy.

32. The work that the rock does on the ground is equal to its PE before being dropped, which is mgh = 100 joules. The force of impact, however, depends on the distance that the rock penetrates into the ground. If we do not know this distance we cannot calculate the force. (If we knew the time during which the impulse occurs we could calculate the force from the impulse-momentum relationship — but not knowing the distance or time of the rock's penetrating into the ground, we cannot calculate the force.)

33. $$(Fd)_{input} = (Fd)_{output}$$

    $$(100 \text{ N} \times 10 \text{ cm})_{input} = (? \times 1 \text{ cm})_{output}$$

    So we see that the output force is 1000 N.

34. The freight cars have only half the KE possessed by the single car before collision. Check:

    $KE_{before} = 1/2 \, mv^2$.

    $KE_{after} = 1/2 \, (2m)(v/2)^2 = 1/2 \, (2m) \, v^2/4 = 1/4 \, mv^2$.

    What becomes of this energy? Most of it goes into heat, the graveyard of kinetic energy.

35. An engine that is 100% efficient would not be warm to the touch, nor would its exhaust heat the air, nor would it make any noise, nor would it vibrate, nor would any of its fuel go unused. This is because all these are transfers of energy, which cannot happen if all the energy given to the engine is transformed to useful work.

36. For the same momentum, the lighter truck must have a greater speed. It also has a greater KE and thus requires more work to stop. Whenever two bodies of different masses have the same momentum, the lighter one not only is the faster of the two, it also has the greater KE. That's because in the formula $KE = 1/2 \, mv^2$, the mass m enters once but the speed v enters twice (that is, it is squared). That means that the effect of higher speed for the lighter truck more than offsets the effect of smaller mass. (See Problem 10.)

Chapter 3 Problem Solutions

1. The answer is 4 km/h. Let m be the mass of the freight car, and $4m$ the mass of the diesel engine, and v the speed after both have coupled together. Before collision, the total momentum is due only to the diesel engine, $4m$(5 km/h), because the momentum of the freight car is 0. After collision, the combined mass is $(4m + m)$, and combined momentum is $(4m + m)v$. By the conservation of momentum equation:

Momentum$_{before}$ = momentum$_{after}$

$$4m(5 \text{ km/h}) + 0 = (4m + m)v$$
$$v = \frac{(20\,m\cdot\text{km/h})}{5m} = \textbf{4 km/h}$$

2. (a) Momentum before lunch = momentum after lunch

$$5 \text{ kg m/s} = 6 \text{ kg } V$$

$$V = \textbf{5/6 m/s}$$

   This reduced velocity after lunch is in the direction of motion of the larger fish.
   (b) Momentum before lunch = momentum after lunch

$$(5 \text{ kg})(1 \text{ m/s}) + 1 \text{ kg } (\text{-4 m/s}) = (5 \text{ kg} + 1 \text{ kg}) 3v$$
$$5 \text{ kg}\cdot\text{m/s} - 4 \text{ kg}\cdot\text{m/s} = (6 \text{ kg}) \, v$$
$$v = \textbf{1/6 m/s}$$

3. At three times the speed, it has nine times (3^2) the KE and will skid nine times as far — **135 m.**

4. At 25% efficiency, we'll get only 1/4 of the 40 megajoules in one liter, or 10 MJ. This is the energy to do work, $F \times d$, where
$$F \times d = 1000 \text{ N} \times d = 10 \text{ MJ}.$$

   So solve for d and convert MJ to J, and we get
$$d = \frac{10 \text{ MJ}}{1000 \text{ N}} = \frac{10\,000\,000 \text{ J}}{1000 \text{ N}} = 10{,}000 \text{ m} = 10 \text{ km}.$$

   So under these conditions, the car gets **10 kilometers per liter.** (A compact streamlined car encounters about half the 1000 N drag force cited here, and will get twice the fuel economy.)

5. From $Ft = \Delta mv$, $F = \dfrac{\Delta mv}{t} = \dfrac{(1000 \text{ kg})(20 \text{ m/s} - 0)}{10 \text{ s}} = \textbf{2000 N}$. (Note this could have been equivalently solved from $F = ma$, Chapter 2, where $a = \Delta v / t$.)

6. Since 3000 J of effort produce 1000 J of work, the efficiency of the pulley system is

   (work output)/(work input) = 1/3, or **33.3%.**

7. We can express efficiency as a ratio of (power output)/(power input), since the times for each are equal [where power = energy/time].

   So, Efficiency = (power output)/(power input) = 100 W/1000 W = 1/10, or **10%.**

8. 1 kilowatt-hour = 1000 joule/second for 1 hour. There are $60 \times 60 = 3600$ seconds in 1 hour, so the total number of joules is 1000 J/s $\times$ 3600 s = **3600000 J = 3.6 MJ.**

9. (a) $v = \sqrt{2gh}$. As an object falls though a distance h, its loss of PE is mgh. This converted to KE (1/2 mv^2). From $mgh = 1/2 \, mv^2$, we see after canceling m and rearranging terms that $v = \sqrt{2gh}$.
   (b) For $2v$, h must be **4 times** as much (because the square root of $4 = 2$).

10. From $p = mv$, you get $v = p/m$. Substitute this expression for v in KE $= (1/2)mv^2$ to get KE $= (1/2)$ $m(p/m)^2 = p^2/2m$. (Alternatively, one may work in the other direction, substituting $p = mv$ in KE $= p^2/2m$ to get KE $= (1/2)mv^2$.)

4   Gravity and Satellite Motion

Answers to Exercises

1. Nothing to be concerned about on this consumer label. It simply states the universal law of gravitation, which applies to *all* products. It looks like the manufacturer knows some physics and has a sense of humor.

2. The reason that a heavy body doesn't fall faster than a light body is because the greater gravitational force on the heavier body (its weight), acts on a correspondingly greater mass (inertia). The ratio of force to mass for a freely falling body is the same — hence all bodies in free fall accelerate equally. (This is illustrated in Figures 2.13 and 2.14 back on page 40 in the text.)

3. Both the plane sheet and the crumpled sheet have the same mass, so they weigh the same. (Although the crumpled sheet will exert a more concentrated force [greater pressure] on your hand and seem heavier.)

4. The closer to the Sun, the faster the planet, and also the smaller the circumference of orbit. So it makes sense that planets closer to the Sun from Earth have smaller periods. Planets farther from the Sun than Earth, go slower and have farther to go to complete orbit, so have longer periods. (This is accord with Kepler's third law, $T^2 \sim R^3$, covered in Chapter 28.)

5. The magnitude of gravitational force on a 700-newton man is 700 N, and the force acts downward, toward the center of the Earth. He calls this force his weight.

6. Nearer the Moon. (At the half-way point, the pull toward the more massive Earth is greater.)

7. The Earth and Moon equally pull on each other in a single interaction. In accord with Newton's 3rd law, the pull of the Earth on the Moon is equal and opposite to the pull of the Moon on the Earth.

8. Your weight would increase if the mass of the Earth increased, because gravitational force is proportional to the product of both your mass and the Earth's mass. If either increases, the force increases also. (Note from the equation $F = G m_1 m_2 / d^2$, there are three ways to increase F: Increase m_1, increase m_2, or decrease d.)

9. By the geometry of Figure 4.3 on page 79, tripling the distance from the small source spreads the light over 9 times the area, or 9 m^2. Five times the distance spreads the light over 25 times the area, or 25 m^2, and for 10 times as far, 100 m^2.

10. The gravitational force on a body, its weight, depends not only on mass but distance. On Jupiter, this is the distance between the body being weighed and Jupiter's center — the radius of Jupiter. If the radius of Jupiter were the same as that of the Earth, then a body would weigh 300 times as much because Jupiter is 300 times more massive than Earth. But Jupiter is also much bigger than the Earth, so the greater distance between its center and the CG of the body reduces the gravitational force. The radius is great enough to make the weight of a body only 3 times its Earth weight. How much greater is the radius of Jupiter? Onward to Exercise 9!

11. Jupiter's diameter is about 10 times that of the Earth's. Our clue to this is our data that bodies on Jupiter weigh 3 times as much as on Earth. If mass were the only factor, weight on Jupiter would be 300 times Earth weight. But Jupiter is bigger than Earth. The greater radius of Jupiter diminishes weight by 100 (because 300/100 = 3). According to the inverse-square law, a 100-fold decrease means that the distance is 10 times as great. Jupiter must have a radius 10 times greater than the Earth's. This means its diameter is 10 Earth diameters also. (More accurately, the mean radius of Jupiter is about 11 times that of the Earth, so your weight is closer to 2.5 times Earth weight.)

12. Normally your insides are supported by parts of your body such as your pelvis. This occurs when you ride in a high-altitude jet plane. You are pulled down by gravity against the seat of the

plane that supports you. But in an orbiting space vehicle, both you and the vehicle are in a state of free fall. The vehicle has no lift to support you, and you feel weightless.

13. Any body that moves in a circular path requires a centripetal force. Objects on the surface of the Earth circle the Earth with a force provided by gravity. The force of gravity is more than enough to hold them to the Earth at its present rotational speed. Beyond certain speeds it is not. For example, if the Earth revolved each 90 minutes instead of each 24 hours, objects at the equator would be traveling at 8 km/s, orbital speed. The Earth's gravity is barely able to provide the centripetal force necessary for them to continue in circular motion. At this speed they would be on the verge of being thrown off the Earth and would not press against its surface. At the poles, weight would be as usual, because there is no tangential velocity there (like being in the center of a rotating turntable). In the middle of the United States, tangential speed would be greater than zero and less than 8 km/s, so objects would still press against the Earth's surface, but much less than at the poles.

14. In a car that drives off a cliff you feel weightless because the car no longer offers a support force. Both you and the car are in the same state of free fall. But gravity is still acting on you, as evidenced by your acceleration toward the ground.

15. The pencil has the same state of motion that you have. Relative to the Earth, you are both falling. Relative to yourself, the pencil does not fall from you.

16. First of all, it is incorrect to say that the gravitational force of the distant Sun is too small to be measured. Its small, but not immeasurably small. If, for example, the Earth were supported so that the Sun's pull showed on a scale, an 85-kg person would see a gain of 1/2 newton on the scale at midnight and a loss of 1/2 newton at noon. The key idea is *support*. There is no "Sun support" because the Earth and all objects on the Earth — people, bathroom scales, and all — are continually falling around the Sun. Just as a person is not pulled against the seat of a car that drives off a cliff, and just as a pencil is not pressed against the floor of an elevator in free fall, we are not pressed against or pulled from the Earth by our gravitational interaction with the Sun. That interaction keeps us and the Earth circling the Sun, but does not press us to the Earth's surface. Our interaction with the Earth does that.

17. As stated in the preceding answer, our "Earth weight" is due to the gravitational interaction between our mass and that of the Earth. The Earth and its inhabitants are freely falling around the Sun, the rate of which does not affect our local weights. (If a car drives off a cliff, the Earth's gravity, however strong, plays no role in pressing the occupant against the car while both are falling. Similarly, as the Earth and its inhabitants fall around the Sun, the Sun plays no role in pressing us to the Earth.)

18. The gravitational pull of the Sun on the Earth is greater than the gravitational pull of the Moon (page 88). The tides, however, are caused by the *differences* in gravitational forces by the Moon on opposite sides of the Earth. The difference in gravitational forces by the Moon on opposite sides of the Earth is greater than the corresponding difference in forces by the stronger pulling Sun.

19. No. Tides are caused by differences in gravitational pulls. If there are no differences in pulls, there are no tides.

20. Ocean tides are not exactly 12 hours apart because while the Earth spins, the Moon moves in its orbit and appears at its same position overhead every 25 hours, instead of every 24 hours. So the two-high-tide cycle occurs at about 25-hour intervals, making high tides about 12.5 hours apart.

21. Lowest tides occur during the same cycle of highest tides — spring tides. So the spring tide cycle consists of higher-than-average high tides followed by lower-than-average low tides (best for digging clams!).

22. Whenever the ocean tide is unusually high, it will be followed by an unusually low tide. This makes sense, for when one part of the world is having an extra high tide, another part must be donating water and experiencing an extra low tide. Or as the hint in the exercise suggests, if you are in a bathtub and slosh the water so it is extra deep in front of you, that's when it is extra low in back of you — "conservation of water!"

23. Because of its relatively small size (it's essentially cut off from the Atlantic by the narrow Straights of Gibraltar), different parts of the Mediterranean Sea are essentially equidistant from the Moon (or from the Sun). As a result, one part is not pulled with any appreciably different force than any other part. This results in extremely tiny tides. This is especially true for smaller bodies of water, such as lakes, ponds, and puddles. In a glass of water under a full Moon you'll detect no tides because no part of the water surface is closer to the Moon than any other part of the surface. Tides are caused by appreciable differences in pulls.

24. Tides are produced by *differences* in forces, which relate to differences in distance from the attracting body. One's head is appreciably closer than one's feet to the overhead melon. The greater proportional difference for the melon out-tides the more massive but more distant Moon. One's head is not appreciably closer to the Moon than one's feet.

25. Yes, the Earth's tides would be due only to the Sun. They'd occur twice per day (every 12 hours instead of every 12.5 hours) due to the Earth's daily rotation.

26. A rocket fired from the Earth to the Moon requires more fuel because the rocket must counteract the stronger gravitational field of the Earth. In going from the Moon to the Earth, only the weaker gravitational field of the Moon must be overcome, and the Earth's field assists motion.

27. (a) True, because the horizontal component of velocity is a constant. (b) False, although the horizontal component of motion is constant, the vertical component changes because of the vertical force of gravity. (c) False! Horizontal components of motion are independent of vertical components.

28. In 1 second a projectile will fall 5 m below where it would have gone without the effects of gravity. For 2 seconds, the vertical distance would be 20 m. These falling distances do not depend on the angle of projection (provided the projectile is still airborne in these times).

29. When the cannonball moves in a circular orbit there is no component of gravitational force in the tangential direction of motion This means there is no acceleration in the direction the ball moves, so therefore, no change in speed. (This is shown in Figure 4.32 on page 94 of the textbook.) Or from a work-energy point of view, no work is done to change its KE.

30. The Moon doesn't crash into the Earth simply because its tangential speed is sufficient to fall around and around the Earth. If it were to stop in its tracks for any reason, then it would crash into the Earth.

31. Neither the speed of free fall nor the speed of a satellite in orbit depends on its mass. In both cases, a greater mass is balanced by a correspondingly greater gravitational force, so the acceleration remains the same (Newton's 2nd law).

32. The rocket departs form a vertical course until it is moving tangentially to the surface of the Earth with a speed of at least 8 km/s. If it traveled only vertically at less than escape velocity, it would fall back to the surface.

33. Rockets for launching satellites into orbit are fired easterly to take advantage of the spin of the Earth. Any point on the equator of the Earth moves at nearly 0.5 km/s with respect to the center of the Earth or the Earth's polar axis. This extra speed does not have to be provided by the rocket engines. At higher latitudes, this "extra free ride" is less.

34. Hawaii is closer to the equator, and therefore has a greater tangential speed about the polar axis. This speed can be added to the launch speed of a satellite and thereby save fuel.

35. The component along the direction of motion does work on the satellite to change its speed. The component perpendicular to the direction of motion changes its direction.

36. In circular orbit there is no component of force along the direction of the satellite's motion so no work is done. In elliptical orbit, there is always a component of force along the direction of the satellite's motion (except at the apogee and perigee) so work is done of the satellite.

37. When the velocity of a satellite is everywhere perpendicular to the force of gravity, the orbital path is a circle (see Figure 4.32c).

38. Consider "Newton's cannon" fired from a tall mountain on Jupiter. To match the wider curvature of much larger Jupiter, and to contend with Jupiter's greater gravitational pull, the cannonball would have to be fired significantly faster. (Orbital speed about Jupiter is about 5 times that for Earth.)

39. If a wrench or anything else is "dropped" from an orbiting space vehicle, it has the same tangential speed as the vehicle and remains in orbit. If a wrench is dropped from a high-flying jumbo jet, it too has the tangential speed of the jet. But this speed is insufficient for the wrench to fall around and around the Earth. Instead it soon falls into the Earth.

40. When a capsule is projected rearward at 8 km/s with respect to the shuttle, which is itself moving forward at 8 km/s with respect to the Earth, the speed of the capsule with respect to the Earth will be zero. It will have no tangential speed for orbit. What will happen? It will simply drop to Earth and crash.

41. This is similar to Exercise 40. The tangential velocity of the Earth about the Sun is 30 km/s. If a rocket carrying the radioactive wastes were fired at 30 km/s from the Earth in the direction opposite to the Earth's orbital motion about the Sun, the wastes would have no tangential velocity with respect to the Sun. They would simply fall into the Sun.

42. Communication satellites only appear motionless because their orbital period coincides with the daily rotation of the Earth.

43. The escape speeds from various planets refer to "ballistic speeds" — to the speeds attained *after* the application of an applied force. If the force is sustained, then a space vehicle could escape the Earth at any speed, so long as the force is applied sufficiently long.

44. The satellite experiences the greatest gravitational force at A, where it is closest to the Earth; and the greatest speed and the greatest velocity at A, and by the same token the greatest momentum and greatest kinetic energy at A, and the greatest gravitational potential energy at the farthest point C. It would have the same total energy (KE + PE) at all parts of its orbit, likewise with angular momentum because it's conserved (mvr is the same everywhere in orbit). It would have the greatest acceleration at A, where F/m is greatest.

176

Chapter 4 Problem Solutions

1. In accord with the inverse-square law, four times as far from the Earth's center diminishes the value of g to $1/4^2$, or $g/16$, or 0.6 m/s^2.

2. $g = \dfrac{GM}{d^2} = \dfrac{(6.67 \times 10^{-11})(6.0 \times 10^{24})}{([6380 + 200] \times 10^3]^2} = 9.27$ N/kg, or 9.27 m/s^2; Compared to g at the Earth's surface, this is 9.27/9.80 = **94%**

   Or we can solve this another way: Since all factors are equal except for distance, the only variable is distance, which follows the inverse-square law. The acceleration g will decrease by the ratio of the squares of the distances:

   That is $\dfrac{(6380 \text{ km})^2}{[(6380 + 200 \text{ km})]^2} = \dfrac{6380^2}{6580^2} = 0.94$, or **94%** of 9.8 m/s^2.

3. (a) Mars: $F = G\dfrac{mM}{d^2} = 6.67 \times 10^{-11} \dfrac{(3\text{kg})(6.4 \times 10^{23})}{(5.6 \times 10^{10})^2} = $ **4.1 $\times 10^{-8}$ N.**

   (b) Physician: $F = G\dfrac{mM}{d^2} = 6.67 \times 10^{-11} \dfrac{(3\text{kg})(10^2)}{(0.5)^2} = $ **8.0 $\times 10^{-8}$ N.**

   (c) The gravitational force due to the physician is about **twice** that due to Mars.

4. $F = G\dfrac{mM}{d^2} = 6.67 \times 10^{-11} \dfrac{(6 \times 10^{24}\text{kg})(2 \times 10^{30})}{(1.5 \times 0^{11})^2} = $ **3.6 $\times 10^{22}$ N.**

5. Nearly 10,000 km thick, not much less than the diameter of the Earth itself! From the ratio 3.6×10^{22} N/x = 5×10^8 N/1 m^2, x = $(3.6 \times 10^{22})/(5 \times 10^8) = 7.2 \times 10^{13}$ m^2. This would be the cross-sectional area of the cable. From the area of a circle, A = $\pi D^2/4$, we find its diameter D = $\sqrt{4A/\pi} = 9.6 \times 10^6$ m = **9,600 km.**

6. $v = \sqrt{\dfrac{GM}{d}} = \sqrt{\dfrac{(6.67 \times 10^{-11})(6 \times 10^{24})}{3.8 \times 10^8}} = $ **1026 m/s.**

7. Speed = distance/time = $2\pi r/1$ year;

   $= \dfrac{2\pi(150{,}000{,}000 \text{ km})}{1 \text{ year}} \times \dfrac{1 \text{ year}}{365 \text{ days}} \times \dfrac{1 \text{ day}}{24 \text{hr}} \times \dfrac{1 \text{ hr}}{3600 \text{ s}} = 30$ km/s = 3×10^4 m/s.

   [note how this is set up so that the units cancel — *dimensional analysis,* — a nice computational technique!]

5   Fluid Mechanics

Answers to Exercises

1. A sharp knife cuts better than a dull knife because it has a thinner cutting area which results in more cutting pressure for a given force.

2. The concept of pressure is being demonstrated. Marshall is careful that the pieces are small and numerous so that his weight is applied over a large area of contact. Then the sharp glass provides insufficient pressure to cut the feet.

3. A woman with spike heels exerts considerably more pressure on the ground than an elephant! Example: A 500-N woman with 1-cm^2 spike heels puts half her weight on each foot and exerts a pressure of $(250N/1 \text{ cm}^2) = 250N/cm^2$. A 20,000-N elephant with 1000 cm^2 feet exerting 1/4 its weight on each foot produces $(5000N/1000 \text{ cm}^2) = 5N/cm^2$; about 1/50 as much pressure. (So a woman with spike heels will make greater dents in a new linoleum floor than an elephant.)

4. More water will flow from a downstairs open faucet because of the greater pressure. Since pressure depends on depth, the downstairs faucet is effectively "deeper" than the upstairs faucet. The pressure downstairs is greater by an amount = density $\times$ depth, where the depth is the vertical distance between faucets.

5. (a) The reservoir is elevated so as to produce suitable water pressure in the faucets that it serves. (b) The hoops are closer together at the bottom because the water pressure is greater at the bottom. Closer to the top, the water pressure is not as great, so less reinforcement is needed there.

6. From a physics point of view, the event was quite reasonable, for the force of the ocean on his finger would have been quite small. This is because the pressure on his finger has only to do with the depth of the water, specifically the distance of the leak below the sea level — not the weight of the ocean. A numerical example should make this point: Suppose the leak were 1 meter below sea level. Then the water pressure would have been = density $\times$ depth = 1000 kg-weight/m$^3 \times 1$ m = 1000 kg-wt/m^2 (slightly more because of the slightly greater density of salt water). That's pressure. Force is pressure $\times$ area: the area of the boy's finger was about 1 square centimeter, which is 1/10,000 square meter. So force = 1000 kg-wt/m$^2 \times$ 1/10,000 m^2 = 1/10 kg-weight; about 1 newton. If, however, the leak were 5 meters below the water line the force would only have been about 5 newtons.

7. Water seeking its own level is a consequence of pressure depending on depth. In a bent U-tube full of water, for example, the water in one side of the tube tends to push water up the other side until the pressures in each tube are equal. The corresponding depths of water contributing to these pressures must also be equal.

8. The use of a water-filled garden hose as an elevation indicator is a practical example of water seeking its own level. The water surface at one end of the hose will be at the same elevation above sea level as the water surface at the other end of the hose.

9. Both blocks have the same volume and therefore displace the same amount of water.

10. A one-kilogram block of aluminum is larger than a one-kilogram block of lead. The aluminum therefore displaces more water.

11. A 10-N block of aluminum is larger than a 10-N block of lead. The aluminum therefore displaces more water. Only for the case of Exercise 9 were the volumes of the block equal. In this and the preceding exercise, the aluminum block was larger. (These exercises serve only to emphasize the distinction between volume, mass, and weight.)

12. Buoyant force is the result of differences in pressure; if there are no pressure differences, there is no buoyant force. This can be illustrated by the following example: A Ping-Pong ball pushed be-

178

neath the surface of water will normally float back to the surface when released. If the container of water is in free fall, however, a submerged Ping-Pong ball will fall with the container and make no attempt to reach the surface. In this case there is no buoyant force acting on the ball because there are no pressure differences — the local effects of gravity are absent.

13. The submerged carton displaces 1 liter of water, or 9.8 N of water. If the weight of the carton is negligible, then 9.8 N of force is required to push it beneath the surface. Otherwise the force required to push it beneath the surface is 9.8 N minus its weight. (Of course if its weight exceeds 9.8 N you will have to exert a force to hold it up!)

14. Ice with 0.9 the density of water floats with a tenth of its volume above water level. Think of it this way: An object half as dense as water floats half way into the water, because it weighs as much as half its volume of water. It follows that objects that float 3/4 submerged are 3/4 as dense as water. So ice, which is 0.9 as dense as water floats with 0.9 below and 0.1 above.

15. Mountain ranges are very similar to icebergs: both float in a denser medium, and extend farther down into that medium than they extend above it. Mountains, like icebergs, are bigger than they appear to be (more on this in Part 7).

16. A mostly-lead mountain would be more dense than the mantle and would sink in it. Guess where most of the iron in the world is. In the Earth's center!

17. Heavy objects may or may not sink, depending on their densities (a heavy log floats while a small rock sinks, or a cork stopper floats while a paper clip sinks, for example). The statement likely implies that dense objects, not necessarily heavy objects, sink in the fluid in which they are immersed. Be careful to distinguish between how heavy an object is and how dense it is.

18. When a ship is empty its weight is least and it displaces the least water and floats highest. Carrying a load of anything increases its weight and it floats lower. It will float as low carrying a few tons of Styrofoam as it will carrying the same number of tons of iron ore. So the ship floats lower in the water when loaded with Styrofoam than when empty. If the Styrofoam were outside the ship, below water line, then the ship would float higher as a person would with a life preserver.

19. The water level will fall. This is because the iron will displace a greater amount of water while floating than submerged. A floating object displaces its weight of water while a submerged object displaces only its volume. (This may be done in the kitchen sink by supposing the boat to be a dish in a dishpan full of water. Silverware in the dish takes the place of the scrap iron. Note the level of water at the side of the dishpan, and then throw the silverware overboard. The floating pan will float higher and the water level at the side of the dishpan will fall. Will the volume of the silverware displace enough water to bring the level to its starting point? No, not as long as it is more compact for its mass than water.)

20. For the same reason as in the previous exercise, the water level will fall. (Try this one in your kitchen sink also. Note the water level at the side of the dishpan when a bowl floats in it. Tip the bowl so it fills and submerges, and you'll see the water level at the side of the dishpan fall.)

21. The balloon will sink to the bottom because its density increases with depth. The balloon is compressible, so the increase in water pressure beneath the surface compresses it and reduces its volume, thereby increasing its density. Density is further increased as it sinks to regions of greater pressure and compression. This sinking is understood also from a buoyant force point of view. As its volume is reduced by increasing pressure as it descends, the amount of water it displaces becomes less. The result is a decrease in the buoyant force that initially was sufficient to barely keep it afloat.

22. You are compressible, whereas a rock is not, so when you are submerged, the water pressure tends to squeeze in on you and reduce your volume. This increases your density. (Be careful when swimming — at shallow depths you may still be less dense than water and be buoyed to the surface without effort, but at greater depths you may be pressed to a density greater than water and you'll have to swim to the surface.).

23. A body floats higher in a more dense fluid because it does not have to sink as far to displace a weight of fluid equal to its own weight. A smaller volume of the displaced denser fluid is able to match the weight of the floating body.

24. Since both preservers are the same size, they will displace the same amount of water when submerged and be buoyed up with equal forces. Effectiveness is another story. The amount of buoyant force exerted on the heavy lead-filled preserver is insignificant, and sinking occurs. The same amount of buoyant force exerted on the lighter Styrofoam preserver is greater than its weight and floating occurs. The amount of the force and the effectiveness of the force are two different things. Think critically.

25. When the ice cube melts the water level at the side of the glass is unchanged (neglecting temperature effects). To see this, suppose the ice cube to be a 5 gram cube; then while floating it will displace 5 grams of water. But when melted it becomes the same 5 grams of water. Hence the water level is unchanged.

26. The weight of a truck is distributed over the part of the tires that make contact with the road. Weight/surface area = pressure, so the greater the surface area, or equivalently, the greater the number of tires, the greater the weight of the truck can be for a given pressure. What pressure? The air pressure in its tires. Can you see how this relates to Home Project 1?

27. We are acclimated so that our bodies push out as hard as the atmospheric pressure pushes in. At higher altitudes where atmospheric pressure is less, our bodies push out a little harder than the atmosphere is pushing in; hence, our ears pop.

28. To begin with, the two teams of horses used in the Magdeburg hemispheres demonstration were for showmanship and effect, for a single team and a strong tree would have provided the same force on the hemispheres. So if two teams of nine horses each could pull the hemispheres apart, a single team of nine horses could also, if a tree or some other strong object were used to hold the other end of the rope.

29. If the item is sealed in an air-tight package at sea level, then the pressure in the package is about 1 atmosphere. Cabin pressure is reduced for high altitude flying, so the pressure in the package is greater than the surrounding pressure and therefore puffs outwards.

30. Unlike water, the density of the atmosphere depends on the depth. Air is compressible, like the foam bricks, and is more dense at the Earth's surface and less dense with increasing altitude.

31. Drinking through a straw is slightly more difficult atop a mountain. This is because the reduced atmospheric pressure is less effective in pushing soda up into the straw.

32. If an elephant steps on you, the pressure that the elephant exerts is over and above the atmospheric pressure that is all the time exerted on you. It is the *extra* pressure the elephant's foot produces that crushes you. For example, if atmospheric pressure the size of an elephant's foot were somehow removed from a patch of your body, you would be in serious trouble. You would be soothed, however, if an elephant stepped onto this area!

33. You agree with your friend, for the elephant displaces far more air than a small helium-filled balloon, or small anything. The *effects* of the buoyant forces, however, is a different story. The large buoyant force on the elephant is insignificant compared to its enormous weight. The tiny buoyant force acting on the balloon of tiny weight, however, is significant.

34. One's lungs, like an inflated balloon, are compressed when submerged in water, and the air within is compressed. Air will not of itself flow from a region of low pressure into a region of higher pressure. The diaphragm in one's body reduces lung pressure to permit breathing, but this limit is strained when nearly 1 m below the water surface. It is exceeded at more than 1 m.

35. The wood has the greater mass. Why? Because the scale reading is weight, *mg*, minus the buoyant force. The wood has a greater volume and therefore a greater buoyant force (displaces more air). To yield the same scale reading it must therefore have a greater mass than the iron. (How much greater? An amount equal to the difference in buoyant force on the wood and iron blocks.)

36. Any object that displaces air is buoyed upwards by a force equal to the weight of air displaced (unless somehow air is prevented from interacting with its bottom surface). Objects therefore weigh less in air than in a vacuum. For objects of low densities, like bags of compressed gases, this can be important. For high-density objects like rocks and boulders the difference is usually negligible.

37. The end supporting the punctured balloon tips upwards as it is lightened by the amount of air that escapes. The weight of air in the inflated balloon (which exceeds the buoyant force acting on it) makes that end move down.

38. The balloon which is free to expand will displace more air as it rises than the balloon which is restrained. Hence, the balloon, which is free to expand will have more buoyant force exerted on it than the balloon that does not expand, and will rise higher.

39. To find the buoyant force that the air exerts on you, find your volume and multiply by the weight density of air (the mass of 1 m^3 of air is about 1.25 kg. Multiply this by 9.8 N/kg and you get 12.25 N/m^3). You can estimate your volume by your weight and by assuming your density is approximately equal to that of water (a little less if you can float). The density of water is 10^{4}N/m^3, which we'll assume is your density. By ratio and proportion:

$$\frac{10^4 \text{N}}{\text{m}^3} = \frac{\text{(your weight in newtons)}}{\text{(your volume in meters}^3\text{)}}$$

If your weight is a heavy 1000 N, for example, your volume is 0.1 m^3. So the buoyant force would be 12.25 N/m^3 × 0.1 m^3 = about **1.2 N**, the weight of a big apple). (A useful conversion factor is 4.45 N = 1 pound.)

40. If you're of average size, your total surface area is about two square meters, so the force of the atmosphere on you is about 2 × 10^5 N (which is about 22 tons, the weight of a freight car!). This is the force of air pressing against your body, to which your body and the air in it pushes back in kind. So the total force of the atmosphere against you is enormous, as enormous as the force with which air in your body pushes back on the atmosphere. Be glad of atmospheric pressure, for without it, you'd bloat to death. The force of the atmosphere is "required" to keep you from bloating outward (which is why astronauts wear strong space suits). In contrast, the buoyant force of the atmosphere on you is very small, being the weight of air you displace. Total force acting by the air is a much different quantity than the weight of air you displace, which is why the and Exercise 36 are asking for entirely different things.

41. The force of the atmosphere is on both sides of the window; the net force is zero, so windows don't normally break under the weight of the atmosphere. In a strong wind, however, pressure will be reduced on the windward side (Bernoulli's Principle) and the forces no longer cancel to zero. Many windows are blown *outward* in strong winds.

42. Air blows over the top of the beach ball and reduces the air pressure there (Bernoulli's Principle). The greater pressure in the non-moving air below pushes the ball upward.

43. Air moves faster over the spinning top of the Frisbee and pressure against the top is reduced. The bowl shape of the bottom contains a relatively dead air space underneath, that exerts near-normal pressure against the bottom. So like the beach ball in the previous exercise, there is a difference in pressures against the Frisbee that produces an upward lift.

44. According to Bernoulli's Principle, the pressure will be less on the side of the car where the air is moving fastest. This is the side of the car nearest the truck, resulting in the car's being pushed by the atmosphere towards the truck.

45. With respect to the car, the interior air is at rest and the air above and outside the roof is in motion. So atmospheric pressure is greater inside the car than it is outside. The canvas roof top is therefore pushed upwards towards the region of lesser pressure.

46. Like the reason for the bulging canvas roof in the preceding exercise, with respect to the train windows, the interior air is at rest and the air outside is in motion. The atmospheric pressure against the inner surface of the window is therefore greater than the atmospheric pressure against the outside. When the difference in pressures is significant enough, the window is blown out.

47. Like an airplane wing, the air moves fastest over the crest. Pressure is therefore lowest at the top of the crests than down below in the troughs. The greater pressure in the troughs pushes the water into even higher crests.

48. Air moves faster past the convex portions of the flag and slower past the concave portions of the flag's surfaces, producing pressure differences as in the last exercise. Increased pressure on the concave side of the flag is met with decreased pressure on the convex side of the flag, with the result that the "waves" increase in amplitude, extending into the wind, which blows them along the length of the flag with the result that the free end flaps to and fro. (We should give some credit to your friend who stated a flag flaps because of Bernoulli's principle. To one who understands Bernoulli's principle, the answer is sufficient. To one who isn't, more explanation should be given.)

49. A solid-walled wharf is disadvantageous to ships pulling alongside because water currents are constrained and speed up between the ship and the wharf. This results in a reduced water pressure, and the normal pressure on the other side of the ship then forces the ship against the wharf. The pilings avoid this mishap by allowing the freer passage of water between the wharf and the ship.

50. According to Bernoulli's principle, when a fluid gains speed in flowing through a narrow region, the pressure of the fluid is reduced. The gain in speed, the cause, produces reduced pressure, the effect. But one can argue that a reduced pressure in a fluid, the cause, will produce a flow in the direction of the reduced pressure, the effect. For example, if you decrease the air pressure in a pipe by a pump or by any means, neighboring air will rush into the region of reduced pressure. In this case the increase in air speed is the result, not the cause of, reduced pressure. Cause and effect are open to interpretation. Bernoulli's principle is a controversial topic with many physics types!

Chapter 5 Problem Solutions

1. (a) The volume of the extra water displaced will weigh as much as the 400-kg horse. And the volume of extra water displaced will also equal the area of the barge times the extra depth. That is, $V = Ah$, where A is the horizontal area of the barge; Then $h = \dfrac{V}{A}$.

   Now $A = 5\text{m} \times 2\text{m} = 10 \text{ m}^2$; to find the volume V of barge pushed into the water by the horse's weight, which equals the volume of water displaced, we know that

   density $= \dfrac{m}{V}$. Or from this, $V = \dfrac{m}{\text{density}} = \dfrac{400\text{kg}}{1000\text{kg/m}^3} = 0.4 \text{ m}^3$.

   So $h = \dfrac{V}{A} = \dfrac{0.4 \text{ m}^3}{10 \text{ m}^2} = 0.04$ m, which is **4 cm** deeper.

   (b) If each horse will push the barge 4 cm deeper, the question becomes: How many 4-cm increments will make 15 cm? $15/4 = 3.75$, so **3 horses** can be carried without sinking. 4 horses will sink the barge.

2. From Table 5.1 the density of gold is 19.3 g/cm^3. Your gold has a mass of 1000 grams, so $\dfrac{1000 \text{ g}}{V} = 19.3$ g/cm^3. Solving for V,

   $V = \dfrac{1000 \text{ g}}{19.3 \text{ g/cm}^3} = \textbf{51.8 cm}^\textbf{3}$.

3. Density $= \dfrac{\text{mass}}{\text{volume}} = \dfrac{2.0 \text{ kg}}{\text{volume of (2.0 - 1.5) kg of water}} = \dfrac{2.0 \text{ kg}}{0.5 \text{ L}} = 4$ kg/L. And since 1 liter (L) $= 10^3$ cm $= 10^{-3}$ m, density $= \textbf{4,000 kg/m}^\textbf{3}$.

   (Or this can be reasoned as follows: The buoyant force on the object is the force needed to support 0.5 kg, so 0.5 kg of water is displaced. Since density is mass/volume, volume is mass/density, and displaced volume $= (0.5 \text{ kg})/(1000 \text{ kg/m}^3) = 5 \times 10^{-4}$ m^3. The object's volume is the same as the volume it displaces, so the object's density is mass/volume $= (2 \text{ kg})/(5 \times 10^{-4}$ m$^3)$ $= 4000$ kg/m^3, four times the density of water.)

4. 10% of ice extends above water. So 10% of the 9-cm thick ice would float above the water line; **0.9 cm**. So the ice pops up. Interestingly, when mountains erode they become lighter and similarly pop up! Hence it takes a long time for mountains to wear away.

5. The displaced water, with a volume 90 percent of the vacationer's volume, weighs the same as the vacationer (to provide a buoyant force equal to his weight). Therefore his density is 90 percent of the water's density. Vacationer's density $= (0.90)(1,025 \text{ kg/m}^3) = \textbf{923 kg/m}^\textbf{3}$.

6. (a) The weight of the displaced air must be the same as the weight supported, since the total force (gravity plus buoyancy) is zero. The displaced air weighs **20,000 N**. (b) Since weight $= mg$, the mass of the displaced air is $m = W/g = (20,000 \text{ N})/(10 \text{ m/s}^2) = 2,000$ kg. Since density is mass/volume, the volume of the displaced air is vol $=$ mass/density $= (2,000 \text{ kg})/(1.2 \text{ kg/m}^3) =$ **1,700 m$^\textbf{3}$** (same answer to two figures if $g = 9.8$ m/s^2 is used).

6   Thermal Energy

Answers to Exercises

1. You cannot establish by your own touch whether or not you are running a fever because there would be no temperature difference between your hand and forehead. If your forehead is a couple of degrees higher in temperature than normal, your hand is also a couple of degrees higher.

2. The hot coffee has a higher temperature, but not a greater thermal energy. Although the iceberg has less thermal energy per mass, its enormously greater mass gives it a greater total energy than that in the small cup of coffee. (For a smaller volume of ice, the fewer number of more energetic molecules in the hot cup of coffee may constitute a greater total amount of thermal energy — but not compared to an iceberg.)

3. If glass and mercury expanded at the same rate with increasing temperature, a mercury thermo-meter would not be feasible. This is because an increase in volume of the mercury would be met with an equal increase in the volume of the glass reservoir, so the level in the tube wouldn't change.

4. Temperature is a measurement of the degree of hotness or coldness of a substance, measured in degrees (or kelvins). More precisely it is a measure of the average kinetic energy per molecule in a substance.

5. Hydrogen molecules will be the faster moving when mixed with oxygen molecules. They will have the same temperature, which means they will have the same average kinetic energy. Recall that $KE = 1/2\ mv^2$. Since the mass of hydrogen is considerably less than oxygen, the velocity must correspondingly be greater.

6. The hot rock will cool and the cool water will warm, regardless of the relative amounts of each. The amount of temperature change, however, does depend in great part on the relative masses of the materials. For a hot rock dropped into the Atlantic Ocean, the change in temperature would be too small to measure. Keep increasing the mass of the rock or keep decreasing the mass of the ocean and the change will be evident.

7. Increasing temperature means increasing KE which means increasing momentum of molecules, which means greater impact and greater pressure against the walls of the container. Simply put, as the temperature of a confined gas is increased, the molecules move faster and exert a greater pressure on the walls of the container.

8. You'll produce the same increase in temperature only if both materials of the same mass have the same specific heat capacity. Add heat to a gram of material with a low specific heat and the temperature will rise higher than the same amount of heat added to a gram of material with a higher specific heat.

9. A watermelon has a high water content, which means it has a high specific heat capacity. So its temperature is more reluctant to change than things with lower specific heat capacities.

10. The climate of Bermuda, like that of all islands, is moderated by the high specific heat of water. The climate is moderated by the large amounts of energy given off and absorbed by water for small changes in temperature. When the air is cooler than the water, the water warms the air; when the air is warmer than the water, the water cools the air.

11. Water has the highest specific heat capacity, so will maintain its high temperature longer than a hot brick. The hot towel is comfortable while the bottle of water or brick is very hot. Then as each cools, the towel can be removed for contact with feet.

12. As the ocean off the coast of San Francisco cools in the winter, the heat it loses warms the atmosphere it comes in contact with. This warmed air blows over the California coastline to produce a relatively warm climate. If the winds were easterly instead of westerly, the climate of San Francisco would be chilled by winter winds from dry and cold Nevada. The climate would

be reversed also in Washington D.C., because air warmed by the cooling of the Atlantic Ocean would blow over Washington D.C. and produce a warmer climate in winter there.

13. The more thermal energy states that a molecule has, the more energy it can absorb in those states. This greater capacity for absorbing potential energy is a higher specific heat.

14. Sand has a low specific heat, as evidenced by its relatively large temperature changes for small changes in thermal energy. A substance with a high specific heat, on the other hand, must absorb or give off large amounts of thermal energy for comparable temperature changes.

15. Natural gas is sold by volume. The gas meter that tallies your gas bill operates by measuring the number of cubic units that pass through it. Warm gas is expanded gas and occupies more space, and if it passes through your meter, it will be registered as more gas than if it were cooled and more compact. The gas company gains if gas is warm when it goes through your meter because the same amount of warmer gas has a greater volume.

16. Every part of a metal ring expands when it is heated — not only the thickness, but the outer and inner circumference as well. Hence the ball that normally passes through the hole when the temperatures are equal will more easily pass through the expanded hole when the ring is heated. (Interestingly enough, the hole will expand as much as a disk of the same metal undergoing the same increase in temperature. Blacksmiths mounted metal rims in wooden wagon wheels by first heating the rims. Upon cooling, the contraction resulted in a snug fit.)

17. Brass expands and contracts more than iron for the same changes in temperature. Since they are both good conductors and are in contact with each other, one cannot be heated or cooled without also heating or cooling the other. If the iron ring is heated, it expands — but the brass expands even more. Cooling the two will not result in separation either, for even at the lowest temperatures the shrinkage of brass over iron would not produce separation.

18. The gap in the ring will become wider when the ring is heated. Try this: draw a couple of lines on a ring where you pretend a gap to be. When you heat the ring, the lines will be farther apart — the same amount as if a real gap were there. Every part of the ring expands proportionally when heated uniformly — thickness, length, gap and all.

19. When a mercury thermometer is warmed, the outside glass is heated before heat gets to the mercury inside. So the glass is the first to expand, momentarily opening (like the ring in Exercise 16) which allows the mercury to drop from the glass tube into the slightly enlarged reservoir. When the mercury warms to the same temperature of the glass, it is then forced up the glass tube because of its greater expansion rate.

20. Poor cold water in the inner glass and it contracts. Dunk both in hot water so the outer glass heats first and expands. Then the glasses will easily slip apart.

21. On a hot day a steel tape will expand more than the ground. You will be measuring land with a "stretched" tape. So you'll get more land. (If you're measuring land *already* staked, then your measurements will be less than the actual land. In this case the land will be measured smaller than it actually is.)

22. Lake Superior has cold winters where water cools to 4°C. This water sinks to the bottom, and due to water's poor conductivity, tends to remain at 4°C year round. Lake Toba, on the other hand, is in the tropics. Water temperature never drops to 4°C, so there's no 4°C water in Lake Toba.

23. Any change in the temperature of 4°C water results in expansion. So if the temperature drops to 3°C, the water expands. If it rises to 5°C it rises. The thermometer is ambiguous in the range of temperatures near 4°C.

24. The combined volume of all the billions of "open rooms" in the hexagonal ice crystals of a piece of ice is equal to the volume of the part of the ice that extends above water when ice floats. When the ice melts, the open spaces are exactly filled in by the amount of ice that extends above the water level. This is why the water level doesn't rise when ice in a glass of ice water melts — the melting ice "caves in" and exactly fills the open spaces.

25. The curve for density versus temperature is:

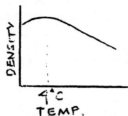

26. It is important to keep water in pipes from freezing because water expands more than the pipe material, which will fracture the pipes if water in them freezes.

27. If cooling occurred at the bottom of a pond instead of at the surface, ice would still form at the surface, but it would take much longer for ponds to freeze. This is because all the water in the pond would have to be reduced to a temperature of $0°C$ rather than $4°C$ before the first ice would form. Ice that forms at the bottom where the cooling process is occurring would be less dense and would float to the surface (except for ice that may form about material anchored to the bottom of the pond).

28. Ponds would be more likely to freeze if water had a lower specific heat. This is because the temperature would undergo more decrease when water gives up energy; water would more readily be cooled to the freezing point.

29. When a wet finger is held to the wind, evaporation is greatest on the windy side, which feels cool. The cool side of your finger is windward.

30. Hot coffee poured into a saucer cools (1) because the greater surface area of the coffee permits more evaporation to take place, and (2) by the conservation of energy, the thermal energy that heats up the saucer comes from the coffee, which subsequently is cooled.

31. When you blow over the top of a bowl of hot soup, you increase net evaporation and its cooling effect by removing the warm vapor which tends to condense and reduce net evaporation. Also, the moving air reduces pressure atop the soup (Bernoulli's Principle) and increases the rate of evaporation.

32. Perfume evaporates rapidly (if it didn't, its aroma would go unnoticed). When applied to one ear, that ear feels noticeably cooler due to the rapid evaporation

33. The key idea here is *net*. There be no net evaporation or no net condensation with the glass of water, but both changes of phase occur continually. If their rates are the same, then there is not net difference. But to say that nothing is occurring is incorrect.

34. If the molecules evaporating from the liquid have no more average kinetic energy than those left behind, there would be no cooling of the remaining liquid. Cooling occurs when the average energy of molecules in the liquid is lowered. If there is not changing of the average energy, there's no change in temperature.

35. In a porous canvas bag, the faster-moving molecules are most prone to seep through the canvas material and evaporate into the air, leaving the slower-moving molecules behind. The motion of the car increases the rate of evaporation and cools the water inside, just as blowing over a hot bowl of soup tends to cool the soup (Exercise 31).

36. A bottle wrapped in wet cloth will cool by the evaporation of liquid from the cloth. As evaporation progresses, the average temperature of the liquid left behind in the cloth can easily drop below the temperature of the cool water that wet it in the first place. So to cool a bottle of beer, soda, or whatever at a picnic, wet a piece of cloth in a bucket of cool water. Wrap the wet cloth around the bottle to be cooled. As evaporation progresses, the temperature of the water in the cloth drops, and cools the bottle to a temperature below that of the bucket of water.

37. The body keeps its temperature a normal $37°C$ by the process of evaporation. When the body tends to overheat, perspiration occurs, which cools the body if the perspiration is allowed to evaporate. (Interestingly enough, if you're immersed in hot water, perspiration occurs profusely, but evaporation and cooling do not follow — that's why it is inadvisable to stay too long in a hot bath.)

38. When water is boiling, it is being cooled by the boiling process as fast as it is being heated by the stove. Hence its temperature remains the same — 100°C.

39. The hot water in a nuclear power plant is under great pressure, so like a pressure cooker, has boiling temperatures considerably greater than the 100°C typical of atmospheric pressure.

40. You could not cook food in low-temperature water that is boiling by virtue of reduced pressure. Food is cooked by the high temperature it is subjected to, not by the bubbling of the surrounding water. For example, put room-temperature water in a vacuum and it will boil. But this doesn't mean the water will transfer more thermal energy to an egg than before boiling — an egg in this boiling water won't cook at all!

41. As in the answer to the previous exercise, high temperature and the resulting thermal energy given to the food is responsible for cooking — if the water boils at a low temperature (presumably under reduced pressure) insufficient energy is given to cook the food.

42. The air in the flask is very low in pressure, so that the heat from your hand will produce boiling at this reduced pressure. (Your instructor will want to be sure that the flask is strong enough to resist implosion before handing it to you!)

43. Cooking time will be no different for vigorously boiling water and gently boiling water, for both have the same temperature. The reason spaghetti is cooked in vigorously boiling water is simply to ensure the spaghetti doesn't stick to itself and the pan. For fuel economy, simply stir your spaghetti in gently boiling water .

44. The lid on the pot traps heat which quickens boiling; the lid also increases pressure on the boiling water which raises its boiling temperature. The hotter water correspondingly cooks food in a shorter time.

45. When snowing occurs, heat is given to the atmosphere by the change of phase of water vapor when it becomes snow. Consequently, snowing occurs on relatively warm days because the act of snowing warms the air. Because people don't experience snowing on cold days, many may incorrectly assume that snowing can't occur when the temperature is low. It certainly can. But it won't stay cold for long.

46. When ice melts, it absorbs energy from the surroundings. It cools the surroundings, which is why you put ice in a picnic cooler.

47. When water freezes, it releases energy to the surrounding air. So the air is warmed by the change of phase from water to ice. Keep water in an igloo when you're in the Arctic. As it freezes, you'll keep the interior of the igloo warmer than if the freezing water weren't there. (See the answer to Exercise 49.)

48. Water vapor in the warm air condenses on the relatively low-temperature surface of the can. Hence a cold can on a hot day very quickly becomes wet.

49. Every gram of water that undergoes freezing releases 80 calories of energy to the cellar. This continual release of energy by the freezing water keeps the temperature of the cellar from going below 0°C. Sugar and salts in the canned goods prevent them from freezing at 0°C. Only when all the water in the tub freezes will the temperature of the cellar go below 0°C and then freeze the canned goods. The farmer must, therefore, replace the tub before or just as soon as all the water in it has frozen.

50. This is an application of Exercise 47. When water freezes, it releases energy to the surrounding air. As temperature drops, more freezing occurs, keeping temperature stable in a way similar to the way boiling water keeps its temperature as it warms the surroundings.

51. The answer to this is similar to the previous answer, and also the fact that the coating of ice acts as an insulating blanket. Every gram of water that freezes releases 80 calories, much of it to the fruit; the thin layer of ice then acts as an insulating blanket against further loss of heat.

Chapter 6 Problem Solutions

1. If a 1-m long bar expands 1/2 cm when heated, a bar of the same material that is 100 times as long will expand 100 times as much, 0.5 cm for each meter, or **50 cm**. (The heated bar will be 100.5 m.)

2. For a $10°C$ increase, the steel bridge will expand 10 parts in 10^5, or one part in 10,000 (10^4). The bridge will expand by one-ten thousandth of 1.3 kilometers, or one-ten-thousandths of 1300 meters, which is **13 centimeters.** So the main span of the Golden Gate bridge expands 13 centimeters when the temperature increases by $10°C$.

   By formula: $\Delta L = L_0 \alpha \Delta T = (1300m)(10^{-5}/°C)(10°C) = 0.13$ m

3. If a snugly fitting steel pipe that girdled the world were heated by 1 Celsius degree, it would stand nearly 64 meters off the ground! The most straight-forward way to see this is to consider the radius of the 40 000 kilometer pipe, which is the radius of the Earth, 6370 kilometers. Steel will expand one part in a hundred thousand for each $C°$ increase in temperature; the radius as well as the circumference will expand by this amount. So one hundred thousandths of 6370 kilometers = **63.7 meters.**

   Or by formula for the Earth's radius, $\Delta L = L_0 \alpha \Delta T = (6370 \times 10^3 m)(10^{-5}/°C)(1°C) = $ **63.7 m.**

4. First, find the number of calories that 10 g of 100°C steam will give in changing to 10 g of 0°C water.
   10 g of steam changing to 10 g of boiling water at 100°C releases 5400 calories.
   10 g of 100°C water cooling to 0°C releases 1000 calories.
   So 6400 calories are available for melting ice.

   $$\frac{6400 \text{ cal}}{80 \text{ cal/g}} = \textbf{80 grams} \text{ of ice.}$$

5. Amount of energy (Q)/rate = time. Q = mcΔT = 1 kg (200 cal/kg·C°)(700°C - 50°C) = 130,000 cal/kg. So 130,000 cal/kg divided by 0.01 cal/kg.yr = **13 million years.**

7   Heat Transfer and Thermodynamics

Answers to Exercises

1. No, the temperature will not rise when a fur coat is wrapped around a thermometer. All the fur coat will do is slow down heat transfer with its excellent insulation.

2. Air at 70°F feels comfortable principally because it is a poor conductor. Our warmer skin is slow to transfer heat to the air. Water, however, is a better conductor of heat than air, so our warmer bodies in water more readily transfer heat to the water.

3. When the temperatures of the blocks are the same as the temperature of your hand, then no heat transfer occurs. Heat will flow between your hand and something being touched only if there is a temperature difference between them.

4. In touching the tongue to very cold metal, enough heat can be quickly conducted away from the tongue to bring the saliva to sub-zero temperature where it freezes, locking the tongue to the metal. In the case of relatively non-conducting wood, much less heat is conducted from the tongue and freezing does not take place fast enough for sudden sticking to occur.

5. Aluminum is an excellent heat conductor, so will conduct heat into the frozen food to be thawed. The black color adds to its ability to absorb. Hence the reason for commercial thawing slabs that are black aluminum alloys.

6. Heat from the relatively warm ground is conducted by the gravestone to melt the snow in contact with the gravestone. Likewise for trees or any materials that are better conductors of heat than snow, and that extend into the ground.

7. The snow and ice of the igloo is a better insulator than wood. You would be warmer in the igloo than the wooden shack.

8. Much of the energy of the flame is readily conducted through the paper to the water. The relatively large amount of water, compared to the paper, absorbs the energy that would otherwise raise the temperature of the paper. The upper limit of 212°F for the water is well below the ignition temperature of the paper, 451°F (hence the title "451" of Ray Bradbury's science fiction novel about book burning).

9. You can hold your fingers quite close to the side of a candle flame without harm because the air between is a good insulator. But you will burn your fingers if you hold them above the flame because of the convection of hot gases in the flame. (Interestingly enough, candle flames will quickly snuff out in orbiting space facilities or any gravity free region. This is because convection depends on gravity, and without convection new oxygen cannot get to the flame.)

10. Air is a poor conductor, whatever the temperature. So holding your hand in hot air for a short time is not harmful because very little heat is conducted by the air to your hand. But if you touch the hot conducting surface of the oven, heat readily conducts to you — ouch!

11. Wood is a poor conductor whatever the temperature, (as John Suchocki demonstrates with his bare feet in Figure 7.2) so you can safely grab a pan by its wooden handle for a short time. Like the hot air in the previous exercise, this is because very little heat will be conducted to your hand. Touching the iron part of the hand is another story, for then heat is readily conducted to your hand. Ouch again!

12. The conductivity of wood is relatively low whatever the temperature — even in the stage of red hot coals. You can safely walk barefoot across red hot wooden coals if you step quickly (like removing the wooden-handled frying pan with bare hands quickly from the hot oven in the previous exercise) because very little heat is conducted to your feet. Because of the poor conductivity of the coals, energy from within the coals does not readily replace the energy that transfers to your feet. This is evident in the diminished redness of the coal after your foot has left

it. Stepping on red-hot iron coals, however, is a different story. Because of the excellent conductivity of iron, very damaging amounts of heat would transfer to your feet. More than simply ouch!

13. The mixture expands when it is ejected from the nozzle, and therefore cools. At the freezing temperature of 0°C, ice forms.

14. Heat transfer is by convection and radiation. Black is the most efficient color for steam radiators. Contrary to the name "radiator," much of the heat produced is by convection, which has to do with its high temperature.

15. The heat you received was from radiation.

16. A good emitter, by virtue of molecular-or-whatever design, is also a good absorber. A good absorber appears black because radiation that impinges upon it is absorbed; just the opposite of reflection. The blackness of materials is evidence for their absorption. By the same token the blackness is also evidence for their emission. The radiation that an object emits at normal temperatures is too low in frequency to be seen by the eye. (A hot black pot will emit more energy in a shorter time than a hot silver pot of the same mass and material.)

17. If good absorbers were not also good emitters, then thermal equilibrium would not be possible. If a good absorber only absorbed, then its temperature would climb above that of poorer absorbers in the vicinity. And if poor absorbers were good emitters, their temperatures would fall below that of better absorbers.

18. A good reflector is a poor radiator of heat, and a poor reflector is a good radiator of heat.

19. Put the cream in right away for at least three reasons. Since black coffee radiates more heat than white coffee, make it whiter right away so it won't radiate and cool so quickly while you are waiting. Also, by Newton's law of cooling, the higher the temperature of the coffee above the surroundings, the greater will be the rate of cooling — so again add cream right away and lower the temperature to that of a reduced cooling rate, rather allowing it to cool fast and then bring the temperature down still further by adding the cream later. Also — by adding the cream, you increases the total amount of liquid, which for the same surface area, cools slower.

20. Heat radiates into the clear night air and the temperature of the car goes down. Normally, heat is conducted to the car by the relatively warmer ground, but the rubber tires prevent the conduction of heat from the ground. So heat radiated away is not easily replaced and the car cools to temperatures below that of the surroundings. In this way frost can form on a below-freezing car in the above-freezing environment.

21. In accordance with Newton's law of cooling, if the Earth's temperature increases, its rate of radiating will increase. And if much of this extra terrestrial radiation is blocked, and the temperature of the Earth increases more, then its rate of radiating simply increases further. A new and higher equilibrium temperature is established.

22. Kelvin and Celcius degrees differ by 273. So whether or not the temperature of the oven is 500 °C or 500 K is quite a different situation. 500 K is actually 500 - 273 = 227 °C, quite a bit different than 500 °C! But for the 50,000 °C or 50,000 K star, the 273 is not significant, and 50,000 K is much the same as a 50,000 °C. (The number 50,273 to two significant figures is 50,000 anyway.)

23. No, for like the previous exercise, a difference of 273 in 10,000,000 is insignificant.

24. Its absolute temperature is 273 +10 = 283 K. Double this and you have 566 K. Expressed in Celsius; 566 - 273 = 293 °C.

25. You do work on the liquid when you shake it back and forth, which increases its thermal energy. This is noted by an increase in temperature.

26. The tire becomes hot for two reasons: 1. The work done in compressing the air increases its thermal energy which is conducted to and shared with the pump. 2. For the increase in temperature involves friction, for the piston rubs against the inner wall of the pump cylinder.

27. A given amount of mechanical energy can be easily and commonly converted to heat; any body moving with kinetic energy that is brought to rest by friction transforms all its kinetic energy into heat (like a car skidding to rest on a horizontal road). The converse is not true, however. In accord with the 2nd law of thermodynamics, only a fraction of a given amount of thermal energy can be converted to mechanical energy. For example, when steam in a steam engine expands against a piston, only some of the thermal energy is converted to work — the rest goes into over-coming friction.

28. If yanked suddenly to the ground, it would be compressed by the greater pressure of air below. This adiabatic compression would heat the confined air by about $10^{\circ}C$ for each kilometer decrease in elevation. If it were 1 km high at a temperature of 0 °C and yanked below, its temperature at ground level would be 10°C. Of if yanked from an altitude of 10 km, where air temperature is typically -35°C, the air would be heated $100C^{\circ}$ and have a ground temperature of about (-35 + 100) = $65^{\circ}C$. (This is $149^{\circ}F$, roasting hot!)

29. This transfer would not violate the lst law because energy has been transferred without loss or gain. It would violate the 2nd law, because thermal energy will not freely transfer from a cooler to a warmer object.

30. The Sun is the energy source for all fossil fuels.

31. The term pollution refers to an undesirable by-product of some process. The desirability or undesirability of a particular by-product is relative, and depends on the circumstances. For example, ejecting hot water into cooler water can be quite desirable from one point of view and undesirable from another point of view.

32. According to the 2nd law, it is not possible to construct a heat engine that is without exhaust. If the exhausted heat is undesirable then the engine is a polluter. If the exhausted heat is desirable, heating a swimming pool for example, then in this sense the heat engine produces no thermal pollution.

33. When the temperature is lowered in the reservoir into which heat is rejected, efficiency increases; substitution of a smaller value of T_{cold} into $(T_{hot} - T_{cold})/T_{hot}$ will confirm this. Re-express the equation as $(1 - [T_{cold}/T_{hot}])$ to better see this.

34. Efficiency will increase, because back pressure is reduced. Efficiency increases (though not noticeably) on a cold day because of the greater ΔT in Carnot's equation.

35. Only when the sink is absolute zero (0 K) will an engine have an ideal efficiency of 100%.

36. Even if the refrigerator were magically 100% efficient, the room wouldn't be cooled because the heat sink is also in the room. That's why the condensation coils are in a region outside the region to be cooled. What actually happens in the case of the refrigerator being operated with its door open in a closed room is that the room temperature increases. This is because the refrigerator motor warms the surrounding air. Net electric energy is coming into the room, heating it.

37. Unlike trying to cool a room by leaving the refrigerator door open, one can certainly warm up a room by operating an oven and leaving the oven door open. In this case energy is being supplied to a larger system — the oven and the room.

38. You *are* cooled by the fan, which blows air over you to increase the rate of evaporation from your skin, but you are a small part of the overall system, which warms.

39. 100%! All the energy in the radiant energy emitted by the lamp is quickly absorbed as heat.

40. Most people know that electric lights are inefficient when it comes to converting electrical energy into light energy, so they are surprised to learn there is a 100% conversion of electrical energy to thermal energy. If the building is being heated electrically, the lights do a fine job of heating, and it is not at all wasteful to keep them on while heating is desirable. It is a wasteful practice if the air conditioners are on and cooling is desired, for the energy input to the air conditioners must be increased to remove the extra thermal energy given off by the lights.

the air conditioners are on and cooling is desired, for the energy input to the air conditioners must be increased to remove the extra thermal energy given off by the lights.

41. It is fundamental because it governs the general tendency throughout nature to move from order to disorder, yet it is inexact in the sense that it is based on probability, not certainty.

42. Most of the electric energy that goes into lighting a lamp turns immediately into thermal energy. In the case of an incandescent lamp, only about 5% goes into light, and in a fluorescent lamp, about 20% goes to light. But all of the energy that takes the form of light is converted to thermal energy when the light is absorbed by materials upon which it is incident. So by the lst law, all the electrical energy is ultimately converted to thermal energy. By the second law, organized electrical energy degenerates to the more disorganized form, thermal energy.

43. Entropy of the overall system, of which the chicken is a small part, increases. So when the larger system is taken into account, there is no violation of the principle of entropy.

44. (a) Yes, very likely. Two heads would come up on average one throw out of four. (b) Not likely. The chance for ten coins to come up all heads is only about 1 in 1000. (c) Extremely unlikely, even with a lifetime of trying. The laws of thermodynamics are based on the statistics of large numbers.

45. Like the previous exercise, the smaller the number of random particles, the more the likelihood of them becoming more ordered increases. But the number of molecules in even the smallest room? Sleep comfortably!

Chapter 7 Problem Solutions

1. If by "twice as cold" she means one half the absolute temperature, the temperature would be (1/2)(273 +10) = 141.5K. To find how many Celsius degrees below $0°$C this is, we first subtract 141.5K from 273K; this is 273 - 141.5 = 131.5K below the freezing point of ice, or **-131.5°C.** (Or simply, 141.5 - 273 = -131.5$°$C.) Quite nippy!

2. Ideal efficiency $= \dfrac{T_h - T_c}{T_h} = \dfrac{2700 - 300}{2700} = \mathbf{0.88}$

3. Converting to kelvins; 25°C = 298 K; 4°C = 277 K. So
   Carnot efficiency $= \dfrac{T_h - T_c}{T_h} = \dfrac{298 - 277}{298} = \mathbf{0.07.}$ This is very low, which means that large volumes of water (which there are) must be processed for sufficient power generation.

4. Seven is most likely because there are more combinations that give seven than any other sum. Of the 36 possible combinations, 6 give seven.

8 Electricity

Answers to Exercises

1. Clothes become charged when electrons from a garment of one material are rubbed onto another material. If the materials were good conductors, discharge between materials would soon occur. But the clothes are nonconducting and the charge remains long enough for oppositely charged garments to be electrically attracted and stick to one another.

2. Electrons are easily dislodged from the outer regions of atoms, but protons are held tightly within the nucleus.

3. The crystal as a whole has a zero net charge, so any negative charge in one part is countered with as much positive charge in another part. So the net charge of the negative electrons has the same magnitude as the net charge of the ions. (This balancing of positive and negative charges within the crystal is almost, but not precisely, perfect because the crystal can gain or lose a few extra electrons.)

4. The electrons don't fly out of the penny because they are attracted to the five thousand billion billion positively charged nuclei in the penny.

5. The law would be written no differently.

6. When a pair of charged particles are brought to half their separation distance the force is quadrupled; to one quarter their separation, the force is increased 16 fold. But four times as far apart, the force is reduced by 1/16. This is in accord with the inverse-square law.

7. (a) For charged pellets, the electric force is likely to be much greater than the gravitational force.
(b) Both change by the same factor (to one-quarter of their original value) because both obey an inverse-square law.

8. The forces they exert on each other are still the same! Newton's third law applies to electrical forces.

9. The leaves, like the rest of the electroscope, acquire charge from the charged object and repel each other because they both have the same sign of charge. The weight of the conducting gold foil is so small that even tiny forces are clearly evident.

10. Cosmic rays produce ions in air, which offer a conducting path for the discharge of charged objects in the vicinity. Cosmic rays are (fortunately!) absorbed to a great degree in the atmosphere. But at higher altitudes where the atmosphere is thinner, there is a greater influx of cosmic rays and a resulting greater amount of ions in the air. Charged objects more quickly lose their charge at higher altitudes.

11. The electrons to be stripped are in the fields of both the positive nucleus and the negative neighboring electrons. Plucking the outer ones is relatively easy, for the electric field set up by the positive nucleus (which attracts electrons) is diminished by the electric field set up by other electrons (which repel electrons) in the atom. As more electrons are stripped, the electric field is predominantly that of the attracting nucleus. When one or two electrons are all that remain, you can imagine the difficulty in pulling them away from the overwhelming field due primarily to 92 or so close-packed positive charges. Only in recent years have researchers at U.C. Berkeley succeeded in removing the innermost electrons of heavy elements like uranium.

12. In both the case of electrical and heat conductors, the conduction is via electrons, which in a metal are loosely bound, easy flowing, and easy to get moving. (Many fewer electrons in metals take part in heat conduction compared to electric conduction, however.)

13. The outer electrons of atoms composing these materials are tightly bound, which makes them good electrical conductors — in contrast with the loose outer electrons (conduction electrons) of conductors.

14. The thickness of the paper contributes to a distance between positive and negative sides of the paper. In accord with the inverse-square law, the farther side with the same magnitude of charge experiences the smaller force. So although the net charge on the paper is zero, there is a net attractive force to the external charge.

15. Planet Earth is negatively charged. If it were positive, the field would point outward.

16. At twice the distance the field strength will be 1/4, in accord with the inverse-square law.

17. 10 joules per coulomb is 10 volts. When released, its 10 joules of potential energy, becomes 10 joules of kinetic energy as it passes its starting point.

18. The molecules in the uncharged bits of paper are induced into alignment with the electric field of the nearby charged balloon. This alignment is charge polarization. So the charges on the balloon interact with the charged sides of the polarized molecules. Closeness wins, and the attraction between the nearer opposite charged side of the polarized molecules is greater than the repulsion between the balloon and farther same-sign charge of the molecules. Charge polarization always results in a net attraction.

19. The metal spikes penetrating into the ground reduce electrical resistance between the golfer and the ground, providing an effective electrical path from cloud to ground. Not a good idea!

20. You are not harmed by contact with a charged balloon, for the same reason you are not harmed by the sparks from a grinder or from a fireworks sparkler. Although both the balloon and sparks have a high ratio of energy per "substance," the total energy in each case is safely small. Electric potential is energy per charge; temperature is energy per molecule — although the ratio of each may be high, if the energy to transfer is small, transfer is safe in both cases.

21. Agree with your friend. The hairs act like leaves in an electroscope. If your arms were as light, they'd stand out too.

22. When you touch the negatively charged dome of the Van de Graaff generator you share some of that charge. Your hair is negatively charged, which is why the strands repel. In brushing a comb through your hair, you remove electrons from your hair and the comb and your hair have opposite charges. But in touching the generator , the excess generator charge is shared with you.

23. The cooling system of an automobile better illustrates the current in an electric circuit because like an electric system it is a closed system. The water hose does not recirculate the water as the auto cooling system does.

24. As the current in the filament of a light bulb increases, the bulb glows brighter.

25. Your tutor is wrong. An ampere measures current, and a volt measures electric potential (electric pressure). They are entirely different concepts; voltage produces amperes in a conductor.

26. A lie detector circuit relies on the resistivity of your body to change when a lie is told. Nervousness promotes perspiration, which lowers the body's electrical resistance, and increases whatever current flows. If a person is able to lie with no emotional change and no change in perspiration, then such a lie detector will not be effective. (Better lying indicators focus on the eyes.)

27. Most of the energy, typically 95%, of the electrical energy in an incandescent lamp goes directly to heat. Heat energy is the graveyard of all forms of energy.

28. Thick wires have less resistance and will more effectively carry currents without excessive heating.

29. (a) The resistance will be half, 5 ohms, when cut in half. (b) The resistance will be half again when the cross-sectional area is doubled, so it will be 2.5 ohms.

30. Current will be greater in the bulb connected to the 220-volt source. Twice the voltage would produce twice the current if the resistance of the filament remained the same. (In practice, the greater current produces a higher temperature and greater resistance in the lamp filament, so the current is greater than that produced by 110 volts, but appreciably less than twice as much for 220 volts. A bulb rated for 110 volts has a very short life when operated at 220 volts.)

31. Damage generally occurs by excess heating when too much current is driven through an appliance. For an appliance that converts electrical energy directly to thermal energy this happens when excess voltage is applied. So don't connect a 110-volt iron, toaster, or electric stove to a 220-volt circuit. Interestingly enough, if the appliance is an electric motor, then applying too *little* voltage can result in overheating and burn up the motor windings. (This is because the motor will spin at a low speed and the reverse "generator effect" will be small and allow too great a current to flow in the motor.) So don't hook up a 220-volt power saw or any 220-volt motor-driven appliance to 110 volts. To be safe use the recommended voltages with appliances of any kind.

32. (a) Electric power in your home is likely supplied at 60 hertz via 110-volt to 120-volt electrical outlets. This is ac (and delivered to your home via transformers between the power source and your home. We will see in the next chapter that transformers require ac power for operation.) (b) Electric power in your car must be able to be supplied by the battery. Since the + and - terminals of the battery do not alternate, the current they produce does not alternate either. It flows in one direction and is dc.

33. Auto headlights are wired in parallel. Then when one burns out, the other remains lit. If you've ever seen an automobile with one burned out headlight, you have evidence they're wired in parallel.

34. There is less resistance in the higher wattage lamp. Since power = current × voltage, more power for the same voltage means more current. And by Ohm's law, more current for the same voltage means less resistance. (Algebraic manipulation of the equations $P = IV$ and $I = V/R$ leads to $P = V^2/R$.)

35. More current flows in the 100-watt bulb. We see this from the relationship "power = current × voltage." More current for the same voltage means less resistance. So a 100-watt bulb has less resistance than a 60-watt bulb. Less resistance for the same length of the same material means a thicker filament. The filaments of high wattage bulbs are thicker than those of lower-wattage bulbs. (It is important to note that both Watts and Volts are printed on a light bulb. A bulb that is labeled 100W, 120V, is 100W *only* if there are 120 volts across it. If there are only 110 volts across it, and the resistance remains unchanged, then the power output would be only 84 watts!)

36. From "Power = current × voltage," 60 watts = current × 120 volts, current $= \dfrac{60W}{120V} = 0.5$ A.

37. The amount of current any device puts through any conductor depends upon the voltage of the device and the resistance of the conductor. Also important is the amount of charge the device can deliver; a relatively large amount of charge at high voltage represents high energy (like that from a power line) while a small amount of charge at high voltage represents low energy (like discharging a balloon rubbed on your hair). The device being warned about is likely highly energized to a high voltage, and should be respected. It possesses no current to be warned about, but because of its high energy and high voltage, may produce a lethal current in anyone offering a conducting path from it to the ground.

38. How quickly a lamp glows after an electrical switch is closed does not depend on the drift velocity of the conduction electrons, but depends on the speed at which the electric field is established in the circuit — about the speed of light.

39. A light bulb burns out when a break occurs in the filament or when the filament disintegrates or falls apart.

40. Bulbs will glow brighter when connected in parallel, for the voltage of the battery is impressed across each bulb. When two identical bulbs are connected in series, half the voltage of the

battery is impressed across each bulb. The battery will run down faster when the bulbs are in parallel.

41. Bulb C is the brightest because the voltage across it equals that of the battery. Bulbs A and B share the voltage of the parallel branch of the circuit and have half the current as bulb C (assuming resistances are independent of voltages). If bulb A is unscrewed, the top branch is no longer part of the circuit and current ceases in both A and B. They no longer give light, while bulb C glows as before. If bulb C is instead unscrewed, then it goes out and bulbs A and B glow as before.

42. As more bulbs are connected in series, more resistance is added to the single circuit path and the resulting current produced by the battery is diminished. This is evident in the dimmer light from the bulbs. On the other hand, when more bulbs are connected to the battery in parallel, the brightness of the bulbs is practically unchanged. This is because each bulb in effect is connected directly to the battery with no other bulbs in its electrical path to add to its resistance. Each bulb has its own current path.

43. Line current decreases as more devices are connected in series. But line current increases as more devices are connected in parallel. This is because the circuit resistance is increased when devices are added in series, but decreased (more pathways) when devices are added in parallel.

44. Yes, there will be a decrease in brightness if too many lamps are connected in parallel because of the excess current that flows through the battery. Internal voltage drop increases with current in the battery, which means reduced voltage to the circuit it powers. If the parallel circuit is powered by a stronger source such as the power utility provides via common wall sockets, no dimming of bulbs will be seen as more and more parallel paths are added.

45. Household appliances are not connected in series for at least two reasons. First, the voltage, current, and power for each appliance would vary with the introduction of other appliances. Second, if one device burns out, the current in the whole circuit ceases. Only if each appliance is connected in parallel to the voltage source, can the voltage and current through each appliance be independent of the others.

46. The 100-watt bulb has the thicker filament and lower resistance (as we discussed in the answer to Exercise 17) so in series where the current is the same in each bulb, less energy is dissipated in going through the lower resistance. This corresponds to lower voltage across the resistance — a lower voltage drop. So the greater voltage drop is across the 60-watt bulb in series. So interestingly enough, in series the 60-watt bulb is brighter than the 100-watt bulb! When connected in parallel, the voltage across each bulb is the same, and the current is greater in the lower resistance 100-watt bulb, which glows brighter than the 60-watt bulb.

47. Agree with your friend, for your electric bill is in energy, kW-h. Its true that your power company delivers power, and in this sense sells power, but they charge you for energy.

48. Open ended.

Chapter 8 Problem Solutions

1. By the inverse-square law, twice as far is 1/4 the force; **5 N.**
   The solution involves relative distance only, so the magnitude of charges is irrelevant.

2. From Coulomb's law, the force is given by $F=\dfrac{kq^2}{d^2}$, so the square of the charge is

   $q^2 = \dfrac{Fd^2}{k} = \dfrac{(20\ \text{N})(0.06\ \text{m})^2}{9\times 10^9\ \text{N m}^2/\text{C}^2} = 8.0\times 10^{-12}\ \text{C}^2$. Taking the square root of this gives $q = \mathbf{2.8\times10^{-6}\ C}$, or **2.8 microcoulombs.**

3. From Coulomb's law, $F=k\dfrac{q_1 q_2}{d^2} = (9\times 10^9)\dfrac{(1.0\times 10^{-6})^2}{(0.03)^2} = \mathbf{10\ N}$ (Like the weight of a 1-kg mass).

4. $F_{(grav)} = mg = (9.1\times 10^{-31}\ \text{kg})(9.8\ \text{m/s}^2) = 8.9\times 10^{-30}\ \text{N}$.
   $F_{(elec)} = qE = (1.6\times 10^{-19}\ \text{C})(10{,}000\ \text{V/m}) = 1.6\times 10^{-15}\ \text{N}$. The ratios of these tell us that the electrical force on the electron is more than 10^{14} times greater than the gravitational force between the Earth and the electron!

5. $F_{(grav)} = G\dfrac{m_1 m_2}{d^2} = (6.67\times 10^{-11})\dfrac{(9.1\times 10^{-31})(1.67\times 10^{-27})}{(1.0\times 10^{-10})^2} = 1.0\times 10^{-47}\ \text{N}$.

   $F_{(elec)} = k\dfrac{q_1 q_2}{d^2} = (9\times 10^9)\dfrac{(1.6\times 10^{-19})^2}{(1.0\times 10^{-10})^2} = 2.3\times 10^{-8}\ \text{N}$.

   The electrical force between the electron and proton is more than
   1,000,000,000,000,000,000,000,000,000,000,000,000,000 times greater!
   (Note that this ratio of forces is the same for any separation of the particles.)

6. a. From $E = \dfrac{F}{q}$ we see that $q = \dfrac{F}{E} = \dfrac{mg}{E} = \dfrac{(1.1\times 10^{-14})(9.8)}{1.68\times 10^5} = \mathbf{6.4\times 10^{-19}\ C}$

   b. Number of electrons $= \dfrac{6.4\times 10^{-19}\text{C}}{1.6\times 10^{-19}\text{C/electron}} = \mathbf{4\ electrons}$

7. From current $= \dfrac{\text{voltage}}{\text{resistance}}$, resistance $= \dfrac{\text{voltage}}{\text{current}} = \dfrac{120\text{V}}{20\text{A}} = \mathbf{6\ W.}$

8. From power = current × voltage, current $= \dfrac{\text{power}}{\text{voltage}} = \dfrac{1200\text{W}}{120\text{V}} = \mathbf{10\ A.}$

   From the formula derived above, resistance $= \dfrac{\text{voltage}}{\text{current}} = \dfrac{120\text{V}}{10\text{A}} = \mathbf{12\ W.}$

9. Two headlights (connected in parallel) draw 6 amps, so the 60 ampere-hour battery will last for about **10 hours.**

10. It was designed for use in a 120-V circuit. With an applied voltage of 120 V, the current in the bulb is I = V/R = (120 V)/(95 W) = 1.26 A. The power dissipated by the bulb is then P = IV = (1.26 A)(120 V) = 151 W, close to the rated value. If this bulb is connected to 220 V, it would carry twice as much current and would dissipate four times as much power (twice the current × twice the voltage), more than 600 W. It would likely burn out. (This problem can also be solved by first carrying out some algebraic manipulation. Since current = voltage/resistance, we can write the formula for power as P = IV = (V/R)V = V²/R. Solving for V gives V = √PR. Substituting for the power and the resistance gives V = √(150)(95) = 119 V.)

11. 100 W = 0.1 kw; so $0.1\ \text{kw} \times \dfrac{\$0.20}{1\ \text{kwh}} \times (30\times 24\ \text{h}) = \mathbf{\$14.40.}$

12. Power absorbed by the water is 24,000 J per 60 s = 402 W.

   Efficiency $= \dfrac{\text{power output}}{\text{power input}} = \dfrac{402\ \text{W}}{500\ \text{W}} = 0.80$. The microwave oven warms the water at 80% efficiency.

9 Magnetism

Answers to Exercises

1. The poles are spread over the flat faces, separated by the thinner dimension of the disk or square. So each "pole" is larger than the space between them. (To see how such a magnet might be made, imagine slicing the bar magnet in Figure 9.2 like a loaf of bread into many thin pieces.)

2. Apply a small magnet to the door. If it sticks, your friend is wrong because aluminum is not magnetic. If it doesn't stick, your friend might be right (but not necessarily—there are lots of nonmagnetic materials).

3. Attraction will occur because the magnet induces opposite polarity in a nearby piece of iron. North will induce south, and south will induce north. This is similar to charge induction, where a balloon will stick to a wall whether the balloon is negative or positive.

4. All magnetism originates in moving electric charges. For an electron there is magnetism associated with its spin about its own axis, with its motion about the nucleus, and with its motion as part of an electric current.

5. All iron materials are not magnetized because the tiny magnetic domains are most often oriented in random directions and cancel one another's effects.

6. Cans contain iron. Domains in the can tend to line up with the Earth's magnetic field. When the cans are left stationary for several days, the cans become magnetized by induction, aligning with the Earth's magnetic field.

7. An electron always experiences a force in an electric field because that force depends on nothing more than the field strength and the charge. But the force an electron experiences in a magnetic field depends on an added factor: relative motion. If there is no relative motion between an electron and a magnetic field in which it is located, no magnetic force acts. Furthermore, if motion is along the magnetic field direction, and not at some angle to it, then no magnetic force acts also. Magnetic force, unlike electric force, depends on the relative velocity of the charge with respect to the magnetic field.

8. The iron and nickel that composes the Earth's core is too hot for permanent alignment of magnetic domains, and therefore does not make up a permanent magnet. The Earth's magnetism more likely originates in electric currents surrounding the Earth's core.

9. A magnet will induce the magnetic domains of a nail or paper clip into alignment. Opposite poles in each material are then closest to each other and attraction results (this is similar to a charged comb attracting bits of electrically neutral paper). A wooden pencil, on the other hand, does not have magnetic domains that will interact with a magnet.

10. The needle is not pulled toward the north side of the bucket because the south pole of the magnet is equally attracted southward. The net force on the needle is zero.

11. Tell your first friend that the magnetic field of the Earth is continuous from pole to pole, and certainly doesn't make a turnaround at the Earth's equator; so a compass needle that is aligned with the Earth's field likewise does not turn around at the equator. Your other friend could correctly argue that compass needles point southward in the southern hemisphere (but the same pole points southward in the northern hemisphere). A compass does no turnaround when crossing the equator.

12. Moving electrons are deflected from their paths by a magnetic field. A magnet held in front of a TV picture deflects the electron beam from its correct path and distorts the picture.

13. Back to Newton's 3rd law! Both A and B are equally pulling on each other. If A pulls on B with 50 newtons, then B also pulls on A with 50 newtons. Period!

14. Newton's 3rd law again: Yes, the paper clip as part of the interaction, certainly does exert a force on the magnet — just as much as the magnet pulls on it. The magnet and paper clip pull equally on each other to comprise the single interaction between them.

15. Just as a nail is magnetized by beating on it, an iron ship is beat upon in its manufacture, making it a permanent magnet. Its initial magnetic field orientation, which is a factor in subsequent magnetic measurements, is in effect recorded on the brass plaque.

16. The electric field in a cyclotron or any charged particle accelerator forces the particles to higher speeds, while the magnetic field forces the particles into curved paths. A magnetic force can only change the direction (not the speed) of a charged particle because the force is always perpendicular to the particle's instantaneous velocity. [Interestingly enough, in some accelerators (e.g., a betatron) the electric field is produced by a changing magnetic field.]

17. Recall that *work = force × distance*, where force and distance are along the same direction. Since the magnetic force that acts on a beam of electrons is everywhere perpendicular to the beam, there is no component of magnetic force along the instantaneous direction of motion. Therefore a magnetic field can do no work on a charged particle. [Indirectly, however, a *time-varying magnetic field* can induce an electric field that *can* do work on a charged particle.]

18. If the particles move in the same direction in the field and are deflected in opposite directions, the charges must be of opposite sign.

19. Yes, each will experience forces because each is in the magnetic field of the other. Interestingly, currents in the same direction attract, and currents in opposite directions repel.

20. The magnetic domains that become aligned in the iron core contribute to the overall magnetic field of the coil and therefore increase its magnetic induction.

21. Work must be done to move a current-carrying conductor in a magnetic field. This is true whether or not the current is externally produced or produced as a result of the induction that accompanies the motion of the wire in the field.

22. A cyclist coasts farther if the lamp is disconnected from the generator. The energy that goes into lighting the lamp is taken from the bike's kinetic energy, so the bike slows down. The work saved by not lighting the lamp will be the extra "force × distance" that the bike will lose to coast farther.

23. Magnetic induction will not occur in nylon, since it has no magnetic domains. That's why electric guitars use steel strings.

24. Part of the Earth's magnetic field is enclosed in the wide loop of wire imbedded in the road. If this enclosed field is somehow changed, then in accord with the law of electromagnetic induction, a pulse of current will be produced in the loop. Such a change is produced when the iron parts of a car pass over it and effectively alter its inductance. A practical application in use for several years now is triggering automobile traffic lights. (You can usually tell if triggered lights make use of this idea by the square-shaped scars on the road surface where the wires have been embedded.)

25. Like the previous answer, inductance of the loop is changed with the presence of iron. When you walk through the loop with a piece of iron and change the inductance of the loop, a changing current activates an alarm.

26. When the ground shakes, inertia of the suspended massive magnet tends to resist such shaking. But the coils of wire are fixed to the Earth and shake relative to the magnet. Motion of the magnet within conducting loops induces a current, which depends on the strength of the Earthquake. So the law of inertia and the law of electromagnetic induction underlie the operation of this device.

27. Electromagnetic induction occurs in the coil. When the tape is moved past a coil, voltage will be induced as the magnetic field in the coil changes via the variations of magnetization of the tape. This is the principle of a tape player.

28. Electromagnetic induction occurs in the coil. This principle is employed with credit cards.

29. The changing magnetic field produced when the current starts to flow induces a current in the aluminum ring. This current, in turn, generates a magnetic field that opposes the field produced by the magnet under the table. The aluminum ring becomes, momentarily, a magnet that is repelled by the hidden magnet. Why repelled? The induced field is opposite to the inducing field (Lenz's Law).

30. If the light bulb is connected to a wire loop that intercepts changing magnetic field lines from an electromagnet, voltage will be induced which can illuminate the bulb. Change is the key, so the electromagnet should be powered with ac.

31. There is no fundamental difference between an electric motor and electric generator. When mechanical energy is put into the device and electricity is induced, we call it a generator. When electrical energy is put in and it spins and will do mechanical work, we call it a motor. (While there are usually some practical differences in the designs of motors and generators, some devices are designed to be either motors or generators, depending only on whether the input is mechanical or electrical.) The similarities are that each has the same components of a magnetic source, and a coil that can be turned in the magnetic field.

32. In accord with Faraday's law of induction, the greater the rate of change of magnetic field in a coil or armature, the greater the induced voltage. So voltage output increases with greater spin.

33. In accord with electromagnetic induction, if the magnetic field alternates in the hole of the ring, an alternating voltage will be induced in the ring. Because the ring is metal, its relatively low resistance will result in a correspondingly high alternating current. This current is evident in the heating of the ring.

34. Energy transfers from the holder to the toothbrush motor by EMI. The system is a transformer.

35. When you electrically turn the rotor of the motor, mechanical energy is the output. If you reverse the roles, and put mechanical work into turning the rotor, its spinning will generate electricity. Then the motor is a generator. (This in fact is the case with a motor; it generates a "back emf" that reduces the net current in its windings, and the net current to run it. This is noted when a motor such as in an electric saw is made to stop by jamming — then the absence of the back emf results in a current that may be too large for the motor and it overheats.)

36. When you mechanically turn the rotor of the generator, electric current is the output. If you reverse the roles, and put electric current into the turns about the rotor, it will spin and do mechanical work. Then the generator is a motor. The principle difference between a generator and a motor is whether electric energy or mechanical energy is the input (or output).

37. The bar magnet will slow down. From a magnetic force point of view, the moving magnet will induce current loops in the surrounding copper as it falls. The current loops produce a magnetic field that tends to repel the magnet as it approaches and attract it as it leaves, slowing it in its flight. From an energy point of view, the energy of the current that is induced in the loop is equal to the loss of kinetic energy of the magnet. The plastic pipe, on the other hand, is an insulator. So no current and therefore no magnetic field is induced to slow the motion of the falling magnet.

38. Such a scheme violates both the 1st and 2nd laws of thermodynamics. Because of inherent inefficiencies, the generator will produce less electricity than is used by the adjoining motor to power the generator. The transformers will step up voltage at the expense of current, or current at the expense of voltage, but it will not step up both simultaneously — that is, a transformer cannot step up energy or power. Like all practical systems, more energy is put in than is put out.

39. Agree with your friend, for light is electromagnetic radiation having a frequency that matches the frequency to which our eyes are sensitive.

40. Electromagnetic waves depend on mutual field regeneration. If the induced electric fields did not in turn induce magnetic fields and pass energy to them, the energy would be localized rather than "waved" into space. Electromagnetic waves would not exist.

Chapter 9 Problem Solutions

1. If power losses can be ignored, in accord with energy conservation, the power provided by the secondary is also **100W**.

2. a. From the transformer relationship,

$$\frac{\text{Primary voltage}}{\text{primary turns}} = \frac{\text{secondary voltage}}{\text{secondary turns}},$$

$$\text{secondary voltage} = \frac{\text{Primary voltage}}{\text{primary turns}} \times \text{secondary turns} = \frac{12V}{50} \times 250 = \mathbf{60V}$$

   b. From Ohm's law, current $= \frac{V}{R} = \frac{60V}{10W} = \mathbf{6A}$

   c. Power supplied to the primary is the same as the power delivered by the secondary;

$$\text{Power} = \text{current} \times \text{voltage} = 6A \times 60V = \mathbf{360W}$$

3. From the transformer relationship,

$$\frac{\text{primary voltage}}{\text{primary turns}} = \frac{\text{secondary voltage}}{\text{secondary turns}},$$

$$\frac{120V}{240 \text{ turns}} = \frac{6V}{x \text{ turns}}$$

   Solve for x: $x = \frac{6V}{120V} \times 240 \text{ turns} = \mathbf{12\ turns}$

4. From , $\frac{\text{primary voltage}}{\text{primary turns}} = \frac{\text{secondary voltage}}{\text{secondary turns}}$, simple rearrangement gives

$$\frac{\text{primary voltage}}{\text{secondary voltage}} = \frac{\text{primary turns}}{\text{secondary turns}} = \frac{120V}{12000V} = \frac{1}{100}.$$

   So there should be **100 times** as many turns on the secondary as primary.

10   Sound Waves

Answers to Exercises

1. Shake the garden hose to and fro in a direction perpendicular to the hose to produce a sine-like curve.

2. To produce a transverse wave with a slinky, shake it to and fro in a direction that is perpendicular to the length of the slinky itself (as with the garden hose in the previous exercise). To produce a longitudinal wave, shake it to and fro along the direction of its length, so that a series of compressions and rarefactions is produced.

3. The fact that gas can be heard escaping from a gas tap before it is smelled indicates that the pulses of molecular collisions (the sound) travel more quickly than the molecules migrate. [There are three speeds to consider: (1) the average speed of the molecules themselves, as evidenced by temperature—quite fast, (2) the speed of the pulse produced as they collide—about 3/4 the speed of the molecules themselves, and (3) the very much slower speed of molecular migration.]

4. Frequency and period are reciprocals of one another; $f = \frac{1}{T}$, and $T = \frac{1}{f}$. Double one and the other is half as much. So doubling the frequency of a vibrating object halves the period.

5. As you dip your fingers more frequently into still water, the waves you produce will be of a higher frequency (we see the relationship between "how frequently" and "frequency"). The higher-frequency waves will be closer together — their wavelengths will be shorter.

6. The frequency of vibration and the number of waves passing by each second are the same.

7. Think of a period as one cycle in time, and a wavelength as one cycle in space, and a little thought will show that in a time of one period, a wave travels a full wavelength. Formally, we can see this as follows:

   distance = speed × time

   where speed = frequency × wavelength, which when substituted for speed,

   distance = frequency × wavelength × time

   distance = $\frac{1}{\text{period}}$ × wavelength × period = wavelength.

   (Rather than formally proving this as above, it is best to visualize it — to "see" that one wave form is generated in each cycle, the time of which is the period — and that the wave form moves outward a distance equal to its own wavelength during this time. Conceptualize physics!)

8. The electromagnetic wave at the same frequency has the longer wavelength — how much longer? About a million times longer because an electromagnetic wave travels about a million time faster than sound.

9. The circular patterns made by expanding waves is evidence that the wave speeds are the same in all radial directions. This is because all parts of the circle have gone equal distances from the center in equal times.

10. The energy of a water wave spreads along the increasing circumference of the wave until its magnitude diminishes to a value that cannot be distinguished from thermal motions in the water. The energy of the waves adds to the internal energy of the water.

11. First, in outer space there is no air or other material to carry sound. Second, if there were, the faster-moving light would reach you before the sound.

12. The speaker would chatter at the resonant frequency and diminish the quality of the sound.

13. The Doppler effect is a change in frequency as a result of the motion of source, receiver, or both. So if you moved toward a stationary sound source, yes, you would encounter waves more frequently and the frequency of the received sound would be higher. Or if you moved away from the source, the waves would encounter you less frequently, and you would hear sound of a lower frequency.

14. No, for there would be no relative motion between sender and receiver. Put another way, the increased frequency the listener would receive if at rest is canceled by the decreased frequency of recession.

15. Oops, careful. The Doppler effect is about changes in *frequency*, not speed. (Careless reading might not spot this!)

16. The Doppler shifts show that one side approaches while the other side recedes, evidence that the Sun is spinning.

17. A boat that makes a bow wave is traveling faster than the waves of water it generates.

18. The conical angle of a shock wave becomes narrower with greater speeds. We see this in the sketches:

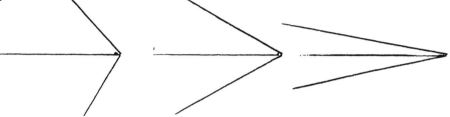

19. Yes, a supersonic fish in water would produce a shock wave and hence a sonic boom for the same reason it would if traveling faster than sound in air.

20. Frequency is twice per second, or 2 hertz. Period is reciprocal frequency, or 1/2 second. Amplitude is 10 centimeters.

21. Bees buzz when in flight because they flap their wings at audio frequencies.

22. The shorter wavelengths are heard by bats (higher frequencies have shorter wavelengths).

23. Light travels about a million times faster than sound, so you see a distant event a million times sooner than you hear it.

24. When sound passes a particular point in the air, the air is first compressed and then rarefied as the sound passes. So its density is increased and then decreased as the it passes.

25. At the instant that a high pressure region is created just outside the prongs of a tuning fork, a low pressure region is created between the prongs. This is because each prong acts as a Ping-Pong paddle in a region full of Ping-Pong balls. Just as a forward motion of the paddle would crowd Ping-Pong balls in front of it, and leave more space between balls in back of it, each prong of the tuning fork that moves into the air molecules creates similar high and low-pressure regions. While a high-pressure region is produced on one side, a low-pressure (rarefied) region is produced on the other side. A half-cycle later when the prongs swing in toward the center, a high pressure region is produced between the prongs and a low-pressure region is produced just outside the prongs.

26. Because snow absorbs well, it reflects little sound, which is responsible for the quietness.

27. The fact that we can see a ringing bell but can't hear it indicates that light is a distinctly different phenomenon than sound. When we see the bell "ringing" in a vacuum, we know that light can pass through a vacuum. The fact that we can't hear the bell indicates that sound does not pass through a vacuum. Sound needs a material medium for its transmission; light does not.

28. The Moon is described as a silent planet because it has no atmosphere to transmit sounds.

29. The pitch of the tapped glass decreases as the glass if filled. This is because the size of the water column increases and vibrates at a lower frequency, just as larger xylophone keys vibrate at lower frequencies. (If you've attempted an answer to this exercise without actually trying it, shame on you!)

30. If the speed of sound was different for different frequencies, say, faster for higher frequencies, then distant music would be distorted, for the higher frequency notes would reach the ear of the listener first. (Be glad this is so, particularly if you like outdoor concerts.)

31. If the frequency of sound is doubled, its speed will not change at all, but its wavelength will be crowded to half its original size. The speed of sound depends only on the medium through which it travels, rather than on the properties of sound itself.

32. Sound travels faster in warm air because the air molecules that compose warm air themselves travel faster and therefore don't take as long before they bump into each other. This lesser time for the molecules to bump against one another results in a faster speed of sound.

33. Sound travels faster in moist air because the less massive water vapor molecules, H_2O, travel faster than the more massive N_2 and O_2 molecules at the same temperature. This faster speed results in sound traveling faster as discussed in Exercise 32.

34. Refraction is the result of changing wave speeds, where part of a wave travels at a different speed than other parts. This occurs in non uniform winds and non uniform temperatures. But if winds, temperatures, or other factors cannot change the speed of sound, then refraction would not occur. (The fact that refraction does indeed occur is evidence for the changing speeds of sound.)

35. The tremor in the ground can be felt before a distant explosion is heard because sound travels faster in the solid ground than in air.

36. Sound is more easily heard when the wind traveling toward the listener at elevations above ground level travels faster than wind near the ground. Then the waves are bent downward as is the case of the refraction of sound shown in Figure 11.13.

37. The short wavelengths of ultrasound allow the imaging of smaller objects. This is similar to the smaller detail seen by short-wavelength blue light in microscopes, and the still smaller detail seen with ultra-short-wavelength electron microscopes (further discussed in Chapter 11. We will also see in Chapter 11 that shorter wavelengths produce clearer images by decreasing a wave effect called *diffraction*).

38. An echo is weaker than the original sound because sound spreads and is therefore less intense with distance. If you are at the source, the echo will sound as if it originated on the other side of the wall from which it reflects (just as your image in a mirror appears to come from behind the glass). It is weaker still because the wall is likely not perfectly reflecting.

39. The rule is correct: this is because the speed of sound in air (340 m/s) can be rounded off to 1/3 km/s. Then, from distance = speed × time = (1/3)km/s × (number of seconds). Note that the time in seconds divided by 3 yields the same value.

40. If a single disturbance at some unknown distance away sends longitudinal waves at one known speed, and transverse waves at a lesser known speed, and you measure the difference in time of the waves as they arrive, you can calculate the distance. The wider the gap in time, the greater the distance — which could be in any direction. If you use this distance as the radius of a circle on a map, you know the disturbance occurred somewhere on that circle. If you telephone two friends who have made similar measurements of the same event from different locations, you can transfer their circles to your map, and the point where the three circles intersect is the location of the disturbance.

41. Marchers at the end of a long parade will be out of step with marchers nearer the band because time is required for the sound of the band to reach the marchers at the end of a parade. They will step to the delayed beat they hear.

42. These devices use interference to cancel the sound of the jackhammer in the ears of its operator. Because of the resulting low jackhammer noise in the ears of the operator, he can hear your voice clearly. But you, however, without the earphones experience no such cancellation of sound, so the voice of the operator is drowned out by the loud jackhammer noise.

43. In addition to pieces of paper at the supporting ends of the string, when a string vibrates in two segments a piece may be placed at the node in its center. For three segments, two pieces can be supported, each one third the total distance from each end.

44. The pitch increases as the glass is filled. To a small degree, standing waves of sound are set up in the glass tube. As the glass fills, the length of the "tube" decreases, favoring reflections of shorter wavelengths.

Chapter 10 Problem Solutions

1. The woman is about **340 meters** away. The clue is the single blow you hear after you see her stop hammering. That blow originated with the next-to-last blow you saw. The very first blow would have appeared as silent, and succeeding blows synchronous with successive strikes. In one second sound travels 340 meters.

2. The skipper notes that 15 meters of wave pass each 5 seconds, or equivalently, that 3 meters pass each 1 second, so the speed of the wave must be
$$\text{Speed} = \frac{\text{distance}}{\text{time}} = \frac{15\text{ m}}{5\text{ s}} = \textbf{3 m/s}.$$
Or in wave terminology:
$$\text{Speed} = \text{frequency} \times \text{wavelength} = (1/5\text{ Hz})(15\text{ m}) = \textbf{3 m/s}.$$

3. To say that the frequency of radio waves is 100 MHz and that they travel at 300,000 km/s, is to say that there are 100 million wavelengths packed into 300,000 kilometers of space. Or expressed in meters, 300 million m of space. Now 300 million m divided by 100 million waves gives a wavelength of 3 meters per wave. Or
$$\text{Wavelength} = \frac{\text{speed}}{\text{frequency}} = \frac{(300\ \text{megameters/s})}{(100\ \text{megahertz})} = \textbf{3 m}.$$

4. Wavelength = speed/frequency = $\dfrac{340\text{ m/s}}{600\text{ Hz}}$ = **0.6 m**.
   So between every beat of its wings, sound travels 0.6 meters.

5. The ocean floor is 4590 meters deep. The 6-second time delay means that the sound reached the bottom in 3 seconds. Distance = speed × time = 1530 m/s × 3 s = **4590 m**.

6. Assuming the speed of sound to be 340 m/s, the cave is 170 meters away. This is because the sound took 1/2 second to reach the wall (and 1/2 second to return).
   Distance = speed × time = 340 m/s × 1/2 s = **170 m**.

7. Assume you hear the highest limit, say 20 kHz. Then from $v = f\lambda$, $f = \dfrac{v}{\lambda} = \dfrac{340\text{ m/s}}{20000\text{ Hz}} = 0.017\text{ m}$
   = **1.7 cm**

8. From $v = f\lambda$, $f = \dfrac{v}{\lambda} = \dfrac{340\text{ m/s}}{1\text{ m}} = $ **340 Hz**.

11 Light Waves

Answers to Exercises

1. Radio waves are longer than light waves, which are longer than the waves of x rays.

2. Sound requires a physical medium in which to travel. Light does not.

3. The fact that the different parts of the electromagnetic spectrum are received simultaneously is evidence for the frequency independence of the speed of light. If wave speed depended on frequency, different frequencies would be received at different times.

4. Radio waves and light are both electromagnetic, transverse, move at the speed of light, and are created and absorbed by oscillating charge. They differ in their frequency and wavelength and in the type of oscillating charge that creates and absorbs them.

5. Energy is spread out and diluted, but not "lost." We distinguish between something being diluted and something being annihilated. By the inverse-square law, light intensity weakens with distance, but the total amount of light over a spherical surface is the same at all distances from the source.

6. Between the Sun, stars, and Earth is the vacuum of interstellar and intersolar space. Since we can see the Sun and stars from Earth is convincing evidence that light travels through a vacuum.

7. The average speed of light will be less where it interacts with absorbing and re-emitting particles of matter, such as in the atmosphere as compared to in a vacuum. The greater the number of interactions along the light's path, the less the average speed.

8. The instantaneous speed of the bullet after penetrating the tree is less than its incident speed, but not so with light. The *instantaneous* speed of light before meeting the glass, while passing through it, and when emerging is a constant, c. A major difference between a bullet fired through a tree and light passing through glass is that the *same* bullet strikes and later emerges. Not so for light. The "bullet of light" (photon) incident upon glass is absorbed by its interaction with an atom or molecule, which in turn then emits, with some time delay, a new "bullet of light" in the same direction. This process cascades through the glass with the result being that the "bullet of light" that emerges is not the same light that was first incident. Between all the interactions of light with matter, the instantaneous speed of light is c. Only its average speed, because of the time delay of the interactions, is less than c. That's why the light emerges with speed c.

9. The greater number of interactions per distance slows the light; hence a smaller average speed.

10. Glass is opaque to frequencies of light that match its own natural frequencies. This is because the electrons in the absorbing medium are driven to vibrations of much larger amplitudes than occurs for non-resonant frequencies. These large amplitudes result in energy transfer to neighboring atoms and an increase in internal energy rather than a re-emission of light.

11. Transparency or opaqueness is determined by the match between incident light frequencies and the resonant frequency of the material. A substance that is transparent to a range of light frequencies will be opaque to those frequencies that match its own resonant frequency.

12. Clouds are transparent to ultraviolet light, which is why clouds offer no protection from sunburn. Glass, however, is opaque to ultraviolet light, and will therefore shield you from sunburn.

13. The sunglasses will be warmer in sunlight than regular reading glasses. This is because the reading glasses transmit most of the light energy that is incident upon them, whereas the sunglasses absorb more light energy, which increases their internal energy.

14. The customer is being reasonable in requesting to see the colors in the daylight. Under fluorescent lighting, with its predominant higher frequencies, the bluer colors rather than the redder colors will be accented. Colors will appear quite different in Sunlight.

15. Either a white or green garment will reflect incident green light and be cooler. The complementary color, red, will absorb green light and be the best garment color to wear when the absorption of energy is desired.

16. Red cloth appears red in sunlight, and red by the illumination of the red light from a neon tube. But because the red cloth absorbs cyan light, it appears black when illuminated by cyan light.

17. A ripe banana appears yellow when illuminated with yellow light (and white light), but appears black when illuminated with red, green, and blue light.

18. The reflected color is the complement of red, which is cyan. So the film of ink will appear cyan by reflection, and red by transmission.

19. You see the complimentary colors due to retina fatigue. The blue will appear yellow, the red cyan, and the white black. Try it and see!

20. White paper reflects all the colors incident upon it — which is why it's white. So it will appear to be the color of whatever color is shone upon it.

21. The color to emerge will be the complimentary color of yellow — blue. (White - yellow = blue.)

22. Shine blue light on the performers and their yellow costumes will appear black.

23. The overlapping blue and yellow beams will produce white light. When the two panes of glass are overlapped and placed in front of a single flashlight, however, no light will be transmitted.

24. Color TV employs color addition. To produce yellow, green and red dots are illuminated; for magenta, red and blue dots are illuminated; for white, red, green, and blue dots are illuminated.

25. Yellow light + blue light = *white* light.
    Green light + *magenta* light = white light.
    Magenta light + yellow light + cyan light = *white* light.

26. Green + blue = cyan = white - *red.*

27. On the negative the sweater is cyan, the opposite or complimentary color of red.

28. If the sky normally scattered orange light, then sunsets would be the complementary color of orange, a "sky blue." (White - Sunset orange = sky blue.)

29. Clouds are composed of atoms, molecules, and particles of a variety of sizes. So not only are high-frequency colors scattered from clouds, but middle and low frequencies as well. A combination of all the scattered colors produces white.

30. Rain clouds are composed of relatively big particles that absorb much of the incident light. If the rain clouds were composed only of absorbing particles, then the cloud would appear black. But its mixture of particles includes tiny high-frequency scattering particles, so the cloud is not completely absorbing, and is simply dark instead of black.

31. If the atmosphere were about fifty times thicker, the sunlight to reach the Earth would be predominantly low frequencies because most of the blue light would be scattered away. Snow would likely appear orange at noon, and a deep red when the Sun is not directly overhead.

32. If we assume that Jupiter has an atmosphere similar to Earth's, in terms of transparency, then the Sun would appear to be a deep reddish orange, just as it would when sunlight grazes 1000 kilometers of the Earth's atmosphere for a sunset from an elevated position. Interestingly enough, there is a thick cloud cover in Jupiter's atmosphere that blocks all sunlight from reaching its "surface." And it doesn't even have a solid surface! Your children may visit one of Jupiter's Moons, but will not "land" on Jupiter itself — not intentionally, anyway. (Incidentally, there are only 4 1/3 planets with "solid" surfaces: Mercury, Venus, Mars, Pluto, and 1/3 of Earth!)

33. During a lunar eclipse the Moon is not totally dark, even though it is in the Earth's shadow. This is because the atmosphere of the world acts as a converging lens that refracts light into the Earth's shadow. It is the low frequencies that pass more easily through the long grazing path through the Earth's atmosphere to be refracted finally onto the Moon. Hence its reddish color.

34. Radio waves are much longer and therefore diffract more than the shorter waves of light.

35. Multiple slits of identical spacings produce a wider and brighter interference pattern. Such an arrangement makes up a diffraction grating (Figure 28.21), which is a popular alternative to a prism for dispersing light into its component parts.

36. Diffraction is the principle by which peacocks and hummingbirds display their colors. The ridges in the surface layers of the feathers act as diffraction gratings.

37. Interference of light from the upper and lower surfaces of the soap film is taking place.

38. Each colored ring represents a particular thickness of oil film, just as the lines on a surveyor's contour map represent equal elevations. Note the colors are predominantly the subtracted primaries, magenta, cyan, and yellow, illustrating that colors have really been subtracted by interference.

39. Glare is composed largely of polarized light in the plane of the reflecting surface. Most glaring surfaces are horizontal (roadways, water, etc.), so sunglasses with vertical polarization axes filter the glare of horizontally polarized light. Conventional non-polarizing sunglasses simply cut down on overall light transmission either by reflecting or absorbing incident light.

40. You can determine the polarization axis for a single sheet of Polaroid by viewing the glare from a flat surface. Glare is most intense when the polarization axis is parallel to the flat surface.

41. Since most glare is due to reflection from horizontal surfaces, the polarization axes of common sunglasses are vertical.

42. You can determine that the sky is partially polarized by rotating a single sheet of Polaroid in front of your eye while viewing the sky. You'll notice the sky darken where polarization is greatest.

43. With polarization axes aligned, a pair of Polaroids will transmit all components of light along the axes. That's 50%, as explained in the preceding answer. With axes at right angles, no light will be transmitted.

Chapter II Problem Solutions

1. From $\bar{v} = \dfrac{d}{t}$, $t = \dfrac{d}{\bar{v}} = \dfrac{d}{c} = \dfrac{1.5 \times 10^{11}\text{m}}{3 \times 10^8 \text{m/s}} = \textbf{500 s}$ (which equals 8.3 min).

2. Roemer found the time it took for light to travel 300,000,000 extra kilometers of distance. Dividing this distance by the 1000 s we have the speed of light:

$$\bar{v} = \frac{300\ 000\ 000\text{km}}{1000\text{s}} = 300,\ 000\ \text{km/s}.$$ Actually, his measurements fell somewhat short of this. And whether he or his followers first made this measurement intrigues history types.

3. As in Problem 1, $t = \dfrac{d}{\bar{v}} = \dfrac{4.2 \times 10^{16}\text{ m}}{3 \times 10^8 \text{ m/s}} = \textbf{1.4} \times \textbf{10}^{\textbf{8}} \textbf{ s.}$

Converting to years by dimensional analysis,

$$1.4 \times 10^8 \text{ s} \times \frac{1\text{ h}}{3600\text{ s}} \times \frac{1\text{ day}}{24\text{ h}} \times \frac{1\text{ yr}}{365\text{ day}} = \textbf{4.4 yr.}$$

12 Properties of Light

Answers to Exercises

1. Only light from card number 2 reaches her eye.

2. Cowboy Joe should simply aim at the mirrored image of his assailant, for the recoiling bullet will follow the same changes in direction when momentum changes (angle of incidence = angle of rebound) that light follows when reflecting from a plane surface.

3. The minimum length of a vertical mirror must be half your height in order for you to see a full-length view of yourself. This is because the light from your feet that reaches your eyes via the mirror meets the mirror halfway up. Then its angle of incidence (from your feet) equals the angle of reflection (to your eyes). Likewise, light from the top of your head meets the mirror halfway down to reflect at the same angle to reach your eyes. Halfway up and halfway down means you can see all of yourself with a mirror that is half your height (and half your width).

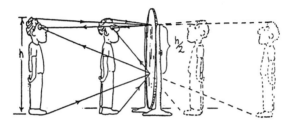

4. The half-height mirror works at any distance, as shown in the sketch above. This is because if you move closer, your image moves closer as well. If you move farther away, your image does the same. Many people must actually try this before they believe it. The confusion arises because people know that they can see whole distant buildings or even mountain ranges in a hand-held pocket mirror. Even then, the distance the object is from the mirror is the same as the distance of the virtual image on the other side of the mirror. You can see all of a distant person in your mirror, but the distant person cannot see all of herself in your mirror.

5. Note in your pocket mirror that the amount of your face you can see is twice the size of the mirror — whether you hold it close or at arm's length. Interesting information!

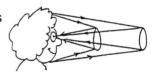

6. The smallest window will be half the height of the person or her twin. Note that this does not depend on distance, providing both subjects are the same distance from the wall. This illustrates Exercises 3, 4, and 5 above.

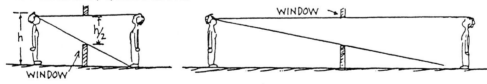

7. We would not see an image of the man in the mirror as shown. If he is viewing himself, then we wouldn't also be able to see his image unless we were in back (or in front) of him. If we are to stand to the side of the man and see him *and* an image of him in the mirror, then the mirror cannot be exactly in front of him. The mirror would have to be located to the man's right, as shown in the sketch. The man's view would miss the mirror completely. Such arrangements are made when staging an actor who is supposed to be viewing himself in a mirror. Actually, however, the actor pretends to be looking at himself. If he really were, his image in the mirror wouldn't be shared by the audience. That's Hollywood!

8. Such lettering is seen in proper form in the rear view mirrors of cars ahead.

209

9. A window is both transparent to light and a reflector of light. Whether it serves principally as a reflector or a transmitter depends on the relative intensities of light being reflected and transmitted. The person outside in the daylight who looks at the window of a room that is dark inside sees only outside light reflected from the window and almost no light transmitted from the room. The glass serves as a mirror. From the point of view of a person inside the dark room, only outside light is seen when looking at the window glass. The situation is reversed at nighttime when it is dark outside and the room is lit up. People in the room cannot see outside, and see only reflections of the room interior when they look at the window glass. The room or the outside does not have to be perfectly dark for this effect. A typical window may only reflect about 8% of the light that is incident upon it, and transmit most of the other 92%. In the daytime 8% of the outside bright daylight reflected from the glass will likely be brighter than 92% of the relatively dim inside light that is transmitted from the room to the outside. [Question for further thought: What should be the relative light intensities outside and inside for equal amounts of reflection and transmission as seen from outside the window? Inside the window?]

10. When the source of glare is somewhat above the horizon, a vertical window will reflect it to people in front of the window. By tipping the window inward at the bottom, glare is reflected downward rather than into the eyes of passers by.

11. Take note that the reflected view of a scene is only *nearly* an upside-down version of the scene being reflected. We don't see the bird's feet in the reflection because the reflected view of the bird is as would be seen from a position below the surface of the water. (See this important idea in the reflection of the bridge in the Practice Sheet on page 52 of the Practice Book.) Clearly, a view and the reflected view are not simply inversions of each other. Take notice of this whenever you look at reflections (and of paintings of reflections — it's surprising how many artists are not aware of this).

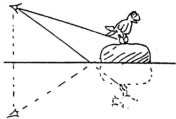

12. When a mirror is rotated, its normal rotates also. Since the angle that the incident ray makes with the normal is the same angle that the reflected ray makes, the total deviation is twice. In the sample diagram, if the mirror is rotated by 10°, then the normal is rotated by 10° also, which results in a 20° total deviation of the reflected ray. This is why mirrors are used to detect delicate movements in instruments such as galvanometers.

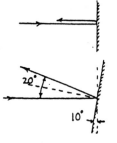

13. If the water were perfectly smooth, a mirror image of the round Sun or Moon would be seen in the water. If the water were slightly rough, the image would be wavy. If the water were a bit more rough, little glimmers of portions of the Sun or Moon would be seen above and below the main image. This is because the water waves act like tiny parallel mirrors. For small waves only light near the main image reaches you. But as the water becomes choppier, there is a greater variety of mirror facets that are properly oriented to reflect sunlight or moonlight into your eye. The facets do not radically depart from an average flatness with the otherwise smooth water surface, so the reflected Sun or Moon is smeared into a long vertical streak. For still rougher water there are facets off to the side of the vertical streak that are tilted enough for Sun or Moon light to be reflected to you, and the vertical streak is wider.

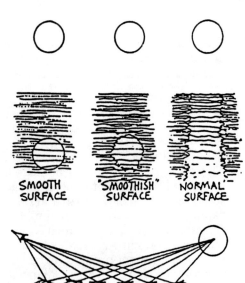

SMOOTH SURFACE   "SMOOTHISH" SURFACE   NORMAL SURFACE

14. When you wave your right hand, the waving hand of your image is not your left hand, but a left-handed version of your right hand. The image of the waving hand is still on the right, just as your head is still up and your feet still down. Neither left and right nor up and down are inverted by the mirror — but *front and back* are. (Consider three axes at right angles to each other as shown to the right of the photo of Marjorie in Figure 12.3 in the textbook. The only axis to be inverted is *z*, the front-back axis, where the image is -*z*.)

15.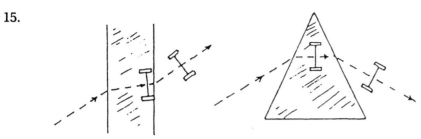

16. If light of all frequencies traveled at the same speed in glass there would be no refraction, no dispersion, and no spectrum of colors. The white light incident upon a prism would emerge as white light.

17. The speed of light in soybean oil is practically the same as the speed of light in glass. Therefore, there is no bending of light as it goes from oil to glass to oil. This results in an invisible glass tube in the soybean oil. (Physicists say the *index of refraction* of glass and soybean oil are the same; the speed of light in both is the same.)

18. In spearing a fish with a laser, make no corrections and simply aim directly at the fish. This is because the light from the fish you see has been refracted in getting to you, and the laser light will refract along the same path in getting to the fish. A slight correction may be necessary, depending on the colors of the laser beam and the fish — see the next exercise.

19. The angle of refraction for blue light is greater than for red, so if you fired your red beam along the line of sight for blue, the beam would pass above the fish. So you should aim slightly below the sighted fish.

20. The two pictures do not contradict each other. In both cases light is bent away from the normal upon emerging from the water. That's why the corner of the immersed square appears to be shallower. Notice that it's easy to confuse the beam of the left-hand picture with the edge of the immersed square in the right-hand picture. Light travels *from* the edge, not *along* the edge of the square.

21. A fish sees the sky when it looks upward at 45°, for the critical angle is 48° for water. If it looks at and beyond 48° it sees a reflection of the bottom beneath.

22. In sending a laser beam to a space station, make no corrections and simply aim at the station you see (like spearing the fish in Exercise 18). The path of refraction is the same in either direction.

23. The "nonwettable" leg of the water strider depresses and curves the surface of the water and effectively produces a lens that directs light away from the eye in the center of the depression which then appears as a shadow. Away from the center the circular lens concentrates a ring of light to your eye which appears as a bright ring. (Interestingly enough, the overall brightness of the shadow and bright ring averaged together is the same whether or not the water is depressed — "conservation of light" — Exercise 30.)

24. We cannot see a rainbow "off to the side," for a rainbow is not a tangible thing "out there." Colors are refracted in infinite directions and fill the sky. The only colors we see that aren't washed out by others are those that are along the conical angles between 40° and 42° to the sun-antisun axis. To understand this, consider a paper-cone cup with a hole cut at the bottom. You can view the circular rim of the cone as an ellipse when you look at it from a near side view. But if you view the rim only with your eye at the apex of the cone, through the hole, you can see it only as a circle. That's the way we view a rainbow. Our eye is at the apex of a cone, the axis of which is the sun-antisun axis, and the "rim" of which is the bow.

25. The fact that two observers standing apart from one another do not see the same rainbow can be understood by exaggerating the circumstance: Suppose the two observers are several kilometers apart. Obviously they are looking at different drops in the sky. Although they may both see a rainbow, they are looking at different rainbows. Likewise if they are closer together. Only if their eyes are at the very same location will they see exactly the same rainbow.

26. Seen from high enough, as from an airplane, the rainbow makes a complete circle. The shadow of the airplane will appear in the center of the circular bow. This is because the airplane is directly between the Sun and the drops or rain cloud producing the bow.

27. Ice crystals floating in the upper atmosphere refract and disperse white Moonlight into a spectrum. Whereas the colors that form a rainbow are from the part of the light *reflected* in the drops, *refracted* light forms the halos around the Moon. Like the primary and secondary rainbow, the ice crystals disperse Moonlight into two halos, the outer one being much fainter than the inner bow.

28. A projecting lens with chromatic aberration casts a rainbow-colored fringe around a spot of white light. The reason these colors don't appear inside the spot is because they overlap to form white. Only at the edges, which act as a ringed prism, do they not overlap.

29. A magnifying lens used as a "burning glass" does nothing more than gather a certain amount of energy and concentrate it at some focal point. The important point is that the lens is considerably larger than the area over which the light is concentrated. But the solar heat sheet is not larger than the surface area of the swimming pool, and doesn't collect any more solar energy than the pool receives anyway. The sheet may help warm the pool by preventing evaporation, as would be the case with any cover, but in no way do the lenses direct additional solar energy to the water beneath. This fraudulent advertising plays on the ignorance of the public.

30. The average intensity of Sunlight at the bottom is the same whether the water is moving or is still. Light that misses one part of the bottom of the pool reaches another part. Every dark region is balanced by a bright region — "conservation of light."

31. A pinhole with two holes simply produces two images. If the holes are close together, the images overlap. Multiple holes produce multiple images. Overlapping can be prevented by placing a converging lens at the holes. Make the holes into one big hole with one big lens, and you have a conventional camera!

32. Your image is twice as far from the camera as the mirror frame. Although you can adjust the focus of your camera to clearly photograph your image in a mirror, and you can readjust the focus to clearly photograph the mirror frame, you cannot in the same photograph focus on both of these. This is because your image and the frame are at different distances from the camera.

33. For very distant objects, effectively at "infinity," light comes to focus at the focal plane of the lens. So your film is one focal length in back of the lens for very distant shots. For shorter distances, the film is farther from the lens.

34. Maps of the Moon are upside down because images of the Moon through the lenses of telescopes show an inverted image of the Moon. The maps then match what the viewer sees.

35. By covering half the lens you cut the light intensity on the film in half, but you do not cut out half the image. Light from all parts of the lens contribute to all parts of the image, so the light through the top half of the lens carries a full image to the film. Similarly, when your pupils contract, the amount of light entering your eye is reduced, but not the amount of image. (Experiment and see!)

36. The near point of vision recedes with advancing age. When you have to hold a book at arm's length to see it clearly, you're really ready for glasses!

37. Chromatic aberration is the effect caused by the different angles of refraction for different frequencies through a lens or transparent medium. Since all frequencies obey the law of reflection, and the angles of reflection are the same for all frequencies, there is no chromatic aberration for mirrors — hence their use in telescopes.

38. The focal point for a lens under water will be longer than for air because of less change in light speed from water to glass, and then from glass to water again. Less refraction occurs and light is not so nearly brought to focus. Nearsighted people see more clearly under water than in air! (Some very nearsighted people with no goggles see underwater views quite clearly.)

39. Goggles ensure that light meeting the eye goes from air to eye. Then the degree of refraction from air to eye is as it is normally above water. Without water, one is farsighted under water.

40. Similar to the previous exercise, since the eyes of a fish are adapted for refraction between water and the fish's eyes, the fish would see better with goggles filled with water. Question: would a fish out of water be nearsighted or farsighted?

41. There is no such thing as a photon of white light. White light is the result of a mixture of multiple photons of different frequencies (colors).

42. Since red light carries less energy per photon, and both beams have the same energy, there must be more photons in the beam of red light.

43. The energy of red light is too low per photon to trigger the chemical reaction in the photographic crystals. Very bright light simply means more photons that are unable to trigger a reaction. Blue light, on the other hand, has sufficient energy per photon to trigger a reaction. Very dim blue light triggers fewer reactions only because there are fewer photons involved.

44. When a photon of ultraviolet light encounter a living cell, it transfers to the cell energy that can damage the cell. When a photon of visible light encounters a living cell, the amount of energy it transfers to the cell is less, and less likely to be damaging. Hence skin exposure to ultraviolet radiation can be damaging to the skin while exposure to visible light generally is not.

45. *Electric eye*: A beam of light is directed to a photosensitive surface that completes the path of an electric circuit. When the beam is interrupted, the circuit is broken, comprising a switch for another circuit. *Light meter*: The variation of photoelectric current with variations in light intensity activates a galvanometer, or its equivalent, calibrated to show light intensity. *Sound track*: An optical sound track on motion picture film is a strip of emulsion of variable density that transmits light of variable intensity onto a photosensitive surface, which in turn produces a variable electric current. This current is amplified and then activates the loudspeaker.

46. The photoelectric effect doesn't prove that light is corpuscular, but rather supports the corpuscular model of light, which is compatible with the particle-like behavior observed. Likewise with interference experiments that support the wave model of light and are compatible with the wavelike behavior of light. We have models to help us conceptualize what something *is*; knowledge of the details of how something behaves helps us to refine the model. It is important that we keep in mind that our models for understanding nature are just that: models.

Chapter 12 Problem Solutions

1. Set your focus for 4 m, for your image will be as far in back of the mirror as you are in front.

2. Relative to the mirror, you and your image walk at 2 m/s, but relative to each other your speed of approach is 4 m/s. So you and your image approach each other at **4 m/s**.

3. If 96% is transmitted through the first face, and 96% of 96% is transmitted through the second face, 92% is transmitted through both faces of the glass.

4. The amount of light transmitted through two sheets of glass is 84.6%. To see this, consider an incident intensity of 100 units. Then 92 units are transmitted through the first pane. 92% of this amount are transmitted through the second pane (0.92 of 92 = 84.6).

13 Structure of the Atom

Answers to Exercises

1. Analysis of light emitted by atoms reveals the atomic structure of atoms. When electrons change orbits about the atomic nucleus, light is emitted. The frequency of the light is proportional to the energy level differences of the orbiting electrons. Most all that we know about the structure of atoms is revealed by the light they emit.

2. The cat leaves a trail of molecules and atoms on the grass. These in turn leave the grass and mix with the air, where they enter the dog's nose, activating its sense of smell.

3. A body would have no odor if all its molecules remained intact. A body has odor only if some of its molecules enter a nose.

4. The age of the atoms in either a newborn baby or in an elderly person are the same; appreciably older than the solar system.

4. The atoms that make up a newborn baby or anything else in this world originated in the explosions of ancient stars (Leslie in Figure 13.1).

5. The atoms that make up a newborn, or the atoms that make up everything in our environment were manufactured in ancient stars that have long since exploded (see Figure 13.1). Interestingly, the atoms that compose us didn't come directly from the stars, but have since cycled and recycled innumerable times in the structures of innumerable creatures, people being one of such, as well as plants and things of many kinds.

6. The finding suggests that the meteorites and the Sun had a common history, which further suggests that the entire solar system probably had a common origin.

7. Atoms are smaller than the wavelengths of visible light, and therefore cannot be discerned by such relatively long waves (just as reeds of grass in water cannot be discerned by the long water waves that pass by). So atoms can't be seen even by the most powerful optical microscopes. The wavelengths of electron beams, however, are different. These wavelengths are more than 1000 times shorter than the wavelengths of visible light, and are short enough to discern atoms.

8. The volume of the oil is like the volume of a very large but very thin pancake, and equal its area multiplied by its thickness. $V = Ah$, where V is the volume (known) and A is the area (known from measurement) and h is the thickness, or diameter of the oil molecule. Solving for the thickness we get $h = V/A$, which produces a microscopic value from the ratio of two macroscopic values. Quite nice! (This is a good lab in the Lab Manual.)

9. You really are a part of every person around you in the sense that you are composed of atoms not only from every person around you, but from every person who ever lived on Earth! Little Manuel Hewitt's statement on page 313 is indisputable. And the atoms that now compose you will make up the atomic pool that others will draw upon.

10. With every breath of air you take, it is highly likely that you inhale one of the atoms exhaled during your very first breath. This is because the number of atoms of air in your lungs is about the same as the number of breaths of air in the atmosphere of the world.

11. Protons contribute more to an atom's mass, and electrons more to an atom's size.

12. If the particles were more massive they would be bent less by the magnetic force — the law of inertia. If the particles had more charge, they would be bent more, for the deflecting force is directly proportional to the charge.

13. Rutherford assumed the nucleus was positively charged because repulsion of the positively charged alpha particles was observed — like charges repel.

14. The very dense nucleus of Rutherford's model of the atom accounts for the back scattering of alpha particles as they ricochet off the gold atoms of the thin foil. This back scattering would not occur if the mass of the atom was spread throughout the volume of the atom, just as a golf ball would not bounce backward when striking a piece of cake. A golf ball will bounce backward if it strikes a massive object such as a bowling ball. Similarly for alpha particles that bounce from the atomic nucleus.

15. Electric forces between the charged parts of atoms prevent the oozing of atoms into one another — straight-forward electrostatic repulsion.

16. It is difficult to compress atoms because their electrons repel one another.

17. Many things and systems that can be represented by both physical and conceptual models. Likely examples of each are: For a physical model — brain, solar system, best friend, gold coin, dollar bill, car engine. Conceptual model — mind, beginning of the universe, stranger, greenhouse effect, virus, spread of infectious diseases. There is crossover between the models, and some can be represented by either model, the solar system and the greenhouse effect, for example.

18. The remaining nucleus is that of Carbon-12.

19. The light emitted by elements comes about via electrons in atoms changing energy states. And the energy states of atoms are characteristic of the atoms themselves, each element having its own states. So the light emitted by atoms carry the "signature" of the atoms themselves, and allow their identity. We know the chemical constitution of the stars because of this.

20. The one electron can be boosted to many energy levels, and therefore make many combinations of transitions to the ground level. Each transition is of a specific energy and accompanied by the emission of a photon of a specific frequency. Thus the variety of spectral lines.

21. Six transitions are possible. The transition from the 4th to the lst level corresponds to the greatest ΔE and therefore highest frequency of light. The transition from the 4th to the 3rd level corresponds to the lowest ΔE and therefore lowest frequency of light.

22. In accord with the conservation of energy, the sum of the combined energies equal the energy of the single transition. (Thus the sum of the frequencies of light emitted by the two steps = frequency of light emitted with the one long step — the Ritz combination principle, specified in the chapter.)

23. Fluorescence is the process where high-frequency (high energy) ultraviolet radiation converts to low-frequency (lower energy) visible radiation with a bit of heat energy left over. When low-energy infrared radiation is incident upon fluorescent material, it cannot be converted to higher-energy visible light, which would clearly be a violation of the conservation of energy — a no-no!

24. If we think of electrons as orbiting the nucleus in standing waves, then the circumference of these wave patterns must be a whole number of wavelengths. In this way the circumferences are discrete. This means that the radii of orbits are therefore discrete. Since energy depends upon this radial distance, the energy values are also discrete.

25. Any fractional-number of de Broglie wavelengths would interfere destructively and fail to form a standing wave. A standing wave, or a stable electron shell, must be composed of an integral number of complete waves (see Figure 13.18).

26. Each proton has a positive charge, which can hold an electron with an equal and opposite negative charge in orbit about the atomic nucleus. It is the number and configuration of electrons in an atom that give it its chemical properties. So the number of protons indirectly affects the chemical properties of atoms. (When the number of electrons about the nucleus is the same as the number of protons within the nucleus, the atom is electrically neutral.)

27. Different atomic numbers means different elements, by definition. But different elements can have the same number of nucleons. An atom with 20 protons and 20 neutrons has the same mass, for example, as an atom with 19 protons and 21 neutrons. Isotopes of different atoms can have the same mass.

28. A major similarity is the enormous empty space between both electrons and the nucleus and between planets and the Sun. Another similarity is the attractive inverse-square forces between both—electrical for electrons, and gravitational for planets. But the nature of the orbits is very different. Whereas there is no restriction for orbital distances for planets, the wave nature of the electron greatly restricts where an electron can orbit. Another difference is the notion of orbiting. For the electron, *orbiting* is a metaphor for the behavior of planets about the Sun. Electrons are smeared about the nucleus, rather than cleanly circling as the planets do around the Sun. There are certainly more differences than there are similarities between the atomic system and the solar system.

29. Atomic mass would be 99 amu, and the element would be technetium, Tc, atomic number 43.

30. Check the periodic table and see that gold is atomic number 79. Taking a proton from the nucleus leaves the atomic number 78, platinum — much more valuable than adding a proton to get mercury, atomic number 80.

31. Lead.

32. Radon.

33. Carbon. (See the periodic table)

34. Arsenic. You wouldn't want to do this, for arsenic is a deadly poison.

Chapter 13 Problem Solutions

1. (a) 10^4 atoms (length 10^{-6} m divided by size 10^{-10} m). (b) 10^8 atoms ($10^4 \times 10^4$). (c) 10^{12} atoms ($10^4 \times 10^4 \times 10^4$). (d) $10,000 buys a small car, for instance. $100 million buys a few jet aircraft and an airport on which to keep them, for instance. $1 trillion buys a medium-sized country, for instance. (Answers limited only by the imagination of the student.)

2. From the hint:

$$\frac{\text{number of molecules in thimble}}{\text{number of molecules in ocean}} = \frac{\text{number of molecules in question}}{\text{number of molecules in thimble}}$$

$$\frac{10^{23}}{10^{46}} = \frac{x}{10^{23}}; \quad x = \frac{10^{46}}{10^{46}} = 1$$

3. There are 10^{22} breaths of air in the world's atmosphere, which is the same number of atoms in a single breath. So for any one breath evenly mixed in the atmosphere, we sample one atom at any place or any time in the atmosphere.

4. First of all, there are about 10^{22} molecules in a breath of air. The total number of people who ever lived ($4 \times 10^9 \times 30 = 120 \times 10^9$ which is roughly 10^{11} people altogether) is enormously smaller than 10^{22}. How does 10^{22} compare to 10^{11}? 10^{22} is $(10^{11})^2$! Multiply the number of people who ever lived by the same number, and you'll get 10^{22}, the number of air molecules in a breath of air. Suppose each person on Earth journeyed to a different planet in the galaxy and every one of those planets contained as many people as the Earth now contains. The total number of people on all these planets would still be less than the number of molecules in a breath of air. Atoms are indeed small — and numerous!

14 The Atomic Nucleus

Answers to Exercises

1. Every element undergoing radioactive decay produces a "daughter" element. In every case, daughter elements are found with all radioactive materials – and in an amount corresponding to the age of the material and the element's radioactive half life. Wherever uranium metal is found, for example, so also is lead.

2. A radioactive sample is always a little warmer than its surroundings because the radiating alpha or beta particles impart internal energy to the atoms of the sample. (Interestingly enough, the heat energy of the Earth originates with radioactive decay of the Earth's core and surrounding material.)

3. It is impossible for a hydrogen atom to eject an alpha particle, for an alpha particle is composed of a pair of hydrogen isotopes (deuterium). It is equally impossible for a one-kilogram melon to spontaneously break into four one-kilogram melons.

4. Alpha and beta rays are deflected in opposite directions in a magnetic field because they are oppositely charged — alpha are positive and beta negative. Gamma rays have no electric charge and are therefore undeflected.

5. The alpha particle has twice the charge, but almost 8000 times the inertia (since each of the four nucleons has nearly 2000 times the mass of an electron). Hence it bends very little compared to the much less massive electrons.

6. The paths of alpha, beta, and gamma radiation bend similarly in both electric and magnetic fields. In both fields, betas bend the most and in the opposite direction of the alphas, and gammas traverse undeflected.

7. Alpha radiation decreases the atomic number of the emitting element by 2 and the atomic mass number by 4. Beta radiation increases the atomic number of an element by 1 and does not affect the atomic mass number. Gamma radiation does not affect the atomic number or the atomic mass number. So alpha radiation results in the greatest change in atomic number, and hence charge, and mass number as well.

8. Because of the fact that like charges repel, and that protons have the same sign of charge (positive) as the target atomic nuclei, the protons must be driven into the target area with enormous energies if they are to bombard the nuclei. Lower-energy protons would be easily repelled by any nuclei they approach.

9. Alpha particles are first of all, much bigger in size than beta particles, which makes them less able to pass through the "pores" of materials. Second, alpha particles are enormously more massive than beta particles. So if beta particles have the same kinetic energy, they must be moving considerably faster. The faster moving and smaller beta particles are therefore more effective in penetrating materials.

10. Within the atomic nucleus, it is the strong nuclear force that tends to hold the nucleons together, and the electric force that tends to mutually repel the nucleons and push them apart.

11. The fact that atomic nuclei composed of many protons exist is evidence that something stronger than electric repulsion is occurring in the nucleus. If there were not a stronger attractive nuclear force to keep the repelling electrical force from driving protons apart from each other, the nucleus as we know it wouldn't exist.

12. At the end of the second year 1/4 of the original sample will be left; third year, 1/8 will be left; and at the end of the fourth year, 1/16 will be left.

13. 1/16 will remain after 4 half lives, so 4 × 30 = 120 years.

14. The half life of the material will be two hours. A little thought will show that 160 halved 4 times equals 10. So there have been four half life periods in the 8 hours. And 8 hours/4 = 2 hours.

15. In accord with the inverse-square law, at 2 meters, double the distance, the count rate will be one-fourth 360, or 90 counts/minute; at 3 meters, the count rate will be one-ninth 360, or 40 counts/minute.

16. Bismuth-213 becomes Thallium-209 when it emits an alpha particle.

17. When radium (A = 88) emits an alpha particle, its atomic number reduces by 2 and becomes the new element radon (A = 86). The resulting atomic mass is reduced by 4. If the radium was of the most common isotope 226, then the radon isotope would have atomic mass number 222.

18. After beta emission from polonium, the atomic number increases by 1 and becomes 85, and the atomic mass is unchanged at 218. However, if an alpha particle is emitted, the atomic number decreases by 2 and becomes 82, and the atomic mass decreases by 4 and drops to 214.

19. Deuterium has 1 proton and 1 neutron; carbon has 6 protons and 6 neutrons; iron has 26 protons and 30 neutrons; gold has 79 protons and 118 neutrons; strontium has 38 protons and 52 neutrons; uranium has 92 protons and 146 neutrons.

20. An element can decay to elements of greater atomic number by emitting electrons (beta rays). When this happens, a neutron becomes a proton and the atomic number increases by one.

21. The elements below uranium in atomic number with short half-lives exist as the product of the radioactive decay of uranium. As long as uranium is decaying, their existence is assured.

22. The Earth's natural energy that heats the water in the hot spring is the energy of radioactive decay, which keeps the Earth's interior molten. Radioactivity heats the water, but doesn't make the water itself radioactive. The warmth of hot springs is one of the "nicer effects" of radioactive decay. You and your friend will most likely encounter more radioactivity from the granite out-croppings of the foothills than would be encountered near a nuclear power plant. Furthermore, at high altitude you'll both be exposed to increased cosmic radiation. But these radiations are not appreciably different than the radiation one encounters in the "safest" of situations. The probability of dying from something or other is 100%, so in the meantime you and your friend should enjoy life anyway!

23. Although there is significantly more radioactivity in a nuclear power plant than in a coal-fired power plant, the absence of shielding for coal plants results in more radioactivity in the environment of a typical coal plant than in the environment of a typical nuclear plant. All nukes are shielded; coal plants are not.

24. Gamma radiation is generally the most harmful radiation because it is so penetrating. Alpha and beta radiation is dangerous if you ingest radioactive material, which is comparatively uncommon.

25. Film badges monitor gamma radiation, which after all, is very high frequency X rays. Like photographic film, the greater the exposure, the darker the film upon photo processing.

26. You can tell your friend who is fearful of the radiation measured by the Geiger counter that his attempt to avoid the radiation by avoiding the instrument that measures it, is useless. He might as well avoid thermometers on a hot day in effort to escape the heat. If it will console your fearful friend, tell him that he and his ancestors from time zero have endured about the same level of radiation he receives whether or not he stands near the Geiger counter. They had, and he has, no better options. Make the best of the years available anyway!

27. Radioactive decay rates are statistical averages of large numbers of decaying atoms. Because of the relatively short half-life of carbon-14, only trace amounts would be left after 50,000 years — too little to be statistically accurate.

28. Stone tablets cannot be dated by the carbon dating technique. Nonliving stone does not ingest carbon and transform it by radioactive decay. Carbon dating pertains to organic material.

29. Nuclear fission is a poor prospect for powering automobiles primarily because of the massive shielding that would be required to protect the occupants and others from the radioactivity, and the problem of radioactive waste disposal.

30. A neutron makes a better "bullet" for penetrating atomic nuclei because it has no electric charge and is therefore not deflected from its path by electrical interactions, nor is it electrically repelled by an atomic nucleus.

31. The average distance increases. (It's easier to see the opposite process where big pieces broken up into little pieces decreases the distance a neutron can travel and still be within the material. Proportional surface area increases with decreasing size, which is why you break a sugar cube into little pieces to increase the surface area exposed to tea for quick dissolving.) In the case of uranium fuel, the process of assembling small pieces into a single big piece increases traveling distance, decreases surface area, reduces neutron leakage, and increases the probability of a chain reaction and an explosion.

32. Because plutonium triggers more reactions per atom, a smaller mass will produce the same neutron flux as a somewhat larger mass of uranium. So plutonium has a smaller critical mass than a similar shape of uranium.

33. Plutonium has a relatively short half life (24,360 years), so any plutonium initially in the Earth's crust has long since decayed. The same is true for any heavier elements with even shorter half lives from which plutonium might originate. Trace amounts of plutonium can occur naturally in U-238 concentrations, however, as a result of neutron capture, where U-238 becomes U-239 and after beta emission becomes Np-239, which further transforms by beta emission to Pu-239. (There are elements in the Earth's crust with half lives even shorter than plutonium's, but these are the products of uranium decay that lie between uranium and lead in the periodic table of elements.)

34. Plutonium builds up over time because it is produced by uranium's absorption of neutrons.

35. The resulting nucleus is $_{92}U^{233}$. The mass number is increased by 1 and the atomic number by 2. U-233, like U-235, is fissionable with slow neutrons. (Notice the similarity to the production of $_{94}Pu^{239}$ from $_{92}U^{238}$.)

36. If the difference in mass for changes in the atomic nucleus increased tenfold (from 0.1% to 1.0%), the energy release from such reactions would increase tenfold as well.

37. To predict the energy release of a nuclear reaction, simply find the difference in the mass of the beginning nucleus and the mass of its configuration after the reaction (either fission or fusion). This mass difference (called the "mass defect") can be found from the curve of Figure 14.27 or from a table of nuclear masses. Multiply this mass difference by the speed of light squared: $E = mc^2$. That's the energy release!

38. Here we distinguish between the mass of a nucleon inside a nucleus and an isolated nucleon. *After* a nucleon has been pulled from a nucleus, it has the same mass as any other isolated nucleon of the same identity. The mass of an isolated proton, for example, is the same as the mass of any other isolated proton, and likewise for neutrons. What is different is their effective masses within atomic nuclei. In that domain they differ according to what nucleus they are a part of.

39. Energy would be released by the fissioning of gold and from the fusion of carbon, but by neither fission nor fusion for iron. Neither fission nor fusion will result in a decrease of mass for iron.

40. If uranium were split into three parts, the segments would be nuclei of smaller atomic numbers, more toward iron on the graph of Figure 14.27. The resulting mass per nucleon would be less, and there would be more mass converted to energy in such a fissioning.

41. Radioactivity in the Earth's core provides the heat that keeps the inside molten, and warms hot springs and geysers. Nuclear fusion releases energy in the Sun that bathes the Earth in sunshine.

42. Minerals which are now being mined can be recycled over and over again with the advent of a fusion-torch operation. This recycling would tend to reduce (but not eliminate) the role of mining in providing raw materials.

43. Such speculation could fill volumes. The energy and material abundance that is the expected outcome of a fusion age will likely prompt several fundamental changes. Obvious changes would occur in the fields of economics and commerce which would be geared to relative abundance rather than scarcity. Already our present price system, which is geared to and in many ways dependent upon scarcity, often malfunctions in an environment of abundance. Hence we see instances where scarcity is created to keep the economic system functioning. Changes at the international level will likely be worldwide economic reform, and at the personal level in a re-evaluation of the idea of scarcity being the basis of value. A fusion age will likely see changes that will touch every facet of our way of life.

44. The lists can be very large. Foremost considerations are these: conventional fossil-fuel power plants consume our natural resources and convert them into poisonous contaminants that are discharged into the atmosphere, producing among other things, acid rain. A lesser environmental problem exists with nuclear power plants that do not pollute the atmosphere. Pollution from nukes is concentrated in the radioactive waste products from the reactor core. Any rational discussion about the drawbacks of either of these power sources must acknowledge that *both* are polluters — so the argument is about which form of pollution we are more willing to accept in return for electrical power. (Before you say "No Nukes!", rational thinking suggests that you first be able to say that you "Know Nukes!")

Chapter 14 Problem Solutions

1. After three half lives, the amount will be $(1/2) \times (1/2) \times (1/2)$, or 1/8 of the original, 0.125 g. After three more half lives, the remaining amount will be 1/8 of 1/8, or 1/64 of the original, 0.016 g. At 10:00 PM, the amount remaining has halved ten times, which leaves $(1/2)^{10}$, or about 1/1000 of the original. The remaining amount will be 0.001 g, or 1 mg.

2. The intensity is down by a factor of 16.7 (from 100% to 6%). How many factors of two is this? About 4, since $2^4 = 16$. So the age of the artifact is about 4×5730 years, or about 23,000 years.

3. The energy released by the explosion in kilocalories is
   (20 kilotons)$(4.2 \times 10^{12}$ J/kiloton)$/(4,184$ J/kilocalorie) $= 2.0 \times 10^{10}$ kilocalories. This is enough energy to heat 2.0×10^{10} kg of water by 1 °C. Dividing by 50, we conclude that this energy could heat 4.0×10^8 kilograms of water by 50 °C. This is nearly half a million tons.

15   Elements of Chemistry
Answers to Exercises

1. Chemistry is the careful study of matter and can take place at a number of different levels including the submicroscopic, microscopic, or macroscopic levels.

2. When looked at macroscopically, matter appears continuous. On the submicroscopic level, however, we find that matter is made of extremely small particles, such as atoms or molecules. Similarly, a TV screen looked at from a distance appears as a smooth continuous flow of images. Up close, however, we see this is an illusion. What really exists are a series of tiny dots (pixels) that change color in a coordinated way to produce the series of images.

3. No, you cannot say that nothing is happening. On the submicroscopic level, water molecules are bustling around, some evaporating into the gaseous phase, while others are moving from the gaseous phase back into the liquid phase. If there is no drop in water level, this means that the rate water molecules move from the liquid to gaseous phase is equal to the rate they move from the gaseous to liquid phase.

4. In all phases, the submicroscopic particles are moving. In the solid phase they vibrate about fixed positions. In the liquid phase, they tumble around one another. In the gaseous phase, they zip about at high speeds with relatively vast distances between them. In general, the higher the temperature the faster the submicroscopic particles are moving.

5. As a gas is compressed its submicroscopic particles come closer together. This decreases the volume of the gas, thereby increasing its density.

6. Imagine trying to get from one side of a crowded convention floor to the other—your path will be anything but a straight line. Instead, because of frequent collisions, you'll find yourself zig-zagging, and your actual path is relatively long. The time it takes you to travel this distance, therefore, is also relatively long. Similarly, gas particles travel in a zig-zag fashion because of all the collisions they experience among themselves. So, although they travel at high speeds, the time it takes them to get between two macroscopically distant points is also relatively long.

7. The distance between atoms in a molecule is very, very small compared to the distance between the molecules of a gaseous material. Thus, a volume of gaseous ozone, O_3, may contain the same number of molecules as an equal volume of gaseous oxygen, O_2.

8. The box in the middle should show all the particles aligned in an orderly fashion. This represents the solid phase of a material. The box on the right should show the particles in a random orientation. This represents the liquid phase. If each particle represents a water molecule, then the box on the right would be showing water at its melting/freezing temperature of 0°C.

9. At room temperature, hydrogen and oxygen are gaseous materials. As a gas, these materials occupy a lot of volume. The hydrogen and oxygen for the space shuttle, therefore, are kept in their liquid phase so as to occupy a minimum volume. To be in a liquid phase, these materials must be brought to very cold temperatures on the order of -200°C. High pressure also helps to keep these otherwise gaseous materials liquid.

10. At the cold temperatures of your kitchen freezer, water molecules in the vapor phase are moving relatively slowly, which makes it easier for them to stick to inner surfaces within the freezer or to other water molecules.

11. That this process is so reversible suggests a physical change. As you sleep in a reclined position, pressure is taken off of the discs within your spinal column, which allows them to expand so that you are significantly taller in the morning. Astronauts returning from extended space visits may be up to two inches taller upon their return.

12. Both chemical properties and personalities are assessed by observing behavior.

221

13. chemical, chemical, chemical, physical, chemical, chemical, chemical, physical.

14. The top set represents a physical change whereby the solid circle molecules have condensed from a gaseous to liquid phase. The bottom set represents a chemical change whereby solid circle molecules and open circle molecules have reacted to form a new type of molecule represented by a solid and open circle paired together. The phase of this new material is indicated to be a liquid phase as the molecules are bunched together in a random orientation. Note that two solid circle molecules remain left-over unreacted.

15. From an introductory chemistry course you are not expected to know how the brain learns. You should, however, be able to make the following assessment: If learning involves the formation of new chemicals in the brain, then learning is an example of chemical change. If learning merely involves the reconnecting of nerve-endings, then learning might be considered a physical change. In actuality, most all biological process, including learning, are examples of chemical changes.

16. The ones that have atomic symbols that don't match their modern atomic names. Examples include iron, Fe, gold, Au, and copper, Cu.

17. The oxygen in water is chemically bonded to hydrogen in a 1:2 ratio. We do not breathe this oxygen. Instead we breath oxygen that is bonded to itself, O_2. H_2O and O_2 are completely different substances. Fish breath the small amount of oxygen, O_2, that is dissolved in water, H_2O.

18. Chemical compounds have physical and chemical properties that are different from the elements from which they are made. Oxygen, for example, is a gas at room temperature, as is hydrogen. These two elements combine, however, to make water, which is a liquid at room temperature.

19. Salt, sodium chloride; classification: chemical compound. Flour, natural product; classification: mixture. Stainless steel, alloy of iron and carbon; classification: mixture. China, glass coated ceramic; classification: mixture. Water, dihydrogen oxide; classification: chemical compound. Sugar, chemical name: sucrose; classification: chemical compound. Vanilla extract, natural product; classification: mixture. Butter, natural product; classification: mixture. Starch, natural product; classification: mixture. Syrup, natural product; classification: mixture. Pepper, natural product; classification: mixture. Aluminum, metal; classification: in pure form— element; sold commercially as an alloy. Ice, dihydrogen oxide; classification: chemical compound. Milk, natural product; classification: mixture. Aspirin, pharmaceutical; classification: in pure form—chemical compound; sold commercially as a mixture with starch filler.

20. Biological processes are very complex resulting in the production of a wide variety of chemicals necessary for sustaining life.

21. The oxygen is a liquid at -214°C while the nitrogen is a solid.

22. Dioxygen oxide O_3 is commonly called ozone, while oxygen oxide O_2 is commonly called oxygen.

23. A compound is a material consisting of submicroscopic units, such as molecules, with more than one type of atom. Water, H_2O, is an example. A chemical mixture is a mixture of chemical compounds, such as sugar water.

24. Box a: mixture. Box b: compound. Box c: element. There are three different types of molecules shown altogether in all three boxes: one with two open circles joined, one with a solid and open circle joined, and one with two solid circles joined.

25. Any macroscopic sample consists of an incredible number of submicroscopic particles— billions of billions of them! To be 100 percent pure means that the material consists of one and only one type of compound. Thus if only one out of a billion billion molecules of a material is different from all the rest, then the material no longer qualifies as 100 percent pure. Practically speaking, it is impossible to maintain a state whereby a macroscopic sample is free of all impurities.

26. Fruit punch is a mixture and mixtures can be separated into their components by differences in physical properties. Initially, freezing water molecules selectively bind to themselves to form ice crystals. This excludes the sugar molecules. The effect is that the liquid phase loses water molecules to the ice crystals. The proportion of sugar molecules in the liquid phase, therefore, increases, which makes the liquid phase tastes sweeter. Upon complete freezing, the sugar become trapped within the ice crystals and the frozen juice can be used as a popsicle. Suck hard on a frozen popsicle, however, and you'll find that only the concentrated sugar solution pulls into your mouth.

27. Because of the greater distance between the submicroscopic particles.

28. Biology is the study of life, which is built upon atoms and molecules. Any biologist, therefore, must be well acquainted with the mechanics of atoms and molecules in order to have a basic understanding of life processes. Chemistry, by contrast, is the study of atoms and molecules, which may apply to either animate or inanimate objects.

29. Chicken noodle soup and soil both consist of many different components all mixed together. In both of these materials one can visually distinguish many of these components.

30. Petroleum we burn as fuel. Lava burns trees and any other organic material in its path down the slopes of a volcano. Water puts out the burning of any organic material.

16   The Periodic Table

Answers to Exercises

1. Calcium is readily absorbed by the body for the building of bones. Since calcium and strontium are in the same atomic group they have similar physical and chemical properties. The body, therefore, has a hard time distinguishing between the two and strontium atoms are absorbed just as though they were calcium atoms.

2. Based upon its location in the periodic table we find that gallium, Ga, is more metallic in character than germanium, Ge. This means that gallium should be a better conductor of electricity. Computer chips manufactured from gallium, therefore, might be expected to operate faster than chips manufactured from germanium.

3. Its low melting temperature of only 30°C.

4. This element may be relatively inert for it would fall under group 18, the noble gases.

5. In order of increasing density:
copper (8.9 g/mL) < silver (10.5 g/mL) < gold (18.9 g/mL) < platinum (21.5 g/mL). For more detail on this periodic trend see page 67 in the Practice Book.

6. Here is a list of sixteen. Aluminum (as in aluminum foil); tin (as in tin foil and tin cans); carbon (as in graphite and diamond); helium (as in a helium balloon); nitrogen (which comprises about 78% of the air we breathe); oxygen (which comprises about 21% of the air we breathe); argon (which comprises about 1% of the air we breathe); silicon (as in integrated circuits for computers and calculators); sulfur (a mineral used for many industrial processes); iron (as in most metal structures); chromium (as in chromium bumpers on cars); zinc (as in the coating of any galvanized nail or as the insides of any post 1982 copper penny); copper (as in copper pennies); nickel (as in nickel nickels); silver (as in jewelry and old silver coins); gold (as in jewelry); platinum (as in jewelry); mercury (as in mercury thermometers).

7. There are two unpaired valence electrons in the third shell of a magnesium atom.

8. There are 7 valence electrons in the second shell of Fl. 6 are paired and one is left unpaired.

9. An electron in the outer shell of neon experiences a greater effective nuclear charge than an electron in the outer shell of sodium because there are fewer shielding inner shell electrons.

10. An electron in the outermost shell of sodium experiences the greatest effective nuclear charge because it is closer to the nucleus (from Coulomb's law, electric forces diminish over distance).

11. Increasing Size: P < Ge < Sn < Tl.

12. Increasing Ionization Energy: Pb < Sn < As < P.

13. Atoms become larger because of a greater number of filled shells. If the first shell had an unlimited capacity, electrons would not occupy outer shells. And with no inner shells to act as shields, the effective nuclear charge would be the same as the number of protons in the nucleus, and would increase with increasing atomic number. The undiminished positive nucleus would pull the lone shell tighter and tighter, and smaller and smaller. If noble gas shells had unlimited capacities, the nature of matter would be entirely different and life as we know it would not exist.

14. One, because it has one vacant space in its valence shell.

15. Sodium ion Na^+ has 10 electrons filling the first two shells. The third shell is empty. Chlorine ion, Cl^-, has 18 electrons completely filling the first three shells. The third shell has 8 electrons.

16. Neon and the calcium ion, Ca^{2+}, both have the electron configuration of a noble gas. They are different in the number of filled shells. Neon has 2 filled shells while the calcium ion has 3.

17. The neutral sodium atom has 11 electrons — 10 filling the first two shells, and the 11th occupying the third shell. Charged sodium ion, Na^+, however, only has 10 electrons, which fill the first two shells. A neutral sodium atom is larger due to a greater number of occupied shells.

18. The second shell of the fluorine ion, F^-, is overcrowded with electrons. This makes the fluorine ion larger than the neutral fluorine atom.

19. Alkali metals (group 1) only lose 1 electron because that is all they have in their outermost shell. Additional electrons won't be lost because they would have to come from the next innershell, which experiences a much greater effective nuclear charge. Similarly, alkali-earth metals (group 2) tend to lose 2 electrons because that is the number of electrons they have in their outermost shell.

20. The electron that is easily pulled away from sodium is the one in the outermost shell where the effective nuclear charge is about +1. A second electron is difficult to pull away because this electron must come from the second shell where the effective nuclear charge is about +9.

21. After oxygen accepts the first electron it becomes a negatively charged ion. This has the effect of making the addition of the second electron more difficult (because of the electrical repulsion between the negatively charged oxygen ion and the negatively charged electron).

22. There is no more room in its outermost occupied shell.

23. The have a greater effective nuclear charge.

24. There are two requirements for electron affinity. 1) The atom must have an effective nuclear charge strong enough to attract additional electrons. 2) There must be room in the valence shell to accommodate the additional electrons. Although the noble gass have strong effective nuclear charges, they lack space in their valence shell to accommodate additional electrons. Therefore they are lacking in electron affinity. With a strong effective nuclear charge, however, it's difficult to remove electrons from them, so they do have high ionization energies. Thus, not all atoms with high ionization energies also have high electron affinities.

25. Just as a room doesn't need people in order to exist, a shell doesn't need to contain electrons in order to exist. A shell is merely a region of space in which an electron may or may not reside.

26. Note carefully the sudden jumps in moving from group 12 to group 13. For atomic size, there is a sudden increase. The reason for this is because of a final filling of the first two subshells (2 electrons in the first and 10 electrons in the second). The 13th valence electron of the group 13 elements is thus forced to reside in the next larger third subshell. Similarly, the ionization energies of the group 13 elements are suddenly lower than the group 12 elements because the 13th electron in the outermost third subshells is relatively easy to remove.

27. The hydrogen on planet Jupiter is under great pressure due to Jupiter's great mass and gravitational forces. This pressure squeezes the hydrogen atoms together close enough so that they lose their electrons in the fashion of metallic bonding.

28. Noble gas atoms tend not to form positive ions because the effective nuclear charge in the valence shell is so strong that electrons have a hard time escaping.

29. The valence electron of a sodium atom is closer to the atomic nucleus than is the valence electron of a potassium atom.

30. The inner transition elements are placed below the main body of the periodic table because they are a unique grouping of elements unlike those of the main body of the periodic table. Ideally, they may be embedded between groups 3 and 4, but that makes for an unusually wide periodic table.

17   Chemical Bonding

Answers to Exercises

1. Metal atoms lose electrons to form a positively charged ions, which are held together by their attractions for the many loose electrons that migrate among them.

2. Brass is not an element (and not found in the periodic table) because it is an alloy, which is a mixture of the elements zinc and copper.

3. Yes, an alloy may contain a nonmetallic element, but the amount of the nonmetallic elements must be relatively small. Steel is an example in that it contains about 1% carbon.

4. A sodium atom loses an electron to become a sodium ion, which is a uniquely different substance. This process, therefore, should be viewed as a chemical change. Furthermore, this process is not easily reversed. As was discussed in the text, sodium metal, which consists of sodium atoms, reacts violently with water. During this reaction the sodium atoms lose electrons to the water molecules thereby creating sodium ions (as in sodium hydroxide) and explosive hydrogen gas.

5. If we consider the diamond to be a large molecule, splitting this molecule requires the breaking of chemical bonds, which is a sign of a chemical change.

6. $MgCl_2$ (Two single negatively charged chlorine ions are needed to balance the one doubly positively charge magnesium ion)

7. Ba_3N_2.

8. The electrical force of attraction between two oppositely-charged ions decreases with increasing distance. Because the chloride ion is larger than the fluoride ion, it cannot get as close to the sodium ion. Thus, the force of attraction between a chloride and sodium ion is weaker. A chloride ion, therefore, is easier to pull away from a sodium ion than is a fluoride ion.

9. A set of oppositely charged ions.

10. Ionic crystals consist of ions. Covalent crystals consist of covalent compounds—molecules!

11. Nonmetallic elements tend to form covalent bonds. This includes most of the elements found in the upper right hand corner of the periodic table.

12. This question is stretching the use of terminology a bit. Chemists do not refer to metallic or ionic bonds as ambivalent. The nature of the term, however, is of interest. To be ambivalent is to be split between two decisions. In the metallic and ionic bonds, the electrons are split from their parent atoms.

13. Four elements that tend to form covalent bonds include carbon, nitrogen, oxygen, and fluorine—all nonmetallic elements.

14. The chemical formula for phosphine is PH_3, which is most similar to that of ammonia, NH_3. Note how phosphorus is directly below nitrogen in the periodic table.

15. Electron affinity is the attraction an atom has for an additional electron. Electronegativity is the attraction that a bonded atom has for a bonding electron. Both are a function of the effective nuclear charge.

16. e) O-H (The greatest difference in electronegativity is between oxygen and hydrogen.)

17. The least symmetrical molecule (c) O=C=S

226

18. The atoms found closer to the lower left-hand corner of the periodic table are those that will bare the positive charge: a) hydrogen b) bromine c) carbon d) neither!

19. In order of increasing polarity: N-N < N-O < N-F < H-F.

20. A selenium-chlorine bond should be more polar. Observe their relative positions in the periodic table. Sulfur and bromine are more equidistant from the upper right hand corner.

21. Compound B: 1; Compound C: 2; Compound A: 3. The greater the number of polar O-H groups, the greater the "stickiness" of the molecule, hence, the higher the boiling temperature.

22. Water is a polar molecule because in its structure the dipoles do not cancel. Polar molecules tend to stick to one another, which gives rise to relatively high boiling temperatures. Methane, on the other hand, is nonpolar because of its symmetrical structure, which results in no net dipole and a relatively low boiling temperature. The boiling temperature of a substance has not so much to do with the masses of its molecules as it does with the interactions that occur between the molecules.

23. O with F: covalent; Ca with Cl: ionic; Na with Na: metallic; U with Cl: ionic.

24. a) The left compound with the two chlorines on the same side of the molecule is more polar and will thus have a higher boiling temperature.

24. b) The left molecule, SCO, with a carbon atoms surrounded by a sulfur and an oxygen atom is less symmetrical, which means that dipoles will not cancel as well as they will in the symmetrical carbon dioxide molecule, CO_2. A material consisting of the left molecule, SCO, therefore, has the higher boiling temperature.

24. c) The chlorine atoms have a relatively strong electronegativity that pulls electrons away from the carbon. In the left molecule, $COCl_2$, this tug of the chlorine's is counteracted by a relatively strong tug of the oxygen, which tends to defeat the polarity of this molecule. The hydrogens of the molecule on the right, $C_2H_2Cl_2$, have an electronegativity that is less than that of carbon, so they actually assist the chlorine in allowing electrons to be yanked towards one side, which means that this molecule is more polar. A material consisting of the right molecule, $C_2H_2Cl_2$, therefore, has the higher boiling temperature.

25. Add up the number of subatomic particles in each of these molecules and you'll find that the carbon dioxide molecule, CO_2, is more than twice as heavy as the water molecule, H_2O. In this case, it is not the mass of these molecules that most influences their physical phase. Rather, it is the polarity, or "stickiness" of the molecules that makes the difference. Water is a polar molecule, which allows water molecules to stick to one another in a liquid phase at room temperature. Carbon dioxide, on the other hand, is a nonpolar molecule, which allows for carbon dioxide molecules to roam about freely in a gaseous phase at room temperature.

26. An electrically neutral hydrogen atoms has a strong affinity for an additional electron. It will readily seek such an electron, which makes is most chemically reactive. The hydrogen ion H-, however, already has its additional electron. It's outermost shell is filled and it is thus more "satisfied".

27. It has only one valence electron to share.

28. Electron affinity is the cause. A filled outer shell is the effect.

29. When bonded to an atom with low electronegativity, such as any group 1 element, the nonmetal atom will pull the bonding electrons so closely to itself so as to form an ion.

30. A small amount of electron sharing occurs even within an ionic bond. Recall that ionic and covalent bonds are two extremes of the same theme of polarity—an ionic bond might be considered as an extremely polar covalent bond, while a covalent bond might be considered as a rather nonpolar ionic bond.

18 Molecular Mixing

Answers to Exercises

1. Because the magnitude of the electric charge associated with an ion is much greater.

2. Just as the atomic nucleus can attract more than one electron, the charged end of a polar molecule can attract more than one molecule. In the liquid phase, the number of molecules that may be attracted is limited by the relative sizes of the molecules.

3. Water induces a dipole in oxygen such that the two can be attracted to each other by dipole-induced dipole interactions, which permit small amounts of oxygen to dissolve.

4. Bromine atoms are larger and this makes the formation of induced dipole-induced dipole interactions more favorable.

5. The molecule on the far left is polar where the O-H bond is located and nonpolar where the carbon and hydrogen bonds are located. Since it is both polar and nonpolar with may best help to bring gasoline and water into a single liquid phase.

6. The boiling points go up due to an increase in the number of chemical interactions between molecules. When we talk about the "boiling point" of a substance we are referring to a pure sample of that substance. We see the boiling point of 1-pentanol (the molecule on the far right) is relatively high because 1-pentanol molecules are so attracted to one another (by induced dipole-induced dipole as well as by dipole-dipole and dipole-induced dipole interactions). When we refer to the "solubility" of a substance we refer to how well that substance interacts with a second substance — in this case water. Note that water is much less attracted to 1-pentanol because most of 1-pentanol is non-polar (its only polar portion is the O-H group). For this reason 1-pentanol is not very soluble in water. Put yourself in the viewpoint of a water molecule and ask how attracted you might be to a methanol molecule (the one on the far left).

7. A high boiling point means that the substance interacts with itself quite strongly. Put yourself in the point of view of a water molecule and you will see that you are attracted to both ends of 1,4-butanediol. In fact 1,4-butanediol is infinitely soluble in water!

8. Two substances that can be mixed homogeneously in any proportion are said to be infinitely soluble. By this definition noble gases are infinitely soluble in noble gases.

9. (a) The nitrogen molecule, N_2, is nonpolar and is held to the fatty tissue to induced dipole-induced-dipole molecular interactions. (b) Dipoles are difficult to induce in helium because it is such a small atom. The dipole-induced dipole attraction between it and the water molecules of blood, therefore, is relatively weak.

10. To tell whether a sugar solution is saturated or not, add more sugar and see if it will dissolve. If the sugar dissolves, the solution was not saturated. Alternatively, cool the solution and see if any sugar precipitates. If it precipitates then the solution was saturated. Because sugar forms supersaturated solutions so easily, however, neither of these methods are always successful.

11. At 10°C a saturated solution of sodium nitrate, $NaNO_3$, is more concentrated than a saturated solution of sodium chloride, NaCl.

12. Salt is composed of ions that are too attracted to themselves. Gasoline is non-polar so salt and gasoline will not interact very well.

13. Chemical interactions form between the water and ethanol molecules. This brings the molecules closer together hence the volume is less. Note that the *volume* is less than you might expect it to be and not the *mass*.

14. Ethanol has a polar hydroxyl group that tends to exclude the purely nonpolar hexane molecules. This exclusion results in a greater volume when the two materials are combined.

15. The polarity of the molecules of a substances has a far greater influence on the boiling temperature of the substance than does the mass of its molecules. Recall that boiling involves separating the individual molecules of a liquid substance from one another. The greater the "stickiness" of the molecules, the harder this is to do. The extra neutron in the deuterium does not affect the chemical bonding within the D_2O molecule, which thereby has the same chemical structure as H_2O. Since they have the same chemical structures, their boiling temperatures are most similar: H_2O, bp = 100°C; D_2O, bp = 101°C. Interestingly, the extra mass of the deuterium has only a small affect on the boiling temperature.

16. The aluminum oxide has a higher melting point because of the greater charges of the ions, and hence the greater force of attractions between them.

17. The greater oxygen content of polar waters permits a greater abundance of life forms upon which the humpback whale feeds. The nutrient cycle of polar waters, however, also has to do with a process known as "upwelling". During the Fall season, surface waters grow colder and thus sink to the bottom of the ocean. This, in turn, forces deeper waters up to the surface. The deeper waters are rich in nutrients because of the decayed matter that has sunk over time. As the nutrient-rich deeper waters reach the surface, edible life forms again begin to flourish.

18. Soap is not at all necessary for removing salt from your hands. The strong ion-dipole inter-actions between fresh water and the salt are most sufficient to lift the salt away from your hands.

19. The edge of the razor blade would effectively cut through the surface tension that holds up the flat-lying razor blade.

20. There is less contact with the surface of the glass compared to the surface area of the water.

21. Mercury sticks to itself (cohesive forces) better than it sticks to the glass (adhesive forces).

22. At higher temperatures water molecules are moving faster, which makes it difficult for them to cohere to one another. This, in turn, decreases the surface tension.

23. Motor oil is much thicker (viscous) than is gasoline. This suggests that the molecules of motor oil are more strongly attracted to one another than are the molecules of gasoline. A material consisting of molecules of Structure A would have greater induced dipole-induced dipole molecular interactions than a material consisting of molecules of Structure B. Motor oil molecules, therefore, are best represented by Structure A, while gasoline molecules are best represented by Structure B.

24. This is a "trick question". Boiling involves the separation of many molecules (plural). With only one molecule, the concept of boiling is meaningless.

25. The arrangement of atoms within a molecule makes all the difference as to the physical and chemical properties. Ethyl alcohol contains the -OH group, which is polar. This polarity, in turn, is what allows the ethyl alcohol to dissolve in water. The oxygen of dimethyl ether, by contrast, is bonded to two carbon atoms: C-O-C. The difference in electronegativity between oxygen and carbon is not as great as the difference between oxygen and hydrogen. The polarity of the C-O bond, therefore, is less than that of the O-H bond. Furthermore, the symmetry of the C-O-C bond results in a cancellation of much of the polarity. As a consequence dimethyl ether is significantly less polar than is ethyl alcohol and is not readily soluble in water.

26. In order to smell something, the molecules of that something must evaporate and reach your nose. If the new perfume doesn't evaporate, it will not have an odor.

27. The oxygen needed for burning is the molecular form O_2, which is not the same thing as the oxygen atom that makes up 88.88% of the mass of water, H_2O.

28. When an ionic compound melts, the ionic bonds between the ions are overcome. When a covalent compound melts, the molecular interactions between molecules are overcome. Because ionic bonds are so much stronger than molecular interactions, the melting points of ionic compounds are typically much higher.

29. These initial bubbles are the gases that were dissolved in the water coming out of solution. Because the solubility of gases in water decreases with increasing temperature, a standing warm pot of water will show more bubbles forming on the inner sides than will a standing cold pot of water.

30. The boiling process removes the air that was dissolved in the water. Upon cooling the water is void of its usual air content, hence, the fish drown.

Chapter 18 Problem Solutions

1. Mass = (Concentration)(Volume) = (3.0 g/L)(15 L) = **45 g.**

2. Concentration in Molarity = $\dfrac{\text{moles}}{\text{Liter}}$

   a) $\dfrac{1\ \text{mole}}{1\ \text{Liter}}$ = **1 Molar (1 M)**   b) $\dfrac{2\ \text{moles}}{0.5\ \text{Liters}}$ = **4 Molar (4 M)**

3. Set up ratios and solve for the unknown by cross multiplying

   a) $\dfrac{1\ \text{mole}}{32\ \text{grams}} = \dfrac{x\ \text{moles}}{0.04\ \text{grams}}$

$$x = \frac{(1\ \text{mole})(0.04\ \text{grams})}{(32\ \text{grams})} = 0.00125\ \text{moles} = \textbf{1.25} \times \textbf{10}^{-3}\ \textbf{moles}$$

   b) $\dfrac{6.02 \times 10^{23}\ \text{molecules}}{1\ \text{mole}} = \dfrac{x\ \text{molecules}}{1.25 \times 10^{-3}\ \text{moles}}$

$$x = \frac{(6.02 \times 10^{23}\ \text{molecules})(1.25 \times 10^{-3}\ \text{moles})}{(1\ \text{mole})} = \textbf{7.525} \times \textbf{10}^{20}\ \textbf{molecules}$$

19 Chemical Reactions

Answers to Exercises

1. This equation is balanced.

2. The coefficients to balance this equation are 8,1,8.

3. a) 2,3,1 b) 1,6,4 c) 2,1,2

4a. Energy to break bonds:
    H-H = 436 kJ
    <u>Cl-Cl = 243 kJ</u>
    Total = 679 kJ absorbed

    Energy released from bond formation:
        H-Cl = 431 kJ
        <u>H-Cl = 431 kJ</u>
        Total = 862 kJ released

    NET = 679 kJ absorbed - 862 kJ released = 83 kJ released (exothermic)

4b. Energy to break bonds:
    C-C = 837 kJ
    H-C = 414 kJ
    C-H = 414 kJ
    O=O = 498 kJ
    O=O = 498 kJ
    <u>O=O = 498 kJ</u>
    Total = 3159 kJ absorbed

    Energy released from bond formation:
        $4 \times$ O=C = 3212 kJ
        $4 \times$ C=O = 3212 kJ
        H-O = 464 kJ
        H-O = 464 kJ
        O-H = 464 kJ
        <u>O-H = 464 kJ</u>
        Total = 8280 kJ released

    NET = 3159 kJ absorbed - 8280 kJ released = 5121 kJ released (very exothermic)

5. Multiple bonds generally have higher bond energies than single bonds because there are more electrons within the bond to which the bonding nuclei are attracted.

6. The nuclei of smaller atoms are able to get closer to the bonding electrons. The closeness translates to a greater electric force of attraction. Recall from Coulomb's law that the closer two oppositely charged particles, the stronger the force of attraction between them. According to periodic trends, atoms get smaller when moving from nitrogen to oxygen to fluorine. So it follows that the H-F bond is stronger than the H-O bond, which is stronger than the H-N bond.

7. Putting more ozone into the atmosphere to replace that which has been destroyed is a bit like throwing more fish into a pool of sharks to replace those fish that have been eaten. The solution is to remove the CFC's that destroy the ozone. Unfortunately, CFC only degrade slowly and the ones up there now will remain there for many years to come. Our best bet is to stop the present production of CFC's and hope that we haven't already caused too much damage.

8. To calculate the percentage of CFC molecules in our air you would also need to know the number of air molecules there are in a single liter of air. Interestingly, on average there are about 25 million quadrillion molecules of air in a liter of air at room temperature and atmospheric pressure. Thus, for every one CFC molecule, there are about 25 million non-CFC molecules such as nitrogen, N_2, and oxygen, O_2. One out of 25 million is about 0.000004 percent.

9. Since this reaction is indicated to need the input of ultraviolet energy in order to occur, it should be viewed as an endothermic reaction.

10. CFCs do not catalyze the destruction of ozone directly. Instead, they are broken down by ultraviolet light into chlorine atoms. They are these chlorine atoms that catalyze the destruction of ozone directly.

11. CFCs were most widely used as refrigerants and as cleansers prior to the bans on their production. Also, CFCs are not naturally occurring chemicals. Rather, human create them. Their presence throughout the Earth's atmosphere is a clear sign of the significant influence we humans can have on our planet's environment.

12. This is an example of a physical change whereby the ammonium nitrate is dissolved in water. Bare in mind, however, that both chemical and physical changes involve the input or output of energy. For a chemical change this is because of the breaking or forming of chemical bonds. For a physical change this is because of the breaking or forming of molecular interactions. Recall that chemical bonds and molecular interactions are both forms of electrical attractions. The difference between the two is magnitude—chemical bonds are stronger than are molecular interactions. Hence, chemical changes typically involve more energy than do physical changes.

13. As the concentration of NO_2 goes up with higher temperatures, so does the chance that NO_2 molecules will collide to form N_2O_4. Remember that in order for two chemicals to react they have to come together. Since there are more NO_2 molecules in the flask, the probability of a collision between two NO_2 molecules is greater. This means that although the amount of N_2O_4 present is very small, it will never completely disappear.

14. High pressure favors reactions that form fewer molecules (this helps to alleviate the pressure). According to the coefficients of the reaction, the forward reaction going from nitrogen and hydrogen to ammonia involves the formation of two ammonia molecules for every four molecules of reactants (1 nitrogen molecule and 3 hydrogen molecules).

15. The greater volume favors the formation of more molecules. Accordingly, reactions that result in a greater number of molecules are favored. For the NO_2/N_2O_4 system, this reaction would be the transformation of N_2O_4 into two molecules of NO_2. Because NO_2 is brown, the chamber of the syringe should get browner as the syringe is pulled outwards. (This shift in color, however, is counterbalanced by the lightening of color that occurs as the gases are diluted over the greater volume.)

16. Only when the number of individuals being born equals the number of individuals dying is a population at equilibrium.

17. They likely contain the same material.

18. 3.322×10^{-24} gram

19. A single oxygen atom has a very small mass of 16 amu.

20. One amu equals 1.661×10^{-24} grams. So, 16 amu must be equal to $(16)(1.661 \times 10^{-24}$ grams$) = 26.576 \times 10^{-24}$ grams or 2.6576×10^{-23} grams.

21. A single water molecule has a very small mass of 18 amu.

22. $(18)(1.661 \times 10^{-24}$ grams$) = 29.898 \times 10^{-24}$ grams or 2.9898×10^{-23} grams.

23. No, because this mass is less than that of a single oxygen atom.

24. Atoms are so small that it is impractical to measure them out one by one. Instead, we work with bulk quantities of atoms. Knowing the relative masses of atoms thus gives us a handle on how many atoms two samples have relative to each other. That oxygen is 16 times more massive than hydrogen, for example, tells us that a 16 gram sample of oxygen contains the same number of atoms as 1 gram of hydrogen.

25. 17.04 grams per mole.

26. They have about the same number of atoms.

27. There is one mole of F_2 in 38 grams of F_2 and one mole of O_2 in 32 grams of O_2. There is one mole of N_2 in 28 grams of N_2. For 32 grams of N_2, there are 32/28 = 1.14 moles of N_2. There are two moles of CH_4 in 32 grams of CH_4, so the answer is **c**.

28. There are two moles of nitrogen atoms in 28 grams of N_2, and two moles of oxygen atoms in 32 g of O_2. There are five moles of atoms in 16 grams of methane, CH_4, and two moles of fluorine atoms in F_2. The greatest number of atoms are in **c**, 16 grams of methane, CH_4.

29. They assumed incorrectly that one hydrogen atom bonds to one oxygen atom to form water with a chemical formula of HO. We know today, however, that two hydrogen molecules (not atoms) react with one oxygen molecule to form water. By a count of molecules—which translates to a count of atoms—we see that the hydrogen and oxygen react in a 2:1 ratio and the formula for water is H_2O. By mass, hydrogen and oxygen still always react in a 1:8 ratio. But because two hydrogen's are needed for every one oxygen, this ratio is better expressed as 0.5 grams of hydrogen to 0.5 grams of hydrogen to 8 grams of oxygen. Comparing one hydrogen atom to one oxygen atom thus shows us that oxygen is actually 16 times more massive as is hydrogen.

30. a) 18 amu b) 42 amu c) 60 amu

Chapter 19 Problem Solutions

1. From their formula masses we find that 60 grams of 2-propanol (60 amu) will form 42 grams of propene (42 amu) and 18 grams of water (18 amu). Six grams of 2-propanol, therefore, should yield 4.2 grams of propene and 1.8 grams of water.

2. Set up a ratio. If 180 grams of aspirin contains one mole of molecules (6.02×10^{23}) then 0.250 grams contains 0.00139 moles of molecules (8.38×10^{20}).

3. In 122.55 grams of $KClO_3$ there is one mole of $KClO_3$. From the chemical equation we find that for every 2 moles of $KClO_3$ 3 moles of O_2 are produced. One mole of $KClO_3$, therefore, should only produce 1.5 moles of O_2. The molecular mass of O_2 is 32 amu. This means that in 32 grams of O_2 we have 1 mole. Multiply 32 grams O_2 by 1.5 to find the number of grams in 1.5 moles O_2: 48 grams. So, 48 grams of O_2 will be produced in this reaction.

20 Acid, Base, and Redox Reactions

Answers to Exercises

1. The potassium carbonate found in ashes acts as a base and reacts with skin oils to produce slippery solutions of soap.

2. The Bronsted-Lowry definition is emphasized greater in this chapter.

3. A hydroxide ion is a water molecule minus a hydrogen nucleus.

4. The positively charged hydrogen ion is the same thing as a proton.

5. The base accepted the hydrogen ion, H^+, and thus gained a positive charge. The base thus forms the positively charged ion. Conversely, the acid donated a hydrogen ion and thus lost a positive charge. The acid thus forms the negatively charged ion.

6. A salt is the *ionic compound* produced from the reaction of an acid and a base. Water is a covalent compound.

7. The corrosive properties are no longer present because the acid and base no longer exist.

8. a) acid, base, acid, base.
   b) acid, base, acid, base.
   c) base, acid, base, acid.
   d) base, acid, acid or base, base or acid.

9. A strong acid solution will conduct electricity better because it contains more ions.

10. Hydrogen fluoride, H-F, has a stronger bond connecting its atoms together than does hydrogen chloride, H-Cl. Thus, H-F does not split apart into hydrogen ions so readily and is a weaker acid. There are other factors that also make hydrogen fluoride a weaker acid. How well a molecule is able to donate a hydrogen ion depends greatly on the stability of the negatively charged ion that results. Recall that as a molecule donates a hydrogen ion, it becomes negatively charged. If the negative charge can be easily accommodated, then the molecule has a greater propensity for donating the hydrogen ion. Both the fluoride and chloride ions carry a -1 negative charge. The chloride ion, however, is bigger and is thus able to distribute the single negative charge over a greater volume. This makes for a fairly stable negatively charged chloride ion, which assists in the acidity of H-Cl. The fluoride ion, by contrast, is small, which intensifies the repulsions among neighboring electrons. This makes for a less stable negatively charge fluoride ion, which detracts from the acidity of H-F.

11. That the value of K_W is so small tells us that the extent to which water ionizes is also quite small.

12. K_W is the product of the hydroxide and hydronium ion concentrations. If K_W increases with increasing temperature, then so does the hydroxide and hydronium ion concentrations. This means that the reaction of a water molecule with a water molecule to form hydroxide and hydronium ions is favored with increasing temperatures. Thermal energy, therefore, drives this reaction forward and energy can be thought of as one of the reactants. The acid/base reaction of two water molecules, therefore, is endothermic.

13. The hydronium ion concentration of pure water is equal to the square root of K_W. If K_W is greater at warmer temperatures, then so is the hydrogen ion concentration, which translates to a lower pH. It should be noted that the hydroxide ion concentration of pure water is also equal to the square root of K_W. Thus as the temperature of pure water is raised, the hydroxide ion concentration increases along with the hydronium ion concentration. Remember that pH is

merely a measure of the concentration of hydronium ions and that a "neutral solution" is one in which the hydronium ion and hydroxide ion concentrations are equal. Thus, with warm water we find an example whereby a neutral solution has a pH less than 7! Strictly speaking, any sample of pure (and neutral) water has a pH of 7 only at about 25°C.

14. The concentration of hydronium ions is typically so small it needs to be stated using scientific notation. The pH scale, therefore, is one of convenience.

15. The sum of the pH and pOH of a solution is always equal to the negative log of Kw, which is 14.

16. $pH = -\log[H_3O^+] = -\log(1) = -(-0) = 0$
    This an acidic solution. Yes, pH can be equal to zero!

17. Use a calculator to find the log of 2 (it's 0.301)
    $pH = -\log[H_3O^+] = -\log(2) = -(0.301) = -0.301$
    This a very acidic solution. Yes, pH's can be negative!!

18. It is the alkaline character of limestone that serves to neutralize waters that might be acidified in the midwestern United States.

19. Add a neutralizing substance such as limestone.

20. The warmer the ocean, the lower the solubility of any dissolved gases such as carbon dioxide, CO_2. Less CO_2 would be absorbed and more of it would remain to perpetuate global warming.

21. A buffer solution is one that serves to neutralize any incoming acids or bases. This is typically achieved by mixing two separate chemicals into a single solution. One chemical serves to neutralize the incoming acid, while the second serves to neutralize the incoming base. It would be quite possible to attach these two chemicals by a covalent bond to make for a single molecule that serves both functions. An example would be an amino acid, $HO-CO-CH_2-NH_2$, which neutralizes any incoming base with the "HO" segment of the molecule and any incoming acid with the "NH_2" side of the molecule. Such a system, however, is limited in its applications. The pH range that a buffering system helps to maintain can be adjusted by changing the relative concentrations of a variety of different buffering components. For a single component buffering system this would not be possible.

22. The hydrogen chloride reacts with the ammonia to form ammonium chloride. The concentration of ammonium chloride in this system, therefore, increases while the concentration of ammonia decreases.

23. The sodium hydroxide reacts with the ammonium chloride to from sodium chloride and ammonia. The concentration of ammonia in this system, therefore, increases while the concentration of ammonium chloride decreases.

24. When the acting buffering component is all neutralized.

25. As an acid, the aspirin reacts with the carbonate ions of the blood stream to form carbonic acid. This carbonic acid decomposes into carbon dioxide and water. By hyperventilating, the body rids itself of the excess carbon dioxide that builds up from the decomposition of carbonic acid. This has the effect of increasing the rate of carbonic acid decomposition, which helps to maintain the blood pH.

26. An oxidizing agent causes another agent to oxidize by accepting electrons. An oxidizing agent, therefore, is reduced. Conversely, a reducing agent causes another agent to reduce by donating electrons and is therefore oxidized.

27. An oxidizing agent causes other materials to lose electrons. It does so by its tendency to gain electrons. Atoms with great electron affinity, therefore, also behave as strong oxidizing agents.

Conversely, a reducing agent causes other materials to gain electrons. It does so by its tendency to lose electrons. Atoms with great electron affinity, therefore, have little tendency to behave as reducing agents. To behave as a strong reducing agent, an atom must have a low electron affinity along with a low ionization energy.

28. To behave as an oxidizing agent, a chemical must have a tendency to gain electrons. This results from a relatively high effective nuclear charge. It is this relatively high effective nuclear charge that makes for a high ionization energy, which is a measure of how much energy it takes to remove an electron from an atom. Thus, the ability of a chemical to behave as an oxidizing agent increases with increasing effective nuclear charge. To behave as a reducing agent, a chemical must have a tendency to lose electrons. This occurs best for chemicals with a lower ionization energy.

29. Fluorine should behave as a stronger oxidizing agent because it has a greater effective nuclear charge in its outermost shell.

30. The electrons flow from the submerged nail to the copper ions in solution.

31. To allow for a balance of charge between the two chambers.

32. The sodium is oxidized as it loses its electron to the aluminum ions.

33. According to the chemical formula for iron hydroxide, there are two hydroxide groups for every one iron atom. Each hydroxide group has a single negative charge. This means that the iron of iron hydroxide must carry a double positive charge, which is no different from the free Fe^{2+} ion from which it is formed. This reaction is merely the coming together of oppositely-charged ions.

34. The Cu^{2+} ion is reduced as it gains electrons to form copper metal, Cu. The magnesium metal, Mg, is oxidized as it loses electrons to form Mg^{2+}.

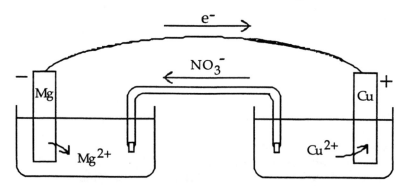

35. Attach a wire to the jewelry to make it an electrode and dip it into a solution of gold ions. In the same container place a gold electrode. Use a battery to drive a current between the two electrodes to force ions from the solution onto the jewelry.

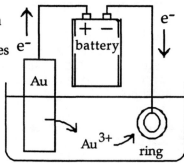

36. How much power a battery can deliver is a function of the number of ions in contact with the electrodes—the more ions, the greater the power. Assuming the lead electrodes (seen as a grid within the battery) are completely submerged both before and after the water has been added,

then diluting the ionic solution of the car battery will decrease the number of ions in contact with the electrode and thus decrease the power of the battery. This effect is only temporary because more ions are soon generated as the battery is recharged by the generator. If the water level inside the battery, however, is so low that the internal lead electrodes are no longer completely submerged, then adding water increases the surface area of the electrode in contact with the solution. This counterbalances the weakening effect of diluting the ionic solution.

37. A heavy duty dry cell battery weighs more because it contains more chemicals. A battery supplies chemical power and so a battery with more chemicals is able to supply more power.

38. Aluminum oxide is insoluble in water and thus forms a protective coating that prevents continued oxidation of the aluminum.

39. As discussed in the answer to exercise 33, each iron atom in iron hydroxide carries a charge of +2. Each iron atom has thus lost two electrons. For two molecules of iron hydroxide, this would correspond to a total of four electrons.

40. They involve the transfer of electrons to oxygen, which accepts the additional electrons with the release of energy.

Chapter 20 Problem Solutions

1. The concentration of hydroxide ions is 1×10^{-4} moles per liter.

2. The pH of this solution is 10, which is basic.

3. The pH is of this solution is 4 and it is acidic.

4. If the pH = 5, then the hydronium ion concentration equals 1×10^{-5}. If the hydronium ion concentration is 1×10^{-5}, then the hydroxide ion concentration is 1×10^{-9}.

5. You know that $[H_3O^+] \times [HO^-] = Kw$. But with a neutral solution, the concentration of the hydronium and hydroxide ions is equal. Thus, the hydronium ion concentration is equal to the square root of Kw, which is 2×10^{-7}. Using a calculator with a log function, you can then find that the pH of the solution is 6.7.

21 Organic Chemistry

Answers to Exercises

1. A saturated hydrocarbon with 5 carbon atoms will have 12 hydrogen atoms. An unsaturated hydrocarbon with 5 carbon atoms will have 10 or fewer hydrogen atoms.

2. Because of greater induced dipole-induced dipole molecular interactions.

3.

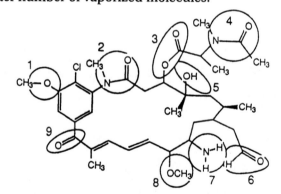

4.

5. The pressure is greater at the bottom of the fractionation tower because of a higher temperature and because of a greater number of vaporized molecules.

6.
   1. ether
   2. amide
   3. ester
   4. amide
   5. alcohol
   6. aldehyde
   7. amine
   8. ether
   9. ketone

7. If the bulk of the "large" alcohol is a nonpolar hydrocarbon chain, then the alcohol may be insoluble in water.

8. The 80 proof vodka is 40 percent ethanol by volume, hence 60 percent water.

9. Ingesting methanol is indirectly harmful to one's eyes because in the body it is metabolized to formaldehyde—a chemical most toxic to living tissue. Methanol, just like ethanol, however, also has inherent toxicity and is thus also directly harmful.

10. Bring the cola to an alkaline pH by adding a base such as sodium hydroxide. This transforms the caffeine salt into its free base form. To remove the caffeine from the aqueous phase add

diethyl ether and mix the two phases by shaking the container. This effectively removes the free base caffeine from the aqueous phase.

11.

12. The caprylic acid reacts with the sodium hydroxide to form a water soluble salt. The aldehyde, on the other hand, is not acidic so it will not form a water soluble salt.

13. No! This label indicates that it contains the hydrogen chloride salt of phenylephrine. This organic salt is not acidic just as the inorganic salt sodium chloride, which is the hydrogen chloride salt of sodium, is not acidic.

14. Don't let the name fool you. Look to the structure to deduce its physical or chemical properties. This molecule is an alkaloid, hence, (b) is the right answer. This molecule has "acid" in its name not because it behaves like an acid, but because it is derived from an acid (lysergic acid)

15. Vanillin is also a phenol and many phenols have antiseptic properties.

16. Aspirin's chemical name is acetyl salicylic acid. It is the acidic nature of aspirin that gives rise to its sour taste.

17. It is the vast diversity of organic chemicals that permits the manufacture of the many different types of medicines needed to match the many different types of illnesses.

18. The side reaction occurs as each 6-aminohexanoic acid molecule reacts with itself rather than with a neighboring molecules. Polymerization, therefore, is favored in a concentrated solution where there molecules have a greater chance of running into a neighboring molecules.

19. Polypropylene consists of a polyethylene backbone with methyl groups attached to every other carbon atom. This side group interferes with the close packing that could otherwise occur among the molecules. As a consequence, we find that polypropylene is actually less dense than is polyethylene—even low-density polyethylene.

20. The combustion of polyacrylonitrile produces hydrogen cyanide. Any of the chlorine containing polymers will produce hydrogen chloride upon combustion. This would include polyvinyl chloride and polyvinylidene chloride.

21. The plastics, along with other combustible trash, could be burned at a power plant for the generation of electric energy. As discussed in the previous exercise, however, the burning of some plastics produce toxic chemicals, such as hydrogen cyanide, or hydrogen chloride. All polymers when burned produce carbon dioxide, which is harmful in that it contributes to global warming. The technology is available, however, to minimize these emissions. Perhaps, though, the ultimate solution is to recycle the plastics. Don't forget that plastics are presently derived from fossil fuels, which are one of nature's finite resources.

22. Place the clothing article in freezer to solidify the chewing gum polymers. Then use a

hammer to "crack" the gum free from the clothing. Residual gum can then be removed by washing with a stain-removing type detergent.

23. A polymer made of long chains is likely to be more viscous because of the tendency of longer chains to get tangled among themselves.

24. A plasticizer decreases the glass transition temperature by interrupting the molecular interactions among polymer molecules.

25. This chemical will work best as a plasticizer because it is the most nonpolar of the three choices. Also, the branching along the carbon chains of this molecule will best inhibit the interactions among polymer chains.

26. All covalent single bonds are able to rotate. This rotation results in a wide number of different possible orientations. The structures of dibutyl phthalate and sodium decanoate, therefore, are able to flop around like cooked strands of spaghetti.

27. Ultimately, this is the energy that was capture from the Sun by photosynthetic plants that turned into fossil fuels after decaying under anaerobic conditions.

28. A fluorine containing polymer such as Teflon.

29. The monomer starting material for polyvinylidene:

30. Recall from Chapter 18 that the larger the atom, the greater its ability to form induced dipole molecular interactions. The chlorine atoms in polyvinyl chloride, PVC, are relatively large, hence, PVC is able to form relatively strong induced dipole interactions. PVC molecules, therefore, are held tightly together by these strong induced dipole molecular interactions. This has the effect of excluding interactions with nonpolar pigment containing oils. In fact, through relatively strong dipole-induced dipole molecular interactions, PVC has a greater preference for water than for nonpolar oils. All-in-all, it is the "polarizability" of the chlorine atoms in polyvinyl chloride that prevents it from being stained by pigment containing nonpolar oils.

22 Rocks and Minerals

Answers to Exercises

1. The properties of minerals are determined by their compositions and their crystal structure. Physical properties include crystal shape, luster, color and streak, specific gravity, hardness, and cleavage and fracture. Chemical properties are less obvious and may require some knowledge and or expensive equipment. Simple chemical tests include reaction to acid (dilute HCl) and the taste test for halite.

2. Volcanic activity: Hawaii Volcanoes National Park, Hawaii, Haleakuala National Park, Hawaii, Crater Lake National Park, Oregon, Katmai National Park, Alaska, Lassen National Park, California, Mount Rainier National Park, Washington, Craters of the Moon National Monument, Idaho.
   Plutonic activity: Yosemite National Park, California, Mount Rushmore National Park, South Dakota, Acadia National Park, Maine.

3. Igneous plutonic rock. If the magma cuts across rock layers, the pluton is referred to as a dike. If the magma spreads out parallel to layering, the pluton is either a sill or a laccolith. The largest pluton is a batholith. Batholiths are generally formed by numerous intrusions over time.

4. Because volcanic rock is extruded at the surface, it cools faster than plutonic rock. The shorter the cooling time, the smaller the crystals.

5. For two magmas that have the same viscosity, a magma that rises slowly is not as buoyant as magma that rises quickly. As such, a slow rising magma is denser than fast rising magma. If one magma is more viscous than the other, it may not so easy to tell which one is denser.

6. Viscosity—magma that rises quickly must be very fluid (low viscosity, low silica content).

7. Basalt can form on both oceanic crust and continental crust. Granite, by definition, is part of the continental crust.

8. Granitic rocks are less dense than basalt. Granitic rocks form the continents, which like icebergs, are buoyant and ride high on the Earth's surface. Basaltic rocks form the oceanic crust, which, because it is more dense, rides low on the Earth's surface.

9. As a batholith moves upward, the rock it intrudes is also pushed upward and aside. In this case, the rock surrounding the batholith is older. Inclusions of rock fragments (xenoliths) from the older, overlying and surrounding rock body become imbedded in the magma and are evidence that the surrounding rock is older than the batholith.

10. The Hawaiian Islands are predominantly made up of igneous rock of volcanic origin.

11. Yes. In order for rock to become metamorphosed it needs to be subjected to heat and/or pressure. The heat source on a volcanic island lends itself to produce either contact metamorphism (rocks surrounding magmas are changed by the heat of the igneous body) or hydrothermal metamorphism (hot fluids that percolate through the rock, changing the rock).

12. Mauna Loa in Hawaii is formed from basaltic magma, which is very fluid. The fluidity allows gases to migrate upward and escape with relative ease. Basaltic eruptions therefore are not very explosive. The eruption of Mount St. Helens is a different story. Volcanoes bordering the Pacific are composed of highly viscous magmas (andesitic magma). High viscosity impedes the upward migration of gases. The gases collect as bubbles and pockets that increase in size and pressure until they explode, ejecting lava and rock fragments from the volcano.

13. Silica content. The internal resistance to flow, is directly related to a magma's silica content. Basaltic magmas, with their low silica contents tend to be quite fluid, while granitic magmas have a high viscosity and flow so slowly that movement is difficult to detect.

14. Chemical composition. There are many kinds of rocks that contain a variety of different minerals, and they do not all melt at the same temperature. Similarly, a magma cools and crystallizes according to chemical composition (fractional crystallization).

15. The Earth likely had similar numerous craters, but nearly all of them have been subjected to the processes of weathering and erosion. Because the Moon lacks an atmosphere and oceans, its surface has not been altered by erosion and weathering.

16. Yes, to some degree, but not a complete cycle in which there is extensive melting of rocks. Moon rocks include: 1) a variety of igneous rocks, 2) breccias (angular conglomerates), and 3) moondust. Igneous rocks of course suggest a magmatic origin; the most common igneous rocks on the Moon are basalt and feldspar-rich rocks. The breccia and moon dust, although igneous in origin, are sedimentary features on the Moon. They are igneous rocks that have been broken and pulverized into breccias and moondust by meteor impacts.

17. Clastic sedimentary rocks are composed primarily of quartz, feldspar, and clay minerals. Clay minerals are the by-product of the chemical weathering of feldspar. Because feldspar is the most abundant silicate, clay minerals are the most abundant clastic sediment. Clastic rocks include shale, sandstone, and conglomerate.

18. Granite, predominantly composed of quartz and feldspar minerals, is resistant to chemical weathering. Marble, on the other hand, is metamorphosed limestone that succumbs more easily to chemical weathering. With time, marble may dissolve from the conglomerate. So we find more granite than marble in conglomerates.

19. The deposition of sediment in a delta environment is due to a stream's inability to transport sediment indefinitely. The settling of grain particles is directly related to inertia. Larger grains have more mass and more inertia; thus larger grains are the first to settle out. Smaller grains have less mass and less inertia and are the last to settle out. Cross bedding is typical in delta environments. In a delta that is actively extending outward has a gradation of sediments that coarsens upward. This happens because with each newly deposited layer of sediment the finer particles will have farther to go before settling out.

20. As a delta grows, the distance traveled by water in the main channel to reach the bay becomes so great that the stream shifts its course and begins cutting new shorter pathways to the bay. This accounts for the radiating branching fingers of a delta. When the fingers get too long, the process begins again. As streams continue to flow to the sea, and as successive beds are deposited one on top of the other, the delta builds itself outward.

21. The steep upper slopes of the fan are characterized by boulders, cobbles, and coarse gravels that are poorly sorted. The base of the fan and the alluvial plain are made up of sand, silt, and mud. So smaller rocks occupy the bottom layers. With each episode of deposition an alluvial fan grows upward and outward. The steep, upper slopes move outward, away from the source area as the fan grows, and covers over areas that were once the site of deposition of finer particles. Thus, the top layers are coarser than bottom layers.

22. The smoothness of the grains that make up the rock indicate travel time, and hence, distance. If its grains are angular, then a short travel time is indicated. Small rounded grains indicate a longer travel time, and hence longer distance.

23. The textural composition (i.e., the size of the sedimentary grains) of gravels and conglomerates indicate sedimentation by strong river currents or high waves on a rocky beach; siltstones, mudstones, and shales indicate sedimentation in quiet waters that allow fine sediments to settle out; sands and sandstones indicate moderate currents, such as rivers, small waves, and winds that blow sand dunes.

24. Principally feldspars and quartz. On a lesser degree, biotite, muscovite, pyroxene, and hornblende.

25. Clastic sedimentary rock's pore spaces between individual sediment grains permits the passage of oil.

26. Halite (d) weathers first since it is composed of NaCl and dissolves easily in a humid environment. Granite (a) weathers last since it is very resistant to all types of mechanical and chemical breakdown.

27. Chemical sedimentary rocks are formed from the precipitation of minerals from a solution, usually water. The process can occur directly, as a result of inorganic processes, or indirectly, as a result of a biochemical reaction. Carbonates are the best example of rocks formed by biochemical reactions, whereas evaporites are good examples of rocks formed by inorganic processes.

28. Sedimentary rock. Petroleum formation begins with the accumulation of sediment in ocean areas rich in plant and animal remains. As the buried organic-rich sediment is heated over a sufficient period of time, chemical changes take place that create oil. Under pressure of the overlying sediments the minute droplets are squeezed out of the source rocks and into overlying porous rocks that become reservoirs.

29. Rock smashed to pieces or moving rock fragments to other places is a form of mechanical weathering. Subjecting a rock to acid is chemical weathering.

30. Sedimentary rock when the previously existing rock is subjected to forces of weathering and erosion. Metamorphic rock when the previously existing rock is subjected to heat or pressure.

31. The most noteworthy characteristic of slate is its excellent rock cleavage. Also, the small crystal size helps make it watertight.

32. Mineralogy. Grade refers to the temperature and pressure conditions. The different metamorphic minerals form in specific ranges of temperature and pressure. Conversely, texture (e.g., large grain size) may only reflect the amount of time over which a mineral crystallized.

33. The micas—muscovite and biotite.

34. Foliation is the realignment of minerals so that they are perpendicular to the direction of compressive forces. Sedimentary layering is the laying down of sediments one on top of the other.

35. Yes, by burial metamorphism. As rocks are buried they slowly heat up due to the geothermal gradient until they are in equilibrium with the temperatures surrounding them. This process alters the mineralogy and texture of the rock. So although metamorphism, both contact and regional, usually involves magma, burial metamorphism can also occur without the presence of magma.

36. (a) Gneiss (b) Quartzite (c) Slate (d) Marble (e) Schist

37. Ingesting asbestos is primarily harmful to the lungs, not to the stomach and intestines. Furthermore, harm depends on the type of asbestos. Whereas the crocidolite variety, blue in color, is harmful, the more abundant white chrysotile asbestos is not. This is the kind found in drinking water. Data from the EPA show that in a liter of drinking water there are often millions of fibers of chrysotile asbestos—deemed safe to drink.

38. First of all, the abundant form of asbestos, chrysotile, is generally not harmful to humans. Left undisturbed, chrysotile fibers typically occur in air at concentrations of 0.001 fiber per cubic centimeter. After a removal process, however, chrysotile fiber content in the air increases to about 40 fibers per cubic centimeter—a 40,000 times increase!

23 Earth's Internal Processes

Answers to Exercises

1. The speed of a wave depends on the type of material it travels through. P-waves (primary waves) are the fastest seismic waves and travel through all mediums—air, solids, and fluids. The denser the material, the faster the movement. S-waves (secondary waves) are slower and can only travel through solids.

2. A primary seismic wave goes though both solids and liquids, whereas a secondary wave goes only through a solid. So when secondary waves fail to traverse part of the Earth's interior, a liquid phase is indicated. By studying the passage of both primary and secondary waves through the Earth, solid and liquid layers can be identified.

3. When a seismic wave encounters a boundary between different layers, reflection and refraction of the wave occurs. The reflected part of the wave tells us about the boundary, and when part of the part that continues into the layer is reflected, that layer is revealed also. Parts that continue without reflection are encountered on another side of the Earth. The relative reflections and refractions reveal a solid inner core, a liquid outer core, a rocky plastic-like mantle, and a rigid and brittle crust.

4. The Earth's solid central core is revealed by the differences in P- and S- wave propagation through the Earth's interior. As these waves encounter the boundary at 2900 km, a very pronounced wave shadow develops. P-waves are both reflected and refracted at the boundary, but S-waves are only reflected. S-waves cannot travel through liquids, implying a liquid outer core. As P-waves propagate through the outer core, there is a depth at which there is a sudden increase in speed. The faster traveling wave indicates a solid inner core.

5. Anyone who has seen a volcano erupt knows that at least some part of the Earth's interior is semi-liquid. This is borne out by seismic wave study. S-waves cannot travel through liquid. Although S-waves travel through the lithosphere quite easily, below the lithosphere the velocity of S-waves decreases as the waves are partially absorbed. This is the asthenosphere which contains a small amount of melt material. At a depth of about 200 kilometers the boundary between the semi-molten asthenosphere and the solid upper mantle can be detected as S-waves increase in velocity.

6. The lithosphere contains the crustal surface—continental and oceanic. As such, it is comprised of the various tectonic plates. The lithosphere is rigid because it is composed of material that has cooled and solidified. The deeper asthenosphere, however, has not experienced the same amount of cooling and is semi-molten. It flows as a semi-liquid plastic. Hence, the lithosphere rides above and "floats" on the asthenosphere.

7. The Earth's mantle is rock, but much of the upper portion (the asthenosphere) is semi-molten rock. So the crust floats on the semi-molten asthenosphere.

8. The mountain requires a large "root" to support the large mass of rock the makes up the mountain. This is analogous to a floating iceberg. The more ice above the water line, the deeper the berg goes underwater. Buoyant forces at work!

9. The principle of isostasy states that the lithosphere floats on the denser mantle. The thick but less dense continents are supported by a buoyant root that projects into the mantle. Seismic waves reveal the existence of these roots. Mountains have even deeper roots to support their weight. The continents stand higher than the ocean basins because the ocean basins are more dense. The pressure exerted on the mantle by the lithosphere must be the same at any given depth. The lithosphere adjusts its position until this state of equilibrium is achieved. This state of equilibrium has the continents standing higher than the ocean basins, due to buoyancy.

10. The continental crust certainly stands higher because it is composed of buoyant granitic material. Like an iceberg, the thicker it is, the further it extends downward. As a mountain range forms it slowly sinks and extends downward as the crust bends downward. Because the oceanic crust is thinner, it doesn't extend as deep into the asthenosphere.

11. Just as shaving off the top of an iceberg would lighten the iceberg, and cause it to float higher, the erosion and wearing away of mountains lightens them and causes them to float higher on the asthenosphere. (This is called the principle of isostasy.) This occurs because material has been removed from the continental crust, and deposited on the oceanic crust. This causes the continental crust to have less mass, so it buoyantly rises. Whether the elevation of the mountain increases or decreases depends on the rate of erosion compared to the rate of isostatic adjustment.

12. If one were to plot the apparent path of polar wandering as determined from North American rocks, it would look different than the path determined from European rocks. A good analogy is two lines plotted on an X-Y plot that have the same slope but different y-intercepts. That is, the apparent polar wander paths are offset. If one were to move North America and Europe back together, then the polar wander paths would overlie each other.

13. Faults and folds are the strain that result from stress. Stress builds up in the lithosphere because it is rigid, broken into plate, and is in motion, just as two cars that crash into each other results in crumpled, broken cars.

14. Most of the stress that builds up in the lithospheric plates does so where two (or three) plates are touching. They touch at their boundaries. When the stress reaches a critical threshold, rocks break, slide past each other, and earthquakes are generated.

15. The Hawaiian Islands are located over what is called a "hot spot". Hot spots originate as plumes of relatively hotter mantle material that rises up through the mantle. The cause of mantle plumes is not well understood at present.

16. Mountain ranges are the result of plate convergence. Since plate margins are typically rather long, the mountains that form along them are long. They are relatively thin because most of the stress and strain related to plate interaction occurs proximal to the plate boundaries.

17. Convergent boundaries. This is so because compressive forces tend to crunch things together, which causes thickening of the crust, which in turn causes isostactic adjustment. Volcanoes also form at convergent margins due to subduction and partial melting.

18. One could find metamorphic rock at all three types of plate boundaries. At convergent boundaries, we expect regional metamorphism involving mechanical deformation and elevated temperatures due to volcanism. At divergent boundaries we might expect to find thermally metamorphosed rocks. At transform boundaries, we might find mechanically deformed rocks. All in all, by far the majority of metamorphic rocks are found associated with convergent boundaries. Metamorphic rocks at the other two types of boundaries represent a small fraction of the total.

19. Possible answers include: The granitic Sierra Nevada range, which are the batholiths left over from subduction-derived partial meting. The occurrence of trench deposits along the coastal areas of Northern California. The occurrence of metamorphic rocks both in the Sierra Nevada and near the trench deposits.

20. Continental drift proposed that continental land was not static—the continents moved. The theory was well supported by the "jig-saw" fit of continental land masses at their margins, and by data in paleo-climatology and paleontology. Although the evidence was quite remarkable, a suitable driving mechanism to produce such crustal movement was lacking. The theory of plate tectonics states that the lithosphere is broken up into about a dozen rigid moving plates that move in response to convection cycles within the planet's interior. The boundaries between these plates—divergent, convergent, and transform boundaries—are the sites where crust is formed (seafloor spreading) and destroyed (subduction zones). Continental drift provided the idea supported by later findings related to plate tectonics.

21. The oceans on our planet have been around since very early in Earth's history. The present ocean basins, however, are not a permanent feature. The present day Atlantic Ocean did not exist when Pangaea was in existence. Then it was a tiny rift area between continental lands. With a spreading center in the middle of the Atlantic, the floor of the Atlantic Ocean is constantly being added to.

22. The present day arrangement of continents is not a permanent feature. Hence, the way a map of the world looks has changed drastically over geologic time. Continents have increased in size over geologic time through magmatic differentiation. Partial melting and fractional crystallization act to increase the silica content of rocks, which decreases their density. The continental crust is made of these less dense rocks. In general, continental crust is not subducted, due to its buoyant nature.

23. The ocean floors are the sites of crustal formation. New crust is generated at a spreading center, as the new crust is formed it pushes the older crust away. In general, continental crust does not get subducted because of its low density. Older oceanic crust has been subducted, while older continental crust has not.

24. Because certain minerals align themselves with the magnetic field, rocks have a preserved imprint of the Earth's magnetism. This is called paleomagnetism. Paleomagnetic data on pole reversals and paleomagnetism provide strong evidence for the concept of seafloor spreading (see the answer to the previous question), which in turn accounts for the motions of the continents and continental drift.

25. A study during the 1950s used paleomagnetism to show that the position of the magnetic poles had gradually wandered around the globe. Since the geographic poles do not wander, it is hard to conceive that the related magnetic poles had wandered. To explain the apparent movement of the magnetic poles it was suggested that it was the continents that had moved and not the poles. This idea was supported by the theory of seafloor spreading and magnetic surveys of the ocean floors. The surveys showed alternating strips of normal and reversed polarity, paralleling either side of the spreading rift areas.

26. Magnetic pole reversals have to do with the fact that the Earth's magnetic field periodically reverses its polarity —the north magnetic pole becomes the south magnetic pole and vice versa. Because certain minerals align themselves with the magnetic field, rocks have a preserved imprint of the Earth's magnetism. Pole reversals and paleomagnetism provide strong evidence for the concept of seafloor spreading. As new basalt is extruded at the oceanic ridge, it is magnetized according to the existing magnetic field. Magnetic surveys of the ocean's floor show alternating strips of normal and reversed polarity, paralleling either side of the rift area. Thus, the magnetic history of the Earth is recorded in spreading ocean floors as in a very slow magnetic tape. Since the dates of pole reversal can be determined by dating rocks that come from the sea floor, the magnetic pattern of the spreading seafloor would document not only the seafloor's age, but also the rate at which it spreads.

27. Divergent boundaries are the dominant feature associated with sea floor spreading. Transform fault boundaries connect offset segments of the divergent boundary.

28. Self explanatory.

29. A fault is defined as a fracture in the Earth's crust along which appreciable movement has taken place. Horizontal movement occurs when two plates slide past one another with no upward or downward movement. This typically occurs along transform faults, which connect offset spreading ridge segments. The most famous horizontal movement in a fault zone is the San Andreas fault in California.

30. The differential separation of elements during Earth's formation resulted in heavier elements migrating toward the center of the planet and lighter elements floating to the surface of the planet. So yes, the greater density of the mantle contributes to its position beneath the crust.

31. J. Tuzo Wilson postulated that the Hawaiian Islands are the tops of huge volcanoes that formed as the floor of the Pacific Ocean moved over a stationary hot spot. Thus the oldest islands are farthest from the hot spot. If on a map you placed an arrow over the Hawaiian Islands with the head at the oldest island (Niihau) and the tail at the youngest island (Hawaii), you would see the direction of plate movement.

32. Any magnetic field has its origin in the motion of electric charge. Most likely, convection currents in the liquid outer core, combined with the rotational effects of the Earth, produce the Earth's magnetic field.

33. Lithosphere is created at spreading centers (divergent plate boundaries) and destroyed at subduction zones (convergent plate boundaries). They are considered to be in equilibrium because the theory of plate tectonics states that the Earth is neither expanding nor contracting. Thus the rate of production of new lithosphere must equal the rate of destruction of old lithosphere.

34. Oceanic crust is more dense than continental crust, so buoyancy inhibits the subduction of continental crust.

35. Mountain ranges, volcanoes, plutonic rocks, metamorphic rocks, folded and faulted rocks are all explained by plate tectonics. The deposition of marine sedimentary rocks on continental crust is explained by higher stands of sea level, which can often be attributed to faster sea floor spreading rates. Virtually all geologic processes can be tied back to plate tectonics, although sometimes the link is quite indirect. For example, consider the formation of a stream valley. As a mountain is growing, the stream gradient increases, which affects the development of the stream valley. The growth of mountains is a result of plate tectonics. Your students may come up with many interesting examples!

36. The Pacific rim is also known as the "ring of fire" because the Pacific Plate has the most subduction zones, and thus the highest potential for tsunami-generating earthquakes. In such a seismically active zone, a reliable warning system is a must.

37. Stratovolcanoes, composed of mostly andesitic lava. This lava is the product of partially melted basaltic oceanic crust.

38. The Himalayan mountains are the result of continent-continent collision between the India plate and the Eurasian plate. The San Andreas fault is a transform fault, it began as a fault that connected spreading ridge segments. The Andes Mountains are the result of volcanic eruptions and uplift related to the subduction of the Nazca plate beneath the South American plate.

39. Horizontal sliding movement between the northwest moving Pacific Plate and the southeast moving North American Plate.

40. The Mid-Atlantic ridge, running essentially north-south in the middle of the Atlantic Ocean, is the world's longest mountain range.

Problem Solutions

1. From distance = speed × time, time = distance/speed. For a numerical value we express km in cm. In 1 km there are 1000×100 cm. So

   time = (5000km / 2cm) $(1000 \times 100$cm $/1$ km) = **250 million years.**

2. Similar to the solution to the previous problem,

   $$\text{time} = \frac{600 \text{ km} \times 1000 \text{ m} \times 100 \text{ cm}}{3.5 \text{ cm per year}} = 17 \text{ million years}$$

3. The comparison is the weight of ocean 3 km deep (the number 3) with the weight of 10 km of crust 3 times as dense (the number 30). How big is 3 compared with 30? One tenth as much. The ocean contributes **10%** of the crust's weight.
   Or by density: Density $\rho = Wt/V$, or $Wt = \rho V$, where volume $V = A \times h$ (cross section area × depth). Let h be depth of crust, and H the depth of ocean. Then by ratio the areas cancel and

   $$\frac{Wt_{\text{ocean}}}{Wt_{\text{crust}}} = \frac{\rho_o V_o}{\rho_c V_c} = \frac{\rho_o AH}{\rho_c Ah} = \frac{\rho_o H}{\rho_c h} = \frac{1 \times 3 \text{ km}}{3 \times 10 \text{ km}} = \frac{3}{30} = \frac{1}{10} \text{ or } \textbf{10\%}.$$

4. Each log unit is an order of magnitude, i.e. one log unit is 10 (10^1), two log units is 100 (10^2), three log units is 1000 (10^3), etc. So an Earthquake of magnitude 8 has 100 times the amplitude of a magnitude 6 quake, and has likewise **100 times more** ground shaking.

24 Water and Surface Processes

Answers to Exercises

1. Fresh water provides the sustenance of life. This includes drinking water, agricultural uses, sanitation, and transportation,

2. Water evaporated from over the oceans produces water vapor rich in salt particles. These tiny salt particles become condensation nuclei. As condensation begins, the salt dissolves, forming a solution. The water vapor droplets will continue to absorb water and grow until they reach a critical size where they are so diluted that they behave as pure water. Thus, the precipitation of fresh water over the oceans is the product of dilution during condensation.

3. Less than 3% of the Earth's water is fresh water, most of it locked in polar ice caps and glaciers.

4. The oceans.

5. Both water on a space station and water on the Earth are essentially finite resources. Although water may undergo different uses, it is not destroyed. It may be filtered, evaporated, or condensed, but the volume remains constant.

6. An artesian system.

7. The water in an unconfined aquifer will rise to the level of the water table, until it is pumped.

8. Gentle, sandy slopes. There are two issues here: 1) runoff vs. infiltration and 2) permeability. Steep slopes tend to have more consolidated material than gentle slopes, which gives them a lower permeability. The steepness enhances runoff, reducing the chance of infiltration. Gentle slopes enhance infiltration (versus runoff) and sandy material is likely to have a relatively higher permeability, which also enhances infiltration.

9. The overall mass balance is not affected much. The only possible affect is evaporation. Water quality is certainly affected, however.

10. The pollution of groundwater is more difficult to detect. The remediation of groundwater pollution is very time consuming and extremely expensive. In most cases the groundwater never resumes back to its original precontaminated state.

11. Metals occur naturally in the ground. In most cases heavy metals that enter the water supply naturally, do so in limited quantities — the balance of nature. Quantities often increase because of human interaction with the environment. Mining tears up the earth. The desired minerals and materials are stripped from the area, with garbage left behind, which may be an unnatural accumulation of loosened heavy metals and minerals that may freely enter the water supply. Industry uses heavy metals, minerals, and chemicals for the various stages of production. Improper management can result in wastes entering the environment.

12. If the water supply is robbed of dissolved oxygen, life forms dependent on oxygen will cease to survive. Pollution of the water supply effects the food chain — plankton, fishes, birds, to mammals. The sources of this type of pollution come from sewage and agricultural waste.

13. Water supply is the major factor. An aquifer will become depleted if the amount of recharge does not equal the amount of discharge.

14. Discharge is the volume of water flowing past a certain point in a given amount of time. Discharge will increase in proportion to the amount of rain that falls. By knowing the area of the drainage basin and the amount of rainfall the change in discharge of a stream can be estimated. (Rainfall rate also plays a role in how discharge changes with time, but this is not discussed in the text.)

15. Water imported from the Sierra Nevada Mountains has solved many problems for the San Joaquin Valley. But, as that water is diverted to the San Joaquin Valley for agricultural

purposes, it is not available for use in other areas. The population of California is growing and people in cities need water. So what is good for the San Joaquin Valley is not necessarily good for the rest of California. This problem has been addressed by new legislator; farmers now sell some of their water to the various cities.

16. Water is a scarce resource in dry areas. The same general answer applies because water for various uses must be allocated by some decision process.

17. When water saturates all the pore spaces in underground rock or soil, we call it groundwater. As water is pumped from the ground, and thus from the pore spaces, the sediments rearrange and partially fill the spaces that used to be occupied by water. This causes the aquifer to compact, and the ground to subside. If groundwater removal is stopped, subsidence will stop. The ground, however, does not return to its original level. Once the aquifer has been compacted it cannot expand to its original level because many parts of the aquifer (interbedded clay aquitards mostly) have compressibilities in expansion that are only one-tenth the value they have in compression.

18. A sinkhole is a large cavity open to the sky. It can form as a cave with a collapsed roof or from the dissolution of carbonate rock by acidic rain or groundwater. So, the factors which contribute to a sinkholes formation include: acidic rain or groundwater, an existing cave or any type of opening that allows the seepage of water.

19. In order for a site to be considered safe it must be located where waste products and their containers cannot be affected chemically by water, physically by earth movements, or accidentally by people.

20. The Mississippi River has a huge water and sediment capacity! With an annual load of 440 million tons of sediment it is no wonder that the Mississippi Delta is moving southward. Each episode of deposition acts to lengthen the course of the river and extend the delta. The Mississippi Delta continues to grow.

21. Ice has the greatest competence. Glaciers moving across a landscape loosen and lift up blocks of rock and incorporate them into the ice. They literally pick up everything in their path. As the ice melts or retreats the rock debris is deposited. Wind has the lowest competence. Wind has a low density and is not capable of picking up and transporting heavy sediments. Sand grains transported by wind move by skipping and bouncing along the surface. Silt and clay sediments are easily transported by the wind, but are not easily lifted by the wind. These types of particles tend to lay flat on the surface. In order to be carried by wind currents they must first be lifted or ejected into the current. For example, wind blowing across a desert road. There is very little dust raised on a quiet road but a road with traffic generates a lot of dust.

22. Wind. Although the force of the wind on the land surface is similar to the force a stream current exerts on its bed, the wind is limited in its ability to transport large grain particles. The combined forces of turbulence and forward motion lift particles into the wind and transport them along, but only for awhile. Although dust and small particles can be carried long distances, it takes higher velocities to carry coarser grain particles.

23. The residence time of groundwater varies from a few hundred years up to thousands of years. The residence time of a lake varies from ten to a hundred years. The difference in these residence times should give a clue as to the problem of groundwater pollution. Because groundwater contamination is in the subsurface it is very difficult to detect. In fact, most cases of aquifer contamination are discovered only after a water-supply well has been affected. The long residence time means that the water is moving at a very slow rate. Therefore long periods of time are required to flush out the contaminant. By the time subsurface water contamination is detected it may be too late for remediation.

24. A dam holds back water. In a lake the water table intersects the land surface and rises when a dam is built, for there is an influx of water from the reservoir into the groundwater.

25. Tampering with the natural work of a river almost always brings unexpected consequences. Evaporation increases as the surface to volume ratio increases, but the effect is very small. Increased evaporation often causes increased soil salinization in the reservoir vicinity.

26. Downstream, water leaving the dam area has increased energy, thus erosion is enhanced.

27. As water enters a reservoir it abruptly slows down and drops its load of sediment. In time the reservoir may fill up with sediment making the dam useless.

28. Water flows from high head to low head. The water flows from the stream into the ground because the water level in the stream is equivalent to the hydraulic head of the stream. We say that the stream is recharging the aquifer.

29. Let us assume that the increased runoff is not enough to cause the banks of the stream to erode. In this case, the cross sectional area of the stream remains constant thus discharge and stream speed increase as runoff into the stream increases. If the cross sectional area of the stream changes, then stream discharge will increase but stream speed may or may not increase. (Speed increase depends on how big the increase in area is compared to the increased discharge.)

30. Glaciers are formed from recrystallized snow. Accumulation of snow slowly changes the individual flakes to rounded lumps of icy material. As more snow falls, the pressure exerted on the bottom layers of icy snow compacts and recrystallizes it into glacial ice. This ice does not become a glacier until it moves under its own weight, usually when the ice is about 50 m thick.

31. A glaciated mountain valley begins its formation in a previously formed stream valley. The glacier carves out the existing features and further accentuates them. A glaciated valley is characterized by sharp, angular features, it is deep and wide with a characteristic U-shape. A non-glaciated mountain valley is characterized by a narrow V-shaped valley.

32. Other sites of glaciated landscapes include Glacier National Park, Montana, The Finger Lakes of upstate New York, Long Island, New York, Cape Cod, Massachusetts, Bunker Hill, Mass-achusetts (drumlin), the Chigmit Mountains in Alaska, and Loch Ness, Scotland to name a few.

33. Frictional drag slows down a glaciers external movement. The glacier experiences this drag as it encounters the bedrock. So, movement is slowest at the base and at the sides of the glacier. Inside the glacier ice flows plastically. The weight of the ice above causes the glacial ice molecules to slide over one another. The internal flow of a glacier exceeds the external flow (due to frictional drag) as the glacier slides over itself without cracking or breaking.

34. One possible answer is that the path of the glacier may be altered if the lava melts all the way through to the ground surface. In this case, erosional and depositional features associated with glaciers would be located in different places. On the other hand, if lava cools on the glacier surface the only long term difference may be in the composition of the morainal material.

35. Glacial ice is simply layers of thick, frozen water. Water is fairly transparent to wavelengths centered in the visible part of the spectrum. The penetration of light waves depends on how clear or how murky the water is, and on the color of the light (in the case of glacial ice, how thick it is). For example, clear ocean water, with wavelengths in the blue-green part of the spectrum, are able to penetrate a depth of nearly 40m before their intensity is reduced by 50%. The extreme ends of the spectrum, red and violet, can only penetrate about 4m before intensity is reduced. This explains why thin layers of water look clear, and thicker layers of water look blue-green. All colors make it through thin layers, but only the blue-green part of the spectrum makes it through thicker layers. Because deep glacial ice is dense thick layers of frozen water, it appears greenish-blue.

36. When water depth approaches half a wave's wavelength, the bottom of the wave's circular path flattens, slowing the wave.

37. The structure itself will not alter the regional scale longshore current, but it will change it on the local scale; that is, on either side of the breakwater. On the upcurrent side, sand that would normally be transported down the coastline will accumulate against the breakwater. On the downcurrent side, energy will be focused at the breakwater causing beach erosion, which is exacerbated by the lack of sand in the current (because it was trapped on the upcurrent side).

38. No, streams can only erode to base level, which by definition cannot be lower than sea level.

25 A Brief History of the Earth

Answers to Exercises

1. The fault is clearly older than the basalt and younger than the sedimentary rock. The sedimentary rock had to be there before the fault in order for the fault to displace it. The reverse argument holds for the basalt.

2. The metamorphic rock had to have been in existence before the sedimentary rock in order for there to be pieces of it in the sedimentary rock.

3. From oldest to youngest the sequence is: G, A, B, C, D, I, H, F, E

4. Geologists used (and still use) the principles of original horizontality, cross-cutting relationships, inclusions, and faunal succession

5. a) Uranium-238 (or possibly Potassium-40, depending on how early)
b) Uranium-235 or Potassium-40 are best, but Uranium-238 will work too (not as precise).
c) Carbon-14 is the only reasonable isotope to use.

6. Uranium has decreased and lead increased (via radioactive decay).

7. The "time clock" can be reset if the mineral is heated during a metamorphic event. The date obtained from that mineral will be the date of the metamorphic event, not the original age of the mineral.

8. The half-life of carbon-14 is only 5730 years. When a material is older than about 50,000 years the amount of carbon-14 that is left is too small to measure, so all we can tell is that the material is older than about 50,000 years.

9. Since the pebbles are clearly older than the conglomerate, the conglomerate is no more than 300 million years old. Since the dike is younger than the conglomerate, the conglomerate can now be bracketed between 200 and 300 million years old.

10. We can say that the average age of the formation is younger than the trilobite and older than the leaves. By average we mean that the formation was deposited over a finite time period, and the age we get via the fossils brackets the beginning and end of deposition of that formation.

11. This sequence must have been overturned by some structural deformation event, such as mountain building. According to the principles of original horizontality and superposition, it could not have been deposited in this manner.

12. The phrase refers to the great diversity of life found in the fossil record that was not apparent in the Precambrian. Almost all major groups of marine organisms came into existence during this time, as evidenced by abundant fossils. The Cambrian saw the development of organisms having the ability to secrete calcium carbonate and calcium phosphate for the formation of outer skeletons, or shells. The preservation of these shells as fossils is why so much more is known about the Paleozoic than the Precambrian

13. A nonconformity is an argument between geologists. A nonconformity is a gap in the rock record represented by sedimentary rocks overlaying the eroded surface of intrusive igneous or metamorphic rocks. This type of unconformity represents large amounts of uplift and an enormous amount of "missing" time. An angular unconformity is tilted or folded sedimentary rocks overlain by younger, relatively horizontal rock layers. This represents a deformational event, such as mountain building, followed by a period of subsidence and deposition.

14. 100 million years.

15. The first atmosphere developed, the ozone layer developed, stromatolites appeared. Stromatolites and certain algae developed photosynthesis.

16. Stromatolites and certain algae developed photosynthesis, which uses sunlight and carbon dioxide and produces oxygen as a byproduct. With the release of free oxygen, a primitive ozone layer began to develop above the Earth's surface. The ozone layer reduced the amount of harmful ultraviolet radiation reaching the Earth. This protection and the accumulation of free oxygen in the Earth's atmosphere permitted the emergence of new life.

17. No, they are not anaerobic. They live partially submerged and partially exposed to air. Since they are exposed to air, they cannot be anaerobic.

18. Stromatolites and other fossils in rocks that are known to be Precambrian in age.

19. Several times during the Paleozoic the continents were flooded by shallow seas.

20. At the time of deposition, the climate of Antarctica was mild enough to support swamps.

21. No they did not. Fossils of humans are not found in the fossil record for millions of years after dinosaurs became extinct.

22. Most of the Earth's iridium is sequestered in its deep interior. The crust is relatively depleted in iridium. Thus large meteorites have a higher iridium concentration than the Earth's crust.

23. Humans have dammed rivers, built irrigation systems, caused pollution, extinctions, etc.

24. If found in granite, the date signifies the age of the granite (when the mineral crystallized from magma). If found in schist, it signifies the age of the metamorphic event, not the age of the original (precursor) rock.

25. Precambrian — first life; stromatolites, bacteria, algae; soft-bodied animals.
Paleozoic — trilobites, shelled animals, first life on land, first fish, first amphibians, first reptiles; major extinctions in the Ordovician and Permian.
Mesozoic.— age of the reptiles, dominance and diversification of dinosaurs, first mammals, first birds and flowering plants; major extinction at the end of the Cretaceous (bye dinosaurs!!)
Cenozoic — age of mammals, diversification of mammals, expansion of flora, emergence of humans; extinction of many large mammals.

26. No, the breakup of Pangaea was for the most part complete by the end of the Cretaceous. (The continents, with some minor differences, were in a very similar arrangement as they are today.)

27. The opening of biological niches left vacant by the demise of the dinosaurs is one possibility. Another possibility is that generally cold climates allowed the evolution of large body size to conserve heat (smaller surface to volume ration means less heat radiation).

28. Sea level rises because a faster spreading rate means warmer ocean crust (same cooling rate as during periods of slower spreading), which is less dense than colder ocean crust. Since it is less dense, the ocean crust "rides" higher, forcing sea water onto the continents.

29. Sea level could be lowered if the climate turned colder, causing more water to be tied up in glacial ice. This could drastically affect shallow water creatures (habitat destruction) and cause many extinctions. The colder climate could also cause the demise of some species through habitat destruction and scarcity of food. Sea level could also be lowered if seafloor spreading rates decreased.

30. Melting of the polar ice caps. This could easily happen if the grim predictions of global warming due to greenhouse gasses were to occur. An increase in seafloor spreading rates could also cause sea level to rise. It is likely that sea level will rise in the future, as it has done so in the past.

31. The lowest elevations, like coastal regions, would be affected first. If the level continued to increase, higher elevations would also be affected, say, major river valleys like the Mississippi valley, etc. It is likely that the habitat destruction caused by rising sea level would cause some extinctions of land-based organisms.

32. Global-scale cooling leading to continental-scale glaciers is most likely caused by the right combination of three things: (1) the arrangement of continents around the globe, (2) the amount of sunlight reflected back into space, and (3) the geometry of the Earth's rotation on its axis and revolution around the Sun. A likely cause of glacial-interglacial cycles is the Milankovitch effect. By definition, we are currently in an ice age because there are continental-scale glaciers present on the Earth.

33. Different characteristics evolved, like skin color, most likely to deal with different intensities of ultraviolet light. Dark skin near the equator to shield from UV light, and light skin away from the equator where dark skin wasn't needed and other selective pressures (such as vitamin D absorption) favored light skin. The effects of these changes are clearly still seen today.

34. We not only adapt to our environment, we manipulate it as well. We could very easily become extinct — from many different causes. Some are obviously beyond our control, but many, unfortunately, are our own doing.

35. Convincing arguments include the huge thickness of sediments in the Grand Canyon compared to sedimentation rates, the immense length of time needed for large crystals to form in igneous and metamorphic rock (compare to crystal size in volcanic rock), great sequences of folded and faulted rocks, etc.

26 The Atmosphere, The Oceans, and Their Interactions

Answers to Exercises

1. It does! The atmosphere is mostly concentrated near the surface because of gravity. Gravity is what holds most of the atmosphere from going off into space. It does, however, thin out as you move away from the Earth's surface until it becomes indistinguishable from the background gas in space. This is why there is no upper limit placed on the atmosphere.

2. The air density would be greater because there is a greater mass of air over a deep mine than at sea level. This greater mass causes the air pressure to be higher, which in turn creates denser air (Pressure is directly proportional to density)

3. The air pressure at higher altitudes is less than at the surface. Time is required for your body to adjust to this new pressure, so the air inside your body pushes outward more than the atmosphere pushes inward, producing that popping feeling.

4. The smoke is initially warmer than the surrounding air so it rises until it equals room temperature At this point the smoke slowly diffuses throughout the room.

5. If more terrestrial radiation were able to leave the Earth than at present, the average temperature at the surface would be lowered. The opposite would be true if less terrestrial radiation escaped.

6. Cooling by radiation prevents the Earth's temperature from rising indefinitely.

7. In January the Northern Hemisphere on the Earth is tilted away from the Sun, so it receives less solar radiation per unit area.

8. The total hours of sunlight (and solar energy) are dependent on the incidence of the Sun's rays on the Earth's surface. In tropical regions the Sun's rays are concentrated as they strike perpendicular to the Earth's surface. As such, tropical regions receive twice as much solar energy as that in polar regions. In polar regions, the incidence of the Sun's rays are at an angle and solar energy is spread out and dispersed. As such, polar regions are cool. The tilt of the Earth allows polar regions to receive nearly 24 hours of sunlight (albeit, dispersed sunlight) for half the year, and nearly 24 hours of darkness the other half of the year.

9. High temperature sources radiate short wavelengths and cooler sources radiate longer wavelengths, The hot Sun emits waves of much shorter wavelengths than the waves emitted by Earth (terrestrial radiation). Radiation from the Sun is mainly in the visible region of electromagnetic waves, whereas terrestrial radiation is infrared.

10. The Earth absorbs short-wavelength radiation from the Sun and reradiates it as long-wavelength terrestrial radiation. Incoming short wave-length solar radiation easily penetrates the atmosphere to reach and warm the Earth's surface, but outgoing long-wavelength terrestrial radiation cannot penetrate the atmosphere to escape into space. Instead, atmospheric gases (mainly water vapor and carbon dioxide) absorb the long-wave terrestrial radiation. As a result, this long-wave radiation ends up keeping the Earth's surface warmer than it would be if the atmosphere were not present.

11. Air temperature is not the factor. Solar radiation is. At high elevations there is less atmosphere above you to filter UV rays, so you are exposed to more high energy solar wavelengths of radiation.

12. Yes, without oceans there would still be weather. Unequal heating of the Earth's surface is responsible for weather, and this is greatly affected by the presence of oceans, but by no means completely dependent upon oceans. Winds and other weather conditions occur on other planets, all without oceans. And weather changes far inland away from bodies of water, such as Chinook winds and tornadoes.

13. Into the oceans. Excess atmospheric carbon dioxide readily dissolves in the ocean, where it undergoes various chemical reactions, most of which lead to the formation of carbonate precipitates such as limestone.

14. The June 1991 eruption of Mount Pinatubo resulted in a cooling of global temperature as the ejection of volcanic aerosols caused an increase in shortwave reflectivity. In fact, average global temperature was lowered for nearly two years. Although volcanic activity generally corresponds to an increase in atmospheric carbon dioxide and/or chlorine which corresponds to climatic warming, the cooling trend (due to increased reflectivity) offset the warming trend. Without an increase in reflectivity, the effects of increased amounts of chlorine would probably have resulted in global warming. In looking at climatic trends it is important to consider all variables.

15. No. Ozone created in cities has a short atmospheric life span (typically less than a day) before it converts to other gases, so wouldn't last long enough to reach the stratosphere, much less the south pole.

16. Although directions are variable, on a non-spinning Earth surface winds would still blow from areas of high pressure to low pressure. Actual Earth at 15° S latitude is in the region of the doldrums where the air is warm and the winds are light. In this region the light winds blow from east to west.

17. Cell-like circulation patterns set up by atmospheric temperature and pressure differences are responsible for the redistribution of heat across the Earth's surface and global winds. Because the winds set the surface waters into motion, atmospheric circulation and oceanic circulation are interrelated. What effects one effects the other. Ocean currents do not follow the wind pattern exactly however, they spiral in a circular whirl pattern—a gyre. In the Northern Hemisphere as prevailing winds blow clockwise and outward from a subtropical high, the ocean currents move in a more or less circular, but clockwise, pattern. The Gulf Stream, a warm water current in the North Atlantic Ocean, is actually a huge gyre.

18. Jet streams are usually found between elevations of 10 to 15 kilometers, although they can occur at higher and lower elevations. As a swiftly flowing westerly wind, the jet streams greatly influence upper-air circulation as they transfer heat from polar regions to tropical regions. As a westerly wind, air travel is faster from west to east and slower from east to west. As such, flights from San Francisco to New York are shorter in time than the return trip from New York to San Francisco.

19. El Niño refers to a warm ocean current off the western coast of South America that typically appears around Christmas and lasts for several months. In normal conditions, high-pressure systems cause the trade winds to blow westward along the equator, dragging warm equatorial surface waters along with them. As warm surface waters move westward, deeper, colder waters to the east rise upward to occupy the space left vacant by the warm surface water. The upwelling of cold waters, rich in nutrients, attract a variety of sea life allowing fishing industries to thrive. In an El Niño year, the trade winds slacken, reversing the normal westward flow of warm tropical surface waters. As the warm surface waters drift eastward, rising warm moist air, low pressures, and storms are found on the eastern side of the Pacific rather than the western side.

20. In normal years the tradewinds are persistent as they blow westward from a region of higher pressure over the eastern Pacific toward a region of lower pressure centered over Indonesia. As the westward moving trades drag cool water from the South America coast, the water is heated and warmed. Consequently in the Pacific Ocean surface water along the equator tends to be cool in the east and warm in the west. During an El Niño, air pressure rises over the region of the western Pacific and falls over the eastern Pacific. This change in pressure weakens the tradewinds causing westward blowing winds to be replaced by eastward blowing winds. A change in winds brings about a change in surface water circulation, and hence a change in the overall weather pattern.

21. The interrelationship between the atmosphere and the oceans is very complex; a change in one effects the other and vice versa. We know that El Niño occurs as air pressure rises over the western Pacific and falls over the eastern Pacific weakening the tradewinds and causing westward blowing winds to be replaced by eastward blowing winds. If global warming also causes such a reversal in pressure systems, we can expect the frequency of El Nino's to increase.

22. Water has a high specific heat thus it retains heat longer than a substance with a low specific heat (like sand or soil). The fact that water takes a long time to cool and that it resists changes in

temperature effects the climate of areas in close proximity to the oceans. Look at a globe and notice the high latitude countries of Europe. If water did not have a high specific heat capacity, the coastal countries of Europe would be as cold as the northeastern regions of Canada, for both are at the same latitude.

23. Water is fairly transparent to wavelengths centered in the visible part of the spectrum. The penetration of light waves depends on how clear or how murky the water is, and on the color of the light. For example, clear ocean water, with wavelengths in the blue-green part of the spectrum, are able to penetrate a depth of nearly 40m before their intensity is reduced by 50%. The extreme ends of the spectrum, red and violet, can only penetrate about 4m before intensity is reduced. This explains why thin layers of water look clear, and thicker layers of water look blue-green. All colors make it through thin layers, but only the blue-green part of the spectrum makes it through thicker layers.

24. The ocean acts to 1) moderate the temperature and weather of coastal lands; and 2) provide a reservoir for atmospheric moisture.

25. Large icebergs come from, or calve off of land glaciers.

26. When evaporation exceeds precipitation salinity increases. In ocean water it is the water that evaporates, the salt is left behind. When precipitation exceeds evaporation salinity decreases as a new influx of fresh water dilutes the salt solution.

27. It will sink until it reaches a point of equilibrium—the point where it encounters water of the same density.

28. When seawater in polar regions freezes only the water freezes, the salt is left behind. The seawater that does not freeze experiences an increase in salinity, which in turn brings about an increase in density. The cold, denser, saltier seawater sinks, producing a pattern of vertical movement. Movement is also horizontal as cold dense water flows along the bottom to the deeper parts of the ocean floor.

29. Evaporation exceeds precipitation.

30. Like the circulation of atmospheric currents, oceanic currents are driven by the heat of the Sun.

31. Tropical regions receive greater amounts of solar radiation. With greater amounts of solar radiation one would expect evaporation to exceed precipitation causing an increase in salinity. Although this is a good assumption, in reality evaporation and precipitation tend to pretty much balance each other. In fact, viewing the world as a whole, 85 percent of the atmosphere's water vapor is water evaporated from the ocean, with 75 percent of the atmosphere's water vapor precipitated back to the oceans. The 10 percent difference is negligible in its effect on salinity as ocean water is able to circulate world wide. In a closed ocean system, such as the Mediterranean Sea, salinity is increasing as the circulation of water is impeded by land barriers.

32. Although salinity varies from one part of the ocean to another, the overall composition of seawater is fairly uniform—a mixture of about 96.5 percent water and 3.5 percent salt. With greater amounts of solar energy at the tropics one would expect evaporation to exceed precipitation causing an increase in salinity. Although this is a good assumption, in reality evaporation and precipitation tend to pretty much balance each other. On a whole, 85 percent of the atmosphere's water vapor is water evaporated from the ocean, with 75 percent of the atmosphere's water vapor precipitated back to the oceans. The 10 percent difference is negligible in its effect on salinity as ocean water is able to circulate world wide.

33. That the prevailing wind direction is a westerly that moves northward from the west to the east.

34. The water level remains the same when the ice melts. Water expands when it turns to ice, which is why part of it sticks above the surface. When it melts, it shrinks back down to its original size, which is why the water level doesn't change. So when floating chunks of ice in the Great Lakes melt, the water level of the lakes doesn't change.

35. Look at the hint: Ice is very much less dense than mercury, and only a tiny part presses into the mercury. Most sticks up above the mercury surface, so when it melts it spills over the surface of the mercury and the level rises. Likewise, but not so dramatic, when floating ice in salt water melts. It sticks up higher in salt water because the salt water is more dense than fresh water. So the level rises a bit when fresh-water ice melts when floating in salt water. But not very much.

36. The polar ice caps are on land and do not displace any water. If they melt the water added to the sea is "new" water and sea level will rise as "new" water is added.

Problem Solution

1. (a) Using the change-in-length formula, $\Delta L = L_0 \alpha \Delta T$, $\Delta L = (1000 \text{ m})(0.07 \text{ m/C}°)(10 \text{ C}°) = 700 \text{ m}$. The 1-km depth of water would expand by **700 m**.

(b) This variation doesn't occur in lakes because the temperature rise occurs only near the surface. Temperature of the deeper parts of the lake remain relatively constant. If the water all the way down expanded, then lakes (and the ocean!) would be appreciably higher in summer than in winter.

27 Weather

1. Weather is the state of the atmosphere with respect to temperature, moisture content, sky conditions, and atmospheric stability or instability at any given place and time. Climate is the consistent behavior of weather over time.

2. The Earth's atmosphere acts as a blanket, it filters short-wave UV radiation entering the lower atmosphere, and it filters and blocks outgoing long-wave terrestrial radiation from leaving the Earth's lower atmosphere. The atmosphere moderates the Earth's surface from temperature extremes.

3. As moist air is lifted or pushed upslope against a mountain it cools adiabatically. As rising air cools, its capacity for containing water vapor decreases, increasing the relative humidity of the rising air. If the air cools to its dew point, the water vapor condenses and a cloud forms. Stable air that is forced upward forms stratus type clouds whereas unstable air tends to form cumulus type clouds.

4. First of all, warm air is able to hold more water vapor before becoming saturated than can cold air. As the relative humidity increases, the water vapor molecules grow larger as they expand. Expansion leads to cooling which leads to condensation. As warm moist air blows over cold water it cools which causes the water vapor molecules to condense into tiny droplets of fog.

5. The ground and objects on the ground are often cooler than the surrounding air. As air comes into contact with these cold surfaces it cools and its ability to hold water vapor decreases. As the air cools below its dew point, water vapor condenses onto the nearest available surface.

6. Greater water content in the air around the Gulf of Mexico makes for more humidity. Arizona, in contrast, has no large body of water to wet the air. Even though both regions may have the same temperature, the prohibiting effect of humidity on bodily evaporation finds one feeling considerably warmer in the Gulf states.

7. First of all evaporation is the change of state from a liquid phase to a vapor phase whereas condensation is the change from a vapor phase to a liquid phase. At the surface of a liquid some water molecules are always leaving (evaporating) while others are always returning (condensing). In a closed container the air directly above the water surface is said to be saturated as it contains the maximum number of water vapor molecules that it can hold. Wind, because it creates a difference between the actual number of water vapor molecules and the number required for saturation, enhances evaporation. Temperature also influences evaporation. The warmer the air temperature the greater the average molecular air speed and the greater the ability of the air molecules to bounce away. Hence, a glass of water will evaporate more readily on a windy, warm, dry summer day.

8. The low cloud cover acts as an insulation blanket inhibiting the outflow of terrestrial radiation.

9. The change in environment from cold to warm. Remember, both environments have the same number of water vapor molecules. As we leave the air conditioned room the warm air outside comes into contact with the cold surface of the sunglasses. During contact the cold surface cools by conduction and the warm airs ability to hold water vapor decreases. As the air cools to its dew point water vapor condenses onto the sunglasses.

10. The change in environment from cold to warm. Remember, both environments have the same number of water vapor molecules. As we leave the cold outdoors the warm air inside comes into contact with the cold surface of the eyeglasses. As the air touching the eyeglasses cools to its dew point, water vapor condenses onto the eyeglasses.

11. Yes! The temperature of an air mass can change without the addition or subtraction of thermal energy— this is adiabatic expansion or compression. Blow on your hand and feel the warmth of your breath. When you pucker your lips and blow, the air expands and when it reaches your hand it is considerably cooler (try it now and see). But no thermal energy was subtracted in this case. Likewise for air that rises and cools. And when air is compressed, like in pumping a bicycle tire, the air is warmed without the addition of thermal energy. So it is with Chinook

winds. If an air mass is lifted up a mountain slope, the temperature will drop because the pressure drops. If an air mass sinks down a slope it's temperature and pressure will go up.

12. Although precipitation actually falls from a descending moist air mass, the production of rain (or snow) requires both descending and rising air or, downdrafts and updrafts. Recall that water droplets in clouds are so small that they evaporate before reaching the ground. Updrafts allow the water droplets more time in the cloud where they can grow in size. Once the weight of the drop is greater than the force of the updraft, the drop descends growing larger as it falls through the moist air. As the drops descend they create a downdraft which, once created, yields precipitation.

13. Recall that water droplets in clouds are so small that they evaporate before reaching the ground. Rising air allows the water droplets more time in the cloud where they can grow in size. Once the weight of the drop is greater than the force of the rising air, the drop descends growing larger as it falls through the moist air, yielding precipitation.

14. First of all, warm air is associated with high atmospheric pressure and cold air is associated with low atmospheric pressure. As air rises it cools by expansion. As air sinks it warms by compression. As air sinks and warms, its capacity for holding water vapor increases. Because more water vapor molecules are required to saturate a warmer air parcel, sinking air inhibits the formation of clouds. On the other hand as rising air cools, its capacity for holding water vapor decreases. Because less water vapor is required to saturate the colder air, rising air enhances cloud formation. Cloudy skies are thus due to rising (cooling) air and low pressure, while clear skies may be the result of sinking (warming) air and high pressure.

15. The eastern side of the Appalachian Mountains are in closer proximity to the Atlantic shore than the western side, thus it is subject to greater atmospheric moisture.

16. As an air mass is pushed upward over a mountain the rising air cools, and if the air is humid, clouds form. As the air mass moves down the other side of the mountain (the leeward slope), it warms. This descending air is dry because most of its moisture was removed in the form of clouds and precipitation on the windward (upslope) side of the mountain.

17. The uneven heating rates of land and water generate convection currents that stir the atmosphere and produce winds. This is especially evident along the seashore. During the daytime, the land warms more easily than the adjacent water and the air above the water remains cooler than the air over land. The effect of this pressure/temperature distribution is a sea breeze—a breeze that blows from water to land. At night the process reverses as the land cools off more quickly than the adjacent water, and then warmer air is over the sea. The effect is a land breeze—a breeze that blows from land to water. Build a fire on the beach and you'll notice that the smoke sweeps inward during the day and seaward at night.

18. Nimbostratus. Nimbostratus clouds are a wet-looking low cloud layer associated with light to moderate rain or snow. They are generally dark gray which makes visibility of the Sun or Moon quite difficult. Although cumulonimbus clouds are also associated with precipitation, they do not produce an overcast sky. You can generally see the top of a cumulonimbus cloud.

19. By a change in atmospheric stability. Altostratus clouds, although varying in thickness, are a layered type cloud that often covers the sky for hundreds of kilometers. Layered clouds are generally stable. If the top of an altostratus cloud cools as the bottom warms the cloud becomes unstable to the point that small convection currents develop within the cloud. The up and down motions make the cloud develop a puffy appearance—the transformation into an altocumulus cloud.

20. The fact that warm air rises and cool air sinks. As cool air sinks, the expansion of warm air beneath it is inhibited, so we usually see single cumulus cloud with a great deal of blue sky between them.

21. The formation of cumulus clouds requires warm thermal bubbles of air. Over cool water the air is cool; there is an absence of warm thermals.

22. Snowfall in Antarctica is very light. The polar cell sits over Antarctica where air tends to sink (recall that you need rising air to produce precipitation). Also the air itself doesn't contain much moisture because it is so cold. So snowfall is usually scarce in the polar regions.

23. In a warm front warm air slides upward over a wedge of cooler air near the ground. Gentle lifting of the warm moist air produces stratus and nimbostratus clouds and drizzly rain showers. In contrast, cold fronts occur as warm moist air is forced upward by advancing cold air. As the air lifts, it expands and cools to the dew-point temperature to a level of active condensation and cloud formation. This abrupt lifting produces cumulonimbus clouds which are often accompanied by heavy showers, lightning, thunder, and hail.

24. When two air masses make contact, differences in temperature, moisture, and pressure can cause one air mass to ride over the other. Such differences are usually accompanied by wind, clouds, rain, and storms.

25. The gradual rise of air means an extended period for the generation of different types of precipitation. In a warm front, less-dense warm air gradually rides up and over colder, denser air producing widespread cloudiness and precipitation way before the actual front. In many respects, a warm front is like a temperature inversion. As the front advances rain or snow develops, and as winds become brisk, the rain or snow changes to freezing rain. At the front, the air gradually warms, and the rain or snow turns to drizzle. Behind the front, the air is warm and the clouds scatter. Change occurs as the air temperature climbs.

26. When an air mass is pushed upward over a mountain range the rising air cools, and if it is humid, clouds form. As the air mass moves down the leeward slope of the mountain, it warms. This descending air is dry because most of its moisture was removed in the form of clouds and precipitation on the windward side of the mountain. Because the dry leeward sides of mountain ranges are sheltered from rain and moisture, rain shadow deserts often form.

27. They simply have more moisture.

28. A very stable air layer may incrementally be converted into an absolutely unstable layer when the lower portion of the layer is moist and the upper portion is dry. If the air layer is forced to rise, the upper portion will cool quite rapidly at the dry adiabatic rate while the lower portion cools more slowly at the moist adiabatic rate. In very little time the upper portion of the layer becomes colder than the bottom portion.

29. First of all the birth of a thunderstorm begins with humid air rising, cooling, and condensing into a single cumulus cloud. As the cloud grows upward it is fed by an updraft of rising warm air from below. Precipitation particles grow larger and heavier within the cloud until they eventually begin to fall as rain. The falling rain drags some of the cool dry air from above along with it, creating a downdraft. The downdraft strengthens as dry air is drawn into the cloud causing some of the raindrops to evaporate. Recall that evaporation is a cooling process, as such the air chills making it colder and denser than the air around it. Thus, although sinking air is generally associated with warming, in a thunderstorm a downdraft is cold.

30. First of all, tornadoes are more prevalent in the Spring when warm, humid surface air is overlain by cooler, dryer air aloft. Such conditions produce an unstable atmosphere. When strong vertical wind shear occurs and surface air is forced upward, large thunderstorms capable of producing tornadoes may form. Because thunderstorms are prevalent in the central part of the United States, so do tornadoes.

31. First of all tornadoes evolve from thunderstorms which form in regions of strong vertical wind shear. Rapidly increasing wind speed and changing wind direction with height cause the updraft within the storm to rotate. Rotation begins in the middle of the thunderstorm and then works its way downward. As air rushes into the low-pressure vortex, it expands, cools and condenses into a funnel cloud. As air beneath the funnel is drawn into the core the funnel cloud descends toward the surface. When the funnel cloud reaches the ground surface it is called a tornado.

32. Moisture from the warm ocean provides the reservoir of energy. When the moisture condenses it releases heat, which provides the energy that the hurricane releases. This is why hurricanes die out over land—they are cut off from their fundamental source of energy — warm, moist air.

33. Hurricanes are a sub-tropical weather system that occurs between 5° and 20° latitude. Hurricanes need warm water. The close proximity to the warm waters of the Gulf of Mexico and the Caribbean provide fuel for the development of hurricanes on the eastern coast of the United States. Although hurricanes do occur on the western coast, the Pacific Ocean is much cooler than the Gulf and the Caribbean. As such it does not provide the proper fuel for a hurricane.

34. A tsunami is generated from disturbances in oceanic or continental crust. The point of origin of a tsunami can be determined by study of seismic waves and when calculated it can be timed so that place of impact can be warned. High waves from both tsunamis and hurricanes are destructive.

35. Answers will vary. More data collection—more points of data, more time increments of data. Faster, more accurate computers.

28   The Solar System

Answers to Exercises

1. The radius of the Sun is nearly twice the distance between the Moon and the Earth! Sun's radius is some 7×10^8 m, and the Earth-Moon distance averages about 3.8×10^8 m.

2. The main advantage of a telescope in orbit is to be beyond the atmosphere and the distortions it imposes on images.

3. The main advantage of a telescope on the Moon is to eliminate the distortions of the atmosphere. There is no atmosphere on the Moon.

4. Gravitation at the Moon's surface is too small; escape velocity at the Moon's surface is less than the speeds that molecules of gas would have at regular Moon temperatures, so any gases on the Moon escape.

5. The fact we see one side is evidence that it rotates; if it didn't rotate, we'd need only wait till it completed a half orbit to see its opposite side.

6. No, even a perfectly spherical Moon would have one side closer to the Earth and therefore have its center of gravity closer to the Earth than the Moon's center of mass. The oblong shape, however, adds to a greater distance between the Moon's center of mass and center of gravity.

7. The positions of the Ping Pong ball held by John Suchocki and the Moon are the much the same with respect to the Sun. The photos support the claim they were made on the same day, but do not prove it. They could have been made at the same time of day on different days.

8. A waning Moon refers to Moon phases after a full Moon; a waxing Moon refers to Moon phases after a new Moon. A gibbous phase shows a more than half-full Moon, whereas a crescent phase shows a less than half-full Moon.

9. Astronomers viewing stars work when the Moonlight does not scatter from the sky and provide unwanted background, which is during the new-Moon half of the month.

10. Unlike the Earth, the Moon wears no makeup! Similar craters on the Earth's surface have long eroded or have been covered by soil.

11. A lunar eclipse is the Earth's shadow on the Moon. Everyone in view of the Moon during this time, which is everyone on the dark half of the Earth, is witness to the lunar eclipse. A solar eclipse, on the other hand, is the shadow of the Moon on only part of the Earth. Because of tapering, the shadow is relatively small. As a result, only the relatively few people in the shadow experience the solar eclipse.

12. A Sun ten times as large and ten times distant makes the Sun the same size in the sky (it subtends the same angle as the Moon), so a solar eclipse would appear much the same as present solar eclipses. Likewise for lunar eclipses. In both cases, the angle of the solar rays would be the same with respect to the Moon and Earth, producing no noticeable difference.

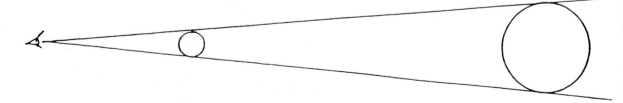

13. Extend the bite to complete a circle, and the patch of the Earth's shadow appears to be a circle with a diameter 2.5 Moon diameters. Does this mean the Earth's diameter is 2.5 Moon diameters? No, because the Earth's shadow at the distance of the Moon has tapered. How much? According to the tapering that is evident during a solar eclipse, by 1 Moon diameter. So add that to the 2.5 and we find the Earth is 3.5 times wider than the Moon.

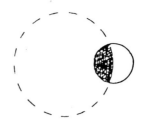

14. The Sun's output of energy is that of thermonuclear fusion. Because fusion in the Sun is triggered by gravitational pressure, we can in this sense say the prime source of solar energy is gravity. Without the strong gravity, fusion wouldn't occur.

15. The answer has to do with contrast. The TV screen appears light gray when illuminated by room lighting, but relative to the brightness of illuminated phosphors on the screen, the non-illuminated regions appear black. Similarly with the Sun, where the relatively low intensity regions appear black relative to the hotter and brighter regions.

16. The disk shape has a greater surface area than a ball shape. Just as a meatball cooks faster when flattened into a burger, and also cools faster than a meatball when removed from the stove, a ball of star material cools faster when in the flattened disk configuration. Increased area leads to increased energy transfer.

17. Mercury has too sparse an atmosphere and therefore cannot have the greenhouse effect that Venus, and to a smaller extent, Earth, have.

18. The cause of winds is unequal heating of the planet's surface, and resulting convection currents.

19. Venus is closer to the Sun than the Earth, so receives more solar energy. Whereas most of Earth's carbon dioxide is locked in limestone rock and the oceans, carbon dioxide on warmer Venus was released into the atmosphere. The resulting greenhouse effect added to surface temperature, releasing more carbon dioxide into its atmosphere. As a result of the greater sunlight on Venus, its atmosphere is now made up of about 95 percent carbon dioxide.

20. Jupiter has no ocean.

21. Jupiter's greater mass would make one's weight at its surface 300 times that of on Earth, but Jupiter's radius is about 10 times that of the Earth, so weight at the surface due to radius would be 100 times less than on Earth (inverse-square law). 300 divided by 100 is 3. So one's weight on the surface of Jupiter would be only about threefold that on Earth.

22. The criterion for floating is that the object weigh less than an equal volume of water; or the object be less dense than water. Less-dense-than-water Saturn would float in a bathtub of water located anywhere. It's weight *compared to* the weight of an equal volume of water would be less in all gravitational fields.

23. The rings of Saturn are in fact individual chunks of matter independently orbiting Saturn, each at a speed that depends on distance ($v = \sqrt{GM/r}$). The greater the distance, the less the speed, which means that outer chunks take a longer time to orbit just as Pluto takes a longer time to orbit the Sun. If the rings of Saturn were solid disks, then the outer part of the disk would travel faster than the inner parts, just as the outside part of a merry-go-round has a greater linear speed than the inside parts. This difference in speeds would be appreciable for a disk about Saturn and shearing forces would tear the disk apart. (James Clerk Maxwell pointed this out when he was 17.)

24. Mechanically, a series of concentric rings could orbit Saturn and compose its rings. Inner rings would revolve at greater speeds than outer rings, just as inner satellites revolve at greater speeds than outer satellites. Space probes, however, show that the rings are not concentric rings (which they *could* be), but are in fact numerous chunks of matter in independent orbits.

25. A planet like Earth rotates through an axis that is slightly non-perpendicular to the orbital plane. This means that the angle that the Sun's rays make with a given part of its surface depends on the time of the planet's year. A slight tilt results in slight changes of season. Uranus, however, is enormously tilted, with its polar axis nearly in the plane of its orbit. Its seasons are very exaggerated, so that when the polar axis is aligned with the Sun, a full summer is at one pole and a full winter at the opposite pole.

26. Neptune was the name given to the first planet to be discovered beyond Uranus, and Pluto the second. Likewise, Neptunium was the name given to the first element discovered beyond uranium, and plutonium the second.

27. The orbit of Pluto is the most eccentric in the solar system. At times it is closer to the Sun than Neptune, in which case we could say Pluto was the eighth most distant planet from the Sun. (Pluto is presently closer to the Sun than Neptune, and after March 4, 1999, Pluto will again be farther away from the Sun.)

28. When meteorites land on common land masses, only careful investigation distinguishes them from ordinary rock. When meteorites land on Antarctica, however, many land on ice masses. Most soon are buried, but when ice melts and they are exposed to the surface they are easily seen.

29. Quite simply, the sky is BIG. A far-away comet occupies a pin point in the sky, and there are oodles of pinpoints!

30. On each pass around the Sun, material and the energy that is associated with it is swept away. This material and energy comprise the comet tails. Since the comet is composed of a finite amount of material, sooner or later it is dissipated entirely.

Chapter 28 Problem Solutions

1.

$$\frac{mv^2}{R} = \frac{G\,mM}{R^2}$$

Multiply both sides by $\frac{R}{m}$, and substitute $\frac{2\pi R}{T}$ for v;

$$\left(\frac{2\pi R}{T}\right)^2 = \frac{GM}{R}$$

$$\frac{4\pi^2 R^2}{T^2} = \frac{G\,M}{R}$$

Rearrange and get $M = \frac{4\pi^2 R^3}{GT^2} = \frac{4\pi^2}{G}\,\frac{R^3}{T^2}$

2. The ratio R^3/T^2 for a satellite about the Earth can be the Moon's (orbital radius)^3/(period of Moon)^2, or (orbit radius of the space shuttle in close orbit)^3/(90 min)^2. Both ratios will be the same, in accord with Kepler's third law (check it out!). Let's do the space shuttle, where its orbital radius is 6.6×10^6 m, only slightly greater than the Earth's radius. To be consistent with the magnitude of $G = 6.67 \times 10^{-11}$, we use SI units, meters and seconds. Then

$$M = \frac{4\pi^2}{G}\,\frac{R^3}{T^2} = \frac{4\pi^2}{6.67 \times 10^{-11}}\,\frac{[6.6 \times 10^6]^3}{[90\ min \times 60\ s/m]^2} = 5.9 \times 10^{24}\ kg.$$

3. From $\frac{4\pi^2 R^2}{T^2} = \frac{G\,M}{R}$ (Problem 1)

simple rearrangement gives

$$\frac{4\pi^2}{GM} = \frac{T^2}{R^3}$$

which is Kepler's 3rd law. Note that

$\frac{T^2}{R^3}$, or its inverse, $\frac{R^3}{T^2}$, is a constant for a particular planet of mass M.

29   The Stars

Answers to the Exercises

1. Stars aren't seen in daytime because their relatively dim light is overwhelmed by skylight.

2. The background of a solar eclipse is the nighttime sky normally viewed 6 months earlier or later.

3. He did not know that the constellations are not always overhead in the sky, but vary with the Earth's motion around the Sun.

4. Both near and faraway stars appear as if on the inner surface of one great sphere, with us at the center. Two stars that appear very close together are on the same line of sight, but may actually be an enormous distance apart, and would not appear close together at all when viewed from the side. Astronomers distinguish between double stars and binary stars. Double stars are on the same line of sight, yet may actually be far apart. Binaries are stars that are both on the same line of sight and are in close interaction.

5. Twelve hours. In 24 hours it makes a complete cycle.

6. The nuclei of atoms that compose our bodies were once parts of stars. All nuclei beyond iron in atomic number, were in fact manufactured in supernovae.

7. The gold in any ring was made in the death throes of stars during supernovae explosions.

8. Since all the heavy elements are manufactured in supernovae, the newer the star, the greater percentage of heavy elements available for its construction. Very old stars were made when heavy elements were less abundant.

9. Too low a mass, and gravitational pressure in the inner core is insufficient to provoke thermonuclear fusion. No fusion, no star.

10. Thermonuclear fusion reactions produce an outward pressure that counteracts the inward pressure that would lead to collapse due to gravity.

11. Thermonuclear fusion powers a star. Only non-fusion energy exists within a protostar.

12. Thermonuclear fusion is initiated by gravitational pressure, wherein hydrogen nuclei are squashed together. Energetic gravitational pressure in the outer layers is insufficient to initiate fusion.

13. Gravitational pressure in massive stars is greater, so fusion rates are correspondingly greater. Like a high roller who soon goes broke, a fast-burning star soon dies.

14. Bigger stars live faster, and collapse more energetically when they burn out.

15. There is insufficient gravitational pressure within the Sun to initiate carbon fusion, which requires greater squashing than hydrogen to fuse.

16. The fewer heavier elements in stars indicates they were formed before the Sun formed, and are older than the Sun — the further back in time, the less the number of heavy elements for star formation.

17. Blue stars have higher temperatures — on the order of twice the temperatures of red stars (because blue light has almost twice the frequency of red light).

18. Large balls are harder to get spinning than small balls — large balls have more *rotational inertia*. Likewise a person with arms extended has more rotational inertia than when arms are pulled in. By the conservation of momentum, a decrease in rotational inertia means a

corresponding increase in rotational speed (like the way a twirling ice skater spins faster when the arms are pulled in). This is what happens when a spinning object shrinks. Its rotational inertia (tendency to remain rotating) decreases, and rotational speed increases. Neutron stars have shrunken enormously, and consequently spin at enormous rates.

19. Just as a spinner skater slows down when arms are extended, a spinning star in formation similarly slows down when material that forms planets is extended. Thus, a slow-spinning star has more likely extended material as planets than a fast-spinning star.

20. Black ink reflect *some* light. A black hole reflects none.

21. The gravitational force you'd experience would not only be enormous, but the difference in force between your near part to the hole and your far part from the hole would also be enormous and tear you apart before you'd make impact.

22. The answer is conveyed in Figure 29.11. If the distance between anything near or at the surface of a collapsed star and the center of the star is less than before collapse, then in accord with Newton's gravitational law, smaller distance means greater force. At distances beyond the original radius of the star before collapse, gravitation is no more intense than before collapse.

23. It decreases with increased mass.

24. During the months before and after July, the dark side of the Earth faces the central part of the milky way.

25. Yes, the central bulge of the Andromeda Galaxy, which covers an area about five times as large as the full Moon, can be seen with the naked eye on a very clear and moonless night. The Magellanic clouds are two galaxies visible to the naked eye in the southern hemisphere.

26. Collisions affect the shapes of galaxies not by the collisions of stars, which are so far apart to make such collisions improbable, but by the collisions of the interstellar gases within the galaxies. Spiral arms are one of the resulting configurations; stars hurled into interstellar space is another; and merger of galaxies into larger ones is another.

27. Galaxies merge. Large galaxies that devour small galaxies in a merger are said to be cannibalistic.

28. Matter was moving fastest immediately after the Big Bang, and has been slowing since. Speed can be determined by a red shift in light emitted by matter. Quasars have extreme redshifts, which indicate they have large recessional velocities, and therefore are luminous objects closer in time to the big bang than other luminous objects.

29. Although there is very likely at least one star in the line of sight of any direction, whether or not that star is seen as luminous is another story. It may be receding fast enough that its light is redshifted below the visual part of the spectrum; it may be burned out and emitting no light; it may be in a protostage and not yet emitting light. If all stars continually and perpetually emitted light, unaffected in frequency by motion, then the night sky would be ablaze with light. This is called Olber's paradox.

30. The blue shift indicates the Andromeda Galaxy is approaching Earth and the solar system.

30 Relativity and the Universe

Answers to the Exercises

1. Radiation at the time of the Big Bang has been bouncing to and fro in the expanding universe, stretching out just as sound waves bouncing from a receding wall stretch out. The amount of stretch conforms to the Big Bang event some 15 billion years ago.

2. Conventional thinking on this matter is that there was no space (or time) before the Big Bang. Rather than thinking of the Big Bang as happening in a space already there, we think of it as the creation and extension of space itself (and time also).

3. Approaching galaxies will show a blue shift in their spectra.

4. The same is true of the universe, or any system undergoing expansion. Energy is dilute, and temperature less.

5. The *average* speed of light in a transparent medium is less than c, but in the model of light discussed in Chapter 25, the photons that make up the beam travel at c in the void that lies between the atoms of the material. Hence the speed of individual photons is always c. In any event, Einstein's postulate is that the speed of light in *free* space is invariant.

6. The velocity relative to us is 87 % the speed of light.

7. Yes, time is dilated from either frame of reference. We each see "the other guy's" clock running slow. We would only see a clock running fast via the Doppler effect when a clock approaches us. Only then would one see our clock running fast also.

8. When you move through space you are also moving in time — at a rate that depends on your rate of movement through space.

9. From $v = d/t$, $t = d/v$. So, (a), $t = 300{,}000$ km$/300{,}000$ km/s $= 1$ s. (b) One thousand times less distance is 1000 times less time; 0.001 s. (c) Yes, as Figure 30.5 suggests.

10. There is an upper limit on speed, but no upper limit on the Lorenz factor, and accordingly no upper limit on either the momentum or kinetic energy of a particle. Since momentum is given by $p = = \dfrac{m\,v}{\sqrt{[1 - (v^2/c^2)]}} =$, p can grow without limit, even though m is constant and v is limited. Similarly, kinetic energy can grow without limit. As p gets larger, so does KE.

11. When we say that light travels a certain distance in 20,000 years we are talking about distance in our frame of reference. From the frame of reference of a traveling astronaut, this distance may well be far shorter, perhaps even short enough that she could cover it in 20 years of her time (traveling, to be sure, at a speed close to the speed of light). Someday, astronauts may travel to destinations many light years away in a matter of months in their frame of reference.

12. If a person travels at relativistic speeds — that is, very close to the speed of light — distances as far as those that light takes thousands of years to travel (in our frame of reference) could be traversed well within an average lifetime. This is because distance depends on the frame of reference in which it is measured. Distances long in one frame may be quite short in another.

13. A twin who makes a long trip at relativistic speeds returns younger than his stay-at-home twin sister, but both of them are older than when they separated. If they could watch each other during the trip, there would be no time where either would see a reversal of aging, only a slowing or speeding of aging. A reversal would result only for speeds greater than the speed of light.

14. Yes, as strange as it sounds, it is possible for a son or daughter to be biologically older than his or her parents. Suppose, for example, that a woman gives birth to a baby and then departs in a high-speed rocket ship. She could theoretically return from a relativistic trip just a few years older than when she left to find her "baby" 80 or so years old.

15. If you were in a high-speed (or no speed!) rocket ship, you would note no changes in your pulse or in your volume. This is because the velocity between the observer, that is, yourself, and the observed is zero. No relativistic effect occurs for the observer and the observed when both are in the same reference frame.

16. In contrast to the previous exercise, if you were monitoring a person who is moving away from you at high speed, you would note a decrease in his pulse and a decrease in his volume. In this case, there is very definitely a velocity of the observed with respect to the observer.

17. Saying she comes back on "the previous night" is inconsistent with relativity theory. A rule for all time effects is that you can extend travel into the future, but not into the past.

18. The stick must be oriented in a direction perpendicular to its motion, unlike that of a properly-thrown spear. This is because it is traveling at relativistic speed (actually $0.87c$) as evidenced by its increase in momentum. The fact that its length is unaltered means that its long direction is not in the direction of motion. The thickness of the stick, not the length of the stick, will appear shrunken to half size.

19. The stick will appear to be one-half meter long when it moves with its length along the direction of motion. Why one half its length? Because for it to have a momentum equal to $2mv$, its speed must be $0.87c$.

20. For the moving electron, length contraction reduces the apparent length of the 2-mile long tube. Because its speed is nearly the speed of light, the contraction is great.

21. At $0.995c$ the muon has ten times as much time, or twenty-millionths of a second, to live. From the stationary earth frame of reference, the muon's "clock" is running ten times slower than earth clocks, allowing sufficient time to make the trip. (Interestingly enough, from the muon's frame of reference, the distance to earth is contracted by ten times, so it has sufficient time to get there.)

22. Just as time is required for knowledge of distant events to reach our eyes, a lesser yet finite time is required for information on nearby things to reach our eyes. So the answer is yes, there is always a finite interval between an event and our perception of that event. (There is even a time interval between touching your finger to a hot stove and feeling the pain!)

23. Matter is made of particles, which have mass. $E = mc^2$ means that energy and mass are two sides of the same coin, mass-energy. The c^2 is the proportionality constant that links the units of energy and mass. In a practical sense, energy and mass are one and the same. In this sense we can say that matter is frozen energy.

24. For the linear acceleration of a space ship, a net force must be provided, which requires the use of fuel. But if the ship is set into rotation, it will spin of its own rotational inertia like a top, once it is set spinning. An astronaut in the ship experiences a centrifugal force that provides a simulated "gravity." No fuel is consumed to sustain this effect because the centrifugal (or centripetal) force is perpendicular to rotational motion and does no work on the astronaut.

25. Your effort in both cases would be the same.

26. Ole Jules called his shot wrong on this one. In a space ship that drifts through space, whether under the influence of moon, earth, or whatever gravitational field, the ship and its occupants are in a state of free fall — hence there is no sensation of up or down. Occupants of a spaceship would feel weight, or sense an up or down, only if the ship were made to accelerate — say, against their feet. Then they could stand and sense that down is toward their feet, and up away from their feet.

27. The separation distance of two people walking north from the earth's equator decreases, and if they continue to the north pole their separation distance will be zero. At the north pole, a step in any direction is a step south!

28. We don't notice the bending of light by gravity in our everyday environment because the gravity we experience is too weak for a noticeable effect. If there were stellar black holes in our vicinity, the bending of light near them would be quite noticeable.

29. We say that a tightened chalk line forms a straight line. It doesn't. We say the surface of a still lake is flat and that a line laid across it is straight. It isn't. But these approximate the straight lines in our practical world. A much better approximation, however, is a beam of light. For distances used by surveyors, a beam of light is the best approximation of a straight line known. Yet we know that a laser beam is ever-so-slightly deflected by gravity. In actual practice, however, we say that a laser beam of light *defines* a straight line.

30. The change in energy for light is not evidenced by a change in speed, but by a change in frequency. If the energy of light is lowered, as in traveling against a strong gravitational field, its frequency is lowered, and the light is said to be gravitationally red shifted. If the energy of the light is increased, as when falling in a gravitational field, for example, then the frequency is increased and the light is blue shifted.

31. Going up in a building is going in a direction opposite to the direction of the gravitational force, and this speeds up time. The person concerned about living a tiny bit longer should live on the ground floor. Strictly speaking, people who live in penthouses live faster lives!

32. Mercury follows an elliptical path in its orbit about the sun, with its perihelion in a stronger part of the sun's gravitational field than its aphelion. If Mercury followed a circular orbit, then there would be no variation of the sun's gravitational field in its orbit.

Chapter 30 Problem Solutions

1. The Lorentz factor $= \dfrac{1}{\sqrt{[1 - (v^2/c^2)]}} = \dfrac{1}{\sqrt{[1 - (0.99)^2]}}$

$= \dfrac{1}{\sqrt{[1 - 0.98]}} = \dfrac{1}{\sqrt{0.02}} = 7.1.$

Multiplying 5 min by 7.1 gives 35 min. According to your watch, the nap lasts **35 minutes**.

2. For small values of v_1 and v_2, the term $v_1 v_2/c^2$ approaches 0, which makes adding these velocities the same as classically. For example we know that $1 + 2 = 3$. Likewise in the relativistic case, where $v_1 = 1$ and $v_2 = 2$. Then we see

$$V = \frac{v_1 + v_2}{1 + \dfrac{v_1 v_2}{c^2}} = \frac{1+2}{1 + \dfrac{2}{c^2}} = \frac{1+2}{1+0} = 3.$$

3. We must use the formula

$$V = \frac{v_1 + v_2}{1 + \dfrac{v_1 v_2}{c^2}} = \frac{0.80c + 0.50c}{1 + \dfrac{0.80c \times 0.50c}{c^2}} = \frac{1.30c}{1.40} = 0.93c.$$

The drone moves at **93%** of the speed of light relative to the earth.

4. A beam of light traveling horizontally for one second in a uniform gravitational field of strength 1 *g* will fall a vertical distance of 4.9 meters, just as a baseball would. This is providing it remains in a 1-*g* field for one second, for it would travel 300,000 kilometers during this second also, nearly 25 Earth diameters away, and well away from the 1-*g* field strength at the Earth's surface (unless it were confined to the 1-*g* region via reflecting mirrors). If light were to travel in a 1-*g* region for two seconds, then like a baseball, it should fall $1/2\ gt^2 = 19.6$ meters in two seconds.

Laboratory Suggestions, with Answers to Lab Manual Questions

Prologue and Part I Activities and Experiments

Introduction

1 [Activity] Tuning the Senses

This activity may be assigned as an "outside experience" (or homework), to be followed up later during classroom discussion.

For the second half of this activity, watching the burning candle, for a large class of 28 students or so you will probably want to use four groups of seven, (or seven groups of four), with one candle per group, as it might be impractical and unnecessary to burn 28 candles, or more, per class. Again, you may choose to assign this as an "outside experience", and avoid clean-up and potential fire problems.

This activity may easily be converted into an experiment by having a student in each group measure and record the candle's length and diameter before and after burning for a recorded time. The hypothesis to be tested could be, "The change in length per minute while burning is not directly proportional to diameter."

2 [Activity] Making Cents

The credit for this activity goes to Brad Huff at Edison Computech in Fresno, CA, who in 1984 discovered there was nearly an equal distribution of pre/post 1982 pennies in circulation. His students discovered the difference in mass as part of an exercise on how to use mass balances. So point out to your students the role of a good scientific attitude in making "accidental" discoveries — this one could have been overlooked as "human error."

The composition of the alloy in pennies was changed in 1982. Pennies since 1982 are 2.500 g; from 1944—1982 pennies were 3.110 g; rare 1943 pennies were 2.700 g; and before 1942, pennies were 3.110 g. Such differences ordinarily escape our notice.

A student can enter data on a data table written on the chalkboard. Students then plot this data as a graph. Alternatively, students can plug their data into an analysis program on a personal computer. If your students have never made a histogram, show them how to set up the values on the horizontal axis for the mass of the coins, using perhaps mass increments of 0.1 gram.

How much copper did the U.S. government save by switching to zinc filled pennies? About 2.6 grams per penny: post 1982: 0.444 g Cu and 2.13 g Zn.

Density of Copper = 8.920 g/cm^3 Density of Zinc = 7.140 g/cm^3

Students see an unexpected result. Ask for more hypotheses. Is it from a change in size or from a change in composition? They can measure size based upon the displacement of water. 100 pennies displace how much water? Time permitting, they can find the density of pennies.

Answers to the Questions
1. Pennies dated before and after 1982 should show a double-humped histogram should result — indicating a change in a penny's material in 1982.
2. Worn cons have less mass than mint ones. Dirty oxidized coins may have more mass.
3. Nails, nuts, soft drink cans, blades of grass, heights of students, etc.

3 [Activity]   Reaction Time

This activity can easily be converted into an experiment by dividing the class into three groups, and recording measurements. A hypothesis could be that there is no significant difference in reaction time for the sense of sight, hearing or touching. Group "A" would measure reaction times for several students using a sight signal — they see the holder drop the bill. In Group "B" they close their eyes, and hear the holder say "Drop!" at the instant of release. In Group "C" they close their eyes, and receive a simultaneous tap on the shoulder from the dropper's other hand.

A fourth group could explore the hypothesis that reaction times would differ between using a wooden 12 inch rule and a wooden meter stick — the meter stick is heavier, and would fall (a) faster? Or (b) slower? Or the (c) same? What if the rule were made of steel?

If you happen to have a sub-group of psychology or political science majors, suggest a hypothesis that persons who believe (a), (b), or (c) will report data that supports their expectations. You may have a future doctor who is ready to understand "double blind experiment"!

Answers to the Questions
1. Evidence ought to be the comparison between sound, sight, and touch on reaction time.
2. For one thing, the individual differences among people.
3. Reaction time can affect measurements that change with time. When the changes are small compared to reaction time, then the effects may be negligible. When they're not, for example in timing a falling object, then choosing the longest time interval lessens the error due to reaction time. Just like measuring the thickness of a page is more accurate when more pages are measured at one time.
4. Reaction time plays an important role in driving. For a reaction time of 0.7 second, a car going 100 km/h (28 m/s) travels nearly 20 m (about 60 feet) in 0.7 s, which is considerable — and has too many times been fatal.
5. In many sports, a single second is a long time. Baseball is an obvious one, where top players must have extraordinary reaction times. Likewise for soccer, football, and even boxing. The winners of races of all kinds usually are discerned in fractions of a second.

4 [Experiment] Graphing with Sonar

Sonic ranging technology is revolutionizing the teaching pedagogy for graph interpretation. The computational power of the computer combined with its ability to make rapid measurements of distance and time enable your students to see the graph on the monitor in real time (where was this when we first learned about graphs!). Sonic ranging kits are available from a variety of sources. Try Pasco Scientific, 10101 Foothill Blvd, Roseville, CA 95678 (800) 772-8700, or Vernier Software, 2920 S.W. 89th St, Portland, OR 97255, (503) 297-5317 [Fax 503 297-1760].

Answers to the Questions
1. Both distance vs time graphs should be straight lines that rise upward to the right. Walking faster away from the detector gives a graph with a steeper slope.
2. Both distance vs time graphs should be straight lines that slope downward to the right. Walking faster toward the detector gives a graph with a steeper downward (negative) slope.
3. The graph should have a positive slope for receding, and then turn around with a negative slope for approaching.
4. Velocity vs time graphs should be positive slopes. Increased speed should produce a steeper slope.
5. Velocity vs time graphs should have a negative slope. Increased speed produces a steeper negative slope.
6. Velocity vs time graphs should have a positive slope as the person recedes and a positive steep slope as the person approaches the sonic ranger.
7. Predictions will vary.
8.

 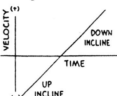

9. Yes, indicating that the acceleration is constant. Important to see that the slope of a velocity vs time graph depicts acceleration.
10. The distance vs time graph will look like a sine curve; the velocity vs time will be 90° out of phase, or a cosine curve.

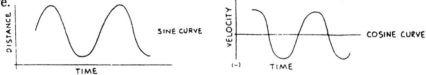

11. Maximum speed occurs at the bottom of a pendulum's swing — at the minimum vertical displacement. Speed is least at the top of its swing — at maximum vertical displacement.

12.

13. Acceleration is that of nearly free fall — a nearly constant *g*.
14. The form of the graphs are very similar; the major difference is the smaller acceleration when the ramp was used. (To investigate the acceleration of free fall, Galileo used inclined planes to better see the relationships between velocity and time — a sort of slow motion version of measuring *g*.)

5 [Activity] Dropping and Dragging - I

This activity is a qualitative version of the follow-up experiment, *Dropping and Dragging II*. Students can work in groups of three or four. With small tables, a group can work at each end, and with large tables, a group can work at each corner. Understanding the role of friction is the least of the objectives of this activity, so the less the friction between the book (or other object you decide to use) the better.

Answers to the Questions
1. Greatest acceleration is the two book drop and the one book drag. Mid acceleration is the single book drop and single book drag, and least acceleration is the one book drop and the two book drag.
2. Two book have both twice the force (gravity) and twice the mass, so accelerate is *g* (Figure 2.13 in the text).
3. Acceleration is less than g because the mass of the system is now twice but the gravity force of one dropping book is the same. Without friction, the acceleration would be one half g. In terms of Newton's second law, ideally,

273

$$a = \frac{F_{net}}{m_{total}} = \frac{mg}{2m} = g/2.$$

4. Acceleration would increase when the force that produces the acceleration increases. When three books are dropped, and drag a single book, acceleration is predictably greater. Ideally,

$$a = \frac{F_{net}}{m_{total}} = \frac{3mg}{4m} = 3/4\,g.$$

5. The upper limit is g! Consider a dropping truck dragging a feather — the feather has negligible influence on the falling truck.
6. Friction was likely very significant, and perhaps greatly masked the idealized results above. Friction of sliding can be reduced by low-friction wheels beneath the dragged books or other objects, or even by using an air track. Friction of the twine at the table's edge can be reduced by pulleys. Onward to these remedies in Dropping and Dragging II.

6 [Experiment] Dropping and Dragging - II

The main difference between D&D-I and D&D-II is the reduction of friction and use of a pulley.

Answers to the Questions
1. Two carts have both twice the force (gravity) and twice the mass, so accelerate is g (Figure 2.13 in the text).
2. With negligible friction, the acceleration would be one half g. In terms of Newton's second law, ideally,

$$a = \frac{F_{net}}{m_{total}} = \frac{mg}{2m} = g/2.$$

3. Acceleration should approach the ideal value of one-third g. That is

$$a = \frac{F_{net}}{m_{total}} = \frac{mg}{3m} = g/3.$$

4. Acceleration should approach the ideal value of two-third g. That is

$$a = \frac{F_{net}}{m_{total}} = \frac{2mg}{3m} = 2g/3.$$

5. This goes back to the case of Question 1. If pulley friction plays a role, the heavier loads here may bring experimental results closer to the ideal one half g.

$$a = \frac{F_{net}}{m_{total}} = \frac{2mg}{4m} = g/2.$$

6. Friction is minimal if this experiment is done on an air track.

7 [Activity] By Impulse

This activity comes from Earl Feltyberger, who in turn got it from rock climber Bill Berner in 1985, who taught in a Catholic high school in the Philadelphia suburbs. Bill used this idea to explain the value of stretch in safety ropes used to stop a climber in the event of a fall. It makes a nice lecture demo — nice enough to be shared with students as an activity.

Answers to the Questions
1. A sudden halt will probably either break the cord, or break the body!
2. Ft = Δmv is central. The impulse that brings the dropped mass to a halt equals the change in momentum the mass undergoes. The breaking force of the string is greatly affected by the "give" of the stick, which lengthens time and reduces the force needed to stop the mass.

3. Less give means less time to stop; less time to stop means more stopping force — more than the string could provide.
4. Ordinarily the strength of a string has to do with its thickness, not its length. The length of the sting plays an important role in that it allows the falling object to fall farther and gain more momentum. So a greater stopping force is needed when the string is long. In short, increasing string length increases Δv, which increases F.
5. The mass of the falling object is directly proportional to the momentum of the falling object; twice the mass at a given speed means twice the momentum, which in turn means twice the needed stopping force. So the greater the mass, the stronger the string needs to be. Just as sheet music guides the musician's tune, Ft = Δmv guides our thinking in answering this and the previous questions.
6. Bending increases the time, so decreases the force that might break the fishing string.

8 [Experiment] Energy Ramp

Students will enjoy this activity. For one thing, they may notice that all balls gain the same speed in rolling down equal-angle inclines. They may not have an explanation for this, and since the textbook does not treat rotational motion, they won't get help there. The explanation for this is not unlike that of the equal accelerations of free fall for objects of different masses — which is that the ratio of weight to mass is the same for all objects — g. Similarly, the ratio of torque to rotational inertia is the same for all balls on the same incline. It is not necessary to get into this with your class, however, for it may obscure the central idea here. And that idea is the value of looking only at the beginning and end points in a problem that involves energy (almost like considering only the limits when doing integral calculus). Question 4 addresses this.

Here they should see that the PE of the raised ball is directly proportional to the work that the rug does in stopping it. In your discussion, your students may be bothered about the idea of the rug doing work on the rolling ball. Ask if the rug exerts a force on the ball. And to answer this, ask if the ball exerts a force on the rug? Then think of Newton's third law, where it was learned that when one object exerts a force on a second object, the second object exerts an equal and opposite force on the first. So we see the rug does exert a force on the ball — which is why the ball slows to a stop!

In discussing this activity, you can emphasize that speed can be measured either as ΔL/Δt, or as Δt/ΔL. A marathon is usually reported as minutes per mile, as "Joe started with a five minute mile, slowed to 10 on the hill, and settled down to a smooth six". You may or may not be surprised to see how many of your students cannot translate these speed into miles per hour in less than 10 seconds.

After Step 3, you may wish to ask this follow-up question: "Would it be incorrect to reverse the axes and plot height vertically on Y, and distance horizontally on X? Why, or why not? Isn't height on Y, and distance on X, more natural?

Point out that in Summary Question 4, we have freedom to choose any level for zero potential energy, table top, or floor, or ceiling, and treat it as a relative signed quantity. Ask, "Where is the absolute level where PE cannot be negative?" [Ans.: Earth's center.] Follow-up question: "What about relative and absolute KE?", and "Does a decrease of 10 J, PE equal an increase of 10 J KE? Why or why not?" [Ans: Yes, because 10 = 10; No, because 10 is 20 more than -10."] We'll have more on "relative" or "absolute" when we get to temperature.

Answers to the Questions
1. The data (or graphs) should indicate direct proportions (straight -line graphs).
2. Yes, because height and ramp length are directly proportional to each other.
3. The speed of the ball was the same for different ramps at the same starting height. ($v = \sqrt{2gh}$). At the same height, the same potential energy changes to kinetic energy.
4. One of the beauties of conserved quantities like energy, is that the beginning amount and the end amount will be the same, regardless of the details involved in the middle. Now the details may be interesting, and have a lot of good physics. But if its the final state we're interested in, we can bypass the details and go straight to it. In this activity, the ball begins with PE, gains KE of translation and KE of rotation (not covered in the text), then spends this gain across the friction enhanced rug. Mechanical energy is completely converted to thermal

energy of the rug (and ball). That is to say, the initial PE is all dissipated along the rug (if we neglect the friction of the ramp — which is reasonable, for ramp friction simply enabled rolling — there was no "dragging" across the ramp and the generation of thermal energy on the ramp). In equation form, we can describe the energy changes of the ball as

$$PE_{\text{top of ramp}} = KE_{\text{bottom of ramp}} = Work_{\text{across rug}}.$$
Note if we are not asked for KE details, then we can simply say
$$PE_{\text{top of ramp}} = Work_{\text{across rug}}.$$

9 [Experiment] Bullseye

This lab provides an interesting challenge to your students. Don't allow "cheating," where trial shots are made before calculations! Trial and error is important, but there are many situations where it is not feasible. Let this experiment be one where it is not allowed!

An important reason for the vagueness of the projecting device in this experiment is the variety of devices that different schools use. Some of you use the ballistic pendulum spring guns, with pendulums raised out of the way; others us similar spring guns without the pendulum to avoid; others use ramps with photo timers at the bottom to record initial speeds, and so on. Pasco Scientific has a new projection gun that works nicely. Whatever your launching device, as long as the launch is horizontal, the lab write-up begins there.

You might point out the similarity of this experiment to Figure 4.25 and the accompanying check question on page 91 in the text.

Answers to the Questions
1. The height of the can makes a very big difference — like the success or nonsuccess of the shot. This is particularly so if the horizontal speed is relatively large and the can is far from the table. The vertical height should be measured from the launching point to the top of the can. Otherwise the ball will hit the side of the can. Furthermore, the can should be moved slightly (one or two centimeters) toward the table so the horizontal distance calculated reaches the can's center (not its near edge).

The equation for the range is $R = v_x, t$, where v_x is horizontal velocity and time t can be calculated from the vertical distance $y = 1/2\ gt^2$. $\quad t = \sqrt{\dfrac{2y}{g}}$, so $R = v_x\sqrt{\dfrac{2y}{g}}$

Summing Up Answers
1. Direct hits are common.
2. Misses can be caused by air friction, misalignment of the launcher, error in measuring vertical distance (and taking the can into account), or using an incorrect launching speed of the ball.
3. Undershooting suggests air drag, or placing the near end of the can at the predicted horizontal distance instead of putting the center of the can there. Also, the launching speed may have been less than used for calculation.

Alternate Summing Up Answers
1. $R = v_x t$; the greater the range, the greater the firing speed — in direct proportion.
2. The 5-m height is quite convenient for it tells you the ball is airborne for 1 second (from $t = \sqrt{2y/g}$). Since it travels horizontally a distance of 18 m, its horizontal launching speed is simply 18 m/s.
3. The complications of an angle in launch is that the time of flight requires more analysis, and the horizontal component of the ball's velocity must be used in determining range. This usually involves some trigonometry.

$R = v_x t$, where $v_x = v\ \text{cosine}\ \theta$, where θ is the angle of launch above the horizontal.

Then time t is found from the more complicated equation for vertical distance;

$y = v (\sin \theta) t - 1/2 \, gt^2$

If the projectile lands at the same level it is fired, the total displacement $y = 0$. This means $1/2 \, gt^2 = v (\sin \theta)t$, or $t = 2 \, v \sin \theta/g$. Then the range is

$R = v \cos \theta \, [2 \, v \sin \theta/g]$.

This can be further simplified by the trig identity that $\sin 2\theta = 2 \sin \theta \cos \theta$. Then the range is

$R = v^2 \sin 2\theta/g$.

This analysis is usually heavy duty for average physical science students. Likely not for the small percentage who are always on top of things, but for the average ones. Use care in deciding how much of your presentation will go into this analysis.

10 [Activity] Sink or Swim

In Step 3, we assume your egg is fresh. With a little planning, you can hide an egg in the back of a cupboard so that it is stale for this experiment. The next-time question is, "Can we use this procedure to separate fresh and stale eggs? Which will float? Why?". We could hard boil a few, and ask the same questions.

Although an egg is denser than tap water, it is less dense than salt water, as evidenced by its floating when salt is added to water.

Diet drinks are appreciably less dense then non-diet soft drinks, as can be evidenced by their floating. Whereas a can of Coke sinks in water, a can of Diet Coke floats. Why? Sugared water is appreciably denser than regular water.

Most people are slightly less dense than water, so most people can float in water. Muscular types, however, are often more dense than water and cannot float. Females usually have a layer of body fat beneath the skin that makes them less dense than water. Very few females are denser than water. For salt water, the difference between floating and sinking is crucial for people who are very close to the density of water. Everybody can float in the Dead Sea, with its high salt content.

Interestingly enough, the reason one can float more easily in salt water is because the volume of water that must be displaced to equal one's weight is less. Buoyant force is the same on a floating body regardless of the density of the liquid.

11 [Activity] Eureka!

One of the goals of Conceptual Physical Science is to help students distinguish between closely related ideas — to nurture critical thinking. The difference between volume and weight is highlighted in this activity. Also highlighted is the concept of displacement, and how it relates to the volume (not the weight) of the submerged object. A distinction between an immersed object and a submerged object can also be made. [You immerse part of your body in the bathtub; you submerge your whole body in a swimming pool when beneath the surface.]

12 [Experiment] Boat Float

Activity 10, Activity 11 and Experiment 12 are all designed to develop a gut feel for Archimedes' Principle. You may want to combine the various elements by doing part of any one, switching to part of another, and then returning, in any pattern as grasp of the concept becomes apparent.

The questions in this experiment will tax your best students, for clear distinctions of concepts developed in the preceding activities are brought to bear. Critical thinking is central to this experiment.

Much of this material is suitable for off campus supplementation, and students should be encouraged create situations, reporting back to the class. Students often enjoy sharing experiences, and today swimming pools are often available. Interesting things can be done in a bathtub!

Answers to the Questions
1. BF equals the weight of water displaced.
2. BF (also) equals the weight of a floating body.
3, 4, and 5. Same.
6. Mass of clay is greater than mass of water displaced.
7. BF on clay less than weight; which is why it sinks.
8. When floating clay displaces more water.
9, and 10. Same.
11. Same, as evidenced by the same amount of water displaced.
12. Yes, pressure is greater with depth (not buoyant force, unless volume of object is reduced by the greater pressure).
13. Answers differ because they address different (but similar) concepts.
14. Water level goes down as boat rises. Low floating boats carry more cargo than high floating boats.
15. Water level goes down. Why? Because when floating, the cargo displaces its weight of water. When submerged it displaces only its volume of water. Since the cargo is denser than water (as evidenced by its sinking) it displaces less water submerged than floating. [Exaggeration helps: consider an enormously dense pea. It's heavy, and when placed in pie pan that floats in your kitchen sink, it displaces considerable water as the pan is pushed deeper. Now consider the amount of water the pea displaces when tossed overboard — only its size, which is very little. So the pie pan raises a lot, and the water level in the sink goes down.]
16. Same as in 15.
17. Aha! The situation is now different, because either way, the cargo floats. So the water level in the canal lock doesn't change.
18. Sea level rises (imperceptibly).
19. No change, because the rowboat displaces its weight whether on board the big ship or floating independently.
20. Simulate this in a small tub of water!

13 [Experiment] Tire Pressure and 18 Wheelers

The primary purpose of this experiment is to distinguish between force and pressure. The secondary purpose is understanding the application of this concept to tire pressure as a measure of a car's weight. It can be time consuming, so you may wish to schedule two lab periods for this one.

Answers to the Questions
1. Whereas the weight stated in the owners manual may list 4 significant figures, the uncertainties in this experiment limit it to about 2 significant figures. Students will usually be within 20% of the published value.
2. Contact area goes down proportionally. In any event, for even distribution, the pressure in the tire multiplied by the area of tire contact approximates one quarter the car's weight. We say approximates because the tire walls contribute to support (much more than in previous years where tire walls were weaker).
3. Total pressure is gauge pressure plus atmospheric pressure.
4. We didn't add atmospheric pressure to our reading because atmospheric pressure does not contribute to supporting the weight of the car. When you have a flat tire, there is still 14.7 lb/in^2 of pressure *inside* the tire (as well as *outside* the tire). The result is no net force by the atmosphere.
5. The pressure in the tires (assumed the same in each tire) multiplied by the total area of tire contact equals the loaded truck's weight. For large weights, you need either great tire pressures, or more tires to provide more area. Too much tire pressure risks blowouts, so additional tires are employed. Hence the 18 wheels. Great!

278

Part 2: Lab Activities and Experiments

Heat

14 [Experiment] Temperature Mix

The distinction between temperature and thermal energy (or quantity of heat Q) is reinforced in this experiment. This experiment is fairly foolproof. Of course a pail of water may get tipped over, so filling no more than two-thirds full may be a good precaution. Also, hot water in the hot pail should not be hot enough to scald anyone who tries to "test the water" by putting their hand in it!

Your students will see that they can average the temperature of two equal volumes of water at different temperatures when mixed — common sense. What they'll discover is that this is not so when unequal volumes of water are mixed. In this case, the final temperature will have an average nearer the temperature of the greater amount of water — refined common sense.

Answers to the Questions
1. Perhaps inaccurate temperature readings.
2. Answers will vary.
3. The cold water changed more because there was less of it, and it absorbs heat from both cups of hot water. By energy conservation heat lost by one part of the system is heat gained at another. The temperature of the mixture is closer to that of the hot water.
4. Answers will vary.
5. The hot water changes more because there is less of it, and it gives off heat to both cups of cold water. The temperature of the mixture is closer to that of the cold water.
6. The amount of water determines final temperature, as seen in Questions 3 and 5.
7. Observations are consistent with $Q = mc\Delta T$; quantity of heat that transfers equals mass of water times its specific heat times the temperature change. We see the direct relation between the mass involved and the quantity of heat it can transfer (or absorb). The transfer is always from high temperature to low temperature; not from the body with the most thermal energy to the body with the less thermal energy.

15 [Experiment] Spiked Water

This lab goes a step beyond Temperature Mix, in that the mix involves substances with different specific heat capacities. Conservation of energy reigns, as in every case the quantity of heat given off by warmer material equals the quantity of heat absorbed by the cooler material (which may be more than the system you're monitoring — hence insulation). Equal quantities of heat do not produce equal temperature changes because of the nature of the substances involved — their specific heat capacities.

Some science types prefer "Specific Heats" or "Heat Capacities" as preferable to "Specific Heat Capacities", holding that "Specific Heat Capacities" is redundant. Let's not get a class into this kind of definition analysis unless in contributes to grasping a key concept. But don't discourage one or two students who show an interest in precise definitions. For example, it may be interesting to suggest that the word "specific" is used because we are choosing the specific substance — water as a ratio scale. Thus some scientists consider these values to have no units because they are just comparing substances to water — calories/gram/degree for the substance divided by calories/gram/degree for water. Others prefer to omit "specific", and always give units.

Answers to the Questions

1. In thermal equilibrium, the temperature of the system is constant; so the temperature of nails and water is the same.
2. Answers will vary. Some students may predict the final temperature to be an average of the two instead of closer to the temperature of the water.
3. Answers will vary.
4. The observation is that the nails cool down a lot while the water warms up a little. The greater change in temperature of the nails is consistent with their lower specific heat.
5. The hot water has more thermal energy than an equal mass of nails at the same temperature, and will give more warmth for a longer time than nails of the same mass and temperature. Water is wonderful!

16 [Experiment] Specific Heat Capacities

Because this experiment requires no special equipment, it is suitable to having several groups, each working with different substances using slightly different procedures so that much can be gained by having groups discuss and compare their results.

Students may not notice much of an increase in temperature for some of the specimens because of their low specific heats. Exercising care, however, their values for specific heat capacities should come within 10% or so of accepted values.

17 [Experiment] Temperature of a Flame

The concept of heat capacity should be addressed in the pre-lab or post-lab lecture. Discuss why in transfers of thermal energy that water changes temperature by only a little while metals change temperature a lot.

Different parts of the flame are at different temperatures. You can, for example, quickly stick the head of a match into the center of the flame and it will not ignite. The hottest part of the flame is normally at the center tip of the inner cone.

Possible sources of error? Energy lost to vaporization; Brass cools down quickly before it is placed in the water; Different parts of the flame at different temperatures; non-perfect insulation; Inaccuracies with the thermometer.

Answers to the Questions

1. Student measurements may range between 400 and 800°C.
2. The faster changing temperature of brass indicates a lower specific heat capacity for brass.
3. A greater change in water temperature implies that the brass had more thermal energy, resulting from a higher flame temperature. (Numerical answer depends on student data.)
4. Possible sources of error include; cooling of the brass before it is dropped in the water, positioning of the brass in the flame (since various parts of the flame has different temperatures), incorrect temperature readings, and some energy lost by evaporation.

18 [Experiment] Taking the Heat

Let students know the purpose of aluminum foil and cardboard piece. Why might the crushed ice be less than 0°C? Is this possible?

Students need to read the thermometer quickly while it is out of the solution. The student bar graphs may look something like this:

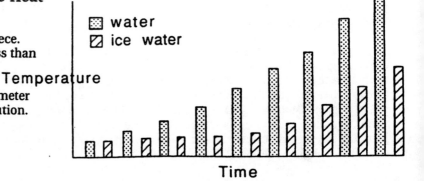

280

Answers to the Questions

1. The heat added to the crushed ice went into changing its phase from solid to liquid.
2. Thermal energy supplied was changing the phase of the ice.
3. Like the change of phase of ice to water, added heat went into phase change rather than temperature increase. Only when all the substance changes phase (ice or boiling water) will continued application of heat produce higher temperature.
4. Ice melts at 0°C. So if heat is added to ice colder than 0°C, the temperature of the ice increases like anything else heated while it is below its change of phase temperature.

19 [Experiment] Cooling by Boiling

Due to the nature of the equipment required, in a sense, this procedure is really not an experiment, but rather a demonstration for a class to observe. It normally requires a laboratory, and cannot easily be done in a classroom.

Boiling depends both on temperature and air pressure. When you lower air pressure in the bell jar, boiling will occur. A strong pump will produce freezing of one or two grams within three or four minutes. Point out to your students that this is how freeze dried coffee is made.

Answers to the Questions

1. To say that boiling is a cooling process is to say that the process of boiling absorbs energy. The water left in the liquid state cools as energy is carried away by the steam.
2. Increase temperature; decrease surrounding air pressure.
3. The reason that applying heat to a vessel of boiling water doesn't increase its temperature is evidence that as much energy is being carried away. By what? By the vapor that leaves the liquid.

20 [Experiment] Warming by Freezing

RE-HEATER packs are available from Arbor Scientific, P.O. Box 2750, Ann Arbor, MI 48106 (800 367-6695). Documentation booklet is included. See page 114 in this manual for a detailed chemical explanation for the heat given off by this change in phase (or the precipitation of a supersaturated solution).

The heat of crystallization for sodium acetate is 4 kcal per mole. Since the molecular weight of sodium acetate is 136, 120 grams is 0.9 mole. When 0.9 moles is multiplied by   4 kcal/mole we have 3.6 kcal, which increases the thermal energy of the water. Point out that the heat gained by the water is not all heat released by the sodium acetate during crystallization because some of the teat went into heating the solid acetate to the final temperature of the mixture.

Answers to the Questions

1. All involve the energy changes when a substance undergoes a change in phase. When the steam in radiators condenses, it releases large amounts of thermal energy which in turn is transferred to the room. Air conditioners operate by liquid refrigerants that absorb thermal energy by vaporizing from liquid to gas. Crystallization in the RE-HEATER is a change of phase where thermal energy is given off.
2. Icing of aircraft flying though clouds of supercooled droplets can change the aerodynamics of the wing surfaces and interrupt flight. To counter this, warm air from engine exhaust is circulated through the wing.
3. Practical applications of the RE-HEATER include being used as pocket warmers for skiers or fans at outdoor winter sporting events.

Part 3: Lab Activities and Experiments

Electricity and Magnetism

21 [Activity] Charging Up

This activity is conducive to dry weather (electrostatics demos in the humidity of Hawaii are unimpressive indeed). It is the polar characteristic of water molecules in the air that is responsible for the bleeding away of charge.

Blown up balloons rubbed on your hair will have the same sign of charge and repel each other. When brought near several kernels of puffed rice or the equivalent, they'll induce an opposite surface charge as molecules in the insulator swing into alignment like magnetic compasses. This is charge polarization. This is the mechanism whereby a charged balloon will stick to a wall, depending on its composition. Plastic walls work well, as mirror charge images are easily induced in plastic. Concrete walls are a bummer.

One's hair stands up when charged for the same reason a pair of charged balloons repel each other. Charged strands of hair simply repel one another, hence they stand out.

You'll produce an impressive shower of puffed rice or Styrofoam chips when they become charged atop a generator! Again, mutual repulsion.

A flame held near a charged Van de Graaff generator will lean toward the generator! The hot ions of the flame are attracted to the generator and form a conductive path. Sometimes a spark will snuff out the match.

All these effects stem from the fundamental rule of electricity — like charges repel and unlike charges attract.

You might add that the reason for a chain dragging the road under a tanker truck, and the invention of current conducting rubber for tires. Observation of the operation of a dry process copier, and discussion of the function of the toner, is relevant. Better yet, obtain a discarded copier, and arrange for a group of students to take it apart and report on how it works. Next time question: "Who invented it, and when?"

22 [Activity] Batteries and Bulbs

This activity introduces circuits. Students know from experience that 1.5-volt cells are not dangerous, but if you're demonstrating with a 12-volt car battery, expect many to feel shorting the terminals with fingers is dangerous. Show this is not the case. A demo with the car battery with extended terminals as described in the Chapter 9 Suggested Lecture is advisable here. Then students can try to duplicate the circuits you show with their own wires and D cells.

Answers to the Questions
1. The bottom of the bulb holder makes contact with the bottom of the bulb when screwed in, and the sides, which are insulated from the bottom, make contact with the sides of the bulb. The bottom and sides of the bulb are connected to opposite ends of the lamp filament.
2. A path is established between opposite battery terminals and opposite sides of the lamp filaments.
3. Brightness dimmer for two bulbs in series compared to a single bulb (more resistance).
4. Brightness greater in parallel circuit (less effective resistance).

5. Unscrew in series and circuit is broken. Unscrew in parallel and the other bulb remains lit.
6. Parallel, as evidenced by the fact that if a bulb burns out the rest of home lighting is unaffected.

23 [Activity] Three-Way Switch

Many students can draw a circuit, and they can "prove" that it will work — but there is no substitute for experience! Here they'll do it.

Begin by asking your students to imagine they are in a multi-story warehouse where stairwell lights are normally off. At the foot of each flight of stairs you want to turn on the light, and turn it off at the top. Now suppose as you start up, someone on the top floor starts coming down. What happens when they are about to pass? Suppose each wants to be the one who does it, and insists? Will they ever go home?

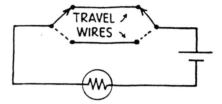

After students have constructed their circuits, compare the two settings on a single-throw double-throw switch to the "up" and "down" settings on a household 3-way switch. The "up" setting closes the circuit between the switch and one travel wire (the wire between the switches). The "down" setting closes the circuit between the switch and the other travel wire.

Next time question: "What can you do with two <u>double</u>-pole double-throw switches?

Answer to the Question
Yes, the switch like all simple switches has nothing to do with the direction of the current, but with the path of the current. A diode, on the other hand, passes current in only one direction.

24 [Activity] Cranking Up - I

Genecon hand held generators are available from Arbor Scientific, P.O. Box 2750, Ann Arbor, MI 48106. The beauty of these is that students can feel the load when they crank. If you don't have such, then any power supply, such as a battery, can be substituted. This activity can be quite enjoyable. Explanation and question-answer elucidation can be postponed to [Experiment] Cranking - II, which follows.

Answer to the Question
1. More effort is required to power more bulbs.
2. Four bulbs in parallel require substantially more effort, as more power output is the result.

25 [Experiment] Cranking Up - II

Whereas the Genecon provided a "feel" for applied voltages in Cranking Up I, the use of batteries in this experiment gives a more reliably constant voltage. However, "constant voltage" is only a close approximation, for the voltage of the battery varies with load. With digital meters this may be evident. The explanation? The battery itself has resistance — *internal resistance.* The terminal voltage of the battery is the ideal voltage (under no load). It is diminished by the product of the current and internal resistance, ir. So the terminal voltage is actually V - ir. Internal resistance is not a constant either, but increases with age in the battery. Its negligible for very small currents, but can be significant for large currents. An analogy is the resistance that builds up in water pipes. Just as water pressure decreases in clogged pipes, current decreases in a "clogged" battery. When there is no flow, the pressure in both pipes and battery is maximum. Resistance is only a factor when there is flow. (That's why a "dead" battery often shows a healthy voltage on a voltmeter — the voltage across its terminals must be measured while a load is across the battery and current flows through it.) Go light on this. You can expect that when 3 volts are applied to a parallel circuit, the voltage of the battery drops about 0.1 volt per lit bulb. Be careful about making a big deal out of this in class. For a student still wondering what the difference is between current and voltage, this would be information overload!

This is, however, a good time emphasize the value of a hypothesis (informed expectation) in science. In each Step students should state the hypothesis (positive or negative) to be tested. It is more difficult to "prove", logically, a negative statement than a positive one, but scientists often prefer the negative form of a hypothesis (null hypothesis) because error is much less likely when concluding that the evidence supporting a negative hypothesis is significant than when the hypothesis is positive. In common speech we often hear the term "scientific proof", but in science there is no proof — only evidence!

Answer to the Questions
1. More bulbs, less brightness.
2. No, the applied voltage remains unchanged. The voltage of the battery is the same whether one or two bulbs are connected. [Actually, the effective voltage of the battery decreases with current, in that the battery resistance increases with heat — this is a second order effect when currents are low.]
3. More bulbs, more resistance, less current.
4. Although values vary with applied voltage, relationships are the same. [Ohm's law holds for all values of voltage, current, and resistance.]
5. No, the brightness of bulbs connected in parallel is independent of the number (as long as the voltage source holds out).
6. No. Each bulb is connected across the same battery terminals.
7. Current increases in direct proportion to the number of bulbs.
8. No, Ohm's law was demonstrated in all cases.
9. Connect them in parallel, for both voltage and current will be more for each. The product of voltage and current is power. The more powerful combination is bulbs in parallel.
10. Answers will vary!

26 [Activity]   Magnetic Personality

Everybody loves to play with magnets. Their actions are mysterious because the explanation of their attractions and repulsions are far removed from simpler phenomena that we do understand. Explanations involve quantum phenomena, so like the similar attractions and repulsions of electrostatics, we simply say they are fundamental.

Don't underestimate the amount of dry iron filings you may need. Students tend to use too much, and to consider used filings as trash to be thrown away. Field patterns should approximate those shown in the textbook figures of Chapter 10. Consider also using some of the many little decorative magnets around — like the kind used to hold notes on a refrigerator door, that can be used to explore magnetism. Small compasses are also intriguing.

The activity concludes with electromagnetic induction (EMI). Cite the role of EMI in generators at power plants, metal detectors at airports, triggers for traffic lights, and that rusty strip of plastic tape that dragged across the head of a tape recorder. Fascinating stuff!

Answers to the Questions
1. Field lines join the attracting magnets; and are swept away from repelling magnets.
2. Current generation depends on the strength of the magnet, the number of turns of wire, and the speed at which the magnetic field is made to change in the turns of wire. Increasing any or all of these increases the amount of current induced.
3. The key idea is that current is generated when the magnetic field in a coil of wire is changed. The magnetic field in a coil of wire, whether it is the earth's magnetic field, or that produced by current-carrying wires, is affected when iron material is introduced. So when one carrying iron material walks through such a coil, the magnetic field in the coil is changed. Although the change may be very slight, if the sensitivity of the apparatus detects it, an alarm is activated. Similarly for the loops of wire buried in a road near traffic lights, that are triggered by an iron car moving over them. Interesting stuff!

Part 4: Lab Activities and Experiments

Sound and Light

27 [Activity] Tuning Forks

All students know the tines of a tuning fork move when they vibrate. They can't see the motion because of the high frequency. But dip a vibrating fork in water and the motion is evidenced in the splashing water. Larger forks work best.

Best evidence is with a strobe light. Caution: Some people have unfavorable reactions to strobe lights (particularly epileptics). Casually ask if strobe lights bother anybody *before* using them.

Air near the vibrating tines is set in vibration — sound. Placing the tuning fork against a table top, or any sounding board, causes the tines to spend their energy faster. Ask your students to explain this in terms of the conservation of energy. Sound energy eventually degrades to thermal energy.

A vibrating tuning fork in outer space would vibrate longer, but its energy would eventually degrade to thermal energy.

28 [Activity] Echo

The speed of sound is about 340 m/s. Good clapping techniques can yield values within 15%.

An alternate technique is done by David Ewing (Southwestern Georgia University) who takes a bass drum outside next to a tall wall. In rhythm with a metronome or a pendulum 25-cm long with a 1-s period the drum is beat once per second. The rest of the class is about 170 m distant, where they hear the beat when the drummer's hand is extended in air exactly 1/2 beat out of phase. If your students walk 340 m, they'll see the motion of the arm and the sound in synch. But when the drummer stops, they'll hear but not see an extra beat. Neat! It's obvious to everyone but the drummer that the speed of sound is 340 m/s.

29 [Activity] Sound Off

This is a great one! It is actually a demo, but so impressive that students will appreciate doing it themselves. They'll one day remember it nostalgically when anti-noise technology is commonplace.

You'll want to have your department invest in a common "boom box" and insert a DPDT switch in one of the speaker wires. This will likely become a routine demo in all courses where interference is taught.

Where does the energy go when sound is canceled? It turns out that each loudspeaker is also a microphone. When the speakers face each other they "drive" each other, inducing back voltages in each other that cut the currents down in each. Thus energy is diminished, but not canceled. So as the speakers are brought closer, and as sound is diminished, the electric bill for powering the sound source diminishes accordingly!

Answers to the Questions
1. Volume is "normal" when speakers are in phase.
2. When out of phase, cancellation of sound occurs as regions of compression from one speaker fill in regions of rarefaction from the other. If the overlap of out of phase waves is exact, then complete cancellation occurs (barring stray waves). Exact overlap cannot occur, however, because of the displacement between the speaker cones. So much of the interference is partial. For long waves, the displacement of the speaker cones is small compared to their wavelength, overlap is relatively exact, and these waves cancel well. But overlap is less exact for shorter wavelengths, producing cancellation that is more partial. For very short waves, reinforcement rather than cancellation occurs. This occurs if the displacement of the cones is a half wavelength of such higher-frequency sound. Then overlap is *in* phase. So for these reasons, high frequency sound survives, giving the music that "tinny" sound.
3. Answers will vary. But interestingly enough, students were asked twenty-five years ago for the practical applications for a laser. Today we ask the same question at the outset period of a growing anti-noise technology.

30 [Activity] Pinhole Image

Both a prism and a lens deviate light because their faces are not parallel (only at the center of a lens are both faces parallel to each other). As a result, light passing through the center of a lens undergoes the least deviation. If a pinhole is placed at the center of the pupil of your eye, the undeviated light forms an image in focus no matter where the object is located. Pinhole vision is remarkably clear. Not magnified, but clear.

Answers to the Questions
1, 2. Yes. Just as the image in a pinhole camera is clear near and far, likewise for this activity.
3. The page is dimmer simply because less light energy gets through the pinhole.

31 [Experiment] Pinhole Camera

The word camera is derived from the Greek word kamara, meaning "vaulted room." Royalty in the 16th century were entertained by the "camera obscura" — a large "pinhole camera" without the film.

Answers to the Questions
1 - 4. Image is inverted in all directions; up and down as well as left and right.
5. All distances are in focus. Actually the consideration is the size of the pinhole compared to the distance to the screen. So openings of a few centimeters act as pinholes if the screen distance is in meters. Openings in the leaves of trees act as pinholes, for example, and cast images of the sun on the ground!
6. A lens gathers more light and is brighter.
7. There is much in common with the eye and a pinhole camera. Image formation is much the same for each.

32 [Activity] Mirror, Mirror, on the Wall . . .

Beware of treating this activity too lightly. Nearly all your students will fail to distinguish between mirror size and image size. They all know image size is less with increased distance — which it is. But mirror size is also, in the same proportion. So a half size mirror lets you see your full size image at any distance. This is evident in a pocket mirror that you can hold near or far. You'll see a part of your face that's twice the height of the mirror.
The question often arises why a mirror inverts left and right but not up and down. Well quite simply, it doesn't reverse left and right; the hand on the east is still on the east — the reason for this misunderstanding has mainly to do with left right convention of the human body. What *is* inverted, is back and front. That person facing you in the mirror points to the east when you do, and looks upward when you do. The only difference is his or her nose is pointing in a direction opposite yours. So front and back are inverted, not left and right.

33 [Activity] Polaroids Ho!

Polaroids are an excellent illustration of vectors. Without a vector way of analyzing their behavior, they seem mysterious.

Answers to the Questions

1. The polarization axes of sunglasses are vertical, so they cut out horizontally polarized light. Since most glare is horizontally polarized reflecting from horizontal surfaces, the vertical-axis sunglasses cut out glare. Non-Polaroid glasses cut down on overall intensity, with no particular attention to glare.
2. Vectors make this comprehensible: Light comes through the first Polaroid aligned in one direction. If the light in this direction has a component that is parallel to the axis of the second Polaroid, light will get through the pair. How much light depends on the relative size of the component compared to the vector. As the angle rotates toward 90°, the component shrinks toward zero.
3. The lower parts of the sky are more polarized, as evidence by the difference in light intensity when view by a rotated Polaroid.
4. Evidence for the fact that the liquid crystals are polarized is the blocking out of the crystal display as a Polaroid in front of it is rotated.
5.

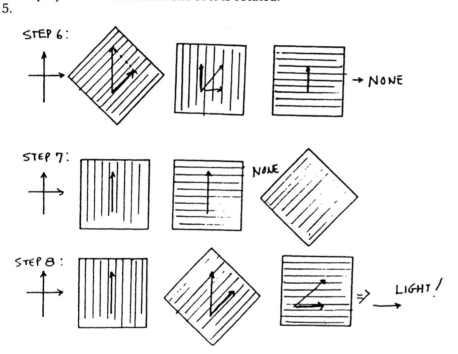

Part 5: Lab Experiments

The Atom

34 [Experiment] Thickness of a BB Pancake

Consider a quick pre-lab activity and show that the diameter of a marble is the same as the thickness of a monolayer of a dozen or more marbles. The volume of the monolayer divided by its top or bottom area equals the diameter of the marble.

Note: Because of the 3-D close packing of BBs in a graduated cylinder, the volume of the same BBs spread into a monolayer is slightly greater. This produces a 5 to 10% higher value than the actual diameter. A typical BB measures about 4.5 mm using a micrometer.

Consider having your students find the density of a rectangular block of aluminum (or look it up in the textbook). Then hand them a sheet of aluminum foil and ask them to find its thickness. From the mass they can calculate the volume, and since volume is simply surface area multiplied by thickness, they can calculate thickness. This sets the stage for this activity and the following experiment.

This experiment presents an opportunity for students to learn to use a micrometer (for those who haven't already).

Answers to the Questions
1. It was assumed that the volume occupied by the BBs in the graduated cylinder and the volume when spread in a monolayer was the same. This is not quite true; since the BBs are spheres, they pack together more compactly than cubes of the same width. Spreading them into a thin layer slightly increases the volume they occupy compared to when packed in the graduated cylinder.
2. Answers will vary; typically, BBs are about 4.3 to 4.7 mm in diameter.
3. Drop a known volume of oleic acid on water and measure the area it covers. Divide the volume of the drop by the area of the monolayer to estimate its thickness.

35 [Experiment] Oleic Acid Pancake

Inform your students that the oleic acid solution will be mostly alcohol with a small amount of oleic acid in it, mainly to allow portioning out less than a drop of oleic acid. When they add a drop of solution to a tray of water, the alcohol dissolves in the water, but the oleic acid floats on top, just as a drop of oil floats on water.

Caution your students not to put too much powder on the water surface, which may interrupt spreading.

The computations that follow treat the oleic acid molecules as a sphere. The conclusion of the lab is an appropriate time to relate that the molecule is actually hot-dog shaped, and they are measuring the *length* of the molecule. Still, the method and the outcome are good.

Sample Calculations

In Step 3, a typical value for the average diameter is 30 cm. **The radius, r is then:**

$$r = d/2 = 30 \text{ cm}/2 = 15 \text{ cm}$$

The area of the circle is:

$$A = \pi r^2$$
$$= (3.14)(15 \text{ cm})^2$$
$$= 706 \text{ cm}^2$$
$$= 7.06 \times 10^2 \text{ cm}^2$$

The number of drops in 1 cm^3 of 5% solution is about 38.

The volume of one drop is:
$$1 \text{ cm}^3/38 = 0.026 \text{ cm}^3$$
$$= 2.6 \times 10^{-2} \text{ cm}^3$$

In Step 4, the volume of acid in a single drop equals 0.005 multiplied by the volume of one drop:

$$(0.005)(2.6 \times 10^{-2}) \text{ cm}^3) = 1.3 \times 10^{-4} \text{ cm}^3$$

In Step 5, the diameter of an oleic acid molecule equals the volume of oleic acid in one drop divided by the area of the circle:

$$\text{diameter} = (\text{volume})/(\text{area})$$
$$= (1.3 \times 10^{-4} \text{ cm}^3)/(7.06 \times 10^2 \text{ cm}^2)$$
$$= 0.18 \times 10^{-6} \text{ cm}$$
$$= 1.8 \times 10^{-7} \text{cm}$$

Good measurements yield values between 1.0×10^{-7} and 2.0×10^{-7} cm. If time permits a second trial, be sure students clean the trays thoroughly before making a second measurement of the diameter.

Answers to the Questions
1. A monolayer is a layer one molecule thick.
2. At full strength, a single drop would cover a huge area.
3. Assume a rectangular shape for simplicity: The volume of one rectangular molecule would be it length multiplied by one-tenth the length multiplied by one-tenth the length. Which means the volume of the long molecule is actually about one-hundredth the volume of a cube of the same thickness.

36 [Experiment] Bright Lights

At the outset of your prelab lecture state the discovery of helium in the sun, and how its spectral patterns did not correspond to any known element. This new element found predominately in the sun was named helium, from the Greek word *helios*.

Spectroscope viewing techniques: Spectroscopes should be held by a ring stand. Students should hold the spectroscope fairly close to the flame, for background light will likely show through the spectroscope. Lights should be dimmed to provide better viewing of colors. The spatula may be taken in and out of the flame for the student to best see the part of the spectrum for which the salt is responsible.

If possible, use a large supply of metal spatulas, one for each element. Residual salts are readily detected and not so readily removed. Alert students to rinse the spatula with water before wiping the spatula on a paper towel, which would otherwise scorch.

Chloride salts tend to glow the brightest. Here's a question you might ask students during the experiment: All the metal salts you are observing are chloride salts. What test might you perform to deduce the effect of the chloride ion on the line spectrum?

Sodium is an impurity found in most alkali and alkali Earth salts, as well as tap water. Students shouldn't confuse the sodium D line with the lines of the other salts. This D line, however, provides a good reference when sketching line spectra using the homemade spectroscope.

Colored pencils work well in this experiment.

Metals in their solid elemental form tend to give continuous spectra because of the numerous interactions that take place within the solid lattice. Spectral "lines" are smudged. A salt works well because when heated it enters a plasma phase, in which it radiates its characteristic frequencies — unsmudged.

Point of info: St Elmos Fire is blue because of the emission spectrum of nitrogen.

Ask students about the relationship between data from Table 1 and Table 2. (in terms of what the flames look like without the diffraction grating)

Answers to the Questions:
1. Make the unknown a mixture of two of the salts! Use a mortar and pestle to finely grind the two salts together.
2. Residual sodium chloride.
3. One reason campfire burn yellow is because of the salt content of the wood. A second reason is the incandescence of rising graphite.
4. Metal salts, typically salts of strontium and barium. If there is an upcoming fireworks display suggest to students that they bring their homemade spectroscopes (cheap but effective diffraction gratings are available at most toy stores as "rainbow glasses".
5. Without the slit the colors from one side of the image merge with colors from the other making the particular frequencies less discernable.
6. No, it's not neon. Probably argon.
7. The hydrogen and oxygen atoms in water are bound together via chemical bonds. These bonded atoms give a different spectra because the electrons are in a completely different environment.

37 [Experiment] Nuclear Pennies

If the penny reflects off the meter stick its the same as though it went right through it and encountered the same density of beakers on the opposite side. It's not so important that the target width W be constant as the density of beakers within the target area remains the same.

Note in student calculations how the only variable with units is W, given in cm. If W is in cm then the radius of the penny must also be given in cm.

A common error for students is that they use the diameter of the penny rather than its radius. Alternatively,

$$R + r = \frac{HW}{2NS}$$ can be simplified to $$D + d = \frac{HW}{NS}$$

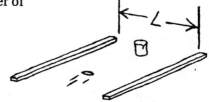

Answers to the Questions
1. 100% probability
2. The number of hits would decline because of the shielding effect of forward beakers. As the number of hits decreases so does the value of R + r. So the calculated probable diameter will be less than the actual diameter. That the electric field of forward nuclei would shield rear nuclei from being hit is one of the reasons why Rutherford needed to work with gold-foil that was ultrathin.

3. Water is in the beaker to provide inertia against the incoming pennies. This also helps to simulate the relatively great inertia of the nuclei in gold atoms.
4. You don't have to see, feel, hear, smell, or touch something directly in order to measure it. Need examples?

38 [Experiment] To Half or Half Not

The simplest version of this lab is tossing coins, and using heads and tails to simulate radio-active decay. Then the half life is each toss. The cubes add variety. Then if you have multifaceted cubes available, so much the better. You can amend the lab by equating each color with one of the facets. For example, the square facet may equal the red color, the triangular facet may equal the blue color, and a square facet with a blue dot in the center may equal the white face.

If not covered in lecture, the pre-lab meeting is a good place to introduce the concept of radioactive dating — carbon-14 dating gets most attention.

Answers to the Questions
1. Answers will vary with the data table. Red should take longest to reduce by half.
2. The unit of half life in this experiment is the number of throws. One half life is the number of throws required for half the cubes to leave.
3. Answers will vary with the data table. Red should take the most rolls.
4. The most radioactive is the one that decays fastest: white.
5. Reroll the cubes that were removed. They will have new half lives.
6. Yes, but not very accurate. Accuracy is increased with number of cubes tossed.
7. The lines should curve, corresponding to a constant rate of decay.
8. a) 10 years: 500 g; 20 years: 250 grams; 50 years: 31.25 grams; 100 years: 0.977 grams.
   b) Yes, substance X will disappear after the last atoms disintegrate.
   An estimate can be made from your graph in Step 8 — between 500 and 1000 years.

Part 6: Lab Activities and Experiments

Chemistry

With all chem labs, there are some basic rules for proper keeping of a laboratory notebook: First, indelible ink should be used. Lab pages must be numbered, dated, and reviewed by the instructor or a fellow student. The notebook ought to be clear enough to be used in a court of law, if so subpoenaed. Its okay to scratch out bad data, but erasure is a no no. Half way messy is okay — meaning that a second person should find sufficient clarity to be able to repeat the procedure based upon what is written.

Students will profit from their mistakes and should not necessarily be penalized for them (to the extent that this is practical).

40 [Activity] Tubular Rust

To take this activity a step further, have students add dilute HCl to the rusted wool. Oxygen is then released back into the atmosphere as evidenced by the bubbling. References: "Percent Oxygen in Air" Martins, G.F. J. Chem. Ed 1987, 64 (9), 809. George F. Martins, Newton North High School, Newtonville, MA 02160.

Answers to the Questions

1. The actual percent oxygen in air is about 21%.
2. The volume of a gas is affected by the pressure exerted upon it. For this reason, it is important that the pressures inside and outside the test tube remains the same. Accomplish this by keeping the water levels even.
3. It would take longer because of less surface area.
4. Use the principle of exaggeration to answer this question. Say the steel wool occupied the entire upper half of the inverted test tube. There wouldn't be so much air in the tube, hence less oxygen to be depleted. This means that the water level wouldn't rise so much. If the volume of the wool is ignored then the calculated percent oxygen would be substantially less than the actual percent oxygen. Taking the volume of the steel wool into account, therefore, would increase the calculated value closer to the actual value.
   Here's another approach: Again say that the steel wool occupies the entire upper half of the inverted tube. This means that air only occupies the lower half of the inverted test tube and the effective tube length is smaller. Shortening the tube length in calculation would have the effect of increasing the calculated percent oxygen.

41 [Activity] Collecting Bubbles

In preparing the set-up, the second flask should be filled with water using water from the beaker, which has been filled close to the brim. This guarantees that water will not overflow as it is being displaced. You may either inform students of this technique or provide sponges and let them discover it on their own.

Many students will want to repeat the CO_2 collection to permit further experimentation.

Challenge students as to how many candles they can extinguish using their 250 mL of CO_2. Creative students might use the stopper with the tubing attached to better concentrate the CO_2 over individual flames.

Students may "pour" some of the carbon dioxide into their mouths. The taste will be familiar to them.

"Going Further" with Step 5 easily changes this activity into an experiment for it requires critical thinking and careful technique. Ideally, the student should dry off the outside of the stoppered flask as much as possible and then measure its mass as precisely as possible. The density of carbon dioxide at 1 atm and 25°C is about 1.80 g/L. This means that about 0.450 grams of CO_2 is contained in 250 mL. The flask should then be emptied of CO_2, filled with air, and reweighed. Since the mass of the air is about 0.290 grams (assuming an air density of 1.17 g/L) students should observe a decrease in mass of about 0.160 grams (0.450 g - 0.290 g). The mass of the air (calculated from its density) plus the difference in mass of the flask and stopper with and without CO_2 should equal the total mass of CO_2 collected.

Students will also need to measure the precise volume of the stoppered flask by filling it with water and then pouring that water into a graduated cylinder. This is the volume (not the size of the flask) that the student needs to use in calculating the mass of air from its density.

Students must be very careful not to lose any water droplets as the carbon dioxide is being released from the flask. One drop of water is about 50 mg, hence, this is potentially a major source of experimental error.

The observation that gases have measurable mass is in itself intriguing to many students.

Answers to the Questions
1. CO_2 is more dense. It pours out of the flask much like water as it extinguishes the candle.
2. The flask was not initially stoppered so that the newly formed carbon dioxide would push the less dense air out. This step helps to increase the purity of the collected CO_2.
3. The displaced water filled up the beaker, which would overflow if it had been filled to capacity.

42 [Activity] Crystal Clear

Note the scant procedure section on crystallization techniques in this activity, which may prompt students the opportunity to discover many of these techniques on their own. A technique you might guide them to is transferring the growing crystal to a freshly saturated solution. You can prod them by asking about the temperature of this fresh solution.

This activity is much like cooking, with students designing their own recipes. So, ask your students about the value of a good recipe if it's not written down. Like recipes, experiments should be well documented. Encourage note taking in everything they do, and when they do it. Consider having them turn in their detailed procedure along with their report.

To stimulate thought you might ask the following question concerning the solvent evaporation method of crystallization: "Might the rate of crystal formation be the same, greater than, or less than the rate of solvent evaporation?" Then ask "How might they test their hypothesis? What experiment might they design?" [If the rates are the same then the mass of the evaporated solvent would be equal to the mass of the crystals that form. If the rate of crystal formation is greater, then the crystals are able to form when the solution is less than saturated (or the saturated solution was really supersaturated). If the rate is less, this means that solute must be precipitating amorphously.]

Students may wish to make more than one crystal. This may be encouraged since it allows more experimentation. The negative aspect is the large quantity of solute that will be used.

The technique of cooling a saturated solution often leads to a "supersaturated" solution, from which crystals form.

Have student use your newest beakers. Crystal growth will often initiate from scratches commonly found in older beakers.

An excellent place to maintain a constant temperature is inside a refrigerator. In fact, the temperature of the refrigerator may be gradually lowered over time to increase the size of the crystals.

Many student tend to think that the dissolution process is instantaneous and will underestimate the importance of stirring diligently.

Many other inorganic salts may be used for this lab. The ones suggested here give seven different crystal systems:

system	inorganic salts
cubic	sodium chloride, $NaCl$
tetragonal	nickel sulfate hexahydrate, $NiSO_4 \cdot 6H_2O$
orthorhombic	nickel sulfate heptahydrate, $NiSO_4 \cdot 7H_2O$
orthorhombic	potassium sulfate, K_2SO_4
triclinic	copper sulfate pentahydrate, $CuSO_4 \cdot 5H_2O$
monoclinic	copper acetate monohydrate, $Cu(CH_3CO)_2 \cdot H_2O$
rhombohedral	calcium carbonate, $CaCO_3$
hexagonal	sodium nitrate, $NaNO_3$

Nickel sulfate hydrates and the copper sulfate hydrate are particularly susceptible to humidity. Students may store these in sealed jars. Alternatively, crystals may be treated with a spray-on polyurethane coat.

As will be discovered in this activity, temperature influences the solubility of some salts more so than others. The solubility of sodium nitrate, for example, is markedly greater at higher temperatures. The solubility of sodium chloride, on the other hand, is not that effected by temperature. Evaporate or boil the water from the solutions to recycle the salts.

Reference: Baer, C.D. J. Chem. Ed. 1990, 67(5), 410.

Answers to the Questions
1. When no more solute will dissolve at a given temperature.
2. Within a crystal there is a regular and repeating arrangement of atoms. Within an amorphous solid such as glass atoms are arranged randomly.

43 [Activity] Circular Rainbows

Chromatography is a technique often used by chemists to separate components of a mixture. In 1906, the Russian botanist Mikhail Tsvett separated color pigments in leaves by allowing a solution of these pigments to flow down a column packed with an insoluble material such as starch, alumina, or silica. Because different colored bands appeared along the column, he called the procedure chromatography. (Note: Color is not a required property to achieve separation of compounds by this procedure.) Because of its simplicity and efficiency, this technique is widely used for separating and identifying compounds such as drugs and natural products.

The basis of chromatography is the partitioning (separation due to differences in solubility) of compounds between a stationary phase and moving phase. Stationary phases such as alumina, silica, or paper (cellulose) have highly polar surface areas that attract the components (molecules) of a mixture to different extents. The components of the mixture to be separated are thought to be continuously adsorbed and then released from the stationary phase into the solvent that moves over the surface of the stationary phase. Because of differences in the attraction of each component for the stationary phase, each component travels at different speeds thus causing their separation.

In paper chromatography, where paper is the stationary phase, a small spot of a mixture is carried by solvent through the paper via capillary action. The solvent and various components of the mixture each travel at different speeds along the paper resulting in the separation of the mixture.

Technique really counts in this activity. Many students will have the tendency to add the solvent too quickly, which will cause the colors to bleed into one another. Point out to students that with a good separation they should be able to cut out individual colors using a pair of scissors. The best separations will show colors with distinct boundaries and white spaces in between colors. Have each student turn in his or her best and most spectacular separation. The name or PIN of each students should be marked on the perimeter in pencil. Base your grading or judging on the degree of separation.

Food coloring is an alternative to pen ink.

Answers to the Questions
1. The ionic component would stick to the paper by ion-dipole interactions and not travel with the solvent.
2. A different hue of blue may be obtained by changing the proportions of a secondary or tertiary color.

44 [Activity] Home Brew Sugar

This activity may take over a month for students to accomplish. Thus it shouldn't be started close to the end of the academic term. Students should know that in making these crystals patience is the greatest virtue. You will need to emphasize the importance of not overcooking the brown sugar. It doesn't take too much cooking time before the brown sugar simply hardens upon cooling. Students should maintain a crystal journal and tape a few of the best crystals they ultimately obtain. How well they keep their journal may be used to assess their grade for this activity. You might also grade them, in part, based upon the colorlessness of their crystals. To make your assessments less arbitrary, exhibit a set of samples along with the number of points you would have assigned to each.

Answers to Questions:
1. Make a concentrated solution of sugar in water. If any molasses is present, it should give the concentrated sugar solution a yellow color, which indeed it does.
2. White sugar is more pure than brown sugar.
3. Brown sugar is more natural than white sugar.
4. The greater the quality (colorlessness) of the sugar crystals, the less of them you have!

Regarding the optional "Further Research", suggest to your students that they also try working with corn syrup, which is a mixture of the sugar-related carbohydrates glucose and fructose.

45 [Activity] Polarity of Molecules

A common error in seeing a running stream of water deflected by a charged rod is assuming the water is somehow charged. If this is the cause of deflection, then holding a charge of opposite sign near the stream ought to produce an opposite deflection. But this is not the case: only attraction occurs. The water is polarized, and oppositely charged sides of water molecules are closer to the charged rod, whatever its charge, and closeness wins in Coulomb's law.

Proper care and ventilation should be exercised when handling these compounds.

46 [Activity] A Roping Experience

Have students work in pairs. This allows for longer strands of nylon and also minimizes the amount of material required — also, less hydrogen chloride is generated. Have students test for the presence of gaseous hydrogen chloride with litmus paper. The nylon can be colored by adding methyl red or bromocresol blue to the solutions. Have a contest to see who can fabricate the longest strand — some good hands-on technique is required. With poor technique, bubbles containing unreacted solution may form within the nylon. While rinsing the nylon under a faucet, be sure to carefully pop any of these bubbles.

Adipoyl chloride should be stored in the refrigerator.

> **Solution A:** Place 5.81 g of hexamethylenediamine (1,6-diaminohexane) in a beaker. Warm until it melts and dilute to 100 mL with 0.5 M NaOH (20 g NaOH per liter).

> **Solution B:** Dilute 4.58 g of adipoyl chloride with cyclohexane to a volume of 100 mL.

Answers to the Questions
1. The strands can be up to several meters in length.
2. It should not, because it involves a physical connection rather than a chemical one.
3. A chain of many molecules chemically linked together.
4. The sodium hydroxide served to neutralize the hydrogen chloride generated during the reaction.
5. Simply put, this is where the two chemical meet. Chemicals have to come together before they can react.
6. There are 6 carbon atoms in each of the starting materials.

47 [Activity] Smells Great

In a pre-lab discussion consider addressing the receptor site model for smelling. Beforehand, however, make sure that students understand that only gaseous chemicals are detected by the nose. An odorous chemical is odorous because it has the right shape to fit within the olfactory receptors in the nose. The chemical fits into the receptor much like a key fits into a lock. Once there, it triggers a neurological signal to the brain. Receptor sites in our nose work in tandem with receptor sites on our taste buds to give distinctive flavor. This receptor site model is the same as the one addressed in Chapter 21 of the textbook.

Essential oils are often formulations of many odorous chemicals. The smell of pineapple, for example, consists of at least 10 chemicals, most of them esters. Artificial extracts reproduce these formulation only close enough to fool most people.

A special note about butyric acid: it has the smell of rancid butter and it stays with you for quite some time. Work with butyric acid under a fume hood only. Interestingly enough, butyric acid is also a component of body odor. Animals can readily detect a human when downwind because of its strong scent. Also, bloodhounds are trained to follow remnant trails of this chemical when tracking humans.
Notes on disposal:
Have students deposit their reaction mixtures into a single waste container such as a 1 liter Erlenmeyer flask. Students may need to rinse their tubes with methanol to make cleaning easier. These rinsings may also be combined in the waste container.

Add a solution of sodium bicarbonate to neutralize the sulfuric acid (it is neutralized when added sodium bicarbonate ceases to cause bubbling). Decant the aqueous layer, which may be poured down the drain. The remaining oils may be sealed in a jar and thrown into the trash.

Table 1.

Alcohol	Carboxylic Acid	Observed Smell
methanol	salicylic acid	Wintergreen
octanol	acetic acid	Oranges
benzyl alcohol	acetic acid	Peach
isoamyl alcohol	acetic acid	Banana
n-propanol	acetic acid	Pear
methanol	o-aminobenzoic acid	Grape
isopentenol	acetic acid	"Juicy Fruit"
methanol	butyric acid	Apple
isobutanol	propionic acid	Rum

Answers to the Questions
1. A chemical reaction that produces heat is exothermic. The heat generated in these esterification reactions comes from the hydration of the concentrated sulfuric acid.
2. Nothing.
3. Molecules have a greater tendency to vaporize at higher temperatures. The assumption here of course is the understanding that a substance has odor because of the gaseous molecules it emits.

48 [Activity]   Name That Recyclable

A main purposes of this short activity is to let students know what those recycling imprints on plastics mean. Cut out small pieces of plastic for the students to work with. One separation scheme is as follows:

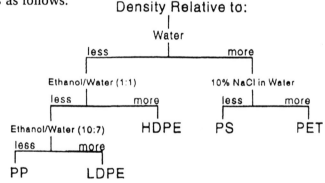

Students may also chose a scheme that separates one plastic at a time.

Students may be expecting all the unknowns to be different. To challenge their trust in their experimental observations, you might consider making two unknowns from the same plastic.

Code 3 (polyvinyl chloride) and code 7 (mixed resins) are not included in this activity because of their variable densities. For your information, since PVC contains a halogen (chlorine), it can be identified using the Beilstein test (touching the plastic with a hot copper wire and then placing the wire in a flame: a blue green flame is positive for a halogen).

Reference: "Method for Separating or Identifying Plastics" Kolb, K.E., Kolb, D.K *J. Chem. Ed.* **1991**, 68(4), 348.

Answers to the Questions
1. Melting points.
2. Throw all the pieces into a large container of water. The less dense polypropylene pieces will float to the top, while the more dense polystyrene pieces will float to the bottom.

49 [Experiment] Chemical Personalities

Perform the sublimation of iodine, in a fume hood. Students may not see the iodine crystals initially form beneath the ice-containing dish. When you point to the crystals, ask what they think the material is. What is the evidence? Show how the crystals appear like iodine. Use a spatula to place a few of them on the hot plate. They will sublime like iodine. Then show how the crystals are insoluble in water and soluble in acetone, just as was discovered with iodine at an earlier station. All this evidence suggests that the crystals are indeed iodine. So the type of change was physical. Note that the opposite of *sublimation* is *deposition.*

Be sure that students use only small amounts of ammonium dichromate and potassium chromate. The potassium chromate should be heated for only a few minutes. It will turn back to the yellow color as it cools, indicating a physical change. The potassium chromate is a known carcinogen and so should be handled with extreme care in the fume hood only. Remind students to continue wearing safety glasses, especially around the ammonium dichromate.

Answers to the Questions
1 a) physical b) chemical c) physical d) chemical e) chemical f) physical.
2. a) physical b) chemical c) physical d) physical.

50 [Experiment] Sugar and Sand

Here it is preferable that each student work alone. Three goals: (1) Learning the limitations of laboratory equipment; (2) Gain first hand experience on how to control variables so as to achieve reliable data; (3) Achieving a certain amount of independence.
There is no way to get reliable data on a single trial of the entire sample. Good science dictates the sample be divided into at least three parts to be analyzed separately. Did students take the precaution of washing sugar solution from filter paper? (Filter paper will turn brown in the oven). How might they know when all the sugar is washed out? Take a few drops of the filtrate and heat to detect residual sugar.

[Journal reference: Richter, E.W. Journal of College Science Teaching 16 (3), 194 (1986).]

Answers to the Questions
2. Sugar and sand is an example of a heterogeneous mixture.
3. The mass of the dissolved compounds in tap water would alter the results of analysis.

51 [Activity] Sugar Soft

You will need to talk about calibrations curves and their function during your pre-lab discussion. A typical calibration curve may look as follows once completed. Regarding this calibration curve, ask your students why it doesn't pass through this origin, even if the origin were shown on the graph. Also ask the students what kind of slope they might expect at sugar concentrations beyond 20%. Stress the importance of being able to relate a graph to the physical reality it is designed to represent. Lastly, you might share with students how it is that beer and wine manufacturers (home ones included) measure the alcohol content by way of the hydrometer. The more alcohol, the less dense the solution and the lower the hydrometer floats. Calibrated properly, the reading of the hydrometer can be translated into percent alcohol.

Answers to Questions:
1. The student's tables may well show that most all soft drink have about the same percentage of sugar. Exceptions include the diet soft drinks. Also, root beer tends to be on the denser side.

2. Perhaps the biggest assumption made in this activity is that of a linear relationship between the height of the hydrometer and the concentration of the sugar. It may be tested by noting how the hydrometer floats in solutions of other known concentrations, including fresh water.

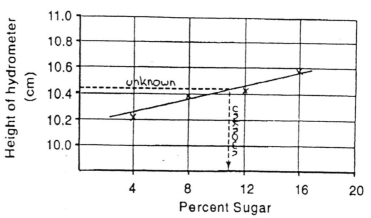

52 [Experiment] Molecules by Acme

There are a couple versions of the model for iron oxide that students might build. Have them keep trying until they get to the one that has no double bonds and looks like a football where the two iron atoms linked together by three bridging oxygen atoms.

Answers to the Questions
1. a) Yes. b) No, you would have hydrogen peroxide.
2. a) Both are tetrahedral. b) Dichloromethane is less symmetrical and more lopsided.
3. Five.
4. Hydrogen, oxygen, nitrogen, carbon dioxide, and acetylene.
5. Oxygen, nitrogen, carbon dioxide, acetylene, acetic acid, benzene.   6. Benzene.

53 [Experiment] Mystery Powders

The most toxic chemical here is the sodium hydroxide. Any skin that gets in contact with the sodium hydroxide should be flushed with water for an extended period of time. Remind students to be careful in working with the unknowns. Safety glasses should be worn.

Use parafilm to cover the test tubes to avoid contact with skin.

The sodium hydroxide is deliquescent and needs to be powdered just prior to the laboratory.

All unknowns are common household chemicals that can be safely poured down the drain

Phenolphthalein can also be obtained from Ex-Lax. Mix on tablet with 100 mL rubbing alcohol and filter several times to remove brown color.

Answers to the Questions
2. Tests # 1, 6, and 7.
3. No, all foods are made of chemicals. Everything is made of a chemical.
5. It's better to split the group in half initially.

54 [Activity] Sensing pH

Have each student prepare his or her small batch of red cabbage pH indicator. A single head of red cabbage should be sufficient for a class of 40 students. Bring dry ice to laboratory and allow students to drop pieces into test tubes of their indicator solution. After the students have become familiar with the colors that the cabbage indicator turns at various pH's have them gather around a 2 L beaker containing about 300 mL of fairly concentrated broth that is a slight shade of red from small amounts of acetic acid. Have students note the color of the broth and then ask them what color the broth might turn to if you were to quickly add 1700 mL of water. Ideally, some will argue that it should stay the same color because no acid or base has been added—only water. Remind the students that pH is a measure of the concentration of hydronium ions. Thus, as you dilute the solution shouldn't the concentration of hydronium ions become less and the pH rise? The color should thus turn from its slight reddish color to purple. Sure enough, if it's not too concentrated with acetic acid, this will be the case. Follow up by asking students whether adding more water will ever bring the indicator to the slightly alkaline green color. Why or why not? Try it and see.

55 [Experiment] Upset Stomach

This is the standard titration experiment. Have students lower burettes to eye-level for easy filling. Make sure that students read from the bottom of the meniscus. Common burettes can be read to the hundredths place.

Spilled acid can be neutralized with baking soda, and spilled sodium hydroxide neutralized with boric acid. Inform students to wash and thoroughly rinse any acid or base away from their skin. The sodium hydroxide will be most apparent due to its slippery feel — slippery because it reacts with skin oils to form a layer of soap. So that students exercise proper precautions you might tell them that the sodium hydroxide *dissolves* flesh and then reacts with skin oils to form a soap-like layer.

Step 4 can be expedited if students know beforehand approximately how much sodium hydroxide should be added. They can get a "ball park figure" by doing a quick trial run before a final more-accurate run.

The burette is well designed to deliver volume — half a drop can be added by quickly turning the valve 180 degrees. At the endpoint, the pink color of phenolpthalein indicator should persist for at least 60 seconds. The color fades away as atmospheric carbon dioxide, which converts to carbonic acid, is absorbed by the solution.

For your information, phenolpthalein indicator is the active ingredient of Ex-lax.

Neutralized solutions may be poured down the drain flushed with plenty of water.

Part 7: Lab Activities and Experiments

Earth Science

56 [Experiment] Crystal Growth

This lab uses thymol which may irritate the skin. Use caution. The seed crystals speed up the process of crystallization, and longer cooling promotes larger crystal size.

Answers to the Questions
1. Crystallization from a solution depends on the concentration of the solution and the rate of evaporation. Crystallization from a melt depends on temperature and the rate of cooling.
2. Yes
3. Under ideal conditions (time, space allotment, temperature, concentration) crystal form provides a useful means for identifying minerals. Unfortunately, ideal conditions are not always possible.
4. Minerals that cool slowly develop larger crystals than minerals that cool quickly. So if you want large, well formed minerals, take your time.

57 [Activity] What's that Mineral?

For the lab on mineral identification use your own collection of minerals (collections from Ward's Scientific or Miners Catalog). The number of minerals you require your students to identify depends on your time schedule and your particular collection of minerals. Please note!! Not all the minerals from the mineral identification tables are necessary for this lab. For example, in a mineral collection composed of quartz, calcite, magnetite, muscovite, and pyrite your students would use hardness to identify quartz, reaction to HCl to identify calcite, a magnet or compass to identify magnetite, cleavage and color to identify muscovite, and streak and probably color and crystal form to identify pyrite.

Answers to the Questions
1. The distinguishing characteristic for the following minerals:

a) halite	chemical — taste
b) pyrite	cubic form with striations, streak
c) quartz	hexagonal form, hardness
d) biotite	cleavage, brown color, soft
e) fluorite	isometric form, hardness
f) garnet	isometric form, dark color, density

2. Physical properties: a mineral's crystalline structure or chemical composition:

a) crystal form	crystalline structure
b) color	chemical composition
c) cleavage	crystalline structure
d) specific gravity	chemical composition

3. Metallic minerals exhibit streak. If there is no streak the mineral is non-metallic.

4. Streak is the more reliable method for mineral identification. Some minerals come in a variety of different colors (Ex: quartz, fluorite, and corundum) and hence cannot be identified by a characteristic color. Weathering may also effect a minerals color. Since streak does not change, it is more useful for mineral identification.
5. Color
6. The physical properties that distinguish plagioclase feldspars from orthoclase feldspars are color and striations. Plagioclase is darker than orthoclase and plagioclase exhibits striations.

58 [Activity] Rock Hunt

This is simply an activity to encourage rock consciousness in the students everyday environment.

59 [Activity] What's that Rock?

This is a lab on rock identification where you use your own rocks or those students have collected. Rock collections can also be obtained from Ward's Scientific or Miners Catalog. Once again the number of rocks you use depends on your collection. If you are using rocks collected by your students, you may find the rocks are all of one type — igneous, metamorphic, or sedimentary — depending on your area. If this is the case, you may want the students to not only identify the rock and rock type but also discuss the environment where the rock was found.

On this note, here's an interesting true story: Students in New York City find that most of the old brownstone buildings are made of Triassic sandstone quarried in Connecticut. Some, however, are built of Scottish sandstones brought across the Atlantic in the 19th century. Its hard to tell which is which. Why? Interestingly enough, both sandstones were formed at the same period under the same circumstances in the same general area. They formed during Triassic times in a northern supercontinent, before the split of the Atlantic Ocean. In the 200 million years since formation, plate tectonics has split this region onto opposite shores of the North Atlantic Ocean — part in Connecticut and part in Scotland. And now civilization has now brought them together in one city. (This tidbit from *The Practical Geologist*, by Douglas Dixon, and Raymond L. Bernor, Editor.)

Answers to the Questions
1. Igneous rocks exhibit both fine and coarse grained textures. Fine grained textures occur when the rock has cooled very quickly. The texture can be so fine that individual crystals are too difficult to identify with an unaided eye. Some fine-grained textures are glassy. Coarse grained textures occur when the rock is allowed to cool slowly. Depending on the rate of cooling, most crystal grains can be easily identified.
2. Slow cooling, recrystallization, and open space. Igneous rocks that have undergone slow cooling exhibit large crystals. Metamorphic rocks subjected to increased pressures and temperatures exhibit large crystals. Sedimentary rocks precipitated from mineral rich water or sedimentary rocks formed from the evaporation of mineral rich water may exhibit large crystals.
3. Bedding planes, fossils, ripple marks, and cross-bedding.
4. By texture and mineral composition. Metamorphic rocks generally exhibit foliation — the realignment of crystals. The process of metamorphism also forms new minerals out of old minerals.

60 [Experiment] Specific Gravity

To follow the experiment as written in the manual, you've got to use an electronic balance. We owe this technique to the note (*Specific Gravity with Electronic Balances*) written by Paul L. Willems, of Minnesoty Valley Lutheran High School in New Ulm, MN, in The Physics Teacher, Vol. 36, Jan. 1998. The electronic balance is nicely used in this experiment.

Answers to the Summing Up

1. There are no units for specific gravity because it is a ratio of densities. The units cancel.
2. Specific gravity values would be the same whatever consistent units are used for densities. Again, the units cancel whatever they are (providing, of course, that whatever units used are consistent with each other).

61 [Experiment] Top This

This is an activity in learning about topographic maps. Students draw contour lines and construct a topographical profile. Supplement this activity by giving your students topographical maps. Ask them to determine the scale of the map and the contour interval. Have them construct a topographic profile in the area that best depicts the overall landscape, and to calculate the vertical exaggeration.

Answers to the Exercises

1. Contour lines should look something like this:

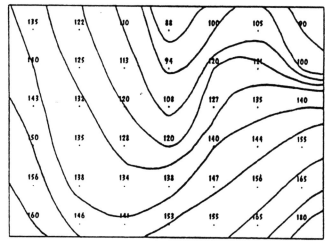

2. Contour lines should look something like this:

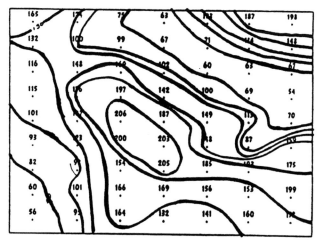

3. Elevations are as shown:

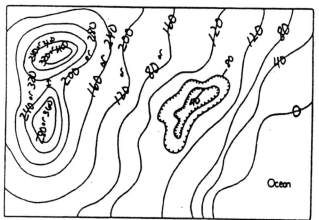

303

4.

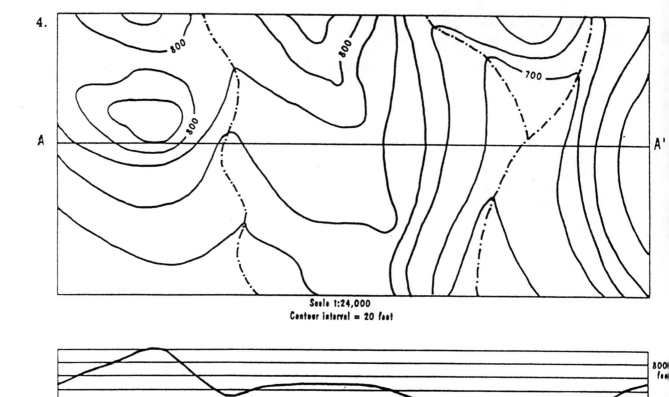

Scale 1:24,000
Contour interval = 20 feet

Topographical profile: Vertical scale is 1 inch = 100 feet = 1200 inches   (1:1200)

$$\frac{1/1200}{1/24000} = \frac{24000}{1200} = 20$$

Therefore the vertical exaggeration is 20 times greater than the true relief.

62 [Activity]   Water Below Our Feet

This is meant to follow the activity on topographical maps, *Top This.* Students will then already know how to draw contour lines. Important here is that the groundwater flow is perpendicular to lines of equal hydraulic head. The lines of equal hydraulic head are *equipotential lines*, completely analogous to the lines of equal potential in an electric field. Electric field lines are perpendicular to equipotential lines, and groundwater flow is perpendicular to the equipotential lines of hydraulic head. Further study of these would lead to *diffusion equations.*

Answers to the Problems

1.

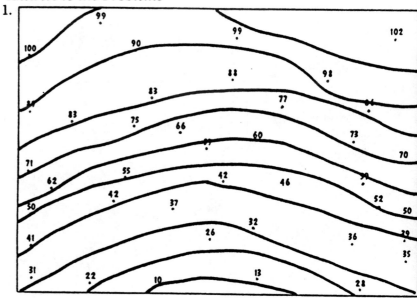

304

2. (shown below)

3. Well C might be affected, but Well E will definitely be affected.

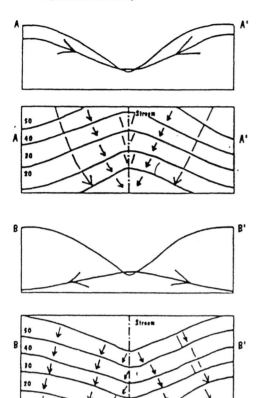

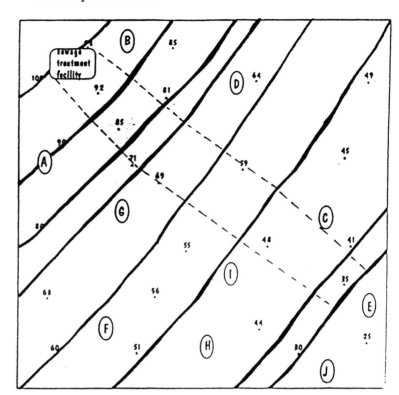

Answers to the Questions

1. The difference between stream A and steam B is the direction of the flow lines. In stream A water flows from the ground into the stream. In stream B water flows away from the stream into the ground. Stream A represents a humid area where water is available to recharge the aquifer. In a humid area the water table slopes toward the stream and water flows into the stream. Stream B represents a dry area where water is scarce. In dry areas precipitation is at a minimum causing no direct recharge of the aquifer. The water table slopes away from the stream bed. When water fills the stream it flows to the aquifer.

2. Yes, excessive pumping at Well H would cause a change in the flow of contamination. Well I would definitely be contaminated. Well G would most likely be affected and Well J may possibly be affected.

3. No. At point 35, however, the contamination would hit an impermeable lens and its flow path would change to go around the lens.

63 [Activity] Darcy's Law

In this lab we use Darcy's Law to determine the hydraulic conductivity of some hypothetical sand samples. We also use it to get the student to think about the impact of porosity on contaminant velocity (by using the analogy of the speed of a water molecule).

Darcy's Law also forms the foundation for the quantitative understanding of groundwater flow and contaminant transport. It is analogous to Ohm's Law and Fourier's Law — a flux response to a gradient. In the quantitative analysis of groundwater flow, Darcy's Law is combined with a conservation of mass equation that enables, for example, the prediction of how a well that is pumping affects the distribution and amount of water in an aquifer. This yields valuable information about the viability of obtaining a water supply from a given aquifer. Furthermore, Darcy's Law tells us the velocity that groundwater continiminants move, which leads to prediction of the extent to which an aquifer may be impacted by contamination.

Answers to the Questions
1. yes

2. K = the slope of the line on the q vs. i graph

$$K = \frac{2.4 \times 10^{-3} - 1.8 \times 10^{-3}}{0.8 - 0.6} = 3.0 \times 10^{-3} \text{ cm/s}$$

3. $K = \frac{q}{i}$

Sand	Flow Rate (cm/s)	Hydraulic Conductivity (cm/s)
1	6.0×10^{-4}	1.0×10^{-3}
2	1.2×10^{-3}	2.0×10^{-3}
3	1.8×10^{-3}	3.0×10^{-3}
4	2.4×10^{-3}	4.0×10^{-3}
5	3.0×10^{-3}	5.0×10^{-3}

4) $K = \frac{q}{i} = \frac{5.0 \times 10^{-3}}{0.8} = 6.25 \times 10^{-3}$;

$Q = 10 \times 6.25 \times 10^{-3} \times 0.8 = 5.0 \times 10^{-2} \text{ cm}^3/\text{s}$

Going Further
Increased porosity yields slower velocity. There are more open spaces for the water to move through. In other words, it is like releasing a hose that is being squeezed.

64 [Activity]   Over and Under

This lab is supplemental rather than essential, so use if time permits. The lab is challenging and heightens student awareness of what lies beneath the earth's surface. Measurement of dip angles can be estimated. Students should be able to tell that a 90° reading is vertical and a 45° is between vertical and horizontal. Dip direction is more important than angle. Students may enjoy coloring in the bed layers with colored pencils.

Answers to the Exercises

1. Structure is a syncline.   2. Structure is an antiline.

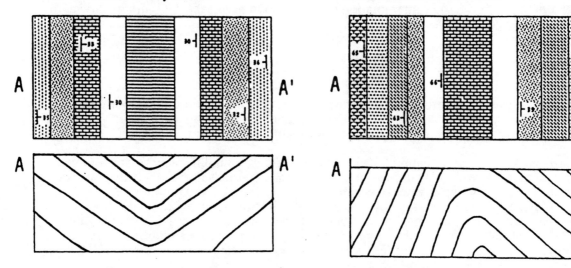

3. Structure is a plunging syncline.

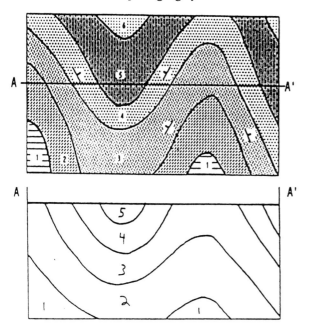

4. Structure is a basin, with youngest bed in center.

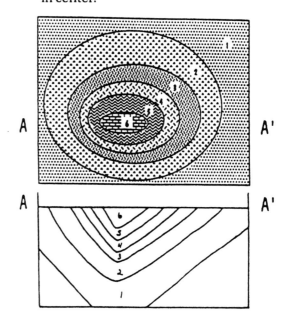

5. Structure is a dome, with oldest bed in center.

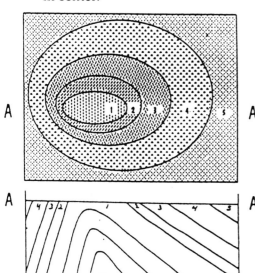

6. A syncline fold is displayed; strike slip fault; oldest structure is fold; youngest is intrusion.

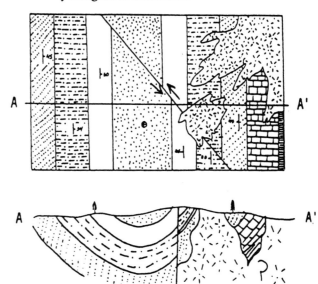

Answers to the Questions

1. A symmetrical syncline is shown in Exercise 2. The symmetry can be determined on the map view by the dip angles and by the apparent thickness of the beds.

2. An asymmetrical anticline is shown in Exercise 3. The lack of symmetry can be determined by the dip angles, which tell us that the beds are dipping in toward the fold axis.

3. A plunging inclines is shown in Exercise 3. The dip direction tells us that the beds are dipping in toward the fold axis.

4. Both Exercises 4 and 5 resemble circular structures in map view. The only way to tell the structures apart is with age sequence or dip direction. Exercise 4 represents a basin with youngest beds in the center. The dip direction would dip in toward the core of the basin. Exercise 5 represents a dome with the oldest beds in the center. The dip direction for a dome would dip outward away from the core of the dome.

5. A strike fault is shown in Exercise 6. Evidence for the fault structure is the horizontal displacement of beds. The fold structure is a syncline. the fold is the oldest structure and the intrusion is the youngest structure.

65 [Activity] Solar Power I

Both Solar Power I and Solar Power II are included here in Part 7 to complement meteorology, but they could as well be in Part 2, Heat; or in Part 8, Astronomy. Use either or both wherever they suit your course.

This is an exercise in the inverse-square law, which needs to be done during bright sunlight during the heat of the day. Amazingly, with some care you can get results reasonably close to the "ideal" data given below. Having the foil in a jar helps to keep foil temperature closer to the inside ambient temperature. If the foil weren't enclosed, cooling by air currents would counteract its temperature rise when illuminated by the lamp or the sun.

Sample Calculations:
Distance from the bulb filament to foil strip = 9.5 cm = 0.095 m and the sun's distance in meters is 1.5×10^{11} m.

So from $\dfrac{\text{sun's wattage}}{\text{bulb's wattage}} = \dfrac{\text{sun's distance}^2}{\text{bulb's distance}^2}$

we find:

$$\text{Sun's wattage} = \frac{[\text{bulb's wattage}][\text{sun's distance}]^2}{\text{bulb's distance}^2}$$

$$= \frac{[100][1.5 \times 10^{11}\text{m}]^2}{[0.095\text{ m}]^2} = 2.5 \times 10^{26}\text{W}$$

Therefore, the number of 100-W light bulbs is

$$\#\text{ bulbs} = \frac{2.5 \times 10^{26}\text{W}}{100\text{W/bulb}} = 2.5 \times 10^{24}\text{ bulbs}$$

Not surprisingly, even if all the electric generators in the world were diverted toward just lighting the calculated number of bulbs, this would constitute only a tiny fraction of the energy radiated by the sun.

Possible sources of discrepancies include: Inaccurate rating of bulb's wattage — inaccurate measurement of distance — atmospheric absorption — non perpendicular alignment of black vanes to solar rays — absorption is only by black paint, that misses energy in other wavelengths.

66 [Experiment] Solar Power II

The amount of solar energy flux just above the atmosphere is 2 cal/cm^2·min — the solar constant. But only three quarters of this reaches the earth's surface after passing through the atmosphere — 1.5 cal/cm^2·min. Since there are 10^4 cm^2 in 1 m^2, the solar energy flux obtained in Step 7 should be multiplied by $(10^4$ cm^2/m$^2)$ for Step 8. So following the sample calculation (next page), the energy reaching each square meter of ground per minute would be 10,000 cal.

Volume of water: 140 mL
Mass of water: 140 g
Initial water temperature: 23°C
Final water temperature: 26°C
Temperature difference: 3°C
Typical top diameter of Styrofoam cup: 6.9 cm
Surface area of the top of a typical Styrofoam cup is:

$$\text{area} = \pi \text{ (diameter/2)}^2$$
$$= 3.14(3.5 \text{ cm})^2$$
$$= 38 \text{ cm}^2$$

The energy collected by the cup was:

$$\text{energy} = mc\Delta T$$
$$= (140 \text{ g})(1.0 \text{ cal/g·°C}) \cdot (3°C)$$
$$= 400 \text{ cal}$$

The solar flux was:

$$\text{solar energy flux} = \frac{\text{energy}}{(\text{area}) \cdot (\text{time})} = \frac{400 \text{ cal}}{(38 \text{ cm}^2) \cdot (10 \text{ min})} = 1 \text{ cal/cm}^2 \cdot \text{min}$$

Factors that might affect the amount of solar energy reaching a location on the earth's surface include: time of day, season of the year, latitude, cloud cover, humidity, air pollution, nearby obstructions.

67 [Activity]   Indoor Clouds

This activity is pretty lightweight, and is probably the least exciting activity in the manual. But it does prompt attention to cloud formation. Consider assigning it as an out-of-class activity.

Answers to the Questions
1. Much the same in that air that is chilled undergoes condensation.
2. In the atmosphere there isn't the confinement that restricts air currents. Relatively little circulation occurs in the capped jar, whereas air more readily rises in the atmosphere. Then expansion rather than ice promotes cooling.
3. Warmer water undergoes more evaporation, which is why warm water was used in this activity.
4. We believe warm air rises from our observation of smoke, the warmer temperature of air near the ceiling in a room, the currents over hot roads in summer betrayed by refraction in the air, and other common occurrences.
5. Air currents are swept upward when heading toward mountains. As a result, the expanding air cools, clouds form, and precipitation follows. Further along, on the other side of the mountains, dry air remains that contributes to a desert area.

Part 8: Lab Activities and Experiments

Astronomy

68 [Experiment] Sunballs

Beauty is not only seeing the world with wide open eyes, but knowing what to look for. Your students have all seen splotches of light beneath the trees. But now you can point out what nearly all haven't seen, and that is that the splotches are circular — or if the Sun is low in the sky, elliptical. For they are images of the Sun. They occur because the holes between the leaves above are small compared to the distance to the ground, and act as pinholes (recall the activity, Pinhole Camera). Its nice to point out the really neat things around us!

Answers to the Questions
1. The shape of the hole has no bearing as long as its size is small compared to the distance to the image.
2. Measure the short diameter, for this is the undistorted diameter needed for the calculation. The long diameter is this same diameter stretched out because of the angle of sunbeams with the ground. Or position the viewing screen perpendicular to the sunbeams and get a circle.
3. The sunball will be the same shape as the eclipsed Sun. And in line with pinhole images, it will be reversed. So if the bottom half of the Sun is eclipsed, the image will show the top half eclipsed.

69 [Activity] Ellipses

Students will enjoy this light activity. It will also very likely be one of the things they'll be sure to remember from your course.

Answers to the Questions
1. The elliptical path of the Earth about the Sun is nearly circular; so the ellipse drawn with pins closest together most likely is the best representation of the Earth's orbit.
2. With pins far apart, a more eccentric ellipse results — one like the path of Halley's comet. The eccentricity of Halley's comet is 0.97, compared to Earth's eccentricity of 0.0167.
3. Evidence that the sum of the distances to the foci is constant is the constant length of string made to construct the ellipses!

70 [Experiment] Reckoning Latitude

This experiment has two parts; building apparatus, and viewing. The viewing segment must be carried out at nighttime. Polaris turns out to be only the 53rd brightest star in the night sky. You'll find students who will expect that it should be brighter, given its importance!

You might point out that Polaris is not only not exactly over the north pole — its almost a degree away from the north celestial pole. For your friends in the Southern Hemisphere, sorry, there is no conveniently placed star above the south celestial pole. Polaris serves navigators well now, and has been in a position to do so for the last several hundred years. But because the Earth precesses about its polar axis, like the wobble of a spinning top, it will remain nearly over the pole only for a few more hundred years. But that should not greatly worry us for the present.

The location of Polaris is easiest to find via the Big Dipper, as described in the text. It can also be located by using the Little Dipper. Polaris is the first star of the Little Dipper's handle. This is seen in Fig. 4 of the lab write-up. Another easily located constellation is Casseopia's Chair, the five-star big W in the sky (Fig. 5).

Answers to the Questions
1. Answers vary according to latitude.
2. Same as the altitude in Question 1.
3. Answers will vary.
4. Answers depend on latitude.
5. If the theolite shows Polaris to be lower in the sky as one moves south, and higher in the sky as one moves north, then this is evidence for a round Earth.

71 [Activity] Tracking Mars

This is a dandy! Students plot the orbit of Mars from measurements of the sky in Tycho Brahe's time. Data is neatly rounded off to the nearest half degree to make plotting straightforward. Corrections have been made to avoid the gap left during the transition from the Julian calendar to the Gregorian calendar now in current use. If you get into this, begin by asking your students what happened between October 5 and October 14 in 1582; the answer is *nothing*! These dates simply didn't exist when the change over in calendars was made.

The plot of this data runs nicely, and the elliptical shape of Mar's orbit is clearly evident. Once your students get the hang of it, they'll find it a pleasant and interesting experience.